Natural Gas and Geopolitics

By most estimates, global consumption of natural gas – a cleaner-burning alternative to coal and oil for electric power and other applications – will double by 2030. However, in North America, Europe, and South and East Asia, the projected consumption of gas is expected to far outstrip indigenous supplies. Delivering gas from the world's major reserves to the future demand centers will require a major expansion of inter-regional, cross-border gas transport infrastructures.

This book investigates the implications of this shift, utilizing historical case studies as well as advanced economic modeling to examine the interplay between economic and political factors in the development of natural gas resources. The contributors aim to shed light on the political challenges which may accompany a shift to a gas-fed world.

DAVID G. VICTOR is Director of the Program on Energy and Sustainable Development at the Freeman Spogli Institute for International Studies, Stanford University.

AMY M. JAFFE is Wallace S. Wilson Fellow for Energy Studies at the James A. Baker III Institute for Public Policy, Rice University.

MARK H. HAYES is a Research Fellow at the Program on Energy and Sustainable Development, Freeman Spogli Institute for International Studies, Stanford University.

Natural Gas and Geopolitics

From 1970 to 2040

Edited by

David G. Victor, Amy M. Jaffe, and Mark H. Hayes

CAMBRIDGE
UNIVERSITY PRESS

CAMBRIDGE UNIVERSITY PRESS
Cambridge, New York, Melbourne, Madrid, Cape Town, Singapore, São Paulo

CAMBRIDGE UNIVERSITY PRESS
The Edinburgh Building, Cambridge CB2 2RU, UK
Published in the United States of America by Cambridge University Press,
New York

www.cambridge.org
Information on this title: www.cambridge.org/9780521865036

First published 2006

Printed in the United Kingdom at the University Press, Cambridge

A catalogue record for this publication is available from the British Library

Library of Congress Cataloguing in Publication data

Natural gas and geopolitics: from 1970 to 2040/edited by David G. Victor,
Amy M. Jaffe, and Mark H. Hayes.
p. cm.
Includes bibliographical references and index.

ISBN-13: 978-0-521-86503-6 (hardback)
ISBN-10: 0-521-86503-4 (hardback)

1. Gas industry – Government policy.   2. Energy policy.   3. Geopolitics.
I. Victor, David G., 1965   II. Jaffe, Amy M., 1958   III. Hayes, Mark H.,
1976–   IV. Title.
HD9581.A2N35 2006
382′.42285–dc22

ISBN-13 978-0-521-86503-6 hardback
ISBN-10 0-521-86503-4 hardback

Contents

Figures

Tables

Boxes

Contributors

JAMES BALL President and Chief Mentor, Gas Strategies Consulting Ltd, London

JOE BARNES Research Fellow, James A. Baker III Institute for Public Policy, Rice University

JAREER ELASS Consultant, James A. Baker III Institute for Public Policy, Rice University

STACY L. ELLER Graduate Student Researcher, James A. Baker III Institute for Public Policy, Rice University

PETER HARTLEY Chair, Department of Economics, Rice University

KOHEI HASHIMOTO Professor, Nihon University

MARK H. HAYES Research Fellow, Program on Energy and Sustainable Development, Freeman Spogli Institute for International Studies, Stanford University

AMY M. JAFFE Wallace S. Wilson Fellow for Energy Studies, James A. Baker III Institute for Public Policy, Rice University

STEVEN W. LEWIS Research Fellow, James A. Baker III Institute for Public Policy, Rice University

DAVID R. MARES Professor, Department of Political Science, University of California, San Diego

KENNETH B. MEDLOCK, III Research Fellow, James A. Baker III Institute for Public Policy, Rice University

FRED VON DER MEHDEN Professor Emeritus, Department of Political Science, Rice University

MARTHA BRILL OLCOTT Senior Associate, Carnegie Endowment for International Peace, Washington, DC

ROB SHEPHERD Senior Consultant, Gas Strategies Consulting Ltd, London

RONALD SOLIGO Professor, Department of Economics, Rice University

DAVID G. VICTOR Director, Program on Energy and Sustainable Development, Freeman Spogli Institute for International Studies, Stanford University

NADEJDA M. VICTOR Research Fellow, Program on Energy and Sustainable Development, Freeman Spogli Institute for International Studies, Stanford University

Foreword

James A. Baker, III

The publication of *Natural Gas and Geopolitics: From 1970 to 2040* could not be timelier. The sharp rise of oil and gas prices that began in 2003 has returned energy to the top of the US public policy agenda. We have been reminded, yet again, of the centrality of energy to our and the world's economic well-being. Discussion has now turned to the domestic policies and international initiatives that can help ensure a stable, reasonably priced supply of energy to global markets through the middle of the twenty-first century and beyond.

One thing is certain: natural gas will play a critical role in meeting the world's energy needs. A series of important economic, political, and technological factors – the growing global demand for energy, the ongoing deregulation of gas and electrical markets, a preference for gas as the cleanest of the hydrocarbons, and declines in the cost of producing and transporting liquefied natural gas (LNG) – have laid the groundwork for an expanded role for natural gas in the world economy.

But there are a host of obstacles to seizing the full potential of natural gas. While increased trade in LNG opens up the possibility of a truly global market for gas, the pace and ultimate scope of this historic development remains very much in doubt. The shift from governments to the private sector as lead players in major pipeline and LNG projects, though welcome, raises important questions of investor confidence, regulatory environment, political risk, and competition from other hydrocarbon fuels and renewable energy sources. The amount of private investment required – by some estimates, up to 3 trillion dollars over the next quarter-century – is simply immense. Any number of factors – from the threat of terrorism to a retreat from market liberalization – could make raising these sums problematic.

James A. Baker, III is honorary Chair of the James A. Baker III Institute for Public Policy, Rice University. He was 61st Secretary of State (1989–1992), 67th Secretary of the Treasury (1985–1988) and White House Chief of Staff for Presidents Ronald Reagan (1981–1985) and George H.W. Bush (1992–1993).

The rise of natural gas also poses thorny geopolitical questions. The lion's share of proven gas reserves are found in areas, like the Middle East and the countries of the former Soviet Union, characterized by regional tensions and political instability. The concentration of these reserves in a relatively few countries raises, at least in theory, the possibility of a producers' cartel or "gas OPEC." These are issues that US policy-makers cannot afford to ignore. Long largely self-sufficient in natural gas, the United States will be increasingly dependent on imports during the years and decades ahead.

Natural Gas and Geopolitics: From 1970 to 2040 marks an important step in addressing these and other crucial issues. It is the result of a multi-year study organized by Rice University's James A. Baker III Institute for Public Policy and Stanford University's Program on Energy and Sustainable Development. The study assembled a team of prominent economists, political scientists, and energy experts from the United States and around the world to address the future of natural gas. Their impressive work includes case studies, economic models, and analytic essays.

I would like to commend editors David G. Victor, Amy M. Jaffe, and Mark H. Hayes for organizing the study and producing this invaluable volume. The national and international debate over the role of natural gas in the global economy is in many ways still in its infancy. *Natural Gas and Geopolitics: From 1970 to 2040* will provide an insightful and comprehensive introduction to these issues for policy-makers, scholars, industry executives, and concerned citizens alike.

Acknowledgments

In 2002, the Energy Forum of the James A. Baker III Institute for Public Policy at Rice University and the Program on Energy and Sustainable Development at the Freeman Spogli Institute for International Studies, Stanford University, began a joint effort to investigate the geopolitical consequences of a major shift to natural gas in world energy markets. We are grateful to our many collaborators and funders for their interest in the long-term evolution of this important industry, its consequences for the economy and environment, and implications for politics and policy.

The Baker Institute Energy Forum thanks project sponsors Baker Botts LLP and Ambassador and Mrs. Hushang Ansary for their generous support of this research. In addition, the Institute thanks its Energy Forum members for their ongoing support and advice for this project. The Program on Energy and Sustainable Development is grateful for core funding from the Electric Power Research Institute and BPplc, which made its participation in this study possible.

We thank the many collaborators and reviewers who have participated in the study. The collaborative research began in earnest at an October 2002 kickoff meeting at Stanford, and we thank the participants for their focused critique of our research plans and methods.

We commissioned several historical case studies, and in November 2003 at Stanford the authors presented drafts for review. (The final versions of these studies are in chapters 3–9 of this book, with more detailed working papers on our websites–http://pesd.stanford.edu and http://rice.edu/energy.) In parallel, the Rice modeling team developed a model to allow projections of gas trade into the future, and initial results were presented at a review meeting in Houston in March 2004. We are enormously grateful to the several dozen participants and reviewers at those two meetings.

We would also like to thank Altos Management Partners for the donation of their software platform *Marketbuilder* for use during this study and to Hill Huntington and the US Department of Energy for their comments and critique of the model through Stanford's Energy

Modeling Forum and during private sessions over the study period. (Final versions of those studies are in chapters 11–13, along with online working papers.)

In May 2004 we convened a major conference in Houston to present the initial findings from the study. We are especially grateful to the many speakers and panelists and especially Baker Botts LLP and Shell Exploration & Production Company that, along with our core funders, made that meeting possible. We would like to thank our conference keynote speakers: the Honorable James A. Baker, III, Baker Institute Honorary Chair; Philip Dingle, President, ExxonMobil Gas and Power Marketing Company; Ambassador Edward Djerejian, Baker Institute director; H.E. Abdullah bin Hamad Al-Attiyah, Minister of Energy and Industry of Qatar; Peter Hughes, Executive Vice President, Group Strategy, BG Group plc (then with BP plc); H.E. Dr. Chakib Khelil, Minister of Energy and Mines, People's Democratic Republic of Algeria; Tomiyuki Kudo, President, Petroleum Energy Center of Japan; James Mulva, President and CEO of ConocoPhillips; and Congressman Francisco Xavier Salazar Diez Sollano, Chairman, Energy Commission, Mexican Chamber of Deputies, for taking the time to share their unique insights on the geopolitics of natural gas. We would especially like to thank Molly Hipp, Sonja Dimitrijevich, Ryan Kirksey and Jason Lyons at the Baker Institute for organizing a seamless event, along with Jack Hogan, Ale Núñez-Luna, and Kassia Yanosek who traveled from Stanford to provide critical support.

In addition to the capstone conference in Houston, we have benefited from comments at various seminars where we have presented the study findings. These include seminars at UC Berkeley, the Graduate School of Business at Stanford, and also Stanford's Center for Development, Democracy, and the Rule of Law.

We owe particular gratitude to George H.B. Verberg, President of the International Gas Union and Bert Panman, Chairman of the IGU Coordination Committee for providing our research a prestigious position at the 23rd World Gas Conference in June 2006.

The breadth and depth of this volume is a product of the extensive contributions of our co-authors. Our conclusions rest upon their in-depth research. Their patience with our lengthy review process is duly appreciated.

This manuscript would not have reached publication were it not for the countless hours of support from the staffs at our respective institutions and the work of our editors at Cambridge University Press. At Stanford—Becca Elias, Josh House, Rose Kontak, Michelle Klippel, and Bob Sherman provided critical support, especially in the busiest times;

Meredith Williams and Becca Newton-Thompson, also at Stanford, deserve full credit for the maps included in the case study chapters. At the Baker Institute, Jill Nesbitt, Jillene Connors, Christina Estrada, and Laura Iszar often burned the midnight oil in aid of this massive project. Our editors at Cambridge, Chris Harrison, Lynn Dunlop, and Elizabeth Davey, and our copy-editor Barbara Docherty, were a pleasure to work with throughout the publication process.

Finally, we thank our family and friends, who supported us through the many evenings and weekends leading up to the production of this effort.

DAVID G. VICTOR
Stanford, California
AMY M. JAFFE
Houston, Texas
MARK H. HAYES
Stanford, California

Acronyms and abbreviations

ADB	Asian Development Bank
ADR	American Depositary Receipts
Agip	Italy's state oil company
AIC	Association of International Cooperation (Russia)
ALADI	Asociación Latinoamericana de Integración
ALNG	Atlantic LNG
AP	alternative project
APCI	Air Products & Chemicals, Inc., with trademark process for natural gas liquefaction
APERC	Asia Pacific Energy Research Center
Apicorp	Arab Petroleum Investments Corporation
ASEAN	Association of Southeast Asian States
BBE	Bahia de Bizkaia Electricidad
BC	Belarus Connector
Bcf/d	billion cubic feet per day
Bcm	billion cubic meters
b/d	barrels (of oil) per day
BIWGTM	Baker Institute World Gas Trade Model
BNDES	Brazilian National Development Bank
Botas	Turkey's monopoly gas importer
BTC	Baku–Tbilisi–Ceyhan (oil pipeline)
BTE	Baku–Tbilisi–Erzurum (gas pipeline)
Btu	British thermal unit
Btu/cm	British thermal unit/cubic meter
CAC	Central-Asia-Center (Turkmen–Russia gas pipeline)
CAF	Corporación Andina de Fomento, Andean Development Corporation
CAMEL	Compagnie Algérienne de Méthane Liquide
CBM	coal-bed methane
CCGT	combined cycle gas turbine
CEE	Central and Eastern European
CEO	chief executive officer

CEPSA	Companía Española de Petróleos SA
CERA	Cambridge Energy Research Associates, Inc.
CGC	Compañía General de Combustibles SA (Argentina)
c.i.f.	cost-insurance-freight
CIPE	Center for International Private Enterprise
CIS	Commonwealth of Independent States
CMEA	Council for Mutual Economic Assistance (COMECON)
CNG	compressed natural gas
CNOOC	China National Offshore Oil Corp.
COMECON	*see* CMEA
Copec	Compañía de Petroleos de Chile
CPI	Consumer Price Index (US)
d.e.s.	destination ex-ship
EBRD	European Bank for Reconstruction and Development
EC	European Community
ECAFE	UN Economic Commission for Asia and the Far East (later ESCAP)
ECE	United Nations Economic Commission for Europe
ECO	Economic Cooperation Organization
EEC	European Economic Community
EFTA	European Free Trade Association
EGU	Enhanced Gas Utility (Qatar)
EIA	Energy Information Administration (US)
EIB	European Investment Bank
EIU	Economist Intelligence Unit
ENAP	Empresa Nacional de Petroleo, Chile's national oil company
ENI	Ente Nazionale Idrocarburi (National Hydrocarbon Corporation, Italy)
EPC	engineering, procurement, construction
ESCAP	UN Economic and Social Commission for Asia and the Pacific
EU	European Union
FBIS	Foreign Broadcast Information Service
FDI	foreign direct investment
FEED	front-end engineering and design
FID	final investment decision
FIESP	Federacão das Indústrias de Estado de São Paulo
FLN	Front de Libération Nationale (Algeria)
f.o.b.	freight-on-board
FSU	Former Soviet Union
Gasbol	Bolivia–Brazil gas pipeline

GCC	Gulf Cooperation Council
GCV	Gross Calorific Value
GdF	Gaz de France
GDP	gross domestic product
GECF	Gas Exporting Countries Forum
GIRI	General Investment Risk Index
GLS	generalized least squares
GME	Gaz Maghreb Europe ("Maghreb pipeline")
GTB	Gas Transboliviano SA
GTL	gas-to-liquids
GW	gigawatt
ha	hectare
HHV	high heating value
IADB	Inter-American Development Bank
ICC	International Chamber of Commerce
ICJ	International Court of Justice
ICRG	International Country Risk Guide
ICSID	International Center for the Settlement of Investment Disputes
IEA	International Energy Agency (Paris)
IFC	International Finance Corporation (part of the World Bank)
IGCC	Integrated gasification combined cycle
ILSA	Iran and Libya Sanctions Act
IMF	International Monetary Fund
IOC	international oil company
IRNA	Islamic Republic News Agency (Iran)
ISOCOTT	Iron and Steel Company of Trinidad & Tobago
IV	independent variable – investment climate, number of transit countries for a particular gas trade project, etc.
JCC	Japanese Customs Clearing Price, often referred to as the "Japanese Crude Cocktail"
JCCME	Japan Cooperation Center for Middle East
J-EXIM	Export–Import Bank of Japan (now Japan Bank for International Cooperation, JBIC)
JILCO	Japan Indonesia LNG Company
JMG	Joint Management Group (Indonesia)
JNOC	Japan National Oil Corporation
JV	joint venture
JVA	joint-venture agreement
kJ/cm	kilojoules/cubic meter
km	kilometer

KOGAS	Korea Gas Corporation
KWh	kilowatt hours
LHV	low heating value
LIBOR	London Interbank Offered Rate
LNG	liquefied natural gas
LPG	liquid petroleum gas
m	meter
Maphilindo	Malaysia, the Philippines, Indonesia
MarAd	Maritime Administration (US)
MBOE	million barrels of oil equivalent
mcm	thousand cubic meters
Mercosur	Mercado Común del Sur, Southern Common Market
METI	Ministry of Economy, Trade, and Industry (Japan)
MFN	most-favored nation
MITI	Ministry of International Trade and Industry (Japan), now METI
MLA	multi-lateral lending agency
mm	millimeter
mmbtu	million British thermal units
mmHg	mm of mercury (measure of pressure)
MNC	multi-national corporation
MNR	Movimiento Nacionalista Revolucionario (Bolivia)
MOU	memorandum of understanding
Mtoe	million tonnes of oil equivalent
mtpa	million tonnes per annum
MW	megawatt
NAFTA	North American Free Trade Agreement
NAR	National Alliance for Reconstruction (Trinidad & Tobago)
NATO	North Atlantic Treaty Organization
NCV	Net Calorific Value
NEGP	North European Gas Pipeline
NGC	National Gas Company (Trinidad & Tobago)
NGLs	natural gas liquids
NGO	non-governmental organization
NIGC	National Iranian Gas Company
NIOC	National Iranian Oil Company
NLNG	Nigeria LNG
NNPC	Nigerian National Petroleum Company
NPC	National Petroleum Council (US)
NPV	net present value
NYMEX	New York Mercantile Exchange

O&M	operating and maintenance (costs)
OAS	Organization of American States
OECD	Organization for Economic Cooperation and Development
OPEC	Organization of Petroleum Exporting Countries
OPIC	Overseas Private Investment Corporation (US)
PDVSA	Petróleos de Venezuela SA., Venezuela's national oil company
PESD	Program on Energy and Sustainable Development (Stanford University)
PG&E	Pacific Gas and Electric Company (US)
PGNiG	Polskie Górnictwo Naftowe Gazownictwo, Polish Oil and Gas Company
PNM	People's National Movement (Trinidad & Tobago)
PSA	production-sharing agreement
PSC	production-sharing contract
PV	present value
QP	Qatar Petroleum (formerly Qatar General Petroleum Company, QGPC)
R&D	research and development
ROE	return on equity
SADC	Southern African Development Community
SADR	Saharan Arab Democratic Republic
SAP	structural adjustment program
SCC	specific capital cost
SCOGAT	Société pour la Construction du Gazoduc Transtunisien (Tunisia)
Segamo	Sociedad de Estudios Gasducto del Mediterráneo Occidental (Spain)
SNOC	Singapore National Oil Company
SOE	state-owned enterprise
Sonatrach	Société Nationale pour le Transport et la Commercialisation des Hydrocarbures (Algeria)
SOTUGAT	Société du Gazoduc Transtunisien (Tunisia)
SPA	sales and purchase agreement
TBG	Transportadora Brasileira Gasoduto Bolivia–Brazil SA
Tcm	trillion cubic meters
TCO	Transport Capacity Option
TCP	Trans-Caucasian Pipleline
TCQ	Transport Contract Quantity
TGN	Transportadora Gas del Norte (Argentina)
TJ	Terajoules

TMPC	Trans-Mediterranean Pipeline Company Limited
TRINGENI	Trinidad & Tobago Nitrogen Company
TSKJ	Consortium of Technip, Kellogg, Snamprogetti, and JGC
TTMC	Trinidad & Tobago Methanol Company
TTP	Turkmenistan Transcontinental Pipeline
TTPC	Trans-Tunisian Pipeline Company Limited
TTUC	Trinidad and Tobago Urea Company
UAE	United Arab Emirates
UES	United Energy System (Russian state electric power enterprise)
UN	United Nations
UNC	United National Company (Trinidad & Tobago)
UOG	UAE Offsets Group
USD	US dollar
USGS	United States Geological Survey
USSR	Union of Soviet Socialist Republics, Soviet Union
VALHYD	Hydrocarbon Development Plan of Algeria
VAT	value added tax
VNG	East German gas transmission company
WACC	weighted average cost of capital
WEC	World Energy Council
WIEE	Wintershall Erdgas Handelshaus Zug AG
WIEH	Wintershall Erdgas Handelshaus GmbH
YABOG	Bolivia–Argentina gas pipeline
YPF	Yacimientos Petrolíferos Federales (Argentine gas consortium)
YPFB	Yacimientos Petrolíferos Fiscales de Bolivia, Bolivian national oil company

Part I

Introduction and context

1   Introduction to the study

Joe Barnes, Mark H. Hayes, Amy M. Jaffe, and David G. Victor

Natural gas is rapidly gaining importance in global energy markets. Prized for its relatively clean and efficient combustion, gas is becoming the fuel of choice for a wide array of uses, notably the generation of electric power. Natural gas is projected to be the fastest-growing major source of primary energy over the coming decades, with global consumption increasing nearly two-fold by 2030 (EIA 2004; IEA 2004). In the next few years, gas will surpass coal to become the world's second most important energy source; by 2050 gas could surpass oil to occupy the number one slot. Recent price increases do not fundamentally challenge the economic viability of this robust gas future.

There is plenty of gas to satisfy these visions of global gasification. The broadest measure of gas available totals about 350 trillion cubic meters (Tcm), or roughly 130 years at today's rate of consumption (USGS 2000). Even "proved reserves," a narrower measure of just the gas that has been detected and is commercial to develop using today's technology, suggest that scarcity is unlikely to impede a global shift to gas. The widely referenced *BP Statistical Review of World Energy* reports 176 Tcm of proved gas worldwide, or nearly 70 years at current production levels (BP 2004).

The geographical, financial and political barriers to gas development, however, will be harder to clear. A high proportion of the most prolific gas resources is concentrated in areas that are remote from the United States, Western Europe, China, Brazil, India, and other areas where demand growth is expected to be strongest. Admittedly, the technological hurdles to moving large volumes of gas over long distances are falling rapidly. Already today, one-quarter of world gas consumption is the result of international trade. Pipelines account for 78 percent of that

The authors would like to thank Barbara Shook of Energy Intelligence Group for her contributions to this chapter, particularly on the historical development of gas markets. Rob Shepherd of Gas Strategies also provided important comments related to the development of the LNG trade. Robert Moore at the Baker Institute also provided invaluable research assistance.

3

trade; ocean-going tankers carrying liquefied natural gas (LNG) convey the rest (BP 2004). However, pipeline and LNG infrastructures are extremely costly to build and require long time horizons and a predictable economic and political context for investors to sink their capital and knowledge. The International Energy Agency's (IEA) comprehensive assessment of future investment in energy found that about 3 trillion dollars in investment will be needed to meet the growing demand for natural gas between now and 2030 (IEA 2003a). Most of the investment will be needed upstream – in exploration, production, and processing facilities – in increasingly remote areas where it has already proved difficult to do business. Two countries alone – Russia and Iran – account for nearly half the world's proven gas reserves (BP 2004).

The growing role for cross-border gas trade will force new political attention on the security of gas supplies. In the past, "energy security" has been debated almost exclusively in terms of oil markets; the shift to gas will force governments and consumers to ask similar questions of an increasingly vital gas supply. Emerging relationships between major gas suppliers and key end-use consuming countries will create new geopolitical considerations rising to the highest levels of economic and security policy.

This book focuses on the political, economic, and security dimensions of the global shift to gas. We look to history to explain why governments and investors have cleared the financial and political barriers for some international pipeline and LNG projects yet failed in many other ventures. And we look to the future – deploying a newly developed economic model of world gas trade – to examine how key political and technological factors may affect the evolution of a global gas market.

In this opening chapter, we offer a brief review of how gas rose to prominence and, at present, is becoming a globally traded commodity. Next, we introduce the two main elements of our study. We look historically at seven case studies that reveal how governments and firms have addressed the geopolitical issues surrounding major international gas trade projects. Then, we look to the future to examine how the business may unfold over the next three decades.

Throughout this book, our quarry is "geopolitics," which is a concept that bears explanation. For many analysts, geopolitics is the competitive zero-sum game played by nation-states in their pursuit of power and security. In this traditional view of international politics, prevalent especially during the Cold War, countries are primarily concerned about gains from trade, investment, and military action *relative* to other national competitors. Greater territory and resources for one party necessarily create a loss for others.

Our concept of geopolitics is broader. It is the influence of geographic, cultural, demographic, economic, and technological factors on the political discourse among international actors. In this definition, relative gains matter, but so do joint gains from possible cooperation. In so far as geography, technology, and political choices direct gas trade along one route at the expense of another, investment and revenues are diverted as well, with considerable political implications. Countries that commit to importing large volumes of gas place the security of their energy systems partly in the hands of others, which in turn gives both suppliers and users of gas a stake in the internal political stability of one another. This is what we mean by "geopolitics of gas" – not simply an endless jockeying for global position, but also the immensely political actions of governments, investors, and other key actors who decide which gas trade projects will be built, how the gains will be allocated, and how the risks of dependence on international gas trading will be managed.

A Primer: From Local to Global Markets for Gas

Humans have been aware of the seepage of natural flammable gases from the earth for at least several thousand years. There is an early reference in ancient China to the use of gas for heating pans of brine water to produce salt. But gas was not used extensively as a fuel source until the nineteenth century.[1] While natural gas was used as early as 1821 to illuminate the town of Fredonia, New York, its widespread use in the United States awaited the rise of the petroleum industry, beginning with the Titusville, Pennsylvania, finds of 1859. Natural gas "associated" with oil was a nuisance for the Pennsylvania oilmen who vented and flared the hazardous byproduct. However, enterprising businessmen soon saw the possibility of transporting it by primitive pipes to nearby industrial centers. By 1890, Pittsburgh was the natural gas center of the United States, with the fuel being used for both industrial and domestic purposes. Natural gas gained an advantage for its high caloric content and for its relative cleanliness compared to coal – an environmental asset that remains a key strength for gas a century later. By 1900, natural gas was used extensively in the Appalachian region, but its broader use remained constrained by the technical difficulties associated with transporting natural gas over long distances.

---

[1] See Castaneda (1999) pp. 3–11 and Peebles (1980), pp. 5–17, for an early history of gas use.

BOX 1.1   WHAT IS NATURAL GAS?

Natural gas is a fossil fuel that contains a mix of hydrocarbon gases, mainly methane (CH_4), along with varying amounts of ethane (C_2H_6), propane (C_3H_8), and butane (C_4H_{10}). Carbon dioxide, oxygen, nitrogen, and hydrogen sulphide are also often present. Natural gas is "dry" when it is almost pure methane, absent the longer-chain hydrocarbons. It is considered "wet" when it contains other hydrocarbons in abundance. Those longer chain hydrocarbons can condense to form valuable light liquids (so-called natural gas liquids, or NGLs). "Sweet" gas possesses low levels of hydrogen sulphide compared to "sour" gas. Natural gas found in oil reservoirs is called "associated" gas. When it occurs alone it is called "non-associated gas." Colorless, odorless, and highly combustible, natural gas is used for fuel in electrical power generation, heating, and cooking. For more on the properties and specific conventions used in this volume, see Appendix: technical notes (p. 484).

Advances in welding, metallurgy, and compression technology in the late 1920s and early 1930s brightened the prospects for gas. A series of long-distance pipelines were laid from new gas fields in the American Southwest, most notably a 1,600 km (1,000 mile), 600 mm (24 inch) pipeline from the Texas Panhandle to Chicago. Natural gas was rapidly becoming a national industry – a trend accelerated by the heavy industrial demands of the Second World War, which saw natural gas consumption increase by over 50 percent in just four years. As part of the war effort, the federal government actively encouraged the construction of additional pipelines linking the Southwest to factories of Appalachia in the East (Castaneda 1999).

Natural gas use in the United States grew rapidly in the years following the Second World War, reflecting robust overall economic growth, continued expansion of the pipeline network, and broad-based technological advances in exploration, transportation, refining, and end-use by industries and households. In 1947, two pipelines built during the Second World War to carry oil from Texas to the Northeast – the so-called "Little Inch" and "Big Inch" – were converted to natural gas to service growing East Coast demand for natural gas. US production rose from 112 Bcm (4 Tcf) in 1945 to 627 Bcm (22 Tcf) in 1970; the national pipeline grid grew from just over 160,000 km (100,000 miles) in 1950 to roughly 400,000 km (250,000 miles) twenty years later. In many ways, the period 1945–1970 marked a "golden age" in gas use in the United States, with natural gas providing a third of total primary energy in the late 1960s and early 1970s, a proportion that has not been reached again to date (BP 2004). By the late 1960s, US policy-makers worried that gas was becoming scarce and began imposing controls on its usage and pricing, which weakened the incentive to look for new gas supplies. Only when US natural gas controls were lifted in 1978 did a boom in gas drilling yield large fresh supplies. Higher decontrolled prices curtailed consumption through the 1980s. More recently, strong demand growth has confronted stagnating US domestic production rates, driving US natural gas prices to unprecedented highs and calling into question the prospects for continued growth in gas consumption.

Before 1950, the development of the natural gas industry was essentially a US phenomenon. In that year, the United States represented roughly 90 percent of the natural gas produced and consumed in the world (Darmstadter, Teitelbaum, and Polach 1971). Subsequent decades, however, saw other key industrial economies shift to gas as well. Natural gas offered a fuel source that was well suited to the rapidly growing energy needs of the industrialized world. Combustion of natural gas is consistent, easily manageable, and cleaner-burning than the key alternatives – coal and oil – making gas ideal for use in industrial boilers, refining, cooking, and space heating. New technologies that were needed to facilitate natural gas growth were developed and rapidly spread throughout the developed world (figure 1.1).

In Western Europe, Italy made the first move to gas with discoveries of natural gas in the Po Valley during the Second World War, developing the largest gas market in Western Europe by the mid-1960s. Later, discoveries in and around the North Sea would make that region the center of Western Europe's gas production. The 1959 discovery of the massive Groningen gas field in the Netherlands set the stage for rapid growth there, and also in neighboring Belgium, Germany, and France in the 1970s.[2] From the earliest years of Khrushchev's rule, the gas-rich Soviet Union (USSR) adopted an industrial strategy that mandated a shift to gas; with pipelines and economic integration, the USSR extended gasification to most Soviet satellite states in Eastern Europe from the late 1960s through the 1970s.

The impetus for increasing the role of gas in the energy supply was enhanced by the 1973 Arab oil embargo. The economies of Japan and Western Europe at the time ran mainly on imported oil. The shortages and spiking prices that resulted from the embargo sent many countries to diversify away from Middle East oil. Japan, in particular, adopted an aggressive policy to diversify its energy sources. Even prior to the oil crises, Japanese planners were looking to import natural gas to replace

---

[2] More detail on European gas markets can be found in chapter 3 and chapter 5 and the references therein.

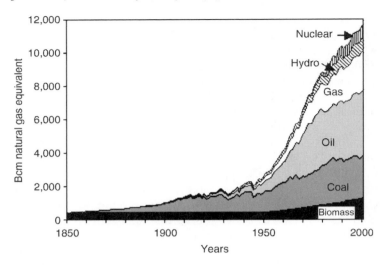

Figure 1.1. Global primary energy consumption, by fuel in Bcm natural gas equivalent.

Source: 1850–1990: IIASA–WEC (1998); for 1990–2001: IEA (2004b) and EIA (2005).

town gas – which was produced from imported coal. Increasingly mindful of the need for ecological protection, the Japanese government orchestrated investment in nuclear power and, especially, natural gas. By the end of the 1970s, Japan was the world's largest importer of LNG. It relied notably on supplies from Indonesia and Brunei (see chapter 4).

As gas consumption grew around the world, North America's share of global gas consumption fell from nearly 90% in 1950 to less than one-third in 2003. Rising consumption in the Former Soviet Union (FSU), Western Europe, and Asia (largely Japan and South Korea) through the 1970s, 1980s, and 1990s brought these regions on a par with the United States in terms of gas consumption. We show this evolution in figure 1.2.

A Global Business: Pipelines and LNG

In tandem with the shift to gas came international trade. In large measure, trade by pipeline was an extension of the same basic pipeline technologies pioneered early in the twentieth century. Improved steel and, especially, compressors made larger and lengthier pipelines both

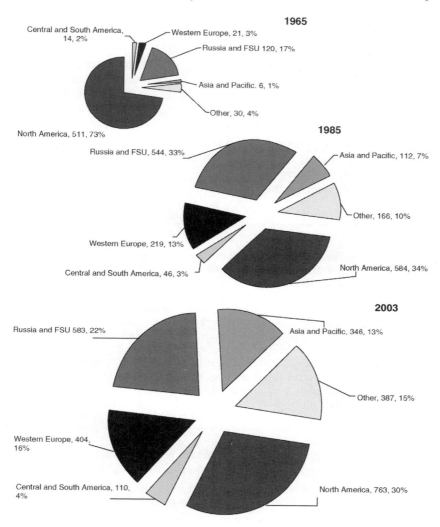

Figure 1.2. Worldwide consumption of natural gas, 1965, 1985, 2003. Pie charts are proportional in size to total consumption. Statistics indicate total consumption in Bcm and share of total.

Source: BP (2004).

technically and economically viable. By the early 1980s, major pipelines linked Canada to the United States, the Soviet Union to Eastern and Central Europe, Norway and the Netherlands to other Western European countries, and Algeria under the Mediterranean to Italy.

Pipelines, nonetheless, imposed severe limitations on the trade in gas. By nature, pipelines are economic for trade over relatively small (though growing) distances, and thus markets made through pipes were regional in nature. These pipeline links created two key large markets – North America and Europe – and many other smaller networks in Latin America, Southeast Asia, and the Middle East (IEA 2004; L'Hagert *et al.* 2004). Denser interconnections and longer pipelines expanded the scope of these regional gas markets, but the emergence of a truly global gas business is taking place only as the development of significant and economical ocean shipping technology – LNG – promotes economical gas trading over very long distances and a flexible business model that encourages arbitrage between these dense pipeline regions.

BOX 1.2   WHAT IS LNG?

LNG is natural gas reduced to a liquid state by cooling it to about minus 260° Fahrenheit (−160° Centigrade). This cryogenic process reduces natural gas's volume by a factor of roughly 600:1. The reduced volume of gas in its liquid state makes transport by ship economically feasible, especially over long distances for which pipelines are increasingly costly to build and operate. (On smaller scales, the LNG process is also used to store gas to meet short-term local needs during periods of peak demand.) LNG is manufactured at liquefaction units or "trains," where heat is removed from natural gas by using a refrigerant. Before LNG can be used as a fuel it must be returned to a gaseous state. This occurs at regasification plants, where LNG is heated before delivery into a pipeline system. All regasification plants today are located onshore, but difficulties with siting have led to numerous proposals for offshore facilities or technologies that would allow regasification on tankers.

LNG took hold in international markets relatively slowly, due largely to the unwieldy and costly technologies associated with producing, storing, and shipping it. The first patent for liquefying natural gas was granted in 1914, and the early applications of LNG technology were for storage. No shipping technologies existed at the time. In the 1940s, there were attempts to use stored LNG during periods of high demand in both the United States and Soviet Union – so-called "peak-shaving," when the pipeline network was inadequate to meet all the demand of final users. These projects were less than successful. Indeed, the first commercial LNG plant in the world – in Cleveland, Ohio – was shut down following a 1944 explosion that killed 128 people (Peebles 1980). Today, much safer LNG storage schemes are widely used for peak shaving.

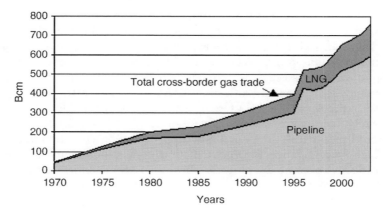

Figure 1.3. World trade in natural gas, 1970–2004. Since the early 1970s gas markets have become increasingly international, with cross-border trade by pipeline and LNG. The share of LNG in imported gas is rising, and the share of imported gas in total gas consumption is also rising. In 2000, for example, 27% of all gas consumed was imported; while in 1970 that fraction was only 4%. 1996 is the first year with reliable data on gas trade within the FSU and the former East Bloc countries. Previously "intra-country" pipeline movements thus became counted as "traded gas."

Source: CEDIGAZ (2000); IEA (2003); BP (2004).

In the late 1950s and early 1960s the technology for shipping LNG was developed and the world's first major LNG export plant opened in Arzew, Algeria, in 1964, exporting gas to buyers in France and the United Kingdom. By 1972, LNG plants were up and running in the United States (Alaska), Brunei, and Libya, with a second plant added in Algeria at Skikda. Rising concern about oil security following the oil crises of the 1970s then set the stage for a boom in new LNG capacity, heralded by major projects in Abu Dhabi (1977) and Indonesia (1977), both delivering LNG to Japan. Algeria and Indonesia emerged as the dominant LNG suppliers, each with nearly 20 million tons per annum (mtpa) of export capacity. New entrants came into the market over the next two decades, including Malaysia (1983), Australia (1989), Qatar (1996), Nigeria (1999), Trinidad & Tobago (1999), and Oman (2000). Today, LNG accounts for about one-quarter of the international trade in gas (see figure 1.3).

For its first three decades from the 1960s to the mid-1990s, the LNG business was a highly conservative enterprise. All participants in the deal – including gas producers, large utilities, and sovereign governments – financed projects on the strength of top-notch credit ratings and long-term sales and purchase agreements. Pricing provisions were mainly tied to oil and inflexible. LNG ships moved from supply source to buyer along fixed routes, regardless of demand fluctuations. Japan, which led the way as purchaser of most of the world's LNG, demanded (and paid dearly for) reliability in gas delivery. As a dominant player, Japan's preference for "gold plating" (via redundancy and overbuilt capacity) became the industry norm for LNG facilities and tankers (see chapters 4 and 8). Outside Japan, the LNG business struggled to gain a foothold and remained a specialized niche activity in most LNG-importing countries. For the US market, LNG projects envisioned in the 1970s faltered as the US government refused to allow domestic buyers to accept price increases sought by Algeria, the main LNG supplier to the US at the time (see chapter 3). In the wake of these troubles, two of the four LNG regasification facilities in the United States were mothballed for over a decade.

Fundamental changes that were remaking the LNG business came to a head in the late 1990s. These changes signaled that in the future LNG would not operate with a business model that depended solely on point-to-point trading in which long-term contracts specified the exact destination of every LNG cargo. Spurred by the shift toward price deregulation and privatization of natural gas businesses around the world, LNG began evolving into a more flexible, competitive, and entrepreneurial business. The chain of infrastructures for delivering LNG – production, liquefaction, shipping, and regasification – did not necessarily require a single integrated operator; rather, the chain could be divided into individual links, each with different owners. The decisions of half a dozen Japanese utilities would no longer define the LNG market or its terms. The first regular "spot" cargoes – completely outside long-term contracts – started from Australia to Spain in 1993. Abu Dhabi and Australia sent their first spot cargoes to the United States in 1996 and 1997, respectively. By 1999, the Atlantic LNG project in Trinidad (see chapter 9) was explicitly structured to take advantage of arbitrage opportunities between the US and Spanish gas markets. A new era of more liquid, flexible international gas markets was rapidly developing.

At least two factors have driven this shift toward a new and more entrepreneurial LNG business model. The first was the development of a competitive market for gas in the United States, spurred by deregulation. From the late 1980s, American gas prices increasingly reflected "gas-on-gas" competition rather than the oil-indexed or administered pricing systems that prevailed in all other major gas markets. The deeply liquid spot market for gas in the United States generated a unique opportunity for LNG sellers (and buyers). In the mid-1990s, investors in the Atlantic LNG project pioneered a new model driven by the realities of the US market. Atlantic's project structure was designed with the flexibility to direct cargoes to either Spain or the United States (via the Everett terminal in Boston). The driver would be gas demand in Spain, where prices – as in the rest of continental Europe – remained linked to oil. The United States would take cargoes essentially when Spain did not want or need them. Such an arrangement was critically dependent on the unique liquidity provided by the US gas market. Active trading on the US gas futures exchange (the New York Mercantile Exchange or NYMEX) allowed US buyers to procure gas to fill any gaps created by LNG cargoes diverted to Spain.[3]

When Atlantic LNG began operations in 1999 it created an active arbitrage market between the United States and Europe, and the Trinidad model has since been replicated by other sellers, mainly serving the Atlantic basin. Cargo swaps in the Pacific are also growing in number in response to market volatility created by unexpected changes in demand, such as during the 1998 Asian financial crisis, the shutdown of Indonesia's Arun LNG plant in 2001 due to civil unrest in province Aceh and during Japan's nuclear crisis in 2003.

Second, over the 1990s especially, LNG has been subject to concentrated technological and commercial innovation that has sharply lowered the cost of moving gas from distant fields to its final users. The improvements are evident in every link of the LNG train, and the total reduction in cost is perhaps as much as one-third in just one decade with trends suggesting continued gains. Some of the improved economic performance has come through removal of "gold plating" that was required by Japanese buyers who imposed certain rules in an effort to raise security, but most of the improvement is a reflection of true innovation. Some of this innovation improved existing processes; some of it allowed the realization of substantial economies of scale (Jensen 2003). As discussed in chapter 9, these cost reductions were critical to developing LNG projects to serve the robust US gas market.

---

[3] For more on this model and the host of innovations—organizational, financial, technological, and political—that made the Trinidad LNG project feasible, see chapter 9. For more on contracting in LNG and the likely development of inter-regional arbitrage see, for example, Jensen (2003, 2004).

Finally, the disintegration of ownership in the LNG value chain has created potential opportunities for middlemen to emerge to take on the risks of buying LNG at the point of export and creating flexible, market-related opportunities for delivery based on immediate market conditions. But heady visions common in the late 1990s of a completely atomized LNG value chain and purely spot market trading have largely disappeared. In part, this vision collapsed with the dwindling of the merchant energy business that intended to be its main market-maker. The promise and much of the capitalization of these merchant companies largely disintegrated in the wake of the Enron accounting and other trading scandals. Some merchant groups such as Tractabel (now Suez LNG) remain, but in large measure, the global gas business is back squarely in the hands of the international energy majors who remained the only players with the strong financial capabilities, global operations, long-term vision, and established relationships with national oil companies in natural gas-producing nations. New LNG projects are risky and costly – requiring, typically, capital investments of $5–$8 billion. The scale of such ventures explains, in part, why the shift to a truly oil-like liquid commodity market will be longer in coming. Nonetheless, integrated major LNG companies have opted to keep some sales volumes from new projects available for spot trading, which is a sign of the rising importance of this activity.

To date, spot trades of LNG cargoes occur relatively infrequently. Historically, LNG was priced off the oil and oil products that it displaced in the offtake market. Japan, as the dominant player in LNG markets, prices its imports via an explicit linkage to a basket of imported petroleum, an index dubbed the "Japanese Crude Cocktail" or (JCC). While the exact indexes and contract terms vary (see chapters 3, 4, and 8), this model continues to be the general rule for most LNG trade around the world. LNG buyers purchase gas inclusive of all transit costs, on c.i.f. (cost-insurance-freight) terms.[4]

The development of a robust market in spot LNG trading will require more standardized pricing mechanisms for LNG cargoes – essential to allowing financial intermediaries to participate more freely in the market. Such structures will likely require the movement to contract structures which explicitly separate the price of LNG at the loading port (sometimes dubbed freight-on-board, or f.o.b.). Currently, most spot trading that occurs is priced off the US NYMEX, owing to the unique depth and

---

[4] Japanese contracts typically dub this pricing arrangement as "destination ex-ship," or d.e.s. A few small Indonesian sales contracts to Japanese buyers do include explicit charges for shipping, thus pricing the LNG pre-shipping.

liquidity of the US market, particularly at Henry Hub. As a larger more global spot market develops, there will likely be additional liquid points for arbitrage (such as Zeebrugge in Europe). Already, there is a market for financial swaps settlements for LNG deliveries – a critical first step in this transition to a more efficient, commoditized marketplace. Over time, total shipments and flexible capacity will continue to grow, driving convergence in prices between regional gas markets, adjusted for transit cost differences.

In most markets – including the largest gas market in North America and the second-largest in Western Europe – LNG plays a small role today. The available spare LNG supply and import capacity are far from the size that would be needed for LNG to force a truly global convergence in gas prices in the near future. But over three decades – the time horizon of this study – it seems likely that the elements of a truly global gas market will come into place.

The focus of this book

The study presented in this book adds a new element to the literature on gas trading through our systematic attention to the interplay between political and institutional forces, on the one hand, and technological and economic opportunity, on the other. Of course, the future for gas is hardly a new topic. There is a large literature on energy scenarios, most of which envision a growing role for gas.[5] In addition to global scenarios, some studies have focused on special regional issues, such as emerging gas grids in Asia.[6] Some projects of special geopolitical interest have also attracted attention, such as the various hypothetical pipeline projects envisioned to China and to India,[7] as well as the Cold War projects that exported gas from the Soviet Union to Western Europe and Russia's special role in gas markets today.[8] Many studies focus on "game-changing" technologies and their possible consequences – today, the literature on such technologies in gas has disproportionately focused on LNG,[9] although "gas-to-liquids" (GTL) technology is also attracting

---

[5] The studies referred to here are (EIA 2004); IEA (2004); Shell International (2002); and IIASA–WEC (1998).

[6] See APERC's studies, at http://www.ieej.or.jp/aperc/. See also the James A. Baker III Institute studies, at http://www.riceedu/projects/baker/Pubs/workingpapers/naturalgas/index.html, and also Klaasen, McDonald and Zhao (2000).

[7] See, for example, Paik (2002) and also the review of the south Asian pipeline options in chapter 7.

[8] For example, see Stern (1980, 1986); Blinken (1987); Stern (2005).

[9] Yergin and Stoppard (2003); for a sobering and (we think) more accurate assessment of the potentials in LNG see Jensen (2003).

attention, as that could allow gas to compete with oil for liquid transportation fuels. Finally, a specialized literature on the investors' perspectives has emerged – an important perspective, as it is private capital increasingly deployed for such projects.[10]

Our methods are two-fold. First, our research team has looked to the lessons of history with the aid of seven case studies, shown in table 1.1 and the map in figure 1.4. We selected our sample with an eye to the factors that we thought were likely to have a large impact on which projects would attract investment. For example, the selection of seven cases includes some where the state played a central role in orchestrating investment and others where private firms led the effort. They include some pipeline projects that linked source and user directly, as well as those that involved transit countries, in an effort to probe whether routes that require transit across third nations pose particularly severe risks. Our studies include LNG and pipeline projects in an effort to probe the differences and similarities in those two clusters of technologies that have quite different investment and operating characteristics. We have selected cases where external institutions – such as international development banks – played a large role and those where they were absent, in an effort to see whether problems of enforcing state-to-state agreements that have often underpinned large international gas projects might be eased with a third party's help.

Chapter 2, which opens part II of this book, offers more detail on the questions that guide our historical research, their importance in the literature, and the methods we deployed to select and conduct the case studies. The case studies themselves are presented in chapters 3–9, and a synthesis of the main findings from history is reported in chapter 10. The latter chapter gives particular attention to the roles for government support and long-term contracts as keystones for investment in gas projects. Traditionally, large international gas projects were the results of state-to-state agreements, where governments provided the financing and often even owned (or controlled) the companies that built and operated the pipeline or LNG infrastructures. Over the last three decades that model has changed; the role of the private sector has grown, and private investors have increasingly relied on contracts to mitigate the

---

[10] See ESMAP (World Bank 1999; ESMAP (2003); see also IEA's efforts, at http://www.iea.org/about/gas.htm. In addition, a much broader and earlier literature exists on investment in infrastructure and the difficulties of investing where contracts are poorly enforced. Raymond Vernon's early work was on the challenges faced by investors in foreign markets; see especially Vernon (1971). More recently, scholars have looked at the institutional barriers to foreign investment (see Levy and Spiller 1994; Henisz 2002; World Bank 2004).

Table 1.1 *Seven historical case studies, with brief descriptions*

Case study (chapter)	Description
3 The Transmed and Maghreb Projects: Gas to Europe from North Africa	The Transmed pipeline from Algeria to Italy advanced in the late 1970s, while a similar project to Spain did not move forward until fifteen years later. This chapter discusses how energy markets in Italy and Spain influenced the decisions to proceed on the Transmed rather than an earlier version of the Maghreb. How did relations with transit countries (Tunisia vs. Morocco) explicitly or implicitly affect the choices available to Algeria as an exporter? What were the key political, institutional and economic factors in Algeria, transit countries, and offtake markets? What changed that allowed the Maghreb to be built in 1996?
4 Liquefied Natural Gas from Indonesia: The Arun Project	In 1978, the Arun Project began shipping LNG across the South China Sea to Japan. The Arun gas could have been utilized for domestic consumption, shipments to the United States were discussed, and a pipeline to Singapore was probably technically feasible at the time. This chapter examines the factors affecting the ultimate decision to advance the Japanese contract, the obstacles that prevented the most likely alternative use for this gas, and the mechanisms used to complete the project.
5 Bypassing Ukraine: Exporting Russian Gas to Germany and Poland	This study analyzes the decision by Russian gas exporters to advance the Belarus Connector (BC) pipeline (also known as "Yamal–Europe") in the 1990s, rather than two alternative projects: (1) expansion of Ukrainian pipeline capacity, or (2) direct export to Germany (and further West) via a sub-Baltic pipeline, bypassing transit countries. The analytical focus of the case study is on the role of transit countries (i.e. Ukraine, Belarus, and Poland) and the shift from monopolistic offtaker to a more market-oriented system in international transportation projects (using the example of Germany).
6 Natural Gas pipelines in the Southern Cone	Large reserves in Argentina and Bolivia were identified in the 1950s and 1960s. In 1972, the YABOG pipeline linked Bolivia to Argentina and demonstrated the feasibility of international pipelines in the region. This study examines a cluster of pipelines built in the late 1990s in the Southern Cone of South America (especially pipelines from Bolivia to Brazil and Argentina to

Chile) and explores the factors that prevented these projects from moving forward earlier.

During the 1990s, Turkmenistan sought alternatives to exporting gas through the Russian pipeline network, engaging in discussions with Iran and Afghanistan and several private investors on possible export alternatives. To date, only a small gas export pipeline to Iran has been constructed. The case explores the key political, institutional, and economic factors that have yielded the current outcome.

Qatargas, the first Qatari LNG export project, was completed in 1996. But Qatar's massive natural gas reserves were well known in the early 1980s. This study investigates why this project was not completed five, ten, or fifteen years sooner and explores the major policy shifts that rendered Qatar a premiere developer of LNG export capacity. The case also looks at what contractual structures were required to overcome obstacles to Qatargas' completion and why LNG was selected over regional and extended pipeline projects.

This case explores the factors that permitted the Atlantic LNG project in Trinidad & Tobago to beat other alternative projects to supply the Northeast US gas market. Alternative supply options at the time were LNG from Nigeria, LNG from Venezuela, or expanded pipeline supply to the United States from the Canadian Maritimes. The case will focus specific attention on the innovations in LNG project structures that occurred from the beginning of the first train in Trinidad to the start of trains two and three.

risks of such international projects. We find that this shift has favored governments that have been able to signal credibly that they offer an attractive and stable context for private investment. Part of that context includes the ability to make and sustain long-term contracts and other provisions (e.g. tax regimes) that affect the financial returns from gas projects.

Second, in part III of this book (chapters 11–13), the research team looks to the future, with the aid of an economic model of global natural gas markets. The model allows analysis of future gas trade flows based on solely commercial considerations including supply costs, cost of capital, level of economic development, and competition with alternative

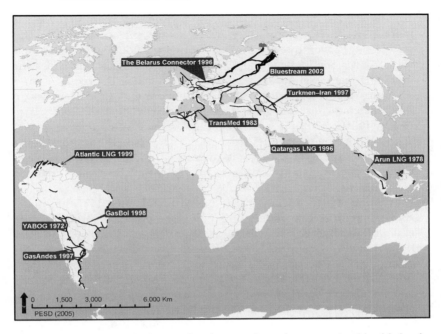

Figure 1.4. The international gas trade projects examined in this book. The Belarus Connector (BC) and Blue Stream are included in chapter 5. YABOG, GasBol, and GasAndes are included in chapter 6.

fuels. A base run – presented in chapter 11 – shows the results of this purely commercial and technological view of world gas. It illustrates how global gas markets may develop over the coming thirty years and predicts, under certain conditions, the future supply sources for natural gas to various end-use markets. Among the conclusions of the model is that Russia plays a pivotal role – not just because it holds vast gas resources but also because it sits astride the large European and emerging Chinese markets and can also deliver LNG to the United States. For LNG exporters, the Middle East emerges over the long term as an important swing producer, with large reserves and geographically positioned to supply US, European, and Asian markets with LNG.

The model also offers a starting point for analysis of geopolitical factors that could affect possible futures of the gas business. Chapter 12 includes the results from a series of scenarios that show the response in gas trading to four geopolitical and economic factors that the historical case studies have revealed to be of considerable importance:

- *Investor risk* The case studies demonstrate that control over gas markets is shifting from governments to the private sector. In this new setting, governments compete to provide a context that is attractive to investors in new supply projects. To reflect this shift, the modeling team examines a "reference case" where the required rates of return are adjusted according to political and economic risk in different countries. We use data from the *International Country Risk Guide* (ICRG 2002), a widely cited assessment of country risk, and World Bank data on country risk premia. The results show how, in the real world, capital for gas projects migrates to countries that are able to combine the availability of gas resources with a hospitable investor environment.

- *Geopolitical supply shocks* In the base run (chapter 11), the model shows outcomes that reflect only commercial considerations; in the real world, however, the fate of major projects also depends on relations between countries. The historical case studies show, for example, how the timing of projects in South America was conditioned strongly by the political relations between gas supplying nations and importers (see chapter 6). To illustrate the sensitivity of trading relationships to such factors, the modeling team examines one illustrative scenario. Pipelines from Russia to Northeast Asia are forbidden – a reflection of political barriers that could prevent the construction of pipelines to ship Russian gas to China and South Korea. As a result, demand for gas in China and South Korea is increasingly satisfied by LNG imports, drawing cargoes that might otherwise go to US or other Pacific basin markets, with corresponding impacts on gas prices throughout the region and world.

- *Demand and technology shocks* The modeling team illustrates the sensitivity of results to different scenarios for critical economic and technological parameters. In one scenario, they examine economic growth in China that is higher than in the base run. In a second scenario, they examine the possible effects on gas markets from more rapid technological innovation that cuts the cost of alternatives to gas (e.g. solar power, coal gasification, or nuclear power).

Chapter 13 examines the prospects for a natural gas export cartel, building on the model scenario results. Importing and exporting countries alike are increasingly sensitive to the prospects for a gas cartel, akin to the cartel for oil, and many members of OPEC are participating in the nascent Gas Exporting Countries Forum (GECF). The authors examine whether a cartel might be organized through the timing of projects, rather than the withholding of short-term supplies and the maintenance of spare capacity, which are the main devices used by OPEC. The high capital cost of gas export projects – notably LNG projects – means that there will be very strong pressure to run projects at capacity rather than to tune operations according to the whims of a cartel. Such pressures will be especially strong where private capital is deployed and where the host countries have large populations that will press for immediate benefits from gas resources rather than distant and uncertain gains from a cartel. Moreover, even if a substantial core group of gas exporters were formed into a cartel, a large competitive fringe (along with competition from non-gas fuels such as advanced coal technologies for electric generation) will make it hard to sustain the cartel, at least during the next two decades. Over the longer horizon, the prospects for a gas cartel improve as the concentration of supply grows over time; however, the prospects for such a cartel also depend on whether new competitively priced clean energy sources, especially for generating electric power, emerge to compete effectively with natural gas.

Conclusion

To a large degree, a rapid shift to a world economy that is increasingly powered by gas will not be constrained by resources or technology. Gas resources are abundant; the technology for extracting and moving them to distant markets is in the midst of a steady revolution that is improving performance and cost. High gas prices in recent years are not evidence that economically attractive sources of gas are limited. Rather, recent high prices signal the need for massive investment in infrastructures that can deliver low cost gas supplies to market. The technological and economic viability of gas is well founded; the central issues are political and institutional.

This study offers a systematic examination of the geopolitical and institutional factors that will shape (in many places, determine) the future of the gas business. We will not address in-depth many of the micro factors that currently dominate discussions about the future of gas, such as technical questions on the safety and siting of LNG terminals. Such issues are important, but our focus is on the long term and on the broad contours of the likely and possible evolution of the industry in its geopolitical context.

We shall show that visions of an expanding role for gas are feasible; however, actual patterns of investment will likely deviate from straight commercial considerations. The ability of governments to assure each other that internationally traded supplies are secure – and their ability to assure private investors about the credibility of promises on taxation and other elements of long-term contracts – will have a significant effect on actual trading patterns. Compared to oil, gas is more capital-intensive; project time horizons are longer; wariness about uncertain political environments appears to be greater. And, unlike oil, gas projects will be exposed to a greater discipline due to the wider array of competing fuels for electric power generation, which is the main expected use for gas growth; oil, by contrast, is still the unrivalled king of energy sources for mobility. The risks to gas investors will place a special premium on countries that are able to combine large gas resources with political and economic environments that are conducive to long-term capital investments.

The study will also debunk several of the "energy security myths" that are likely to rise to the policy forefront with growing dependence on imported gas. Among those is the assumption that long-term contracts create security for investors and governments; we shall show several instances where such contracts have, in fact, not held. We expect to see growing worries about the prospects for a gas exporters' cartel much like OPEC; this study examines such concerns and finds that such a grouping will be hard to sustain in the immediate term but may emerge over time with the right conditions. As a global gas market emerges and gas supplies become more flexible, the fungibility of supply could enhance security, but whether this potential advantage is realized will depend, in part, on achieving robust investment in gas transport infrastructures.

Although we find that visions for a robust shift to gas are credible, it is far from certain that the full potential for natural gas will be realized over the next three decades. Gas resources are plentiful and industry can, in principle, deliver the needed volumes. In the final chapter 14, in part IV, we return to this question and identify some of the most severe obstacles on the horizon that could stall gas growth. Prominent among them is uncertainty surrounding the organization of the electric power sector, which is expected to be the largest user of gas. In many countries, the power sector is in the midst of reforms – and, in general, those reforms have been halting. With the confidence of private investors shaken, the key advantages for gas – a relatively clean and economic option for generating electricity – may erode as well.

REFERENCES

Blinken, Antony J. (1987). *Ally versus Ally: America, Europe, and the Siberian Pipeline Crisis*. New York: Praeger
BP (2004). *Statistical Review of World Energy*, available at http://www.bp.com

Castaneda, Christopher J. (1999). *Invisible Fuel: Manufactured and Natural Gas in America, 1800–2000.* New York: Twayne

CEDIGAZ (2000). "CEDIGAZ news report September 2000" (November 16, 2001). http://www.ifp.fr/TXT/CE/CE400TH2.html

Darmstadter, Joel, Perry D. Teitelbaum, and Jaroslav G. Polach (1971). *Energy in the World Economy: A Statistical Review of Trends in Output, Trade, and Consumption since 1925.* Baltimore: the Johns Hopkins Press Resources for the Future

EIA (2004). "International energy outlook 2004." Washington, DC: US Energy Information Administration

(2005). "International Energy Annual 2003.' Washington, DC: US Energy Information Administration; available at http://www.eia.doe.gov

ESMAP (2003). "Cross-border oil and gas pipelines: problems and prospects." Washington, DC: Joint UNDP/World Bank Energy Sector Management Assistance Programme, p. 130

Henisz, Witold Jerzy (2002). *Politics and International Investment: Measuring Risks and Protecting Profits.* Northampton, MA: Edward Elgar

ICRG (2002). *International Country Risk Guide.* Political Risk Services (IBC USA, Inc.). New York: International Reports

IEA (2003a). *World Energy Investment Outlook (WEIO) 2003.* Paris: International Energy Agency

(2003b). "Historical gas statistics." Paris: International Energy Agency

(2004). *World Energy Outlook (WEO).* Paris: International Energy Agency

IIASA–WEC (1998). *Global Energy Perspectives*, N. Nakicenovic, A. Grübler, and A. McDonald (eds.). Cambridge: Cambridge University Press

Jensen, James T. (2003). "The LNG revolution." *Energy Journal*, 242, pp. 1–45.

(2004). *A Global LNG Market: Is It Likely and if so, When?* Oxford: Oxford Institute for Energy Studies

Klaasen, G., A. McDonald, and J. Zhao (2000). "The future of gas infrastructures in Eurasia." *Energy Policy*, 29, pp. 399–413

Levy, Brian and Pablo T. Spiller (1994). "The institutional foundations of regulatory commitment: a comparative analysis of telecommunications regulation." *Journal of Law, Economics, and Organization*, 102, pp. 201–246

L'Hagert, Guilliame, Boris Silverstova, and Christian von Hirschhausen (2004). *International Market for Natural Gas? A Cointegration Analysis of Prices in Europe, North America, and Japan.* Cambridge, MA: MIT Center for Energy and Environmental Research

Paik, Keun-Wook (2002). "Natural gas expansion in Korea", p. 188–229 in I. Wybrew-Bond and J. P. Stern (eds.), *Natural Gas in Asia: The Challenges of Growth in China, India, Japan, and Korea.* Oxford, Oxford University Press

Peebles, Malcolm W. (1980). *Evolution of the Gas Industry.* New York: New York University Press

Shell International (2002). "Global scenarios to 2020: energy needs, choices and possibilities." Royal Dutch Shell, Inc.; available at http://www.Shell.com

Stern, Jonathan P. (1980). *Soviet Natural Gas Development to 1990: The Implications for the CMEA and the West.* Lexington, MA: Lexington Books

(1986). *International Gas Trade in Europe: The Policies of Exporting and Importing Countries.* Aldershot: Gower

(2005). *The Future of Russian Gas and Gazprom.* Oxford: Oxford University Press

USGS (2000). "World petroleum assessment." Washington, DC: United States Geological Survey

Vernon, Raymond (1971). *Sovereignty at Bay: The Multinational Spread of US Enterprises.* New York: Basic Books

World Bank (1999). "Natural gas: private sector participation and market development." Washington, DC: World Bank Group

(2004). *Reforming Infrastructure: Privatization, Regulation, and Competition.* Washington, DC: World Bank Group

Yergin, Daniel and Michael Stoppard (2003). "The next prize." *Foreign Affairs,* November–December

Part II

Historical case studies

2 Introduction to the historical case studies: research questions, methods, and case selection

Mark H. Hayes and David G. Victor

International transport of gas on a large scale is hardly a new phenomenon; since 1970, especially, governments and private investors have chosen to build and operate ever-larger gas trade projects, involving both pipelines and trains of tankers hauling LNG. This part of the book (chapters 2–10) looks to that historical experience to glean useful lessons about the factors that determine where governments and private firms have built international gas projects. In Part III, (chapters 11–13) we look to the future, building on our insights on the factors that affect expansion of gas trade infrastructures with economic models to project the development of global gas trade over the coming decades.

In probing history, we have focused on projects that extend outside the sphere of the advanced industrialized nations. If gasifying the world involved building more projects such as the pipelines that export gas from Canada to the United States, or from Norway and the Netherlands to the rest of Europe, the barriers to gasification and the geopolitical consequences of new interconnections would be few. Governments and firms have demonstrated ample interest in building and managing risks in such projects, and the advanced industrialized nations are already richly interconnected in myriad ways. What makes the shift to gas challenging – and potentially seismic in geopolitical importance – is that it requires securing supplies that originate in, cross and arrive in countries where contracts are difficult to enforce, regulatory systems are immature, and investors have been wary in deploying capital. In such settings, the benefits from gas trade may be difficult to realize. Yet every study that envisions a massive shift to gas – including the model results in Part III of this book – reveals that "risky" countries will play pivotal roles. They include large potential gas suppliers – Russia, Iran, Saudi Arabia, Qatar, Nigeria, Algeria, Indonesia, Venezuela, Trinidad, and Bolivia; key potential transit countries – Ukraine, Turkey, Pakistan, and Chile; and new centers for potential gas demand – the rapidly growing economies of China, India, and Korea. In looking to history for lessons, we focus on projects that are most relevant to investing in such settings.

This chapter outlines the questions that we aim to answer using the method of historical analysis; we explain the selection of the sample of cases that are presented in chapters 3–9; and we elaborate on methods employed in the case studies to avoid some common pitfalls in such historical research. We have aimed for brevity here; additional detail is presented in Hayes and Victor (2004).

Questions to Answer

Our central aim in these historical studies is to identify the factors – beyond simply technological and economic potential – that explain why certain large-scale gas transport projects are built. In the early stages of this project, we surveyed the literature and canvassed experts, with the aim of identifying the factors that could prove to be powerful explanations for the observed patterns of investment in gas trade projects over the next four decades. That process led us to four factors.[1] Each of the seven case studies focuses on these four factors as well as the more particular aspects of each project and region that ultimately influence the observed outcomes.

First, we focus on the *investment context*. Historically, most countries that are large gas suppliers have put gas projects into the hands of state-owned enterprises (SOEs), such as state petroleum companies. Many countries that are large gas users have also created state firms to manage the distribution and marketing of gas. Where state enterprises dominate, the key contextual factors relate to their financing and interests, as well as to the governments and managers that control them.

In our discussions of key factors, we explored whether the shift in investment context – away from an "old world" where state enterprises dominated to a "new world" where private firms increasingly bear the burden of making investments – affects the locations and types of projects ultimately constructed. In this new world, investment decisions are increasingly guided by relative risks across countries rather than by direct state engagement. Investors contemplating gas trade projects pay particular attention to the "sunk cost" nature of the capital investment in these fixed infrastructures, which requires long periods of predictable

---

[1] An outline of the research protocol for the case studies was presented at a meeting of academic and industry experts in November 2002 (PESD 2002). The current selection of factors and study design reflects feedback from that meeting and subsequent revision. The IEA and the World Bank listed similar concerns in recent publications and conferences on the subject. See in particular (Appert 2002; ESMAP 2003).

operation to recover the original investment and to yield acceptable returns. Long-term contracts therefore usually play a central role in such projects. However, the balance of bargaining power that existed at the time of contract negotiation shifts to favor the offtakers or regulators once the infrastructure is built, a condition referred to as the "obsolescing bargain" (Vernon 1971). Thus, investors pay attention to the enforceability of contracts, the stability of the business environment and tax codes, and exposure to regulatory takings – factors often loosely lumped together as the "rule of law" – as well the factors that are particular to individual deals, such as the rights for repatriation of profits and provisions for managing exchange rate risks.[2]

Second, preliminary evidence suggested that *transit countries* can present a significant obstacle to creating viable cross-border gas pipelines. Many pipeline routes involve one or more of these transit points, which may complicate the task of negotiating original deals and create additional risks for the enterprises that operate the project once their capital is sunk.[3] To date, no major LNG projects have involved transit countries; although LNG tankers ply the territorial waters of transit nations, in most cases they have a variety of routes available should a transit country aim to hold up a trading project. However, a few LNG projects contemplated for the future would involve transit countries – for example, Bolivian LNG exports could involve pipeline transit via the West (e.g. Chile) or East (Brazil).

Third, project investors may have special concerns about *offtake market risks*. Risks arise around both the quantity and price of the gas that can be sold from a given pipeline or LNG project. Success in introducing large quantities of gas into immature offtake markets depends on large complementary investments by potential customers in gas-using technologies. Gas suppliers (and buyers) are also exposed to variations in price, depending on the particular contractual and regulatory arrangements. Preliminary evidence suggested that the uncertainty and risks for new gas project sales were particularly acute where the infrastructure for utilizing gas was poorly developed. In such instances, there is considerable uncertainty about whether the necessary

---

[2] A large body of extant literature has demonstrated the importance of stable legal and political institutions for attracting private and foreign investment. Henisz (2002) provides an overview of work in the field: For particular reference to infrastructures, Levy and Spiller (1994) demonstrate the impact of institutions on investment in telecommunications grids. No comparable empirical work has tested the impact of "investment climate" on the decisions to sink capital in natural gas trade infrastructures.

[3] The additional complexity introduced by transit countries is discussed by ESMAP (2003) and many other sources.

investments in gas-using technology will be made, how gas prices will be regulated, and the rate of growth in end-use gas demand relative to the volumes delivered from the proposed project and other new supplies.

Fourth, governments and private investors alike may be attuned to the *geopolitical relationship* between supply, transit, and offtake countries. If the countries have already developed a broader relationship – through, for example, trade and cross-investment – then the state-to-state agreements that back gas projects may be easier to sustain and governments may be willing to intervene to prevent unattractive outcomes. However, where such inter-state relationships do not exist, governments may be willing to use their market power to drive up prices or cut off supplies for political purposes; wariness of this " gas weapon" may lead some investors and governments to shun projects that might expose them to unpredictable neighbors. We particularly explored whether international institutions could help ease problems of international coordination by reducing transaction costs and building confidence. The absence of institutions can be both symptom and cause of the inability to make investments in collective infrastructures.

These four factors – investment climate, transit countries, offtake risks, and geopolitical relationships – are broad. As the case studies show, each project is replete with many complicated and important factors that explain ultimate outcomes. Yet we have identified these four broad factors often cited by experts, so that we can ensure the cases selected for historical analysis will cover the range of relevant explanations and thus be appropriate for discussion of possible futures.[4]

Selection of Cases

Selection of cases from the historical set of cross-border gas trade projects is a three-step process. First, we must identify the key supply countries, transit routes, and prospective gas importers that are implied in future scenarios for high consumption of natural gas. Second, we seek to identify the full universe of historical studies relevant to the types of countries and trading relationships that are likely to prevail in the future. Third, we select a sample from that universal set. In-depth analysis of each case requires immense attention to detail to unravel complex

---

[4] For those concerned with research methodology, we refrain here from fully developing hypotheses for the effect of each of these "factors" on the selection or rate of investment in gas-trade projects. Rather, we posit only that these are important factors, based on both academic and trade literature. In turn, these factors are used to select and guide research on the historical cases. We revisit these four factors in the conclusion of chapter 10.

pathways of cause and effect. Thus, it is only practical to examine a relatively small number of cases, and the selection of which historical projects to study becomes extremely important. Any biases in that selection could skew our results.

The first step is to look at the trading relationships that are likely to be essential to realizing a global shift to gas. That task is not easy to fulfill. If we knew which broad factors were most important in determining gas investments, then we could include such factors in techno-economic models and identify the most important trading relationships. The study reported in this book exists because we don't know which factors are critical, and thus the selection of case studies must begin with plausible estimates of the new gas trading relationships that are likely to be vital for a vision of world gasification. Table 2.1 shows our estimate, which we derived by looking at the estimates for rising demand and inter-regional trade reported in the International Energy Agency's *World Energy Outlook (WEO) 2002* (IEA 2002); we then checked those broad expectations against the model results that are detailed in chapters 11 and 12.

Our aim in table 2.1 is to represent typical projects, not to offer excessive detail on what is, *a priori*, an unpredictable phenomenon. We are mindful that typical projections, such as from the WEO, offer only regional patterns that obscure the particular trading routes between projected demand centers and the locations of gas reserves at the sub-regional level. Our interest here is focused on cross-border trade. In defining the types of countries that will be critical to future gas trade development, table 2.1 shows our selections of representative countries from within each WEO region.

Next, we identified four simple "proxy" variables that correspond broadly with the four main factors identified earlier, and we assign values to the proxy variables for each of the typical future trading relationships (table 2.1). This process of looking at the characteristics of *future* projects is essential to inform our selection of *historical* case studies. The historical case studies were chosen from a set broadly representative of the range of factors that, we hypothesize, will determine where (and if) future gas-trade projects are to be built. Hayes and Victor (2004) offer extensive detail on the proxy variables and their coding for both prospective and historical case studies. Briefly, the four variables are:

- *Investment context* We use a composite of scores from the *International Country Risk Guide* (ICRG 2002), a widely known source of investment risk information for foreign investors. Our composite

Table 2.1 *Projected major inter-regional trade and representative country routes*

Trading regions (from IEA–WEO) Supply country	Transit countries	Offtake countries	Pipe/ LNG	Investment climate (GIRI, 0–10)	Gas share of primary energy (2003) (%)	Strength of institution for Economic Cooperation (0–5)	Institution referenced
1 Transition economies –> OECD Europe							
(a) Russia						3	ECE
	Belarus		Pipe	5.5			
	Poland		Pipe	5.5			
			Pipe	7.7			
		Germany	Pipe	8.8	22		
(b) Russia			Pipe	5.5		3	ECE
	None	Turkey	Pipe	5.7	17		
2 OECD Europe –> OECD Europe							
Norway			Pipe	9.2		5	EFTA
	None	Germany	Pipe	8.8	22		
3 Middle East –> OECD Europe							
Iran			Pipe	5.8		2	ECO
	None	Turkey	Pipe	5.7	17		
4 Africa –> OECD Europe							
Algeria			Pipe	4.7		0	None
	Morocco		Pipe	7.4			
	Spain		Pipe	8.3			
		Spain	Pipe	8.3	12		
		Portugal	Pipe	8.3	21		

		Mode				
5 Transition Economies -> China						
(a) Russia None		Pipe	5.5		0	None
	China	Pipe	6.5	3		
(b) Kazakhstan none		Pipe	6.5		0	None
	China	Pipe	6.5	3		
6 Transition Economies -> South Asia						
Turkmenistan Afghanistan	Pipe	Pipe	NA		0	None
Pakistan		NA				
	Pakistan	Pipe	5.1	42		
	India	Pipe	5.1	8		
		Pipe	6.1			
7 Middle East -> South Asia						
Iran Pakistan		Pipe	5.8		0	None
		Pipe	5.1			
	Pakistan	Pipe	5.1	42		
	India	Pipe	6.1	8		
8 North America -> North America						
Canada None	United States	Pipe	8.9		5	NAFTA
	United States	Pipe	8.7	26		
9 Latin America -> North America						
Venezuela None	United States	LNG	4.3		2	OAS
	United States	LNG	8.7	26		
10 Africa -> North America						
Nigeria None	United States	LNG	2.8		0	None
	United States	LNG	8.7	26		

Table 2.1 (*cont.*)

Trading regions (from IEA–WEO) Supply country	Transit countries	Offtake countries	Pipe/ LNG	Investment climate (GIRI, 0–10)	Gas share of primary energy (2003) (%)	Strength of institution for Economic Cooperation (0–5)	Institution referenced
11 Middle East –> North America							
Iran			LNG	5.8		0	None
	None	United States	LNG	8.7	26		
12 Latin America –> Latin America							
(a) Bolivia			Pipe	5.8	6	3	Mercosur
	None	Brazil	Pipe	5.5			
(b) Argentina			Pipe	5.3		3	Mercosur
	None	Chile	Pipe	8.0	24		
13 Africa –> Africa							
Mozambique			Pipe	5.4		3	SADC
	None	South Africa	Pipe	5.5	1		
14 Middle East –> OECD Pacific							
Iran			LNG	5.8		0	None
	None	Japan	LNG	9.0	14		

score combines ICRG's scores for government stability, investment profile, internal conflict, corruption, law and order, ethnic tensions, and bureaucratic quality – what we call the "General Investment Risk Index (GIRI)," with possible values ranging from 0-10.[5]

- *Transit countries* We simply code the number of transit countries involved in a project – zero where country A sells gas directly to country B, one where a pipeline passes through a country *en route* to its destination etc.

- *Offtake market risk* We assign a value to each case study based on the fraction of gas in the total primary energy supply of the offtake country in 2003, as reported in BP (2004). Admittedly, this measure does not incorporate market rules or pricing considerations that are important determinants in driving project decision-making (especially those that are privately funded). However, simple measures of these more complex issues are not readily available for our purposes of assessing such risks in cross-border gas trading. Thus, we use the more readily available gas market share data and leave the more complex analysis to the historical case studies. In looking forward here to setting bounds on the range of variables we should be interested in studying, we include both virgin and more developed gas-using markets. We are interested in how investment will be realized in potential supply countries that will serve both developing and developed markets.

- *Geopolitical relationships* There is no simple measure of such relationships, so we focus on the presence of collective institutions that are both indicators of and aids to longer-term stable relationships between potential gas-trading nations. Using a scale of zero to 5, we offer high scores to institutions such as the North American Free Trade Agreement (NAFTA) that integrate a wide array of activities and offer, in part, mechanisms for enforcement of obligations. We offer a zero score for projects that span countries with no current institutional interconnections – for example, a project connecting Iran to India and transiting Pakistan.[6]

---

[5] Unstable countries with virtually no government such as Somalia had a GIRI of 2.3, while Sweden had a GIRI 9.4. For more detail on coding of all variables, see appendix A of Hayes and Victor (2004).

[6] More on the subjective assignment of values for strength of geopolitical relationship can be found in Hayes and Victor (2004). The quantification of these variables also allows us to set somewhat objective standards for the types of gas-trade routes that we exclude from this study – namely, those involving trade entirely within the advanced industrialized nations where investors are able to secure contracts, governance is relatively

Table 2.2 *Range of relevant values for major projected international gas trade routes*

Variable	Range of values
1. Investment climate (GIRI)	2.8–9.0
2. Number of transit countries	0–2
3. Offtake quantity risk	3%–42%
4. Institutions for cooperation	0–3

Source: table 2.1.

For convenience, we have summarized in table 2.2 the range of values for these proxy variables for representative prospective gas-trade projects. In selecting the seven historical case studies for in-depth analysis we ensure that the sample is broadly representative of this range.

The second step is to identify the range of available historical experiences – the "universe of cases." In probing the "universe" of experience we have, again, excluded projects that trade gas entirely within the sphere of advanced industrialized nations. We presume that projects connecting countries with welcoming investment environments are relatively easily conceived, or are constrained by a different set of factors than the focus of this study (see note 6). For this study, a "case" is a large international gas-trade project (pipeline or LNG) that was built at any time from 1970 to the present. Table 2.A in the appendix (p. 44) lists the results of an exhaustive effort to identify all such historical projects, reviewed for completeness by several experts in the field.

Assembling such a list is relatively easy because built projects leave long paper trails. However, simply selecting cases for study from that list

transparent, and robust international institutions are omnipresent. We exclude such "easy" cases from further study. Quantitatively, we have excluded projects that meet the following criteria:

- *Stable investment climate* (all involved countries have GIRI scores greater than 8)
- Relatively strong cooperative institutions (scoring a 4 or 5 in our ranking of institutional strength).

This approach excludes pipeline exports from Canada to the United States as well as pipeline exports from the North Sea fields to Europe. Note that the exclusion of such "easy" cases from table 2.1 does not exclude very much. Some trade routes, such as Russia to OECD Europe, include relatively unattractive investment climates in the supply country (Russia GIRI = 5.5), combined with varying conditions in transit countries (Belarus GIRI = 5.5, Poland GIRI = 7.7), and relatively attractive offtake countries (Germany GIRI = 8.8). Other prospective trade routes span countries with relatively unattractive investment climates in the upstream, transit, and offtake countries (e.g. Turkmenistan, Afghanistan, Pakistan, India).

would bias our sample because the set of built projects is, by definition, strongly shaped by governments and investors who have sought to identify projects that they thought would be successful. In making their decisions about where to sink capital and commitments, they had in mind factors akin to the four main factors we have already identified. Defining a "case" in this way is appropriate only if the goal is to study the factors that affect the construction and operation of a pipeline *after* the decision has been made to invest in the project.[7] Our goal is to probe the factors that explain the *original* decision to invest. Observable outcomes (i.e. built projects) from these decisions represent only a fraction of the possible outcomes.[8] We solve this problem by ensuring that every case selected for study in this project is paired with at least one plausible, but unbuilt, "alternative project," or "AP." For pipelines, the AP is a substantially alternative route, such as a route through

---

[7] For example, the World Bank study, *Removing Obstacles to Cross-Border Oil and Gas Pipelines* (ESMAP 2003) focuses solely on built projects and the "major factors" that led to their successful completion and operation. That study is an invaluable guide to the mechanisms at work within any particular infrastructure investment, and it is not our purpose to reproduce its findings here. However, the approach of selecting already built projects is not valid for analyzing why some deals go forward and others do not. That sample of cases does not, by definition, include any deals that have not gone forward.

[8] We have excluded two other approaches to defining a "case" in a way that would avoid the bias of selecting from built projects. One would involve collecting data on all pipeline and LNG projects that have been technologically and economically feasible and then selecting from that a sample of hypothetical (and built) projects. That approach is infeasible in practice because the array of hypothetical projects is practically infinite, and the tools do not exist to identify that universe objectively. Selecting cases at random from that universe would yield only a very tiny fraction of cases that have been built, and thus such a study would not take us far past the starting point of this project: there is a large array of barriers to constructing gas transportation infrastructures and a large array of techno-economic potentials. A second strategy would appear to be more feasible, but it, too, leads to a dead end. We could catalog all projects for which a MOU was signed or similar declaration to develop a project was made by relevant parties. It is much easier to compile that universe of possible cases because such declarations are usually covered in the trade press. The problem with this approach, however, is that MOUs cost little to compile and are not a proper reflection of the range of possible projects or of the parties' intentions. Moreover, using MOUs as the universe would introduce a bias into the sample that is similar to the bias that exists in starting with "built" projects, as well as possibly additional biases. The sample of MOUs includes a host of possible projects that have been nominated for a host of uncontrolled reasons – political signaling, dreams in particular regions, etc. Mindful of this difficulty, it might be tempting just to select MOUs that had attracted some substantial investment and then try to explain why some went all the way to completion and operation whereas others get stalled. But that route, also, is a dead end because investment in these infrastructures is lumpy – once the investor gets to a certain point they go all the way. We are unaware of any project that gets partially built and then fails; the key decision point lies at the first substantial investment that, once made, is sunk and transforms the project into one dominated by marginal operating costs.

different transit countries or to a different offtake country.[9] In selecting the APs, we focused on three options:

1. The AP is a *pipeline constructed substantially later than the "built" project under study*. The alternative follows a substantially different transit route, and/or flows to a different offtaker. The fact that such a project was built later is often evidence that the project is *technically* feasible; we seek to determine why that project was not constructed earlier and why the "built" project was constructed first. If no such "considered alternative" exists, then we seek to identify the plausible alternative following a second strategy . . .

2. The AP is a *pipeline or LNG project that was the subject of serious attention at the time the built project was negotiated and constructed*. This "plausible alternative" should have a signed memorandum of understanding (MOU), substantial background studies, and if constructed would have involved capital expenditure and operating costs within about 50 percent of the project that was built. The case study seeks to explain why that alternative was not built and why the built project was selected instead. If no such "considered alternative" exists then we seek to identify the plausible alternative following a third strategy . . .

3. The plausible alternative is a *hypothetical pipeline or LNG project* involving capital expenditure and operating costs within about 50 percent of the project that was built. The case study seeks to explain why that alternative was not built and why the built project was selected instead.

In some cases a plausible alternative project may not exist – notably LNG projects in countries that are remote from any center for gas demand. In those cases, it is difficult to get variation in outcomes, although it may be possible to explore in a case study why the LNG project was not built earlier. For example, why did Qatar, sitting on its vast gas reserves that are far from markets yet convenient to the ocean, not build LNG export facilities earlier than 1996?

The third and nearly final step in selecting cases for in-depth study is to select projects that reflect the range of historical experiences and also the range of experiences likely to be relevant for the future. Table 2.3 shows the selection of seven cases, each with an appropriate AP.

Once the "built" historical projects were selected, the AP is selected using either the first, second, or third option described above. Figure 2.1

---

[9] We focus on alternative projects that involve international trade in gas. In practice, an alternative domestic use always exists, although price and quantity may be lower than for international trade.

Table 2.3 *Proposed case study pairs/clusters: built projects selected from the larger "universe of cases"*

Chapter and built/ AP pair or cluster	Description	Investment climate (0–10)	Number of transit countries	Gas as % total primary energy consumption	Strength of Institution for economic cooperation (0–5)
3 *Built Transmed pipeline;* Not built early Maghreb	Gas pipeline built to Italy in 1980; no pipeline built to Spain until 1996; Spain LNG export built in 1976;	5–7	1–2	0–17	0
4 *Built Arun LNG;* Not built Indonesia–Singapore pipeline; Other options included domestic consumption and export to United States	Malaysia–Singapore pipeline completed in 1992	3–9	0	0–3	2
5 *Built Belarus Connector;* Not built Ukrainian expansion or Baltic export pipeline	Series of export options for Russian gas in 1990s	5.5–9.5	0–3	10–20	3
6 *Built Southern Cone pipelines c.a. 1970s;* YABOG built; no other projects for twenty years; built and not built alternatives to supply Chile and Brazil in 1990s	YABOG provides historical context; then in 1990s GasAndes built; Transgas not built; GasBol built; Argentina to Brazil via Uruguay not built	3–8	0–1	0–19	2–4
7 *Built Turkmenistan–Iran 1997;* Not built Trans-Afghan pipeline;		2–7	0–2	7–40	0–2
8 *Built Qatargas 1996;* Not built earlier	Alternative pipeline proposals also analyzed	4.0–8.5	0–2	13–40	0–2
9 *Built Atlantic LNG;* not built Nigeria and Venezuela LNG	Nigeria completed shortly after in 1999.	5.5–9	NA	10–25	0–2

Note:
NA = Not available.

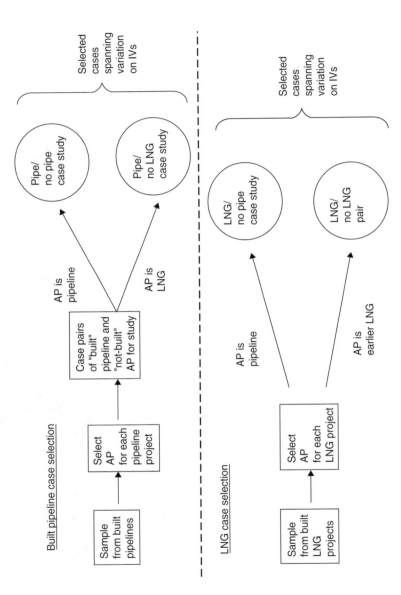

Figure 2.1. Case selection: ensuring variation in outcomes.

Note: AP = Alternative project.

IV = Independent variable. The IVs are the key factors – such as investment context, number of transit countries, offtake market risk, and geopolitical relationships – that we hypothesize are potentially important determinants in affecting whether or not a gas trade project is built. The IVs are represented by the proxy variables shown in table 2.2.

summarizes this approach to defining a case for built pipeline (top panel) and LNG (bottom panel) projects. The plausible alternatives for pipeline projects include LNG terminals and pipelines, while an LNG project is paired with either a plausible pipeline alternative or an alternative LNG export option.

As summarized in table 2.3, the seven cases that are analyzed at great depth in chapters 3–9 largely cover the variation in proxy variables deemed representative of critical future gas-trade projects. Our selection includes pipeline as well as LNG projects. Among the pipeline cases are projects that include no transit countries and projects that span as many as three transit countries. The pipeline projects span the full range of international institutions that we expect to exist in the future: some projects include countries engaged in cooperative trade agreements, and other projects join countries with practically nonexistent inter-govermental institutions. The selected projects also include countries with essentially no gas consumption prior to the construction of the gas-trade project and those with significant gas consumption at the time of project investment (up to 40 percent of total primary energy consumption as gas).

Chapter 3 pairs the Transmed gas pipeline, built in 1980, with an alternative route that later became the Maghreb pipeline in 1996. The case study will seek to explain why a project was chosen in the late 1970s to deliver gas to Italy and Slovenia (i.e. the Transmed project) rather than to Spain (i.e. the Maghreb project). How did energy markets in Italy and Spain influence the decisions to proceed on the Transmed rather than an earlier version of the Maghreb? How did relations with transit countries (Tunisia vs. Morocco) affect the choices available to Algeria as an exporter? What changed that allowed the Maghreb to be built in 1996?

Chapter 4 examines the Arun LNG export project, completed in 1977. LNG from the Arun project was liquefied and shipped across the South China Sea to Japan. The AP for the Arun case is a pipeline to neighboring Singapore – a technically feasible, but unconsidered alternative in the late 1970s. The case study also considers the decision to not utilize the Arun gas for Indonesian domestic consumption, as well as the viability of an actively considered proposal to sell LNG to the United States.

Chapter 5 pairs the Belarus Connector (BC), completed in the 1990s to deliver Russian gas to Poland and Germany, with two alternative projects: (1) expansion of Ukrainian pipeline capacity and (2) direct export to Germany (and further west) via a sub-Baltic pipeline, bypassing transit countries. The analytical focus of the case study will be on the role of transit countries (i.e. Ukraine, Belarus, and Poland) and the shift from monopolistic offtaker to a more market-oriented system in international transportation projects (using the example of Germany).

Chapter 6 examines a cluster of pipelines built in the late 1990s in the Southern Cone of South America (especially the pipelines from Bolivia to Brazil and Argentina to Chile). Large reserves were identified decades earlier in Argentina and Bolivia and a 1972 pipeline linking Bolivia to Argentina demonstrated the feasibility of international pipelines in the region. The study examines the factors that prevented these projects from moving forward earlier and the mechanisms that finally allowed the projects to come to fruition.

Chapter 7 weighs the export options of Turkmenistan in the post-Soviet era. During the 1990s Turkmenistan sought alternatives to its sole option of exporting gas through the Russian pipeline network. The Turkmen government engaged in discussions with Iran and Afghanistan and several private investors on possible export alternatives. Yet, to date, only a small gas export pipeline to Iran has been constructed. The case explores the key political, institutional, and economic factors that have prevented a more lucrative outcome for the gas-rich, but land-locked country.

Chapter 8 considers the timing of Qatargas, the first Qatari LNG export project completed in 1996. Why was this project not completed five, ten, or fifteen years sooner? What unique contractual structures were required to overcome obstacles to its completion? The case also considers proposals for a gas pipeline to ship gas to the neighboring United Arab Emirates (UAE), and potentially on to Pakistan.

Finally, chapter 9 looks at the Atlantic LNG project in Trinidad & Tobago. The case explores the factors that allowed this project to beat alternative projects to supply the Northeast US gas market. Alternative supply options at the time were LNG from Nigeria, LNG from Venezuela, and expanded pipeline supply from the Canadian Maritimes. The case focuses specific attention on the innovations in LNG project structures that occurred from the beginning of train 1 in Trinidad & Tobago to the start of trains 2 and 3.

Methods

Each case study employs in-depth historical analysis to understand why the project was built, and uses APs as a foil to help the authors assess which factors were critical to explaining the observed outcomes.

The first stage of each case study involved working with the author(s) to assess whether the selected AP met the criteria indicated earlier. The final case studies do not report the details on that process. Instead, they focus on the historical record of the built project and the AP. Each case study examines the general investment context in the key countries, the role of the state in managing gas infrastructure investment, provisions for enforcing contracts, the maturity of the gas markets to be served, transit country risks, and the geopolitical relationships among the key countries. In addition, each chapter gives attention to a variety of project-specific factors, such as particular contractual provisions, the specific arrangements for financing, and a host of other factors that are part of any real world assessment of large, costly, and politically visible projects such as gas infrastructures.

The detailed protocol employed in the case research is offered elsewhere (Hayes and Victor 2004). In the final case studies presented here, the authors have removed much of the superstructure from that protocol. They present the cases as histories, and focus their attention on explaining cause and effect. The authors offer their own conclusions on the key factors in their respective cases. In chapter 10 we revisit these key factors to present some general lessons based on our analysis of the entire sample. In turn, those lessons inform the scenarios that are applied to the model in part III of this book, so that we can probe how key lessons from history may mold visions for the future.

APPENDIX : THE UNIVERSE OF CASES

Table 2.A Universe of built projects that involve difficult investment environments (see n. 6)

Project/Type	Source	Destination	Completed (year)	Supply Country	Transit Country	(#1) Investment Climate (GIRI) Rating (1-10)	End-Use Country	Rating (1-10)	(#3) Offtake Quantity Risk — Gas as % of Total Primary Energy Consumption: Country	Pre-Project	(#5) Strength of Institution for Economic Cooperation (0-5)	Institution Referenced in (#5)
1 USSR-Poland Pipeline	USSR	Poland	1950 c.a.	USSR	⋯	NA	Poland	NA	Poland	NA	5	COMECON
2 Afghan-USSR Pipeline	Afghanistan	USSR	"late 1960's"	Afghanistan	⋯	NA	USSR	[4.5]	USSR	NA	0	NA
3 Arrow (Camel GL4Z) LNG	Algeria	UK, later France	1964	Algeria	⋯	NA	UK, later France	[8.5] [2]	UK, later France	0%	0	NA
Algeria-Spain LNG	Algeria	Spain	1969	Algeria	⋯	[4.5]	Spain	[8]	Spain	2%	0	NA
Algeria-U.S. LNG	Algeria	U.S.	1970	Algeria	⋯	[4.5]	U.S	[9]	U.S	32%	0	NA
4 a-Marsa El Brega LNG	Libya	Barcelona, Spain	1971	Libya	⋯	NA	Spain	[6.5]	Spain	0%	0	NA
b-Marsa El Brega LNG	Libya	La Spezia, Italy	1975	Libya	⋯	NA	Italy	[7]	Italy	10%	0	NA
5 IGAT-I Pipeline	Iran	USSR	1970	Iran	⋯	NA	USSR	[4.5]	USSR	NA	0	NA
4 Skikda (GL1K-1) LNG	Algeria	France	1972	Algeria	⋯	NA	France	[8]	France	4%	0	NA
6 Bolivia-Argentina Pipeline	Santa Cruz Fields, Bolivia	Campo Duran, Argentina	1972	Bolivia	⋯	[2.5]	Argentina	[4.0]	Argentina	19%	2	ECLA
7 Lumut LNG	Brunei	Japan	1972	Brunei	⋯	NA	Japan	[9]	Japan	1%	0	NA
8 Transgas Pipeline Network (incl. Brotherhood, Northern Lights & below)												
a - USSR-Czechoslovakia	Shebelinka, Ukraine, West Siberia	Czechoslovakia	1968	USSR	Czechoslovakia [6]	[4.5]	Czechoslovakia, Austria	[6] [9]	Czechoslovakia, Austria	1% 12%	1	ECE
b - TAG-I,II (Trans-Austria-Gasleitung)	West Siberia	Austria	1974	USSR	Czechoslovakia, Austria [6]	[4.5]	Czechoslovakia, Austria, Italy	[6] [9] [7]	Czechoslovakia, Austria, Italy	3% 16% 10%	1	ECE
MEGAL (Mittel-Europäische Gasleitung) **c - USSR-FRG (Ruhrgas)**	West Siberia, West Siberia	Western Europe, FRG	1979 [1], 1974	USSR	Czechoslovakia [6]	[4.5]	Austria, GDR (East Germany), FRG (West Germany)	[9] [7] [8.5]	Austria, GDR, FRG	16% NA 7%	1	ECE
d - USSR-France	West Siberia	France	1976	USSR	Czechoslovakia, FRG [6] [8.5]	[4.5]	FRG, France	[8.5] [8]	FRG, France	11% 10%	1	ECE
9 USSR-Finland Pipeline	Leningrad	Finland	1974	USSR	⋯	[4.5]	Finland	[9.5]	Finland	0%	1	ECE
10 Orenburg ("Soyuz") [1] Pipeline	West Siberia	Eastern Europe	1975	USSR	Czechoslovakia, Romania [6] [4]	[4.5]	Bulgaria, Hungary, Romania	[6] [6] [4]	Hungary, Bulgaria, Romania	18% 1% 52%	5	COMECON

Project/Type	Source	Destination	Completed (year)	(#1) Investment Climate (GRI)[1] Supply Country	Rating (1-10)	Transit Country	Rating (1-10)	End-Use Country	Rating (1-10)	(#3) Offtake Quantity Risk — Gas as % of Total Primary Energy Consumption — Country	Pre-Project	(#5) Strength of Institution for Economic Cooperation (0-5)	Institution Referenced in (#5)
11 Das Island LNG	Abu Dhabi	Japan	1977	Abu Dhabi	[3]	...		Japan	[9]	Japan	2%	0	NA
12 Bontang-Japan LNG	Indonesia	Japan	1977	Indonesia	[3.0]	...		Japan	[9]	Japan	2%	2	ESCAP
13 Arun LNG	Indonesia	Japan, South Korea, Taiwan	1978	Indonesia	[3.0]	...		Japan[7]	9.0	Japan	3%	2	ESCAP
14 Bethioua (G1.1Z) (Near Arzew) LNG	Algeria		1978	Algeria	NA								
15 Bethioua (G1.2Z) (Near Arzew) LNG	Algeria		1981	Algeria	NA								
16 Skikda (G1.1K-1) LNG	Algeria		1981										
Algeria-Belgium LNG	Algeria	Belgium	1982	Algeria	[4.5]	...		Belgium	[9]	Belgium	20%	0	NA
Algeria-Italy LNG	Algeria	Italy	1989	Algeria	[5]	...		Italy	[7]	Italy	17%	0	NA
17 Transmed-1 Pipeline	Algeria	Italy, Slovenia, Tunisia	1983	Algeria[5]	[5]	Tunisia[5]	[5]	Tunisia[8] Italy[9] Slovenia[8]	[5] [7] [5]	Tunisia Italy Slovenia	[10%] 17% [NA]	0	NA
18 Urengoy Pipeline	Urengoy, USSR	West Europe via Czechoslovakia	1985	USSR[6]	[4.5]	Czechoslovakia[6] FRG Austria	[7] [8.5] [9]	Austria-1.5-2.5 bcm/yr [7] FRG-10.5 bcm/yr [8.5] France-6-8 bcm/yr [9] Switzerland-0.36 bcm/yr [9.5] Italy-6 bcm/yr [7]	[9] [8.5] [8] [9.5] [7]	Czechoslovakia Austria FRG[4] France Switzerland Italy	9% 19% 14% 12% 5% 17%	2	ECE
19 USSR-Turkey Pipeline	West Russia	Turkey	1986	USSR	[4.5]	...		Turkey	5.4	Turkey	0%	0	NA
20 Bontang-South Korea LNG	Indonesia	South Korea, Taiwan	1989	Indonesia	2.7	...		South Korea[7]	6.0	South Korea	3%	2	ESCAP
21 Bintulu LNG	Malaysia	Japan, South Korea, Taiwan	1991	Malaysia	5.8	...		Japan[7]	8.1	Japan	11%	2	ESCAP
22 Malaysia-Singapore Pipeline	Peninsular Malaysia	Singapore	1992	Malaysia	5.0	...		Singapore	7.6	Malaysia	0%	2	ASEAN
23 STEGAL Pipeline	Russia	Germany/France	1992	Russia	[6.2]	Czechoslovakia FRG	[7] 9.0	FRG France	9.0 8.3	FRG[4] France	17% 12%	3	ECE

Project/Type	Source	Destination	Completed (year)	(#1) Investment Climate (GIRI)[1]						(#3) Offtake Quantity Risk		(#5) Strength of Institution for Economic Cooperation (0-5)	Institution Referenced in (#5)
				Supply Country	Rating (1-10)	Transit Country	Rating (1-10)	End-Use Country	Rating (1-10)	Gas as % of Total Primary Energy Consumption Country	Pre-Project		
24 Algeria-Turkey LNG	Algeria	Turkey	1994	Algeria	4.0	---		Turkey	6.7	Turkey	8%	0	NA
25 Transmed-2 Pipeline	Algeria	Italy, Slovenia, Tunisia	1995	Algeria	4.0	Tunisia	5.9	Italy / Slovenia	7.2 / 2.2	Tunisia / Italy / Slovenia	[NA] / 27% / [NA]	0	NA
26 Ringpipeline Pipeline	Bulgaria	Macedonia	1995	Russia	4.5	Ukraine, Romania, Bulgaria	4.5 / 5.0 / 6.5	Romania, Bulgaria, Macedonia[a]	5 / 6.5 / 1.9	Ukraine, Romania, Bulgaria, Macedonia	45% / 50% / 17% / [NA]	3	ECE
27 Maghreb Pipeline	Algeria	Spain, Portugal	1996	Algeria	4.3	Morocco	6.5	Spain, Portugal	7.3 / 7.5	Spain, Portugal	7% / 0%	0	NA
28 Methanex-PA Pipeline	Tierra del Fuego	Methanex, Methanol Plant	1996	Argentina	5.3	---		Chile	6.3	Chile	12%	0	NA
29 Qatargas LNG	Qatar	Japan	1996	Qatar	6.6	---		Japan	8.0	Japan	11%	0	NA
30 Yamal-Europe 1 Pipeline	Russia	West Europe	1996	Russia[a]	5.5	Belarus[a], Poland	5.5 / 7.7	Belarus[a], Poland, Western Europe	5.5 / 7.7 / [9]	Belarus, Poland, Western Europe	57% / 10% / [20%]	3	ECE
31 Gas Andes Pipeline	La Mora, Argentina	Santiago, Chile	1997	Argentina	6.8	---		Chile	9.8	Chile	9%	3	Mercosur
32 Korpezhe-Kurt-Kui Pipeline	Korpezhe, Turkmenistan	Kurt-Kui, Iran	1997	Turkmenistan[a]	[4.2]	---		Iran	7.1	Iran	34%	2	ECO
33 Bulgaria to Greece Interconnect Pipeline	Russia	Greece	1997	Russia	4.2	Ukraine[a], Moldova[a], Romania, Bulgaria	[4.2] / [4.2] / 5.8 / 6.4	Greece	7.8	Greece	1%	3	ECE
34 Myanmar-Thailand Pipeline	Yadana	Ratchaburi, Thailand	1998	Myanmar	5.3	---		Thailand	7.2	Thailand	19%	2	ASEAN
35 Argentina-Uruguay Pipeline	Entre Rios, Argentina	Paysandu, Uruguay	1998	Argentina	6.8	---		Uruguay	5.3	Uruguay	0%	4	Mercosur
36 Bolivia-Brazil Pipeline	Santa Cruz, Bolivia	Sao Paulo and Curitiba, Brazil	1999	Bolivia	4.8	---		Brazil	6.0	Brazil	3%	4	Mercosur
37 Cuiba Gas Pipeline	Bolivia	Central Brazil	1999	Bolivia	4.8	---		Brazil	6.0	Brazil	3%	4	Mercosur
38 Norandino Pipeline	Northwest Argentina	Antofagasta region, Chile	1999	Argentina	6.5	---		Chile	8.1	Chile	11%	4	Mercosur

Project/Type	Source	Destination	Completed (year)	(#1) Investment Climate (GIRI) Supply Country	Rating (1-10)	Transit Country	Rating (1-10)	End-Use Country	Rating (1-10)	(#3) Offtake Quantity Risk Gas as % of Total Primary Energy Consumption Country	Pre-Project	(#5) Strength of Institution for Economic Cooperation (0-5)	Institution Referenced in (#5)
39 Gas-Atacama Pipeline	Salta Province, Argentina	Norte Grande, Chile	1999	Argentina	6.5	---		Chile	8.1	Chile	11%	4	Mercosur
40 Gasoducto del Pacifico Pipeline	Neuquen, Argentina	Concepcion, Chile	1999	Argentina	6.5	---		Chile	8.1	Chile	11%	4	Mercosur
41 Methanex-2 & 3 Pipeline	Tierra del Fuego	Methanex Methanol Plant	1999	Argentina	6.7	---		Chile	6.3	Chile	9%	3	Mercosur
42 Ramgas LNG	Qatar	South Korea	1999	Qatar	7.0	---		South Korea	7.6	South Korea	6%	0	NA
43 Bonny LNG	Nigeria	Italy, Spain, Turkey, France	1999	Nigeria	5.4	---		Italy[7]	8.4	Italy	30%	0	NA
44 Atlantic LNG LNG	Trinidad	U.S., Spain	1999	Trinidad	5.9	---		USA	8.8	USA	26%	2	OAS
45 Soyuz-Romania Interconnect Pipeline	Russia	Romania	1999	Russia[9]	5.5	Ukraine[9]	5.7	Romania	6.3	Romania	40%	3	ECE
46 Transportadora de Gas del Mercosur Pipeline	Parana, Argentina	Uruguaiana, Brazil	2000	Argentina	7.4	---		Brazil	5.8	Brazil	4%	4	Mercosur
47 Myanmar-Thailand Pipeline	Yetagun	Ratchaburi, Wangnoi	2000	Myanmar	4.5	---		Thailand	6.2	Thailand	25%	2	ASEAN
48 Oman LNG LNG	Oman	South Korea	2000	Oman	7	---		South Korea	7.3	South Korea	8%	0	NA
49 Iran-Turkey Pipeline	Iran	Turkey	2001	Iran	6.6	---		Turkey	5.5	Turkey	15%	2	ECO
50 West Natuna–Singapore Pipeline	West Natuna, Indonesia	Jurong Islands, Singapore	2001	Indonesia	3.9	---		Singapore	9.1	Singapore	5%	2	ASEAN
51 Cruz del Sur[10] Pipeline	Neuquen Basin, Argentina	Montevideo, Uruguay and Porto Alegre, Brazil	2002	Argentina	7.6	Uruguay	6.8	Uruguay / Brazil	6.8 / 5.2	Uruguay / Brazil	1% / 5%	4	Mercosur
52 Bluestream Pipeline	Russia	Turkey	2002	Russia	3.6	---		Turkey	5.3	Turkey	17%	3	ECE

Notes:

1 For a complete description of the methods and sources for calculating the indicator variables see Appendix A, "Notes on Coding of Variables".

2 [Bracketed] values indicate estimated data.

3 MEGAL was fully completed in 1979, but shipments began earlier.

4 The source of the energy consumption data, BP Global, combines data from the FRG (West Germany) and GDR (East Germany). No attempt is made here to disaggregate the data.

5 Country risk data for Algeria, Tunisia and Slovenia (Yugoslavia) are estimated from 1982 ICRG indices, as 1982 is the first year of the dataset.

6 ICRG index was first calculated for these countries in 1984. Thus, 1984 data is used, rather than two years prior estimation.

7 For purposes of simplicity, proxy variable data is provided for the largest project off-taker.

8 Yugoslav data is used as proxy (even post-independence in 1991) where Slovenia or Macedonia data is unavailable.

9 The ICRG dataset provides only one index for the former Soviet Union.

10 Connection to Brazil is not yet completed.

REFERENCES

Appert, Olivier (2002). *Cross-Border Gas Trade Conference: Concluding Remarks.* Paris, IEA

BP (2004). *Statistical Review of World Energy*, available at http://www.bp.com

ESMAP (2003). *Removing Obstacles to Cross-Border Oil and Gas Pipelines: Problems and Prospects.* Washington, DC: UNDP/World Bank, p. 130

Hayes, Mark H. and David G. Victor (2004). *Factors that Explain Investment in Cross-Border Natural Gas Transport Infrastructures: A Research Protocol for Historical Case Studies.* Stanford, CA, Program on Energy and Sustainable Development; available at: http://pesd.stanford.edu/gas.htm

Henisz, Witold Jerzy (2002). *Politics and International Investment: Measuring Risks and Protecting Profits.* Northampton, MA: Edward Elgar

ICRG (2002). *International Country Risk Guide. Political Risk Services* (IBC USA, Inc.). New York: International Reports

IEA (2002). *World Energy Outlook (WEO).* Paris: International Energy Agency

Levy, Brian and Pablo T. Spiller (1994). "The institutional foundations of regulatory commitment: a comparative analysis of telecommunications regulation." *Journal of Law, Economics, and Organization*, 10(2) pp. 201–246

PESD (2002). "Rapporteur's report." *Geopolitics of Gas Meeting*, Stanford: Program on Energy and Sustainable Development, October 17–18; available at: http://pesd.stanford.edu/gas.htm

Vernon, Raymond (1971). *Sovereignty at Bay: The Multinational Spread of US Enterprises.* New York: Basic Books

3   The Transmed and Maghreb projects: gas to Europe from North Africa

Mark H. Hayes

Introduction

A snapshot of the central Mediterranean region starting in the 1970s provides an ideal case for the analysis of decision making in cross-border natural gas-transport projects. During this period the massive size of Algeria's gas reserves were well known and the Société Nationale pour le Transport et la Commercialisation des Hydrocarbures (Sonatrach), Algeria's state-owned oil and gas company, actively sought to monetize this gas through exports. Across the Mediterranean, both Italy and Spain were seeking to expand natural gas consumption. Projects to import gas from Algeria were proposed, studied, and discussed at the highest levels of government and in state-owned energy companies. Starting in the early 1970s, Ente Nazionale Idrocarburi (ENI), Italy's state-owned energy company, began to pursue a sub-sea pipeline to bring Algerian gas across the Mediterranean. The option of using ships to bring LNG from Algeria was also discussed, but the parties ultimately decided in favor of the "Transmed" pipeline and deliveries finally began in 1983. Spain also discussed numerous proposals for a gas pipeline under the Mediterranean with Sonatrach and potential French partners. However, by the mid-1980s two LNG import projects to bring gas to Spain from Algeria and Libya had been attempted and largely aborted. Only in 1996 did the Gaz Maghreb Europe[1] pipeline transport Algerian gas under the Mediterranean to Spain (see the map in Figure 3.1).

The author is indebted to Jack Hogan for his invaluable research assistance. Amy M. Jaffe, James Jensen, Giacomo Luciani, Moustefa Ouki, Jonathan Stern, and David Victor provided many constructive comments. Becca Elias and Rose Kontak provided editorial assistance. Responsibility for any mistakes, in fact or interpretation, is solely my own.
[1] In 2000, Algerian President Abdelaziz Bouteflika renamed the two trans-Mediterranean gas pipelines. The Transmed was renamed the *Enrico Mattei* gas pipeline and the GME pipeline was renamed *Pedro Duran Farrel* in honor of the late chairman of Spain's Gas Natural. I continue to use the names *Transmed* and *Maghreb* pipelines throughout this text.

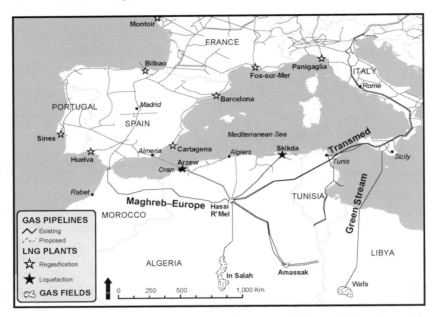

Figure 3.1. Gas pipelines and LNG facilities: Algeria, Italy, and Spain.

What factors explain these different outcomes? A natural gas-export pipeline spanning international borders and deep ocean waters was an enormously complex political, economic, and technical undertaking at the time these projects were proposed in the 1970s. Pipeline routes from Algeria to Italy and from Algeria to Spain involved transit countries, massive investments, and the technical challenges of laying the world's deepest sub-sea pipelines at the time. But LNG provided its own set of challenges. Liquefaction and regasification technology was still in its infancy – and Algeria, in particular, was plagued by high capital costs and reliability problems in its existing LNG liquefaction plants. LNG, however, did avoid difficult negotiations with transit countries (Tunisia or Morocco) and was more scaleable than the pipeline alternatives.

Ultimately, politics and energy security concerns dominated techno-logical and economic considerations in determining which projects were built and at what time. Basic economics favored gas moving from Algeria to both Spain and Italy throughout this period. The Transmed pipeline was completed rapidly in the early 1980s because Italy had a strong and politically mobilized company, ENI, which pushed the project. ENI

favored pipelines as part of an energy security and technology imperative, and had the financial backing of the Italian and other European
governments to make it happen. Spain and its gas company, Enagas, had
none of these characteristics in the late 1970s and 1980s and thus could
not mobilize the resources required to create a successful gas-import
project during this period.[2]

Post-Independence Energy Policy in Algeria

The bumpy history of post-colonial Algeria is deeply intertwined with
the development of the country's oil and gas sectors. Major gas discoveries in Algeria date back to 1956 during the period of French
colonial rule. In 1961, the giant Hassi R'Mel field commenced production, initially to supply the cities of Algiers and Oran and some electric
power stations (Sutton 1978). After a long and vicious war to evict the
French colonialists, Algeria achieved its independence from France in
July 1962. Within eighteen months the first state enterprisee Sonatrach
was founded to engage in the oil and gas businesses.

Domestic consumption of natural gas grew slowly through the 1960s
and 1970s, remaining below 1 Bcm per year until 1974 (see figure 3.2).
Meanwhile, gas exports quickly became a focus of the Algerian government as it increased its control over the country's oil and gas resources.
The world's first commercial gas liquefaction plant was completed
at Arzew in 1964, with the Algerian company CAMEL (Compagnie
Algérienne de Méthane Liquide) shipping LNG to the United Kingdom
and later France.[3] Under the leadership of President Houari
Boumediene, Algeria pursued an aggressive policy to implement
national control of all "strategic" interests – with Sonatrach as the
instrument to achieve this goal in the energy sector. From 1965 until
1969, Algeria nationalized the holdings of most small companies and
continued bitter negotiations with the French over their companies'
remaining interests, mainly in the hydrocarbon sector.[4] By 1971 the
government had assumed control over most of the hydrocarbon industry. Sonatrach assumed complete control of gas production and

---

[2] As all of these factors changed for Spain and Enagas in the mid-1990s and, in turn, the
  Gaz Maghreb Europe was completed by 1996 finally delivering Algerian gas to Spain via
  pipeline. See the p. 77 for more details.
[3] CAMEL was jointly-owned by early pioneers in the LNG business; including the
  US-based Continental Oil Company (later Conoco), Shell, and Total, among others.
  Sonatrach would later assume control of both operation and contract.
[4] The legacy of Algerian bitterness toward France from the colonial period – and French
  bitterness over nationalization of oil and gas assets – would taint relations for decades
  to come.

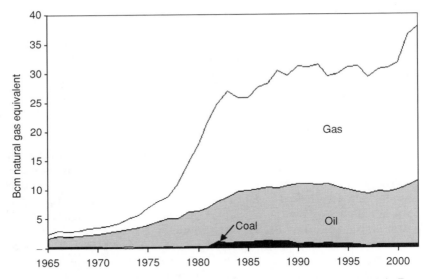

Figure 3.2. Algeria: primary energy supply, by fuel, 1965–2004, in Bcm equivalent.

Source: BP (2005).

transmission, and directly controlled 70 percent of crude oil production in Algeria (Aïssaoui 2001).

Through the 1970s the Boumediene government aggressively pursued investment in gas-export infrastructure as a means to lift the country from a "vast legacy of political and economic backwardness left by the colonizing power" (Entelis 1999). The government realized that its endowment of gas resources was much larger than oil and thus sought to increase utilization of gas. At the prodding of Belaïd Abdesselam, the Minister of Industry and Energy, the corresponding policies were incorporated into the 1976 *Charte Nationale* (National Charter) and marked the shift from oil to natural gas as the main focus of energy policy (FLN 1976):

Natural gas reserves represent one of Algeria's most valuable assets. Proved reserves are among the biggest in the world. Thus, the valorization of natural gas represents an important source of capital accumulation. Revenues generated by such an activity will enable the financing and economic development in the country and the creation for the foundation for the state's financial independence.

(Translated from the French version in Aïssaoui 2001)

Sonatrach, in turn, commissioned the US firm Bechtel to produce a financial plan to operationalize Abdesselam's policy prescription.

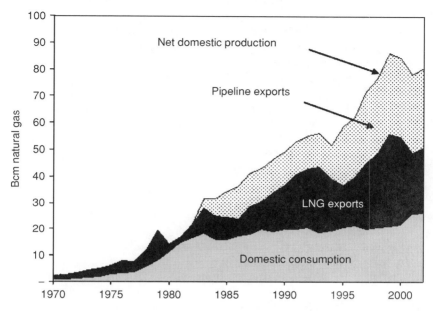

Figure 3.3. Algeria: natural gas production, consumption, and exports, 1970–2004.

Note: That net domestic production does not include gas flared or re-injected for oil production. See Aïssaoui (2001, p. 139) for a complete breakdown.

Source: Moraleda (2002); BP (2003); Domenico Dispenza, personal communication, July 31, 2003.

VALHYD, the "Hydrocarbon Development Plan of Algeria" was the culmination of Abdesselam's planning. VALHYD called for the production of all of the known oil reserves and most of the known gas reserves between 1976 and 2005. This extremely aggressive export growth was to be financed by foreign exchange earnings (Aïssaoui 2001). LNG exports were to grow rapidly. By 1978 Algeria was shipping out 10 Bcm of LNG per year on tankers to Europe and the United States, the latter being Algeria's largest single customer at the time (see figure 3.3).

Expanding LNG exports required massive capital investments and posed technical challenges that ill-conceived foreign technical assistance programs did not efficiently tackle (Aïssaoui 2001). Rising interest rates combined with major cost overruns both in constructing and operating the liquefaction facilities at Arzew and Skikda placed increasing fiscal pressure on the Boumediene government in the late 1970s.

Simultaneously, a burgeoning population of young Algerians placed a huge burden on the government to provide increased access to education and employment (Stern 1986).

On the international front, the 1970s saw the rise of OPEC with Algeria as a leading price-hawk of the oil exporters' cartel. Algeria, like other gas exporters, sought better terms for its gas sales, more in line with the rapidly rising cost of oil and oil products. Led by its Vice-President for Marketing, Nordine Aït Laoussine, Sonatrach began the push to price its gas off alternative energy sources in the consuming markets (fuel oil or syngas from coal). This "net-back" pricing strategy replaced earlier pricing formulas in the early US and UK contracts which sought to provide a fixed return on investment to Sonatrach and contracting parties (Aïssaoui 2001). However, the US and UK contracts did not provide for price increases to compensate for cost overruns in the construction and operation of the liquefaction facilities – and rising prices for oil made the earlier contracts look even worse.

In this environment Italian, Spanish, and French companies were in discussions with Sonatrach about plans to pipe gas under the Mediterranean. By 1973, productive relations with ENI had produced an agreement between the two companies to build a sub-Mediterranean pipeline to ship 12 Bcm of gas per year to Italy for twenty-five years.

Italy's Early Move to Natural Gas

Italy is not a country well endowed with energy resources. Throughout the post-war period the country has been dependent on imported energy sources (first coal and oil and later natural gas). In the mid-twentieth century, Italy followed the rest of Europe in the switch from a coal- to a petroleum-based energy system – with the significant caveat that Italy took an early lead in utilizing gas resources (see Figure 3.4).

In the process of searching for oil during the Second World War, the state oil company Agip made significant gas discoveries in the Po Valley of Northern Italy. After 1945, Agip came under the leadership of Enrico Mattei, a man with little experience in the energy industry but whose position as former commander of the opposition partisans in the struggle against the fascists made him one of the most powerful political figures in Italy. As the Po (and Italy) was endowed with gas resources but little oil, Mattei turned this apparent weakness into strength, advancing the strategy that natural gas must not be a mere substitute for petroleum, but a cheaper and more functional substitute for imported coal for the growing industrial activities of Northern Italy (see figure 3.5):

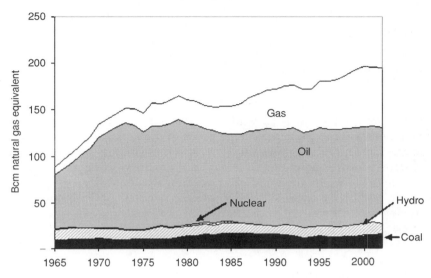

Figure 3.4. Italy: primary energy supply, by fuel, 1965–2004, in Bcm equivalent.

Source: BP (2003).

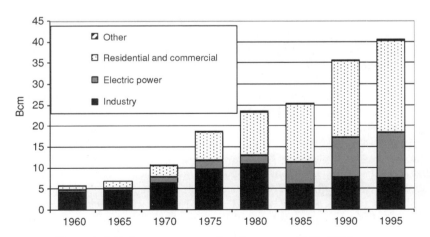

Figure 3.5. Italy: gas consumption, by sector, 1960–1995.

Source: IEA (2003).

Large reservoirs in the Po Valley allowed (or, better, impelled) the creation of pipeline facilities to reach the major factories in northern Italy. That choice determined a virtuous circle of growth: the major Italian firms expanded enormously in the 1950s and 1960s, high profits from natural gas sales were plowed back into exploration, production, the expansion of pipelines, and the acquisition of new customers. (Pozzi 2003)

Ente Nazionale Idrocarburi (National Hyrocarbon Corporation) (ENI) was created in 1953 with fresh financing from the government and a mission to supply the energy needs of the rapidly growing Italian economy. The Agip drilling and production operations were folded in under the new ENI holding company. The company was granted exclusive rights to exploration and production in the Po Valley, providing a stable profit core on which ENI could grow. Later, ENI would gain a monopoly position over gas imports, transport, and sales, though it was never exclusively granted this right by regulation (Pozzi 2003).

By 1965, Italy was the largest gas producer and consumer in Western Europe (Darmstadter, Teitelbaum, and Polach 1971). Gas met over 10 percent of the country's total primary energy demand, while other European countries such as Germany, Spain and the United Kingdom had nascent gas industries. (Dutch production from the massive Groningen field was just beginning to take off.) Under Mattei's aggressive leadership, and with strong backing from the state, ENI announced plans to build a national gas grid. However, it soon became apparent that Italy's domestic resource base would not be sufficient to meet the country's growing energy needs.

Recognizing the need to secure foreign supplies and driven by his goal to make ENI a player on a par with the Exxons and Totals of the world, Mattei saw a strategic imperative to expand abroad. Bold, yet realistic, in his assessment of the company's resources, Mattei developed a strategy to forge partnerships that other major oil companies could not. His talent for creating good relations with producing countries led ENI first to Egypt (1955), Iran (1957), Morocco (1958), Libya (1959), Sudan (1959), Tunisia (1961), and Nigeria (1962) (Pozzi 2003).

Mattei visited Moscow in 1959, where he brokered the first oil import deal with the Soviets over heated protests from NATO and the United States. His public position in support of independence movements against colonial powers allowed ENI to take advantage of post-colonial bitterness in places such as Algeria. Indeed, several units of ENI were busy in the country in the years immediately following Algeria's independence, notably Snamprogetti and other engineering/consulting units.[5]

---

[5] Giacomo Luciani, personal communication, April 4, 2004.

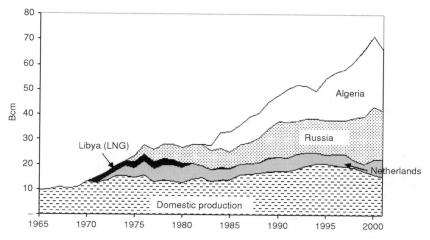

Figure 3.6. Italy: sources of natural gas, 1965–2002.

Note: Italy also took LNG shipments from Qatar and Abu Dhabi in the late 1990s, but total deliveries from these sources are negligible relative to overall volumes shown here.

Source: BP (2003); IEA (2003).

Mattei's leadership of ENI came to an end when his private plane crashed in 1962. His dealing with the Soviets and his courtship of the insurgent Front de la Libération Nationale (FLN) in Algeria led many to suspect Western intelligence agencies or bitter French colonialists in the "accident." Nevertheless, ENI's drive toward internationalization had begun and would continue in his absence.

The Transmed Gas Pipeline

In the early 1970s, ENI secured gas imports from the Soviet Union and the Netherlands, and began to take shipments of Libyan gas into an LNG regasification facility at Panigaglia, near Genova (see figure 3.6). Seeking to diversify its rapidly growing gas imports and building on the historically warm relations with Algeria and Sonatrach, in 1973 ENI signed a contract with Algeria for 11.75 Bcm of gas per year over twenty-five years (Petroleum Economist 1977a). The volume and offtake arrangements in the Algerian contract were similar to deals that ENI had struck with the Soviets and the Dutch. However, the daunting technical challenge of crossing the Mediterranean made the new "Transmed" project a radically different proposal.

Pipeline vs. LNG

The debate between using ship-based LNG technologies or a direct pipeline link to Algeria was a hotly debated subject within the ENI group during the 1970s.[6] The decision to pursue the pipeline was founded on multiple strategic considerations.

Proposals to import gas from Algeria dating back to the 1960s envisioned using existing LNG technologies. However, construction and operation of LNG facilities were expensive and encouraged ENI to explore the feasibility of a pipeline connecting Italy with North Africa. A preliminary feasibility study was carried out for the sub-sea pipeline in 1969, followed by the first route survey in 1970. Simultaneously, Snam was testing its abilities in the LNG business. In 1971, Snam delivered LNG from Libya on its own tankers to Italy's first regasification facility at Panigaglia. The project was troublesome from the start. Marcello Colitti, then ENI Director of Planning, recalls "near accidents, fires, and many delays" at the Panigaglia facility (Marcello Colitti, interview, October 10, 2003). Many of the problems in fact originated at the source, as the Libyan gas was too "rich" in heat content. Managing these quality problems would have required additional refining investments either in Libya or more likely at the Italian end (Domenico Dispenza, interview, October 7, 2003). Algeria – despite being the first to utilize LNG technology – was having its own share of problems with its liquefaction facilities. Existing LNG export facilities at Arzew and Skikda experienced protracted operating difficulties and cost overruns (Petroleum Economist 1976).

The strategy for developing ENI's core technical competencies was also a major consideration. Transportation technology looked to be critical to the future of the gas business. According to Marcello Colitti, ENI planners realized that the current leaders in LNG – including Total, Mobil, and Exxon – would hold tightly to their proprietary technologies and capabilities. Rather than be beholden to the incumbent LNG leaders, Colitti adopted the view that through the Transmed project ENI could create its own strategic niche in sub-sea pipelines. Such a

---

[6] The ENI group consisted of the following companies circa 1970: Mattei's prized Agip maintained all upstream responsibilities; Snam was the importer, transporter, and wholesaler of natural gas within Italy; Italgas (40 percent owned by ENI) was the distributor of gas to commercial and retail customers. Snamprogetti and Saipem were subsidiaries focusing on engineering and construction, respectively. All except Italgas were 100 percent owned by the ENI holding company, which in turn was owned 80 percent by the Italian government.

project was a risky venture, but it could create many future business opportunities for ENI subsidiaries Saipem and Snamprogetti. After much discussion and debate – including with a Snam management that was loath to see its existing LNG tankers sit idle – early plans for the pipeline pushed forward (Marcello Colitti interview, October 10, 2003).[7]

Commercial considerations and supply security were also factored into the LNG vs. pipeline debate within ENI. Snam studies at the time showed that the delivered cost of pipeline gas to Northern Italy would be greater than LNG transport and regasification (Petroleum Economist 1976). However, these studies did not consider that a share of the pipeline costs could be borne by newly connected gas users in southern Italy. Under the plan for the "Gasification of the Mezzogiorno," the Transmed pipeline was to bring gas to the underserved south of the country. Such a plan would not have achieved rapid returns for ENI, however the potential benefits to the new customers was great. Some of these "social benefits" could be counted against the incremental costs of piping the gas to the north of Italy and would later become an important part of providing political (and, in turn, financial) support for the project.

With regard to security, supporters of the pipeline argued that the "marriage" of partners would ensure greater supply stability (Marcello Colitti, interview, October 10, 2003). A new Algerian liquefaction train could – in theory – fill a ship heading in any direction, while pipeline gas could go only to Italy. (Tunisian transit risks were perceived to be minimal, and thus not affecting the security benefits of the pipeline, as is discussed in more detail on p. 63.)

The pipeline option was also strongly favored by Sonatrach and the Algerian government. Their costly experience with LNG exports in the 1970s made the pipeline option attractive. A pipeline from the Hassi R'Mel gas field to the Tunisian border was shorter than a new pipeline to the northern Mediterranean coast to deliver gas to an LNG liquefaction terminal (Arzew, Skikda, or some new plant). Most importantly from the Algerian perspective, at the end of a Transmed pipe would be a cash payment from ENI – not a multi-billion dollar investment in a liquefaction terminal.

As the strategic and motivating force behind the project, ENI set out to develop the needed technical capabilities. In the early 1970s the

---

[7] It is worth noting that Colitti's and ENI's bet paid off handsomely. Saipem and Snamprogetti remain leaders in the field of designing and building pipelines worldwide, and particularly for deep-sea pipe laying.

worldwide experience in the design, construction, and maintenance of offshore pipelines was limited to water depths of less than 150 m, using diver-assisted procedures. Thus, new technologies needed to be developed for marine surveying, remote controlled seabed preparation equipment, and pipe-laying procedures adapted to the much greater depths and pressures that a Transmed crossing would demand (Caroni 1992). The research and development (R&D) program for these new technologies was tasked almost completely within the ENI group. Engineering and construction problems were tasked to ENI subsidiaries Snamprogetti and Saipem, respectively.

In 1974 Saipem laid the first test pipe 350 m under the Straits of Messina, linking Sicily with the Italian mainland. Its engineers then moved to the Sicilian Channel where, in 1975, at a depth of 550 m they artificially buckled a pipe to prove that it could be recovered and repaired (Business Week 1977). In parallel with the successful testing program Saipem developed a new ship, the CASTORO 6, to be used in the Transmed and other major pipelaying operations (Caroni 1992).

1977 Contract

As technical tests proceeded apace, troubles negotiating the transit fee with Tunisia forced ENI, Sonatrach, and the Tunisian government back to the bargaining table to craft a new contract.[8] In the context of rising oil prices, the growing commitment from ENI to the Transmed project, and with the only feasible route passing through their territory, the Tunisian government sought to take advantage of its strategic geographic position. In 1975, the government demanded 12 percent of the value of the gas that entered its territory as payment for transit rights – essentially holding the project hostage. ENI first sought a reduction in the price of gas delivered to the Tunisian border to compensate. Sonatrach, supported by the rising oil price environment, was unwilling to cede further price breaks to ENI.[9]

ENI responded to the Tunisian demand by publicly exploring the option of "abandoning" the Transmed project and negotiated a contract

---

[8] Tunisia did not want Sonatrach to have any role in the Tunisian section of the pipeline. Negotiations were thus conducted separately, between Sonatrach and ENI and between ENI and the Tunisians.

[9] Sonatrach was initially offering gas to ENI at a price below the f.o.b. price Sonatrach was earning for its LNG – but more profitable for Sonatrach since it did not have to bear the cost of the liquefaction facilities needed for LNG exports. However, the further reduction sought by ENI in response to Tunisian demands was deemed too low (Nordine Aït Laoussine interview, December 11, 2003).

to import 8.5 Bcm of LNG per year from Sonatrach instead (Petroleum Economist 1977a). Ultimately, this maneuver forced Tunisia to settle for a payment of 5.625 percent of transported gas volumes, in cash or in gas, less than half of its original demand.

The new transit agreement, signed in July 1977, involved only ENI and the Tunisian government (Petroleum Economist 1977a). Tunisia was reluctant to include Sonatrach in its segment of the project. Sonatrach would sell the gas at the Tunisian border to a newly created project company financed entirely by ENI (see table 3.1).

Separately, Sonatrach and ENI then needed to make an agreement for gas shipment. On October 22, 1977, the two parties signed a contract for gas imports, elaborating the structures necessary for the financing, construction, and future operation of the pipeline. A review of both Algeria's and Italy's precedent gas trade deals – in the context of the broader events in the world energy markets – is necessary to better understand the framing of the 1977 Transmed contract.

The Transmed was the first pipeline export project for Sonatrach, but the company had been selling LNG to several European buyers and the United States for over a decade.[10] The company's first LNG contracts were with British and American customers. These were long-term, fixed-volume contracts with prices based on capital and operating costs indexed only to macroeconomic indicators, with no clauses for renegotiating the pricing formula. The aim was to provide the LNG seller with a stable return on investment. However, major cost overruns in the construction and operation of the liquefaction plants continually eroded positive margins to Sonatrach (Aïssaoui 2001).

The 1970s saw many gas sellers seek to bring natural gas export prices in line with sky-rocketing oil prices (see figure 3.7). The Boumediene-era Sonatrach leadership sought pricing formulas that reflected the rising costs of competing fuels (usually fuel oil) in the offtake markets (Aït Laoussine 1977). Sonatrach was able to obtain these gains in its contracts with European buyers in the mid-1970s, including Spain, France, and Belgium. The prices in these contracts escalated from $1.30 per mmbtu in 1975 to $1.60 per mmbtu in 1978 – compared to the earlier fixed price El Paso (US) contract that started deliveries in 1978 at $0.37 per mmbtu (see figure 3.7). Although the El Paso contract was subsequently revised to $1.75 per mmbtu, the contract became a point of contention between rivals in the Algerian government. When Algerian president Boumediene died in 1978 opponents used the apparent

---

[10] The LNG contract with the United Kingdom was first signed with CAMEL. Later, Sonatrach took complete control of both operation and contract.

Table 3.1   *Transmed: technical details*

Segment	Length (kms)	# Pipes × Diameter (in.)	Number of compressors	Maximum depth (meters)
Algeria	550	1 × 48	1	
Tunisia	370	1 × 48	3	
Sicilian Channel	155	3 × 20	0	610
Italian Section				
Sicily Overland	340	1 × 48	1	
Straits of Messina	15	3 × 20	0	270
Italian Mainland	1,055	1 × 42–48	4	
Total	**2,485**		**9**	

Source: Sonatrach, Snam.

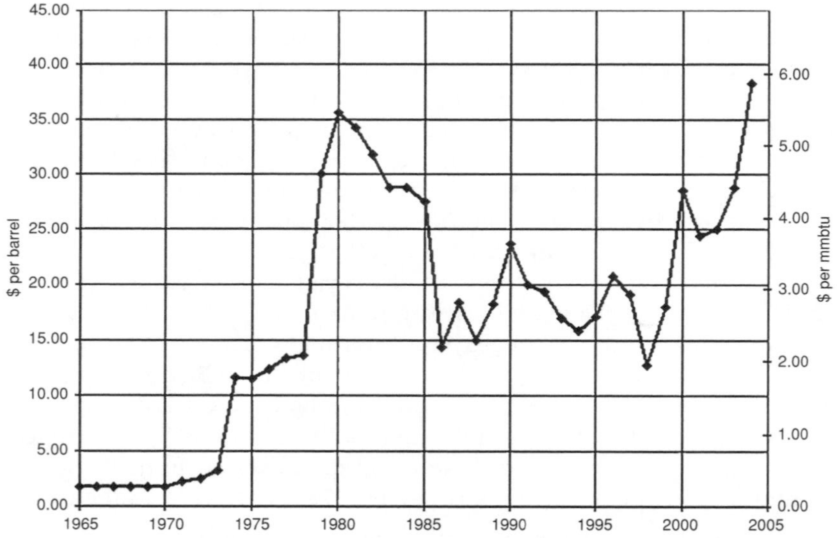

Figure 3.7. International oil prices, 1965–2004.

Note: The right axis shows price based on heat content, as natural gas is priced for LNG sales. 1965–1983 reflect Arabian Light prices posted at Ras Tanura and 1984–2004 are Brent dated. Algerian gas sales generally track these levels, though the Transmed and Sonatrach LNG contracts were explicitly priced off other indices.

Source: BP (2005).

failure of the El Paso contract as a platform from which to launch an aggressive campaign to rapidly raise Algerian gas export prices (Aïssaoui 2001).

The price of ENI imports from other suppliers was also rising. From 1974 to 1977, Gasunie of the Netherlands – which supplied nearly 40 percent of Italy's gas imports – more than doubled the price of its pipeline-delivered gas, from $0.62 per mmbtu to over $1.30 per mmbtu. Soviet gas export prices during the period are harder to discern. Anecdotal evidence suggests that the Soviet Union likely maintained a somewhat lower price level seeking to increase volumes and market share, but nevertheless also secured significant price increases during this period (Stern 1986).

When the negotiations settled on the 1977 contract with Snam, Nordine Aït Laoussine, the Vice President of Marketing for Sonatrach, had secured a price of $1.00 per mmbtu for gas delivered to the Tunisian border – at a time when Gaz de France was paying $1.30 per mmbtu c.i.f. for its LNG. The escalation formulas in both contracts were identical, using the "net-back" formula that linked the gas price to competing fuels in the offtake market (PIW 1982a). The 1977 natural gas sale and purchase agreement between ENI and Sonatrach was signed for a period of twenty-five years with deliveries to begin in 1981. The contractual build-up is shown in table 3.2.

Transit Risks

Serious mention of the additional risks posed by the 370 km of pipeline that crosses Tunisian soil is notably absent from published reports and interviews with key players on the Italian or Algerian sides. Tunisia's failed attempt to squeeze an oversized share of the rents from the project nearly stalled the whole project in its early stages. Few analysts, either internal or external to the project, seem to have considered the range of events that might affect the continued operation of the pipeline once it was built. Presumably, planners considered Tunisia a necessary risk in choosing the pipeline route.[11] Hindsight is perfect, and indeed history shows that Tunisia has been a stable partner in the project. But a brief

---

[11] It is worth noting that more recent proposals by Algeria to expand gas pipeline capacity to Italy seek to avoid Tunisia and pipe directly to the European continent. Libya avoided Tunisia and piped gas directly to Italy with the Greenstream pipeline. These decisions apparently have more to do with avoiding Tunisia's transit fees than an explicit risk management strategy. Twenty-five years of technological improvements make long deep-water pipes less of a hurdle than political negotiations with Tunisia.

Table 3.2 *Transmed: contracted volumes, 1977*

Year	Volume (Bcm per year)
1981–1982	3.9
1982–1983	7.4
1983–1984	10.5
1984–	12.4

review of the Tunisian historical context reveals that this outcome was far from predetermined when the 1977 contract for the Transmed pipeline was signed.

Habib ben Ali Bourguiba led Tunisia with a heavy hand from its independence in 1956 through the late 1980s when he was deposed in a bloodless *coup*. Bourguiba's reign was marked by numerous twists and turns in foreign and domestic policy as the president sought to maintain power and steer the country between its two much more powerful neighbors, Algeria and Libya. Bourguiba first supported the insurgent FLN in their fight for independence from France, but later sided against Algeria in its heated dispute with Morocco over the Western Sahara. He then leaned toward the rising radical Colonel Qaddafi in 1974, briefly entertaining the idea of a union with Libya after a proposed "merger" between Libya and Egypt had failed (Knapp 1977).

At the time of the 1977 contract negotiations, ENI negotiators must have been relatively at ease in Tunis, a favorite tourist destination for Europeans with an open economy that welcomed foreign investment. Still, the future stability of the country was not assured. President Bourguiba was in his mid-70s in 1977 and had suffered from years of bad health. By 1977 economic malaise and social unrest unleashed massive street protests in Tunis – which were brutally repressed by the military. Regional experts argue that any destabilization of Tunisia would not have lasted long before Libya and Algeria would have become engaged – with the outcome of such meddling far from certain (Parker 1984).

The 1977 agreement between ENI and the Tunisian government rewarded Tunisia handsomely for its location at the edge of the Sicilian Channel. Bourguiba did not obtain the 12 percent share of the gas he had sought in 1975. However the 5.625 percent share of total gas shipments provided as a transit fee still tripled the country's existing gas supplies – while Tunisia bore no financial or operational responsibility for any part of the project. President Bourguiba just had to decide how he wanted to receive payment – in gas or in cash.

The following extract contains the main terms of the agreement for the construction and operation of the 370 km Tunisian pipeline, as reported in ENI internal documentation (Domenico Dispenza, personal communication, July 31, 2003):

Construction activities had to be carried out by SCOGAT (Société pour la Construction du Gazoduc Transtunisien), a Tunisian company fully owned by ENI. SCOGAT retained the ownership of the new facilities until the beginning of operations and was wholly financed by TTPC (Trans-Tunisian Pipeline Company Limited) was a company wholly owned by ENI and based outside Tunisia (in Jersey, the Channel Islands); it was established with the purpose of financing the pipeline and holding exclusive transportation rights.

The agreement establishes that, once the pipeline becomes operational, the ownership shall pass from SCOGAT to TTPC – against the settlement by TTPC of all debts connected with the construction – and then from TTPC to the state-owned Tunisian company SOTUGAT (Société du Gazoduc Transtunisien). TTPC would retain exclusive rights to transport gas, including the right to conclude transportation contracts with third parties, subject to the previous approval of the Tunisian Government.

ENI had to conclude a transportation contract with TTPC, in order to transport natural gas bought from Sonatrach through the Tunisian section. The "ship-or-pay" transportation charges due by ENI to TTPC represented the security for the TTPC lenders.

The agreement between ENI and the Tunisian Government dealt with taxation as well. The Tunisian Government was granted a yearly global fiscal charge determined in proportion to the actual gas throughput and payable in kind or, at the sole discretion of the Tunisian Government, in cash. ENI and related companies were exonerated from all tax payments, including royalties, excise and custom duties, during construction and operation.

ENI did receive concessions on taxes for the construction and operation of the Tunisian section, but with transit fees worth $25 million per year Bourguiba could be quite content with his bargain.[12]

Sonatrach was not involved in the Tunisian segment – at the behest of the Tunisians – but the Algerians did acquire a stake in the Sicilian Channel crossing. The 1977 contract between ENI and Sonatrach also established the Trans-Mediterranean Pipeline Company Limited (TMPC). TMPC was jointly funded by ENI (50 percent) and Sonatrach (50 percent) and given responsibility for the finance, construction, and operation of the Sicilian Channel section of the Transmed. TMPC financing was, in turn, supported by a long-term transit contract with ENI (Snam).

---

[12] The $25 million estimate is based on the 1977 Italian contract price of $1.00 per mmbtu and full capacity of 12 Bcm per year of flow.

Discussions with ENI officials suggest that Sonatrach was given a role in the TMPC to increase its stake in the project, given that almost all of the other risks except price were squarely borne by ENI (Domenico Dispenza., interview, October 7, 2003). However, Sonatrach also benefited from the transfer of technical knowledge from its involvement in the TMPC. Such experience would have been valuable for Sonatrach's potential participation in other deep-sea pipelines, such as a pipeline to Spain.[13]

ENI had no offshore experience prior to the Transmed project. Indeed, a gas pipe had never been attempted at the depths required for the Transmed. The risk of technical failure on the sub-sea section of the pipeline was significant. Newham (1979) notes the four strategies Snamprogetti engineers utilized to mitigate the risk of catastrophic failure through robust design:

1. Each pipeline was *overbuilt* to allow for capacity increases on two lines to compensate for a failure on one of the others.
2. Two pipelines were run together in a southern route from Cape Bon on the Tunisian coast to Sicily, while the *third pipeline* will start and end at the same points, but will be as far as *20 km from the other pair*, thus minimizing the risk that all three could be damaged in one event.
3. In shallow depths near the coast, pipelines were *encased in cement* to protect against ships' anchors.
4. Saipem conducted tests of its own *repair capabilities* in advance of laying any of the pipes.

Financing

ENI assumed liability for nearly all of the financing for the Transmed project. The company assumed responsibility either through ownership of the project companies (as in the Tunisian segment and half of the Sicilian Channel crossing) or by directly guaranteeing the financing, as in the Algerian section of the pipe. Where feasible, the project companies sought international lending, as interest rates on foreign borrowing were around 9 percent at the time, while Italian domestic borrowing costs were significantly higher at 15 percent per year (Newham 1979). International – and, in particular, European – lending agencies lined

---

[13] Sonatrach's involvement in the sub-sea project was mostly in the operation of the pipeline, after construction was completed. Snam and Snamprogetti long retained their leadership in the deep-water pipe-laying.

Table 3.3 *Transmed: financial details*

Segment	Investment (millon Y2000 USD)	Ownership	Debt financing (Y2000 USD)
Algeria	2,000	100% Sonatrach	2 billion total; 1.2 billion from Italian banks backed by guarantee from ENI – Sonatrach shall use to buy Italian services and equipment; 800 million from international consortium of banks
Tunisia	1,000	SOTUGAT, Tunisian government; Leased to TTPC – 100% Snam-owned	950 million total; 650 million from export credit agencies; 300 million from international consortium of banks
Sicilian Channel	1,700	TMPC, 50% Snam, 50% Sonatrach	1.5 billion total; 700 million from export credit agencies; additional financing from international consortium of banks
Italy	4,000	100% Snam	1.8 billion total from EIB
Total	**8,700**		**6,250**

Note:
All numbers are rounded and adjusted to Y2000 USD.
Sources: Newham (1979); Dispenza (2002).

up to finance the Transmed project, despite the many technical challenges and the turbulent energy markets of the late 1970s and early 1980s (see table 3.3).

Ultimately, however, ENI's financial position was backed by the Italian government. The company was largely government-owned and though the company had long been self-sustaining, the government was still the guarantor of all its financial obligations. The policies of ENI and the government were thus strongly connected. The European Community (EC) also provided major financial backing through the European Investment Bank (EIB), by providing financial support for the planned expansion of the main gas trunk line in Italy, and the gasification of the Mezzogiorno.

Supply Risks

The super-giant Hassi R'Mel field was the planned source of gas for the Transmed pipe. Hassi R'Mel was discovered in 1956 and entered into production in 1961, supplying gas mainly to LNG export facilities and also to domestic users. In 1976, the massive field was estimated to contain 2,000 Bcm of gas reserves, over half of Algeria's known total reserves at the time (Sutton 1978). At the time of the Transmed signing, Sonatrach already had future commitments for gas deliveries rising to over 70 Bcm per year by the mid-1980s. The aggressive target under Boumediene's VALHYD was to increase exports to over 100 Bcm per annum through the end of the century (Aïssaoui 2001). Even if ENI planners took the Algerians' hyper-aggressive targets seriously the Hassi R'Mel field alone would not have been depleted for twenty years.[14]

Technical and political risks were more pressing concerns for the long-term stability of the gas supply into the Transmed pipeline. Sonatrach's technical and organizational capabilities were largely unproven, and were thus an area of potential concern for Italy and ENI. However, the recent history of nationalization and the potential for continued swings in government energy policies – played out directly through Sonatrach operations and planning – should also have been primary concerns for the Italian partners. History shows that ENI was not well prepared to protect itself from these risks. ENI had fronted the vast majority of the capital invested in the project, yielding Sonatrach and the Algerian government tremendous bargaining power once the pipeline was completed. The Italians later became acutely aware of this asymmetric bargaining situation.

Offtake Risk

ENI, through Snam, held a monopoly position over the import, transport, and sales of natural gas in Italy. As the state gas company, ENI worked with the Ministry of Industry to develop the National Energy Plan and then sought to meet the targets it established. Gas consumption growth (like overall energy consumption) grew rapidly over the period 1960–1977, increasing almost 9 percent per year (IEA 2003). When the 1977 Transmed contract was drafted Italy expected growth in gas demand to continue, albeit at the slower pace of 4 percent per year through 1990 (IEA 1978). Rapidly rising prices for oil and oil products and the clean-burning characteristics of gas relative to coal made gas a favored fuel.

---

[14] This is a reference calculation only. Gas from Hassi R'Mel was also to be utilized for domestic gas supply, petrochemical production, etc. Additional fields could also have been brought on-line to meet Italian demands.

ENI's dominance of domestic gas production, imports, and domestic supply afforded it the position to effectively manage the entire gas supply chain. Domestic production allowed ENI to take a steady stream of gas imports, managing fluctuations in demand by varying domestic production and storage. Domestic production could be slowed and imports used to fill storage during the warm summer months in the north. In the winter, domestic production could be increased and storage utilized, while maintaining continued flows on the expensive gas import pipelines.

ENI had both an obligation to the state and a commercial incentive to deliver gas to meet the expected demand. ENI also secured major political and financial support for the Transmed project by promising to use the new pipeline supplies for the "gasification of the Mezzogiorno," a bold plan to expand the gas network to the previously unserved south of Italy.

As the monopoly gas importer and seller, ENI (Snam) was relatively protected by price risks in its domestic market. Consumer prices were set by the company, with oversight by the Ministry of Industry. The industrial users lobby was the strongest advocate for lowered prices (Marcello Colitti, interview, October 10, 2003). Again, ENI was ultimately backed by the resources of the Italian state.

Pricing Dispute

With the construction of the Transmed project about to begin, major events both within and outside Algeria began to set the stage for what would eventually become a contentious dispute among Sonatrach, ENI and their respective governments. President Boumediene died unexpectedly in December 1978. In the transition, the more conservative wing of the ruling FLN sought to grab power. Colonel Chadli Benjedid emerged from the FLN conservatives in March 1979 to assume the presidency. Wresting firm control over the distribution of petroleum rents was the first goal of the new administration. "Sonatrach was at the heart of the political struggle in the course of the transition from the Boumediene to the Benjedid regime. The new political leadership maneuvered through the apparatus of the FLN to secure control of the main source of income and power in the country" (Aïssaoui 2001). Sonatrach was to be restructured to ensure that the hydrocarbon sector would be controlled at the "suitable political level" (Benachenou 1980, in Aïssaoui 2001). The FLN majority in Parliament strongly backed the Sonatrach restructuring. In March 1979, Minister of Energy and

Industry Abdesselam was replaced by Belgacem Nabi.[15] Nabi in turn forced out the entire top management at Sonatrach, including Aït Laoussine.[16]

Abdesselam and the Boumediene technocrats were particularly vulnerable because of the dismal performance of the LNG export projects, in particular the El Paso contract. The pricing arrangement in the original El Paso contract meant that the first LNG deliveries in 1978 from the new liquefaction plant at Arzew earned only $0.37 per mmbtu f.o.b. (Zartman and Bassani 1987). More recently contracts signed with Spain, France, Belgium, and Italy were garnering $1.60 per mmbtu f.o.b. for the same gas. The pricing terms with El Paso were actually revised before Nabi took over – but the record left the incumbent energy leaders vulnerable. Nabi established a Commission of Enquiry to investigate former Sonatrach CEO Sid Ahmed Ghozali and the El Paso contract (Aïssaoui 2001).

Rising domestic pressures were also a significant factor affecting the new Algerian leadership's changes in energy policy. Boumediene had pursued a program of rapid industrialization, financed by dramatic increases in oil exports and austerity measures that curtailed domestic consumption. The expansion of gas export infrastructures (especially gas liquefaction terminals) absorbed huge volumes of domestic investment and were slow in yielding returns. Heavy industry received the bulk of attention and resources, while ill-designed, and underfunded agricultural policies moved Algeria from domestic surplus to a food importer by the end of the Boumediene era (Aïssaoui 2001). The new Benjedid government thus saw a political imperative to abandon this investment strategy in favor of the immediate needs of agriculture and education, in particular (Stern 1986).

New energy guidelines were adopted by the FLN Central Committee in 1980, which put particular emphasis on "guaranteeing long-term domestic energy requirements," rationalizing energy demand within an "energy consumption pattern," and conserving energy resources by establishing "strategic reserves" of hydrocarbons. While couched in a

---

[15] Responsibilities for industry and energy were split, so Nabi actually became Minister of Energy.

[16] Nabi and his fellow conservative members of the FLN were also settling scores with the technocrats who had dominated during the Boumediene era. The dispute between Nabi and Abdesselam was largely personal, dating back to the formation of Sonatrach in the pre-Boumediene era. Nabi was previously the chairman of SN-Repal, the Algerian–French partnership that was squeezed out of lucrative oil and gas to the benefit of the Abdesselam-led Sonatrach. The removal of Aït Laoussine also marked the displacement of the bulk of commercial experience in Sonatrach.

rational framework, the new policies were in large part politically motivated and a direct refutation of Abdesselam's export-oriented VALHYD policy – particularly with respect to natural gas.

External events also favored this radical shift in gas export policy. Rising OPEC power in the late 1970s and the aftermath of the Iranian Revolution resulted in sky-rocketing oil prices. The volumes of Algerian oil and oil product exports remained relatively constant, but surging prices created overflowing export revenues (see figure 3.8). The mindset among petroleum exporters was that greater export revenues could be generated from higher prices rather than from higher export volumes (Aïssaoui 2001). Oil producers were also placing increasing emphasis on the distribution of rents from the resource trade. Framed in terms of the "North–South" dialogue, the argument was intertwined with post-colonial development and the rise of OPEC. Producing countries were demanding a larger share of rents for their resource exports. In this broad context – and supported by overflowing oil revenues – the new Algerian and Sonatrach leadership saw the opportunity to push aggressively for price increases for its gas exports in line with sky-high oil prices.

Despite the radical changes in the political regime, construction on the Transmed project officially began with a ceremony in Algiers in June 1979. By the end of 1980, the three pipes spanning the Straits of Sicily were completed. The 1981 target for first gas deliveries appeared technically achievable.

Toward the end of the pipeline construction, in mid-1980, Algeria notified Italy that it would demand more than $5.50 per mmbtu for gas delivered to the Tunisian border, $2 more than the price as determined by the formula in the 1977 contract ($3.50 per mmbtu).[17] After transit charges this would yield a cost of gas to ENI of $6.32 per mmbtu at the Italian border and a cost to Italian buyers of more than $7 per mmbtu. ENI flatly refused, and argued that the 1977 contract provisions should hold (Zartman and Bassani 1987). When ENI refused to accept the new pricing terms, Sonatrach and the Algerian government quickly escalated the dispute. Sonatrach stopped payments on its project-related debts to Italian banks and the Algerian government ordered a halt to all Italian industrial contracts and construction projects in Algeria.

The new price demands for Transmed gas were part of a broader shift in gas pricing policy sought by Minister of Energy Nabi. Nabi was directing Sonatrach to demand from gas buyers an immediate increase

---

[17] The formula price in the 1977 contract rose with oil product prices in the Italian market – but not as fast or as much as the Algerians desired.

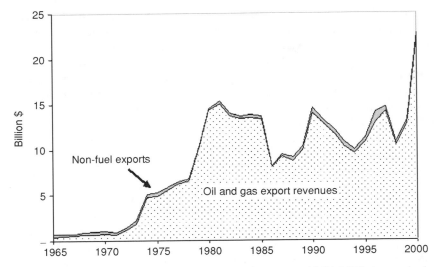

Figure 3.8. Algeria: export revenues, by source, 1965–2000, in nominal USD.
Source: World Bank (2003).

to f.o.b. parity with Algeria's own high-grade crude oil. This was a major jump in price and a radical departure from the Aït Laoussine strategy of pricing gas off competing fuels in the offtake market, the so-called "netback pricing" scheme. Such a strategy ensured that gas was able to compete and gain market share relative to oil products. The earlier strategy would price gas near oil on a c.i.f. basis. Under Nabi's new formula, the *de facto* high transportation costs of gas made gas a premium fuel relative to most alternatives. The new *political* leadership of Sonatrach would demonstrate unprecedented willingness to withhold supplies to achieve these price demands.

When negotiations stalled in Rome, the Algerian government pushed Sonatrach to pursue price increases with each of its LNG buyers. Negotiations with US buyer El Paso began – and ended – rapidly. The US Department of Energy and Department of State effectively represented El Paso in the negotiations. The Reagan administration would not allow a price significantly above that for imports from Canada and Mexico. The US government feared that a higher Algerian price would encourage Canadian and Mexican suppliers to use "most-favored nation" (MFN) treatment clauses in their contracts to seek similar price increases (Mortimer 1984). Algerian imports accounted for a small fraction of the US market, and the government determined that it was better to curtail Algerian supplies completely than see across-the-board price increases. Algerian imports were much more critical to Belgium and France than to the United States. In the early 1980s, Algerian LNG imports accounted for over half of Belgian gas demand and nearly a quarter of French gas consumption, while the sum of Algerian contracts with US buyers amounted to less than 1 percent of the US gas market (BP 2003).

With the Transmed pipeline sitting empty – and its new $2 billion dollar LNG facility at Arzew shut down with the cancellation of the US contracts – Sonatrach sought to use its leverage over Belgium's Distrigaz to achieve Nabi's price goals. Distrigaz acquiesced, seemingly protected by a "most-favored company" clause that allowed the Belgians to claim any lower prices subsequently negotiated with Sonatrach's other buyers. While this seemed advantageous to Distrigaz, Sonatrach instead used the Belgian contract to increase the leverage on the French and Italians (Zartman and Bassani 1987).

Gaz de France first tried to ignore the new Algerian gas price demands and continued to send payments only for the originally contracted price. Sonatrach responded by sending only a fraction of the obligatory gas shipments. The French bargaining position was further weakened as the Netherlands also sought increases in its pipeline delivered gas from $2.54 to $4.10 per mmbtu. The Soviets also sought price increases from their Western European buyers (Zartman and Bassani 1987).

The French Socialist government ultimately intervened in the negotiations and agreed to provide a direct subsidy to add to the commercially viable price (as determined by Gaz de France) to meet the oil–gas f.o.b. parity price sought by Algiers. The French Socialist government's intervention had as much to do with addressing post-colonial guilt as it did with energy security concerns. On February 3, 1982, the French signed a twenty-year agreement for 5.15 Bcm per year with a formula price of $5.12 per mmbtu f.o.b. or $5.85 per mmbtu c.i.f., based on the $30 per barrel oil prices of the day. In return for the "political subsidy" from the French government, Algeria provided guarantees for future industrial import orders totaling $2.13 billion (PIW 1982a).

After the French had signed, ENI had little negotiating leverage left. Both France and Belgium had caved in to Sonatrach's demands and ENI was stuck with virtually all of the loan payments on an empty multi-billion-dollar gas pipeline. ENI's one remaining bargaining chip was the negotiations that were taking place simultaneously for new Soviet gas imports.

The Soviets – more focused on securing markets – used Italy's weakened negotiating position to their advantage, but did not seek the aggressive price indexing demanded by the Algerians.[18] An agreement was reached between ENI and Moscow in January 1982 for a base price of $4.53 per mmbtu indexed 20 percent on a basket of crude oils, 32 percent on domestic gasoline, and 48 percent on domestic fuel oils – yielding a border price at the time of $4.73 and a distributors' price of $5.38, a 30 cent increase over previous Soviet gas contracts (Zartman and Bassani 1987).

The French government's intervention in the LNG import contract made it nearly inevitable that the Italian government would also become involved in the Transmed pricing dispute. Italian businesses with contracts frozen in Algeria saw the French "goodwill" gas price as paving the way for more French imports into the country at the expense of Italian goods and services (Financial Times 1982). Separately, political pressures were rising for the delivery of the promised gas to the millions of new customers to be connected in the Mezzogiorno.

On September 23, 1982, ministerial meetings opened in Rome, and in only four days the Italian Minister of Foreign Trade, Capria, and the Algerian Minister, Nabi, signed a ministerial agreement for the delivery of Algerian gas to Italy, based on a formula similar to that imposed on Gaz de France (GdF) in 1981 (Buxton 1982).

1983 Contract

As in France, it was the willingness of the Italian government to guarantee to pay the "political price" demanded by the Algerians that kept the Transmed project from sitting indefinitely idle – or, at least, empty until oil prices came back to earth. Before it would sign any contract with Algiers, ENI demanded a legislative commitment to cover the difference between what it would define as the "commercial" price for gas and the larger price demanded by Algeria. The law was to be renewed annually and did not specify the commercial price, and thus the direct cost of the subsidy borne by the Italian government was to be determined.

With this legislative guarantee, Sonatrach in turn received its f.o.b. oil-linked pricing formula, yielding $4.41 per mmbtu at the Tunisian border based on the crude prices still in the $30 per barrel range. The price was less than the $4.80 Algeria had most recently demanded. But it was substantially above the $3.67 Italy would have paid under the original

---

[18] The Soviet contracts were a source of significant geopolitical tension during this period of the Cold War. The United States was staunchly opposed to increased European dependency on Soviet gas supplies – ultimately creating a significant trans-Atlantic rift. Italian politics had their own dynamics related to the gas pipelines, with the opposition Socialists seeking to displace the Christian Democrat chairman of ENI.

1977 contract. Including $0.72 in pipeline charges, $4.41 f.o.b. translated into $5.13 c.i.f. delivered into Italy. In its negotiations with the legislature, ENI argued for a substantially lower "commercial price." After a tumultuous battle, the government agreed to provide a subsidy to ENI of $0.53 per mmbtu (PIW 1983). Finally, after a conquering a monumental technical challenge and a political battle that ultimately proved more costly, the first btus of gas were delivered through the Transmed pipeline in June 1983.

History shows that Algeria's aggressive pricing gains did not come cheaply or last long. Rising energy prices were showing signs of slowing demand growth worldwide in the early 1980s, and the Italian economy was no exception. After gas deliveries were held hostage for two years by Sonatrach, ENI still sought reductions in the base contracted volumes for the Transmed when the project started up in 1983. The new contract with Sonatrach included take-or-pay provisions for only 19.7 Bcm for the first three years, down from 22 Bcm in the 1977 agreement (see table 3.4). Furthermore, the new contract contained flexibility provisions for revising all aspects of the accord – not only the price – after the first three years (PIW 1982b).

The delayed start-up of the Transmed had mixed impacts on ENI. Obviously, ENI was not earning revenues from the sale of Transmed gas. However, to accommodate the surge in gas from the Transmed, ENI had originally planned to restrain domestic production while the domestic gas market expanded to utilize full Transmed imports along with other contracted deliveries (Soviet and Dutch). With the economic slowdown in Italy, this would have meant even greater cuts in domestic gas production – ENI's most profitable business segment. Thus, the Algerian cutoff allowed domestic production to continue at near full volume, offsetting some of the damages of its idle investment in the Transmed. Soviet and Dutch gas imports continued largely as planned. In the long term, the biggest impact of the whole "gas battle" was the tarnished reputation of Algeria and Sonatrach as a stable gas supplier – a subject to be revisited in the chapter epilogue (p. 86).

Table 3.4 *Transmed: revised contract volumes, 1983*

Year	Volume (Bcm per year)
1983	3.5
1984	6.5
1985	9.7
1985–	12.4

The Gas Imperative for Spain in the 1970s

Like Italy, Spain is not endowed with plentiful domestic energy resources. At the start of the 1960s, Spanish oil and gas production were
non-existent. Coal production at the time provided half of total primary
energy supplies, yet Spain's domestic coal supplies were limited, of poor
quality, and relatively expensive to mine (see figure 3.9). Hydropower
provided nearly half of the electricity supply in 1960. Yet growth
prospects for hydropower were limited as most of the best sites had been
already exploited by that time. Thus, the rapid industry-led growth that
Spain experienced in the 1960s during an era of cheap world oil prices
was fueled in large part by imported oil.

Between 1960 and 1973, Spain's total primary energy demand grew
nearly three-fold, at an annual rate of 8.5 percent per year. With stagnating coal and hydropower supplies and nascent domestic oil production,
oil imports soared. By 1973, imported oil supplied nearly two-thirds
of the country's energy needs (IEA 1978). Thus, the Spanish economy
(like many other European economies) was dangerously exposed to
the 1973–1974 oil embargo and resultant spike in world oil prices.
The tab for foreign oil created a balance of payments crisis, increased

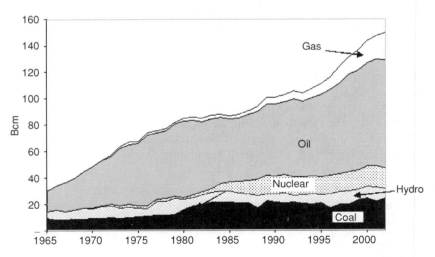

Figure 3.9. Spain: primary energy supply, by fuel, 1965–2004, in Bcm
equivalent.

Source: BP (2003).

interest rates and inflation, and ultimately stalled economic growth. Such problems plagued oil-dependent economies around the world during this period.

Despite the six-fold increase in world oil prices between 1970 and 1975, Spanish oil imports and consumption continued to grow steadily throughout the period. Relative to its European peers such as Italy, Spain was unique in its near total lack of policy response to the oil crisis. However, natural gas imports were on the agendas of foreign companies operating in Spain, and to a somewhat lesser extent the main Spanish state natural gas company, Enagas. In Spain, as in the rest of Europe, the gas imperative was strong and growing. The macroeconomic costs of growing oil imports could not be ignored.

Spanish Pipeline and LNG Import Proposals in the 1970s and Early 1980s

Pipelines to bring Algerian gas to Spain and on to France were proposed as early as 1963 by French companies, with French government support (Pawera 1964). Two basic routes are described in Pawera's early report on Algerian infrastructure (see map, figure 3.1). The first pipeline route would run from the Hassi R'Mel field west across Algeria and Morocco, under the 40 km of sea at the Straits of Gibraltar at depths up to 450 m, and then north into Spain. If this pipe continued through to Strasbourg to serve the French market, the pipeline would have spanned some 3,200 km (Pawera 1964).[19] The second proposed gas pipeline route would also tap the Hassi R'Mel field, follow an existing pipeline route toward the Arzew liquefaction terminal, and then head straight under the Mediterranean for nearly 200 km at depths of up to 2,500 m before terminating in Spain near Almeria. Finally, LNG imports from Algeria were also an option. Algeria was the world's leading LNG exporter at the time and the closest potential supplier to Spanish markets.

Both of the pipeline routes faced major technical hurdles during the 1960s and the 1970s. Industry experience with sub-sea gas pipelines at the time was very limited. The Transmed pipeline, completed in 1981, was the first sub-sea gas pipeline completed below depths at which divers could do most of the construction and maintenance. Maximum depths on that project were similar to the Gibraltar route. As discussed on p. 60, a major R&D initiative by ENI was required to make the construction of

[19] This is the basic route that the GME pipeline would eventually take, shown in the map in figure 3.1. To date, however, there is no significant capacity to deliver gas to France. Instead the GME connects to the Portuguese market.

the Transmed pipeline possible in the late 1970s. However, the edge of the technological envelope was probably not so obvious for decision-makers in Spain or elsewhere at the time. Engineering reports by Bechtel and Williams Bros. suggested that both the Gibraltar and Almeria routes were technically feasible in the 1970s (Pawera 1964; Petroleum Economist 1976, 1977a). However, trade press banter and optimistic consulting reports were not backed by capital investment – on either sub-sea pipeline routes to Spain or other deep-sea projects at the time. The Transmed pipeline experience suggests that: (1) the shorter and shallower Gibraltar pipeline would have required a major financial commitment from either the governments or companies to make it technically feasible; and (2) the deeper Almeria route would not have been possible to construct at this time without major technological breakthroughs.[20]

Despite the additional technological challenge of building the much deeper Almeria pipeline, this is the only pipeline project that was the subject of serious attention during the early 1970s. In November 1973 the direct Almeria route was the route chosen by the Sociedad de Estudios Gasoducto del Mediterráneo Occidental (Segamo), a consortium comprised of Sonatrach (50 percent), Spain's Enagas (25 percent), and GdF (25 percent) (Petroleum Economist 1977a). The Almeria route did indeed provide a shorter path to reach the French market – about 500 km less pipe. However, as discussed above, the technical challenges of the deep-sea route would likely have made it at least as costly as the Gibraltar route. Indeed, it was non-economic factors that derailed any progress on a trans-Morocco Gibraltar route at any time in the 1970s, and thus made the deep and technically challenging Almeria route the only option available to technical planners.

Regional Political Tensions Prevent the Gibraltar Pipeline

Two disputes created political tensions that stalled any serious discussion of a gas pipeline crossing Morocco to Spain during the 1960s and 1970s. First, Algeria and Morocco had long had uneasy relations. The border between the two countries had been contested ever since Algeria

---

[20] The record set by the Transmed gas pipeline at 600 m in depth remained unchallenged for many years, and was in fact only beaten by the Blue Stream, connecting Russia to Turkey across the Black Sea at depths of over 5,000 m. Laying the Blue Stream pipeline was only made possible by the introduction of a novel pipe-laying method (J-lay as opposed to S-lay), which could be adopted following adaptation of the special pipe-laying vessel, the Saipem 7000. Today, this is history. The boundaries of feasibility are never so obvious with time running forward, rather than looking in retrospect.

won its independence in 1962, leading to armed conflict in the 1963 "War of the Sands." The border dispute can also be framed more broadly in the struggle for regional dominance in North Africa. On-again, off-again tensions between the two countries long made Algerians uncomfortable with any gas export pipeline transiting Morocco.

Still, the Transmed example demonstrates that a Spanish company could have – in theory – conducted separate negotiations in Algiers and Rabat and established separate project companies in each country and for the sub-sea segment. Such a structure would have required a strongly motivated Spanish player with firm government and financial backing (as was the case with ENI in the Transmed). However, a separate regional political dispute which developed in the mid-1970s made any bilateral agreement between Spain and Morocco unlikely.

Until the early 1970s, Spain controlled a section of the Western Sahara, south of Morocco and along the Atlantic coast. The region was sparsely populated, with a people known as the Sahrawi, and was a valuable source of phosphate for fertilizers. An independence move-ment began in the 1960s, actively supported by Morocco, Mauritania, and Algeria, each seeking to assert territorial dominance. By 1974 Morocco and Mauritania were conspiring to carve up what became known as the Western Sahara against Spanish interests. King Hassan II of Morocco launched a diplomatic campaign to gain support for Mo-rocco its dispute with Spain. The United Nations (UN) and the Inter-national Court of Justice (ICJ) became involved (Parker 1984). Spain was simply seeking the best exit strategy, and in May 1975 announced its evacuation from the Western Sahara.

The Western Sahara dispute also incited a decade of tensions between Algeria and Morocco. Algeria supported self-determination for the Sahrawi and a close friendship with Algiers. Morocco was angling to split the country with Mauritania. In 1975, King Hassan organized the "Green March," a movement of 300,000 Moroccans to lay claim to the Western Sahara region. Hassan's tactic forced Spain out, and weak statements from the international community could not prevent Morocco and Mauritania from quickly carving up the former colony. Algeria – seeking to protect its regional position and advance its commitment to liberation movements everywhere – soon began to funnel fuel and weapons to support insurgent guerillas dubbed the "Polisario" in their struggle against Morocco. Algeria officially recognized the Polisario's Saharan Arab Democratic Republic (SADR) as an independent state in March 1976 – although Morocco retained *de facto* control of the country. Morocco, in turn, terminated diplomatic relations with Al-geria. A proxy war ensued through the early 1980s, with Algeria supporting the Polisario with weapons and diplomatic support (Entelis 1983; Parker 1984). Diplomatic relations between Morocco and SADR are not normalized to date. A UN-brokered cease-fire was negotiated in 1991, but a referendum on the sovereignty of the country has been delayed.

Ultimately, the high-level and at times heated disputes between Algeria, Morocco, and Spain prevented any proposal of a pipeline across Morocco. No evidence of any serious discussions of a trans-Morocco pipeline can be found in the trade press through the mid-1980s.

Domestic Political Economy and Energy Policy in Spain

With external political relations stalling any progress on the Morocco–Gibraltar route, two options for bringing Algerian gas to Spain remained: (1) the deep-sea pipeline route to Almeria; and (2) LNG imports.[21] Despite the Segamo proposal and supposed positive findings from seabed surveys and consulting studies, no concrete or steel was ever put on the Mediterranean floor to test the technical feasibility of this pipeline route. If regional political tensions were the key factor preventing progress on a trans-Morocco–Gibraltar gas pipeline during the 1970s and 1980s, Spain's domestic political economy, with strong oil concerns and no proponent for natural gas, may be viewed as a critical factor stalling Spanish gas imports more generally during this period.

Any pipeline route to Spain would have needed to deliver at least 10 Bcm of gas per year to be economically viable. The country's total gas consumption in 1973 amounted to less than 2 Bcm per year, delivered across a gas network of less than 2,000 km of pipelines. The near total lack of residential gas supply connections meant that the majority of initial gas supplies would first connect to industrial and commercial users. Industrial users are less costly per unit gas sales to bring onto the gas grid, however the absence of a viable residential market limited the potential volume of sales. Significant new capital investments in gas-burning equipment would have been needed to switch consumers of

---

[21] Other proposals were offered during this period to bring Nigerian gas north across Africa to mainland Europe. Spain also could have expanded connections to the European gas grid via France. The first option was a fanciful proposal of diplomats, never receiving serious attention from investors. The second option to build connections to France (and thus potentially to Dutch and Soviet gas) was stalled in Spain–European Community politics that were cold during the Franco period, but then warmed considerably afterwards. Nevertheless, interconnections between the Spanish and French gas markets have been limited to date.

other fuel types to using gas to create a robust market for gas consumption. In total, the expansion of infrastructure to distribute and consume 10 Bcm of new gas supplies demanded bold moves on the part of Enagas and local gas companies, likely requiring financial backing from the Spanish government and probably international lenders. Together, the cost of expanding the pipeline grid and investing in gas-burning equipment in Spain would have been comparable to the total estimated $4 billion cost of building the main pipeline to Almeria from Algeria (Petroleum Economist 1977b).

However, in the 1970s, Enagas was in no position to mobilize its own capital or secure support from the Spanish government to undertake such an expansion. During the Franco period and the transition to democracy, the Spanish gas industry had mixed capital (state and private) in a manner similar to the country's petroleum refining industry. Unlike the petroleum industry, however, the structure of the Spanish gas industry was dispersed and lacked cohesion (Lancaster 1989). Enagas did not enjoy the financial resources or political clout of the major petroleum companies, such as Repsol or Companía Española de Petróleos, SA (CEPSA). Repsol was able to secure subsidies to support LPG sales as oil prices climbed. As a result, the expansion of capital-intensive natural gas transport and distribution infrastructure was slow, while sales of Repsol's bottled LPG, refined from imported oil, soared.

The relative weakness of Enagas may also explain the lack of attention given natural gas in the National Energy Plan (PEN-75) drafted in the last years of the Franco regime. Drafted in an attempt to respond to the first oil crisis, PEN-75 sought to reduce Spain's petroleum dependence by substituting coal, hydroelectricity, and nuclear energy – with little attention to natural gas (Lancaster 1989).

The Franco regime ended with the Generalissimo's death in November 1975. The transition to democracy that followed was peaceful, but nevertheless stalled most major policy-making decisions (Lancaster 1989). Interim energy policy objectives were included in the broader Moncloa Pacts signed between representatives of business, labor, and the state in 1977. It would be nearly two years later, in July 1979, before the new Spanish parliament would debate and approve PEN-79, yielding initiatives to expand natural gas infrastructures (IEA 1980).

Lacking the political and financial support necessary to pursue a major gas import pipeline, Enagas and other players in the Spanish market from the 1960s were forced to look to LNG as the only viable supply source. Gas Natural, SA was formed in 1966 by a consortium of banks, the Catalunya Gas Company, and US-based Exxon to import LNG from Exxon's Libyan fields (Lancaster 1989). But due to delays in the

Libyan project, it was the Enagas regasification terminal at Barcelona that first brought LNG to Spain in 1969. These first shipments came from Sonatrach and would presage a larger future contract. The first Libyan shipments did not arrive until 1971, and these supplies later dwindled when Libya nationalized its petroleum industry.

For Enagas, LNG was the option best suited for the limited Spanish market and its limited financial resources at the time. Sonatrach and Algeria bore over a third of the total capital cost of the gas trade project in the liquefaction terminal on Algerian soil. Enagas also partnered with Norwegian and private Spanish companies in the LNG tankers. The LNG project allowed Enagas to deliver smaller initial volumes to customers into the Barcelona gas grid, with limited connection to the rest of the country.

By the mid-1970s, the impetus for expanding gas imports – rising oil consumption and prices – drove Enagas to more aggressive measures for gas. With the Gibraltar route blocked by politics and a deep-sea route beyond the company's technological or financial capacity, Enagas signed a contract with Sonatrach in 1975 to take 4.5 Bcm (3.3 mtpa) of LNG per year for twenty-five years. The contract had the typical rigid take-or-pay terms of the day, with indexing to a basket of oil products.

The failure of the only major foray by Enagas into LNG in the 1970s is instructive of the broader limitations on Spanish gas imports during this period. From the inception of its twenty-five-year contract, Enagas never took more than 1.5 Bcm per year, nor did it pay for the full 4.5 Bcm of contracted volume in the period of 1975 through 1980.[22] Enagas was unable to market all of the gas for which it had agreed to take delivery. Gas distribution expansion plans were proposed, but the distribution network was very slow to expand outside of Barcelona (Petroleum Economist 1977a). The policy uncertainty of the post-Franco transition period did not provide the regulatory and financial support needed to expand the gas grid.

Sonatrach, under Aït Laoussine's leadership, was probably hesitant to press Enagas on its contractual violations, realizing the fragile state of the gas business in Spain. As in other markets, the goal of Sonatrach pre-1979 was to build markets, with a view toward long-term gas sales and securing a foothold in European markets. Sonatrach's strategy changed markedly after Algerian President Boumediene died in late 1978.

---

[22] Enagas non-performance in the early stages of the project did not leave them in a solid negotiating position when Algeria later sought rapid price increases. International arbitrators would later order Enagas to pay $200 million in damages for breach of contract.

The aggressive "gas battle" waged by the post-Boumediene leadership in Algiers and Sonatrach dealt a deadly blow to the possibility for gas imports to Spain. Enagas, in its weakened position, had been unable to sell what volumes it was taking from Algiers (under 2 Bcm per year). When Nabi and the Sonatrach leadership began to threaten to withhold gas deliveries without price increases, Enagas was more inclined to not take the gas at all than to pay higher prices for gas it could not sell. Unlike Belgium, France and Italy, Spain did not cave in to the Algerian price demands for it had much less at stake.

Ultimately, the political and economic contexts of the period did not support the complex cooperation and clear policy initiatives required to complete an international gas pipeline connecting Algerian gas reserves to the Spanish market. Fractious political relations between all of the countries potentially involved in the more technically feasible Gibraltar pipeline stalled any progress on this route. The mid-to-late 1970s were also a period of major political uncertainty in Spain, as the new democratic government struggled to gain stable footing after the death of Franco. Just as a new Spanish energy policy began to take shape in the late 1970s and early 1980s, the political transition in Algiers significantly changed Sonatrach's perspective on gas exports. The new Algerian administration may have favored pipelines over costly LNG exports, but this policy preference was overshadowed by the contentious "gas battle" being waged by Algiers in demand of higher prices for all gas sales. Whatever the political challenges, the key limiting factor for a major project delivering Algerian gas to Spain was the absence of a single actor like ENI with the resources and the mettle to push any such project through to fruition.

Conclusions

The design of this study facilitates comparison across the Italian and Spanish cases. Both ENI and Enagas sought to bring gas from Algeria to their respective European markets. Both Italian and Spanish energy demands were growing rapidly leading up to and into the energy crises of the 1970s. Many of the economic and political factors mentioned above are hard to measure empirically, particularly for the unbuilt pipelines to Spain that exist only hypothetically (or were realized only when the Gaz Maghreb Europe pipeline was completed thirteen years later).

Working from the assumption that the factors identified here as common hold constant across the two cases, logic instructs that the factors that differ between the Spanish and Italian cases are those critical to project completion. Casual observers – including those very knowledgeable about the region and the projects – may at first glance find this a trivial exercise. Indeed, in retrospect it does seem obvious that the Spanish gas market was limited and that troubled relations between Morocco, Algeria, and Spain spoiled any hope of a trans-Gibraltar route in the late 1970s. In hindsight, it is simple to say that the deep-water Almeria route was impossible at the time. However, when the lens of analysis is turned to the perspective of decision-makers at the time, rather than to *ex post* storytelling, questions that ask *why* a particular project succeeds become much more interesting.

The course of events that led to the construction of the Transmed and the numerous innovative mechanisms used to complete the gas project are worthy of closer examination. Gas transport technologies have advanced considerably since the 1970s and will continue to do so over the coming three decades, which later chapters of this book pontificate. However, many of the political and strategic considerations that affected ENI's decision to proceed with the Transmed project and the Enagas decision to pursue limited LNG imports in the 1970s will continue to play an important role in gas import decision-making in the future.

Tables 3.5 and 3.6 list common and contrasting factors for the Transmed project and the proposed project to pipe gas from Algeria to Spain. Starting with the historical perspective, the success of ENI (Snam) with natural gas in Italy's Po Valley in the 1950s and 1960s propelled the company into a national powerhouse. With its success came the expansion of the Italian gas grid and, in turn, a stable and rapidly growing market, eventually demanding more gas than domestic resources could provide. The company then set out to secure imports from Algeria, among other suppliers. Critical to the company's success in signing contracts for long-term gas import purchases was the company's complete monopoly of the offtake market and the critical financial backing of the Italian government. All these factors made ENI a favorite of international lenders, which in turn provided financing for projects such as the Transmed pipeline.

Spain's Enagas was nearly at the opposite end of the spectrum. Endowed with neither domestic resources nor a power base in the national government, the company struggled to expand the gas network and gain markets for its contracted shipments of LNG from Algeria and Libya.[23] The limited size of the Spanish market at the time necessitated French involvement in a pipeline project to make it economically viable. However, the French market would come only with the added expense

---

[23] Domestic gas discoveries in the 1980s provide further evidence that state support may have been the critical limiting factor in building the Spanish gas market.

Table 3.5 *Factors common to both projects*

Factor	Transmed	Not built pipeline/ LNG imports
1 Policy drivers	Italy 79% dependent on imported oil in 1973; very limited supply of domestic energy resources	Spain 73% dependent on imported oil in 1973; very limited supply of domestic energy resources
2 Supply risk (Algeria)	Sonatrach offered secure access to massive reserves	Sonatrach offered secure access to massive reserves
3 Transit country involvement	No direct disputes between Italy or Algeria and Tunisia; Tunisia did stall deal in attempt to squeeze rents	Difficult relations between both Morocco and Spain and Morocco and Algeria during the 1970s and 1980s; direct route to Spain would have avoided transit country issue – but also greatly increased technical complexity
4 Technical challenge *(depth for sub-sea pipe)*	610 m maximum depth	450 m max. depth for Gibraltar crossing; approx. 2000 m for direct route
5 Total capital cost/ Scope	$4 billion in 1977/2,500 km pipeline	$4 billion in 1977; rough estimate depending on route/ 3,200 km to France via Gibraltar; 2,400 km via direct route
6 Legal environment	Legal risk relevant only in Tunisia as other players were state-owned and operating domestically	Legal risk only in Morocco for Gibraltar route as other players were state-owned companies operating domestically
7 Regulatory	State-owned monopolies	State-owned monopolies

of a longer pipeline and the increased complexity of another party in the negotiations.

Beyond these fundamental factors, other historical and political events were at work. The Algerian nationalization of French energy assets in 1971 tempered any French interest in engaging again with Sonatrach in a pipeline project. In the mid-1970s, the dispute over the Western Sahara between Morocco and Algeria, and Morocco and Spain raised obstacles to a Gibraltar route, while the transition from dictatorship toward democratic rule in Spain stalled major energy policy decisions until the end of that decade. Just as these distractions were clearing, a new regime in Algiers started Sonatrach on a "gas battle" that soured commercial and political relations with most of its gas buyers and made new gas export

Table 3.6 *Factors varying across the two projects*

Factor	Transmed	Not-Built Pipeline / LNG imports
1 Domestic political economy	The ENI group was the dominant player in both the energy market and policy-making, with strong political and financial backing	Enagas is a poor step-child to Spanish oil companies; domestic policy instability/void in post-Franco transition
2 Offtake risks	Monopoly pricing subject to ministerial approval; 22 Bcm domestic gas market in 1977	Monopoly pricing subject to ministerial approval; less than 2 Bcm domestic gas market in 1977
3 Financing	ENI had no problem with financing based in large part on domestic political economy	Enagas had limited ability to raise funds, a product of domestic political economy
4 Resource base/ path dependence	Domestic gas resources, though limited, spawned the development of ENI's core competence in gas and the company's growth	Spain still trying to rationalize its coal subsidies in the 1980s; no domestic gas industry
5 Multiple offtakers / transit countries	Slovenia signed contract for deliveries in follow-on deal; minimal effect on original deal complexity	Spain's limited gas market necessitated French involvement, multiplying political and commercial complexity

projects unattractive to importers. Moreover, gas priced on parity with oil would not have been a solution to Spain's energy security issues, particularly as Sonatrach showed its penchant for withholding deliveries.

The Transmed pipeline, however, was never a forgone conclusion. Strong financial backing and political support were necessary to bring the Transmed pipeline to completion. Enagas enjoyed neither of these strengths during the 1970s, and it was thus left with the limited LNG option for gas imports until the 1990s.

Epilogue: Italian and Spanish Gas Import Projects Through the 1990s

This research is focused on the factors that affect the initial decision to invest in and build a cross-border gas trade project – in this case, comparing projects to move Algerian gas to Italy and to Spain. Many will also be interested to know about the performance of the projects after that initial decision was made. A complete analysis of the private and social returns on these projects would be a daunting task for those that were actually completed, and a hypothetical exercise for the Algeria–Spain pipeline that was ultimately built in a different era (1996 rather than 1980). Such an analysis is beyond the scope of this study. Some general insights are offered here on the history of operations in the region and the current status of these and other new projects.

The "gas battle" waged by Nabi and Sonatrach ultimately turned into the "gas fiasco."[24] The abrogation of the 1977 Transmed contract and the ensuing dispute over prices were costly for all parties involved: Algeria and Italy, Sonatrach, and ENI. Nabi's pursuit of oil price parity at the Algerian coast – by any means necessary – proved rather quickly to be shortsighted. By November of 1985, with oil prices falling to $25 per barrel, the gas price in the Transmed contract fell to $3.50 per mmbtu f.o.b. By mid-1986, oil prices fell to $10 per barrel and the pricing formula – if it had held – would have yielded a negative f.o.b. price. More conservative pricing formulas, such as that included in the earlier 1977 contract, would have included a higher base price and a less direct oil–gas linkage, ultimately reducing the exposure to these downward price swings. However, ENI was keen to keep the Transmed project viable and renegotiated the contract months before the price fell toward zero. The revised 1986 contract replaced the OPEC official oil price as an index and used the old and reliable net-back formula instead. The base price was reinstated at $1.30 per mmbtu (Aïssaoui 2001).

However, the pricing issues had a relatively short-term effect compared to the longer-term impact on the Algerian market share and reputation that resulted from the "gas battle." Sonatrach almost completely lost its US market for LNG and stunted its growth possibilities in Europe. As a result, Sonatrach's already built LNG export facilities operated significantly below design capacity through the 1980s and 1990s (Zartman and Bassani 1987; Aïssaoui 2001). Sonatrach later had trouble keeping its LNG facilities properly maintained over this period, and only in the late 1990s was it able to invest in the necessary plant refurbishments to bring its export facilities at Arzew and Skikda back to designed capacity.

The goal of ENI in the Transmed project was to secure a long-term, stable, and economic supply of gas. Excepting Sonatrach's early performance, the project has proven been to be surprisingly reliable in

---

[24] The "gas fiasco" was so called by Aït Laoussine, who had earlier been forced out by Nabi and thus some obvious bitterness remained. Still, even to the objective analyst the title does not seem inappropriate.

delivering gas to Italy, especially given Algeria's troubles with its LNG exports and the tumultuous decade of civil unrest and terrorism of the 1990s. ENI was suitably pleased with Algerian supply that it partnered with Sonatrach to add new compressors and an additional sub-sea line to expand Transmed capacity to 24 Bcm per year in 1995. In the fall of 1997, terrorists did attack the pipeline, severing one section of it on Algerian soil and stopping deliveries for five days.[25] Italian consumers were not significantly affected as ENI had adequate storage at the time to cover the shortfall (WGI 1998).[26] Despite these challenges, the Italian gas market continues to expand. The Galsi pipeline project is its early stages, and if completed it will bring more Algerian gas to Italy via Sardinia.

On the Spanish side, when Sonatrach tried to raise its selling price in 1982, Enagas was not interested in any "political subsidy" to keep its LNG deliveries coming, as ENI sought for Transmed deliveries. Enagas did not want to lift its full contract amount in the future, nor would it pay for any of its liftings by the new formula agreed to by France and Belgium yielding $5.12–$5.28 per mmbtu for LNG at that time. Sonatrach and Enagas were soon deadlocked. Algeria eventually pursued arbitration under the International Chamber of Commerce (ICC) and won $200 million in damages as compensation for breach of the original LNG contract with Enagas (Zartman and Bassani 1987).

Given the Spanish experience with LNG, it is hard to imagine Spain's gas demand growing rapidly enough in the 1980s to justify pipeline imports without a very different policy approach by the government. Expanding gas infrastructure required major public support in the form of both regulation and financing. Nevertheless, the steep drop in oil prices after 1982 allowed Spain to easily continue its dependence on imported oil.

It was not until the mid-1990s that the Spanish government was able to stimulate a burgeoning gas market. The opening of the Spanish gas and electric power markets spurred new investment, particularly in new gas-fired power generation. The drivers and context had changed completely. Liberalization of the Spanish market had spawned a new

---

[25] LNG shipments have also been interrupted by terrorism and accidents. In the spring of 1998 supply pipelines to Arzew were blown up, reducing LNG exports from the facility to 50 percent of capacity for approximately a week. In September 2003 a fire at the Arzew complex disrupted production at one train for several weeks. Then, in January 2004, a massive explosion at the Skikda complex completely destroyed two of six liquefaction trains. Four workers were killed and sixty injured in the worst LNG-related accident since the Cleveland disaster in 1944 (see chapter 1).

[26] Italy has total storage capacity of 17 Bcm, on 73 Bcm annual consumption. The amount of gas in storage varies seasonally (IEA 2003; BP 2005).

powerhouse in Gas Natural. With support of the European Union (EU), the new Spanish company pushed through an agreement with Sonatrach and Morocco for the long-troubled Gibraltar route.

In 1996 the Gaz Maghreb Europe (GME) pipeline was finally built, spanning Morocco and passing under the Straits of Gibraltar to bring Algerian gas to Spain and on to Portugal. The critical importance of the shifting Spanish policy context (and the rise of Gas Natural) can be seen as the GME project was completed in the midst of the persistent violence that plagued Algeria during the 1990s. The empowered Gas Natural still pushed forward, despite the civil unrest and continued difficult relations between Rabat and Algiers. The Maghreb gas pipeline has since been expanded and LNG deliveries to Spain have grown rapidly since the late 1990s (from Algeria, Qatar, and Trinidad, among others). The direct under-sea pipeline from Algeria to Almeria, Spain is back on the drawing table, now as the "Medgaz" project, with plans to deliver gas on to France as well. The Spanish gas market in 2005 is still relatively small, however, when compared to the well-established Italian gas system (27 Bcm vs. 73 Bcm, respectively).

REFERENCES

Aïssaoui, Ali (2001). *Algeria: the Political Economy of Oil and Gas.* Oxford: Oxford University Press
Aït Laoussine, Nordine (1977). "LNG exports – a contribution to world energy supplies in the decades to come." *OPEC Review.* 1–7, pp. 21–35, October
Benachenou, A. (1980). *Planification et développement en Algérie.* Algiers: Enterprise Nationale "Imprimerie Commerciale"
BP (2003). *Statistical Review of World Energy,* available at http://www.bp.com
(2005). *Statistical Review of World Energy,* available at http://www.bp.com
Business Week (1977). "Italy's costly undersea pipeline." December 26
Buxton, James (1982). "Italy agrees to gas price with Algeria." *Financial Times,* September 28
Caroni, G. (1992). "The Transmed: an energy 'highway' across the Mediterranean." *Revue de l'energie,* 441, pp. 561–566
Darmstadter, Joel, Perry D. Teitelbaum, and Jaroslav G. Polach (1971). *Energy in the World Economy: A Statistical Review of Trends in Output, Trade, and Consumption since 1925.* Baltimore: Johns Hopkins Press, for Resources for the Future
Dispenza, Domenico (2002). "International pipelines across the Mediterranean," IEA Cross Border Gas Conference. Paris: IEA, March 26
Entelis, John P. (1983). "Algeria in world politics: foreign policy orientation and the New International Economic Order." *American–Arab Affairs*
Entelis, John P. (1999). "Sonatrach: the political economy of an Algerian state institution." *Middle East Journal,* 53–1, pp. 9–26
Financial Times (1982). "Italy's gas needs: a tale of two pipelines." February 25

FLN (1976). *Charte nationale*. Algiers: FLN Press

IEA (1978). *Energy Policies and Programmes of IEA Countries: 1977 Review*. Paris: International Energy Agency

(1980). *Energy Policies and Programmes of IEA Countries: 1979 Review*. Paris: International Energy Agency

(2003). "Energy statistics of OECD countries." Paris: International Energy Agency

Knapp, Wilfrid (1977). *North West Africa: A Political and Economic Survey*. Oxford and New York: Oxford University Press

Lancaster, Thomas D. (1989). *Policy Stability and Democratic Change: Energy in Spain's Transition*. University Park, PA: Pennsylvania State University Press

Moraleda, P. (2002). "How the major barners to cross-border gas trade were overcome in the case of the Maghreb Pipeline." IEA Cross Border Gas Conference, Paris, March 26. Paris: International Energy Agency

Mortimer, Robert A. (1984). "Global economy and African foreign policy: the Algerian model." *African Studies Review*, 27–1, pp. 1–22

Newham, Mark (1979). "ENI and Sonatrach team up for trans-Mediterranean pipeline." Offshore Engineer, May, pp. 87–90

Parker, Richard Bordeaux (1984). *North Africa: Regional Tensions and Strategic Concerns*. New York: Praeger

Pawera, John C. (1964). *Algeria's Infrastructure: An Economic Survey of Transportation, Communication, and Energy Resources*. New York: Praeger

Petroleum Economist (1976). "Gas pipelines to Europe." June

(1977a). "Bold plan to pipe Algerian gas." May

(1977b). "Three routes for Algerian gas pipe." September

Petroleum Intelligence Weekly (PIW) (1982a). "Algerian gas price disputes." February 15

(1982b). "Italy, like France to pay 'political' Algerian gas price." October 4

(1983). "Algerian gas prices to ease in Europe if oil comes down." March 7

Pozzi, Daniele (2003). "Techno-management competencies in Enrico Mattei's Agip: a prolonged accumulation process in an international relationship network (1935–1965)." 2003 BHC/EBHA Meeting, Lowell, MA

Stern, Jonathan P. (1986). *International Gas Trade in Europe: The Policies of Exporting and Importing Countries*. Aldershot: Gower

Sutton, Keith (1978). "The Algerian natural gas industry." Unknown Source

WGI (1998). *World Gas Intelligence*. 26 February

World Bank (2003). "World development indicators." Washington, DC: World Bank

Zartman, I.William and Antonella Bassani (1987). *The Algerian Gas Negotiations*. Washington, DC: Distributed by Institute for the Study of Diplomacy School of Foreign Service, Georgetown University

4 Liquefied natural gas from Indonesia: the Arun project

Fred von der Mehden and Steven W. Lewis

Introduction

The Arun natural gas project in Northern Sumatra is probably the most lucrative LNG operation in the twentieth century. This chapter analyzes the issues involved in the transmission of that gas to potential buyers and why Japan became Arun's only foreign market in its first two decades. Following a description of the development of the Arun field and its LNG facilities, we review the agreements made with the initial buyers. To explain the context in which these contracts evolved, we analyze Pertamina, the Indonesian national oil company, and the political and economic conditions in the Republic at the time. We give considerable attention to the long-term impact of this trade on the Japanese and Northeast Asian gas markets, the contractual relations between Pertamina and Japanese buyers, and competition among those buyers.

The basic thrust of this analysis is that Japan was the only viable customer for Arun's gas in the initial decade after discovery. Japan had a need for clean energy, was prepared to use LNG, and was willing to finance the project in Indonesia. There was not a sufficient domestic market in Indonesia at the time and Arun was perceived to be geographically too far from its population center. The rest of East and South Asia had not developed to the point of usefully importing LNG and did not have the ability to finance these operations. Singapore was later to become an importer of gas piped from Indonesia, but at the time was not interested in Arun. The only other viable alternative was California, where environmental and other concerns aborted efforts to develop that market.

The authors would like to thank the following for their help: the researchers and staff of PESD, our colleagues at the Baker Institute, our field research interviewees in Japan and Southeast Asia, two anonymous reviewers, case study authors and other participants at workshops in Palo Alto and Houston, many anonymous officials and industry experts in Southeast Asia, Japan and North America, and especially Don Emmerson and Al Troner.

Development of the Arun and Asian LNG Market

Indonesia (then the Dutch East Indies) was an early producer of petroleum, with drilling for oil beginning in the 1870s. Major companies involved in exploration and production included Royal Dutch Shell, the dominant early oil firm, Stanvac, and Caltex. Prior to the Second World War, the Indies was producing 148,000 barrels of oil per day. The war brought a scorched earth policy by the colonial government, with more destruction from a four-year-long nationalist conflict that did not end until late 1949. Pre-war production levels were not reached again until 1951 (Arndt 1983; Hunter 1966). Independent Indonesia became increasingly suspicious of foreign investors, and although oil production increased through the 1950s there was little new exploration. Political pressures for nationalization forced Royal Dutch Shell to leave its Indonesian operations, and by the mid-1960s it appeared that all foreign enterprises were endangered by the threat of nationalization.

During this period natural gas played little or no role. Small amounts had been used for fuel by an oil industry that had also utilized gas injection to enhance oil production since the 1920s. It was not until 1963 that gas was first used as feedstock in a fertilizer plant. As late as 1973 as much as 60 percent of gas was either flared or vented (Ooi Jin Bee 1980, p. 172).[1] The Indonesian government, however, was becoming increasingly cognizant of the potential for the export and, to a lesser extent, the domestic use of gas. Meanwhile internal events in the Republic were making the development of the oil and gas industry more feasible.

An aborted *coup* attempt in 1965 led to the ultimate attainment of power by a pro-foreign investment government under President Suharto, and by the late 1960s exploration was developing again with the involvement of foreign companies. As part of these new conditions, in 1967 the Mobil Oil Corporation had secured a production-sharing partnership with Pertamina. Mobil began searching for oil in northern Sumatra, and by 1971 it discovered a vast natural gas field in the province of Aceh, approximately 12 miles southeast of the port of Lhoseumawe and 200 miles north of the major city of Medan (Pertamina 1979; Ooi Jin Bee 1980, 1982; Sugiono 1997). This discovery became known as the Arun field and plant (see the map in figure 4.1).

The original oval shaped field was 4.8 km wide, 18.5 km long, and on average 153 m thick. According to Ooi Jin Bee, using the terminology,

---

[1] It was claimed that by 1979 only 23 percent was lost in this manner, with the percentage dropping to 8.9 by 1984 (Migas 1984).

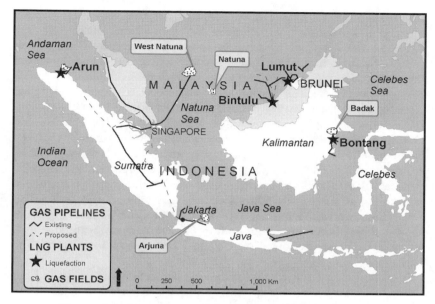

Figure 4.1. Natural gas infrastructure: Indonesia, Malaysia, and Brunei.

analytical methods, and standards of that period, it was a find large enough to warrant development of LNG:

The gas reservoir is carbonate of Early and Middle Miocene age, underlain by a clastic sequence resting on basement rock of pre-Tertiary age. The reservoir is effectively enclosed in shales which, together with the organic material in the reef, are probably also the sources of hydrocarbons. The reservoir covers an area of about 17,000 ha. The average depth of the formation is about 3,048 m, while the net pay thickness varies from 102 to 316 m. Gas produced from the reservoir has a methane content, of 72 percent, a carbon dioxide content of nearly 15 percent, a small nitrogen content and a trace of hydrogen sulfide. The high potential of the reservoir is indicated by well productivities of over a billion ft^3 per day, with significant quantities of condensate. Wet gas-in-place has been calculated at 17.15 trillion standard ft^3 (486 Bcm), or the equivalent of 3 billion barrels of oil. This will be sufficient to produce 2 billion ft^3 per day (21 Bcm per year) of gas (or 15 mtpa LNG) for a twenty-year period
(Ooi Jin Bee 1982, pp. 165–166)

Initially, the Arun plant, built some 12 miles from the field, cost $940 million in 1973–1974 ($3.6 billion in 2005 dollars), with four storage tanks and three production trains of liquefaction facilities. Ultimately, after three more trains were added in the early 1980s, Arun had a design capacity of 9 mtpa, with working capacity of more than 10 mtpa.

The partners developing Arun established companies specifically to handle the operation of the field, and brought in other partners from Indonesia, Japan, Europe, and North America to finance the enormous cost of the project and to transport the LNG to Japan. Pertamina contracted out the construction and operation of the liquefaction plant and pipelines to a joint Indonesian–Japanese company, PT Arun Natural Gas Liquefaction Company (55 percent of which was owned by JILCO – Japan Indonesia LNG Company – a Japanese firm owned by a large group of utilities, manufacturers, trading houses, and banks). In 1978, Pertamina and JILCO invested another $187 million, with a European syndicate putting up a $50 million dollar loan and the Indonesian government providing another $100 million. Burmah Tankers of Britain chartered seven cryogenic ships built by General Dynamics and operated by Energy Transportation of New York. The first LNG was shipped to Japan in 1977.

It was initially reported that Indonesia was negotiating with the Far East Oil Trading Co. to ship just 40 percent of Arun's production to Japan (*International Petroleum Encyclopedia* 1973, p. 108). Ultimately an agreement was signed in December 1973, with five Japanese companies covering LNG exports from both Arun and its sister project, Bontang (initially called Badak) in East Kalimantan. The original buyers were Chubu Electric Power Company, Kansai Electric, Osaka Gas, Kyushu Electric, and Nippon Steel. The contract was for 8.18 mtpa from August 1977 to December 1999, with an extension of 8.45 mtpa from January 2000 to December 2010.

Even as it was negotiating with Japanese buyers, Pertamina signed a twenty-year contract with Pacific Lighting Corporation of Los Angeles in 1973, with shipments to start in 1978. This became a joint venture between Pacific Lighting and Pacific Gas and Electric (PG&E) called Pacific Gas. When the agreement with Pacific Gas fell through in 1979–1980, Pertamina and Mobil looked for new buyers. During 1980–1981 there were new negotiations between Pertamina and Tohoku Electric Power Company and Tokyo Electric. These discussions were complicated by the Indonesian desire that the expansion of the Arun facilities be done without their financial involvement, and a newly focused Japanese desire to direct government lending and negotiating support to Japanese buyers and trading firms (Chapman 1985). In the end, it was agreed that the Japanese would borrow funds from the then Export–Import Bank of Japan (J-EXIM) and other sources to pay in advance for LNG equal to the funds required to finance the Arun and Bontang expansions. Other aspects of the agreement included a higher LNG sales price, completely tied to the price of Indonesian export crude. By the early 1980s, Japanese firms were increasingly interested in controlling access to LNG imports. Shipping responsibility for the new Arun cargoes was thus transferred from Pertamina to the buyers, and Japanese trading firms began building the vessels in the shipyards of their fellow *keiretsu* members.

Arun was not the only major gas discovery in Indonesia during the 1970s and 1980s. At approximately the same time, another American company, Huffco, had found and developed Bontang in East Kalimantan. Initial Pertamina gas and LNG policies were formulated with both Arun and Bontang in mind. In fact, in 1976 a Joint Management Group (JMG) was formed with Mobil, Huffco, and Pertamina to coordinate both operations after gas delivery. The JMG was to oversee "the flow of funds between the purchaser, the transporter, the lenders, the tax authorities, the plant operators and the equity interests in the gas" (Chapman 1985, p. 80). Smaller gas finds occurred in the 1970s in Sulawesi and in the Java area. It was not until the 1980s and 1990s that there were other major gas discoveries in Irian Jaya, the Natuna area, Java, and other parts of Sumatra.

In the end, after many years of negotiation and expansion of the project plans, the complex financing of Arun and Bontang involved considerable Japanese government support, investment from commercial banks, the group of five major Japanese buyers, a wholly new Japanese firm owned by a large group of utilities, manufacturers, trading houses, and banks (JILCO), and the Indonesian government. Most directly, the Japanese government made loans from the Overseas Economic Cooperation Fund to the Indonesian government and Pertamina. The Indonesian government itself also made direct loans to Pertamina. Representing the bulk of the project financing, however, J-EXIM and a group of associated commercial banks loaned funds to JILCO, with 60 percent of these guaranteed by the state-owned Japan National Oil Corporation (JNOC), and 40 percent guaranteed by the consortium of five major buyers, which in turn had support from the Ministry of International Trade and Industry (MITI) in the form of overseas investment insurance. JILCO also loaned money for project development to Pertamina. Finally, payment on LNG from the five major buyers was sent to an escrow account, with funds sent to Pertamina and repayment back to J-EXIM Bank through JILCO (Miyamoto 2002, p. 125).

Arun and Bontang were among the world's largest LNG projects for two decades, with Arun initially considerably larger. Because of their production, Indonesia had become the largest exporter of LNG in the

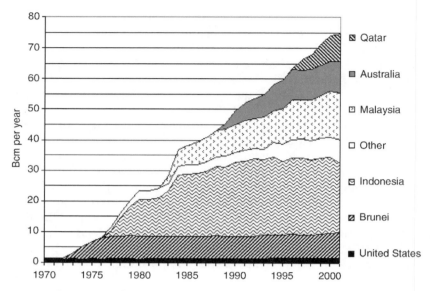

Figure 4.2. Japanese imports of LNG, by country, 1969–2001.

Source: IEA (2003), p. 164. "Other" includes shipments from Abu Dhabi beginning in 1977, limited cargoes from Algeria in 1989 and shipments from Oman beginning in 2000. Volumes converted to Bcm of gas equivalent.

world, providing some 40 percent of the commercial market in 1988. Likewise, Japan became the largest importer of LNG, with increasing efforts to diversify its sources of supply across Southeast Asia and the Gulf (see figure 4.2).

Although the Japanese gas market is relatively underdeveloped in comparison with some other OECD countries (notably the United Kingdom, Germany, or the United States), with gas representing only some thirteen percent of its primary energy supply in 2003. LNG played a key role in shifting Japan's energy mix away from coal, and in slowing its rising dependence on imported oil (see figure 4.3).

Prices for Indonesian gas and LNG changed over time, depending upon evolving relationships with major buyers. Prior to entering into LNG export contracts, natural gas was sold domestically to the Pusri Fertilizer plants in Palembang at prices ranging from $0.15 to $0.65 per mmbtu, depending upon the amount of pipeline required to reach the

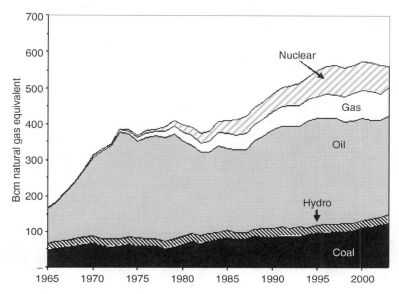

Figure 4.3. Japan: primary energy supply, by fuel, 1965–2003, in Bcm natural gas equivalent.

Source: BP (2004).

buyer. LNG prices differed from domestic gas, and between the Japanese and prospective US buyers. The Japanese price was originally set at $2.35 per mmbtu c.i.f. This was indexed on the price of Indonesian crude (90 percent indexation in the 1973 contract and 100 percent in the 1981 agreement) and had an annual 3 percent escalation factor (putting the price at $2.40 in 1978) (Ooi Jin Bee 1982, p.168). After the 1978–1979 oil crisis in the wake of the fall of the Shah of Iran, oil prices spiked, leading to a 50 percent increase in LNG prices over the following eighteen months. As oil (and thus LNG) prices sky-rocketed, Japanese buyers sought to keep gas competitive at the burner tip in Japan while Pertamina sought an f.o.b. linkage to its export crude (see figure 3.7 p. 62). As in the Transmed project discussed in chapter 3, this was really a veiled dispute over price, with Pertamina simply seeking a higher price for the gas. Like the Transmed contract, all of these were conditions renegotiated over time.

Initially, American buyers were to pay $0.63 per mmbtu, but later negotiations increased the price to $1.36 per mmbtu f.o.b. This was the result of a 1978 agreement that placed the US price at half the US wholesale price index for fuels and half the price of Indonesian crude.

All of this came to naught when the contract was later dropped. Later in 1983 an agreement was reached with the Korea Electric Power Corporation to purchase approximately 2 mtpa of LNG for twenty years. This contract followed the lines of the earlier agreements with the Japanese buyers.

The Arun LNG case neatly illustrates the problems in using prices to compare the nature of emerging and developed markets. When the LNG contracts with Japan were initially negotiated there were few suppliers and little transparency in prices. In 2003, as Indonesians and Japanese re-negotiated long-term contracts initiated in the 1970s, governments, producers, shippers, and buyers were much more conscious of regional and global variations in gas prices. Gas project developers in Indonesia today feel they must consider the projected price of LNG from Qatar, Russia and Australia, and from natural gas piped from Malaysia to Singapore (*Jakarta Post* October 3, 2003; *Xinhua News Agency* October 9, 2003). As interviews with the former JNOC and Japan LNG managers in 2003 reveal, Japanese investors in a deregulating energy market believe they must now take into account not only the potential price of gas piped in from Sakhalin, but also the effect on prices caused by new LNG buyers in California and China. The large Japanese trading firms, the most likely players in a regional spot or short-term contract market, are adopting a "wait-and-see" attitude in response to such perceived uncertainty.[2]

The Japanese and Indonesians did not face this type of uncertainty about prices in the 1970s. Indonesian suppliers then viewed prices primarily as a measure of projected income, which they preferred to be steadily expanding and, for reasons mainly of organizational consistency, to be linked to similar sources of revenue, notably oil. The prices eventually negotiated with the Japanese could also have included side payments between governments, individuals, and corporations, both legal and illegal. Consider the conclusions of recent research demonstrating that Chevron and Texaco, through Caltex, had a perfectly legal arrangement with Pertamina such that a combination of excessive prices and extra-contract oil transfers allowed these two companies to avoid paying nearly $9 billion in US federal and local income taxes between 1964 and 2002 (Gramlich and Wheeler 2003). Some research by Japanese scholars speculates about the existence of side payments to individuals in governments and corporations (Kunio 1982).

Even if there were side payments in these initial LNG projects, Japanese buyers were primarily concerned with reducing supply uncertainty.

---

[2] Interview with S. Shimizu, formerly of Nissho Iwai, September 2003.

Interviews in 2003 with Osaka Gas, the lead buyer of the "Western Group" of gas utility, electricity, and industrial buyers, suggest that Japanese investors in the 1970s and 1980s were most focused on overcoming the significant technological and safety obstacles in order to transition away from using town gas manufactured locally from coal. This meant finding ways to guarantee a steady, safe supply of LNG; price concerns were secondary. Because there was no domestic competition in gas transmission, gas utilities in the 1970s, as today, felt that the high cost of imported LNG could be passed easily to consumers. Competition between regions–especially Tokyo and Osaka–was focused on obtaining long-term overseas sources of LNG, even at a high cost.

Japan's central planners, who had played such a strong role in the 1960s in coordinating domestic investment across economic sectors, and in controlling foreign trade and investment through tariffs, currency controls, and investment programs, may have inadvertently contributed to this situation through inaction. As Chalmers Johnson has argued, MITI saw a period of diminished control over much economic planning in the early 1970s because of reforms in the political administration of the bureaucracy in general, public antipathy in the light of environmental disasters, and individual scandals involving politicians and ministerial officials (Johnson 1982). Although MITI, J-EXIM Bank, and JNOC later came to play an important role in guaranteeing the financing of the Arun project, in the 1970s regional competition was the key driver for major Japanese buyers. Even as the Japanese economy slowed after the first and second oil shocks, none of the negotiating partners questioned the long-term demand for natural gas in western Japan.

Before returning to an examination of why Arun gas was developed as LNG and not as piped gas, it is worthwhile examining other ways that the Arun project affected the long-term development not only of production in Indonesia and consumption in Japan, but also the development of the infrastructure supporting the regional and global LNG market. This includes institutions supporting project finance, the intergovernmental and business–government means to deal with uncertainties in supply security and legal disputes, and the elimination of technological challenges of LNG. Ironically, although the establishment of such uniquely large and intimate energy relations between Indonesia and Japan was intended to develop the economies of both nations, scholars and energy experts can agree that it has also contributed to the underdevelopment of supply in Indonesia and broader consumption in Japan.

On the Indonesian side, for reasons discussed later in this study, the perceived success of the Arun project ultimately resulted in the underdevelopment of a piped gas system for domestic and foreign users, even when changes in the national economy and relations with its neighbors favored this alternative to LNG. This dependence on LNG not only constrained the ability of government and corporate policy-makers to balance international energy ties in a way that promoted national economic goals, it also made it hard to balance local versus national and public versus private development plans. On the Japanese side, the Indonesian LNG projects, because of their high cost and long-term institutional influence, established the structure for the most advanced LNG-receiving infrastructure in the world. In the 1970s and 1980s this enabled the rapid growth of competing, regional economies within Japan – part of the "Japanese Miracle." By the 1990s, however, it had created significant institutional obstacles to the development of a national gas transmission system (Miyamoto 2002), and in doing so created constraints on the ability of local and national, government and private policy-makers to promote national economic plans in an increasingly liberal and globalizing economic environment.

Because Arun and Bontang were largely viewed as successful, they presented a new model for international energy project development. These two LNG projects created a blueprint for how national governments, state-owned oil and gas companies, and multinational corporations in the energy industry (including subsidiaries of companies dedicated to exploration, production, shipping, trading, and construction) could negotiate long-term contracts across diverse legal systems and in an environment of considerable political and economic risk. Remarkably, even when political uncertainty in both the producer and consumer markets would seem to call into question the ability of the actors to commit themselves to maintaining the contracts, the producers and buyers were able to identify third-party institutions – including international arbitration and courts in "neutral" countries such as the United States – to conclude negotiations.[3]

Furthermore, competition between buyers in the offtake market, and also among traders supplying that market, may have established credibility in periods of uncertainty. The existence of such competition was made clear to the Indonesians in the negotiations in the early 1980s, when the switch from c.i.f. to f.o.b. was initiated and driven by a trading firm, Nissho Iwai, that wanted to develop its own tanker fleet and associated technology in order to more effectively compete with the other Japanese trading firms. It saw the switch to f.o.b. as a means to

---

[3] Chapman (1985) and interview with S. Shimizu, formerly of Nissho Iawai, September 2003.

constrain competition in shipping.[4] This competition among the Japanese trading firms continued to play a strong role in the selection and development of LNG projects for the Japanese market, continuing through the mid-1990s and the Qatargas LNG project (see chapter 8).

At the same time, the Japanese government, through MITI and J-EXIM Bank (now Japan Bank for International Cooperation), expanded the investment tools and strategies for working with foreign governments and corporations as it went about developing the Japanese gas market. The earliest LNG imports for Japan were either completely financed by foreign actors (e.g. Phillips and Marathon in the Kenai, Alaska LNG project which began operations in 1969), or involved loans from J-EXIM Bank directed through the trading firms: Mitsubishi and Brunei LNG in 1972, and Mitsui and Abu Dhabi LNG in 1977. Arun and Bontang's development reflected the strong coordinating role of Nissho Iwai, responding in competition with Mitsubishi and Mitsui. But because Arun also included direct government-to-government loans from Japan to Indonesia, overseas investment insurance by MITI, and import credit loans from J- EXIM Bank to JILCO, it reflected an expansion of investment tools for working with foreign governments, foreign companies, and such new diverse forms of domestic incorporation as JILCO. Later LNG import projects, including to Malaysia in 1983, Australia in 1989, and Qatar in 1997, saw even more loans by the Japanese government to both foreign governments and foreign members of joint ventures (Miyamoto 2002). Overall, such government policies to support a greater number of actors in order to develop a gas market may indirectly provide a source of credibility in periods of uncertainty in negotiations between producers and buyers. Put more succinctly, Japanese government support of multiple competing import groups increased the potential number of chairs at the negotiating table. The success of the Arun case established the credibility of such policies.

The Arun case also made clear the range of technological obstacles involved in the establishment of long-distance, long-term LNG ties, and in doing so lowered the perceived cost of future LNG projects. Only after many years of successful operation did the Arun project establish expectations of safety and environmental awareness in the minds of the Japanese public in western Japan. Californians might still question the safety of LNG offtake facilities, but the Japanese now know that it is possible to have operations without accidents and little environmental

[4] Chapman (1985) and interview with S. Shimizu, formerly of Nissho Iawai, September 2003.

impact. Consequently, Japanese buyers are able to expand existing facilities with little popular opposition.

Producers, shippers, and buyers have also used the Arun projects to identify and develop new sources of revenue. These include the production and sale of condensates,[5] which Mobil later found to be lucrative, and the development of ancillary industries for LNG buyers, including manufacturing (industries using freezing), and industrial technology consulting, which Osaka Gas found to be lucrative. As mentioned above, gains from the development of shipping technology were also valued by Nissho Iwai. Finally, offtake market gas utility buyers also benefited from LNG technology by exploiting the higher calorific value of LNG in comparison with gas produced from existing sources (especially coal). This enabled them to expand supply capacity – Tokyo Gas estimated it could double capacity – while using much of the existing transmission systems.[6]

Profile of Pertamina

To understand the main actors in the development and transmission of Indonesian gas, it is essential to analyze the character, history, and powers of the national oil and gas company, Pertamina (Bartlett *et al.* 1972; Pertamina 1974; Goldstone 1977; Arief, 1977; ASEAN 2000). Prior to the 1965 attempted *coup* and the subsequent establishment of the "New Order" government under then General Suharto, there were three state oil companies, Permina, Pertamin and Permigan. Permigan was allegedly tied to the Communist Party and folded under Suharto. By 1968, under the aegis of Ibnu Sutowo and the New Order leadership, Permina and Pertamin were integrated into a new organization, Pertamina. It has been Pertamina that has dominated the Indonesian oil and gas world since that period.

At the time of the discovery and development of the Arun field, Pertamina was based upon Indonesian Law No. 8 of 1971. Under this law, Pertamina was headed by a President Director and Chief Executive Officer (Ibnu Sutowo) appointed by President Suharto and managed by a Board of Directors. Following a serious case of financial malfeasance in the mid-1970s, the management of Pertamina became responsible to a Board of Commissioners composed initially of three, then four, cabinet ministers. Overall, the Ministry of Mines was given responsibility for

---

[5] Longer-chain hydrocarbons such as propane found in association with methane in many gas fields (see box 1.1, p. 6).

[6] Miyamoto (2002, p. 120) and interviews with Osaka Gas, September 2003.

energy, and within the Ministry the Director of Oil and Gas had control over the petroleum industry. Energy policy was the purview of the National Energy Coordinating Board. The right of Pertamina to control Indonesian oil and gas has been based upon Article 33 of the country's constitution which states that all riches of land and water shall be used for the greatest welfare of the people. Under Law No. 44 of 1960, oil and natural gas are strategic enterprises to be controlled by the state and exploited by a state-owned enterprise. Article 6 of Law No. 8 of 1971 assigned Pertamina to explore, process, transport, and market oil and gas, and to enter into agreements with other parties as necessary. These laws charged Pertamina to conduct oil and gas exploration, earn revenues from oil and gas, and supply domestic markets.

Under Sutowo, Pertamina perfected its production sharing arrangements in oil and gas (Arief 1977; Rochmat 1981). As formulated during the period when Arun was being developed, foreign firms were to be contractors for Pertamina, which maintained managerial control. Pertamina was to retain a share of the oil or gas produced, the contractor was required to provide the financial and technical assistance for the operation and be responsible for the costs and risks. Once initial costs, including capital investments, were recouped, the balance of production was divided between the Indonesian government and the contractor in a ratio of 65:35. The contractor's corporate tax liabilities were included in the government's share. There were some modifications to this system in 1976 to meet generally accepted US accounting principles. The typical contract term was thirty years with an option to terminate or extend if no petroleum was discovered. (Since 1960, "petroleum" has meant oil and gas.) If natural gas utilization was not economical it could be flared. If economical, the production-sharing was to be the same as crude oil.

Initially, the larger foreign firms were reluctant to sign production-sharing contracts and only smaller independent companies agreed. However, by 1971 all the majors were engaged in Indonesia and subsequently found the system to be profitable. Pertamina was flexible in how it handled contractual provisions and companies were able to take 40 percent off the top to recover costs. In practice, cost recovery allowances sometimes exceeded 40 percent and Pertamina's weak supervision allowed contractors leeway in determining initial costs. Contractors were limited to their allotted fraction of production. For Arun and Bontang, Pertamina maintained sole control over all marketing of gas production.

The first decade of operations of the Arun project was one of transition for Pertamina. While Sutowo proved to be innovative in the development of the national oil company, he also showed himself to be an unwise manager. His emphasis upon growth rather than profits, reckless borrowing for his multitude of projects in and out of oil and gas interests, and inability to judge the market, all led to financial crisis for Pertamina in the early 1970s (Goldstone 1977). The depths of Sutowo's mistakes were exposed in 1975 when the government called for an investigation and found that Pertamina's debts had reached $10.6 billion. Ibnu Suwoto was replaced, many of Pertamina's non-oil and gas activities were transferred to other agencies, settlements of debts were formulated, and the system was streamlined.

The "Pertamina crisis," combined with changing external conditions, affected foreign petroleum firms. Pertamina gave major emphasis to increasing exploration and production, but the need for further revenues brought changes in the production-sharing contracts in 1976. Instead of 65:35, the government take was increased to 85 percent, leaving only 15 percent for the contractors. When exploration quickly declined, the government was forced to offer new incentives, including a 50:50 split in exploration costs, before returning to the restrictive 85:15 split. Exploration recovered by 1978–1979. The Arun field development avoided this roller-coaster policy environment as the Pertamina leadership considered it necessary to maintain the 65:35 ratio for gas. The events of the mid-1970s did not appear to have a negative impact on government LNG revenues, which reached $1.7 billion in 1980–1981 and $3.9 billion in 1985–1986.

Political and Economic Context

The third major background element to be discussed is the Indonesian political and economic context within which the Arun operation developed. Greater national stability combined with isolated problems of local security characterized the political context of Indonesia during the period 1971–1985 when the Arun project was developing. Nevertheless, this was a period of transition during which many investors displayed caution regarding major involvement in Indonesia's economy. The decade of the 1960s had been an era of instability, violence, serious threats of nationalization of foreign enterprises, and the transition from a socialist-oriented government to one that was more market-oriented. The first half of that decade saw an Indonesia led by an increasingly anti-Western government under the then President Sukarno. He had significant backing from a large Communist Party whose labor wing made life difficult for foreign firms. Sukarno established "Guided Democracy," which eschewed Western-type competitive politics and emphasized consensus and nationalism. The legislature was emasculated and key political opposition parties were outlawed. Internationally, the

Sukarno government allied itself with more radical elements of the Third World and even presented Indonesia as a leader of those in opposition to Western political and economic interests. Opposed to these policies were the majority of the country's military officers, political activists outside Java, and conservative Muslim elements.

Economically, the first half of the 1960s was characterized by high inflation, a severely weakened local and national financial system, a deteriorating physical infrastructure, and declining foreign involvement. Rampant inflation began in the early 1960s and the government made individual agreements with embassies and foreign firms regarding currency exchange rates. It became increasingly difficult to import foreign goods, and factories found it almost impossible to import needed machinery and parts. Non-Indonesian firms faced the threat of state nationalization or takeover by militant political or labor groups. In the outlying provinces, where petroleum projects were primarily to be found, largely autonomous military units tended to control the local economy. The import and export of goods in these areas became the purview of corrupt military and civil authorities. Finally, in a display of nationalist ideology, President Sukarno declared that Indonesia did not need foreign aid, and external official economic support largely dried up.

In sum, the decade prior to 1965 was not one conducive to foreign investment or the development of new entrepreneurial projects. In the petroleum business, Dutch and British firms were being forced out and American companies feared that they would be next. Political and economic stability left new exploration for oil and gas largely at a standstill.

Anti-Western and anti-foreign investment policies changed after the failed *coup* of 1965. The *coup* attempt by a group of military officers in which President Sukarno and the Communist Party became implicated yielded a turning point in Indonesian history. The Communist Party was eliminated by combined military and Muslim activist actions, leading to the death of hundreds of thousands of communists and alleged communists and the imprisonment of many others. Sukarno died of natural causes in 1970, two years after having been slowly eased out of power. The so-called "New Order" replaced "Guided Democracy" and for the next more than thirty years Indonesian politics was dominated by the military under the leadership of General and then President Suharto.

During the 1970s, and 1980s, when the Arun project was being implemented, Indonesia was far friendlier to foreign oil firms than was true under Sukarno. Instead of socialist-oriented policies, the military brought in the "Berkeley Mafia," a group of University of California, Berkeley-trained technocrats with market-oriented ideas. Efforts were made to attract foreign investment into the country and US oil firms took advantage of the new economic climate. This employment of technocrats became a hallmark of the Suharto regime, as the military largely left the daily administration of the country to the civil service. The capabilities of the bureaucracy gradually improved from the previous administration, although corruption and inefficiencies were not eliminated. While those around Suharto became wealthy from these actions and corruption played a large part if the economic system, there was also a general "rising of all boats." During the 1970s gross domestic product (GDP) grew 8.1 percent a year and there were major increases in private and public consumption (Poot, Kuyvenhoven, and Jensen 1996). Improved economic conditions after the débâcle of the latter Sukarno years helped to weaken political opposition and reinforce stability until the financial disasters of the late 1990s.

Yet, the perceptions of the strength and stability of the economy during much of the 1970s were not uniformly favorable. Memories of the problems of the later Sukarno years were fresh. The initial liberalization of investment was followed from 1974 to 1986 by protectionist policies. Some sectors were closed to foreign investments, new regulations were put into place, and there were increased nationalist reaction to expanding Japanese economic power (Setiawan 2002, pp. 3–10). Inflation remained a problem, though much better than the 85 percent of 1968. In the early 1970s inflation ranged from 20 to 33 percent after a period of low rates and increased again in the late 1970s. The Pertamina crisis of the mid-1970s, and perceived dangers of national bankruptcy, did not inspire confidence in a bureaucracy that was already infamous for its corrupt tendencies. Thus, while real economic progress took place, foreign investors tended to be wary.

A second result of the new regime was that a more stable political system was established. The "New Order" provided what could be termed a "façade democracy" replete with regular elections, an elected executive and legislature, and most of the institutional elements of a democratic system. However, this was a tightly controlled democracy with the military limiting political activity, the legislature holding little power, and the President (Suharto) indirectly elected with little or no opposition. This "façade democracy" had two elements conducive to stability. It provided a means of "letting off steam" by an opposition that at least had the opportunity to participate in the electoral process and it helped to forestall criticism from Western governments that were supplying major economic aid to the Republic.

Opposition to the New Order during this period came from three elements, two of which had little impact on the overall economy or the oil and gas industry. At the national level, opposition political parties sought to expand their political power and to participate more fully in the operation of the state, but the government limited their role and eventually prohibited political party activity. Student groups were a second critic of this undemocratic system and its ties to foreign investors and corrupt practices. In spite of demonstrations and other vocal criticisms, they were unable to coalesce with other groups to develop an effective opposition until the late 1990s.

The third element of the opposition that did have a direct impact on the Arun operation came from local dissidents, and particularly from those in Aceh that sought greater autonomy and even independence (Hill 1989; Kell 1995; Ross 2002). Aceh had a cherished history of independence prior to its final conquest by the Dutch at the beginning of the twentieth century, it had been a real power in the region that had cooperated militarily with the Ottoman Empire against the Portuguese in Malacca. With its historic heritage, ethnic homogeneity, strongly conservative Muslim roots, and isolation from the rest of the Republic, it has long been a problem for the central government in Jakarta. Immediately after independence some Acehnese Muslim activists had joined the Java-based Dar ul Islam rebellion that had demanded the formation of an Islamic state. However, a generally strong economy in the province, the provision of greater provincial autonomy, and the ability to migrate across the Straits to Malaysia and Singapore for jobs mitigated some of the previous dissatisfaction.

During the initial years following the discovery of gas at Arun there was general peace in Aceh. At first, political leaders in the province did not actively oppose the Arun project. Although the government had wanted the processing plant and harbor to be built outside Aceh, this was rejected by Mobil. The Arun construction employed 8,000–12,000 and daily operations ultimately employed 5,000–6,000. Mobil publications regularly emphasized the opportunities provided to the Acehnese by the Arun projects.

However, by the mid-1970s there was increased dissatisfaction in Aceh. The Acehnese perceived that the Suharto regime had weakened the provincial powers they had enjoyed under Sukarno, as the special autonomy that had been granted had been effectively lost. In addition, the province did not support the government Golkar Party and instead gave their vote to the Muslim opposition. More directly related to Arun was the view that non-Acehnese had been given management positions. A problem that foreign firms have wrestled with for some time has been confusion over the meaning of "Indonesianization." For people like the Acehnese, Indonesianization often meant the hiring of Javanese for upper-level positions. In addition there was objection to the fact that revenues from the exploitation of local natural resources went to the central government with little or no return to the provinces. According to the leader of the autonomy movement, Hasan M. di Tiro, "our country has been laid bare by the Javanese colonialists at the feet of the multinationals to be raped. Our mineral and forest resources have been put up to the world markets for clearance sale for quick cash for Javanese generals and their foreign backers" (Ross 2002, p. 17). Mobil was increasingly identified with an oppressive government based in Jakarta. In the initial years of the Arun project, the Aceh problem did not have a major impact on its development. There were minor irritations such as the stealing of a payroll and sabotage, but in those early years they did not lead to a suspension of activities. However, these grievances ultimately led to a series of violent and non-violent attacks on Indonesian forces, Mobil assets, and those opposing the rebels. These began in 1976, lasted for several years and were rekindled in later years. Since 1998 the conflict has become aggravated, leading to the temporary suspension of Arun operations and finally to full-scale central government military operations against the Acehnese rebels in 2003. The violence and sabotage accompanying these activities had serious repercussions on the Arun operation and Indonesian LNG prospects in general.

Similar to perceptions of Indonesia's economic stability, there was a certain disconnect between the growing political stability of the system and external views. Suharto's stability was not characterized by many observers as democracy. Human rights observers and many foreign academics criticized the undemocratic nature of the regime and highlighted opposition activities. Serious problems of corruption and bureaucratic inefficiency tainted perceptions. However, the geographic isolation of most oil and gas operations tended to insulate them from many of these issues. Given the new opportunities for exploration and production, the demise of the socialist-oriented Sukarno regime, and increased corporate profits, foreign petroleum firms had a generally positive perception of the "New Order."

Regional, NGO, and Corporate/MNC Energy Initiatives in the 1970s

During the decade following the Arun discovery, there was little influence from either regional organizations or non-governmental organizations (NGOs) on the development of the project. Regional official organizational energy initiatives were in their infancy in Southeast Asia in the 1970s and remained more in a planning than an implementation mode throughout the 1980s. There were United Nations regional economic organizations such as ECAFE (later called ESCAP).[7] However, their tasks were primarily information gathering and dissemination and did little to initiate actual regional energy programs.

Nor were there any regional political organizations with effective economic programs. During the 1960s Indonesia participated in the largely symbolic bloc called Maphilindo (for Malaya, the Philippines and Indonesia), but this loosely knit grouping had no real economic agenda, and folded over issues involved in the formation of Malaysia in 1963. In 1967, the Association of Southeast Asian States (ASEAN) was formed and initially included Indonesia, Singapore, Malaysia, Thailand, and the Philippines. In 1984 Brunei joined, but it was not until the 1990s that the other four Southeast Asian states (Cambodia, Laos, Myanmar and Vietnam) became members. The development of a trans-Asian gas pipeline system was the first major regional effort in the energy field and today is seen as the future for regional gas development. During the 1970s ASEAN was primarily a politically oriented bloc with a weak economic agenda. It played no important role in energy cooperation during the first two decades of its existence. Marcello Colliti, a senior executive of Italy's ENI (see chapter 3), initially presented detailed ideas of a trans-ASEAN pipeline in 1989 and in that same year S. Talisayon published a book called *Designing For Consensus*.[8] However, it was not until 1988–1990 that the ASEAN Council on Petroleum even launched a study on the potential for gas pipelines in the region. In 1989 there was discussion of cooperation between ASEAN and the EEC on a Trans-ASEAN gas line. By 1996 the ASEAN Ministers of Energy endorsed a "Master plan" on natural gas development and utilization and the next year there were statements of cooperation on an ASEAN electric power grid and a Trans-ASEAN gas pipeline. In 1999 ASEAN Energy Ministers agreed on a regional pipeline "Plan of Action" and the Trans-ASEAN Gas Task Force was created. However, by the turn of the century there was no consensus on technical standards or general principles.

Meanwhile, even bilateral cross-border pipeline construction in the region was slow to progress. Negotiations for a Singapore–Malaysia pipeline began in the early 1980s, but were delayed by disputes over prices. It was not until the 1990s that Malaysian gas was piped to Singapore, and after 2000 before gas pipelines were completed between West Natuna in Indonesia and Singapore. Malaysia and Thailand signed

---

[7] UN Economic Commission for Asia and the Far East (ECAFE), later the UN Economic and Social Commission for Asia and the Pacific (ESCAP) in the early 1970s.
[8] On the trans-ASEAN gas line, comments by Al Troner, 2003.

an MOU to explore cooperation in developing their gas reserves in 1979, and later committed to a $2.42 billion contract for a 255 km pipeline (Allison 2000). Environmental, economic, and political roadblocks have slowed development of pipelines between the two countries. Nevertheless, two pipelines between Myanmar and Thailand were successfully completed in 1999 and 2000. These efforts were initiated long after the Arun project was implemented and, in fact came to fruition at a time when Arun's gas production was diminishing. In reality, there was no effective regional energy program or completed cross-national gas pipeline or LNG system within Southeast Asia for two decades after Arun's gas was first discovered. According to a private gas industry analyst, important impediments to the earlier development of pipelines also included the immaturity of markets, national jealousy, a lack of government support, the cost of developing a gas infrastructure, and an inability of gas suppliers to organize gas markets.[9]

NGO activities in the 1970s also had little significant impact on either the development of the Arun field or the transmission of its gas. This is in contrast to later years when a variety of politically and environmentally oriented NGOs became far more involved in events in Aceh. Weak NGO reactions in the 1970s were later followed by a wide array of publications, web sites, petitions, and other pressures on governments and corporations. These variously supported Acehnese efforts to gain autonomy, criticized activities that were perceived as environmentally damaging by Western industries in Sumatra, attacked what was described as capitalist exploitation, and assailed the human rights records of the Indonesian government and the Mobil Corporation. However, in the 1970s these critics had as yet not organized themselves sufficiently to provide significant impediments to the Arun operation.

Alternatives

An important aspect of this case study analysis is the consideration of possible alternative buyers of Arun's gas. As we have noted, Arun's natural gas initially was delivered to only one bidder, a group of Japanese firms. This section seeks to assess what other possible alternative uses there were to Japanese exports at the time of the project's development. Three major alternatives will be explored, although none of them could ultimately seriously compete with the Japanese. The first possibility was the sale of LNG to California utilities, an expectation rooted in a

---

[9] Comments by Al Troner, 2003.

contractual arrangement signed between Pertamina and Pacific Gas in 1973, although this became increasingly questionable in the ensuing years. The second possible alternative was the large-scale provision of natural gas to domestic buyers, either through the development of petrochemical facilities in the Aceh region or via pipelines or LNG shipments to other parts of the archipelago for home and industrial use. Finally, what were the advantages and obstacles to the provision of natural gas to Singapore, either by pipeline or LNG?

The reason for limiting possible alternatives to these three is a realistic assessment of development and industrialization elsewhere in Asia during the initial ten–fifteen years after the discovery of Arun. The rest of South and Southeast Asia remained primarily agricultural and economically underdeveloped. The rare more developed countries in the region, such as Malaysia and Thailand, had their own gas resources. In Northeast Asia, China was still coming out of the Cultural Revolution, while the Republic of Korea and Taiwan were in a process of development that would make them limited customers for Indonesian gas a decade later.

The Demise of the California Connection

As previously noted, the second party to the sale of Arun LNG to Japan was the Pacific Lighting Corporation (later Pacific Gas). In 1973 Pacific Lighting signed a MOU to take 1.4 mtpa starting in 1978 and rising to over 3.8 mtpa. This would necessitate the construction of three more trains in Arun and would result in the largest single purchase of gas by a California utility in history (Howell and Morrow 1973). There were extraordinary claims at the time regarding the economic costs and gains of this project, although at an early date critics questioned the viability of the agreement.

However, in the early 1970s this arrangement appeared desirable for both parties. For Jakarta, it provided a counterbalance to Japan, which was becoming increasingly dominant in the Indonesian economy. This was an era of Southeast Asian suspicion of Japanese economic hegemony in the region and there was political and popular opposition expressed through demonstrations, speeches, and editorials. In addition, elements in the Indonesian leadership considered that having Japan as the only buyer of LNG could place Indonesia in a difficult bargaining position on price and the California contract could be a useful bargaining chip (Sacerdoti 1981).

There also were hopes for massive American investments in the development of Arun and other gas fields in the islands that could bolster a weakened Indonesian economy. On the California side, a coalition of business and labor interests, backed by then Governor Jerry Brown, saw LNG imports as having sound economic and environmental elements. Some have argued that more questionable factors behind this support including the alleged economic interests of the Brown family in Indonesian oil and gas. Also noted were the hopes of American bankers that the revenues from the sale of LNG would bolster an Indonesian government that had defaulted on billions in loans (Walters 2001). Under Governor Brown's leadership and against the opposition of environmentalists and consumer advocates, legislation was passed to build a LNG terminal at Point Conception, near Santa Barbara, California.

However, a series of forces finally led to the abandonment of this and other LNG projects in California. There were initial disputes over pricing that were not settled until the late 1970s. The Point Conception site was found to be prone to earthquakes and seismologists made dire predictions of future disasters. Environmentalists launched attacks on the safety of LNG tankers and argued that they might explode or run aground. Even the local Chumash Indians got involved, identifying the chosen site as sacred ground. Placing any US LNG import project in further jeopardy was the deregulation of natural gas that produced surplus gas supplies, making LNG appear less attractive economically. Lower-cost gas supplies and alternative fuels from Canada also looked comparatively attractive, while economists at the time estimated that shipping costs from Southeast Asia to the US West Coast would be prohibitively high.[10] Interestingly, to this day no LNG import terminal has been sited on the California coast, although multiple projects are currently proposed.[11]

During the latter 1970s Indonesia waited for the expected fruition of the California project. Jakarta established a number of deadlines and upheld the legality of the contract, apparently still hoping to fulfill the original agreement. A review of oil and economic journals in the late 1970s finds numerous discussions about the probability of success or failure of the arrangement. It was not until the end of 1980 that the US utility was formally released from the agreement to purchase gas from Indonesia. By that time, it was obvious that a LNG terminal in

---

[10] Interview with David Hudson, former chief economist for Esso Eastern, February 2004.

[11] As of late 2005, multiple proposals are competing to site LNG terminals onshore and offshore in the state of California. Most analysts predict that at least one terminal in the Mexican state of Baja California will be the first western North America LNG import terminal. Substantial volumes of gas from the Baja terminal are expected to ultimately reach California markets as natural gas, or as electricity produced from power plants on the Mexican side of the border.

California was impossible. Other pressures and incentives remained on the Indonesian side. The Japanese were anxious to guarantee a major stake in Indonesia's gas and were prepared to provide the financing needed to obtain such an exclusive contract. As a consequence, they put pressure on Jakarta to cut its ties with the potential US buyer. Declining oil production had made gas a greater foreign exchange earner than crude, making more desirable the Japanese offers to help build more trains and purchase expanded LNG production.

The long series of negotiations and continued Indonesian hopes for California sales might have helped to preclude any other efforts to find alternatives for the sale of Arun's gas. However, it should also be noted that the 1973 contract the Japanese gave the option for any surplus from the Arun field. Theoretically, this could have been a crucial period for other possible buyers. By the early 1980s, Malaysia was in the process of developing its own natural gas pipeline system and Singapore could look to the possibility of purchasing gas from Malaysia or from new fields in Indonesia. Yet, given Japanese desires to obtain a secure supply and the weak market elsewhere in Asia, it is doubtful that the seven-year wait between the signing of the California contract and its final abrogation would have brought other possible buyers.

Domestic Distribution

The initial decision to sell Arun's gas overseas was based upon the understanding among Indonesian policy-makers at the time that there was an insufficient domestic market within Indonesia. In the early 1970s the island of Java had almost two-thirds of the total population of Indonesia and was the center for the country's limited manufacturing activities. The rest of the populace was spread throughout an archipelago 3,000 miles long. Aceh was far from the Javanese center of population and industry. The projected high front-end investments needed to bring gas to Java suggested that other energy sources would be more economical (Reksohadjiprodjo 1980, p. 303). The shallow oil and gas fields of Central and South Sumatra were also less expensive than the deep reservoir in North Sumatra at Arun. Additionally, developing a consumer gas infrastructure would also have required major capital investment. In 1978 Indonesian official energy policy sought to exploit the export of gas and depend more upon coal, hydropower, and geothermal sources to meet its energy needs. Heavily subsidized gas was available on a limited basis for government-sponsored projects, yet the very low price of gas for state enterprises discouraged foreign companies from selling domestically (Wijarso 1988). By the end of the century there was still no gas pipeline from Sumatra to Java, although there was discussion of a pipeline grid to connect Sumatra, Kalimantan, and Java and a pipeline from Natuna to Java (Rahardjo 2000, pp. 549–553).

There was also the expectation that there would be a major development of a petrochemical industry in Indonesia, including fertilizer plants and industrial products, as well as electric power generation. There were large-scale plans for petrochemical activities in the Aceh region employing Arun's gas resources. An integrated complex for ethane, polyethylene, a glycol plant, and vinyl chloride nomomer production was envisioned at an estimated cost of $1.6 billion (*Petromin* March 1980; Ooi Jin Bee 1982, p. 164). There were regular projections of such activities throughout the 1980s. Yet, by the end of the 1980s Indonesia had firmed up plans only for an aromatics plant producing benzene, toluene, p-xylene, and ethylene supposedly to start up in 1992. In reality, the high cost of development of petrochemical plants and the limited market in Asia at the time made such projects difficult to implement.

At the end of the twentieth century only a small amount of Arun's gas went to the regional petrochemical industry by way of a local fertilizer plant. Technically, the low liquids fraction of Arun gas was not ideal for manufacturing petrochemicals such as ethane and ethylene. In fact, medium and large-scale manufacturing was rare in Aceh and in 1980 it engaged only 2,500 workers. According to the World Bank, plans were delayed by Pertamina's financial problems, the lack of a long-range development program, a poor balance of payments situation, and confusion about feedstock availability (Vergara and Babelon 1990, p. 128). The Bank noted that the base and resources were already present to develop major projects. Foreign investors, however, remained cautious in funding large-scale manufacturing in Indonesia. Suffice to say, the domestic utilization of Arun's gas for transmission to major population centers or the development of a petrochemical program in Aceh proved more a vision than a reality. While these ideas may have been technically plausible alternatives to foreign sales, they failed in their implementation.

Under a different policy regime, Arun's gas could have served other domestic needs. During the 1970s and early 1980s, oil was the major energy source. At the end of the first National Development Plan (1969–1970 through 1973–1974) the national electric company reported that some 61 percent of electric power was produced with fuel oil. By the late 1970s, 90 percent of energy came from oil and 8 percent from gas. Other sources of energy at that time were more hypothetical than actual. There was considerable discussion of using Indonesia's plentiful reserves of coal, but the availability of oil and the long distance of coal deposits from Java (coal was primarily in Sumatra) limited its use (Reksohadjiprodjo 1980).

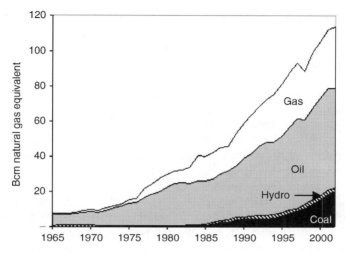

Figure 4.4. Indonesia: primary energy supply, by fuel 1965–2003, in Bcm natural gas equivalent.
Source: BP (2004).

In fact, although coal production increased from 175,673 metric tonnes in 1968 to an estimated 265,000 metric tonnes in 1978, coal consumption remained below pre-1945 levels and was not expected to be a significant player in energy production. As shown in figure 4.4, in spite of increased production, coal only accounted for 8 percent of Indonesia's energy consumption by 1992. Hydroelectric power has been important in Indonesia, but again sources were largely off Java. Geothermal-based power was not expected to be a major contributor. In sum, energy requirements for Indonesia were not large at the time of the development of the Arun project. In 1970 total energy use was the equivalent of only some 8 Bcm of natural gas. (The Arun LNG plant, by comparison, produced over 13 Bcm per year throughout the 1980s). Domestic use was thus not a competing alternative to the project.

The Singapore Alternative

Singapore would appear to be a possible alternative buyer of Arun's gas in the decade after its discovery, for a number of reasons. The city-state's economy was the envy of its neighbors. While its population had grown from 2 million in 1970 to 2.6 million in 1985, during that same period its GDP had risen from $5 billion to $39 billion. GDP *per capita* rose from S$2,462 in 1970 to S$6,565 in 1984. From 1965–1984 nominal GDP growth averaged 7.8 percent per annum, outstripping every other country in Asia and by 1984 it had the highest gross savings rate in the world (Sandhu and Wheatley 1989; Sharma 1989). Singapore would thus appear to be a viable market in economic terms.

Second, the city-state also had a long history in utilizing gas, although total gas consumption remained small until the 1990s. The Singapore Gas Company was formed in 1861 and the first gasworks was built in 1862. Coal carbonizing plants were used until catalytic gasification plants came on line in 1958. By 1972 there were 861 km of gas mains, 104,900 gas consumers, and a steady increase in gas production and sales. Gas was the major source for Singapore's electricity generation and from 1970 to 1976 electricity generation grew by 7.5 percent per annum.

The 1970s also saw Singapore move into the petrochemical business in a major fashion. Plans were initiated at that time to build an artificial island off Singapore for a major project to be completed in 1982, although commissioning took place some time later. Much of the development was in joint ventures with Japanese companies and was seen as only the beginning of a new economic program for Singapore. While the initial feedstocks were naphtha and LPG, as the petrochemical industry grew it became more apparent that large supplies of natural gas would be desirable.

Thirdly, Singapore had shown an interest in importing natural gas from its neighbors since the early 1970s. The 1973 world oil crisis had a major impact on the city-state as it experienced oil shortfalls and increased prices. This brought into consideration both nuclear power and natural gas as long-run energy alternatives. The government conducted feasibility studies at the time, but no investment in alternatives followed. A decade later Singapore actively explored importing natural gas from its neighbors. Although Singapore–Indonesia relations had frequently been unhappy in previous decades, by 1982 there was considerable discussion in the press of building pipelines from Indonesia and particularly from Natuna (*Straits Times* September 10, 1982; *Far Eastern Economic Review* 1982). In 1982 Singapore's Prime Minister, Lee Kuan Yew, met with President Suharto concerning the issue, and there were reports of negotiations between Pertamina and the Singapore National Oil Corporation (SNOC). The hope was that Indonesian natural gas would come into Singapore within ten years, although little progress was made in the 1980s. In 1982 Singapore began discussions with Malaysia to bring in gas from off Trengganu on the East Coast of the peninsula. Representatives from SNOC and Malaysia's national oil company Petronas met in 1982 and discussed a pipeline that was to reach Singapore by 1990.

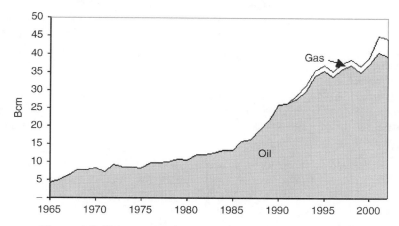

Figure 4.5. Singapore: primary energy supply, by fuel, 1965–2003, in Bcm natural gas equivalent.

Source: BP (2004).

This was also a period when Singapore and Indonesia were looking to develop the latter's Batam Island, some 20 km south of Singapore. In the late 1960s, Pertamina decided that it would turn Batam into a logistical base for petroleum activities in Sumatra and Natuna. Then in 1973 a Presidential Decree set up the island as an industrial zone with a planned oil refinery, storage facilities, and a harbor for supertankers (Murray and Perera 1996; Regnier 1991). The developing Pertamina scandal and economic problems in Indonesia shelved the petroleum part of the project, although Singapore and Indonesia became partners in building Batam as an industrial zone for Singaporean interests. In the late 1980s, Batam came to the fore again, this time as a base for future natural gas projects and Singapore began developing its "Chemical Island" of Jurong. When the pipeline from West Natuna was finally built to supply Singapore 2001, Batam was its western terminus and much of the impetus for the project came from those involved in developing Natuna.

Given these forces, why didn't Indonesia export gas to Singapore? It needs to be emphasized that any import of Arun gas by Singapore would not have been sufficient to replace the California contract, let alone Japanese planned purchases. As seen in figure 4.5, even in the late 1990s Singapore's gas imports from Malaysia represented only a small part of the city-state's primary energy supply, less than 1 mtpa of equivalent LNG. In contrast, as early as 1980 Japan was importing nearly 9 mtpa of LNG from Indonesia, and Arun alone could produce nearly 10 mtpa in the early 1980s. According to the contract with California, Arun was supposed to supply 4 mpta by the early 1980s. In 1980, Singapore's total primary energy supply, predominantly met through oil, was the equivalent of just 7 mtpa. It is also unlikely that Singapore had the capital available to develop the Arun LNG project in the 1970s that the Japanese buyers ultimately provided.

Beyond the centrality of the relatively small Singapore market, there appear to be a number of obstacles which kept the Republic from pursuing Arun gas in the 1970s and 1980s. Six key negative points expressed by public or private observers were:

1. A pipeline from Arun to Singapore was questioned in the 1970s on the grounds that it would cross one of the busiest sea-lanes in the world and its rupture might harm shipping. The issue was not a technologically difficult problem ("armored" pipelines, similar to those used in the Transmed were feasible); nevertheless, the shallow and narrow Straits of Malacca were a key security concern for ship traffic and Singapore's livelihood.

2. Mobil corporate strategy was not enamored with pipelines. Among reasons given for this stance were negative experiences with sabotage and cross-national delays in the Middle East and the perception that pipelines required captive customers.[12]

3. LNG for Singapore faced several problems. Bringing LNG ships into the ports of Singapore itself was deemed risky. LNG was also costly – proposals for developing LNG facilities in the 1990s were delayed after it became apparent that cheaper natural gas would be coming by pipeline from Malaysia and Natuna.

4. As noted previously, the long and fruitless effort to sell Arun's LNG to California had closed a door of opportunity for other buyers at a crucial time, even if Singapore had been interested. However, the city-state did not appear to be ready to act expeditiously on any LNG or pipeline operation. As later shown in the Malaysia and Natuna contracts, there was a lengthy period between initial discussions and the first gas deliveries.

5. In the late 1970s and early 1980s Singapore was in the process of becoming the third largest oil refining center in the world, receiving crude from the Middle East, Indonesia, Malaysia, and Thailand. These refining operations yielded large volumes of naptha, which itself is a relatively inexpensive fuel for generating electricity. In general, the emphasis given by Singapore on refineries came at the expense of alternative energy sources such as natural gas or nuclear power.

---

[12] Interviews with Al Troner, 2003.

6. Singapore has not had a centrally directed petroleum policy, although there have been official studies and suggestions. SNOC was really a small energy department in the government: it does not make long-range forecasts and does not regulate oil prices (Fesharaki 1989, p. 301–302). In this largely free enterprise system, the private sector sets priorities, with some guidance from the government. Given Singapore's small size, the expenditure of large up-front capital for building pipelines or LNG facilities and a change from traditional gas sources did not appear to be sufficiently profitable. Strong financial support from the government was not forthcoming.

In sum, a combination of factors appears to have made the Singapore alternative unattractive at the time. If Arun had been discovered a decade later, Singapore would have been a natural alternative to Japanese exports. Singapore's energy needs evolved over the next decade as its petrochemical industry was expanding. Later in the 1980s the city-state began negotiations with both Malaysia and Indonesia for the development of natural gas pipelines. The Arun gas might then have tied into the Malaysian pipeline developed in later years.

Conclusions

The ultimate transmission of Arun's natural gas to its major users was a factor of place and time. Arun, like its sister project Bontang, was perceived to be too far from both probable domestic and regional users to make pipelines appear economically feasible. In the 1970s neither Singapore nor the Indonesian government considered the cost of building such domestic gas infrastructure an acceptable alternative to other energy sources.

Perhaps more importantly, the timing of Arun's development dictated the primary buyers. At the time of Arun's discovery in 1971, Japan was the only East Asian economy that could successfully utilize large quantities of natural gas and provide the necessary financial support for the project. The industrial growth success stories of countries such as Republic of Korea, China, Taiwan, and Singapore were still in their infancy: Korea would not import its first LNG until 1986 and Taiwan in 1990. With the withdrawal of the California contract, there was only one real market for Arun gas. Ultimately, the only competition that took place was between buyers within Japan.

If Arun had been developed ten–fifteen years later, several other countries would have competed with Japan and domestic consumption would also have been a more attractive alternative. In the 1990s Arun gas could have plugged into the evolving Malaysian pipelines. By this time, however, Indonesia would also have been competing with new LNG suppliers coming online in Australia, Southeast Asia, and the Middle East.

REFERENCES

Books and articles

Allison, Tony (2000). "The Trans Thai–Malaysia natural gas project." *Asia Times On Line*, August 5
Arief, Sritua (1977). *Financial Analysis of the Indonesian Petroleum Industry*. Jakarta: Sritua Arief Associates
Arndt, Heinz Wolfgang (1983). "Oil and the Indonesian economy." *Southeast Asian Studies*, pp. 36–150
ASEAN (2000). "Profile of Pertamina." Jakarta: ASEAN Council on Petroleum
Bartlett, Anderson. III *et al.* (1972). *Pertamina: Indonesian National Oil*. Jakarta: Amerasian Limited.
BP (2004). *Statistical Review of World Energy*; available at http://www.bp.com
Chapman, John (1985). *Hands Across the Sea*. Jakarta: Pertamina
Energy Data and Modeling Center (2003). *EDMC Handbook of Energy & Economic Statistics in Japan*. Tokyo: Energy Conservation Center Japan
Fesharaki, Fereidun (1989). "Singapore as an oil centre," in Kernial Singh Sandhu and Paul Wheatley (eds.), *Management of Success: The Moulding of Modern Singapore*. Singapore: Institute of Southeast Asian Studies, pp. 300–313
Goldstone Anthony (1977). "What was the Pertamina crisis?" *Southeast Asian Affairs*. Singapore: Institute of Southeast Asian Affairs, pp. 122–132
Gramlich, Jeffrey and James Wheeler (2003). "How Chevron, Texaco and the Indonesian government structured transactions to avoid billions in US income taxes." *Accounting Transactions*, 17(3), pp. 107–122
Hill, Hal (1989). *Unity and Diversity*. Singapore; Oxford University Press
Howell, L. and M. Morrow (1973). "Natural gas: the invisible gold hunt." *Far Eastern Economic Review*, 82, p. 39
Hunter, Alex (1966). "The Indonesian oil industry." *Australian Economic Papers*, 5, pp. 59–106
IEA (2003) *Historical Gas Statistics*. Paris: International Energy Agency
Johnson, Chalmers (1982). *MITI and the Japanese Miracle: The Growth of Industrial Policy, 1925–1974*. Stanford: Stanford University Press
International Petroleum Encyclopedia (1973). Tulsa, OK: Petroleum Publishing Company
Kell, Tim (1995). *The Roots of the Acehnese Rebellion, 1889–1992*. Ithaca: Cornell University Modern Indonesia Project
Kunio, Yoshihara (1982). *Sogo Shosha: The Vanguard of the Japanese Economy*. Oxford: Oxford University Press
Migas (1984). *Oil Statistics of Jakarta*. Jakarta
Miyamoto, Akira (2002). "Natural gas in Japan," in Ian Wybrew–Bond and Jonathan Stern (eds.), *Natural Gas in Asia: The Challenges of Growth in China, India, Japan and Korea*. London: Oxford University Press, pp. 106–87

Murray, Geoffrey and Audrey Perera (1996). *Singapore: The Global State*. New York: St. Martin's Press

Ooi, Jin Bee (1980). "Natural gas in Indonesia." *Asian Profile*, 8(2), pp. 171–180
(1982). *The Petroleum Resources of Indonesia*. Kuala Lumpur: Oxford University Press

Pertamina (1974). *Pertamina: Indonesian State Oil Enterprise*. Jakarta: Pertamina
(1979). *Pertamina Today: A Review of Indonesia's Petroleum Industry*. Jakarta: Pertamina

Poot, Huib, Arie Kuyvenhoven, and Jaap C. Jensen (1996). *Industrialisation of Trade in Indonesia*. Jogjakarta: Gadjah Mada University Press

Rahardjo, Irawan (2000). "The development of a natural gas pipeline in indonesia." Kuta, Bali: Proceedings of the Sixth AEEEAP Triennial Conference, pp. 549–553

Regnier, Philippe (1991). *Singapore: City-State in South-East Asia*. London: Hurst

Reksohadjiprodjo, Sukanto (1980). "Oil and other energy resources for development: the Indonesian case." *The Journal of Energy Development*, 2, pp. 289–325

Rochmat, Rudioro (1981). *Contractual Arrangements in Oil and Gas Mining Enterprises in Indonesia*. Alpha aan den Rijn: Sijthoff & Noordhoff

Ross, Michael (2002). "*Resources and Rebellion in Indonesia*." Los Angeles: UCLA

Sacerdoti, Guy (1981). "Contracts." *Far Eastern Economic Review III*

Sandhu, Kernial Singh and Paul Wheatley (eds.) (1989) *Management of Success: The Moulding of Modern Singapore*. Singapore: Institute of Southeast Asian Studies

Setiawan, Grace (2002). "The impact of foreign investment on Indonesia's economic growth." Kiddi School of Public Policy and Management

Sharma, Shankar (1989). *Role of the Petroleum Industry in Singapore's Economy*. Singapore: Institute of Southeast Asian Studies

Sugiono, M.P. (1997). *Pancaran Rahmat Dari Arun* (The Blessing Broadcast from Arun) Lhokseumawe, Aceh: Public Relations PT Arun NGL Co.

Talisayon, Serafin (1989). *Designing for Consensus: The ASEAN Grid*. Singapore: Institute of Southeast Asian Studies

Vergara, Walter and Dominique Babelon (1990). *The Petrochemical Industry in Developing Asia*. Washington, DC: World Bank

Walters, Dan (2001). "Natural gas – an old story." *Sacramento Bee*, March 14

Wijarso (1988). "Gas utilization in Indonesia." Singapore: First Asia-Pacific Gas Conference, February 1

Journals and newspapers

    Far Eastern Economic Review
    Jakarta Post
    Petromin (PetroMin & Petromin Asia)
    Straits Times
    Xinhua News Agency

5   Bypassing Ukraine: exporting Russian gas to Poland and Germany

Nadejda M. Victor and David G. Victor

Introduction

In the early 1990s the giant Soviet enterprise of Gazprom began work on a new project to export gas across Belarus to Poland and Germany. Close examination of this project offers crucial insights into the potential for Russia's future gas exports because it was the first (and so far only) large new Russian gas pipeline project constructed after the dissolution of the Soviet bloc of nations (the Council for Mutual Economic Assistance, CMEA, also known as COMECON) and the Soviet Union itself. The Russian government envisions that total gas exports to Western Europe will rise to 200 (Bcm) per year by 2020 (up from more than 130 Bcm in 2005); whether, and how, such ambitions are realized depends on the practical experiences with this project – the first constructed in an era where markets have played a larger role than state-controlled financing in determining the size and route of pipelines.

This project remains the single largest expansion of gas transmission through Belarus. Whereas nearly all Russian gas exports to Western

The authors are grateful to Jack Hogan for stellar research assistance and to Mark H. Hayes, Josh House, and Amy M. Jaffe for comments on drafts, insightful discussions and editorial assistance. We are particularly grateful to Catherine Locatelli and Jonathan Stern for detailed critical reviews of a draft, and we also thank reviewers at a November 2003 meeting – notably Ed Chow, Ira Joseph, and Julie Nanay. Thanks also to more than a dozen unnamed experts who participated in and studied these projects in Germany, Poland, and Russia for interviews and background information. The Carnegie Endowment for International Peace and Centre for Energy Policy (Russia) organized a helpful meeting in February 2004 in Moscow where we presented some preliminary findings for critique. For simplicity, we have used the most common and convenient names when referring to key actors. Thus we speak of Ruhrgas throughout this text, although recently the firm was bought by electric conglomerate E.On. Similarly, throughout we refer to Gazprom although the exact ownership structure and formal name of the firm has changed in significant ways – where relevant, we use the particular names and detail the changes. When discussing the role of Wintershall we focus on the firm's actions although, in fact, it is a wholly owned subsidiary of BASF, and much of its financial muscle comes from BASF itself: where it is important to discuss BASF's particular role, we do that.

Europe traveled through Ukraine (and still do today), by the mid-1990s theft and risk of interruption of gas during Ukrainian transit had focused Russian minds on finding alternative routes. Finally, although this project was mainly conceived to serve the German market, it also was pursued partly with the aim of supplying the largely virgin gas market in Poland. Unlike most other CMEA nations, Poland had not been part of the centrally mandated gasification in the 1960s to 1980s; coal retained a vastly dominant share of Polish primary energy supply, and very few gas import pipelines from Russia served Poland. Although market forces did not yet rule in the Polish energy system in the mid-1990s when this project was conceived, the subsequent liberalization of Poland's energy markets in the 1990s meant that gas would have to penetrate without strong direction from the central government; in contrast, in all other CMEA nations gasification had been directed by the state in an era of central planning.

We call this project the Belarus Connector (BC). In Gazprom's vision, this project would have originated in the giant gas fields on the Yamal Peninsula and supply large volumes of gas to European markets. So far, development of the Yamal fields – a venture that would cost more than $25 billion for exploration and development alone – remains stillborn. Nonetheless, Gazprom and many analysts often call the built pipeline the "Yamal–Europe" project, but we avoid that terminology since production from the Yamal fields is still a dream rather than reality. Instead, Gazprom and its partners created the BC by connecting to existing trunk gas pipelines in Russia and running these new pipes through Belarus then Poland and into Germany. That smaller vision began with two large pipelines, but so far just one has been built with compressors that deliver a smaller volume than its potential.[1]

The Belarus connection projects are quite distinct from the large gas pipelines that the Soviet Union built from the 1960s through the 1980s that already have been the subject of extensive analysis (e.g. Stern 1980; Stent 1982; Gustafson 1985; Stern 1993). Those projects crossed territory that was either part of the Soviet Union (e.g. Belarus and Ukraine) or was firmly under the Soviet thumb (e.g. Czechoslovakia) – creating essentially no transit risk. Those projects were financed as grand state projects – either by Western European banks with state guarantees or by the Soviet Union itself. In the Soviet Union, the Soviet Ministry for the

---

[1] At the time of writing, (mid-2005) discussions are under way to build four additional compressor stations on the line, which would bring the system to full capacity; however, disputes over land leases and gas pricing in Belarus has delayed the compressors in the Belarusian section.

Gas Industry (Gazprom's predecessor) rewarded managers for the size of their visions rather than for commercial performance. In the consuming countries, as well, Soviet-era gas projects were conceived as vital state missions – Germany, for example, supplied concessionary loans, implicit state guarantees, and used the power of the government to assure deliveries of key technologies such as pipe and compressors. In that era of state control, project planning was relatively easy because the political and financial resources of a few large governments could be mobilized and coordinated for grand projects; governments not only eased the construction of these projects but they also directed state-owned enterprises to accept long-term agreements that specified the quantity and (usually oil-linked) pricing formulas.

We make two arguments. First, the experience with building the BC contrasts sharply with the era of complete state control over gas markets. The 1990s were a period during which the German gas market slowly saw the introduction of very limited competition, and the role of the state as maker and guarantor of markets declined, not least because political and financial resources of the German government were distracted by the task of unification with the former East Germany. Actual construction of the BC began when the largest single user of gas in Germany (BASF) sought alternative supplies that would be less costly than those of state monopolist Ruhrgas. Gazprom welcomed this overture since it, too, sought to bypass Ruhrgas, but for different reasons; it thought that alternative marketing arrangements could recover some of the rents that had traditionally gone to Ruhrgas by boosting the prices that Gazprom received for its exports. The German state played little positive role in making this project happen; it cautiously welcomed competition but stood ready to intervene if these new entrants caused too much harm to the well-connected incumbent Ruhrgas. The Russian state favored the project but had few political or economic resources to offer; it welcomed a project that circumvented troublesome Ukraine, but it had little ability to direct the project nor did it anticipate the troubles it would later have with Belarus. The Polish state favored the project but contributed little as well; Poland remained wary of any scheme that would raise dependence on Russia, but at the same time gas figured in a vision for new cleaner electric power generation and the project would also help to tie Poland to Germany's gas market. The practical effect of this relatively weak involvement of key governments was to raise the risk for commercial investors, slow the pace at which this project actually proceeded (in contrast with the earlier massive Soviet gas export projects), and favor elements of the BC that could be brought on-line with relatively low risk and greater ease once the key sponsors decided to allocate the capital. Thus the smallest and most scaleable aspects of the project were pursued, while those that required the grandest visions and the largest capital expenditures languished. As Polish investors found that demand for gas was smaller than originally anticipated, they unilaterally downscaled the project by installing fewer costly compressors than was planned originally, with more compressors to be added later with market-driven demand for the pipeline's gas.

Second, we argue that commentators on Russian gas exports have been prone to overstate the risks associated with crossing transit countries. Threatened and actual shutoffs of gas crossing Ukraine attracted much attention in the mid-1990s, but the logic for a pipeline crossing Belarus was driven principally by the logic of serving the North and Eastern German market (and, to a lesser degree, Poland). Avoiding Ukraine was convenient and helped to keep Gazprom's attention on the project, but simple bypass was not the primary motivating force. (Ironically, Belarus has proved to be an equally problematic transit country; in February 2004 Gazprom shut the BC for eighteen hours as part of a dispute with the Belarusian government about ownership of the pipeline segments in Belarus, theft, and gas prices.) Disputes with transit countries have affected the allocation of rents between producers and transit nations but have not affected gas prices for offtakers who have priced Russian gas with reference to oil. Russia and Gazprom are pushing other projects to bypass Ukraine, including notably the Blue Stream pipeline from Russian territory on the Black Sea directly to the Turkish market. In that case, too, the perception of a commercially viable Turkish market was a keystone to the effort – not simply the bypass of Ukraine. Also essential to the Blue Stream project was a willing partner who had deepwater pipeline expertise (ENI). We argue that the credible threat of bypass exerted considerable discipline on Ukraine in the mid-1990s and on Belarus in recent years, but the root cause of these countries' behavior have been internal political developments that caused their political and industrial leadership to focus on immediate survival and thus discount the long-term consequences of their actions. Most of the bypass threats exerted by Russia and also wielded by Poland when it feared dependence on Russia and Belarus for imported gas were not fully credible, but they had sufficient plausibility that they probably averted greater vulnerabilities to transit country risks. Russia exerted such threats against Ukraine with a proposed pipeline through southern Poland that would serve no purpose except to bypass Ukraine – a project that was never built. Poland exerted such threats against Belarus and Russia by contracting with Norway to deliver gas by pipeline across the Baltic Sea – a project not yet consummated.

We begin the story with an overview of the rise of gas in the Russian economy, as that explains both the emergence of Gazprom (and its structure) as well as the design of the gas pipeline network that was bequeathed to Russia as the Soviet Union broke apart in the late 1980s. We include a brief review of major gas export routes and then focus on the deals surrounding the three different aspects of the BC and the alternative projects that might have been pursued at the same time.

Soviet Energy Strategy and the Dash to Gas

1819 saw the first use of gas in Russia – for lamps on Aptekarsky Island in St. Petersburg. By the end of the nineteenth century the major cities of Moscow and St. Petersburg and many others were supplied with gas networks. Although lighting was the first widespread application of gas, industrial applications such as glass melting and metal hardening soon followed. In Baku, where oil pipelines were first laid in 1872 as the city emerged at the epicenter of Russia's largest oil-producing region, annual natural gas consumption rose to 33 million m^3 by the eve of the Russian Revolution in 1917 (Gazprom 2004). Wherever gas was used in large quantities the supplies were local, as the Soviet Union did not lay many long-distance gas pipelines until well after the Second World War – several decades after the appearance of the first long-distance gas pipelines in the United States. By the early 1930s the Soviet economy consumed 10–15 million m^3 annually; a decade later this figure had grown to 3.4 Bcm. (For comparison, the United States consumed about 50 Bcm in 1935.) During this period, the inflexibility of central planning, along with Stalin's iron grip, impeded the utilization of gas. Job-intensive hydropower and coal dominated in an industrial system that emphasized large industrial projects and electrification. Gross technical inefficiencies coupled with rapid industrial growth – both hallmarks of Stalin era central planning – caused a rapid and dramatic rise in total primary energy consumption, growing at about 6 percent per year from 1913–1940 and more than 9 percent annually from 1945–1960.

Not entirely by coincidence, 1953 marked the peak for coal's share in the Soviet economy and also the end of Stalin's rule; the share of primary energy supplied by gas that year stood at only 2 percent (see figure 5.1). In 1955, the USSR produced just 9 Bcm of gas from fields that were dispersed across the European part of Russia and in Ukraine (Kosnik 1975). Khrushchev set the goal of catching the United States economically within twenty-five years; modern industry, Khrushchev and his planners reasoned, required modern fuels. Oil was Khrushchev's principal focus, but gas also occupied a prominent role in his modernization –

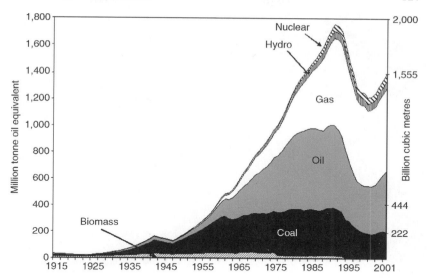

Figure 5.1. Primary energy production on Soviet territory, 1913–2002.
Source: 1913–1954: Elliot (1974); 1955–1964 Goskomstat (various years); 1965–2002: BP (2003); 1970–1990: UN (1993).
All fuels converted to Bcm natural gas equivalent.

the desire to develop a gas industry was officially inserted into the sixth Five-Year Plan (1956–1960) and advanced with the Seventh Plan (1959–1965)[2] (AIC 1995). Not only were modern fuels more flexible and efficient, but some keystones to modern industry demanded the fine-tuned combustion uniquely provided by gas and oil. A modern chemical industry, for example, requires petrochemical feedstocks and Soviet industry arrived quite late to that cluster of innovations. Investment in long-distance pipelines and gas fields in the northern Caucusus, Ukraine, and Turkmenistan followed.

Just fifteen years later (in 1968) persistent state sponsorship of the oil industry had catapulted oil to the top of the Soviet Union's primary energy supply.[3] (In the United States, for comparison, oil rose to the top

[2] The Sixth Five-Year Plan was discarded in 1957 primarily because it overcommitted available resources and could not be fulfilled, and was replaced by a special seven-year plan.
[3] The share of oil production rose from 21 percent of all primary energy produced in the USSR in 1955 to 38 percent in 1968. Coal retained a large share because it had entrenched itself in the electric power sector. At the same time, gas production rose from 2 percent in 1955 to 17 percent of total primary energy in 1968. These data are

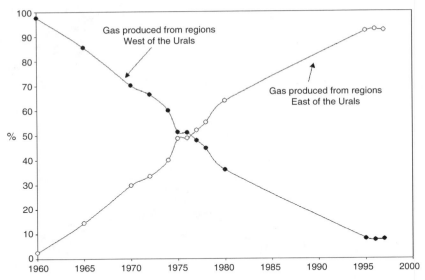

Figure 5.2. The shifting geography of Soviet and Russian gas production, 1960–1998.

Source: 1960–1974: Kosnik (1975); 1975–1980: calculated from Stern (1980), table 2–5, p. 28; 1995–1997: Goskomstat (1998).

Estimated gas production from regions West and East of the Urals. Early production focused on fields close to demand centers as they were easiest to tap and long-distance transportation proved to be especially difficult without access to Western technology. Operating fields in Arctic permafrost conditions, which characterized the most lucrative fields east of the Urals, was also very challenging as it required special anchors and procedures such as cooling systems so that post-compression gas would not melt the surrounding permafrost, creating a jelly-like slush in which the pipes would float and heave along the tundra surface.

spot in 1950.) Gas rose more slowly because gas was harder to handle and, unlike oil for petrochemicals and internal combustion engines, gas was not uniquely qualified for any particular major use.

Khrushchev's Eighth Plan, which began in 1966, recognized the potential importance of the vast Siberian gas reserves to the east of the Ural mountains; production from these fields began slowly, as shown in figure 5.2. This plan marked the beginning of the "Siberian period" with

calculated on the basis of primary energy production estimates that include biomass fuels (e.g., wood) and thus are somewhat non-comparable with estimates made for Western countries, which typically exclude "traditional" biomass fuels. (Kosnik 1975).

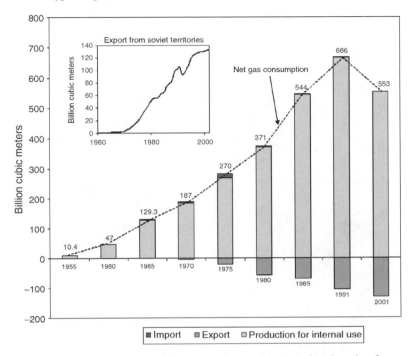

Figure 5.3. Production, consumption and international trade of gas on Soviet territory, 1965–2001.

Sources: 1955–1960: Stern (1993); 1965–2001: BP (2003).

Imports from the late 1960s are from Afghanistan (beginning in the late 1960s) and Iran (the IGAT pipeline, beginning in 1970). The IGAT pipelines linked via Georgia to the pipelines that had tapped gas reserves in the Caucasus and delivered gas north to Moscow and other centers, but the Iranian revolution effectively shut this import route in 1979. A series of pipelines mainly for the European market (summarized in this chapter) provided substantial exports starting in the early 1970s. The effect of the massive pipelines connected to the large new Urengoy field in Northwestern Siberia is evident.

the opening of the world-class fields in Urengoy – discovered in 1966 and brought into first service in 1978. As the small and dispersed fields West of the Urals and close to demand centers became depleted and the slow process of working in the arctic conditions of Western Siberia yielded viable fields, net production shifted east. These new Siberian supplies were injected into the existing network of pipelines that had been established earlier to link the now depleting gas fields to major centers of demand. The export routes from the new Siberian fields thus

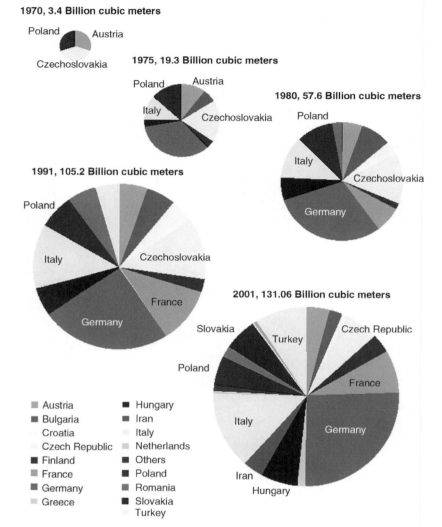

Figure 5.4. Composition of Soviet gas exports to Europe, 1970–2001.

Source: BP (2003).

travelled southwest and linked to Moscow-bound pipelines that then traversed the industrial heartland and gas fields of Ukraine.

As shown in figure 5.3, through the 1970s gas remained predominantly for domestic use. International trade was minimal; in fact, the

USSR was a slight net importer of gas (from Iran and Afghanistan). Soviet planners extended this same industrial model to other members of CMEA. The first such pipeline – "Brotherhood" – began operation in 1968, linking the Shebelinka gas field east of Kiev to Czechoslovakia. A small extension later linked that pipe to Austria, the first Soviet gas exports to the West; a small pipeline also served Poland. As shown in figure 5.4, that was the sum total of Soviet gas exports in 1970. That same year, total hydrocarbon exports (nearly all in the form of oil) amounted to $US 444 million, or 18.3 percent of the Soviet Union's total hard currency earnings (Stent 1982). In the early 1970s a few additional pipelines were being considered for other CMEA members as well as extensions to Western nations that were geographically and politically close to the Soviet Union, such as Finland, Austria, and Germany.

The oil shock of 1973 changed this strategy. Higher oil prices put a premium on boosting production of gas to replace oil while also lifting the price that the Soviet Union could charge for the gas that it exported. Internal gas and oil prices remained low, and thus the planning mechanism rather than price incentives was needed to direct gas resources to their most advantageous purposes. Planners took up the task by drawing long lines on maps – linking the West Siberian fields with demand centers in central Europe and in the West. When the Soviet Union was planning for internal consumption it created a grid; when it planned for massive exports it sought to match output (from the wellhead) to input (the offtaker).

The gas projects that followed during the 1970s through the mid-1980s followed two basic scripts. Projects for CMEA nations involved

Caption for Figure 5.4 (*cont.*)
Around 1970 the only exports were from small pipes to Poland (dating from 1949) and via a small pipeline from Ukraine to Czechoslovakia and Austria. Offtake diversified in the 1970s with the creation of two large pipeline clusters that first tapped the "warm" West Siberian fields (i.e. the fields not in the permafrost region): (1) the "Transgas" pipeline network, which included the TAG I and II pipelines to Czechoslovakia, Austria, and Italy (1974) and the MEGAL pipelines to Austria, the two Germanies and France (1974, 1976, 1979); (2) the Orenburg ("Soyuz") pipelines to Bulgaria, Hungary, and Romania (1975). Ever since those large exports began, Germany has been the dominant off-taking country. The dominant German position as offtaker has remained even as large new fields in the permafrost region of Northwest Siberia – notably the Yamburg and Urengoy fields – have been tapped.

the Soviet parent selling gas at discounted prices and through complex barter exchanges. Projects for Western nations involved hard prices for the gas – usually indexed to the price of oil, which gas was replacing. The financing arrangements included hard currency loans offered at concessionary terms and secured by the physical shipments of gas delivered to the state-owned Western European gas companies. The 1970s atmosphere of détente meant that West European nations shared a common interest with the Soviet Union in advancing commercial exchange. Shared infrastructure would bind the two blocs together; from the Western perspective, they would give the Soviet Union a stake in the West and make it a less threatening country. At the same time, deals involving hard currency and Western technology served the Soviet interest – not only was the currency useful, but Western technology made possible the fuller development of West Siberian fields. The effect of all this investment in gas exports was dramatic – in 1980, the year that détente came unstuck, the Soviet Union earned $14.7 billion from gas and oil exports, or 62.3 percent of its total hard currency earnings. As shown in figure 5.5, from 1975 to 1980 both the volume and (oil-indexed) price of gas can he tound in the *exports tripled*, yielding a nine-fold increase in total earnings (data on more recent earnings can be found in appendix table 5.A, p. 166).

The Soviet invasion of Afghanistan (1979), along with Ronald Reagan's assumption of power in the United States (1980), refroze the Cold War and erased the Western consensus on Soviet oil and gas exports. US sanctions initiated under the Carter administration and enhanced by Reagan sought to limit the hard currency that the Soviet Union could earn through exports and also to block exports of grain and essential high technology from the West to the Soviet Union. Natural gas provided an immediate test of the US sanction effort and revealed the difficulty of sustaining an anti-Soviet coalition of Western nations. In the early 1980s the West German government, working through its gas monopoly Ruhrgas, launched negotiations to build new pipelines to carry Soviet gas to Europe. The new German projects would expand Russia's export capacity, with two key differences.

One was the new political climate; the other was the size of the projects: rather than tapping into the existing Russian gas production capacity, these new projects would include upstream investments to develop the giant Urengoy gas fields in north western Siberia (see the map in figure 5.6). In exchange for gas, German banks (backed by the German government) would supply capital; German firms would provide pipe and compressors. For the German government, the project promised not only to reduce import bills by replacing oil but also to

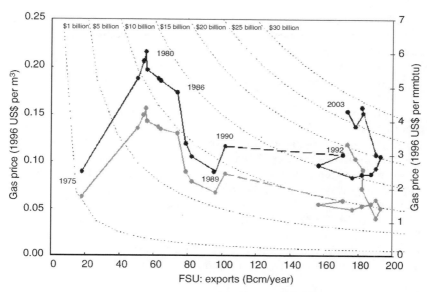

Figure 5.5. Soviet and Russian earnings from gas export, 1975–2003.

Source: Total volumes from BP (2003) for 1970–1990; EIA (2003) for 1992–2003. Prices from BP (2004).

The dark line shows the total volume of trade computed using European c.i.f. prices in constant 1996 dollars. However, trade with the CMEA countries and (after 1992) the CIS countries occurred mainly at prices far below the Western rate. For these countries, we estimated prices and made allowances for barter payment of transit fees in gas (rather than cash). The lighter line reports total value of exports from the USSR (pre-1992) and Russia (post-1992) revised downward to account for these lower prices. These estimates are based on a simple division of importing countries into three groups: CMEA, Western Europe, and CIS. We assume that gas prices for Western Europe are the same as those reported by BP; for CMEA, 50 percent of Western levels; for CIS, 25 percent. Barter trade is especially difficult to estimates and can lead to substantial error, although our estimates for the total value of Russian gas exports in recent years are quite close to the actual values reported by the Central Bank (see appendix, p. 166).

employ thousands of German workers in making the huge (1,400 mm (56 inch) diameter) rolled steel pipes and compressors. Some of the compressor technologies were subject to collective export controls that were in place in Western countries, and thus the US attempted to exert veto control. From the European perspective the US objection was rooted in an imagined geopolitical threat; nonetheless, the risk of US sanctions slowed the project and forced closer attention to constructing a deal that could be tolerated by the Reagan administration. The threat of delay or cancellation led the Soviets to develop their own (quite inferior) compressors, and when the pipeline eventually began operation in 1985 it deployed a combination of Western and Soviet technology (Gustafson 1985).

When finally completed, this huge pipeline network delivered 180 Bcm of gas from the Urengoy fields to many Soviet destinations, paid for with the 30 Bcm per year exported to Germany, France, Italy, Austria, and Switzerland. When it reached fully capacity in 1991 this single project increased Soviet exports to the West by roughly half. Soviet exports to the West (Germany, Italy, France, Austria, Turkey, Finland, and Switzerland, in order of volume that year) reached 63 Bcm, up from 31 Bcm in 1985 (BP 2003). In the same model of operation – US-led but ineffective sanctions, West European semi-soft financing and technology bartered for gas, and backing of Western governments – German and French state-owned gas firms led a coalition of Western investors to expand Soviet gas exports with another pipeline ("STEGAL") that began operation in 1992.

The sudden dissolution of the Soviet bloc had three effects that have altered the environment for Russian gas exports to the West. The first change was the disintegration of the CMEA bloc – a process that began in the mid-1980s with Hungary's moves for independence, and continued through the fall of the Berlin Wall and the Czechoslovak Velvet Revolution in 1989. These political changes created transit countries – each with its own distinct interests – where previously there had existed a somewhat unified bloc. Although these new transit countries created new uncertainties for gas supply, in most cases there were strong incentives not to disrupt Soviet-era gas export arrangements. Most Russian gas exports to the West traveled through Czecholovakia, which soon broke into two distinct countries, the Czech Republic and Slovakia. Both these countries were in the midst of developing close ties with Western Europe; if they had caused trouble for gas exporters then they would have harmed the interests of their new allies in the West whose consent was essential for membership in the European Union and NATO.[4] In fact, both countries saw their gas bills rise sharply as they

---

[4] Slovakia would have been an interesting case for scholars studying transit countries if its government had continued down a track that was hostile to the West, the Czech Republic, and markets – especially as Western governments sought to marginalize the Slovak president Meciar. But that affair lasted only a short while, and today the Slovak Republic is behaving like a country that has a stake in the West.

were charged Western rather than CMEA discount prices. The Czech Republic quickly moved to the higher West European price as that country sought rapid integration with West European institutions. Slovakia's internal gas prices remained lower for longer, but then rose sharply in the first half of 2000 and in 2005 are at Western levels. Both countries have reliably paid their increased bills for gas imports.

A second and more important change was the creation of politically distinct states within the Soviet Union itself. The European part of the Soviet Union formally disintegrated in 1992 into seven states – Russia, Belarus, Ukraine, Moldova, and the three Baltic states. Thus instantly transit countries (Belarus and mainly Ukraine) appeared on the routes of all the pipeline projects connecting the European part of Russia to the outside world. (The only exception was a small pipeline to Finland that began operation in 1974 and, until the Blue Stream project started pumping gas in 2002, was Russia's only direct gas connection to any non-Soviet market.) In figure 5.3, nearly all of the 60 percent jump in gas exports from 1990–1992 is the consequence of reclassifying internal Soviet transfers (pre-1992) as external trades (1992 and beyond), notably to Ukraine.[5] At the time that the Soviet Union dissolved, about 90 percent of Russia's gas exports traveled through Ukraine.

Third, the collapse of the Soviet Union caused economic shockwaves that dramatically lowered the internal demand for Russian gas. The Soviet economy shrank by about 40 percent and total energy consumption declined by about one-third (OECD 1997). With a shrinking economy, gas consumption in Russia declined over 16 percent – from 420 Bcm in 1990 to 350 Bcm in 1997 (BP 2003). Gas exports to the CIS (Commonwealth of Independent States)[6] also declined (by 31 percent or from 110 Bcm in 1990 to 76 Bcm in 1998), in part because these countries' economies were intertwined with the Soviet economy and thus suffered severe economic recession. In addition, they were now forced to purchase gas at semi-hard export prices, which were higher

---

[5] In 1992 Ukraine consumed 104 Bcm of gas and produced only 40 Bcm – the rest (64 Bcm) it imported from Russia. Add to that the 17 Bcm of consumption in Belarus (which produces no gas and imports all its needs from Russia) and the result is essentially all the increase in Russian exports. For the CIS Customs Union, the price in 1992 was about $50 per 1,000 m^3, or $1.39/mmbtu; for a Western European country, the full market price was charged, which was close to $100 (or $2.78/mmbtu) (Cohen 2001). The actual prices charged to CIS members varied, and barter and theft tolerance also varied which makes it hard to assess true relative prices (Kuzio 2003).

[6] The CIS was created in December 1991. It unites all of the former Soviet states except the Baltic Republics. Members include Azerbaijan, Armenia, Belarus, Georgia, Kazakhstan, Kyrgyzstan, Moldova, Russia, Tajikstan, Turkmenistan, Uzbekistan, and Ukraine.

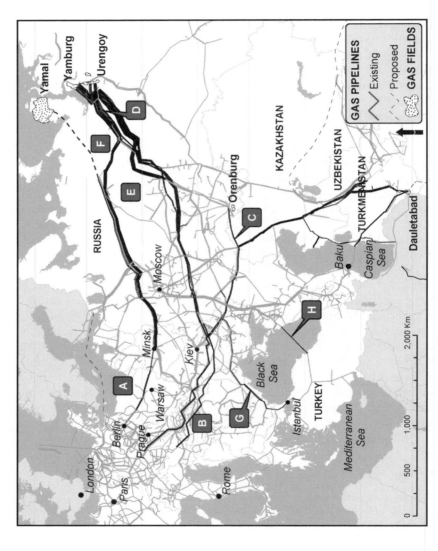

Figure 5.6. Major Soviet and Russian gas export routes, 2003.

than the internal Soviet price but lower than the price charged for Western exports, and those higher prices discouraged gas consumption and promoted efficiency (Garipov, Kozlovsky, and Litvinenko 2003; Zhiznin 2003). Even as consumption shrank, reported gas production declined only slightly (about 8 percent) from 1992 to 1998 (Russia's total oil production, by contrast, fell nearly 23 percent during the same period).[7] In principle, this large and growing surplus in the 1990s was available for export – allowing Russia to expand its role as the world's largest exporter of natural gas and earn additional hard currency.

Crossing Belarus and Poland

The 1990s offered Russia both the possibility of exporting more gas to the West and the urgent need to earn additional hard currency. Whether those potentials would be realized requires us to look at the incentives and organization of the exporter (Russia's Gazprom) and the importers (notably the German gas importers). We address each in turn.

Gazprom: a State within a State

The collapse of the Soviet Union brought turmoil to the organization of the gas operations that spanned its territory. The Soviet Gas Ministry, which had coordinated all production and transmission of gas, was reorganized in 1989 as a state-controlled committee. By presidential decree following the dissolution of the Soviet Union, it was reorganized

---

[7] Reports in the West at the time claimed that gas production did not decline with the same severity as the rest of Russian industry because gas production required relatively low levels of ongoing investment in equipment and maintenance (CERA report, cited in PIW 1992). This underinvestment was not sustainable, as evident is today with the deterioration of the gas infrastructure, a problem to which we return shortly.

Caption for Figure 5.6 (*cont.*)
Note, in particular, the large parallel pipelines extending from the Urenguoy and Yamburg fields in Northwestern Siberia past Moscow and across Ukraine. The dominance of Ukraine as a transit country reflects not just geography but also path-dependence. Early fields in Ukraine yielded a gas infrastructure in the region, and the first pipelines to Central and Eastern Europe tapped that infrastructure, supplying Czechoslovakia and Austria. The majority of projects serving European customers in the 1970s followed these routes—including all the projects serving Germany, France, Austria, and Italy. The few exceptions include generally smaller pipelines across Romania to Bulgaria and Turkey, as well as across Hungary to Yugoslavia.

into a joint-stock company, with the assets divided among Belarus (1.5 percent), Ukraine (9.5 percent), and Russia (89 percent) – each controlled by its respective government. The Russian joint-stock company Gazprom ("RAO Gazprom") was then to be privatized over three years, forming an open joint-stock company ("OAO Gazprom"). The privatization decree required the government to reduce its stake in the company below 40 percent, and most of the government's stake was sold to Gazprom employees (in practice, senior managers); a small fraction over the years has been sold to non-Russian investors, who by 2005 held about 11.5 percent of all shares.[8] The Russian state retains 38 percent ownership of the company, but through insiders the state has probably retained a controlling interest.

During this period Gazprom's managers faced two often incompatible tasks – retaining control over the enterprise and boosting profits. Retaining control required Gazprom's managers to integrate all of the functions of gas production, transmission, and marketing completely within their grasp so that others could not capture the monopoly rents for themselves.[9] During the highly turbulent period from 1989 through the mid-1990s, when much in Russia was reorganized, Gazprom was not completely successful in this effort. Key gas-processing facilities in Siberia, for example, fell into alien hands. For a brief period in 1990 the central government retained control over *Soyuzgazexport* – the state entity responsible for marketing all gas exports – thus putting the most lucrative Western sales contracts outside Gazprom's control. Gazprom's managers responded by creating their own export marketing arm (*Zarubeshgaz*).[10] Gazprom also purchased stakes in gas distribution and marketing companies in Europe, notably in the privatization of

---

[8] In 2005 about 4.4 percent traded openly on Western markets in the form of American Depository Receipts (ADR) (i.e. instruments that carry the promise of exchange for normal Gazprom shares, in this case on a 1:10 basis, although it is illegal for non-Russians to own Gazprom shares directly); the rest of the non-Russian shares (7.1 percent) are owned by non-Russian strategic investors, notably Ruhrgas (which owns nearly 6 percent). Until 2005, Russian legislation limited foreign ownership in Gazprom to 20 percent; at the time of writing, a series of measures to liberalize trading in Gazprom shares is set to raise the limit, in principle, to 49 percent while assuring that the Russian state retains a majority share. At the same time, the Russian government will, in effect, repurchase outstanding shares so that it owns 51 percent of the company.

[9] The government of Prime Minister Yegor Gaidar tried to open the gas industry to competition, and in February 1992 it presented an idea of establishing independent gas-producing companies. The Minister of Oil and Energy, Vladimir Lopukhin, made an effort to realize this idea, but became an enemy of Gazprom's head, Viktor Chernomyrdin. In 1993 Lopukhin was sacked and replaced with Chernomyrdin, who was also given a rank of Vice-Premier responsible for oil and energy complex.

[10] By then, however, it had already set in motion the creation of its own export marketing arm and strategy.

central and east European gas pipelines and distributors. Russian gas officials had long thought that Western importers – notably Ruhrgas, the largest single customer for Russia's exports – paid prices that were too low and retained large markups for themselves. Control over transit pipelines, export marketing, and a firmer role in final user markets were all part of a strategy to lift revenues. Gazprom eventually obtained control over *Soyuzgazexport* and consolidated control over nearly all Russian gas exports in the early 1990s.

For Gazprom's managers to retain control also required actions that would appear to undermine the firm's profitability yet were essential to making the firm uniquely indispensable to Russia's economy and society, so that political authorities would be reluctant to reorganize the firm or change management. Like all large Soviet-era industrial conglomerates, Gazprom had a large array of non-essential assets and functions – agricultural lands (for producing food for Gazprom employees), equipment manufacturers, banks, and so on; whereas most other Russian conglomerates sought to sell those sprawling assets and focus on core business, through the 1990s Gazprom actually purchased larger amounts of non-core assets. Some of the Gazprom menagerie could be transformed into useful entities – Gazprombank, for example, became the collecting agent when Gazprom sought to squeeze local gas distributors in Russian cities by billing customers directly for gas. Although often lamented by Gazprom's management, low gas prices have been essential to the firm's control strategy. In the Soviet era and in Russia today, revenues from natural resources largely accrue to the regional authorities where production occurs, which in principle is a potentially huge windfall that could shift revenues and power from Gazprom and the central government to the regions. However, natural gas producer prices are regulated at low levels. Gazprom sets the fees charged for transit on its pipeline network, also at low levels (in the 1990s, about one-fifth the level in the West), and final prices to consumers are also regulated at low levels. In this system, control over the market flows not to the most efficient producers and marketers but to those who control physical access to the pipeline network.[11]

---

[11] Real Gazprom transit fees were largely unknown to Western analysts until the firm started renegotiating contracts with the newly independent FSU. Over the 1990s, Gazprom adopted a more complex transit fee structure, which allowed it to retain control over access to its pipeline network and, especially, to the export pipelines. Thus transit fees have risen more rapidly than the spread between producer and offtaker tariffs – in essence, allowing Gazprom to ensure that as controller of the pipelines it extracted as much of the rent for itself. For example, in 1992 a hypothetical seller of contract gas from the Yamburg gas fields to Latvia would pay 33 cents per mmbtu for the 3,300 km of

Low producer prices and uncertain access to pipelines prevented most independent producers from entering the market. Thus Russian gas production includes only minuscule quantities of associated gas, even though Russia's oil industry is one of the world's largest and large amounts of associated gas are vented or flared. Lukoil, for example, claims that it costs 57 cents per mmbtu to process its associated gas; yet oil companies are given only 6.7–40 cents per mmbtu (2002 figures, quoted in WGI 2002). A few independent producers have arisen in this market, but principally when they have been able to use political connections at Gazprom to ensure access to the pipeline system. The most prominent example – Florida-based Itera – thrived through its political connections with Gazprom's early management and occupied a niche selling Russian and Turkmen gas (some of it produced by Itera and some bought from state enterprises) to Belarus and Ukraine. As Itera's connections to Gazprom's management have waned so has their ability to operate in the market, with other independents arising to fill other special niches (e.g. Novatek). Oil producer Lukoil has sharply lifted its gas production while trying to force access to Gazprom's export pipelines; other firms, including Shell, are exploring joint ventures with Gazprom itself for producing and transmitting gas to profitable markets. All the while, Gazprom sits at the center of a rigged competition – an outcome much more convenient to Gazprom than guaranteed third-party access to pipelines with transparent tariffs. Periodically, reformers such as Sergei Kiriyenko (Prime Minister from 23 March 1998 to 23 August 1998 under President Yeltsin) would envision sweeping reform of the gas sector, including guaranteed access for independent gas producers and regulated access to the pipeline network. But the reformers' rule has been punctuated by longer tenures of more Gazprom-friendly rulers, notably former Gazprom chairman Viktor Chernomyrdin (Prime Minister from 1992 to 1998). In Putin's Kremlin still another new group of Gazprom advocates has ruled.

To boost profits, Gazprom's managers in the 1990s had in principle a plethora of options, but few were practical to implement. Gazprom

---

transit from field to market and would receive $1.47 per mmbtu for the gas in Latvia, leaving $1.14 for production and profit, which probably would be profitable for an independent producer if they could have gained access to the market (WGI 1992). If Western transit fees were charged on the whole Gazprom pipeline system it is unlikely that Russian gas would be competitive with alternative European supplies. *World Gas Intelligence* calculated the transit fee at Western levels for gas shipped from Urengoy in Western Siberia across 500km of permafrost (where pipelines are more expensive to build and operate) and then 3500km of rolling hills to the German border. Their estimate was $2.50/mmbtu – or almost exactly the price that Gazprom got that year for contract sales to Ruhrgas (WGI 1992).

could attempt to raise internal prices and improve collections, which would both lift revenues and "produce" gas by inducing conservation. That tree was ripe with fruit, but the political obstacles were many. Moreover, rapid movement on that front might have gone against Gazprom's own interests since a more visibly profitable domestic gas sector could amplify calls for a breakup or reallocation of the firm's assets. Even after many sharp price rises through the 1990s, by 2003 the government-approved price for residential gas was just 68 cents per mmbtu, which was roughly one-fifth the level of wholesale prices for Western exports. Moreover, 90 percent of households do not have gas meters and residents pay for gas on a *per capita* basis. While oil product prices in Russia now approach world levels, gas lags far behind. Gazprom could also improve collections from Russian and non-Russian customers alike, in the mid-1990s only one-quarter of Gazprom customers actually fully paid their bills, and accumulated debts (including amounts owed, by former Soviet republics) totaled $2.5 billion (WGI 1995a, 1995b). But Gazprom had few tools for extracting these billings – cutting off internal customers was politically impossible.[12] Cutting off external customers, especially those along key transit routes (notably Ukraine) could cause collateral damage to Gazprom's more lucrative customers further along the pipeline, as the experiences with Ukraine and Belarus both revealed. Gazprom could improve the efficiency of its own operations and shed non-core assets. Its pipeline system was leaky and inefficient – an early 1990s study by the European Bank for Reconstruction and Development (EBRD) estimated that 15 percent of the pipeline throughput went just to operate the system, and improving the system could free 60 Bcm in production (EBRD 1995). But with low producer prices it actually made little sense for Gazprom to invest in its own efficiency. Projects such as replacing pipe that had been installed in the Soviet era with poor anti-corrosion coatings or installing more efficient Western compressors would require capital (which was unavailable) and a long planning horizon (which did not characterize Gazprom's management approach). A few such projects went ahead where they were attractive to Western contractors who could be repaid

---

[12] It is politically impossible to cut off internal Russian customers (the population of entire regions could easily freeze to death during Russia's long winter), but summer curtailments have occurred. Russian electricity monopolies' United Energy System (UES) has had gas supplies for power generation cut off periodically, with the result that electric trams and subways stopped working as some regions plunged into darkness (Higgins 1998; Aris 2000).

with gas and were financed, in part, with export credits from their home countries.

The quickest way to boost profits was to lift the price and volume of Western exports. Gazprom's closet was full of projects that could be rekindled. For example, in the 1970s the "Northstar" joint project of the US firm Tenneco and the Soviet Gas Ministry would have shipped gas from a port just east of Murmansk to Philadelphia, but that effort remained stuck in the planning stages – running foul of unfavorable economics that closed two other LNG reception terminals that had been built at the same time in the United States as well as the geopolitical fallout from the 1979 Soviet invasion of Afghanistan.[13] In the 1990s the opportunities for LNG exports were expanding as technologies improved, but most of the options were far outside the realm of Gazprom's experience and not competitive with other LNG ventures such as those in Indonesia, Qatar, Trinidad and Tobago (see also chapters 8 and 9). Projects on Sakhalin were under consideration in the 1990s, but none of the major projects was conceived by Gazprom; Sakhalin was outside the firm's traditional zone of influence, and none of these projects went forward until after the year 2000.[14]

Gazprom's existing pipeline network offered four broad routes to the West, as summarized in table 5.1. In the far south, routes crossed Ukraine to serve markets in Southeastern Europe – the former CMEA nations (Romania and Bulgaria) along with Yugoslavia, Greece, and Turkey. Romania and Yugoslavia were potentially significant markets for the future. Greece was seen as attractive, and Gazprom created a financially disastrous joint venture ("Prometheus Gas") to operate and market gas transmission services and generate electricity. (The Greek market may yet prove lucrative as gas consumption is rising sharply.) In

[13] For background on the Northstar project see Kosnik (1975). This idea, updated for new supply and port options, is now being considered actively.

[14] Today, arctic fields are again under consideration for LNG exports to Europe and the United States; so far, however, Gazprom has not allocated significant capital to such ventures, although Lukoil has more actively explored a possible LNG project to export Yamal gas. Pipelines from Siberia to China or Korea had been discussed periodically in the 1990s and were considered serious options in the late 1990s (Paik 1995, 2002; APEC 2000; IEA 2002a). None, however, has advanced to construction because of the lack of serious interest by offtakers, the huge capital requirements, and special geopolitical problems with China for any project that would involve crossing Mongolia. (The most likely project at present is from the Kovytka field near Lake Baikal, and the current plans envision traveling hundreds of extra km to avoid Mongolia.) The Chinese are increasingly enthusiastic about these ideas, and Gazprom is agitating for a role in the projects, but is not the lead player. From the vantage point of the early 1990s, if Gazprom wanted to export to Western markets it would need to concentrate on its traditional markets using the traditional pipeline method of transmission.

Table 5.1 *Russia's major international gas export lines, 2003*[a]

Route	Capacity volume
1 From Russia direct, via the North	
Finland Connector	20 Bcm/year
2 From Russia via Belarus to Western Europe	
(a) Belarus Connector ("Yamal–Europe")	
Belarusian section	33 Bcm/year
Polish section	20 Bcm/year
3 From Russia via Ukraine to Western Europe	
(b) Brotherhood (Bratstvo)	30 Bcm/year
(c) Orenburg (Soyuz)	30 Bcm/year
(d) Urengoy Center	40 Bcm/year
(e) Yamburg (Progress)	30 Bcm/year
(f) Northern lights (Siyaniye Severa)	25 Bcm/year
4 From Russia South to Turkey	
(g) Bulgaria, Romania and Turkey	20 Bcm/year
(h) Blue Stream	16 Bcm/year

Note:
[a] All these routes were constructed prior to 1990 except the BC (a) and Blue Stream (h). Volumes shown are export potential attributed to each project.
Source: EIA (2004b).

the early 1990s Turkey, especially, was seen as a reachable prize. The Turkish population was large, and in the 1980s Turkey's economy grew some 4 percent per year on average (only 1.7 percent per capita), while demand for primary energy rose at more than 7 percent per year. Russian gas first entered the Turkish market when a pipeline linking Bulgaria to Ankara was completed in the late 1980s, and the capacity of the trans-Bulgaria pipelines were expanded in the 1990s to accommodate the expected surging demand in Turkey. While Turkey offered great potential, demand was slow to rise as it depended, in part, on reorganization of the Turkish energy system and creating incentives for private investment in gas power plants – a process that was under way but slow to take shape. Gazprom formed a marketing joint venture with Turkey's monopoly importer Botas; part of the gas would be sold to two planned power plants where Gazprom was part owner. (Just one is being constructed at present – a joint venture with Entes and ABB near Ankara.)

Blue Stream

The Blue Stream project was rooted in a 1997 inter-governmental agreement between Russia and Turkey and financially organized under a 1999 agreement between Gazprom and ENI to form Trustco to build, own, and operate the undersea section of pipeline – the Blue Stream (see figure 5.6). That project was as much a demonstration of ultra deep-water gas pipeline technology and a potential spearhead into the Russian market as it was an attempt to create a commercially viable enterprise. Indeed, the project has since run foul of the glut in the Turkish gas market, created by poor strategic planning and a faltering Turkish economy, which raises doubts about whether the $3.2 billion project was ever needed at all. Botas estimated in the mid-1990s that gas demand in Turkey would rise six-fold by 2010 (WGI 1995c); in reality, gas consumption had risen to about 17.4 Bcm by 2002 and was increasing at about 10 percent per year – a rapidly growing market, but well below Botas' projected trajectory.

Turkey could eventually become the transit point to Europe and thus become a competitor to Belarus (and the Baltic Sea pipeline and eventually LNG exports from the Arctic). But the distances are long and the route is a lot less attractive until the Turkish market itself becomes a major destination for Russian gas. Russia is not the only option for Turkey. Iran, too, has explored pipelines to the West that would put Iranian gas into direct competition with Russian exports for Central and Southern Europe. The Central Asian Republics, too, could use Turkey as a transshipment point.

The total cost of the Blue Stream pipeline was $3.2 billion, including $1.7 billion to construct the marine section and the Beregovaya compressor station. Though the project qualified as an engineering triumph, it seems far less likely to be a commercial success. Turkey's gas demand was expected to more than double and reach 45 Bcm by 2006, but this amount, in fact, was reduced due to the Turkish economic crisis. It became clear in 2001 that the Blue Stream project would face financial problems.[15] Turkey had previously committed to buy from Russia over 60 percent of its total gas import, but analysts have been warning for years that Turkish gas demand forecasts have been far too optimistic.

Gas deliveries to Turkey through the Blue Stream stopped in April 2003, with Turkey demanding a price revision and lower supplies. Turkey thus shut down the flow of gas from Russia less than a month after commercial supplies started on 20 February 2003. Even before the cutoff, Turkey had negotiated with Gazprom to reduce by half the flow contracted to start in 2003. It is unclear whether the new government is simply trying to deal with

---

[15] Turkey's financial crisis of 2001, followed by a severe recession, sharply decreased its gas requirements calculated in the 1990s. Facing a free fall of its economy in 2001, it neither needed nor could afford huge amounts of gas imports.

a gas glut, save money, spread its energy sources, or perhaps steer more business to Iran.[16] In 2002 Turkey also stopped importing Iranian gas on a pretext of quality problems until it negotiated a lower price. Turkish demand is now recovering and Blue Stream's full capacity (and expansions) will be invoked – but much later than expected.

Routes through Ukraine

The central routes through Ukraine corresponded most closely to Gazprom's experience – indeed, nearly all Russian gas traveled to Western markets via these routes, and most of that went through Slovakia along the "Transgas" cluster of pipelines then south to Austria and Italy or directly West to the Czech Republic, Germany, Switzerland, and France. The Transgas system was rated for 79 Bcm per year; in 1990, 73 Bcm moved along the route (WGI 1991a). Gazprom could have created additional capacity along these lines by boosting pressure on existing lines, or even building new lines in bottleneck areas. However, Russia was already selling as much gas as it could along these routes. The industry press at the time was filled with articles about the European "gas bubble" – created by the arrival of large volumes of gas from the giant Norwegian Troll field, which was piped directly to the continent and made inroads deep into the German market with new pipelines. In the early 1990s Ruhrgas designed its expansion of gas transmission lines into East Germany explicitly to allow interconnection with Norwegian and Dutch gas supplies. In the large and growing Italian market, Gazprom faced competition from Sonatrach, which sold large new volumes as LNG in addition to the Transmed pipeline (see chapter 3). By the mid-1990s gas marketers in continental Europe were also expecting the arrival (in the late 1990s) of UK gas through the "Interconnector."[17]

Ukraine also presented a problem. The 1990s saw a constant simmering battle between Gazprom and Ukraine over the latter's repayment of accumulated debts and demands for more favorable gas contracts and the former's desire to cross Ukrainian territory with its

---

[16] Like Russia and Azerbaijan, Iran has tried to turn the problem of Turkey's gas glut into an advantage by seeking transit routes through the country that could supply Greece and other countries.

[17] Indeed, as part of its strategy to invest in downstream pipelines and distribution companies, Gazprom took a small stake in the Interconnector. By the late 1990s Gazprom had stakes in twenty pipeline and trading companies in the European market, including incumbents such as Gaz de France (GdF) as well as upstarts such as Wingas. In addition, Gazprom sought stakes in major gas users, such as power plants in Turkey and a chemical company in East Germany, which it bought along with a subsidy from the German Treuhand privatization agency.

gas. The effects of these battles were occasionally felt in Western nations when contracted gas supplies fell short. The first incident was in October 1992 when unusually cold weather and a shortfall in supplies from Turkmenistan caused a 45 percent shortfall in gas delivered to the West from trans-Ukraine pipelines (WGI 1992, 1993), Ukraine's problems were compounded by the country's own inability to get its gas customers to pay their bills (WGI 1995d).

That left two routes by which gas could move to Western markets. One was the far north. Russia had built a small pipeline directly to Finland that had opened in 1974, but by 1990 the Finnish market was already tapped and further expansion West into Scandinavia was un-attractive – existing suppliers already found it difficult to profit in that market. A possible export route via a pipeline along the Baltic seabed had been discussed (we analyze this option later), but that was not really a credible option in the 1990s because underwater pipelines were not within Gazprom's competence at the time, and Gazprom did not have any partner willing to finance such a project.

These factors explain the obsessive attention of Gazprom to the one remaining route – a new pipeline network that would bypass Ukraine and, instead, cross Belarus and serve Poland and Germany. Essentially no gas followed that route: even the large pipelines that moved gas across Belarus turned south to join the central corridor, as shown in figure 5.6.

Delivering gas to Europe via the northern route had been under discussion in the Soviet Union as early as 1978, driven by keen interest in tapping the large Yamal fields.[18] The Yamal project was delayed again in 1981 in favor of focusing on the Urengoy field, already under devel-opment and at the time the largest production gas field in the world.[19] Once Urengoy was in production, next in line logically was the Yamburg field just to the northwest, which once again left the more complicated to

---

[18] The name "Yamal–Europe," which is often applied to this project, reflects the supply orientation of the Russian planners and namers. In all the big gas export projects of the Soviet era, the Soviet government sought to couple downstream interest in gas with their upstream interest in developing large new fields. Thus most export projects to the West include a large field in their name, despite the fact that the particular origin of the gas is physically irrelevant to the transit and offtake market.

[19] The Soviet government probably could have developed dispersed fields closer to existing lines before its big new venture in Yamburg; indeed, it probably underutilized easier fields before it sought to exploit Urengoy in the 1980s. But the Soviet system rewarded managers who built grand projects, as importance in the Soviet bureaucracy was measured by the flow of investment resources and jobs rather than efficiency. Strategically, the coupling of multi-billion-dollar upstream projects with new pipelines probably also made sense since it eased the task of leveraging downstream technology and capital for use in developing the fields.

develop Yamal field a bridesmaid. In the gas industry's equivalent of the standard QWERTY keyboard, once infrastructures are in place it is costly to move far from the main line. From the 1970s, whenever large new potential exports to the West came on the Soviet and Russian agenda the lines crayoned on maps often started in Yamal. In the late 1980s the state ministry that was the predecessor of Gazprom funded exploratory drilling in Yamal but suspended operations in 1989, since developing the fields would be extremely expensive and there was no market for the gas. Throughout the 1990s, public statements by senior Gazprom officials would nearly always include the following script: gas export prices must be higher to raise the revenue needed to develop the Yamal fields, and development of those fields was always about five years on the horizon.[20] (Next on this wish list was usually the Shtokmanovskoye field in the Barents Sea.) Thus the project to move gas across Belarus became called "Yamal–Europe" because the crayons on maps usually started there; in fact, that project today moves no gas from the Yamal fields nor is it likely to any time in the near future.[21]

Belarus Connector

The original plan was to build six 56 inch pipelines from the giant gas fields of Bovanenko (onshore) and Kharasevey (offshore) at the Yamal peninsula. These pipes would travel to Ukhta, where they would join the existing 56 inch pipelines that already traveled West from the Urengoy field north of Moscow. From there, two 56 inch pipelines would follow the existing "Northern Lights" route through Belarus where they would connect at Brest, allowing an expansion of Russia's export potential along this route by about 67 Bcm/year. As the 1990s progressed the project kept being pushed into the future and the export potential reduced. By 2005, just one pipeline had been built along the final segments from Belarus to Poland and Germany; with a reduced number of compressors from the original plan, the export capacity at the Belarus border is only 20 Bcm/year. (However, additional compressors are planned for the next few years.) Table 5.2 shows the gas balances for the key countries involved in this project, along with Ukraine.

---

[20] For one of many examples of the Gazprom party line on the urgent need for upstream development, and therefore higher export contract prices, see excerpts of the January 28, 1993, press conference by Gazprom Chairman Rem Vyakhirev (WGI 1992, pp. 16–17).

[21] Plans regarding the development of the Yamal gas fields have been undergoing near-constant revision during recent decades. Gazprom is considering gas production on the Yamal fields as early as 2008; the initial production level has been put at 15 Bcm, rising to 45–60 Bcm by 2010.

Table 5.2 *Gas balances for key countries along the BC, 2001*

	Main flows (Bcm)	Sub-totals (Bcm)
Russia		
Production	574	
Imports (from Turkmenistan)	10	
– *of which are barter transit fees/theft*		*0*
– *of which are purchased*		*10*
Exports of Russian production	188	
Consumption	394	
Transit (at exit gates), Turkmen –> Ukraine	5	
Ukraine		
Production	18	
Imports	56	
– *from Turkmenistan*		*5*
– *from Russia*		*51*
– *of which are transit fees/theft*		*38*
– *of which are purchased*		*13*
Exports	1	
Consumption	74	
Transit (at exit gates)	122	
Belarus		
Production	0.3	
Imports	16	
– *of which are transit fees/theft*		*11*
– *of which are purchased*		*5*
Exports	0	
Consumption	17	
Transit (at exit gates) to Poland	18	
Transit (at exit gates) to Ukraine	24	
Poland		
Production	4	
Imports	9	
– *of which bought from Russia*		*7.3*
– *of which are barter transit fees from Russia*		*0*
– *of which from Uzbekistan*		*0.7*
– *of which from Germany*		*0.4*
– *of which from Norway*		*0.3*
Exports	0	
Consumption	13.8	
Transit (at exit gates)	11	
Germany		
Production	22	
Imports	79	
– *of which Russia*		*33*
– *of which Norway*		*21*
– *of which The Netherlands*		*20*

Table 5.2. (*cont.*)

	Main flows (Bcm)	Sub-totals (Bcm)
– *of which others*		5
Exports	7	
Consumption	94	
Transit (at exit gates)	7	

Note:

Data show gross consumption and production from IEA (IEA2002b). For IEA member countries (Germany and Poland), available energy balances report trade in gas as well, but for non-member countries the data are more scarce and we have made estimates. Russian gas imports are difficult to estimate for 2001: we show 10 Bcm of imports from Turkmenistan, as reported to IEA. We are mindful that potential Turkmen exports are much larger. A new gas deal between Turkmenistan, and Itera will deliver 6–7 Bcm annually to Russia (via Uzbekistan and Kazakhstan) starting in 2004, and rising to 10 Bcm in 2006. In addition, Turkmenistan has committed to supply (via the same route and then across Russia) 36 Bcm to Ukraine starting in 2004, which (if true) would resolve a long-standing dispute about exorbitant transit fees. In both those deals, payment would be a combination of cash and barter goods. Turkmenistan has also made loose plans to supply tens of Bcm to Russia by around 2010 and beyond (120 Bcm total some time after 2010), a commitment that seems implausible. 2001 shipments from Turkmenistan to Russia may have been as small as 2 Bcm; official Turkmen data show total exports for 2001 at 37 Bcm, which we assume were consumed mainly in Iran, Ukraine, and Russia. We have estimated Ukraine imports from Russia; purchases of that gas we get from Gazprom and Itera reports. Transit is reported by the EIA (EIA 2004a), although we lack confidence in that number as it appears to be much higher than the reported imports by the major importers downstream, as shown in IEA (2002b); one source of difference may be the inclusion of pipeline fuel and leaks in gross transit volumes reported by the EIA. (In figure 5.4, we show a lower number of 99 Bcm actual exports, which is the amount actually consumed at burner tip downpipe.) For Belarus we get imports from the IEA and consumption from BP, and we estimate sold gas from Itera's reports, which leaves the rest of consumed gas as barter or theft. Total transit in Belarus is reported by the EIA at 42 Bcm, and we estimate the portion exported via the BC at 18 Bcm, with the rest in transit to Ukraine. For Poland, all data are from the IEA except the transit, which is drawn from the EIA. German data are from IEA balances; German transit is estimated from known purchases (reported by EIA) by down-pipe countries from suppliers that are up-pipe of Germany.

To understand the scaling back of this project requires looking at the demand for gas and the changing markets in Poland and, especially, Germany. During the brief period when Gazprom did not control export contracts the Russian giant found common interest with Wintershall, the largest independent oil and gas producer and marketer in Germany. Created originally as a mining company, BASF, Germany's largest chemical producer, bought Wintershall in 1969 as part of its effort to gain control over its main oil and gas feedstocks. BASF and Gazprom shared

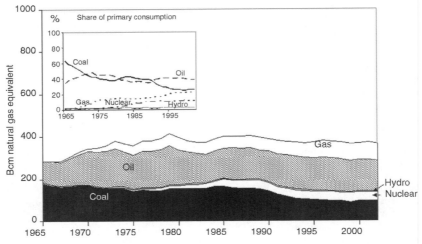

Figure 5.7. Germany: primary energy consumption, by fuel,
1965–2003, Bcm natural gas equivalent.

Source: BP (2004).

their dislike of the monopoly position that Ruhrgas enjoyed and thus
sought to break open the German gas market, creating three joint ventures – Wingas (a pipeline and wholesale marketing company) along with
two companies, German-based Wintershall Erdgas Handelshaus GmbH
("WIEH") and Swiss-based Wintershall Erdgas Handelshaus Zug AG
("WIEE") that both marketed gas in central Europe. Wintershall
produces a small amount of its own gas that is accessible to the German
market, but the only way to become a significant player in the German
market was to secure its own imports, which required both pipelines and
a foreign supplier. BASF helped secure Gazprom's role in Wintershall's
attempt to break open the regional fiefdoms and the Ruhrgas monopoly
in gas transmission by agreeing in 1993 to build a huge ($500 million)
chemical complex in Western Siberia; in return, Gazprom pledged that
WIEH would hold exclusive marketing rights for the Yamal output – a
decision that shocked the industry. By 1994 Gazprom and Wintershall
had invested about $2.6 billion (in 1994 currencies) in the Wingas
pipeline system and contracted 14 Bcm of imports from Gazprom, of
which only half was sold for 2000 (WGI 1994a, pp. 1–2). It was implausible that Wintershall could sell perhaps another 50 Bcm that would
come to Germany and the rest of Western Europe if the full Yamal plan
were realized (see figure 5.7 for the scale of German gas and energy
market). Gazprom's public infrastructure investment plans were simply

unbelievable, but the much smaller volumes that Gazprom directed around Ruhrgas to its partner Wintershall were real. These joint ventures would allow Wintershall to sell directly to large customers (such as BASF itself) and to gas distributors. Costs for new pipelines were shared. The segments on Russian soil were built with traditional very large-diameter Russian pipe and funded by Gazprom with loans from Russian banks and from Wintershall that would be repaid with gas revenues (WGI 1994b, p. 10, 1996, p. 5). Segments in other countries were developed by local affiliates in Belarus (Beltrangas) and Poland (EurPolGaz), with each relying on bank financing secured with portions of the transit revenues.[22] The German section was developed by Wingas, with financing from BASF via Wintershall (WGI 1994c, p. 2).

Gazprom saw bypassing Ruhrgas as a way to get higher export prices (which benefited Gazprom directly) and to secure (through its joint venture with Wintershall) part of the wholesale markup that Ruhrgas had traditionally kept for itself. In the mid-1990s, for example, Ruhrgas paid about $2.70 per mmbtu for Russian gas, while average consumer prices approached $6 per mmbtu – Ruhrgas kept much of the difference for itself, which explains why it earned an extraordinary 25 percent after-tax profit margin (PIW 1995, pp. 3; WGI, 1995e, p. 6). Wintershall's interests were slightly different – for it, Gazprom was a convenient initial supplier, but Wintershall eventually built pipelines and secured contracts with other key suppliers, and this divergence in interests explains why Gazprom's strategy for circumventing Ruhrgas backfired badly. Gazprom probably achieved higher export volumes through its Wingas partnership with Wintershall, but Wingas secured user markets by cutting prices (WGI 1994d, p. 1–2).

The Gazprom strategy through this period was exposed in a rare case where export contract prices and markups were released to the public in a pricing dispute involving the East German gas transmission company VNG. Created from the East German state Gas Ministry, VNG was crafted as a German joint-stock company in 1990 and then privatized by Treuhand in 1991. At the time of privatization, VNG assumed the CMEA-era contracts for gas supplies, which made Gazprom its only supplier. Gazprom handed the task of renegotiating the main supply contracts to WIEH, and in 1994 the firm created new contracts with prices that were only slightly higher than the pre-existing arrangements –

---

[22] The Polish entity (EuroPolGaz) was owned 50 percent by the Polish government-owned Polskie Górnictwo Naftowe and Gazownictwo (PGNiG), 48 percent by Gazprom, and 4 percent by a Polish marketing company (Gaz Trading).

a huge disappointment for Gazprom, which had originally joined WIEH with the central goal of obtaining much higher margins.

The net effect of this competition between Wintershall and Ruhrgas was to drive down prices for distribution companies and for final consumers. As wholesale contracts between Ruhrgas and distributors expired, WIEH would attempt to entice the distributors with rebates, only to find that Ruhrgas would match the offers and in most cases win the contracts. Margins for Ruhrgas declined, and Wintershall struggled to gain market share. It is hard to assess whether Gazprom would have obtained different prices or volumes in the absence of its role in the Wintershall joint ventures. Our assessment is that Wintershall could have pursued its strategy with any large-volume supplier – Gazprom was most convenient but hardly the only one.[23] Throughout this process, Gazprom nonetheless sustained a close relationship with Ruhrgas as its largest customer; Ruhrgas bought the largest non-Russian share of Gazprom (nearly 6 percent by 2005) and occupied the only non-Russian position on Gazprom's eleven-member board of directors (Gazprom 2002).

Reflecting the interests of its two main advocates – Wintershall and Gazprom – construction began in the mid-1990s on the two opposite ends of the Belarus Connector (BC). With resources on hand, Gazprom starting building the first (and so far only) export line on Russian territory without having lined up firm contracts for hardly any of the output – it built the line because it was part of a larger strategy to lift both volumes and prices while deploying little of its own capital. Through the mid-1990s gas exports accounted for about 15 percent of the total value of Russian exports. In the West, Wingas (with financial support from BASF) focused on building pipelines that led East but would be of immediate utility for Wintershall's plan to attain 15 percent of the German gas market by 2000. Thus Wingas gave priority to scaleable investments that could rapidly bring new supplies into its network while also bringing Wingas-controlled gas closer to big industrial customers and distributors. By that logic, Wingas opened the first pipeline in the BC in 1996 – a connection between Poland and Germany that allowed small quantities of gas to flow as WIEH lined up buyers.

Although the project began as part of a grand strategy in Germany, the market for gas in Poland gave additional impetus for building the project along the Belarus corridor rather than simply expanding the corridor

---

[23] Absent Gazprom, Wintershall would have faced severe but not impossible difficulties in securing gas supplies, such as through acquisitions (which Wintershall did pursue later) and contracting from alternate suppliers.

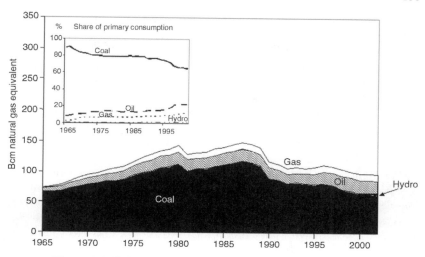

Figure 5.8. Poland: primary energy consumption by fuel, 1965–2003, Bcm natural gas equivalent.
Source: BP (2004).

that passed through Ukraine and Slovakia (i.e. the Transgas pipelines). Whereas the CMEA nations in Central and Southern Europe were all gasified by Soviet supplies, the role of gas in the Polish and East German economies remained much lower. In the early 1990s gas accounted for less than 10 percent of Poland's primary energy (figure 5.8). Displacement of the dominant coal supplies offered a potentially large market; the environmental consequences of coal-burning created an incentive for the Polish government (often with assistance from the West) to create space for gas.

The investment in Poland, like that in Germany, proceeded in a scaleable fashion – capacity was adjusted as the market demanded. Even as Gazprom scaled back its export pipelines from two (a total capacity of 66 Bcm) to one (for 33 Bcm), achieving the full 33 Bcm required compression, and the original plan called for five large compressor stations in Poland. As the project developed, Polish demand did not grow as rapidly as expected, making it difficult to justify the expense of building all the compressor stations. Polish compressor stations were actually constructed in Włocławek and Kondratki; three more compressor stations – at Szamotuły, Ciechanów and Zambrów – were never built owing to a dispute over financing rooted, fundamentally, in the financiers' valid concern that the demand for gas in Poland and the lack of more success by

WIEH in obtaining contracts in Germany could not justify additional capacity. The pipeline became operational with these three compressors in 2000 and its annual throughput in 2005 amounts to 20 Bcm.[24]

All told, the Polish market has been disappointing for Gazprom. A forecast by the Polish Academy of Science (upon which the original plan for Poland's offtake of the BC was justified) predicted that gas consumption in Poland would grow from about 10 Bcm per year in 1993 to around 20 Bcm per year by 2010. In reality, the total market has risen from 9.9 Bcm in 1990 to just 11.4 Bcm in 2001. The bottleneck is not supply but demand for gas. In electricity, new independently built power plants have had to compete with incumbent coal-fired generators that have much lower costs. Gas prices indexed to oil, even when oil was inexpensive, made little sense for Poland's coal-dominated power system. Just one of Poland's two independent generators built during the 1990s is fired with gas (the other burns coal), and electric power modernization projects have focused on ways to improve the existing coal-fired fleet rather than replace them with gas. This experience is somewhat distinct from that of East Germany, where the industrial stock in 1990 was similarly coal-based, but the rapid integration with West Germany (along with huge infusions of German redevelopment cash) facilitated a more decisive shift to gas.

Alternative Projects

The BC was the largest expansion of Russia's export capacity in the 1990s. Here we examine three other options that were considered at the time but did not attract investment – first, a large pipeline that would move additional volumes of gas around Ukraine (what we call the "Ukraine bypass"); second, expansion of the Ukraine export route, which would make it unnecessary to build new pipelines across Poland; and third, a Baltic Sea pipeline that would make it possible to bypass all the Commonwealth of Independent States (CIS) and CMEA transit

---

[24] Interestingly, pipeline corridors offer the possibility of transmitting more than just gas. With the pipeline, Gazprom and EurPolGaz also laid a state-of-the art fiber optic cable consisting of twenty four optic fibers that could transmit 2.4 trillion bits of information per second – about 38 million telephone calls simultaneously. When reports of the cable leaked out in 2000 it was clear that the Polish Communications Ministry had not authorized a telecommunications system as part of the gas project. EurPolGaz claimed that the line was essential for pipeline control and did not require special authorization from the Communications Ministry. The Polish government, which does not have a controlling stake in EurPolGaz, is poised to lose millions of dollars in telecommunications transit fees (RFE/RL 2000).

countries and serve the lucrative Western markets directly. By comparing these "alternative projects" to the one that was actually built, our aim is to reveal more fully the factors that explain why some projects are constructed while others languish.

Bypassing Ukraine

In the Soviet era, pipelines were built without regard to internal borders. Moscow controlled the entire Soviet Union, and even where pipeline planners knew of possible long-term political risks, internal borders were not factors to be considered in the planning process. Invariably, pipelines followed straight-line routes. Thus the trunkline that carries gas from the Caucusus north to Moscow links several cities on straight-line paths that carry the line a few miles inside Ukraine's territory – an irrelevant fact in Soviet times and now a source of substantial transit revenues for Ukraine

When the giant Urengoy fields in Northwestern Siberia were developed from the early 1980s, it would have been shorter (and thus cheaper) to send their gas straight to Germany. That direct routing might have avoided Ukraine altogether and bequeathed to Russia a very different pipeline network today. However, three factors pushed the line south through Ukraine – one would have been easy to resolve, but the other two were politically immovable. The easy problem to solve was assuring adequate quantities of gas to all the destinations (Austria, France, Germany, Italy, and others) that had been crafted into the Urengoy financing and technology deal. Planners could have branched the export lines in Soviet territory and sent just some of the gas south through Ukraine and Slovakia, which was the gateway to Austria and Italy, while sending the rest directly to Germany along a more northern route. Indeed, the Soviet Union built the "Northern Lights" pipelines to follow a direct export route, and in Western Belarus the line takes a sharp turn south into Ukraine, joining all the other lines that carry gas from Urengoy West.

The immovable objects, however, were political. A straight line to Germany would have required crossing Poland, where the government in the early 1980s was focused on crushing the highly visible Solidarity movement – a severe political liability for any project that relied on Western financing and technology. (US sanctions had threatened the Urengoy deal when it followed the Slovak route; if the Urengoy plan had enriched martial law in Poland the United States probably would have found it easier to build an opposing coalition that included West European countries. Instead, the US sanctions were undercut by the Reagan government's failure to engage any significant West European offtaker.) Second, whether by Poland or Slovakia, a straight route to central or northern Germany would have crossed East Germany – a political impossibility for West German politicians. The political signage thus all pointed south. This was convenient to Ruhrgas and German distributors who kept the German gas market highly segmented into regional fiefdoms. The capacity to move gas between north and south was highly limited until the 1990s – the north German market was based on supplies from Dutch, North Sea and other imports. The south German market was dominated by Russian gas. Interconnections between the two were limited until Wingas helped broker the Stegal pipeline to connect West and East in the newly unified Germany and the Midal pipeline (which linked North and South and began operation in 1993).[25]

Around 1990, when Gazprom's joint ventures in Germany first put a focus on the need for new supplies in northern and central Germany, the problems with Soviet transit countries were not pressing. The Soviet Union was still a single entity, and the joint venture with Wintershall to supply gas across Poland and Belarus was initiated as part of a grand strategy to change how Russian gas was marketed in Germany. As the risk of stoppage by Ukraine rose in importance from 1992 to 1995, Gazprom also explored the possibility of building a spur from Belarus (where the "Northern lights" pipeline turned south and headed to Ukraine, see figure 5.6), to the closest point downstream of Ukraine, in Slovakia. This Ukraine bypass spur would be cheaper to build (approximately $1 billion) than the whole BC since it would be much shorter, but it would not serve any new markets.

Gazprom would have been happy to bypass Ukraine if others paid for it. But most other possible partners did not favor the bypass. In Germany, Gazprom's buyers either sought diversification away from Russia entirely or – such as Wintershall and buyers in the north and east of Germany – sought new gas volumes outright and did not worry as much about the possible transit risks.

Politically, the bypass would be difficult to construct. Poland's consent would be needed since the spur from Belarus to Slovakia would cross Polish territory. Poland and Ukraine had both suffered under Soviet rule and there was enormous concern among Polish politicians that potential allies against Russian meddling – Ukraine, first and

---

[25] The Midal pipeline was commissioned in 1993, runs from Emden to Ludwigshafen, and transports gas from Western European sources to the north of Germany. The pipeline is owned by Wingas and has a capacity of 13 Bcm. Midal is linked at Phillipstal/Heringen to the STEGAL pipeline which was commissioned in 1992 and runs from the Czech Republic to transport gas from Russia to the new East German Länder. The Stegal pipeline is also owned and operated by Wingas and has a capacity of 8 Bcm. The RHG pipeline is connected to Midal and supplies greater Hamburg.

foremost – not be split over commercial deals. Polish politicians at the highest level undertook direct negotiations with Ukraine to avoid Russia playing the two countries off each other. A spur through Poland could deliver useful transit fees, but that was a distant and uncertain prospect; such a spur would do little to serve Poland's nascent gas market. Moreover, by the late 1990s 90 percent of Polish gas consumption was imported from Russia, and the Polish government feared greater Russian domination. As the 1990s progressed and Poland became ever more engaged with the mission of joining the European Union it had further incentive to diversify away from Russia – European planners typically set a benchmark of about 25–30 percent for the maximum single-source dependency of energy imports. (That goal was somewhat arbitrary but, conveniently, was identical to the value that German planners had long been using to gauge whether their dependence on Soviet and Russian imported gas was excessive.) Indeed, in 2001 Poland announced a speculative long-term deal to import gas from Statoil, which would supply gas starting in 2008 and rise rapidly to 5 Bcm.[26] That deal has since collapsed since Poland has already attracted much more gas than it can use, and Russia is by far the least costly supplier. For Poland, the key to keeping Russia in line is the potential for alternative supplies through interconnections with the West rather than the actual contracting of those supplies. The same logic partly helps to explain why the Ukraine Bypass was never built. For Gazprom, putting Ukraine into line required the credible threat of bypass – not actually building the bypass itself. We remain skeptical that Gazprom was ever in a position to make the threat fully credible, not least because it never had a serious plan for building costly storage facilities on the Belarus line as a hedge against the periodic disruptions that had been experienced on the Urengoy and Yamburg lines; in contrast, Ukraine had 30 Bcm in storage available that was essential to ensuring uninterrupted contracted supplies to Western offtakers.

---

[26] Poland's Buzek government signed a long term gas supply agreement in September 2001 with Norwegian suppliers for 5 Bcm per year, starting in 2008. The contract was to be on a take-or-pay basis, was to run for sixteen years, and was reported to have a total value of about $11 billion. An average value for the gas of around $140/per thousand cubic meters ($3.9/mmbtu) was significantly more than Poland was paying Gazprom in a 10 Bcm per year take-or-pay contract that runs to 2020. Since Poland presently imports slightly more than 8 Bcm per year from all suppliers, contracting new supplies makes little sense. Thus, in 2003 this deal appeared unworkable. But when Russia cut off natural gas to Belarus in February 2004 a Polish gas official announced that Poland had signed a MOU with Norway's Statoil for gas supplies. Gas supplies from Norway, estimated at 2–2.5 Bcm annually, would come through an existing pipeline that crosses German territory (Interfax 2004; Renik 2004).

Transiting Belarus did not really solve the Ukraine problem, for at least two reasons. First, the West European gas system had neither the capacity nor the markets to hedge against potentially huge shortfalls from Ukraine. Building a much larger BC would be costly, and delivering another 10 (if the first Connector pipeline had been built with full compression) to 40 Bcm (if both Connector pipelines were built at full compression), on top of the 20 Bcm already available starting in 2000, could not be utilized in northeastern Germany. A full shutoff from Ukraine would harm Central Europe, and there wasn't the spare pipeline capacity to move the hypothetical gas from the BC south into those markets. Ukraine would suffer from the reputation as an unreliable transit partner, but Russia was even more exposed. When the two countries settled the matter of Ukraine's past debts to Russia for gas they did so on terms that nearly mirrored Ukraine's interests – $1.4 billion in arrears (not the much higher value claimed by Russia), a moratorium on principal repayments for three years, and repayment at LIBOR plus 1 percent (nearly the same rate that Ukraine had negotiated with its Western creditors) over ten years. Russia had no choice but to find an accommodation. Gazprom continues to push Ukraine to accept higher prices, but that has been a slow process.

Second, Belarus was hardly a paragon of stability itself. Most attention on problematic transit countries has focused on Ukraine because most Russian export gas moves across Ukraine. Problems similar to those with Ukraine beset Belarus as well – having accumulated $300 million in arrears, Belarus saw its supply from Gazprom reduced sharply in 1994 (WGI, 1994e, p. 2). In February 2004, Gazprom cut all exports to Belarus for eighteen hours and partly reduced exports through the BC to Poland. (Poland offset the loss, in part, through another pipeline from Ukraine.) In the wake of these incidents, calls in Poland to diversify importers (i.e. reduce the role of Russia) again gained momentum.

Thus the Ukraine bypass was a weapon that Gazprom periodically brandished but it never made sense to utilize. Moreover, Gazprom never had the capital nor the political support in Belarus or Poland (the key transit countries for the bypass) to make the threat fully credible.

Boosting Ukraine's Exports

A second major alternative was to pursue the opposite of bypass – rather, to entice or bludgeon Ukraine into becoming a more reliable partner and then to raise export volumes along the Ukraine transmission system while boosting the capacity of Transgas in Slovakia and the Czech Republic. This option was impractical at the time that the key decisions to build the BC were made because Ukraine was far from a reliable partner. Political turmoil in Ukraine had produced short time horizons and in that context the risk of poor reputation had little effect on Ukrainian behavior. Incentives to bring Ukraine into line could have included higher transit fees, but the 1994 deal already put Ukraine's fees at nearly Western levels, once the cost of barter gas and tolerated theft were included. These extra fees came out of Gazprom's share of gas sales and could not be passed on to customers in the West where Gazprom found even stiffer competition. Moreover, having Wintershall as Gazprom's Western partner required a direct route to Wintershall's own nascent pipeline network in Northern Germany and its attempts (through VNG) to secure a share in Eastern Germany. There was little advantage to following the existing export routes since the German portions were controlled by Ruhrgas; the German market in the mid-1990s did not have provisions for third-party access nor the capacity to move additional volumes of gas from the Czech border to northern and eastern German markets.

Over time, this option has become more viable. A series of political changes within Ukraine – themselves unrelated to gas – created the internal conditions needed for Ukraine to settle its debts and become a more "normal" country for investors, which in turn has probably made downstream countries less wary of relying on Ukraine as a transit route provided that the physical infrastructure in Ukraine is adequate to the task. Some analysts estimate that Ukraine's transit capacity could decline sharply in the coming decade without overdue maintenance and upgrades. Thus the alternative project for investment would entail not so much an expansion of transit capacity but, rather, to invest in avoiding deterioration of the existing system (Füeg 2001). With this aim, Gazprom and the Russian government have assembled an "international consortium" of Western governments and firms to invest in Ukraine's transmission and storage system.[27] At the time of writing (mid-2005)

---

[27] Had the "international consortium" been only Gazprom's idea it probably would not have earned Ukraine's consent. However, key governments – notably Germany – were keen to tame the Ukraine problem. Moreover, foreign firms had already been involved in efforts to invest in Ukraine's pipelines. A British independent gas firm (JKX Energy) produced gas in Ukraine in the 1990s, and Shell had attempted to make a $1.5 billion investment in Ukraine's gas pipeline system; BP was also considering similar investments (WGI 1997, pp. 6–7). Other gas companies made similar investments along the Russian export route, such as Italy's ENI in Slovakia – in part to secure their exports and in part to earn a direct return (WGI 1998, p. 1).

Gazprom has mainly used the consortium in an effort to entangle West-ern interests in Ukraine, thus making it harder for Ukraine to meddle with exports; Ukraine, by contrast, has sought to make the consortium into a gas marketing agent (thus bypassing the downstream marketing companies in which Gazprom has invested since its pathbreaking deal in 1990 to market gas in Germany through WIEH). Western companies, starting with Ruhrgas, appear ready to invest in the system because it holds the promise of yielding higher contract security for affordable Russian gas. Until a concrete commercial framework for the consortium is settled the Western companies are unlikely to do much. Systems for monitoring storage and pipeline systems, settling disputes, and creating transparency in the Ukraine transit system are envisioned but remain to be created. Among the first projects in the system will be an additional pipeline that travels West across Ukraine, lifting Ukraine's export cap-acity by up to 30 Bcm and also making it easier to import and transit gas from the Central Asian republics.

The Baltic Pipeline

A third alternative project would have involved building a trans-Baltic pipeline (the North European Gas Pipeline, or "NEGP") that would extend from nearby St. Petersburg underwater, offering the possibility of direct connection to connect, especially, to the German markets and eventually the United Kingdom (see figure 5.6).[28]

So long as the Soviet Union was one country there was little need to consider a Baltic Sea pipeline route. Underwater pipelines are difficult to lay and maintain and were not within Gazprom's expertise; the route would be about 50 percent more expensive than a traditional overland route. Nonetheless, the idea has been around for a while. Around 1990 a British–Russian joint venture (*Sovgazco*) was established to investigate

---

[28] The various proposals envision a pipeline capacity that ranges from 19 up to 55 Bcm annually. Gazprom has arranged European partners to pay for this pipeline, whose price is estimated at between $8 billion and $10 billion, which makes it an expensive way for Russia and its European partners to avoid transit countries. In its most recent incar-nation, known as the North European Gas Pipeline (NEGP), this pipeline system would be a grand joint venture – with 51 percent ownership by Gazprom and 24.5 percent each for major German buyers BASF and E.On with a cost of $5 billion. At year-end 2005, Gazprom was forging ahead with NEGP plans, encouraged by continuing tensions with Ukraine over gas transport fees. Construction of the onshore segments of the project have already begun. First deliveries are targeted for 2010 at 27.5 Bcm per year, rising to 55 Bcm per year by 2012. Such massive volumes would necessitate signing up plenty of buyers outside Germany – with limited progress on this front to date (WGI 2005).

the Baltic options with the principal aim of serving the UK market. At the time, UK demand was 55 Bcm and set to rise rapidly as gas was the favorite fuel for the newly liberalized electric power system. *Sovgazco* worked with a projection of 100 Bcm demand in 2000 (actual demand was 96 Bcm) and on that basis found that the project would be economic. They examined the option of piping gas via Belarus then the Russian enclave of Kaliningrad or directly offshore at St. Petersburg. The final cost for gas from either route was about the same. All told, the landed cost of gas in the United Kingdom would be about $4.50/mmbtu, which was only slightly higher than forward gas contracts in the UK market at the time (WGI 1991b, p. 5). That idea fell apart, however, as Gazprom was a risky partner for a complicated consortium that would need to rely on hard financing and strict timetables if it were to compete successfully in the UK market.

The Baltic route periodically resurfaced during the 1990s. Was it a real proposal, or only a negotiating ploy to get Belarus, Poland, and Ukraine to make concessions? For Western participants, the problem with the Baltic route then and now was uncertainty about supply. A small pipeline would not be economic – the *Sovgazco* project would have been 10 Bcm and probably not economic even before considering the large political and investment risks in Russia (and in Belarus and Kaliningrad, if that route were followed). A large pipeline (say, 20–30 Bcm capacity) along with a decade of technological advances in underwater pipelines (in part arising from the Blue Stream experience) would require a credible plan for long-term supply. In turn, that would require a vision for developing the Yamal fields or the Shtokmanovskoye field in the Barents Sea.[29] Until the mid-2000s, Gazprom's vision for offsetting the decline in its existing fields has been higher imports from Central Asia (notably Turkmenistan), which is less costly because the gas transmission infrastructure is already in place, but incurs the risks of developments in that region. As outlined earlier, there are also options for improving operational efficiency, offering access for utilizing the large amounts of associated gas available, or in lowering domestic demand

---

[29] The Shtokmanovskoye field contains more than 3 trillion m^3 of gas, one of the biggest known offshore gas fields in the world. A consortium, led by Gazprom, has been working on an assessment of the field and production options, with the leading candidate an LNG plant that would be located on the coast and able to export gas by tanker to the Atlantic Basin LNG market. Annual production potential is estimated at 60 Bcm (over fifty years), and total field development is estimated to cost $18–$30 billion. Yamal, by contrast, is thought by Gazprom to be easier to develop (because it is on land and within the realm of Gazprom's experience) and less costly.

through efficiency. But all these options turn mainly on the uncertain prospect of reform of Gazprom.

At the time of writing, EBRD is performing an environmental assessment of the Baltic export route. We are confident that all the technical issues can be resolved – they include not only environmental impacts but also the laying of pipe on a seabed that has unexploded ordnance. But the environment is not attractive for outside investors until there is greater certainty about the future of Gazprom's role in the Russian pipeline system. As a threat against Belarus during the 1990s the Baltic route, we think, played no role – it was not an option that was attractive to either Gazprom (the supplier) or Wintershall (the user). Even today, the project is probably not an option except with substantial political guarantees that might come, for example, with the prominent involvement of EBRD and with the creation of a gas market in Russia that is more attractive to outside investors.

Analysis and Summary

We summarize by returning to the five factors to be addressed by each case study in this book:

1. General investment climate
2. Transit countries
3. Risk in the quantity of gas sold
4. Risk in the price of gas sold
5. Roles for international institutions in securing contracts and hedging risks.

For most of the countries involved in this project the general investment climate was terrible. Private investors had no way to secure investments in the gas sector; tariffs and transit fees were controlled by governments that often changed course and had no clear policy strategy. In the Soviet era such large infrastructure projects were controlled directly by the state, but neither the state nor state-controlled enterprises such as Gazprom had the capital on hand to make such strategic decisions. The general investment climate in Germany was more attractive, but in the gas sector the risks were enormous because the BC was conceived as part of an effort to break the highly profitable German gas monopoly, Ruhrgas. Thus the new entrant was trying to market gas in competition with a deep-pocketed, well-connected incumbent. In this climate, the multi-billion-dollar vision for developing the Yamal fields – even if the European market could have absorbed such large quantities of gas – was not practical. Instead, the project proceeded in a manner that corresponded closely to each party's narrow interests. Gazprom built what it could to export gas from existing fields and largely utilized the existing gas network, while attempting (albeit with an ill-conceived strategy) to boost profits by getting higher export prices. From Wintershall's perspective, contracting with Gazprom made sense because it was the easiest source of the new volumes that would be needed in their attempt to break open the market – a task that corresponded narrowly with BASF's interest in low-cost gas and Wintershall's interest in becoming a viable German gas company. This was not a climate for strategic long-term investments; the result, not surprisingly, was an export project that was much smaller than Gazprom's original vision, corresponded with each party's narrow and relatively short-term interests, and was highly scaleable.

Regarding transit countries, our study reveals little evidence of deploying the "gas weapon" by Russia or transit countries. The main argument levied against the large Soviet era projects – especially by the Reagan administration in the period of tension after détente – was concern that Russia would use the gas weapon against the West à la OPEC and the oil embargo. That never happened; rather, gas was priced – as in most other markets – by reference to oil. From October 1973 when the first gas crossed the Czech–German border until October 1992 when Ukraine first interrupted supplies, the Soviet system never used the gas weapon. In the 1990s Russia (in the name of Gazprom) did cut off fellow-CIS countries when they failed to pay their bills or siphoned extra gas during transit, but only as a final measure in long-standing disputes where Gazprom was arguably in a proper legal position to demand higher prices and payment. The only times that the "weapon" of shutting off supplies has been applied has been by weak states that are bankrupt and beset by internal turmoil that makes it hard to pursue long-term strategies – in those cases, their actions have caused interruptions to users further down the pipeline, but that was not the goal. In contrast with the LNG imports to Japan (see chapters 4 and 8), we find little evidence that countries have been willing to pay much of a premium to diversify their suppliers. There is some evidence that when major gas distributors diversified their sources in the 1990s they may have paid some suppliers (notably Norway and the Netherlands) more than the price at which Russia was willing to sell. Russia's strategy, however, was to maximize volumes and ultimately, the difference between Russian prices and landed gas in the same markets from other suppliers was not substantial. Poland depended heavily on Russian gas for its small gas market; it was willing to sign deals with alternative Norwegian suppliers at prices that were about 20 percent higher than those charged by Russia; in practice, though, none of those supplies has been delivered – rather, the threatened diversification mainly served an imposed discipline on Russia as the low-cost supplier. In Germany, interconnection with the rest of the Western market made it easier to hedge against transit risks in the Russian supply, and premia for non-Russia supply were small or zero.

The BC is often seen as an effort to move gas around Ukraine. In reality, the project made sense mainly on commercial terms for the markets it served – in particular, it was the most direct path on Wintershall's effort to break open the German market. This was a project that incidentally avoided Ukraine; the projects conceived solely to bypass Ukraine were not credible. Nor has Belarus proved to be a reliable transit country. The Baltic Sea pipeline would avoid both these troublesome partners, and Gazprom is now pursuing that option.

We suggest that the traditional notion of "transit countries" is prone to oversimplification. The Ukraine case is one of a transit country that also had substantial gas storage facilities. Storage was crucial to Russia's strategy for exporting gas from Urengoy and Yamburg and other technically complicated areas – poor construction and harsh environments made for unstable supply, but huge storage areas made it possible to assure deliveries and track seasonal loads. Ukraine was thus much more important than simply a transit nation – it also leveled supply.

Regarding risk in the quantities of gas sold, in both the German and Polish markets Gazprom and its partners badly overestimated demand, but for different reasons in each market. In Germany, total demand for Gazprom gas rose slightly during the 1990s, but most of that was sold by Ruhrgas. Actual demand through the Wintershall/Wingas/WIEH arrangement (which Gazprom favored because it held the promise of higher prices) was much lower than anticipated because it proved difficult for the new entrant to create a market for itself. Competition did force lower end-user prices (although it probably did not greatly affect import prices, as they were set through the emerging gas-on-gas competition), but in most cases the contracted volumes stayed with Ruhrgas as the supplier. Wingas' position continued to improve, albeit slowly, garnering 15 percent of German gas sales in 2004. In Poland, gas volumes fall far short of expectations because the energy system was dominated by coal and there was no strong central direction to move away from it, since it was much less costly than imported gas. This experience contrasts sharply with the gasification of the Soviet Union, which moved rapidly once central planners gave the word.

Price risks were a regular feature of the European gas market and did not play a significant role in the outcome of this project. While Gazprom had thought it would get higher margins for export, both Gazprom and Wintershall would have gone ahead with the project if export prices had been unchanged – for Gazprom, the goal was higher volumes and export earnings, and for Wintershall it was obtaining supplies outside the Ruhrgas monopoly. These risks were not appreciably different from those that gas exporters had borne in the European market. Traditionally, Soviet gas export contracts were inter-governmental agreements that set terms for volumes, with price formulae renegotiated every three years and indexed against oil. During the 1990s there was much discussion about a change to gas-on-gas competition, but in practice oil-linked contracts still dominate the continental European gas market.

Finally, each study in this book has explored the role of international institutions. During the CMEA era, the CMEA itself played a substantial role in assuring transit of gas and in gasification of the CMEA members. When the Soviet grip weakened and CMEA dissolved, gas projects required much closer attention to the narrow interests of a much large number of individual entities. The scaling back of the BC from Gazprom's original grand "Yamal–Europe" vision reflects that atomization of interests. The European nations had attempted to create a special framework for energy projects that could facilitate collective long-term infrastructure investments – known as the Energy Charter – but that institution figures nowhere in the history of the BC. Progress towards Russia's long-awaited ratification of the Energy Charter Treaty is determined to a large extent by the outcome of the negotiations on a Transit Protocol.[30] However, the Energy Charter is aspirational in its attempt to create a context for investment. It has no authority nor collective funds, nor much influence inside its member states. The "international consortium" now taking shape in Ukraine may turn out to be an important international institution if it truly fosters collective investment and control of Ukraine's vital gas transmission and storage infrastructure, but at present it is too early to make an assessment.

---

[30] The aims of the Transit Protocol are to build on the existing transit-related provisions of the Energy Charter Treaty, by developing an enhanced set of rules under international law governing energy transit flows across national borders. There remained a few outstanding issues to be resolved before the Protocol could be finalized, all of which related to differences in position between the European Union and Russia. Gazprom has put forward two main arguments against ratifying: first, ratification would undercut Gazprom's position on European markets by forcing Russia to open up its network for cheaper gas from Central Asia and, second, ratification would place in jeopardy the system of long-term contracts for supplies of Russian gas to Europe.

APPENDIX

Table 5.A *Russian earnings from oil and gas export, 1994–2004*

| Year | Oil and oil products | | Natural gas | | Total export |
	Million US$	% in total export	Million US$	% in total export	Million US$
1994	14,615	22	10,591	16	67,379
1995	18,348	22	12,122	15	82,419
1996	23,412	26	14,683	16	89,685
1997	22,060	25	16,414	19	86,895
1998	14,507	19	13,432	18	74,444
1999	19,606	26	11,352	15	75,551
2000	36,191	34	16,644	16	105,033
2001	34,364	34	17,770	17	101,884
2002	40,366	38	15,897	15	107,301
2003	53,739	40	19,981	15	135,929
2004	77,600	43	22,400	12	182,000

Note:
[a] 2003 data were estimated on the basis of the first nine months.

Source: Bank of Russia (2004).

REFERENCES

AIC (1995). *Russian Oil and Gas (History and Perspectives)*. Moscow: Association of International Cooperation (in Russian)

APEC (2000). *Natural Gas Pipeline Development in Northeast Asia*. Tokyo: Asia Pacific Energy Research Center

Aris, B. (2000). "Power wars: Gazprom cuts off UES" *Alexander's Gas & Oil Connections*, 5(8); available at http://www.gasandoil.com/goc/company/cnr01973.htm

BP (2003). *Statistical Review of World Energy*; available at http://www.bp.com

BP (various years) *Statistcal Reveiw of World Energy*; available at http://www.bp.com

Bank of Russia (2004). *The Central Bank of the Russian Federation*; available at http://www.cbr.ru (last visited March 20, 2004)

Cohen, A. (2001). The New Tools of Russian Power: Oil and Gas Pipelines; available at http://www.cdi.org/russia/johnson/5003.html##16 (last visited March 20, 2004)

EBRD (1995), *Russian Gas Supply System Study*. London: The European Bank for Reconstruction and Development

EIA (2003). *Country Analysis Briefs*; available at http://www.eia.doe.gov/emeu/cabs/russexp.html#GAS (last visited October 20, 2003)

(2004a). *Country Analysis Briefs*; available at http://www.eia.doe.gov/emeu/cabs/ (last visited March 20, 2004)

(2004b). *World Oil Transit Chokepoints*; available at http://www.eia.doe.gov/emeu/cabs/choke.html (last visited May 19, 2004)

Elliot, I. F. (1974). *The Soviet Energy Balance: Natural Gas, Other Fossil Fuels, and Alternative Power Sources.* New York, Praeger

Füeg, J.-C. (2001). *Ukraine – An Important Energy Supply Corridor to Europe.* International Energy Agency; available online at http://spider.iea.org/papers/kievcwc1.pdf (last visited March 10, 2004)

Garipov V. Z., Kozlovsky E.A., and Litvinenko V.S. (2003), *Reserves Base of Russian Energy Sector.* RAS Moscow: *Moscow,* (in Russian)

Gazprom (2002). *Annual Report*; available at http://www.gazprom.ru/documents/annual_eng.pdf (last visited 20 March, 2004)

(2004). *History of the Gas Branch*; available at http://www.gazprom.com/eng/articles/article8518.shtml (last visited March 20, 2004)

Goskomstat (varous years). *Narodhoe Khozyaistro SSR.* Moscow (in Russian)

Gustafson, T. (1985). *Soviet Negotiating Strategy: The East–West Gas Pipeline Deal, 1980–1984.* Santa Monica, CA: The Rand Corporation

Higgins, A. (1998). "Twilight economy". *The Wall Street Journal* 27 August, 1998; available at http://www.pulitzer.org/year/1999/international-reporting/works/twlight_economy.html

Interfax (2004). *Poland and Norway sign memo on Norwegian Natural Gas Supply,* February 20, 2004; available at http://www.interfax.com/com?item=search&pg=10 &id=5698867&req=gas

IEA (2002a). *Developing China's Natural Gas Market: The Energy Policy Challenges.* Paris: OECD/IEA

(2002b). *Russia Energy Survey 2002.* Paris: OECD/IEA

(2003). *World Energy Outlook.* Paris: OECD/IEA

Kosnik, J. T. (1975). *Natural Gas Imports from the Soviet Union.* New York: Praeger

Kuzio, T. (2003). *Russia: Ukraine Squeeze,* for Oxford Analytica; available at http://www.ualberta.ca/~cius/stasiuk/st-articles/an-squeeze.htm (last visited 20 March, 2004)

Narodnoe khozyaistvo SSSR. Moscow: Goskomstat, various years (in Russian)

OECD (1997). *Short-Term Economic Indicators: Transition Economies.* Paris: The Centre for Cooperation with the Economies in Transition, OECD

Paik, K.-W. (1995). *Gas and Oil in Northeast Asia: Policies, Projects and Prospects.* London: Royal Institute of International Affairs

(2002). "Natural Gas Expansion in Korea", in Ian Wybrew-Bond and Jonathan Stern (eds.), *Natural Gas in Asia: The Challenges of Growth in China, India, Japan and Korea.* Oxford: Oxford University Press, pp. 188–229

PIW (1992). *Petroleum Intelligence Weekly.* 27 January, pp. 6–7

(1995). *Petroleum Intelligence Weekly.* 13 November, p. 3

Renik, K. (2004). "Nothing in the Pipeline." *Warsaw Voice*, February 25, 2004; available online at: http://www.warsawvoice.pl/view/4899

RFE-RL (2000). *Mysterious Telecommunications Cable Crosses Poland. Radio Free Europe/Radio Liberty*; available online at http://www.rferl.org/reports/pbureport/2000/11/43-211100.asp (last visited 20 March, 2004).

Stent, A. E. (1982). *Soviet Energy and Western Europe*. Washington, DC: Center for Strategic and International Studies. New York: Gertown University

Stern, J. P. (1980). *Soviet Natural Gas Development to 1990: The Implications for the CMEA and the West*. Lexington, MA and Toronto Lexington Books D. C. Heath and Co

(1993). *Oil and Gas in the Former Soviet Union: The Changing Foreign Investment Agenda*. London: Royal Institute of International Affairs

UN (1993). *Human Development Report*. Oxford and New York: UN, UNDP

WGI (1991a). *World Gas Intelligence*, p. 4

(1991b). *World Gas Intelligence*, October, p. 5

(1992). *World Gas Intelligence*, November, p. 1

(1993). *World Gas Intelligence*, March, p. 5

(1994a). *World Gas Intelligence*, April 15, pp. 1–2

(1994b). *World Gas Intelligence*, June 30, p. 10

(1994c). *World Gas Intelligence*, August 26, p. 2

(1994d). *World Gas Intelligence*, August 26, pp. 1–2

(1994e). *World Gas Intelligence*, March 11, p. 2

(1995a). *World Gas Intelligence*, August 11, p. 2

(1995b). *World Gas Intelligence*, January 27, p. 6

(1995c). *World Gas Intelligence*, August 11, p. 5

(1995d). *World Gas Intelligence*, May 26, p. 5

(1995e). *World Gas Intelligence*, July 14, p. 6

(1996). *World Gas Intelligence*, February 9, p. 5

(1997). *World Gas Intelligence*, July 20, pp. 6–7

(1998). *World Gas Intelligence*, May 14, p. 1

(2002). *World Gas Intelligence*, August 7, pp. 1–2

(2005). *World Gas Intelligence*, December 14

Zhiznin, S. (2003). *Fundamentals of Energy Diplomacy*: Moscow. Moscow State Institute of International Relations, Ministry of Foreign Affairs of the Russian Federation, International Institute of Fuel and Energy Complex (in Russian)

6   Natural gas pipelines in the Southern Cone

David R. Mares

Introduction

Discussions of trade in natural gas in South America's Southern Cone (Argentina, Bolivia, Brazil, Chile, Paraguay, and Uruguay) began as early as the 1950s. But it was not until 1972 that the first international gas pipeline in the region, linking Bolivia and Argentina, was built. It was twenty years later before significant gas pipeline projects integrating Chile and Argentina were proposed, followed by one large project connecting Bolivia and Brazil (see the map in figure 6.1.)

This chapter examines three historical cases to understand why there was a twenty-five-year lag between the first international pipeline project and the others, and to uncover the key factors that determine why particular pipeline projects were built while similar proposed pipelines languished. The 1970s pipeline, "YABOG," linked Bolivia and Argentina and competed with an alternative project to send Bolivian gas to Brazil. Information on this pipeline project is limited, as the main financier of the project, the World Bank, has not yet released its records. The YABOG case thus serves mainly as historical background for the contemporary projects. This chapter examines in detail competition in two major gas trade projects in the 1990s. First, it examines the GasAndes pipeline and the competing alternative, Transgas – both projects would transport Argentine gas to Chile. Second, it analyzes the decision to supply Brazil with Bolivian gas (via a pipeline known as GasBol) rather than Argentine gas (via the Paraná–Porto Alegre project).

Among the findings in this comparative study is that private investors can be attracted to a virgin gas market (in this case, Chile) if government policies for that particular sector offer the possibility of making a profit.

The author wishes to thank Mark H. Hayes and David G. Victor for their comments, Monica Herz of IRI–PUC and Francisco Rojas of FLACSO–Chile for their assistance and Eduardo Dubin, Pablo Pinto, Kati Suominen, and Andrés Villar for research support. Meredith Williams created the map in figure 6.1. Responsibility for all views presented here is my own.

169

Figure 6.1. South America: international gas pipelines.

In Chile's case, the government adopted a credible policy to favor gas to offset the vulnerability of hydropower to unpredictable weather patterns.

The general investment climate was favorable in all four countries at the time of the contemporary projects, but the investment climate was generally poor during the early period of YABOG. Pricing risks were fundamental to the Bolivia–Argentina and Chile–Argentina projects. In GasBol, the Brazilian government and World Bank intervened to mitigate the risks to private investors. The "early" YABOG project was driven by the well-developed Argentine gas infrastructure and offtake market, whereas the contemporary projects to Brazil and Chile had to overcome hurdles of limited gas infrastructures. International institutions for economic cooperation were important only when they provided financing, as in YABOG and GasBol; regional institutions for economic cooperation were marginal to all the pipeline decisions. Finally – and important to the subject of this chapter – governments see cross-border gas pipelines as influencing interstate relationships. Geopolitical relationships in the Southern Cone have been, and continue to be, fundamental factors in shaping the development of regional energy markets.

The first section of this chapter provides a brief history and analysis of the YABOG pipeline project, and competing alternatives at the time. The second and third sections analyze in greater detail the economic, legal, and financial aspects of the two projects in the 1990s. The conclusion briefly reviews the evolution of the gas markets after the pipelines were built and elaborates on the lessons that can be drawn from these three case studies for understanding trade in natural gas.

YABOG (Bolivia–Argentinia) Pipeline: 1972

The first discussions concerning a natural gas pipeline in southern South America revolved around two competing Bolivian gas export projects, one to Brazil and the other to Argentina. Argentina and Brazil had been competing for influence over their smaller neighbors Uruguay, Paraguay and Bolivia since the mid-nineteenth century (Kelly and Child 1988). Bolivia began discussions with Brazil and Argentina in the 1930s to develop a regional energy market fueled by Bolivian petroleum. Bolivia, a poor country, hoped that its neighbors would finance exploration and development, with Bolivia using crude sales to repay its debts.

Bolivia experienced a revolution in 1952 in which mobilization by miners and peasants played a major role. Yet the country remained significantly stratified by race and income after the revolution (Malloy 1970; Gamarra 1996). These economic and social tensions combined with the willingness of frustrated citizens to engage in massive and prolonged demonstrations and dramatically limited the ability of government to follow through on many public policies. In a pattern that continues today, ever since the 1950s Bolivian governments searching for investment and prospective buyers have had to walk a fine line, lest their policies provoke popular protests and counter-reaction by civilian and military sectors fearful of public protest.

Bolivia's revolutionary government, led by the Movement of the National Revolution (Movimiento Nacionalista Revolucionario, or MNR), quickly broadened the search for capital to develop its energy resources. In 1956, legislation permitted private foreign investment in the petroleum sector. Gulf Oil invested in Bolivian oil fields and quickly asserted its rights to associated natural gas, provoking a nationalist uproar. The government of Brazil also expressed its interest in natural gas imports from Bolivia at the time. In 1958, seeking to attract more private investment, Bolivia offered Brazil all the natural gas from Bolivian fields developed by private Brazilian investors (Vargas Salguiero 1996; Calvo Mirabal c. 1996).

Brazil had growing energy needs, but it also had options. In 1964, oil finally caught up with wood and charcoal as the main source of primary energy consumed in Brazil. The rising price of petroleum even before the 1973 oil shock, however, led national policy-makers to switch their focus away from oil and promote hydropower. By 1972, hydropower had more than doubled its contribution to primary energy consumption compared with 1964 (21 percent, up from 13 percent) (Santiago 1989). In this context, a hydropower complex at Itaipú was an attractive alternative for Brazil. The waters between Brazil and Paraguay had been a source of disagreement, but in 1966 the two countries decided to jointly develop the waterway and share the benefits. The Itaipú Treaty, signed in 1973, authorized the construction of a massive dam and world's largest hydroelectric power plant at the time.[1]

Despite its success with the Itaipú agreement with Paraguay, Brazil continued to woo Bolivia both for geopolitical reasons and to keep Bolivian energy resources as a potential reserve for the future. These were the years during which the Brazilian "economic miracle" was in full bloom and future energy supplies were problematic in the wake of OPEC's damaging oil embargo of 1973. In 1974, Brazil and Bolivia signed a cooperation and industrial complementary accord that committed Bolivia to sell 2.5 Bcm per year of gas over the next twenty years in return for Brazil's intent to purchase steel, petrochemicals, fertilizer, and cement from a new Bolivian industrial complex to be built on the border. Brazil also agreed to finance electric power plants and infrastructure in Bolivia to support the industrial complex. In 1978, the gas agreement was reaffirmed with volumes increased to 4.1 Bcm per year. Domestic

---

[1] Construction commenced in 1975, the dam began filling in 1982, electricity was first produced in 1984, and the eighteenth and final generating unit came on line in 1991. Fifty percent of Itaipú is owned by Electrobrás, Brazil's national electric power company; essentially all of Itaipú is Electrobrás/Brazil financed. The $18–20 billion project generates 75 billion kwh of electricity per year. Brazil has first call on the output, using 95 percent of it and Paraguay uses the remaining 5 percent (Itaipú Dam and Environment (1996)).

opposition to the export of gas erupted in Bolivia (Vargas Salguiero 1996), as the poor majority of Bolivians began to feel betrayed by YABOG's inability to spur development and by Argentine efforts to reduce the price and quantity of imports from Bolivia. Once again, the agreement remained on paper only.

In contrast to Brazil, Argentina had a developed market for natural gas years before seeking Bolivian supplies. Domestic policies controlled the price of gas in Argentina, initially benefiting both middle-class consumers and industrial users, but these policies starved the gas sector of capital. By the late 1960s, both civilian politicians and military dictators feared the political fallout of gas shortages for middle-class homes and industry. The Comodoro Rivadia pipeline from Argentina's northern gas fields to Buenos Aires, in particular, was underutilized (Davison, Hurst, and Mabro 1988), making Bolivian gas an attractive option for Argentina.

Gulf Oil, meanwhile, had begun to export petroleum from Bolivia in 1966 via the Sicasica–Arica pipeline through Chile, and naturally sought export markets for its natural gas. With its developed gas market and declining domestic reserves, Argentina was a more attractive market than Brazil. Gulf Oil created a company (Bolsur) to negotiate the terms of a contract, and in September 1967 signed a Letter of Intent with the Argentine parastatal Gas del Estado to supply it with Bolivian natural gas for twenty years.

Bolivia's national oil company (Yacimientos Petrolíferos Fiscales de Bolivia, or YPFB) produced gas from its own fields and also targeted the Argentine market. Within Bolivia, this competition between Gulf and YPFB over export markets sparked large protests against Gulf Oil. The Bolivian government responded by putting the Army on alert. The Argentine Foreign Minister insisted that the Bolivian government and Gulf Oil resolve their differences before Argentina would buy any gas from Bolivia (Calvo Mirabal 1996).

The administration of General René Barrientos was doing a delicate balancing act: retaining the interest of private investors in Bolivia while increasing government revenues from the exploitation of natural gas to pacify the nationalist opposition. Faced with increasing civil unrest in Bolivia and the possibility of losing the Argentine market, Gulf agreed to discuss an increase in royalty payments. The Barrientos government issued a decree permitting the sale of gas to Argentina through a new entity, YABOG, with equal ownership between YPFB and Gulf Oil. A contract among the three parties was signed in August 1968. The twenty-year agreement stipulated that Bolivia would provide 1.5 Bcm per year for the first seven years, rising to 1.7 Bcm per year in the subsequent thirteen years. Williams Bros., a partner of Gulf Oil, was selected to build the pipeline (Calvo Mirabal 1996).

Discussions between Gulf Oil and the Bolivian government failed to produce an agreement regarding royalty payments. After a military coup by General Alfredo Ovando, the issue was settled via the nationalization of Gulf's Bolivian holdings in October 1969. (Nationalization was a constant threat in the Southern Cone countries at the time. Bolivia had nationalized the tin companies in 1952, Peru nationalized the IPC oil company in 1968, and Chile progressively squeezed copper companies through a process known as "Chileanization," then nationalized them in 1971.)

The nationalization of Gulf Oil slowed construction but did not terminate the YABOG pipeline project. Financing for the project was provided by the World Bank and US private firms. Construction began in 1970 and the pipeline began operating in 1972 (Calvo Mirabal 1996). The 441 km, 600 mm trunk line has a total capacity of 2.2 Bcm per year and connects Río Grande, Bolivia to the Argentine pipeline network in Salta. The Argentine portion is operated by Transportadora Gas del Norte (TGN).

The Bolivian–Argentine agreement that produced the YABOG pipeline proved contentious as the market in Argentina evolved in a manner unforeseen by either government at the time the original agreement was signed. The new Argentine military government (1976–1984) began adopting neo-liberal policies to attract both domestic and foreign investment (Ramos 1986). Private investment rushed in and by 1978 large new gas reserves were being developed in Argentina. An expansion of the Argentine natural gas transport and distribution system followed, increasing gas supplies and lowering internal prices below the rate negotiated with Bolivia (Bechelli 1989). The contracted volumes of Bolivian gas were no longer competitive.

The Bolivian economy collapsed in the early 1980s (inflation peaked at 11,700 percent in 1985), producing a foreign debt crisis and making the country ever more dependent upon its exports. Disagreements developed over the price Argentina paid for Bolivian gas, the proportion of currency and in-kind payments, and Bolivia's failure to make its debt payments to Argentina, its largest bilateral creditor. The two nations negotiated a comprehensive agreement in 1987. Under the accord, Bolivia agreed to cut its gas price by 20 percent and also to periodically readjust from the gas price to an index of imported fuel oil prices (c.i.f.) in Buenos Aires, with allowances of $0.71 per mmbtu for transport from the wellhead to the Argentine border (see figure 6.2). To avoid abrupt price fluctuations for Bolivia, Argentina agreed to a final price that

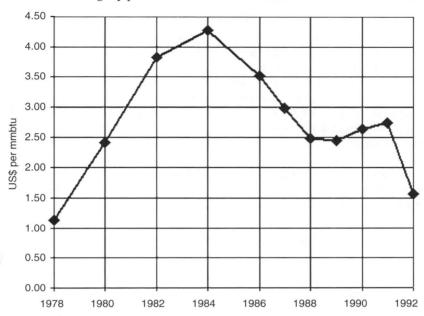

Figure 6.2. Evolution of YABOG gas prices, 1978–1992, nominal US$ per mmbtu.
[a]Assuming the heat content of Bolivian gas at 36,908 btu/m^3 (see Appendix: Technical notes, p. 484).

Source: Muller & Associates, *Estadísticas Socioeconómicas* as cited in Vargas Salguiero (1996).

would be a combination of a new formula price (70 percent) and price paid in the past period (30 percent). Argentina resumed its gas payments to Bolivia with 80 percent of its payment in convertible currencies and 20 percent in goods, such as wheat (Givogri, García and Bastos 1990; Library of Congress 1999).

The long-term contract with Argentina expired in 1992, but the two governments agreed to several consecutive extensions (although at a much lower price) providing income to Bolivia until the start of gas exports to Brazil. The contract expired on July 31, 1999; Argentina subsequently purchased only small amounts of gas via two short cross-border pipelines owned by the Argentine company, Pluspetrol. Over the life of the relationship, Bolivia exported almost 50 Bcm of natural gas to Argentina, worth about $4.3 billion (in nominal dollars) for an average price of $2.21 per mmbtu (Vargas Salguiero 1996).

The early Brazilian bid for Bolivian gas was driven largely by geopolitical interests in extending Brazilian influence in the region and was limited by the existence of energy alternatives that fit better into the Brazilian energy matrix than did natural gas. Brazil opted to pursue greater influence over Paraguay and additional hydropower resources at Itaipú during the 1970s rather than to invest in a Bolivian gas pipeline. Argentina pursued its project (the YABOG pipeline) to completion. Not only did Argentina have geopolitical interests similar to those of its rival, Brazil, but its domestic market for natural gas was already developed and domestic supplies were expected to become insufficient. Gulf Oil's Bolivian company originated the project, but the pipeline was developed by the two governments, in conjunction with the World Bank, after Gulf was nationalized by Bolivia.

Contemporary Projects

Argentine Gas to Chile circa 1997

In the early 1990s, Chile had an interest in importing cheaper and cleaner natural gas and Argentina was seeking to promote its natural gas exports. Two pipeline projects competed fiercely to bring Argentine gas to Chile's major energy market. The GasAndes pipeline would run directly across the Andes into Santiago, tapping into an existing Argentine pipeline extending north of the Neuquén gas fields from which the gas would originate. The Transgas pipeline, in contrast, would begin at Neuquén and cross into south–central Chile, servicing a number of smaller urban and industrial centers before heading north to Santiago (see the map in Figure 6.1).

Argentine reserves of natural gas continued to expand after the 1978 discoveries, turning the country from a gas importer into a potential gas exporter. By 1993 Argentine proven reserves had reached 517 Bcm (Secretaría de Energía, as cited in IEA 2003). The Argentine gas market was further liberalized in the 1990s, producing a robust domestic gas market with very competitive prices. The dominant question at the time was whether the availability of that supply for foreign trade should be subordinate to domestic demand.

Chile, a neighbor with a booming economy and an interest in diversifying its energy sources, provided a potential market for Argentine exports. Chile's energy sector did not use much natural gas in 1994 – less than 2 Bcm or about 9 percent of total primary energy (see figure 6.3). However, natural gas became an attractive energy source in Chile for multiple reasons. Concern over the potential for petroleum prices to rise again

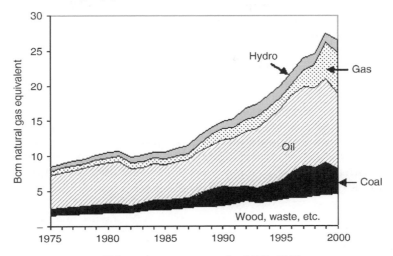

Figure 6.3. Chile: primary energy mix, 1975–2000.
Source: IEA (2003).

stimulated government efforts to diversify energy supplies. Also, severe air pollution in the nation's capital and industrial center provoked the new democratic government to promulgate more stringent environmental regulations (Jadresic 1999).[2] Concerns were also voiced over the possibility of prolonged drought and the ensuing shortage of hydroelectric supplies.

But before Argentina and Chile could pursue closer economic relations, especially in a sector considered to be as strategically important as energy, the two countries had to overcome a legacy of mistrust and rivalry. Resolution of the Beagle Channel dispute in 1984, after near-war in 1978, opened the way for improved relations between the Southern Cone neighbors.[3] The 1984 Treaty of Peace and Friendship reaffirmed the need to promote economic relations as the building blocks for a lasting peace.

Argentina returned to democracy in 1984 and Carlos Saúl Menem became President in 1990. Menem was able to use his control of the Justicialist (Peronist) Party to attain almost complete dominance over

[2] Santiago has a population of 5 million and lies in a basin 1,700 ft above sea level.
[3] Argentina and Chile sent their maritime boundary dispute to arbitration in 1971. In 1977, the British monarch awarded three disputed islands in the Beagle Channel to Chile. Argentina rejected the decision and attempted to militarily coerce Chile into negotiating a division of the islands that would produce a maritime boundary consistent with Argentine claims.

the Legislature and Supreme Court during his tenure (1990–1998), implementing the most far-reaching changes to the economy in Argentina's history. Under the guidance of Economy Secretary Domingo Cavallo, SOEs were virtually all privatized in a process heavily criticized for having little transparency. A constitutional amendment pegged the peso to the dollar and made it freely transferable, which appeared to eliminate foreign exchange risks. The Heritage Foundation ranked Argentina's economy as among the "freest" in the world in 1999 (Corrales 2002). For most of the 1990s the Argentine economy boomed, fueled by large infusions of foreign investment. The Menem administration had great support at home and abroad. The indirect tax imposed by the vast network of corruption was easily overshadowed by the rapidly growing economy.

In contrast to the tumultuous history of Argentina, Chile had a long history of democratic rule that was interrupted by a military coup in 1973. The military government overhauled much of Chilean legislation to make the country attractive to foreign investment, thereby creating in 1978 the first neo-liberal economy in Latin America, long before the so-called "Washington Consensus" of 1990 initiated a wave of market reforms across Latin America. When the country returned to democracy in 1989, the military government's constitution was revised to include "authoritarian enclaves" (a number of designated Senators, Senators for Life, a national security council in which the military occupied half the seats, etc.). The constitution and its reforms played a major role in convincing the Armed Forces and the political Right that the Left could not make major changes even if they won elections.

The new democratic government of Chile was significantly constrained in its policy by the constitution. In addition, it needed to produce growth because it faced public comparison with the previous dictatorship that had overseen a booming economy. As recently as the 1988 plebiscite on military rule, the dictatorship garnered 43 percent of the vote.

The credibility of both the Argentine and Chilean governments *vis-à-vis* private investors was high during the 1990s, though for completely different reasons. In Argentina, Menem's free market ideology and political power convinced private investors that the investment climate would remain favorable. In Chile's case it was the restricted policy space within which the Center-Left governments could move that gave private investors confidence.

Once both countries had redemocratized in the 1990s, they embarked on a flurry of bilateral agreements, quickly settling twenty-two of the twenty-four remaining territorial disputes and signing agreements promoting trade and integration. On August 2, 1991 the countries signed the Acuerdo de Complementaridad Económica under the auspices of the ALADI (Asociación Latinoamericana de Integración) Montevideo Treaty of 1980, which provided a basis for permitting bilateral agreements exempt from most-favored nation (MFN) clauses that would automatically extend similar benefits to third parties.[4]

Political leaders in both Chile and Argentina saw economic integration not only as a means of promoting growth but also a way of consolidating democracy – on the logic that a diminished external threat environment would undercut the military's influence at home. Chilean President Patricio Alwyn proposed an energy agreement with another traditional rival, Bolivia, in 1992. Projects with both Bolivia and Argentina were viewed as complementary by the Alwyn administration: Bolivia would supply the north while Argentine gas could meet Chilean gas demand in the center of the country. There was also discussion about integrating electrical grids, but Chile's National Energy Commission decided to pursue integrating the natural gas markets first.[5] However, Alwyn's initiatives towards Bolivia could not overcome the stumbling block of Bolivia's demand that Chile provide it with a sovereign outlet to the Pacific Ocean to compensate for the littoral province seized by Chile in the War of the Pacific (1879–1883).[6]

The governments of Chile and Argentina prematurely called for international bids on a gas pipeline project linking the two countries. Investors initially stayed away primarily because neither the rules for deciding among competitive bids nor those guiding the project's operation after construction were clear. This uncertainty was rectified when the

---

[4] MFN clauses in trade agreements speed the process of decreasing trade barriers by making the benefits provided by one country to another automatically applicable to all countries. But because it is automatic, countries lose the ability to negotiate adjustments with those third parties. ALADI has twelve members; any lowering of trade barriers between Chile and Argentina would have to have been extended to the other ten members if the MFN clause had not been circumvented. ALADI adopted this treaty circumventing MFN because it believed that progress on lowering trade barriers could proceed faster among sub-sets of its membership than if all members had to be included.

[5] The Commission concluded that natural gas imports would not be profitable if electricity were imported. While lowering electricity prices was a goal of the Commission, they wanted to decrease energy prices for industry, domestic consumption and transport first (FLACSO–Chile 1996).

[6] Bolivian passions about the Chilean border dispute run deep. In 2003 massive and violent protests forced the resignation of Bolivian President Sánchez de Lozada and the rejection of a gas export project that would have traversed Chilean territory to reach a proposed LNG export facility. LNG was to be shipped to Mexico and the United States. In 2004, when Argentina faced domestic shortages of natural gas, Bolivia signed an emergency agreement to export gas to Argentina but stipulated that "not one molecule" could be re-exported to Chile.

Gas Interconnection Protocol (1991) stipulated that gas exports from Argentina would be subject to a maximum level, and Chile could import gas only from the Neuquén Basin in Argentina (Gallardo 1995).

The 1991 Protocol reflected both Argentina's move under President Menem to adopt the neo-liberal economic policies that had produced sustained economic growth in Chile, as well as the Argentine fear that the domestic market might be undersupplied if exports competed with domestic demand. Under the legal stipulations of the original Protocol, Chile would likely confront a monopolistic supplier, resulting in higher prices to the consumer because only one pipeline consortium could ship gas from Neuquén and domestic Chilean supplies were very limited.

Chile's newly democratic government, tied to a constitution favoring private markets and politically in favor of lowering energy prices, wanted market forces to determine who would build which pipeline. The Alwyn administration recognized the need to set the context through both a better treaty for supply from Argentina and the establishment of a regulatory regime under which transportation and distribution of gas would operate. But the administration was not yet ready to revise the regulations governing the natural gas sector and thus investors confronted the risk that major investments had to be legally committed to the projects before the reforms were settled (*Business Latin America* 1995).

The decision to modify the Gas Interconnection Protocol in 1995 and allow Chile equal access to Argentine gas was a major step towards permitting private investors to compete on a level playing field set by the bi-national market. Within this framework two consortia (Transgas and GasAndes) competed to build the major pipeline that would bring Argentine gas to Chile. Although the playing field was level, the two competing consortia structured themselves in fundamentally different ways, and this would make an enormous difference in their competitiveness in what came to be known in Chile as the "pipeline wars" (Figueroa and Smith 2002).

The "pipeline wars"   In 1992 the Argentine government began receiving requests for permits to export Argentine natural gas. Shell Argentina presented a rudimentary proposal, which was seen as only an expression of interest and it was told to flesh out the details. The petition of Gas Natural, SA, a Chilean company, was rejected because its application for a permit did not specify where and how it was going to get the gas to export. The proposal of an Argentine consortium led by YPF (Yacimientos Petrolíferos Federales, owner of 70 percent of Argentine natural gas reserves) and including Astra, Bridas, Petrolera San Jorge, and Pluspetrol, was accepted for the full 1.8 Bcm per year that the Protocol authorized for export. But the deadline for the proposal had to be extended a number of times until the consortium could find suitable buyers for the gas in Chile (Secretaría de Hidrocarburos y Minería 1992).

Chile's Enersis group (including the country's largest electricity distribution company, Chilectra) and Chile's national oil company, ENAP (Empresa Nacional de Petróleo) became the Chilean partners in the Transgas consortium along with the YPF-led Argentine group. The pipeline project was to be financed by equity participants and had two components–the pipeline itself and a distribution network. Shareholding in the pipeline was to be Chilectra/Enersis 35 percent, US-based Tenneco 25 percent, ENAP 10 percent, YPF 10 percent, and the remaining 20 percent to be allocated among Astra, Bridas, Pluspetrol, and Petrolera San Jorge. Financing of the distribution network, "Gas de Chile," was to be divided among the operator British Gas (46 percent), Chilectra (27 percent) and Enersis (27 percent). Transgas participants did not formalize their partnership and had no separate management council; their coordination was affected by the lack of institutionalized collaboration throughout the negotiation process (Figueroa and Smith 2002). On the Argentine side, pipeline owner Transportadora Gas del Norte (TGN) contracted to transport the gas but did not wish to become a shareholder (Cameo 2003).

The proposed Transgas pipeline was to begin in the Neuquén Basin, Argentina, and run a total of 1,381 km, feeding the cities of Concepción, Santiago, and Valparaíso, Chile. Because the consortium on the Chilean side was dominated by hydropower producers, Transgas chose a circuitous path (1,200 km) to the main industrial and population center, Santiago. One advantage for Chile of this indirect route was that it would supply a greater area of the country. But the longer pipeline would also make gas prices higher in Santiago, thus reducing gas-generated power's ability to compete with hydropower in the lucrative Santiago market.

The Transgas pipeline was anticipated to cost $490 million to reach Santiago, $90 million for branches to regions along the way, another $90 million for compression stations, and $330 million for investments in the distribution network, requiring a total of $1 billion in direct investment. Another $700 million would be needed for new combined-cycle gas turbines to burn the gas for electric power generation, and $100 million for conversion of industrial and residential consumers to gas. In total, mobilization of nearly $1.8 billion in capital was needed to make the project viable (Figueroa and Smith 2002).

Transgas was especially vulnerable to the two governments' regulatory policies. Essentially, the consortium was gambling that the project's positive externalities for regional gas market development would lead both countries to allow it a monopolistic position as sole importer of gas from Argentina in the central region and with closed access for the pipeline in Chile. This result, however, required that Argentina adopt policies that restricted the export market (one supply source and a limited volume), and that Chile regulate the domestic market in ways that protected Transgas' early market position (a *de facto* closed system for transportation). In short, Transgas wanted public policy to protect its gains under the original Protocol.

A second pipeline project emerged without seeking many of these regulatory protections. NOVA Corporation of Canada, two Chilean firms (Gasco, a gas distributor and Gener, the country's second largest power generating company and its largest thermoelectric generator) and two Argentine companies (Compañía General de Combustibles and Techint Compañía Ténica Internacional) formed a competing project, GasAndes. This proposed pipeline tapped into an existing Argentine pipeline north of the Neuquén basin and went directly to Santiago. The shorter pipeline route (463 km) meant a significantly lower cost, initially estimated at just $284 million for the pipeline itself.

Recognizing the risks posed by both an evolving government policy and the immature Chilean natural gas market, the GasAndes partners structured the terms of their relationship very clearly. NOVA Corporation committed to increasing the capacity of the Central-Oeste pipeline owned by TGN in Argentina to feed the proposed GasAndes pipeline. (The Canadian firm held 11 percent of TGN shares in 1994 and had increased its stake to 19.1 percent by 1997.) NOVA held 70 percent of the shares in the GasAndes project, with the two Chilean partners splitting the remaining 30 percent as they saw fit (see table 6.1). The option of adding institutional investors to the deal later was kept open. Any sale of shares had to be offered first to partners and then to outsiders, subject to agreement by the rest of the group (Figueroa and Smith 2002).

Gener committed to modifying its thermoelectric power plant at Renca to accept natural gas and Gasco was to organize and operate a distribution company in Santiago (Metrogas). They set up a Management Committee and bound themselves to not participate in competing projects for a period of two years unless the MOU had been dissolved; this stipulation applied even if a company withdrew from the project. The agreement was governed by Chilean law and disputes among the partners were to be settled by the Rules of Conciliation and Arbitration

Table 6.1 *GasAndes: ownership structure*

Pipeline (Gasoducto GasAndes SA)	(%)
NOVA Gas International	56.5
Gener	15.0
Metrogas	15.0
CGC, Argentina	13.5
Nueva Renca Thermal Power Plant (Sociedad Eléctrica Santiago SA)	
Gener	51.0
Duke Power	24.0
NOVA Gas International	15.0
Companía General de Electricidad (majority owner of Gasco)	10.0
Santiago Distribution system (Metrogas SA)	
Gasco	40.0
Copec	22.5
Gener	10.0
NOVA Gas International	10.0
Lone Star Gas	10.0
Enagas	7.5

Source: Figueroa and Smith (2002).

of the ICC, in a process to be held in Paris. Cooperation among the GasAndes partners was further promoted by cross-investments in these ventures. The project was solely equity financed, with the pipeline totaling $325 million, new power plants $235 million, and the distribution system estimated to be $600 million over eight years (Figueroa and Smith 2002). Thus the project would require mobilization of just over $1 billion, 60 percent of the Transgas proposal.

GasAndes' feasibility study showed that, with a competitive pricing structure, demand for natural gas in its potential area of service would double between 1997 and 2000 and increase by almost 900 percent in the twenty-year time frame relevant for the pipeline project. The study also anticipated that the composition of demand would undergo important changes. Rapid growth in gas use for generating electric power was projected to make the electric sector the dominant gas buyer, consuming over 70 percent of total gas supplies by the end of the twenty-year project lifetime. The feasibility study projected industrial gas demand to grow relatively slowly, and thus the industrial share of the gas market was projected to decline from 45 percent to just 12 percent (GasAndes 1994).

GasAndes was also vulnerable to political decisions. However, whereas Transgas bet that governments would allow it a monopolistic position, GasAndes' gamble was that the Chilean government would choose a regulatory scheme that would allow market forces to decide which project should proceed. GasAndes' studies had convinced the developers that if the government let the market decide which pipeline should be built, prices would be competitive enough for natural gas for GasAndes to compete effectively against other energy sources. The bet on the Chilean government choosing a regulatory scheme that would err on the side of letting the market work was an acceptable risk, given the record of economic growth under Chile's free market reforms and the constitutional/legislative limits on the Executive's ability to implement important economic changes (Aguila 2003).

The Menem administration in Argentina was split over the Gas Interconnection Protocol. YPF's director argued for limiting and regulating access to Argentine gas; the Secretaries of Energy and Economy favored creating open markets. Once Menem decided to favor Economy Secretary Domingo Cavallo's dramatic liberalization of the economy, YPF's opposition ceased (Bastos 2003). In 1995, the Gas Interconnection Protocol was renegotiated, allowing exports from any Argentine gas field and providing for open access to any pipeline built. A small 356 mm, 83 km pipeline, *Methanex PA*, was immediately built to supply a methanol producing plant in the far south of Chile. The pipeline began operations in 1996 with an initial capacity of 0.73 Bcm per year (IEA 2003).

Once the Argentine and Chilean governments agreed to let the market decide which pipeline would be built, GasAndes' advantages gave it a tremendous benefit in securing downstream clients. Both groups sought commitments from buyers for their supply. GasAndes' lower pricing attracted sufficient buyers to justify their pipeline, while Transgas failed to sign up enough clients; even a subsidiary of one of the Transgas partners wound up signing with GasAndes (Qué Pasa 1995).

The GasAndes pipeline, with a capacity of 3.3 Bcm per year through a 610 mm pipe, runs 463 km from La Mora, Mendoza, to San Bernardo on the outskirts of the Chilean capital, Santiago. Operations began in August 1997. Total investment in the GasAndes project, including the pipelines, distribution grids, and thermal power plants, was $1.46 billion (Jadresic 1999).

Brazilian Gas Import Options (1997–1999)

The third gas pipeline in our study connects Bolivia and Brazil. In a repeat of the earlier Bolivian search for an outlet for its energy resources,

Argentina was a player in the discussions of the 1990s. This time, however, Argentina had its own surplus gas to sell and the question was whether Brazil would be supplied by a pipeline from Bolivia (GasBol) or Argentina (Paraná–Porto Alegre, see figure 6.1). The GasBol project would ultimately beat out its Argentine competitors because of price and the Brazilian government/World Bank interest in promoting the political and economic development of Bolivia.

Macroeconomic and environmental concerns raised the profile of natural gas in Brazilian policy-makers' eyes. In the early 1990s, hydropower, petroleum, and wood/sugar cane derivatives each accounted for about one-third of Brazil's primary energy supply, with natural gas contributing only 2 percent (see figure 6.4). Not only was increasing the supply of these existing sources expensive, but fuelwood contributed to deforestation and fuel oil's high sulfur content worsened the industrial city of São Paulo's notorious pollution problems (de Franco 2001). Brazil's macroeconomic problems, particularly its fiscal deficit and inflation, were heavily influenced by the country's efforts to increase the domestic supply of petroleum, hydroelectricity, and alcohol (as a fuel produced from sugarcane).

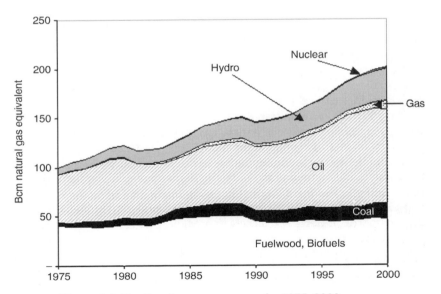

Figure 6.4. Brazil: primary energy supply, 1975–2000.
Source: IEA (2003).

Table 6.2 *Brazil: gas market assessment, circa 1993*

Sector	Consumption (Bcm)	Share of total (%)	Growth prospects within sector	Determinants of prospects
Industrial	2.1	69	Good	Price/environmental policy
Fertilizers/feedstocks	0.7	23	Good	Price/environmental policy
Residential	0.2	8	Good	Inherent limits on growth
Transportation (CNG)	0.0	0	Good	Inherent limits on growth
Electric power	0.0	0	Good	Structural constraints; requires policy stimuli

Source: Author's analysis based on Deffarges and Maurer (1993); IEA (2003).

The reforms of the 1988 Brazilian constitution did not disrupt the monopoly of state-owned Petrobrás over Brazil's petroleum markets. (Petrobrás maintained exclusive responsibility for the import, refining, and wholesale of all petroleum and petroleum products including transport fuels, LPG, and natural gas). Even after the 1988 reforms petroleum prices continued to be controlled by the government. Policy-makers used petroleum prices to combat inflation, often subsidizing LPG and fuel oil, to the detriment of natural gas (de Franco 2001). Brazilian industrialists as well as private investors worried that Petrobrás was biased against natural gas.

The 1990 "Reexamination of the National Energy Matrix" report advocated increasing the use of natural gas to 6 percent of all primary energy by 2010. In 1993 President Fernando Henrique Cardoso approved the Gas Commission's recommendation of doubling that goal to 12 percent by 2010 (Salles Abreu Passos 1998). The state governments of São Paulo and other industrialized states were pressuring the federal government in the early 1990s for greater supply of natural gas, through domestic production or imports (Deffarges and Maurer 1993). At the beginning of pipeline discussions with Bolivia and Argentina, the goal was primarily to supply the industrial sector in Brazil (ESMAP 2003) (see table 6.2).

The Argentine Option Brazil and Argentina had signed an accord in 1987 committing the two countries to trade in natural gas.

But the two countries were far apart on price, with Brazil insisting that it would not pay more than $1.70 per mmbtu and Argentina insisting on $3.40 per mmbtu. Talks among representatives of both governments continued without agreement for years.

Industrialists in Rio Grande do Sul were attentive to the looming energy shortage. They were also aware that the Argentine government and industrialists were concerned that the trade liberalization proposed under the Mercosur regional integration project (to be inaugurated in 1994) would produce a trade surplus for Brazil. Brazilian industrialists worried that their products might get locked out of the Argentine market to compensate for the trade imbalance. Importing natural gas from Argentina thus met both their energy and their trade concerns.

In 1989, the industrialists' association Federacão das Indústrias do Estado de São Paulo (FIESP) mobilized their state government to promote a pipeline project directly with the provincial government of Entre Rios, Argentina. A technical feasibility study was presented to the state governments by a bi-national consortium led by the Brazilian firm Mendes Junior. The proposed pipeline would run from Paraná to Entre Rios on the Argentine side, to Porto Alegre and then on to Rio Grande do Sul, on the Brazilian side. Along its 1,140 km path it would also provide gas to the Brazilian cities of Alegrete, Santa Maria, Santa Cruz do Sul, and Montenegro. The 460 mm pipeline would have a capacity of up to 3 Bcm per year at a cost of $600 million (Bem David 1989; Wells 1989; Zero Hora 1989).

The Argentine national government favored the resumption of talks and indicated flexibility on price. Petrobrás claimed to support the project in principle as early as 1990, but insisted that it would not finance the project and that the prices offered by Argentina were not acceptable. (Despite a fall in Argentina's asking price to $2.70 per mmbtu, the two sides still remained far apart because Brazil in turn lowered its preferred price to $1.10 per mmbtu). Brazilian industrialists, however, believed that the price issue could be resolved and accused Petrobrás of opposing the pipeline (Teixeira 1990; Thompson 1992).

GasBol Bolivia, because of its problems with exports to Argentina via its existing export pipelines, looked once again to Brazil as a potential buyer. In 1988, Presidents José Sarney of Brazil and Victor Paz Estenssoro of Bolivia signed an agreement under which Brazil would purchase power from a 525 megawatt (MW) thermal plant fed by a 500 mm pipeline from the Bolivian gas fields to Puerto Suarez, Bolivia, near the border with Brazil. Brazil also committed to purchase 10 Bcm of natural gas, 100 million tons of nitrogen fertilizer, and 500 million tons of high-, medium- and low-density polyethylene annually (Petrobrás 1999). This agreement continued the earlier characteristic of negotiations between the two countries, in which gas sales were part of a larger economic integration project under which Brazil would also invest in and purchase from Bolivian industrial development projects.

However, there were some initial concerns about the adequacy of Bolivian reserves. Initial projections suggested that only 80 percent of the capacity of the pipeline could be filled (Law and de Franco 1998).[7]

A series of agreements hammered out by the SOEs YPFB and Petrobrás in 1992, 1993, and 1994 were signed by the respective Presidents of Bolivia and Brazil. The 1992 Paz Zamora–Collor de Mello and 1993 Paz Zamora–Itamar Franco agreements stipulated six principles:

1. A 710 mm pipeline extending 3,280 km from Rio Grande, Bolivia to Curitiba, Brazil;
2. A twenty-year contract;
3. Petrobrás received first option to build and own the Bolivian side of the pipeline;
4. Petrobrás received exploration rights in Boomerang, San Alberto, and other undeveloped Bolivian fields;
5. Shipments of 2.9 Bcm natural gas per year, increased to 8 Bcm per year within seven years and maintained for the remainder of the contract period; and
6. A commodity price of $0.90 per mmbtu at the start of the pipeline in Rio Grande.

Seeking to continue the neo-liberal reforms he had promoted as Bolivian Planning Minister in 1985, President Gonzalo Sánchez de Lozada (whose first term ran from 1973 to 1977) undertook major political and economic reforms to decentralize government, attract private investment, and increase earnings from non-coca exports. The Popular Participation Law of April 1994 required that a significant portion of national revenues be transferred to municipalities to fund projects selected locally. The Administrative Decentralization Law of 1995 gave Bolivia's nine departments greater autonomy from the central government.[8]

---

[7] Major finds would begin in 1995 after policies were adopted to attract foreign investors. Barbara Pando, TED Case Study: Bolivia; available at http://www.american.edu/projects/mandala/TED/bolpipe.htm.

[8] The irony of these reforms is that they empowered people at the local level, which Sánchez de Lozada wanted, but they also made central government policy more

Reforms were implemented to attract foreign direct investment (FDI). President Sánchez de Lozada removed exchange controls, restrictions on the repatriation of capital, dividends, interests, and any other remittances abroad. Most public enterprises were privatized and the five major state-owned companies in the energy, transport, and telecommunication sectors were "capitalized."[9]

To promote foreign investment specifically in the energy sector, the Bolivian government introduced legislation removing restrictions on foreign ownership of property within 50 km of its borders and created tax-exempt areas for energy export projects. YPFB was reorganized into several independent business units – two upstream units, a transport unit, two refining companies, and a marketing company.

Capitalization of YPFB was limited to 50 percent of shares, but Sánchez de Lozada offered Enron 55 percent of YPFB's shares. Massive protests erupted when this offer was made public, and on March 22, 1996, the Army occupied refineries and natural gas facilities to prevent workers from sabotaging them. Tensions were relieved when Enron invited Royal Dutch Shell to purchase some of the disputed shares (Ladouceur 2000; Pató 2000). Capitalization of YPFB's upstream and transportation units took place in 1996 and 1997. Prior to these reforms, about 25 percent of the country's natural gas production originated from fields operated by private companies.[10]

Sánchez de Lozada also sought to increase export earnings. He threatened to withdraw his country from the gas project unless three conditions were met: (1) increased gas sales; (2) higher prices; and (3) a bigger share of the Brazilian side of the project (*Oil Daily* 1994). The first addendum to the GasBol agreement was negotiated in 1994. YPFB and its partners negotiated an 85 percent interest in the pipeline in Bolivia and 20 percent in Brazil, while Petrobrás and its partners would own the corresponding 15 percent and 80 percent shares. The diameter of the pipeline was increased to 810 mm with a capacity up to 11 Bcm

---

vulnerable to opposition. (Sánchez de Lozada would later be overthrown by popular protests against his natural gas policies during his second term in 2003).

[9] In this uniquely Bolivian program the government sets up "mixed capital corporations," to which a private partner contributes a 50 percent capital investment; the remaining 50 percent of the shares are transferred to a Bolivian pension fund. The foreign investment is used to expand the production apparatus or the capital stock of the companies, rather than to solve budget deficit problems. The program was hailed as a model for privatization worldwide and attracted unprecedented levels of foreign investment to Bolivia (IEA 2003).

[10] Today, all natural gas production is in the hands of private companies, which have shared-risk contracts with YFPB. There are efforts to nationalize the industry once again.

per year. The new agreement was also extended until financing could be arranged.

Financing the pipeline project was complicated by the uncertainty introduced by the reforms of the state and energy sector regulations in both countries, and the immature gas market in the offtake country. Petrobrás' initial foray into the commercial financial markets in 1994 came up dry.

These financing difficulties produced a second addendum in 1995, raising gas prices at Rio Grande, the start of the pipeline, and establishing that Petrobrás would pay YPFB to supply the compressor stations. The base price was raised from $0.90 to $0.95 per mmbtu for the first 5.8 Bcm per year, with volumes above that at $1.20 per mmbtu. The base price was determined via a formula that included a basket of three internationally priced fuel oils and was to be adjusted each trimester.

Under the 1995 addendum, the transport fee was the responsibility of Gas Transboliviano SA (GTB) and Transportadora Brasileira Gasoduto Bolivia–Brazil SA (TBG). The transport fee is set in US dollars and is the sum of two other fees, the Capacity Fee and the Conveyance Fee. The Capacity Fee is adjusted annually at the rate of 40 percent of the change in the US Consumer Price Index (CPI) through 2007, and 15 percent thereafter. The Conveyance Fee is revised yearly at 100 percent of the US CPI. The final city-gate price is subject to value added and other taxes (Gama Coutinho 2000).[11] The parties agreed to review prices every five years. Petrobrás also purchased a Transport Capacity Option (TCO) for an additional 2.2 Bcm per year above the base contract volume of 5.8 Bcm per year for $383 million. $81 million of this would finance the Bolivian side of the pipeline, with the remainder dedicated to the Brazilian portion.

The TCO negotiation also involved Eletrobrás and the Brazilian National Development Bank, BNDES. These additional volumes were earmarked for thermoelectric plants that were to be installed in Mato Grosso do Sul and São Paulo. According to an agreement between Petrobrás, Eletrobrás, and BNDES, Mato Grosso do Sul plants were expected to consume about 0.73 Bcm per year and the plants in Corumbá, Campo Grande, and São Paulo 1.5 Bcm per year. BNDES financing of the TCO value spurred a significant increase of gas demand by the electrical sector.

1996 brought more formal agreements and contracts. A bilateral agreement on August 5 exempted the pipeline construction from taxes

---

[11] IEA (2003) reports that gas sales contracts are not in the public domain and reports a city-gate price for GasBol customers of "around US 3.20 mmbtu" at that time.

in both countries. The Definitive Contract for the sale and purchase of natural gas and a contract for pre-payment were signed on August 16. The key new features were three-fold: (1) YPFB would supply gas volumes under the Transport Contract Quantity (TCQ), starting at 3.3 Bcm in year one, ramping up to 6.6 Bcm by year eight, and remaining at this level for twelve years thereafter; (2) Petrobrás would take on a 0 percent take-or-pay commitment in year one, 60 percent in year two, and 80 percent in year three and thereafter; and (3) Petrobrás would receive preferential access to the first 11 Bcm per year of available Bolivian production, as well as the option to supply gas to the pipeline from those Bolivian fields where Petrobrás (or its subsidiaries) would have a participating interest. Petrobrás also committed to finance the Bolivian portion of the pipeline to the tune of $280 million over fifteen years (Petrobrás 1999; Pató 2000; de Franco 2001; Andersen and Faris 2002).

Petrobrás played a major role in securing financing for the overall project, despite doubts in the company's management about its viability. Brazilian President Cardoso had reined in Petrobrás with elimination of its oil and gas monopoly in 1994 and a 1995 Law that required all public concessions for services, including gas distribution, to be awarded via competitive bids. Cardoso and the Foreign Ministry wanted GasBol to proceed because they believed in the future of natural gas, they wanted to help Bolivia in a time of need (exports to Argentina had slowed dramatically), and they wanted to strengthen Brazil's geopolitical influence in the region. Petrobrás was pressured by the Brazilian government to rescue the project. Not only did it agree to oversee pipeline construction in Bolivia, it "basically passed through financing terms which it obtained for an equivalent amount of borrowing in the market, based on its own balance sheet" (Law and de Franco 1998; de Franco 2001; Sauer 2003).

The World Bank had been working with Brazil to develop projects for its emerging natural gas market and had already approved a São Paulo natural gas distribution project in 1989. Talks between Brazil and the World Bank about a pipeline from Bolivia to Brazil had been initiated as early as 1992 (Mauro Arbex 1992). The Paraná–Porto Alegre pipeline was also included in the Brazilian negotiations with the World Bank for financial backing of a gas pipeline.

When the completed proposal was submitted to the World Bank for consideration in December 1996, the Bank had chosen to back GasBol. Argentina's gas prices were indeed higher than Bolivia's. However, this was not the only, and perhaps not even the largest, factor in the Bank's consideration. The World Bank, and its partner, the Inter-American

Development Bank (IADB), examine multiple factors in considering projects.

The World Bank had an interest in helping to create an export alternative for Bolivian gas in the wake of its loss of the Argentine market. Increasing the participation of private investment and promoting the creation of efficient regulatory agencies in both Bolivia and Brazil were also important Bank objectives. Argentina was already relatively advanced on this path. In addition, the project had social and environmental implications that allowed the World Bank to play a larger role in human development in Bolivia and in the Amazon. Given the length of the GasBol pipeline within Brazil, there were possibilities of inter-connections to help boost the development of local and regional economies in Brazil. The international financial institutions also considered GasBol to be a key factor for creating a Southern Cone gas transportation infrastructure (Salles Abreu Passos 1998; de Franco 2001; ESMAP 2003; Sauer 2003). Argentina's attraction to the development banks on all these other points lagged significantly behind Bolivia's.

The Brazilian federal government preferred GasBol as well. Prices were obviously a factor, however, given that GasBol was over twice as long as the proposed Paraná–Porto Alegre pipeline (3,280 km vs. 1,140 km) it seems likely that the Argentine option should have been at least cost competitive. Brazilian industrialists believed the government had not been motivated to lower Argentina's prices. Brazil's agenda to bolster Mercosur and its own role as regional heavyweight also favored GasBol, albeit indirectly. Argentina was already a firm member of the regional trade zone and the promise of GasBol gave Brazil a carrot with which to further entice Bolivia to enter into the pact. For Brazil, the decision was sealed once the IADB and the World Bank (hereafter multilateral lending agencies or MLAs), opted to finance the Bolivian project (Sauer 2003).

The GasBol pipeline was built and operated by the two consortia: TBG and GTB. Each is the owner of its respective side of the pipeline, and each has Petrobrás as partner through its subsidiary Petrobrás Gas SA (Gaspetro). The large equity participation of the private sector was in part due to the demands of the main project lenders, the MLAs. The shares of different companies of TBG and GTB are presented in table 6.3.

These public companies, private enterprises, and pension fund administrators each had differing goals and stakes. To deal with this diversity of interests they created a structure for the entire project that comprised a certain degree of cross-ownership by each sponsor group. All sponsors were represented on oversight committees. However, legal

Table 6.3 *GasBol: ownership structure*

TBG (Brazilian section)		GTB (Bolivian section)	
Partners	%	Partners	%
Gaspetro: Petrobrás Gás SA	51	Gaspetro: Petrobrás Gás SA	9
BBPP Holdings Limited	29	BBPP Holdings Limited	6
Enron	4	Enron	17
Shell	4	Shell	17
Transredes	12	Transredes	51
of which: Bolivian Pension Funds	6	of which: Bolivian Pension Funds	25.5
Enron	3	Enron	12.75
Shell	3	Shell	12.75

Source: TBG website.

responsibilities for operating decisions rested with Petrobrás until TBG was solidly established (de Franco 2001).

The MLAs played a fundamental role because of the nature of Brazil's energy market and the magnitude of the project itself. Costs of the pipeline were expected to exceed $2 billion. The short maturities and terms characteristic of commercial loans on this large amount of debt would have resulted in a price level for gas that would have severely limited its ability to penetrate the market (de Franco 2001).

Accessing the resources of the MLAs was complicated. The Bolivian government's privatization push and restructuring of YPFB's role in the energy sector had produced a transportation company, GTB, in which private capital overwhelmingly predominated. Consequently, the government could not offer the sovereign guarantees required by the MLAs.

The total cost of GasBol was ultimately $2.15 billion, of which $1.72 billion was spent on the Brazilian segment and $435 million on the Bolivian segment. TBG was the main debt-holder for the project, financed with 64 percent debt and the remainder in equity. Since financing draw-downs from the MLAs occurred only one year after construction was launched, private shareholders had to absorb the initial construction costs; they also had to accept restrictive and uncertain terms for reimbursement (Gama Coutinho 2000). Table 6.4 summarizes the sources of finance for the full project.

Participation in the mega-GasBol project was inherently risky for all the parties involved. Investors had to gauge the degree of risk and seek mechanisms to hedge those risks. Despite the potential of the Brazilian

Table 6.4   *GasBol: sources of funding*

Sources	million USD	% total
IADB	240	11.1
World Bank	310	14.4
IFC	126	5.8
CAF	80	3.7
EIB	60	2.8
Finame	285	13.3
Export credit agencies	286	13.3
Total external financing (loans)	**1,387**	**64.4**
Petrobrás (BNDES–TCO)	383	17.8
Petrobrás	165	7.7
TBG and GTB Shareholders	219	10.1
Internal financing (equity)	**767**	**35.6**
Total financing requirements (internal and external)	**2,154**	**100.0**

Note:
Full detail on the terms of the loans is included in the appendix (p. 198).

Source: Gama Coutinho (2000).

natural gas market, investors faced a considerable risk in the country's gas pricing policies. The GasBol contract priced gas in US dollars and linked the price to a basket of international fuel prices. When international oil prices rise or the Brazilian currency falls, gas becomes too expensive for end users, but suppliers are caught in long-term contracts.[12]

The MLAs were arguably less concerned, as they took the long view, confident that Brazil's energy demand would grow strongly over time, despite the potential pitfalls. Private investors and Bolivian pension funds hedged their risks of investing in the pipeline itself by getting direct Brazilian government support for the project. First, they required take-or-pay contracts with Petrobrás. Still, this was not enough security and they dragged their feet on the project until multilateral financing was secured and Petrobrás assumed the major financial risks of the project (Law and de Franco 1998). With regard to investing in thermal power plants, private investors largely stayed out until the Brazilian government assumed the foreign exchange risks and Petrobrás became a co-investor. Even then, new investment in power generation was slow in coming (de Oliviera Pató 2004).

---

[12] In 2003 city-gate gas prices along the GasBol pipeline were well above prices for domestically produced Brazilian gas and Brazilian prices for fuel oil or coal at around $3.20 per mmbtu.

Petrobrás attempted to shift these risks by locking downstream parties into long-term gas purchase agreements. In addition, in 1998, when the pipeline was half-built, Petrobrás negotiated an arrangement with TBG to allow for periodic revisions of the capacity amounts reserved under the Brazil Transportation Capacity Extra (TCX) Transportation Agreement, as needed by Petrobrás. Ultimately, the capacity of the TBG pipeline to be utilized by Petrobrás in 2000, 2001, and 2002 was reduced, while the capacity usage by Petrobrás for 2004, 2005, and 2006 was increased. These adjustments left TBG exposed in the early years, but did not eliminate Petrobrás' exposure to volume risk, as it faced challenges selling even the reduced offtake requirements at the prices it was paying for the Bolivian gas (de Franco Pató 2001).[13]

Construction of the giant GasBol pipeline began in 1997 and was completed in 1999. The Petrobrás-guaranteed market for Bolivian natural gas (along with the privatization of the sector) encouraged massive investments in exploration and pipeline construction in Bolivia, which in turn produced certified (proven and probable) natural gas reserves that increased from a level around 170 Bcm before 1997 to 1,481 Bcm by January 2001 (IEA 2003). Since natural gas and petroleum are often found together, petroleum reserves also increased dramatically, from 200 million barrels in 1997 to 892 million barrels by January 2001. During the construction of the GasBol project, new reserves were discovered by a number of companies, such as Chaco, a subsidiary of BP Amoco (UK); Perez Companc (recently purchased by Petrobrás); Pluspetrol, and Andina (both Argentina); Maxus, a subsidiary of YPF (now controlled by Repsol of Spain); Petrobrás; Total (France); Mobil Oil and Tesoro (both United States). Bolivia now has the second largest gas reserves in Latin America after Venezuela and the most non-associated gas (ESMAP 2003; Andersen and Faris 2002; IEA 2003). Bolivia's reserves now make it possible to exceed the volumes that can be shipped via the GasBol pipeline. Total and Petrobrás are studying the feasibility of constructing a second gas pipeline to Brazil or doubling the capacity of the GasBol pipeline (IEA 2003) – a proposal that seems rather fanciful given the current financial woes of GasBol.

Conclusion

In the 1970s case (YABOG), the developed nature of Argentina's gas market drove Bolivian gas to Argentina instead of Brazil. At the time, Brazil's government would not invest to develop Bolivia's natural gas

[13] Petrobrás' losses on the GasBol project totaled some $1 billion in 2002 (Sauer, 2003).

exports because it perceived other options as preferable (including investment in hydropower at Itaipú and alternative energy sources such as biomass, gasohol, and domestic exploration for petroleum, which were all firmly in national hands).

Moving to the 1990s and the shift to markets in the Southern Cone, the GasAndes project beat the Transgas project because it was designed to compete. When the "market" decides, individual buyers make decisions based on price. GasAndes sought to deliver gas to a small group of customers as cheaply as possible. The Transgas project sought government protection to serve an expanded grid of customers, serving a range of objectives other than price. When the Chilean government decided to allow the "market" to decide – or more accurately *not* to provide the regulatory concessions sought by Transgas – the GasAndes project became the clear winner. Geopolitical goodwill and rising confidence in the relations between Chile and Argentina was an important factor in the two governments' willingness to let the market determine how much gas would move across their borders, at what price, and under the control of which companies.

Governments and MLAs played a larger role in the GasBol project. The Brazilian government and the World Bank sought to intervene to push forward a project that would not have advanced otherwise. Government and MLA intervention subsidized the project via preferential financing and contract guarantees. MLAs funded the GasBol project because it was seen as an important lever to induce Bolivia and Brazil to undertake economic and political reforms and spur development of the entire Southern Cone region. Because Argentina already had a mature gas market and the government's role in the economy had already been scaled back dramatically, the MLAs perceived a greater payoff in the long run for GasBol than for its Argentine rival. The decision by the World Bank not only added support to Brazil's geopolitical interests in Bolivia, but also attracted private investors to GasBol – and away from the Paraná–Porto Alegre project to bring Argentine gas to southern Brazil. Brazil pushed Petrobrás to support the GasBol project as part of its broader regional objectives and at the behest of domestic industrialists. Critically, however, the Brazilian government did not provide a domestic energy regulatory regime to support an economically viable GasBol project.

Epilogue

The Southern Cone gas markets are currently in a state of great uncertainty. In 2003 the future looked bright – the failed Transgas project was reincarnated and completed as "the Gasoducto del Pacífico," and the

Paraná–Porto Alegre project began to progress in piecemeal fashion. A project was also proposed to reverse the flow of the YABOG (as well as build a parallel pipeline), in order to send Argentine gas to Rio Grande, where it could then intercept the GasBol pipeline and supply Brazil (IEA 2003).

The collapse of the Argentine economy in 2002 produced concerns in Chile that the free market orientation of future governments in Argentina would be diminished. Chileans wanted to ensure transparency in the energy sector and equal treatment for Chilean consumers – e.g. that Argentine supplies to Chile would not be cut off (XXXVII Reunión 2002). An additional protocol to the gas agreements between the two countries was signed in 2002, creating a national information system to induce transparency in both countries.[14]

However, Chile's worst fears came to fruition in 2004, when Argentina restricted exports to Bolivia to address its own domestic gas shortage. (The shortage resulted from domestic price controls in Argentina, which in turn reduced the incentive to maintain supply.) Not only did the price of natural gas rise in Chile – along with the specter of blackouts – but a political debate developed concerning the appropriateness of depending on energy imports from Argentina.

Meanwhile, Bolivia staggered through domestic turmoil in 2003–2004 as a project to export LNG to the United States and Mexico via Chile rekindled geopolitical animosity. First, President Sánchez de Lozada was run out of the country for attempting to implement the export plan. Then, Bolivia insisted that no Bolivian gas would pass through Chilean territory until Chile provided Bolivia with some type of sovereign access to the sea as compensation for the territory lost in the War of the Pacific. Faced with Chilean refusal to discuss the issue and Argentine shortages of natural gas, Bolivia signed a contract with Argentina to supply it so long as "not 1 btu" of Bolivian gas was diverted to Chile.

The Southern Cone gas markets seem to have come full circle. If the gas markets are to recover their path towards regional integration, governments will have to pay more attention to the social and economic consequences of their energy promotion policies for their citizens. If private investors wish to tap into this bounty they will need strategies to facilitate a broader distribution of the benefits of natural gas exports.

---

[14] Government entities (the Secretary of Energy and ENERGAS in Argentina, Comisión Nacional de Energia in Chile) will be responsible for maintaining updated information and providing it in a timely fashion to those who request it. The topics covered include all regulations, participants, prices and tariffs, future plans and all new contracts, except for confidential provisions (Protocolo Adicional 2002).

APPENDIX: TERMS OF MULTILATERAL LOANS FOR GASBOL

World Bank

In December 1998, the World Bank and Petrobrás signed a loan of $130 million. The loan is for a fifteen-year period and amortized in twenty-four bi-annual portions after a three-year grace period. In December 2000, the World Bank approved partial credit guarantee (PCG) notes worth $180 million. TBG issued these notes in the US capital market. The privately placed notes are fixed-rate instruments with an eighteen-year maturity. The principal would amortize over a three-year period (years 16–18) in three equal installments. The guarantee covers 100 percent of the amortizing principal repayment at scheduled maturities on a non-accelerable basis. In addition, the World Bank would also guarantee two annual coupons on a rolling basis, which cannot be accelerated. The negotiated price has been 435 basis points (4.35 percent) above thirty-year US Treasury Notes, which is extremely advantageous to the project finances and indicates the high value added by the Bank instrument. This is the first Bank guarantee operation for Brazil.

IADB

Under Resolution No. DE/152–97 of December 17, 1997, the IADB Board of Directors authorized a loan of $240 million from the Bank's Ordinary Capital to TBG.[15] The loan was signed December 15, 1998 and had a disbursement period of three years, ending December 15, 2001. The loan is for twenty years, with amortization in thirty-three biannual installments with a three-and-a-half-year grace period. The IADB was scheduled to partially finance the construction and installation of the Corumbá–Campinas Segment of 1,256 km, and the purchase and installation of the monitoring and control system, SCADA, for the entire Brazilian portion of the pipeline.

EIB

Petrobrás' loan with the EIB, agreed to in November 1998, is over twenty years, with a five-year grace period and repayment in thirty bi-annual installments. The loan is provided in the context of the European Community's cooperation policy with third countries that have concluded cooperation agreements.[16]

---

[15] de Franco, 2001.
[16] Gazeta Mercantil (1998); Financial Times Energy Newsletters (1998).

CAF

In November 1998, the Corporación Andina de Fomento (CAF) and Petrobrás agreed on a $80 million loan to finance construction of the Bolivia–Brazil natural gas pipeline. The financing would be paid back in fifteen years with eighteen payments to be made after a six-year grace period and fixed interest rates of approximately 8 percent, based on the US Treasury rate plus an annual spread of 3 percent. The loan covers a fifteen-year period, with payments made by the Brazilian state energy company every six months after a six-year grace period. Petrobrás had earlier, in August 1998, reached a similar $85 million financing accord with CAF in order to secure rights to transport natural gas through the Bolivian section of the pipeline (Gazeta Mercantil 1998; Financial Times Energy Newsletters 1998).

OPIC

In June 1999, the US Overseas Private Investment Corporation (OPIC) approved $200 million in concessional financing to Enron for the pipeline project (Library of Congress 1999).

REFERENCES

XXXVII Reunión de Altos Ejecutivos de Empresas y Organismos de la CIER (2002). Mesas de Trabajo Distribución meeting, Chile, November

Aguila, Guillermo (2003). Marketing Director, GasAndes, interview by David Mares, Santiago, January

Andersen, Lykke E. and Robert Faris (2002). "Reducing volatility due to natural gas exports: is the answer a stabilization fund?," Andean Competitiveness Project, February

Bastos, Carlos (2003). Secretary of Energy, Government of Argentina, 1991–1996, interview by Eduardo Dubín, Buenos Aires, August

Bechelli, Carlos M. (1989). "Gas del Estado," in Centro Internacional de Información Empresaria, *Petróleo y Gas '88: Argentina, País Para Inversiones Petroleras*. Buenos Aires: Ediciones CIIE, pp. 27–33

Bem David, Lilian (1989). "Governo gaúcho assina protocolo com Argentina para construir gasoduto," *Gazeta Mercantil* May 24, p. 15

Business Latin America (1995). "Chile: Gassing up." April 24

Calvo Mirabal, Tristán (c. 1996). *Transnacionales Petroleras en Bolivia*. La Paz: Impresiones La Amistad

Cameo, Fredy (2003). Director General of Transport, TGN 1992–1997, interview by Eduardo Dubín, Buenos Aires, August

Corrales, Javier (2002). "The politics of Argentina's meltdown," *World Policy Journal*, 19(3); available at http://www.worldpolicy.org/journal/articles/wpj02-3/corrales.html

Davison, Ann, Chris Hurst, and Robert Mabro (1988). *Natural Gas: Governments and Oil Companies in the Third World*. Oxford: Oxford University Press
de Franco, Nelson (2001). "Project report: GAS SCTR DEV PROJECT," *L/C/ TF Number:* SCL-42650, World Bank, June 27
Deffarges, Etienne H. and Luiz T.A. Maurer (1993). "Growing Brazilian demand to spur gas network in South America," *Oil & Gas Journal Online*, January 19, 1993, accessed September 7, 2002
ESMAP (2003). "Cross-border oil and gas pipelines: problems and prospects." ESMAP Technical Paper, 035, June
Figueroa B., Eugenio and Birgitta Smith (2002). *Natural Gas Across the Andes: A Case Study of an International Pipeline Venture*. Edmonton: University of Alberta
Financial Times Energy Newsletters (1998). "Power In Latin America," December 1
FLACSO–Chile (1996). "Informe integración Chileno/Argentina: las dimensiones energéticas." Report, March
Gallardo, Mauricio (1995). "Gasoducto Chile–Argentina: la hora decisiva," *El Mercurio (Santiago)*, September 4
Gama Coutinho, Edna Maria B. (2000). "Infrastructure report," BNDES, Infrastructure Projects Division, 45, April
Gamarra, Eduardo A. (1996). "Bolivia: managing democracy in the 1990s," in Jorge I. Domínguez and Abraham F. Lowenthal (eds.), *Contructing Democratic Governance: South America in the 1990s*. Baltimore: Johns Hopkins University Press, pp. 72–98
Gazeta Mercantil (1998). August 17, November 24, November 26
GasAndes (1994). "Gas natural para Chile: estudio de factibilidad, resumén," September
Givogri, Carlos A, Raúl E. García, and Carlos M. Bastos (1990). "Integración gasífera con los países limítrofes," manuscript, June
IEA (2003). *World Energy Outlook*. Paris: International Energy Agency
Itaipú Dam and Environment (1996); available at http://www.american.edu/ted/Itaipú.htm
IEA (2003). *South American Gas*. Paris: OECD/IEA
Jadresic, Alejandro (1996). "Investment in natural gas pipelines in the Southern Cone of Latin America," Executive Director Jadresic Consultores Ltda. Former Minister of Energy of Chile (1994–1998). Paper presented at the Annual Conference of the Harvard–Japan Project on Energy and the Environment, Tokyo, January
Kelly, Philip and Jack Child (eds.) (1988). *Geopolitics of the Southern Cone and Antarctica*. Boulder, CO: Lynne Rienner
Ladouceur, Micheline (2000). "As petroleiras e o assalto ás terras indígenas na América Latina: os megaprojetos de gasoduto no Brasil e na Bolivia." Geografia cultural, Brasil e globalizacão, available at http://resistir.info/energia/gasoduto.html
Law, Peter and Nelson de Franco (1998). "International gas trade – the Bolivia–Brazil gas pipeline." *Viewpoint* (World Bank), Note 144
Library of Congress (1999). *Petroleum and Natural Gas*, available at http://countrystudies.us/bolivia/60.htm

Malloy, James M. (1970). *Bolivia: The Unfinished Revolution.* Pittsburgh: University of Pittsburgh Press

Mauro Arbex, José (1992). "Missão do BIRD e do BID virá ao Brasil para estudar como financiar o gasoduto." *Gazeta Mercantil,* July 1

Oil Daily (1994). August 18

de Oliveira, Adilson (2004). "Political economy of the Brazilian power industry reform." Program on Energy and Sustainable Development, Stanford University

Pató, Zsuzsanna (2000). "Piping the forest: the Bolivia–Brazil gas pipeline." CEE Bankwatch Network, January; available at http://www.bankwatch.org/downloads/pipeline.pdf

Petrobrás (1999). *Gasoducto Bolivia-Brasil.* Santa Cruz de la Sierra: PETROGASBOL, June

Protocolo Adicional al Ace No. 16 (2002). Sobre información de los mercados de petróleo y gas, y decisiones de la Autoridad con relación al intercambio energético entre las Repúblicas de Chile y Argentina." October 29

Qué Pasa (1995). "El precio de una derrota." July 22

Ramos, Joseph (1986) *Neoconservative Economics in the Southern Cone of Latin America, 1973–1983.* Baltimore: Johns Hopkins University Press

Salles Abreu Passos, Maria de Fatima (1998). "Bolivia–Brazil pipeline." *Economy and Energy,* 2(10)

Santíago (1989), in Emílio Lèbre La Rovere and Marcelo Robert (eds.), *Energia e desenvolvimento: a política energética no Brasil.* Rio de Janeiro: FINEP

Sauer, Ildo Luis (2003). Director, Gas and Energy, Petrobrás Rio de Janeiro, interview by David Mares, August

Secretaría de Hidrocarburos y Minería, Government of Argentina (1992). "Otorga autorización para exportar gas producido en la Cuenca Neuquina con destino a Chile." Resolution SHyM 61/92, June 26

Teixeira, Waldoar (1990). "Gasoduto no Sul 'é disafio á iniciativa dos gauchos'." *Gazeta Mercantil,* May 10

Thompson, Carlos (1992). "Nova investida para garantir o gasoduto." *Zero Hora,* April 19, p. 5

Vargas Salguiero, Augusto (1996). *YPFB entre nacionalistas y liberales.* La Paz: editorial, "Los Amigos del Libro"

Wells, Milton (1989). "Gás da Argentina para o Brasil?" *Gazeta Mercantil,* December 7

Zero Hora (1989). "Mendes Júnior apresenta seu projeto para gasoduto." December 12

7 International gas trade in Central Asia: Turkmenistan, Iran, Russia, and Afghanistan

Martha Brill Olcott

Introduction

This chapter describes how the landlocked energy-rich state of Turkmenistan has failed to successfully develop its vast gas reserves because of a combination of incompetent leadership, an unattractive investment climate, and competing geopolitical goals of the United States and Russia, which compounded the difficulties caused by a lingering civil war just beyond Turkmenistan's borders.

When Turkmenistan became an independent country in 1991, its President, Saparmurad Niyazov, had little preparation for the tasks that he faced. A senior Communist Party functionary, Niyazov became president of the Turkmen Soviet Socialist Republic on October 27, 1990, and was then elected to the post on June 21, 1991. In January 1994, Niyazov prolonged his rule until 2002, and on December 28, 1999 he was named President for life. The Turkmen leader likens himself to Atatürk, taking the name Turkmenbashi in 1993, but his rule is more analogous to Josef Stalin's. Niyazov's face is broadcast constantly on state television, his picture put on the front page of newspapers and on posters at principal intersections of the country's roadways. There is even a 12 meter gold-plated statue of Niyazov that is solar-driven to cast his countenance on much of downtown Ashgabat. He is the country's political and spiritual leader, the self-proclaimed author of *Rukhname* – part history, part biography, part spiritual guide, which is studied one day a week in Turkmenistan's schools.

For all the idiosyncrasies of its ruler, Turkmenistan was and still is eager to attract foreign investment in its oil and gas sectors, among the country's most bountiful resources. Turkmenistan has 2.9 Tcm of proved gas reserves and 500 million barrels of proved oil reserves (BP 2004). In the early years after the breakup of the Soviet Union,

The author wishes to thank Kate Vlatchenko for the enormous amount of work she did researching the materials in this chapter.

numerous representatives of Western firms came to Turkmenistan to assess what was on offer, and judged Turkmenistan's gas an attractive prize if new transport routes could be found to bring the bounty to foreign buyers.

Two new routes appeared to be commercially viable. The first would take Turkmen gas across Iran and then on through Turkey to markets in Europe. The second, a project originally led by Unocal, would send Turkmen gas through Afghanistan to markets in Pakistan and India. A third possibility, which offered long-term potential as new pipeline technology became available, would send Turkmen gas across Central Asia to the ports of eastern China and then possibly on to Japan. In addition, there was strong US government support for a fourth route: across the Caspian Sea then to Western markets via Baku and Tbilisi, parallel to the Baku –Tbilisi – Ceyhan oil pipeline (see the map in figure 7.1).

In the end, only a single new international pipeline was built in the 1990s, which moves Turkmen gas from Korpedzhe, on Turkmenistan's Caspian coast, to Kurt-Kui in northern Iran. Larger Turkmen – Iranian and trans-Afghan pipeline projects were put on hold. At least for now, Turkmenistan is forced to market the bulk of its production through Russia, under terms that favor Russian interests over Turkmen ones (EIU 2003).

The case of Turkmenistan is an interesting one. Geopolitical considerations have played an enormous role in the postponement of Turkmenistan's two major new pipelines, through Iran and through Afghanistan, as well as fueling the decision to build the smaller Korpedzhe – Kurt-Kui export line. Plans for the larger Turkmen – Iranian – Turkish pipeline collapsed largely because of the near impossibility of getting international financing for projects in Iran due to continuing US sanctions against that country. Building the smaller pipeline became a way of asserting the importance of Turkmen – Iranian friendship and economic cooperation and signaling the goal of reducing dependence on Russia. Unocal abandoned its plans for oil and gas pipelines to move oil and gas across Afghanistan in 1998, largely because of unstable internal conditions. Even in the absence of these geopolitical factors, Turkmenistan's new pipeline projects still would have faced enormous challenges given the number of political and economic risks associated with doing business in Turkmenistan as well as in the transit countries.

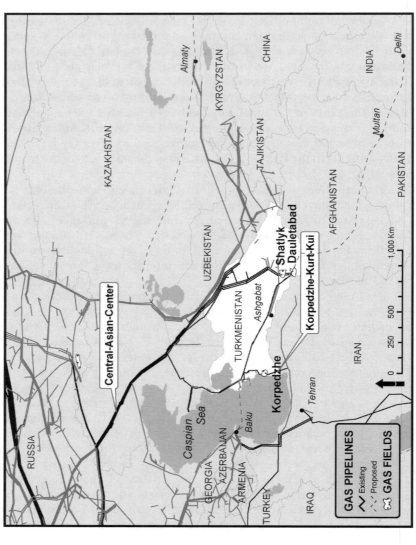

Figure 7.1. Existing and proposed Turkmen gas export pipeline routes.

Turkmenistan's Economic and Political Life

Turkmenistan became an independent country on December 25, 1991, following the dissolution of the Soviet Union.[1] Its constitution (adopted in May 1992 and amended in 1995, 1999, and 2003) concentrates political power in the office of the President. There is no provision for a Vice President or a Prime Minister. In the event of the death of the President, power is handed over to the chairman of the legislature, who must hold new elections within two months. The President nominates all the candidates for the People's Council (Halk Maslakhaty), a cumbersome 2,507-member body that superseded the fifty-member Parliament in 2003; he chooses the members of the Cabinet of Ministers, the country's leading judges, and the heads of the provincial, municipal, and local administrations.

Niyazov frequently fires political appointees to ensure the loyalty of those that remain. An alleged *coup* against him in November 2002, purportedly led by former Foreign Minister Boris Shikhmuradov, led to the arrest of dozens of prominent figures and many members of their families. There have been periodic arrests and smaller purges since. Shikhmuradov had been instrumental in attracting foreign investment to Turkmenistan's oil and gas sector. After his dismissal,[2] Niyazov further increased his direct control of the country's economy. No decision on foreign investment can be confirmed without his approval, and the allocation of foreign exchange credits requires his personal consent. Niyazov, who is said to take advice from a changing coterie of foreign businessmen,[3] is generally distrustful of international economic advice.

The country's GDP is export-driven, with the principal commodities – gas, oil, and cotton – all still largely under state control (see figures 7.2 and 7.3). After several years of declining GDP, Turkmenistan has begun to report high rates of economic growth due to increased gas exports

[1] Turkmenistan declared its independence on October 27, 1991, but did not seek to exercise the powers of a sovereign nation until December 25, 1991. Until this time Turkmenistan's oil and gas sectors were under the direct supervision of Moscow.

[2] Shikhmuradov became Deputy Prime Minister in 1992 and Foreign Minister in January 1993. In July 2000 he was appointed as Turkmenistan's special representative on Caspian affairs, and later served as ambassador to China. He resigned his posts in October 2001 and formed an opposition party, the National Democratic Movement of Turkmenistan.

[3] Shortly after independence this circle included former Secretary of State Alexander Haig, then it was said to be dominated by Yosef Maiman, head of Israel's Merhav corporation, and more recently it is rumored to be centered around a small group of Turkish businessmen.

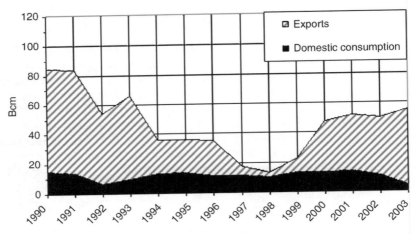

Figure 7.2. Turkmenistan: natural gas balance, 1990–2003.
Consumption and exports are roughly equivalent to net gas production, not including gas used in oil production or flared. Precipitous declines in gas exports in 1995 and 1998 resulted from disputes with Russia over payments and prices. In late 2004, negotiations with Russia again stalled gas shipments completely and reliable data for shipments are not available. New contracts were signed with Gazprom in 2005 and Ukraine in 2006 for future gas exports. Consistent and reliable data are difficult for Turkmenistan.

Sources: EIA (2003); IEA (2003); BP (2004).

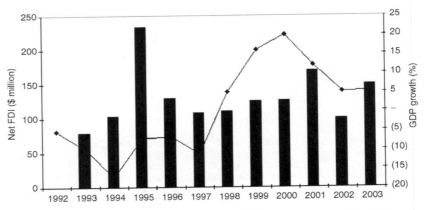

Figure 7.3. Turkmenistan: key economic indicators, 1992–2003.
Solid bars are net FDI in million $US, shown on the left-hand axis. Annual growth in GDP is represented by the line with units on the right-hand axis.

Sources: IMF (1999); EIU (2001b); EBRD (2003); WEC (2003).

Table 7.1 *Turkmenistan: trade balance, 1997–2001*

Exports of goods (million US$)	1997	1998	1999	2000	2001
Natural gas	274	72	392	1,250	1,490
Share of total (%)	*35*	*12*	*33*	*50*	*57*
Oil and refined products	284	264	365	750	680
Share of total (%)	*37*	*43*	*31*	*30*	*26*
Cotton fiber	87	135	214	300	80
Share of total (%)	*11*	*22*	*18*	*12*	*3*
Total including all other goods	**774**	**614**	**1,187**	**2,506**	**2,620**

Source: EIU (2003).

through Russia, but all economic data coming from the Republic should be viewed with suspicion.

In recent years, Russia's Gazprom has generally purchased Turkmen gas on a half-barter, half-cash basis, with the price of gas set through accords. But the real price of the gas is very difficult to measure, given the opaque nature of the barter transactions; the Russians provide the evaluations of the technical assistance and consumer goods that constitute the trade. Turkmen gas exports to Ukraine are also on a partly cash, partly barter basis (ICAR 2003). Until 2003, the trade with Ukraine was largely conducted through the Florida-based International Trading Energy and Resources Association (Itera) (Moscow Times 2003), the key officials of which are from Turkmenistan.[4] But in December 2004, Turkmenistan began aggressively pushing both countries to move to a cash-only basis of payment.

Agriculture, especially cotton cultivation, remains the country's major source of employment, and most agricultural workers continue to live on Soviet-era collective farms. The Turkmen government sets production quotas for farmers, as well as a low state purchase price for raw cotton. This maximizes profit from transfer pricing, and much of the international trade in cotton is said to be controlled by the President's family.

In recent years, the amount of cotton harvested has been substantially less than what the state projected, but the Turkmen government continues to report increases in the standard of living (see table 7.1). The average *per capita* income in Turkmenistan is $950 USD, and this includes the market value of a host of state subsidies on communal

---

[4] These include its president Igor Makarov and Valery Otchertsov, Chairman of Itera's management board, who served as Minister of Economy and Finance and Vice-Chairman of the Cabinet of Ministers of Turkmenistan. For details on Itera see the company's website: *http://66.129.88.179/index2.htm* and chapter 5 in this volume.

services, foodstuffs, and energy supplies (EIU 2003; World Bank 2003). These generous subsidies, combined with the dilapidated state of infrastructure in the gas and power supply system, have created unsustainable increases in domestic natural gas consumption.

According to the IEA, Turkmenistan depends upon natural gas for 80 percent of primary energy supplies; about 55 percent of the electric power generated in the country goes to various industrial usages with the remainder largely absorbed by subsidized residential use (IMF 1999; EIU 2003; IEA 2003). Current domestic gas consumption is about 10 Bcm per annum, and the World Bank estimates that the Turkmen government spent $600 million on subsidies to the energy sector in 2000, money the Bank feels would be better spent addressing the country's deteriorating energy infrastructure (EIU 2001a). But as recently as August 2003, President Niyazov reaffirmed that natural gas would be supplied to Turkmenistan's population free of charge (RFE/RL 2003).

Turkmenistan's private sector accounts for less than a third of the country's GDP and the participation of ordinary Turkmen in the private sector is severely hampered by sharp restrictions on access to foreign exchange. The difference between offered and market exchange rates provides a valuable "rent" for a privileged few. The banking sector is weak and state-dominated. Nominally, the Turkmen government is committed to both privatization and land reform, and the government has promulgated a series of laws designed to encourage private investment in the country; in practice, however, Turkmenistan's legal system offers little protection for private property. This environment has stifled FDI, even in the attractive oil and natural gas sectors; FDI has been flat since the mid-1990s (see figure 7.3). Regardless of legal provisions to the contrary, the government insists on maintaining majority stakes along with managerial control of all major projects.

Turkmenistan's oil sector is less attractive than that of either Azerbaijan or Kazakhstan. Of the three, it has the smallest proved oil reserves and the lowest annual oil production.[5] Turkmenistan's two largest oil projects both have foreign partners, but none of the oil "majors" is currently involved in the country (see appendix Table 7.A).[6] The

[5] Estimates range from 0.5 billion to 1.7 billion barrels of proved oil reserves, and Turkmenistan may have potential oil reserves of 38 billion barrels, making estimated Turkmen oil reserves slightly smaller than Azerbaijan's. Turkmenistan produced 159,000 B/d in 2001, with estimated production slated to grow to 1 million b/d by 2010 (EIA 2003).

[6] Cheleken, being developed in cooperation with Dragon Oil, produces 10,000 b/d, and Nebit Dag, in which average production is 13,650 b/d, is being worked in cooperation with Burren Oil. For a list of foreign firms involved in the oil and gas sector in Turkmenistan, see appendix Table 7.A.

government has repeatedly stated that its major oil and gas assets will not be privatized for at least ten to fifteen years (RFE/RL 2001).

The unresolved legal status of mineral rights in the Caspian Sea has further slowed foreign investment in offshore oil and gas resources. In May 2003, Russia, Azerbaijan, and Kazakhstan divided the northern two-thirds of the sea into three parts, giving Kazakhstan 27 percent, Russia 19 percent, and Azerbaijan 18 percent. Turkmenistan and Iran both refused to sign the May 2003 agreement (EIA 2003). Turkmenistan claims ownership of the Kyapaz and Chirag fields, which Azerbaijan says lie within its sector of the Caspian Sea. There have also been disputes over the boundaries between the Iranian and Turkmen sectors of the Caspian Sea. Uncertainty over borders and the sharing of revenues has stalled development of any of Turkmenistan's offshore oil and gas reserves. Interest in the thirty different blocks that the Turkmen government placed on offer has been minimal (EIU 2003). The Turkmen government has been more successful in attracting investment in improving its refining capacity. The Turkmenbashi refinery, with a throughput capacity of 116,500 b/d is currently in the second stage of its $1.5 billion modernization process.

Overview of Turkmenistan's Gas Industry and the Legal Regime that Governs It[7]

Turkmenistan has proven gas reserves of approximately 2.86 Tcm in assets spread across some 150 separate oil and gas deposits (EIA 2002) (see appendix Table 7.B). The exploitation of Turkmenistan's gas fields began in earnest in the 1950s, well after the gas industry was established in the Russian Volga region (AIC 1995; IEA 1998). New fields continue to be discovered, and since the mid-1990s the Turkmen government has identified seventeen new natural gas deposits, some of which have begun to be developed (EIA 2002). In addition, the President's economic program also calls for Turkmengaz, the state-run company, to step up exploratory work for the identification of new sites.

The Turkmen government has sought to provide a legal regime that would attract foreign investment in its oil and gas sectors. Despite the promulgation of laws, the government provides no real protection for investments. The existing legislation includes a Law on Foreign Investment, enacted in May 1992 and amended in April 1993. This

---

[7] In-depth detail on the legal regime for Turkmenistan's oil and gas resources can be found in Olcott (2004).

law guarantees that foreign investments shall not be subject to nation-alization or requisition. Foreign firms are granted concessions of between five and forty years for onshore and offshore areas containing natural resources, as well as for investment in enterprises that explore, develop, extract, and use natural resources. Foreign firms may carry out their operations based on licenses extended through tenders, as well as through direct negotiations. Foreign firms working with domestic companies are eligible to receive licenses in the "Program of Social and Economic Development of Oil and Gas Industry through 2010" that was adopted by the government in 2001 (World Oil 2001).

The Law on Foreign Investment offers foreign investors an anti-discrimination pledge, promising that they will not be subject to government-imposed conditions that are less favorable than those applied to national investors. The Law also includes a stabilization clause that provides foreign investors with a ten-year grace period during which they will not be affected by changes in the legal regime.

The Law on Hydrocarbon Resources (the Petroleum Law) of March 1997 declares hydrocarbon resources to be national property and assigns the right to manage them to the Cabinet of Ministers, which is also responsible for an overall strategy for the development of the country's hydrocarbon reserves. The law permits foreign companies to be involved in oil exploration and production, through the negotiation of production-sharing arrangements (PSAs) and joint-venture agreements (JVAs), and describes various types of licenses that can be issued on the basis of either a tender or through direct negotiations.

A June 1997 Presidential decree on "The steps to be taken in order to implement the Law of Turkmenistan on Hydrocarbon Resources (the Petroleum Law)" provided for the creation of a "competent body" that would be responsible for negotiations in this sector, headed by a deputy Chairman of the Council of Ministers, which was to establish rules and regulations for the development of hydrocarbon fields. But in reality no one but the President is involved in these key decisions.

Turkmen legislation also sets the tax structure for projects, but leaves wide room for negotiation. Legislation stipulates a maximum profit tax of 25 percent and enumerates tax-deductible expenses. However, the law also allows taxable profit to be determined via licensing and individual PSAs. The size of royalties is also to be determined in each agreement, and has ranged from 3 to 15 percent. The government also provided investors with model PSA agreements and provides that the state pipeline company set a transportation tariff.

Turkmenistan also has a value added tax (VAT) of 20 percent. While oil and gas production are generally not subject to VAT, exports can be. However, oil exported by a company working under a PSA or JVA regime is supposed to be free of VAT assessment. The law is not clear about the export of production, however, and lawyers who have worked in Turkmenistan have found difficulties applying the law to the oil and gas sectors (Varanese and James 2001).

Foreign investors in Turkmenistan are guaranteed the right of international arbitration.[8] However, Turkmen legislation sharply limits the applicability of these rights. Both the Rules and Regulations and the Petroleum Law fail to provide a specific provision binding Turkmenistan to the enforcement of awards rendered in the arbitration of disputes, and there is no express sovereign immunity waiver contained in either of these pieces of legislation, or in any other law of the Turkmen republic (Varanese and James 2001). Lawyers working in the Caspian oil sector are also mindful of the initial weak track record of the Turkmen government, which has been subject to – or threatened with – international arbitration in a number of its early contracts, including some related to the Trans-Afghan pipeline projects discussed below. Turkmenistan is a contracting party to the International Center for the Settlement of Investment Disputes (ICSID) and is also a signatory to the 1994 Energy Charter Treaty.

The warnings of the US government to those wanting to do business in Turkmenistan could not be more explicit. The following is an excerpt from the August 2002 investment climate statement from the US Embassy in Ashgabat (US Embassy 2003):

The government of Turkmenistan has a history of capricious and arbitrary expropriation of property, local businesses and individuals, including foreign investors. Such actions have included declaring ownership certification granted by former government officials invalid without supporting reason. Further, the government has often refused to pay any compensation, much less fair market value, when exercising the right of eminent domain. Most notably, the government expropriated a Western oil company's compound in Ashgabat in response to doing an arbitration case with the company in an internationally recognized forum . . . Finally, a change in the leadership of the government entity that signed

---

[8] Article 55 of the Petroleum Law gives contractors protections that are "in accordance with international law" in addition to the protections that are stated in the license and agreements that they negotiate. Most importantly, the investor's tax liabilities are considered to be "frozen" at the moment of signing a petroleum operations agreement. Similarly, Article 56 expressly allows parties to seek international arbitration for resolution of any disputes "associated with issuance, refusal to issue, suspension of effect and/ or annulment of a license, as well as associated with performance of a contract."

the original contract often triggers a government call for reevaluating an entire contract including profit distribution, management responsibilities, and payment schedules.

Building New Pipelines from Turkmenistan

Turkmenistan – Iran – Turkey

The government of the Islamic Republic of Iran looked at the independence of Turkmenistan as creating new opportunities for its own gas industry. Like the Russians, the Iranians believed that the potential synergies between their country and Turkmenistan could help promote the expansion of their own role as a global gas provider. The construction of a pipeline linking the Kricheh (Korpedzhe) gas deposit in western Turkmenistan to Kurt-Kui in northern Iran was intended to be the first step in creating a long-lasting energy partnership between the two countries.

Iranian officials viewed the collapse of the Soviet Union as an opportunity for major geopolitical realignments in the region, and they worked hard to ensure that Teheran would be at the center of them. They recognized that Turkey had competing views of how these geopolitical alignments might evolve, but Iranian officials believed that Turkmenistan's gas created an opportunity for the two countries to work in concert.

The Turks were not averse to considering Iran as a potential source of gas for the Turkish market and for transit across Turkey to European markets. To this end, Turkey and Iran signed a $23 billion agreement for the supply of gas from Iran (including Turkmen gas) to Turkey in August 1996. This was an agreement in principle only; it created no real financial obligation on either side.

The first formal Iranian proposal for a pipeline came in August 1994, was finalized in January 1995, and was initially conceived in the context of discussions on building a gas pipeline to link Turkmenistan to Turkey along a 1,400 km route through Iran which would allow a subsequent link to European gas markets. The broader project was one that had strong support in both Iran and Turkey. The 1420 mm pipeline was expected to take between four and eight years to build, with an eventual capacity of 28 Bcm per year (18 Bcm for the Turkish market and 10 Bcm for the European market). The overall project was estimated to cost between $1.6 and $2.5 billion. The pipeline project designers envisioned that Turkmen gas would provide 2 Bcm per year in the start-off phase, growing to 7 Bcm per year, and that this would be supplemented by 3 Bcm per year of Iranian gas.

Turkey was the major intended offtaker for the proposed project. The country's demand for gas was expected to rise rapidly, from 9 Bcm in 1997 to 52 Bcm in 2010, and studies suggested that gas would be delivered to the Turkish border at prices of $2.60–$2.70 per mmbtu (Lelyveld 1997; Joseph 1998). After the Turkish economic crisis of the late 1990s, such estimates were scaled sharply downward, and the Turkish market faced a glut of supplies.

Interestingly, one of the first discussions of the Turkmenistan – Iran – Turkey pipeline was sponsored by former US Secretary of State Alexander Haig, who helped arrange a visit by President Niyazov to Washington, DC in 1993, and who formed a consortium to advance the idea of building a small pipeline to carry modest amounts of Turkmen gas across Iran, to Turkey. Haig was reported to have sought and won endorsements from energy ministers in Kazakhstan, Iran, and Turkey for his venture, which was registered in the British Virgin Islands (Ottaway and Morgan 1998).

The Turkmen were keen on the project to ship gas to Iran. In February 1995 the Interstate Council on Export of Oil and Gas, a committee formed of the energy ministers of Iran, Kazakhstan, Russia, Turkey, and Turkmenistan, as well as representatives from Chevron, Mannesmann, and Mobil Oil, formed an international joint-stock company, the Turkmenistan Transcontinental Pipeline (TTP), to plan, finance, construct, and operate this 1400 km pipeline with an expected capacity of 15 to 25 Bcm per year (FBIS 1995). Thirty-five percent of financing was to come from the Interstate Council and 65 percent from international sources, including the World Bank, the European Bank for Reconstruction and Development (EBRD), and J-EXIM of Japan (Albion 1995). But in 1996, the Turkmen government backed away from the project when it became clear that continued US opposition to projects involving Iran meant that it would not get international funding (EIU 1997a).

In October 1995, certain that the larger pipeline project would be slow to develop, the National Iranian Oil Company of Iran (NIOC) decided to begin construction of the Korpedzhe – Kurt-Kui pipeline (IRNA 1996). It signed a twenty-five-year contract with the Turkmen government to ensure its supply (CBR 1998).

The Korpedzhe–Kurt-Kui pipeline had a very limited goal – to facilitate the supply of gas to a remote part of Iran, where annual demand was 6 Bcm per year (Lelyveld 1997). The project was a modest one, to build 200 km of 1,000 mm diameter pipeline, at a cost of roughly $190 million. The pipeline would initially carry 4 Bcm per year (8 Bcm at peak capacity) and with the potential to later expand to 13 Bcm with added compression (PFC 1997a). The cost of the

Korpedzhe – Kurt-Kui pipeline was less than building a new pipeline to link northwestern Iran to the nearest domestic natural gas source in Iran.

Iran agreed to finance 90 percent of the cost of the pipeline, to be paid back through gas deliveries over a three year period (IRNA 1997). The contractual price for Turkmen gas was set at $1.20 per mmbtu ($40 per 1,000 m^3), with 35 percent of the gas allocated for repayment of the loan during the first three years. The loan related solely to the 140 km of pipeline in Turkmen territory. Iran also agreed to bear the cost of further developing the Korpedzhe gas field, and the NIOC constructed a facility at the Korpedzhe field to process gas prior to pipeline transport; the payback for the loan has yet to be announced. The financial terms for the Iranians were even better than the paperwork of the transaction implies: the $190 million cost was computed in inflated local currency but was paid for in gas, which the Iranians planned to sell to Turkey through a series of gas swaps. Turkmen gas would be used in Iran, freeing Iran's domestic supplies for export.

The pipeline was opened in December 1997. But the amount of gas transported through the pipeline has fallen short of the Turkmen government's planned goals. In 2000, Iran imported 3 Bcm; Iranian imports rose sharply in early 2003 (to about 6.5 Bcm) and total shipments from Turkmenistan to Iran were set to top 7 Bcm in 2004, but the pipeline is not consistently filled to its 10 Bcm annual capacity (EIU 2003; Turkmenistan Oil and Gas Industry 2003).

For the Iranian government, the size of this project was so small that it was able to view it as a form of development aid, effectively offered to cement relations between the two states. But the construction of the pipeline did little to satisfy Iran's desire to be a major regional player in Central Asia and to use its relationship with Turkmenistan as a launching pad for this goal.

Iran had hoped that the revitalization of the Economic Cooperation Organization (ECO) would help facilitate Teheran's plans for dominance in the region in general and for marketing Turkmenistan's gas supply in particular. Charter members Iran, Pakistan, and Turkey founded ECO for the purpose of sustainable socio-economic development of the Member States. In 1992, the ECO was expanded to include seven new members: the Islamic State of Afghanistan, Republic of Azerbaijan, Republic of Kazakhstan, Kyrgyz Republic, Republic of Tajikistan, Turkmenistan, and the Republic of Uzbekistan. The May 1997 ECO summit in Ashgabat was used as an occasion for the Presidents of Turkmenistan, Turkey, and Iran to sign a MOU which provided for the eventual export of up to 30 Bcm per year of Turkmen gas to be transited across Iran to Turkey. Turkmenistan's gas was to come from the large Dauletabad gas field (near Turkmenistan's border with Afghanistan and Iran), the resource for any major new pipeline from Turkmenistan (this field also figured in the Unocal pipeline proposal that was being developed at the same time).

This underscores the degree to which the development of pipelines from Turkmenistan was a zero-sum game throughout, in which one route (be it Russia, Iran, or Afghanistan) would "win" and all other major pipeline schemes would be abandoned.

From the Iranian point of view, the planned pipeline was particularly attractive as it would have maximized the profitability of Iranian gas via the planned gas swap arrangement. Thus, the Iranians pushed this planned pipeline project more than the Turkmen did. From the onset, the Turkmen seemed at least as interested in the Afghan route as in the prospect of transit across Iran. Although Teheran might have had the ability to fund the Turkmenistan – Iran pipeline using its own resources, it is a major point of contention among members of that country's oil industry that Iran decided to seek the development of the pipeline through the creation of an international consortium, and to integrate this pipeline into the broader plans for the development of Iran's own vast reserves. The alternative would have been to "capture" Turkmen reserves through a stage-by-stage process of building new pipeline links, something that the Iranian government might well have had the resources to support through the first stage of long-term Turkmen asset "capture."

The Iranian government had correctly assessed the level of international interest in the project. Royal Dutch Shell was quick to express interest in the project, as did Snamprogetti (Italy) and GdF. This made the project vulnerable to US censure, the United States having in 1996 banned foreign investment of more than $40 million in the Iranian energy sector as part of the Iran and Libya Sanctions Act (ILSA).

In August 1997 Shell submitted its proposal for construction of a natural gas pipeline to President Niyazov. Despite Washington's announcement in October 1997 that ILSA sanctions applied to the project, in December 1997 Iran, Turkmenistan, and Turkey signed an agreement with Royal Dutch Shell for the latter to prepare a feasibility study and an export scheme for this pipeline project. That same month, President Niyazov publicly endorsed the idea of Shell taking the lead in the construction of this project, and in February 1998 Shell began a formal feasibility study for this project (CBR 1997; EIU 1997b). The feasibility study for the 3,800 km gas pipeline running from the Shatlyk gas field across northern Iran, on to Dogubayazid in Turkey, and then through to Bulgaria to allow it eventual access to the German market was completed by 1999. But after years of maintaining a small office in Turkmenistan, Shell withdrew from the country in April 2003 (Vremya Novostey 2003).

Many factors contributed to Shell's decision. Turkmenistan was certainly a difficult country to do business in, and there was little incentive for Shell to remain in Ashgabat solely to try to gain control of transit rights to Turkmenistan's reserves. But Iran was a much bigger prize, and the small investment in Turkmenistan would prove to be a bargain if it helped Shell even marginally to position itself to take a commanding role in Iran.

At first it looked as if Washington would support the pipeline project, as it was in line with the Clinton administration's policy of creating multiple pipelines for the export of Caspian oil and gas. Moreover, the design of the project allowed the administration to view this as construction of a pipeline that transited Iran, rather than supporting the development of Iran's gas industry itself. Part of the reason for the optimism on the part of the pipeline project sponsors was that in early July 1997 the US Department of State dropped its earlier objections to a new section of pipeline between Iran and Turkey, which was promoted by the Turkish state gas company Botas, as well as National Iranian Gas Company (NIGC).

The Turkish proponents of the plan successfully argued that in fact three separate pipelines were being built, two across Turkey and one across Iran. The Iranian pipeline went from Tabriz to the Turkish border – some 270 km – and was to be financed by the Iranian government and state companies. The first Turkish pipeline, a 300 km pipeline from the Iranian border to Erzurum, had a price tag of $117.5 million and would be financed and constructed by a local Turkish consortium. The longer Turkish pipeline, from Erzurum to Ankara via Sivas, a route of 874 km, cost roughly $500 million, and was to be financed by bids sought both locally and internationally (Alexander's Gas and Oil Connections 1997). Botas began construction on the Turkish pipeline in November 1998. The construction works, undertaken under five sections (Dogybayazit – Erzurum, Erzurum – Sivas, Sivas – Kayseri, Kayseri – Anakar, and Kayser – Konya), were completed and gas delivery from Iran was initiated on December 10, 2001 (Lelyveld 1999). But by the time the pipeline opened, the market for Iranian (and Turkmen) gas in Turkey was declining, in part due to the Turkish economic crisis. Even more importantly there were competing sources of gas planned that were potentially more attractive to Turkey, such as through the US-supported Baku – Tbilisi – Erzurum gas pipeline (to be operational by 2006), and Gazprom's "Blue Stream" pipeline under the Black Sea (operational since February 2003). For a detailed description of the Turkish "gas bubble", see chapter 5.

The Trans-Afghan Pipeline

Washington's posture on Iran made plans for the development of a Trans-Afghan pipeline more attractive than exports through Iran, although not necessarily more feasible. The Clinton administration was very supportive of the idea that a US firm could help the Turkmen government break Russia's hold on the export of their gas, for much the same reason that it was supporting the transport of Azerbaijan's (and if possible Kazakhstan's) oil and gas via Turkey.

The initial proposal for the development of a Trans-Afghan pipeline, though, was made by Bridas for an Argentine firm whose chief executive officer, Carlos Bulgheroni, began courting Turkmenistan's President Niyazov in 1991. The entire saga of Bridas in Turkmenistan is steeped in controversy.

Bridas acquired a 75 percent stake in the Yashlar natural gas field in southeastern Turkmenistan after an international tender in 1991, as well as the rights to develop the Keimir oil field. Bridas claimed that Yashlar held 736 Bcm of reserves (Gopul and Ivanov 1997; Pope 1998); Keimir was reported to have 89 million barrels of oil and 18 Bcm of natural gas (Alexander's Gas and Oil Connections 2001). Shortly thereafter, in 1993, Bulgheroni began lobbying the Turkmen president to build a $1.9 billion pipeline along a 1,400 km stretch from Yashlar across Afghanistan to Pakistan. The projected price of this pipeline eventually rose to $2.5 billion (PFC 1997b).

According to *The Wall Street Journal's* Hugh Pope, Bulgheroni was sent to Pakistan in June 1994 as a special emissary of the Turkmen government, and in March 1995 Turkmenistan and Pakistan agreed to conduct a feasibility study on the pipeline (Pope 1998). Bridas committed to complete the pipeline within two-and-a-half years of beginning construction, with the expectation that it would be operational by early 2001. Bridas signed a contract to deliver 20 Bcm of gas to Pakistan on a take-or-pay basis and planned to supplement Yashlar gas with gas from Iran, Uzbekistan, and Afghanistan (*AFT* 1997).

But in October 1995 President Niyazov signed an agreement with Unocal and its partner in the project, Delta Oil of Saudi Arabia, providing support for Unocal and its partners to explore a trans-Afghan pipeline project to move Turkmenistan's gas to south Asia (World Press 2000). These negotiations came as a surprise to Bridas, which thought it had a firm commitment from Turkmenistan's government for it to lead a pipeline consortium.

Bridas' problems with the Turkmen government preceded, but were likely not wholly unrelated to, Unocal's growing interest in Turkmenistan. The Argentine firm was prevented from exporting oil from the Keimir block in 1994, although exports resumed again in 1995 after the share of profits to Bridas was lowered. Then, in November 1995, the Turkmen government declared Bridas' licenses and contracts to be "unacceptable," and announced that the Keimir joint venture would be terminated in 2000 rather than 2018, insuring that Bridas' investment would never return a profit (Pope 1998). In December 1995 Bridas was forced to halt oil exports from Keimir, which was producing over 15,000 barrels of oil per day. Finally, in early 1996 the Turkmen government began to seize Bridas' wells.

The Argentine firm, which had invested over $400 million in Turkmenistan, decided to take its case to international arbitration, and also filed suit against Unocal in a Texas court, alleging that the company had unfairly influenced the Turkmen government against them (EIA 1997). An international arbitration court dismissed the claim on October 5, 1998, but in September 2000 the court ruled in favor of Bridas in its claims against the Turkmen government, which was ordered to pay the firm $600 million in damages (Alexander's Gas and Oil Connections 2001). Although Bridas sold off most of its assets in Argentina to Amoco in 1996, it continues to keep its plans for a Trans-Afghan Pipeline on its website and to seek payment of damages.

While legal action was still pending, in August 1996 Unocal, Delta, Gazprom, and Turkmenrosgaz signed a memorandum on a $2 billion project to ship gas from Turkmenistan's Dauletabad field to Pakistan via Afghanistan, and established a consortium to control this trade. Unocal and Delta jointly held an 85 percent interest, Gazprom a 10 percent interest, and Turkmenrosgaz a 5 percent interest (OMRI 1996). In July 1997 officials from Turkmenistan and Pakistan, as well as representatives from Unocal and Delta, signed a formal agreement to build a 1,450 km pipeline to move 20 Bcm per year from the Dauletabad field to Pakistan. The agreement called for a formal consortium to be formed by October 1997 and for construction of the pipeline to begin by December 1998, with all work to be completed by 2001. The agreement also made reference to the building of a possible 640 km spur to New Delhi. The total cost of the project was estimated to be between $2 billion and $2.7 billion (EIA 1997).

Table 7.2 *CentGas: ownership structure*

Shareholder	%
Unocal	54.1
Delta Oil	15.0
Inpex	7.2
Itocho	7.2
Government of Turkmenistan	7.0
Huyundai Engineering of South Korea	5.5
Crescent Group of Pakistan	4.0
Total	**100.0**

Source: Newsbase (1999).

In September 1997, Unocal and Pakistan concluded a thirty-year gas pricing agreement, in which Pakistan agreed to pay an upper limit of $2.05 and a lower limit of $1.60 per mmbtu of gas delivered to Multan, Pakistan (see figure 7.1). The price of gas included a 15 cent per mmbtu transit fee for Afghanistan, a preliminary figure reached without consultation with members of the Taliban government. The Taliban took offense at this, and were subsequently quoted as saying that this transit fee was too low and that they would not negotiate further with Unocal (PFC 1997b).

Unocal, though, continued to try and solidify the project. In October 1997, it formed the Central Asian Gas Pipeline consortium (CentGas), in which Gazprom originally had a 10 percent interest before it withdrew. The final project ownership was apportioned as shown in table 7.2.

The CentGas pipeline was to have a diameter of 1,200 mm and to extend 1,271 km from the Afghanistan – Turkmenistan border, generally following the Heart–Kandahar road through Afghanistan, crossing into Pakistan in the vicinity of Quetta, and terminating in Multan, where it would be connected to an existing Pakistani pipeline system (see figure 7.1). As part of the project, Turkmenistan pledged to construct a pipeline that would link with the CentGas line at the border and stretch 169 km to the Dauletabad field. The complete pipeline was to have five compressor stations, and was priced at $1.9 billion with an additional $600 million necessary for an extension into India.

Pakistan was strongly supportive of the project, as the Pakistanis expected that demand for natural gas would rise by 50 percent between 2003 and 2006, and the government of Pakistan hoped to make gas "the fuel of choice" for future electric power generation projects (Kabir

2003). Meeting this goal required that imports of natural gas increase sharply. Official Pakistan estimates of the time put the need for imports at 10 Bcm per year by 2002 and 31 Bcm per year by 2010 (EIA 1999).

The trans-Afghan pipeline was only one of the gas import options that the government of Pakistan was considering. An alternative pipeline, known as the Dolphin Project, was proposed to run from the North Dome gas field in Qatar across the Arabian Peninsula to Oman, then under the Arabian Sea to Pakistan, a total distance of some 1,610 km. The United Offsets Group, a UAE state-owned corporation, signed a preliminary MOU for this project with Qatar, Oman, and Pakistan in 1999. The Qatar – UAE – Oman segment of the plan has moved forward, but with little serious progress on the onward connection to Pakistan (see chapter 8).

There are also ongoing discussions about building a pipeline from Iran's huge South Pars offshore gas field to Pakistan, which could carry 17 Bcm per year. Shell, Statoil, and Broken Hill Proprietary (BHP) are all hoping to partner with Iran's NIOC in a consortium for this project. Shell also hopes to win Phases 13 and 14 of the project for LNG production and GTL development (EIA 2003).

Pakistan's domestic gas market is also being transformed by the discovery of new gas fields within the country, which has weakened demand for imported gas in Pakistan and increased the need for access to the Indian market to insure the profitability of any trans-Afghan pipeline. Most analysis suggests that Indian natural gas demand is sufficient, as Indian demand for imported gas is expected to soar. According to Indian government projections made in 2001, gas consumption was projected to rise from 19 Bcm per year in 1995, to 23 Bcm in 2000, 57 Bcm in 2005, and 75 Bcm per year in 2010 (Government of India 2000). However, recent domestic finds in India, along with the opening of two LNG terminals there, will probably blunt some of the drive for imported pipeline gas.

The CentGas project was introduced at a time when there was a lot of government and international interest in creating an environment of confidence-building between these two states in the hope that this would contribute to resolving the crisis in Kashmir. However, relations between India and Pakistan deteriorated somewhat in the period during which the CentGas pipeline project was being actively considered as the Kashmir tensions rose.

There remain a number of contending projects being developed to serve the Indian market, most of which have less political risk than the Trans-Afghan pipeline. There are variations of development plans for South Pars in Iran that call for shipping gas to India via Pakistan, in which the Iranians would bear the contractual responsibility for assuring India its gas supplies. Another version of the same plan would link Iran to India directly (without transiting Pakistan) through an undersea pipeline. There are also discussions of importing gas from Bangladesh with both Unocal and Shell involved in these projects, and a route from Myanmar is also in the planning stage.

The CentGas project spurred a lot of rumors over the years, including unsubstantiated accusations that Unocal was an agent of the US government, and also that it had funneled vast sums of money to the Taliban forces. There were also reports that Delta Oil was linked the Saudi royal family and to Osama Bin Laden.

Unocal never signed a formal agreement with any Afghan authorities, but tried to develop close ties to all the competing Afghan groups.[9] Unocal representatives did have contact with members of the Taliban government, in both Afghanistan and in the United States. A Taliban delegation traveled to the United States in February 1997 in search of diplomatic recognition. Later, this same delegation went to Argentina to visit Bridas' headquarters.[10] A second delegation came to the United States during November and December 1997, reportedly at Unocal's invitation, and traveled to Texas (Coll 2004).

Regardless of any putative Unocal lobbying, the Clinton administration was debating the possibility of de facto and de jure recognition of the Taliban forces independent of questions relating to the creation of a Trans-Afghan pipeline. But by 1998, as the Taliban's position towards women hardened, there were powerful lobbying efforts by women's groups against US recognition of the Taliban, and against Unocal (Levine 1998).

Eventually the unresolved nature of the Afghan conflict led to Unocal's decision to withdraw from the CentGas project in 1998. Moreover, according to at least one Unocal insider, former US Ambassador John Maresca, the actual spark was Unocal's concern about links between Taliban leaders and al-Qaeda forces based in Afghanistan. At the same time that it withdrew from CentGas, Unocal also abandoned a planned 1,600 km pipeline project designed to transport Turkmen, Uzbek, and Kazakh oil to Pakistani ports through Afghanistan.

---

[9] In 1997 and 1998 this author served as a member of a group of regional experts that did a political risk analysis for Unocal on a quarterly basis. My responsibility was summarizing press accounts about political and economic developments in Central Asia.

[10] For a detailed, and seemingly quite accurate, timeline of the events surrounding the plans for a Trans-Afghan pipeline, see http://www.worldpress.org/specials/pp/pipeline_timeline.htm. This was prepared by the World Press Organization, a project of the Stanley Foundation, Muscatine, Iowa.

The Transport of Turkmen Gas: Existing Alternatives

Unocal's withdrawal from the Trans-Afghan pipeline project worked to Russia's advantage. This was certainly seen by US policy-makers as an unintended and undesirable outcome, and Washington began pressuring Ashgabat to commit Turkmen resources to a planned Trans-Caspian pipeline, a project the Russian government strongly condemned, citing the unsettled legal status of the Caspian Sea and the potential environmental impact of undersea pipelines.

There must have been a sad sense of inevitability among the leadership in Ashgabat when the Turkmen government turned back towards Moscow. Moscow had always taken a proprietary interest toward Turkmenistan's gas reserves and the leadership in the Kremlin never accepted the idea that the collapse of the Soviet Union meant the end of a privileged position for Moscow in this tiny – and in their minds, inconsequential – Caspian state.

Turkmenistan's gas reserves were critical to Russia's domination of the European gas market. Turkmenistan's Dauletabad field had low production costs and was closer to the European markets than the east Siberian or Far Eastern fields. After the breakup of the Soviet Union, Moscow wanted to retain control over the gas spigots of several CIS states, including fractious Georgia and independent-minded Ukraine. Buying and then reselling Turkmen gas allowed Moscow to supply these states while keeping the lucrative markets of Europe largely to itself (see chapter 5).

In the first days of independence, the Russian government and Gazprom, its vertically integrated gas conglomerate, believed that it would not be a difficult task to continue their domination of the Turkmen gas industry. Gazprom, which underwent a formal reorganization in 1992, was made up of senior members of the Soviet gas industry (see chapter 5). Those serving in the gas industry of Turkmenistan were both their colleagues and their subordinates, and Moscow hoped that such relationships would serve it well, and that they would be institutionalized through a series of formal, as well as informal, agreements.

The principal route for the export of Turkmen gas is the Central-Asia-Center (CAC) pipeline system, which was built in stages from 1960 to 1974 (see figure 7.1). The CAC system moves gas about 2,000 km from supply regions in Central Asia and has a maximum capacity of 90 Bcm of gas per year. The construction of the CAC pipelines began after a discovery of the Dzharkak field, and the first section was completed in 1960. The second section reached Tashkent in 1968 and was extended to Frunze (Bishkek) in 1970 and to Alma-Ata (Almaty) in 1971. By the mid-1970s the CAC transmission system, totaling 13,750 km of pipes, had been completed, including four parallel lines from the junction point of Beyneu in northwest Kazakhstan, two lines going northwest to Moscow, and two others proceeding westward across the Volga river to the North Caucasus – Moscow transmission system (Dienes and Shabad 1979). In 2001, 32 Bcm of Turkmen gas was moved along the CAC pipelines.

In 1992 Gazprom asserted formal ownership of the old Soviet-era gas transport network located in Russia, limiting Turkmen access to the markets of Europe (Sagers 1995). By 1993, President Niyazov was also becoming highly suspicious of the motivation of the management in Turkmenistan's gas industry. One of the first to go was former Deputy Prime Minister and Minister of Oil and Gas Nazar Soiunov who in the early days of independence traveled abroad, seeking potential investors in Turkmenistan's gas industry. After his demotion in 1994, Soiunov now lives in exile in Moscow, where he reportedly enjoys close ties to the beleaguered Russian independent gas company Itera (see chapter 5).

Until 1996, Gazprom purchased its gas from Turkmenistan's Ministry of Oil and Gas under a series of short-term inter-governmental agreements that left neither side satisfied. Gazprom, which was slow to receive payment from its customers, was slow to pay the Turkmen as well, and Ashgabat was displeased with the purchase price on offer. Russia's government lobbied hard for the signing of a long-term agreement and for the creation of a JV that would allow it to hold the rights to the transport of Turkmen gas. Russia's President Boris Yeltsin played a direct role in the negotiations and in the process negotiated a series of side agreements designed to sweeten the deal, including the acceptance of a dual-citizenship treaty. At one point Yeltsin formally posed holding a Turkmen passport.

Since January 1, 1996 Turkmenistan's gas exports have been governed by direct arrangement between trading entities. At that time Turkmenistan entered into a joint venture, Turkmenrosgaz, in which Gazprom controlled a 45 percent stake, Itera held 4 percent, and the newly organized Turkmenneftegaz (the production and trading company) held the remaining 51 percent. In 1996, Turkmenneftegaz and Turkmenneftegazstroy (a construction company) were created to succeed the Ministry of Oil and Gas (Ebel 1997).

Under the 1996 agreement Itera was designated the marketing agent for Turkmen gas, and paid Turkmenistan $1.26 per mmbtu ($42 per 1,000 m^3) at the border, with 47 percent due in cash and the rest offset by barter trade. However, the end result of this agreement was actually worse than the previous arrangement. Turkmenistan stopped all gas shipments to Russia at the end of March 1997 and unilaterally abrogated their association with Turkmenrosgaz in June 1997 (IMF 1999).

In 1999 Turkmenistan resumed its natural gas exports to Ukraine, in a trade managed by Itera, in which Russia was paid for transit, and the gas trade itself was used to cover unpaid fees. Under this new agreement Turkmenistan was reportedly paid $1.08 per mmbtu, with 40 percent paid in cash and the rest in barter. This was an increase over Gazprom's originally reported offer of $0.90 – $0.96 per mmbtu, with 30 percent to be paid in cash. The Turkmen claim that they received 50 percent in cash in the Itera deal (WPS – Business Oil 1999). By this time, Gazprom was eager to re-enter the Turkmen market, as it needed 20 Bcm of Turkmen gas in 2000 to maximize the profitability of its European gas contracts (Kortes 2000).

After Vladimir Putin took over the presidency in 2000, Gazprom's interest in Turkmenistan increased. Partly this was a result of increased scrutiny of Gazprom by the Kremlin, which sought to end the long-rumored corrupt practices of the Russian gas giant. A new management was chosen for Gazprom, headed by Alexei Miller, and the company was charged with reasserting control of "dissipated" assets, some of which had come under the control of Itera (Alexander's Gas and Oil Connections 2004).

As part of this effort Gazprom sought to bring Turkmenistan's gas back into its fold, as well as to extend its reach into other Central Asian countries. After several years of negotiation, Niyazov and Miller signed a new long-term contract in April 2003. This agreement called for the Turkmen side to supply gas to Gazprom until 2028, a total of 2 Tcm over 25 years. It set up a 50 percent cash, 50 percent barter payment structure, with gas priced at $1.32 per mmbtu ($44 per 1,000 m^3) in the first three years. This was to make way for a new formula in 2007, when Turkmenistan is to be compensated at world prices according to terms similar to those offered by Western companies (Blagov 2003). This agreement, while technically still in force, was effectively abrogated by Turkmenistan in December 2004, when shipments to Russia were cut off as part of a Turkmen demand for increasing the price of their gas by nearly 50 percent. Shipment of Turkmen gas to Russia resumed in April 2005, reportedly at the originally negotiated price but payable fully in cash.

Ukraine has increasingly become a spoiler between Gazprom and Turkmenistan, particularly since the government of Viktor Yushchenko came to power in December 2004. In April 2005 Ukraine announced the intention to purchase 50–60 billion cubic meters of gas from Turkmenistan – about the same amount as Gazprom intended to purchase – for a start price \$0.48 per mmbtu (\$16 per 1,000 m^3) higher than Moscow was offering (*Nezavisimaya Gazeta* 2005). The agent of this sale was reportedly Igor Makarov and his Itera Group, once a favorite of Turkmenistan, but now reported to be allied with Yushchenko and Ukraine's backers in the US (*Nezavisimaya Gazeta* 2005).

The consequences of adding Ukraine to the equation became clear in late 2005, when Yushchenko's government threatened to throttle the flow of gas across its territory if Gazprom continued to insist on high delivery prices to Ukraine, thus directly threatening supplies to western Europe, a situation that was further exacerbated by Europe's dependence on Russian gas and the unusually cold winter there. In late 2005 the Ukrainians and the Russians entered a three-sided bidding war over Turkmen gas, with the Russians seemingly coming out on top, agreeing to pay the Turkmen \$1.95 per mmbtu (\$65 per 1,000 m^3), and they in turn would trade this gas to Ukraine for \$1.20 per mmbtu (\$40 per 1,000 m^3) more, for a total price to Ukraine of \$3.15 per mmbtu (\$105 per 1,000 m^3). While shipments to Gazprom resumed in 2006 (Interfax 2006), the Turkmen began talking about renegotiating the six-month pricing agreement in early February, and entered into formal plans with the Pakistani government to divert large supplies to that country in the not so distant future.

Turkmenistan's gas is critical to Russia's plans for the development of a unified gas system across Central Asia. In the case of both Kyrgyzstan and Kazakhstan, Gazprom has taken equity interests in either existing or newly organized local gas companies.

For example, in June 2002 Gazprom and KazMunaiGaz established a joint venture, "ZAO KazRosGaz," with Gazprom initially owning 38 percent of the shares. In July 2003 Gazprom's stake in KazRosGaz went up to 50 percent. KazMunaiGaz holds the other 50 percent. The agreement with Kazakhstan will allow 3 Bcm of Kazakh gas to reach European markets through the KasRosGaz joint venture with Gazprom (Alexander's Gas and Oil Connections 2002). The arrangement with Kyrgyzstan is designed to protect the Kyrgyz from alleged price gauging by the Uzbeks. Under this agreement Gazprom will be buying gas from Uzbekistan and Turkmenistan and then selling it to Kyrgyzstan. So payments for gas will be made to Gazprom, not the Uzbek government, which in the past insisted on charging Kyrgyzstan world prices for gas instead of the favorable rates it had initially granted its neighbors (ICAR 2003; RFE/RL 2003). But Gazprom has also become a major investor in Uzbekistan's gas industry since 2003, and reached a new ten-year transit accord with UzNefteGaz (the Uzbek state gas company) making Tashkent far more important in Moscow's plans than Bishkek.

But Gazprom's plans may outstrip the company's current capacity. There is serious concern about how much gas can actually be moved through the CAC pipeline system in its current state. The new agreement between Russia and Turkmenistan calls for capacity to be increased to 60 Bcm by 2007, 70 Bcm per annum by 2009, and eventually 80 Bcm. There are also plans for new pipelines to be laid that will give Turkmenistan more direct access to the Kazakh pipelines system. In 2003, Gazprom and Turkmenistan were planning to build a new gas pipeline that would run mostly on land parallel to the CAC system. It would have an annual capacity of 30 Bcm of gas, cost about $1 billion USD, and be 1,745 km long. Turkmenistan was to pay for construction of the pipeline segment on its territory, something that seemed unlikely in the current state of relations between the two countries, while Gazprom currently lacked the money for this. As for the grand remodeling of the CAC pipeline system, there was also no immediate likelihood that the company would undertake the kind of corporate reorganization necessary to raise international investment capital. Moreover, should the reorganization take place, and the capital be raised, the planned Central Asian projects would have to compete with a number of other investments that Gazprom is contemplating (see chapter 5). Lacking alternatives, Turkmenistan will remain wedded to the Russian pipeline system, with or without its modernization.

Conclusion

Twelve years after independence Turkmenistan has made little progress in maximizing the economic value of its vast gas reserves. Having spent nearly ten years trying to reduce dependence on marketing gas through Russia, Niyazov signed yet another long-term agreement with Gazprom in 2005, which promises Turkmen deliveries to the Russian pipeline system for the next thirty years.

At the same time, Turkmenistan continues to hope that other alternatives will become available. Since the fall of the Taliban government in 2001, the governments of Turkmenistan, Pakistan, and Afghanistan have signed accords that support the construction of a gas pipeline across their three countries, and the Asian Development Bank (ADB) funded a major feasibility study for the project, which was completed in mid-2005. This study is intended to stimulate commercial interest in the project. Although there has been some expression of interest by Japanese firms, as of June 2005 there has been no commercial activity generated in support of this project. In part, this is because questions of long-term stability in Afghanistan have not been resolved, and also because of the increased competition in the South Asian gas market (e.g., new gas finds in Pakistan and India, and LNG imports to India).

The Turkmen continue to reject the idea of shipping their gas through an undersea TransCaspian pipeline, an idea that the United States began to press for in 1998, when Washington was seeking sources of additional oil and gas to help facilitate the construction of the Baku – Tbilisi – Ceyhan (BTC) oil pipeline and a parallel gas pipeline, known as Baku – Tiblisi – Erzurum (BTE), along the route (Caspian Development 2003; Alexander's Gas and Oil Connections 2004). This pipeline is scheduled for completion by the end of 2006.

The decision to go ahead with the BTE gas pipeline – which became irreversible when the BTC was opened in May 2005 – will impact the development of both the Iranian and the Turkmen gas industries. Turkish gas demand will be supplied by Shah Deniz (Azerbaijan), as well as Iranian gas. Moreover, surplus import capacity created by the Blue Stream project and slower-than-expected growth in Turkish gas demand means that Turkmen gas will not find a market west of the Caspian for some time. Even today Turkey is not buying all the Iranian gas available to it, removing any economic incentive for the development of a major east – west gas transit project across Iran.

As the development of Iran's gas reserves moves forward, the Iranians will certainly seek greater integration of their assets with Turkmenistan, and will continue to advocate projects that will maximize profitability of Iranian reserves. However, the Iranian export route is unlikely to serve to maximize Turkmenistan's export capabilities. Similarly, over the long run Turkmen gas may find ready markets in East Asia, but development on any of these routes is currently only a pipe dream.

It is hard to know the most important lessons to take away from Turkmenistan's experiences in trying to build gas pipelines in the past twelve years, or how much we can generalize from the Turkmen case. The environment for doing business was not favorable for private investors. The government of Turkmenistan under President Niyazov was and is an unquestionably unreliable partner, offering little protection to ensure the sanctity of contracts. The political future of the country is very uncertain, and the successor regime to that of Niyazov may well try to overturn the decisions of its predecessor.

In addition to poor leadership, the Turkmen people are cursed with a very poor geographical location, particularly with regard to being able to market their gas reserves. Turkmenistan's two easiest routes to market are through large gas-producing states, Russia and Iran, and both these countries have a strong interest in harnessing Turkmenistan's reserves only insofar as they amplify the value of their own gas assets.

Over the past twelve years Russia has held the stronger hand of the two, and may well have effectively tied up Turkmen reserves for the foreseeable future, especially given Moscow's ability to provide security guarantees to the internally divided Niyazov regime. But if Moscow's interest should wane, Teheran would be eager to step in, and questions of better integration of the gas assets of Turkmenistan and Iran are certain to come up again when Western oil companies at some point become more active in Iran.

Turkmenistan's only other "easy" exit is through Afghanistan, and anyone who has paid the slightest attention to developments in the south Asian region over the past three decades realize that "easy" and Afghanistan are rarely uttered in the same sentence. It is also not simply a question of providing security for a pipeline across the country, but of finding customers for the gas. The key to the financial success of the project increasingly depends on being able to reach India's expanding gas market, especially since Pakistan has increased its domestic production of gas in recent years. It is all well and good to talk about "peace" pipelines, but for a Trans-Afghan pipeline to be economically viable there has to be some realistic prospect of sustained peace in the region, in Afghanistan, and between India and Pakistan as well.

APPENDIX

Table 7.A *Foreign firms involved in the Turkmen oil and gas sectors*[a]

Company	Remarks
Technip (France)	In 2001, Technip was awarded a contract to build a lubricants blending plant, which is scheduled for completion in 2004. This unit has a capacity of 36,150 barrels per day.
Bridas Sapic (Argentina)	Turkmenistan's largest foreign investor and the first Western company to become involved in the gas and oil sector; the main project is the Yashlar field, which reportedly contains 770 Bcm in gas reserves and 165 million barrels of oil.
Burren Energy (UK)	Operates under a twenty-five-year PSA contract at the onshore Nebit-Dag oilfield in Western Turkmenistan. Since 1997, it has invested $200 million to develop the Burun oil field.
Dragon Oil PLC (Ireland, UAE) 70% owned by the UAE's Emirates National Oil	Signed a twenty-five-year PSA for the Cheleken contract area in the Turkmen Caspian Sea. Dragon Oil has four wells under production in the Caspian Sea, following a new well coming onstream at Jeytun field that produces about 3,950 barrels per day of oil. It has invested about $315 million to develop two offshore oil fields in the Caspian Sea since 1993.

Table 7.A (*cont.*)

Company	Remarks
Exxon Mobil (US)	Left reportedly after disappointing well tests at its Garashsyzlyk-2 project.
Larmag Energy Associates (Netherlands)	Major investor in Turkmenistan. The Turkmen government has twice suspended Larmag's export licenses as a means of renegotiating its contract. It has also failed to pay Larmag for oil sent to the Turkmenbashi refinery.
Maersk (Denmark)	Maersk Oil and Turkmenistan signed a PSA in 2002 to develop blocks 11 and 12 in the Caspian Sea and it plans to invest about $10 million in 2003.
Petronas Carigali Overseas (Malaysia)	Petronas is developing part of the Turkmen sector of the Caspian Sea under a PSA signed in 1996, and in late 2002 it extended its exploration and production license for three years until November 2005. The company has invested more than $190 million in the exploration and development of three offshore oil fields in the Caspian sea since 1996.
Shell	In 2002, it reduced its presence in Turkmenistan to a minimum. The company had hoped to become involved in the upstream development side of the Trans-Caspian Pipeline (TCP) project.

Note:

[a] Turkmenistan has 127 prospected natural gas deposits, thirty-nine of which are under development (Alexander's Gas and Oil Connections 2001, Turkmenistan Oil and Gas Industry 2003).

Sources: EIA (2003); US Embassy (2003).

Table 7.B   *Turkmenistan: major natural gas deposits*

Name	Development/Reserves
Byashkyzyl gas deposit	11 Bcm. Development is under way with a total investment of $62 million. This project is to be serviced through the construction of a 90 km Byashkyzyl – Uchaji pipeline, under the auspices of Turkmenneftegazstroy (the state oil and gas construction company), to link the field up with the main Central Asian gas pipeline system.
Darganata field in Northeastern Turkmenistan	Turkmengaz started exploration in May 2001.

Table 7.B (*cont.*)

Name	Development/Reserves
Dauletabad – Donmez/Sovetabad field, located near Seraks on the border with Iran	700 Bcm. Discovered in 1974 with its reserves initially put at 1,626 Bcm. The Central-Asia-Center I, II and IV (CAC) pipeline originated at this field. About 417 Bcm has been extracted since its development. Residual reserves are 1,209 Bcm. It is now estimated that this deposit could produce 15 Bcm of gas per year for a minimum of thirty years. About 80 percent of the recoverable reserves are still untapped. Unocal's planned Trans-Afghan pipeline was intended to send gas from this highly attractive deposit to the South Asian markets.
Gagarinskoye deposit in Zaunguz Karakum	Turkmengaz has recently started commercial exploration.
Karakum and Kyzylkum fields	Exploratory work is being planned by the Turkmen government.
Krichen or Korpedzhe gas deposit	It is at the start of the Korpedzhe – Kurt-Kui gas pipeline. Initial reserves were at 141.85 Bcm. About 22 Bcm has been extracted since its development. The residual reserves area is about 121 Bcm. The construction of the pipeline was completed in December 1997 at a cost of $190 million. Initially, the pipeline was to carry 2–4 Bcm per year of gas from Turkmenistan to the Neka power stations in Iran.
Lebansky, Maryinsky, and Deashoguzsky regions of the country	Seventeen new natural gas deposits have been discovered in this area in the last ten years.
Mayskoye field in the Murgab gas region in the South	It was discovered in 1964. In 1970 it began supplying Ashgabat via a 53 mm pipeline.
Samantepe field on the right bank of the Amu Dar'ya in Eastern Turkmenistan	Initial reserves were 102 Bcm. About 16 Bcm has been extracted since its development. Residual reserves are 84.95 Bcm. Prior to 1991 this field supplied up to 4 Bcm of gas to the Murabek gas-processing field in Uzbekistan. Turkmenistan plant to construct a gas-processing plant and a gas pipeline at the field with an annual design capacity of 3 Bcm. In 1998 a construction contract was signed with Lurgi (Germany).
Shatlyk gas field in the Amu–Daria basin	1 Tcm. Discovered in 1963 and at the time had 894 Bcm of recoverable gas reserves. The field began producing in 1973 when the

	first of two 1420 mm pipelines were laid from Khiva, connecting with the Central Russia transmission system. By 1985 the field had produced a cumulative total of over 340 Bcm of gas. It remains an important producer and a key pipeline junction.
Yashlar deposit in the Margab river basin	750 Bcm. Bridas acquired a 75 percent interest in the field in 1992 and invested around $120 million, including a $15 million bonus to the Turkmen government for its participation in the field.

Sources: IEA (1998); EIU (2001a); RFE/RL (2001); EIA (2002); Oil and Gas Journal (various years).

REFERENCES

AFT (1997). *Asian Financial Times*, May 4

AIC (1995). *Russian Oil and Gas (History and Perspectives)*. Moscow: Association of International Cooperation

Albion, Adam Smith (ed.) (1995). "Playing geopolitics in Central Asia: the Turkmenistan – Iran – Turkey gas pipeline project". ASA-4, February, p. 10

Alexander's Gas and Oil Connections (1997). 21:5, May 26
    (2001). 6:5, August 14
    (2002). 7:14, June 12
    (2004). 9:7, April 7

Blagov, Sergei (2003). "Russia gains big in Central Asian gas game." Asia Times Online, April 12

BP (2004). *Statistical Review of World Energy*, available at *www.bp.com*

Caspian Development (2003), available at http://www.caspiandevelopmentand-export.com/ASP/BTC.asp

CBR (1997). *Caspian Business Report* 1.6. December 18
    (1998). *Caspian Business Report*. September 18

Coll, Steve (2004). *Ghost Wars*. New York: Penguin

Dienes, F. and Shabad, L. (1979). *The Soviet Energy System*. Washington, DC: John Wiley

Ebel, Robert E. (1997). "Energy choices in the near abroad." *CSIS*, April

EBRD (2003). "Transition Report." *European Bank for Reconstruction and Development*

EIA (1997). "Turkmenistan," available at http://www.converger.com/eiacad/turkmen.htm
    (1999). "Country Analysis Brief: Pakistan." June
    (2002). "Central Asia: Turkmenistan Energy Sector." Washington, DC:US Energy Information Administration

(2003). "Caspian Sea Region Country Analysis Brief." US Energy Information Administration, August available at http://www.eia.doe.gov/emeu/cabs/caspian.html

EIU (1997a). "Turkmenistan Country Profile." London: Economist Intelligence Unit

(1997b). "London: Turkmenistan Country Report." London: Economist Intelligence Unit

(2001a). "EIU Country Report." London: Economist Intelligence Unit, September 1

(2001b). *EIU Country Data.* London: Economist Intelligence Unit

(2003). "Turkmenistan Country Profile." London: Economist Intelligence Unit

FBIS (1995). "Pipeline to supply gas to Europe via Iran, Turkey." *Foreign Broadcast Information Service*, January

Gopul, Philip and Pavel Ivanov (1997). "Learning the rules of Central Asia's energy game." *Asia Times*, April 29

Government of India (2000). "Report of the Group on India: hydrocarbons vision 2025." November 16, 2001, available at www.nic.in/indiabudget/ed99-2000/infra.htm

ICAR (2003). *Interfax Central Asia Report*

IEA (1998). *Caspian Oil and Gas.* Paris: International Energy Agency

(2003). "Energy balances of non-OECD countries." Paris: International Energy Agency

IMF (1999). "Staff country report." International Monetary Fund, 99/140, December

Interfax (2006). January 1

IRNA (1996). Islamic Republic News Agency, Tehran, October 14

(1997). "Turkmenistan: new gas pipeline to Iran to be financed within six months." Islamic Republic News Agency, Tehran, March 17

Joseph, Ira (1998). "Gas exports: stranded resources in a unique predicament." Houston, TX: James A. Baker III Institute for Public Policy, Rice University

Kabir, Aamir (2003). "Security risks to gas import." *The News*, 3 March, Business and Finance Review; available at http://www.jang.com.pk/thenews/mar2003-weekly/busrev-2031-2003-2003/p2005.htm

Kortes (2000). *Oil & Gas Spectator: Macro.* November 4

Lelyveld, Michael (1997). "Russia/Turkmenistan: the race to Turkey's energy market." *RFE/RL*, October 21

(1999). "Iran: Turkey seeks to avoid gas penalties." *RFE/RL*, December 30

Levine, Steven (1998). "Unocal quits Afghanistan pipeline project." *The New York Times*, December 5

Moscow Times (2003). "Gazprom gives way to Turkmenistan–Ukraine sales." *Moscow Times*, February 28

NewsBase (1999). April 29

Nezavisimaya Gazeta (2005). April 23

Oil & Gas Journal. Various years

Olcott, Martha (2004). "International gas trade in Central Asia: Turkmenistan, Iran, Russia, and Afghanistan." Working Paper, 28. Stanford, CA: Program on Energy and Sustainable Development

OMRI (1996). "Daily Digest." August 14

Ottaway, David B. and Dan Morgan (1998). "Gas pipeline bounces between agendas." *The Washington Post*, October 5, p. A-1

PFC (1997a). "Petroleum Finance Company Memorandum." August 6, Petroleum Finance Company Limited

  (1997b). "Report on the Turkmenistan – Afghanistan – Pakistan pipeline." October, Petroleum Finance Company Limited

Pope, Hugh (1998). "Pipeline dreams: how two firms fight for Turkmenistan gas landed in Texas court." *The Wall Street Journal*, January 19

RFE/RL (2001). *Radio Free Europe/Radio Liberty.* June 8

  (2003). "Central Asia Report." *Radio Free Europe/Radio Liberty.* August 22

Russian Petroleum Investor (2003). *Russian Petroleum Investor.* 80, March

Sagers, Matthew (1995). "The Russian natural gas industry in the mid-1990s." *Post-Soviet Geography*, 369 (555), November

Turkmenistan Oil and Gas Industry (2003). "Government plans."

US Embassy (2003). "Turkmenistan: 2003 Investment Climate Statement, July 22, 2003." Ashgabat

Varanese, Jonathan H. Hines and B. James (2001). 'Turkmenistan's oil and gas sector: overview of the legal regime for foreign investment.' (eds.) *International Energy Law and Taxation Review*

Vremya Novostey (2003). "Shell leaves Turkmenistan." April 10

WEC (2003). World Energy Council

World Bank (2003). *World Development Indicators* Washington, DC: World Bank

World Oil (2001). Interview with Kurbannazar Nazarov, Minister of the Oil and Gas Industry and Mineral Resources of Turkmenistan

World Press (2000). "Timeline of competition between Unocal and Bridas for the Afghanistan pipeline." June 3, 2005, available at http://www.worldpress.org/specials/pp/pipeline_timeline.htm

WPS – Business Oil (1999). April 12

8   Liquefied natural gas from Qatar: the Qatargas project

Kohei Hashimoto, Jareer Elass, and Stacy L. Eller

Introduction

The Qatargas LNG project is suggestive of the many political, economic, and technical challenges inherent to first-in-country LNG export projects. In this chapter we examine the myriad factors that stalled the export of Qatar's massive gas resources for over twenty-five years from their first discovery in 1971 – as well as the alignment of political and economic interests that ultimately moved the project forward in the early 1990s. The Qatargas case is also a study of a "last-of-a-kind" LNG project. This case and the earlier Arun study (chapter 4 in this volume) bookend the period of Asia Pacific LNG projects characterized by the sole dominance of Japanese gas buyers with robust Japanese government support.

The North West Dome (now North Field) gas structure was discovered off the coast of Qatar by Shell in 1971, in the course of the company's prospecting for oil (see the maps in figures 8.1 and 8.2). An oil field would have been a much-preferred find at the time; gas was not a priority for the newly independent country awash in oil revenues. Oil exports were garnering the tiny country of 130,000 people $2 billion per year in 1975, growing to over $5 billion per year in 1980.

Only when the oil revenues started to wane in the early 1980s did gas exports slowly rise in importance to the Emir. Still, progress proceeded slowly. The Emir sought analysis and input from foreign advisers. Early plans prioritized domestic gas development over gas export projects. However, as the enormity of the North West Dome became more apparent, proposals were developed to export gas both as LNG and via a pipeline to Gulf neighbors and beyond.

The authors would like to thank Amy M. Jaffe for her contributions to the research and the editing of this chapter. We also thank Baker Institute research interns Laura Szarmach and Andrew Rosenblatt for their assistance. Rob Shepherd at Gas Strategies Limited provided invaluable comments on the current chapter, and earlier drafts.

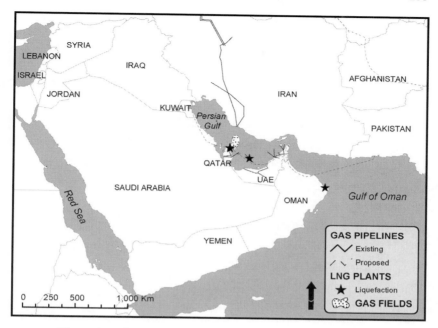

Figure 8.1. Greater Persian Gulf region.

A joint venture was finally established in 1984 to export Qatari gas as LNG. Japanese buyers expressed interest, but before a deal could close an escalation of the Iran–Iraq War spread to regional shipping traffic in the Persian Gulf. In the spring of 1984, Saudi and Kuwaiti oil tankers were sunk as both Iraq and Iran escalated the conflict into the Gulf. The incidents heightened Japanese concerns about security of supply and the ability to protect the costly LNG infrastructure and ships.

LNG exports to Japan were also forestalled by stagnating Japanese energy demand that left limited room for new project supply. The signing of the sales and purchase agreement for Australia's North West Shelf project in 1985 filled a narrow niche for new LNG supply to Japan during this period of the late 1980s. Qatar and the foreign partners waited nearly another decade for security in the Gulf region to settle – and for a new opening to develop in the Japanese market large enough to take the lumpy deliveries from another new greenfield LNG project.

Regional tensions played an important role in forming Qatar's natural gas export strategy. In 1984, the Iran–Iraq War was in its fourth year, and the fledgling Gulf Cooperation Council (GCC) was in its relative

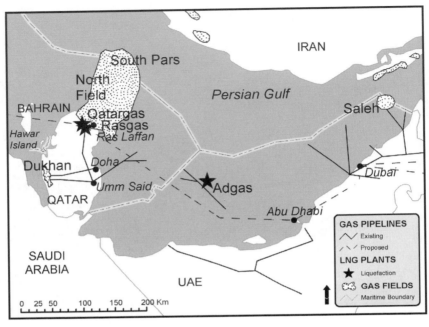

Figure 8.2. Qatar: gas infrastructure.

infancy, having been formed in 1981 as a political entity of six Arab neighbors (Qatar, UAE, Bahrain, Kuwait, Saudi Arabia, and Oman) to protect themselves from the two powerhouses in the region – Iraq and Iran. The sinking of Saudi and Kuwaiti oil tankers during the Tanker War was ample evidence to the Qataris that the GCC lacked the collect-ive military capabilities to ward off threats from its warring neighbors. Indeed, in those early years, the GCC's central focus was on serving as the mediator in the conflict between Iraq and Iran. The GCC's preoccu-pation with mediation efforts for the war also left it with little time to establish the kinds of economic institutions that might have promoted regional gas pipeline development until the war ended in 1988.

The Iran–Iraq War and the escalation to the tanker attacks convinced Qatar that alliances with Saudi Arabia could not protect the tiny Emirate from either a territorial attack by a belligerent Iran or Iraq or from the economic catastrophe should the Emirate's oil exports be cut off, as oil revenues comprised some 90 percent of government income during this period. Qatar began to feel that sitting passively as a satellite of the Saudi Kingdom, in effect having to blindly follow the Gulf producer's lead in political and economic policies, was not in the country's best long-term interests.[1]

The Kuwaiti experience in the Tanker War suggested to Qatari leaders that alliances beyond the GCC might best provide for the country's security needs. As Kuwaiti tankers were increasingly targeted around Gulf Arab ports, the Kuwaiti government aggressively sought international intervention in the Fall of 1986. Under Operation Earnest Will, the United States began escorting reflagged Kuwaiti vessels in July 1987 (Partin 1998; Al-Akim 2001). It soon became evident to the Qatari leadership that gas resources might allow it to cultivate important ties with foreign powerbrokers, both East and West.

Border disputes and bilateral political tensions between Qatar and some of its key GCC neighbors stymied the development of cross-border gas pipeline projects to export Qatari gas through most of the 1980s and into the 1990s. Ambitious plans to send natural gas to Israel and then on to Southern Europe also ran up against political barriers as the project was considered contingent on the Arab–Israeli peace process which has made only uneven progress.

Production of gas from the giant North Field ultimately did not begin until the early 1990s. Qatar General Petroleum Corporation (QGPC, now QP) initiated a three-phase plan to: (1) develop gas production for domestic consumption (in power, desalination, fertilizer, and petrochemicals), (2) build an export pipeline to deliver gas to neighboring Dubai, Bahrain, Saudi Arabia, and Kuwait, and (3) build a liquefaction facility for the export of LNG.

Phase one of North Field development was inaugurated in 1991, financed with calls on future oil revenues. Phase two of the North Field development called for a $2 billion pipeline to supply 10 Bcm per year to the east and 16.5 Bcm per year to the west. The project was dubbed the GCC pipeline, as it was discussed at the GCC, the forum of countries that was to be connected by the pipeline grid. The GCC pipeline was hampered from the very outset by a number of political obstacles. Saudi Arabia made major gas finds in 1990 and was reluctant to grant transit rights for the pipeline; Kuwait was invaded by Iraq later that year. A border dispute frustrated relations between Bahrain and Qatar. Finally, Dubai was not willing to pay much for gas largely to be used for miscible injection to enhance its oil production.[2] Two other

---

[1] Authors' interviews with regional leaders.

[2] Dubai was reportedly willing to pay only $1 per mmbtu in the early 1990s, a price that was not suitably attractive to Qatar. Abu Dhabi was also less than cooperative on the transit of an undersea pipeline through its waters to Dubai, as it had aims in selling its own gas to its neighboring Emirate.

pipelines were also discussed during this period–a 1,600 km pipeline under the Gulf from Doha to Karachi and an even more politically ambitious pipeline to Israel. Neither project advanced beyond early proposals.

The LNG export facility that became Qatargas was to be phase three of the North Field development. The large-scale gas export project would not have succeeded had it not been for the intervention of US major Mobil, which came to the rescue of Qatargas following the abrupt departure of BP in 1992, as well as the symbiotic relationship of Japanese trader Mitsui Bussan and Japanese utility Chubu Electric, which produced key financial backing and concrete long-term sales agreements. As a major American oil firm with expertise in LNG, Mobil brought strong financial backing as well as the political security of a US firm that appealed to the Qataris. Mitsui and Chubu, through their relationship with Qatargas, saw the project as an important new foothold for them into the global gas market.

Qatargas set the stage for a continuing series of major investments by Mobil (later super-major ExxonMobil). Important ties have been built between Qatar, the United States, and Japan as the major offtaker from the project.

The GCC pipeline and other pipeline export alternatives remain in various stages of discussion and design. Qatar's conflicts inside the GCC, especially with Saudi Arabia, closed off any possibility of a gas pipeline that would transit the GCC, or Saudi Arabia in particular, until recently. These political problems gave impetus to alternative plans to export gas as LNG which did not require transit through any GCC-neighboring countries. A fuller discussion of related events that affected the progress of the GCC pipeline and alternative gas export pipelines follows later in this chapter (see appendix Table 8.A, p. 265 for a timeline of events related to the Qatargas project).

Qatar: From Independence to Oil Bust (1971–1983)

Qatar has been inhabited for millennia, a part of the Persian Gulf trade route connecting Mesopotamia to the Indus Valley. The country was briefly under Turkish Ottoman rule from 1872 until the end of the First World War, when it became a British protectorate. The British recognized as ruler Sheikh Abdullah bin Jassim Al-Thani, a member of the Al-Thani family that had previously ruled the region of Doha, the present-day capital city.

Later, when Britain announced its withdrawal from East of Suez in 1971, it proposed that Qatar merge with Bahrain and other Emirates on

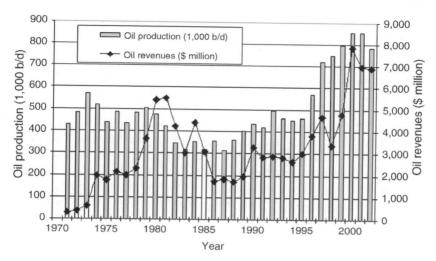

Figure 8.3. Qatar: oil production and revenues, 1971–2002.
Source: OPEC (various years); BP (2004).

the shore of so-called Trucial Oman. But due to rivalries with Abu Dhabi and Bahrain, Qatar chose to become a separate, independent Emirate in 1971 under the rule of Ahmad Al-Thani. In February 1972, the Deputy Ruler and Prime Minister, Sheikh Khalifa bin Hamad, deposed his cousin, Emir Ahmad, and assumed power. This move was supported by the key members of Al-Thani family and took place without violence or signs of political unrest. A provisional constitution was enacted on April 19, 1972 (Kelly 1980).

In his first acts, Emir Khalifa expanded free public housing, introduced price controls on consumer goods, and set up subsidized food cooperatives. He poured large amounts of money into education, health care, and other social programs to benefit less wealthy Qataris and to solidify his support among the population of 130,000 (Crystal 1990).

Rapidly rising oil prices during this period provided the new Emir with ample funds to distribute. Oil revenues doubled from $300 million in 1971 to $600 million in 1973, and rose to nearly $2 billion in 1974 – on basically flat production (see figure 8.3). In 1974, Qatar followed the trend toward nationalization with other OPEC producers, establishing the state-owned QGPC, with responsibility for exploration, production, refining, transportation, and sales of Qatari oil and gas. By 1977, all privately held oil assets and claims had come under the control of

QGPC, although foreign companies, such as Shell and BP, stayed on as contractors and advisors.

Khalifa used the swelling oil revenues to initiate a rapid phase of industrialization focused on three areas: fertilizers, steel, and petrochemicals. Throughout this oil-boom period, a rapid growth of employment in the government administration continued, which would later become a serious problem for Emir Khalifa (Crystal 1990).

Toward the end of the 1970s it became apparent that the glory days for Qatari oil production might not continue. International oil companies (IOCs) became dissatisfied with the service contracts awarded by QGPC, convinced that the potential for oil recovery was not there in the aging oil fields. Oil production peaked in 1979, but revenues were temporarily propped up by the second oil crisis, a product of the revolution in neighboring Iran. When oil prices also began to fall in 1982 and 1983, the Emir found his promises to the population outstripped the country's limited oil endowment.[3]

After years of surpluses, in 1983 the government had a deficit of nearly QR8 billion ($2.2 billion in 2004 dollars). Major state investments in petrochemicals and steel floundered amid stiff competition and ailing global markets (Crystal 1990). Financially, the Qatari government was struggling with budget deficits and there were few signs that oil production would recover. Many other oil producers responded to the falling prices in the 1980s by raising output. With oil reserves down to 3.3 billion barrels in 1983, Qatar was forced to pursue alternative policies (BP 2004).

The Emir cut departmental expenditures, reduced state employment, and delayed several major development projects. In May 1983, the first charges for the health care, water, and electricity were introduced. By November 1983, the government had announced the layoffs of 3,000 state employees. These austerity measures were unpopular among a previously pampered population, creating opposition in the general population and also in the ruling family itself, making the Emir's position vulnerable.

Gas Exports in the 1980s: A Missed Opportunity

Until 1980 the leadership of Qatar was not prepared for export-oriented gas development plans. Oil was flowing and its price rising, while the

---

[3] Qatar was never endowed with overwhelming oil resources. In 1980, Qatari reserves were estimated at 3.6 billion barrels, compared to 30 billion barrels in neighboring UAE (BP 2004).

costs of developing any gas project were large. However, when oil production began to decline Qatar's massive gas reserves – estimated to be in excess of 3 Tcm in 1980 – became an obvious target to offset falling oil earnings (BP 2004).

The Qatari government had expropriated the North Field in the late 1970s, although Shell continued to provide technical support. In this context, Shell was asked to evaluate alternatives for exploiting the North Field. As the natural gas business was entirely new to the Qataris at that time, the studies in 1980 entailed providing estimates of requirements for domestic gas consumption – e.g. electricity and water – before any thought could be given to exports. Comparative studies were made of many different LNG configurations, a methanol plant, an aluminum smelter, and a further petrochemical complex.[4]

Several sources suggest that the lack of institutionalized decision-making in Qatar likely stalled progress in negotiating the complexities of LNG development during this period. Emir Khalifa maintained a commanding position in every corner of Qatari politics, society, and economy. The Emir strictly controlled the money supply in such a personal way that Khalifa himself signed all checks over $50,000 (MEED 1983). Lack of institutionalization was pointed out as a reason for delay in decision-making in every corner of Qatari society; all operations ceased if the Emir was not available or willing to focus on an issue (US Embassy Doha 1983). One of Shell's executives involved at the time notes that discussions on the gas utilization were "further delayed by the presence of a number of expatriate Arab advisers who were [naturally] intent on protecting their positions and so raised question after question to justify their presence which often planted seeds of doubt and confusion in the Qatari decision-makers' minds."[5]

The outcome of the lengthy discussions among Shell, Qatari ministers, and expatriate Arab advisors was a plan that sought to optimize the management of the country's gas resources for both domestic consumption and LNG exports. Because of QGPC's lack of gas experience, foreign partners were required to proceed on any of the development plans.

In 1982, Shell, BP, and CFP (now Total) were each offered 7.5 percent equity stakes in a joint venture with QGPC to develop the North Field and an LNG export project as a result of a competitive selection process. The understanding was that the foreign players would provide their much-needed technical services at cost. Shell, however, exited

---

[4] Personal communication with Ian Wybrew-Bond, December 2003.
[5] *Ibid.*

Qatar for a variety of reasons, focusing their efforts on the development of more promising resources in Australia, while BP and CFP stayed on in Qatar.[6]

Shell's exit further shook up progress on gas development plans, given the company's close involvement since discovering the North Field in the 1970s. Still, in 1984 a joint venture agreement was signed between QGPC, BP, and CFP (Total) officially establishing Qatar Liquefied Natural Gas Company Limited ("Qatargas") and laying plans for the development of North Field. The search was on for a buyer.

Early Japanese Interest in Qatargas

First expressions of interest in LNG exports from Qatar came from Japan. The Japanese economy had boomed in the post-war period, with energy demand growing at over 10 percent per year through the 1960s (see figure 4.3, p. 97). The oil price shocks of the 1970s stalled this rapid growth – as nearly 80 percent of the Japanese economy depended on imported oil. The legacy of this experience made the Japanese government steadfast in its determination to move away from dependence on Middle East oil. At the same time, new air pollution regulations forestalled increases in coal consumption. With gas (and nuclear) the only remaining major energy supply options, Japanese gas and electric companies garnered government support to bankroll a number of new LNG gas supply projects in the late 1970s and early 1980s.

Japanese players were key drivers in all of the international LNG projects serving the Asia Pacific region during this period. Financially secure Japanese electric and gas companies offered long-term contracts for purchases, and the Japanese government offered favorable financing via loans and export credits. With this support, the first shipments of LNG to Japan came from Alaska in 1969. Later the Japanese supported LNG projects in Brunei (1972), Abu Dhabi (1977), Indonesia (Badak and Arun, 1977, see chapter 4), and Malaysia (1983). Nearly three-quarters of global LNG shipments went to Japanese buyers in the first half of the 1980s (CEDIGAZ 2000).

In 1984, the drive to continue to expand LNG imports led two groups of the Japanese trading companies – one comprising Mitsubishi Shoji, Mitsui Bussan, and Itochu and the second Marubeni and Nissho Iwai – to enter negotiations with QGPC for the acquisition of the remaining 15 percent equity stake in the $6 billion Qatargas LNG export venture (MEES 1996). The Qatargas negotiations did not occur in a vacuum,

[6] *Ibid.*

however. As negotiations proceeded slowly with Japanese buyers in Qatargas, events both near and far ultimately forestalled the project for nearly a decade.

Security was a primary concern. Since its discovery, the boundary of the North Field has been a subject of contention with Iran.[7] More importantly, the Iran–Iraq War (1980–1988) increased Japanese concerns about the security of further energy imports from the Persian Gulf. When oil tankers in Qatar's neighborhood became a favorite target of both warring parties in 1984, the short-term prospects for Qatargas dimmed considerably. Thirty-nine commercial ships were attacked in the Persian Gulf in 1984, with the attacks escalating through the end of the war in 1988 (El-Shazly 1998). Although no LNG shipments from Abu Dhabi to Japan (over 2 mtpa) were disrupted in 1984 or later in the war, Japanese LNG buyers had other options that did not involve sending more $300 million LNG tankers into war zones.

With Qatargas plodding ahead in a hostile neighborhood, the North West Shelf LNG project in Australia was also angling to serve the Japanese market. Shell, BP, Chevron, and Japan's two largest trading houses, Mitsubishi and Mitsui – both with extensive experience in the LNG business – were all deeply involved in the project. In 1981, the Japanese LNG buyers had committed in principle to long-term sales contracts from the North West Shelf. However, slower-than-expected growth in gas demand caused Japanese buyers to be timid in signing a new contract, temporarily delaying the Australian project (Feltham 2002).

The energy price increases of the early 1980s stalled energy demand growth in Japan, just as both the North West Shelf and the Qatargas projects were mobilizing to secure long-term contracts with Japanese utilities. Japanese gas consumption, supplied almost entirely by imported LNG, had grown at a blistering 25 percent per year in the period 1972–1980. Then from 1981 to 1983, gas growth slowed to a relatively anemic 2 percent per year and the projected needs for new LNG imports deflated considerably (JCCME 1991).

---

[7] Tensions with Iran over rights to the North Field have clouded development of the North Dome since its inception. When Shell suggested, at the very beginning of the North Field development, that the field might extend into Iranian territory, orders were given from the highest levels of the Qatari government to exclude any such possibility from any maps. The North Field/South Pars gas reserves were clearly demarcated in a maritime border deal in the late 1980s. In April 2004, Iran accused Qatar of overproducing its share of natural gas from the giant offshore North Field that straddles the Qatari–Iranian border, warning that Iran would resort to "other ways and means of resolving the issue" if Qatar did not enter new negotiations about regulating production from the field (Oil Daily International 2004).

Thus, when eight major Japanese gas and electric utilities finally signed long-term sales and purchase agreements in 1985 with the North West Shelf project for massive 6 mtpa deliveries (later expanded to 7 mtpa), Qatargas was forced to wait until a new opening for gas deliveries again developed in Japan.

Late 1980s: Gas Development Begins to Take Shape

Domestic Production and Pipeline Options

Discussions on LNG and pipeline export projects continued in the latter half of the 1980s, albeit slowly. In the summer of 1987, QGPC began the "Phase 1" development of the North Field for domestic consumption. Short on cash, QGPC used an innovative financing technique introduced in the 1980s, obtaining loans backed by future oil sales. In 1987 and 1988 QGPC announced plans to use proceeds from 40,000 b/d of oil exports (one-tenth of total production) to fund the development of the North Field. As planned costs rose on Phase 1 through 1990, the remaining two-thirds of financing for the $1.3 billion project came from a $400 million syndicated Euroloan and a $400 million loan from Arab Petroleum Investments Corporation (Apicorp) (*Arab Oil and Gas Directory* 1994).[8]

Phase 1 of the North Field development faced several delays prior to its targeted startup in 1990 due to technical problems and Iraq's invasion of Kuwait. Fourteen of the sixteen production wells in Phase 1 suffered from cement casing leaks. Then, a week prior to the revised startup on August 3, 1990 it was discovered that chemicals had leaked into an onshore pipeline and the North Field had to be shut (*WGI* 1990). The exodus of contractors from the region during the Second Gulf War further postponed the start of production (Oil & Gas Journal 1991). Finally, on September 3, 1991, the twentieth anniversary of Qatari independence and twenty years after the discovery of the North Field, gas production was underway (see figure 8.4). Phase 1 production produced about 8.6 Bcm per year of raw gas, yielding 7.8 Bcm per year of lean gas and 35,000 b/d of condensate. Most of the dry gas was supplied to local power stations and industrial plants and the remainder was injected in the Khuff reservoir underneath the onshore Dukhan oil field, Qatar's only other source of non-associated gas which is now used as a strategic reserve.

---

[8] These upstream investments (and financing) would later prove critical to the development of the Qatargas LNG project.

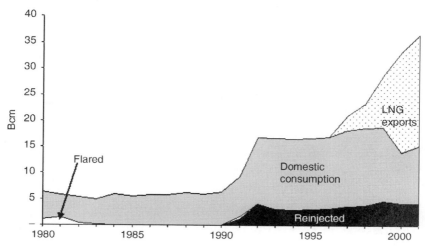

Figure 8.4. Qatar: natural gas output, 1980–2001.
Source: OPEC (various years); BP (2004).

Phase 2 of the North Field development was to export gas via a pipeline to nearby GCC countries Saudi Arabia, Kuwait, Bahrain, and Dubai (UAE), starting in 1996. The construction cost of $2 billion was to be divided among the six participants. This was considered a much more feasible undertaking compared to LNG facilities requiring investments of the order of $5 billion (twice total Qatari national income in 1991) to produce 4 mtpa (less than 6 Bcm per year).

The original plan of a Qatari gas export pipeline was advanced at a GCC summit meeting in November 1989. In the following year, Saudi Arabia, Kuwait, Bahrain, and Dubai (UAE) showed an interest in importing some 20 Bcm per year of North Field gas; these four nations were expected to approve the project at the GCC summit of December 1990.

Ultimately, political barriers stalled the pipeline project. The project was planned during one of the most difficult periods in the history of the Persian Gulf. Saudi Arabia, once said to be interested in importing natural gas for domestic consumption, made major domestic gas finds in early 1990. As a result the country was reluctant to grant transit rights for Qatari gas, which effectively killed off the Kuwait option even before Kuwait was invaded by Iraq in August 1990. Demand from Bahrain was small and a border dispute with Qatar over the Hawar Islands raised tensions. These factors stalled pipeline export proposals well into the 1990s.

The political problems surrounding a regional pipeline grid in the 1980s and early 1990s gave further impetus to plans to export gas as LNG. By shifting its energy export portfolio to natural gas, Qatar was able to move away from heavy dependence on oil, a commodity whose fate was dominated by Saudi Arabia. Saudi Arabia had little influence in the world of LNG, and Qatar's move to become a major gas exporter fit with the Emir's desire to be more independent of the Saudi orbit and to attain economic and security relationships that were outside direct Saudi influence.

Qatargas Makes a Comeback

BP and Total (formerly CFP) remained engaged in Qatar after the LNG project stalled in 1985, hopeful for an opportunity to move forward again. By the late 1980s projections began emerging from Japan and Asia suggesting that a window was opening for new LNG shipments. New buyers were entering the market. South Korea and Taiwan started importing LNG in 1986 and 1990, respectively, increasing pressures on Japanese buyers to lock up future supplies. Total LNG demand in the Asia Pacific region was projected to grow to 57 mtpa by 2000, while maximum production capacity of existing LNG facilities was estimated at only 42 mtpa. The 15 mtpa gap suggested a healthy window of opportunity for Qatargas (Ohashi 1989).

The Japanese trading company Mitsui Bussan re-entered discussions with the Qatargas partners in 1989, while Marubeni had never strayed far from Qatar, peddling the country's oil. Mitsui had helped to develop the Abu Dhabi LNG and the North West Shelf Australia projects and brought much-needed coordinating experience and influence to the proposed Qatargas project.

The important role of the trading companies (*Sogo Shosha*) and their relationship with Japanese buyers (in this case, Chubu Electric) can hardly be overstated. Japan's public electric and gas utilities were the main buyers of LNG in the world at the time and thus had a commanding position in determining the success of any new LNG projects as Qatargas organizers were trying to get their project off the ground in the late 1980s. The great credit strength and influence of *Sogo Shosha* and financial institutions were also critical to promote a successful grassroots LNG project in the 1980s.

Still, Qatar was a relatively poor country with less important reserves of oil and no experience in the LNG business. The risks of a new venture in unproven Qatar – and in the volatile Gulf region – led Japanese importers to look at other sources of gas production, such as Canada, Alaska, and Iran.

Sogo Shosha played a decisive role in building Japanese buyers' confidence, especially between long-term purchasers and investors in the Qatar greenfield project. In Qatargas and previous Japanese LNG import projects, *Sogo Shosha* acted as the "glue" to connect LNG users and the supplier as well as financial institutions, both official and private, to form the critical chain of actors. Involvement of Mitsui Bussan was one of the most decisive factors for the success of the Qatargas LNG project.

In the 1970s, Japanese customers initially enjoyed competition among rival suppliers, while they prioritized buying LNG *en bloc*. But by the mid-1980s and early 1990s, Japan began to experience regional buyer competition. In Japan, domestic rivalries shape three distinct groupings in the world of electric power generation companies. Each of three major electric power companies in Japan – Tokyo Electric Company, Kansai Electric Company, and Chubu Electric Company – built relationships with specific trading firms for LNG supply. Tokyo Electric had long been a recipient of LNG from Brunei and Malaysia through trader Mitsubishi Shoji. Kansai Electric had special relations with Nissho Iwai through developing Indonesian LNG (see chapter 4), and Chubu Electric had long sought its own LNG project through Mitsui Bussan.

Each of the electric companies did buy gas from "competing" projects – as Chubu did from Australia and Indonesia at the time. But Chubu Electric sought a project where it could assume the role as lead buyer, a position it sorely lacked.

Throughout the 1980s, Chubu Electric in vain eyed resources in Western Canada (where it had come close to agreement on the Dome LNG project in 1985 before it ultimately failed), Alaska, Russia (Sakhalin), Thailand, Burma, Papua New Guinea, and Iran. Excluding Russia and Iran, these countries could not support the long-term provision of large gas volumes that Chubu demanded. Sakhalin had potential, but due to the territorial dispute between Japan and Russia over the Northern Territories talks stalled until the Soviet Union crumbled.[9] No viable option was proposed in Iran during this period, due to the war with Iraq and subsequent reconstruction.[10] Removing these alternatives

---

[9] The Sakhalin project came alive after the collapse of the Soviet Union in 1991, and current plans are to export LNG to Japan, starting in 2007.

[10] Iranian LNG projects were later halted when the United States imposed sanctions, which began in 1993 and were tightened in 1996.

rendered Qatar's North Field an increasingly attractive option, despite regional security concerns. Chubu had essentially shopped around the Pacific Basin and come back to Qatar again.

It was felt that the North Field was one of the only viable projects of the day that could satisfy Chubu Electric's desire to import 4–6 mtpa of LNG for twenty years. The fact that it was a greenfield project that required a huge investment even encouraged Chubu's interest. Chubu's sales and purchase agreement for all of the initial capacity, and its relationship with Mitsui, would give it substantial control, at least during the early stages of field development. Also, in Chubu's eyes, committing to a project that was struggling to find a buyer meant that the Japanese firm might gain an upper hand in price and transport cost negotiations.[11] Security concerns were also somewhat allayed by the massive US military presence in the Gulf (especially Qatar) for the liberation of Kuwait. This "security umbrella" likely comforted Chubu as it signed a letter of intent for long-term deliveries from the Qatargas project in 1991 on the same day the US offensive to recapture Kuwait began.

Now with an interested buyer, pressure was on the partners of the Qatargas LNG project to finalize the long-negotiated project structure. The major stumbling block for BP and Total was access to the potentially lucrative gas production segment of the project. The 1984 joint venture agreement provided each with a 7.5 percent stake in the LNG plant and no share in the upstream gas production. QGPC had allocated a block within the North Field to supply Qatargas and did the initial feasibility study work on the upstream development itself.

Early plans to supply Chubu called for a 4 mtpa scheme expandable to 6 mtpa. Based on interviews with BP executives involved at the time, the economics of the project under the existing tax and 1984 joint venture agreement were not promising. "Even with a $0.50 per mmbtu into plant gas price (indexed to LNG price), a 35 percent tax rate and a 10-year tax holiday the 4 mtpa scheme was marginal," said one BP manager involved with the project at the time.[12] BP's analysis suggested that participation in gas production would improve their position, and thus sought improved tax terms and an integrated project where BP and Total would a share in the upstream and LNG plant. According to this same BP manager, the Qatari government "was making progress" on creating such an "integrated project," and did improve the terms for gas

[11] Interview with former J-EXIM official, March 2003.
[12] Personal communication with Rob Shepherd, Gas Strategies Consulting Limited, October 2004.

sales to the project. Before new terms could be agreed upon, Total unilaterally negotiated its own PSC with QGPC – giving it a commanding role among the outside investors in the upstream segment of the project. Total sought to persuade BP and the Japanese trading houses to take a share, which they all refused.

BP was suffering a cash crisis which imposed severe restrictions on its ability to invest in new projects, and was frustrated by the lack of progress in achieving suitable terms and unwilling to take the share in the PSC offered by Total; it announced its withdrawal from the Qatargas consortium in January 1992. The project appeared in jeopardy when the first cash calls for front-end engineering and design (FEED) were on the horizon. Chubu Electric persisted, however, signing the sales and purchase agreement in May 1992 with the remaining Qatargas partners (Total, Mitsui, and Marubeni) to buy 4 mtpa of LNG over a twenty-five-year period beginning in 1997 (Oil & Gas Journal 1992).

Just as the Qatargas project was getting under way, another consortium was lining up to take Qatari gas to Europe. The Qatar Europe LNG Company ("Eurogas") was formed in late 1991 as a partnership between QGPC (65 percent), US Hunt Oil (5 percent) and Italian conglomerate ENI's Snamprogetti (30 percent). The consortium planned to construct two liquefaction trains at the largely Italian-built port of Ras Laffan,[13] and ship 5.7 mtpa of LNG through the Suez Canal to a new terminal in Ravenna on Italy's northern Adriatic coast. Snam and Italian state power generator Enel were to be the main gas buyers.

Eurogas also proposed future increases in capacity to raise total gas output to 10 mpta per year in order to supply gas to central Europe and planned to use larger 200,000 m^3 capacity tankers to cut transport costs. An agreement was made with the Suez Canal authorities to provide for discounted tolls.

At the time, Eurogas appeared to possess several advantages to the established Qatargas consortium looking to sell to Japan. The equity stake of Snam gave Eurogas an apparent jump on Qatargas, which – despite a purchase commitment from Japan's Chubu Electric – was dogged by organizational problems and foot-dragging by foreign

---

[13] Although the Eurogas LNG project would ultimately fail, the development at Ras Laffan did not. As early as 1990, the Qatari government began promoting a major new industrial development to be called Ras Laffan Industrial City. Plans were developed by Bechtel, and Ras Laffan was to be the site of all the new major gas developments, including Qatargas. The extra cost of the Ras Laffan development ($900 million) further frustrated BP. The Ras Laffan project ultimately went forward, with the government footing the bill for the port development costs and providing a significant stimulus to the Qatargas and subsequent Rasgas projects. The preceding is based on personal communication with Rob Shepherd, see n. 12 above.

partners (WGI 1992a).[14] The exit of BP had left the Qatargas consortium without leadership from a player with greenfield LNG experience. Coincidentally, energy major Mobil Oil was looking for a new LNG project to replace the Arun project where reserves were facing decline (see chapter 4).

Mobil to the Rescue

As Qatargas was struggling to move forward, now without BP, Mobil Oil was facing a dilemma of its own in Indonesia. Mobil was an early and successful entrant in the LNG business with its 35 percent interest in Indonesia's Arun field, commissioned in 1978 (chapter 4). Having paid off its capital costs by the early 1980s, Arun was an important contributor to Mobil's corporate cash flow. However, Arun's remaining gas reserves were depleting quickly, totaling only 255 Bcm in 1992. This resource base was insufficient to extend existing Mobil LNG supply contracts to Japan, and options to expand the Arun project were limited (*WGI* 1992b).[15]

By contrast, Mobil executives saw Qatargas as a viable alternate supply source. In addition to diversifying its LNG holdings away from the declining Arun field, an investment in Qatargas could be utilized to expand its global customer base. Qatar's reserves in 1990 were estimated to be over 6 Tcm (BP 2004), which would offer a sufficiently long project life and opportunities to expand annual export volumes over a long period of time from a geographic location that would make deliveries to Europe feasible.

---

[14] It is worth noting that Italy's purchase of 6 mtpa of LNG from Qatar could have set a new benchmark for European gas prices. Italy's probable acceptance of a base price of well over $3 per mmbtu not only shifted markets up to a level where costly LNG schemes were economic, but also struck a blow at long-distance gas pipeline projects from Iran and Russia (PIW 1992a). The Eurogas project was eventually abandoned when Enel, initially a buyer of 40 percent of Eurogas' LNG, began to scale back its gas-buying plans in 1994. Enel was about to be privatized, and was thus tightening its expansion plans, which would no longer be state-financed. Snam opted for increasing the purchase of Russian piped gas from 6 Bcm to 20 Bcm out to 2000, further reducing the need for LNG imports.

[15] Indonesia's state-owned Pertamina approached Mobil about taking a large minority stake in its Natuna island LNG project. Pertamina's idea was to pipe Natuna gas to Arun, allowing it to expand exports. But since the Natuna project was previously structured with then-independent Exxon Corporation possessing the other 50 per cent interest, and the Natuna field contained in excess of 70 percent carbon dioxide, making it a very expensive proposition to develop, Mobil steered clear. Understandably, Mobil was not interested in a project to liquefy Exxon's gas, and the high project costs were unlikely to persuade it otherwise (WGI 1992b).

Table 8.1 *Qatargas: ownership structure*

	Gas production PSC Contractors (%)	Qatargas LNG plant and sales (%)
QGPC	65.0	65.0
Total	20.0[a]	10.0
Mobil	10.0	10.0[a]
Mitsui	2.5	7.5
Marubeni	2.5	7.5

Note:
[a] Responsible for leading operations.

In August 1992, Mobil announced its entry into the Qatargas project with a 10 percent interest and improved terms. Total retained its 20 percent share in the upstream segment of the project through its PSC; Mitsui and Marubeni maintained their original 7.5 percent stake in the downstream and were also awarded small 2.5 percent stakes in the PSC (see table 8.1). To meet Mobil's demands for a greater interest in the development of the North Field, they were awarded a 30 percent stake in a second LNG project to be developed in the future. This second LNG export project would later be dubbed Ras Laffan LNG or Rasgas (WGI 1992b). When the structure was finalized in January 1993, Mobil was assigned the lead role in all liquefaction operations. The original shareholding structure was maintained for the Qatargas plant and sales.

Project Economics

Acquiring the final sales and purchase agreement from Chubu Electric in May 1992 was essential in moving the project forward from the initial planning stage, but accommodating the needs of the Japanese electric utility and investors provided its own challenges. The structure of the contract was designed to emphasize security of supply over price and lifting flexibility. The Japanese partners insisted on a very conservative design philosophy using tried and tested frame 5 gas turbines and emphasizing redundancy over innovation and cost savings. Initial plans called for two 2 mtpa liquefaction trains,[16] adding a third 2 mtpa train when Chubu exercised its option for these additional volumes in

---

[16] Interviews with one industry analyst suggests that larger trains might have been feasible and more economical (interview with Al Troner, October 2003).

Table 8.2 *Qatargas: sales contracts, 1994*

	Volume (tonnes/year)
Train 1 (1997–2021)	
Chubu Electric	2,000,000
Train 2 (1997–2021)	
Chubu Electric	2,000,000
Train 3 (1998–2021)	
Tohoku Electric Power	520,000
Osaka Gas	350,000
Tokyo Gas	350,000
Kansai Electric Power	290,000
Tokyo Electric Power	200,000
Toho Gas	170,000
Chugoku Electric Power	120,000
Train 3 Total	2,000,000

Source: MEED (1995).

September 1993. Chubu then brokered the additional 2 mtpa to seven other Japanese companies to retain its leadership (see table 8.2).

Chubu was offering take-or-pay terms on nearly all 6 mtpa from the eventual three-train project. However, the buyers for the last 2 mtpa could not agree to a pricing formula for Qatargas deliveries. As construction got under way in 1994, Mobil and the project lenders sought financial security in the form of a guaranteed minimum floor price. There was no precedent for such a floor price in Japanese LNG purchases, and with little pressure to accept the non-Chubu buyers refused these terms and a contract price remained elusive (WGI 1994). The final price was left to be determined shortly before first delivery, on the expectation, according to insiders, that it was to be "competitive" with other LNG sold to Japan.[17]

Lacking a floor price, Qatargas partners faced increased pressures to keep costs down. The project benefited from playing suppliers off each other to lower fixed costs for the project. Qatargas' tender for the liquefaction plant led to a successful award to Japan's Chiyoda, who bid to do the work for $1.39 billion, well below competitors

[17] Personal communication with Rob Shepherd, Gas Strategies Consulting Limited October 2004.

Table 8.3 *LNG shipping costs to Japan (Sodegaura), when Qatargas was being negotiated, early 1990s*[a]

	$/mmbtu
Arun	0.51
North West Shelf	0.54
Kenai	0.55
Oman	0.81
Qatar/Abu Dhabi	0.91

Note:
[a] Includes cost of LNG consumed during transport, does not include port costs.

Source: (CERA 1992).

M. W. Kellogg Co. and Foster Wheeler, who were used to winning such construction projects (WGI 1993; Hillman 1994).

Transportation was anticipated to be nearly 40 percent of delivered costs. The longer distances from Qatar to Japan – which increased fuel consumption and required more tankers – placed further pressures on the project to cut costs (see table 8.3). After getting quotes of about $300 million for each of the seven LNG tankers needed for the project, Qatargas persuaded Japanese firms Mitsubishi Heavy Industries, Mitsui Engineering, and Kawasaki Heavy Industries to reduce the price in line with the $250 million levels Abu Dhabi had previously been able to attain from Finland's Kvaerner, when shipyards had spare building capacity and were therefore particularly competitive (WGI 1993).

In addition to these cost savings, condensate sales were essential to project economics. Proceeds from 50,000 b/d of condensate stripped from gas produced in the North Field were used to fund upstream development costs borne by the PSC partners and QGPC.

Financing

The Japanese government played a critical role in ensuring that the Qatargas project was able to find adequate financing – following in the tradition of almost every previous LNG project built to serve the Japanese market (see box 8.1). The engagement of Japanese firms in every segment of the project – from investors to construction firms to transporters to key buyers – enabled Japanese financial institutions to provide the vast bulk of financing (PIW 1994). Financing plans for the first two trains of the Qatargas venture were finalized in December 1993. The Export-Import Bank of Japan (J-EXIM) agreed to provide the bulk of financing for the original 4 mtpa $2.9 billion liquefaction train to be constructed at Ras Laffan. J-EXIM provided $1.6 billion in loans, with the remaining $400 million provided by a consortium of Japanese banks including Bank of Tokyo, Industrial Bank of Japan, Fuji Bank, and Sakura Bank. The remaining 30 percent of the cost of the liquefaction train was to be covered by the shareholders (FT 1996).[18] The project represented a major commitment of the Japanese government to Qatar and the Middle East, through its support of the J-EXIM loans.

Seven new LNG tankers were dedicated to the Qatar–Japan route. Qatar Shipping Company was established as a new private company, owned by National Navigation & Transport (15 percent), QGPC (10 percent), and 300 private investors (75 percent) (WGI 1992b).

Finally, upstream investment costs for the project – drilling, wells, and a pipeline to deliver gas to Ras Laffan – were projected at $1.2 billion. European banks were to provide $700 million in commercial loans with the $500 million of equity contributions from the PSC partners (Hillman 1994).

BOX 8.1   JAPANESE FINANCING FOR LNG PROJECTS: FROM BRUNEI TO QATARGAS

Historically, LNG development and trade has required integrated contracts, with sellers, buyers, and financiers bound together in long-term agreements for up to twenty-five years. In the case of Japanese involvement in the LNG affairs in the past there are three key players: (1) a purchase commitment from Japanese users; (2) official financial agencies to support the investment; and (3) Japan's *Sogo Shosha* that served as lead organizers or "the glue" for the project.

An examination of all greenfield LNG projects (except Alaska) built to serve the Japanese market – from Brunei and Indonesia in the late 1970s through Qatargas – shows three general patterns. In the first kind of structure, a single Japanese sponsor provides a third-party loan, as in the case of Abu Dhabi and Malaysia, or a loan in accordance with the sponsor's share, as in the case of Brunei. In these cases, financial risk was borne by the sponsors in proportion to their share. There are also cases, as in Malaysia, in which J-EXIM directly financed the gas-producing country's portion of the sponsor loan, with a guarantee provided by the host country's government.

The second type of LNG project structure uses a Japanese special-purpose company to provide loans to the LNG venture party. This structure is unique to the Bontang and Arun LNG projects in Indonesia (see chapter 4). In these cases a Japanese special-purpose finance company, JILCO, provided direct

---

[18]   J-EXIM later provided all of the $550 million debt financing (70 per cent total cost) for the third 2 mtpa train. Shareholders provided the remaining 30 per cent (FT 1996).

loans to Pertamina to finance the liquefaction plant investment. Financing for JILCO came directly from J-EXIM and a group of associated commercial banks. The main shareholders of JILCO – and thus the guarantors of the J-EXIM loans – were Japanese electric power and gas enterprises, whose investments were in turn backed with overseas investment insurance provided by MITI. The unique Indonesian structure required the strong backing of the Japanese government, which was readily available after the 1973 oil shock.

Finally, there is a case in which funds are shared by multiple unincorporated joint ventures. This is the case in the North West Shelf Australia LNG project, where each sponsor bore one-sixth of the funding required for each of the development phases – gas field development, liquefaction plant, and shipping. This project also included the first use of J-EXIM for project finance to cover the Japanese sponsor's portion (Aoki 1995).

In each of three financing arrangement styles, the Japanese government contributed some form of financial support. In fact, of all the LNG supply projects in which Japanese companies have participated – nearly 30 liquefaction trains in total in Abu Dhabi, Alaska, Australia, Brunei, Indonesia, and Malaysia – all (with the exception of Train F of Bontang in Indonesia and the early Kenai terminal in Alaska) have been principally supported by J-EXIM. In addition to its direct support, cofinancing from J-EXIM has played an important role in securing the participation of Japanese commercial banks in financing the projects.

Additional government support is also evident in the form of insurance provided by MITI and guarantees provided by JNOC.

Price Revisited

The long-running battle over prices was not easily finalized. With construction proceeding on the liquefaction trains and loading terminal in 1994 and 1995, there were signals that gas demand in Japan was again stagnating. The Japanese economy was in recession and low oil prices had Japanese buyers rethinking their preference for LNG. Japanese LNG buyers uniformly campaigned against the proposed new pricing formula which included price floors, arguing the method was not justified by efficiency gains in power generation, the environmental advantages of gas, nor higher project costs (WGI 1994).

Japanese buyers were also hesitant to pay a premium for Middle East gas because of perceived concerns of security of supply from the Gulf. Memories of two regional wars in the 1980s left a lasting impression, and internal events in Qatar in 1995 likely heightened concerns further. In June of that year, Crown Prince Sheikh Hamad Bin Khalifa Al-Thani, armed forces commander and defense minister, staged a bloodless *coup* while his father, Emir Sheikh Khalifa Bin Hamad Al-Thani, was *en route* to a vacation in Geneva. The *coup* shook Qatar's relations with its Gulf neighbors, but the Qatargas project itself was not disrupted. In fact, the new Emir Hamad was a strong advocate of expanding gas exports and ties to the West – although the uncertainty around the *coup* no doubt made negotiating a pricing deal that much harder for the Qatargas partners.

The challenge was that Qatargas was seeking to continue the old practice of the newest project getting the highest price, while Japanese buyers were trying to engineer a downward movement in LNG prices.[19] Qatargas had been started in the "old" era of Asian LNG projects, where Japanese buyers were willing to pay a hefty premium for supply security. By 1997, Asian LNG markets were awash with new offers from proposed projects in Sakhalin, Yemen, Oman, and Australia. New buyers in South Korea and Taiwan (and later India and China) were competitively shopping among these new potential suppliers, and Chubu and the other offtakers were not keen to accept prices that would place Qatargas deliveries at the price pinnacle of a declining Asian market.

Qatargas was in a bind. In late 1996, Korean Gas Corporation (KOGAS) demanded the elimination of the minimum price in its contract as a precondition to doubling its planned purchases from what was to be the second major Qatari LNG export facility – Rasgas. When KOGAS obtained these terms from Rasgas leaders QGPC and Mobil, it became increasingly unlikely that a similar provision would apply to purchases from Qatargas (APS 1997). When the first cargo from Qatargas arrived in Japan aboard the tanker *Al-Zubbarah* in January 1997, there was still no agreement on a pricing formula. A provisional price of $4.10 per mmbtu delivered (c.i.f.) was agreed upon for the first three months of deliveries.

Based on the January 1997 index of Japanese crude oil import prices (the Japanese Customs Clearing price, or JCC) of roughly $23/barrel – to which the price of all other Japanese LNG was linked – the prevailing price for the rest of Japan's LNG was around $4.40 per mmbtu. In these conditions, Chubu was well- positioned to negotiate a pricing formula in its favor. Perhaps not surprisingly, the provisional price of $4.10 was extended through September 1997 when the parties still could not agree on a formula price. However, the incentive for Chubu to move to the traditional oil-price linkage was raised considerably during the summer of 1997, when the JCC price dropped to $17 per barrel and with it the price of other oil-linked LNG deliveries to Japan fell to around $3.50 per mmbtu. The pressure to settle the pricing terms eventually brought

---

[19] Personal communication with Rob Shepherd, Gas Strategies Consulting Limited, October 2004.

Qatar's Energy Minister to Japan in October of 1997 to negotiate on behalf of Qatargas. Finally, near the end of 1997 a price was agreed that brought Qatargas to Japan near the middle of the market, in line with prices from Australia's North West Shelf project, but just below the most recent Adgas project in Abu Dhabi (MEES 1996; APS 1997; Reuters 1997).[20]

Alternative Projects: Politics Outweighs Economics

GCC Pipelines

In the 1980s, as Qatar began to look seriously at gas export projects, it was proposed that 8 Bcm a year of North Field gas could be exported via a GCC pipeline network to nearby countries such as Saudi Arabia, Kuwait, Bahrain, and Dubai. However, the project was blocked by political considerations and economic factors. A related project to pipe Qatari gas to neighboring states and then on to Pakistan also remained stalled through the 1980s and 1990s because of similar economic and political challenges.

In the late 1980s, other factors came into play to delay the GCC network project. Saudi Arabia made significant domestic gas discoveries, and the Gulf War and the subsequent reconstruction period complicated Kuwait's participation.

Qatar was thus left with few regional options. A smaller project to Dubai was proposed, but the high costs of bringing only 6.2 Bcm per year of gas via pipeline to Dubai made the project uncompetitive with the alternatives. Dubai sought 3 Bcm per year of gas for a miscible gas injection project to slow the decline in its oil production and ensure sufficient supply for its own industries and utilities, but was willing to pay less than $1 per mmbtu, insufficient to cover the pipeline capital costs of a line from Qatar. Plans for a project to pipe Qatari gas on from neighboring Gulf States to Pakistan also languished with the setbacks to the initial proposals for a GCC network.

At the time Qatar was moving ahead with its ambitious gas agenda, it was facing a series of territorial conflicts with Saudi Arabia, putting pressure on the already fractious relationship. In September 1992, a confrontation between Bedouins resulted in a minor clash of the two neighbors, the death of two Qataris, and the kidnapping of a third

---

[20] According to industry analysts, the formula price in Qatargas was set according to 14.85 JCC + 90, where JCC is in $US per barrel and the resultant price in US cents per mmbtu. Based in part on personal communication with Rob Shepherd, Gas Strategies Consulting Limited, October 2004.

(Cordesman 2003). This small incident reflected Qatar's contention that the Kingdom was infringing on Qatari territory by building roads and facilities in the border area and it prompted Qatar to suspend a 1965 border agreement between the two sides that had never been ratified. Qatar also pulled its participation in the GCC's ongoing Peninsula Shield exercises, which were designed to protect the borders of Saudi Arabia and Kuwait against Iraq.

Despite mediation efforts, there were further clashes, including an incident in October 1993 that resulted in several more deaths and a handful of border skirmishes that occurred in 1994. A diplomatic row caused Qatar to boycott the November 1994 GCC summit conference (Cordesman 2003).

In 1995, relations between Saudi Arabia and Qatar boiled over again when the Emirate questioned the choice of a Saudi candidate to take over the position of Secretary General of the GCC. Although the GCC had no formal rules regarding the nationality of the Secretary General, Doha claimed that the rotation should be conducted alphabetically, which conveniently would favor a Qatari choice, as the previous job holders had been Kuwaiti and Omani, respectively. Faced with strong opposition by Saudi Arabia and its allies, the new Emir and his foreign minister walked out of the GCC meeting (Cordesman 2003).

There were other political reasons behind the opposition to the Qatari candidate. Emir Hamad had angered the Kingdom and other GCC states by being the first Gulf state to establish economic ties with Israel, agreeing in October of 1995 to a letter of intent to supply Qatari gas to Israel. This was a bold indication of Qatar's pursuit of a maverick foreign policy that would be at odds at times with the GCC and evidence that Qatar would pursue alternative markets for its gas if the closest markets via the GCC were not available.

Following the December 1995 GCC meeting, Saudi Arabia made a public statement of welcome to the deposed Qatari emir, Sheikh Khalifa, as did the governments of Bahrain and the UAE, which gave the former ruler the opportunity to claim that he was determined to come back to power.

Ties between Doha and Riyadh degenerated even further in February 1996, when Qatar's Emiri Guard arrested hundreds of supposed *coup* plotters suspected of having support from neighboring states (MEES 1996). Before things could spiral further, Qatar came to an agreement in March 1996 with the other GCC states that the position of Secretary General within the organization would be selected through an alphabetical rotation and that the Secretary General would serve no more than two three-year terms. Unfortunately, for Qatar, the fact that a Saudi then held the post meant that every other member state of the GCC would have a representative in the post before Qatar came up through the alphabetical rotation. This strategic decision apparently led the way for Saudi Arabia, Bahrain, and the UAE to endorse Sheikh Hamad's rule and for Bahrain to agree to Qatar's request that the long-standing Bahrain–Qatari dispute over territorial ownership of the Hawar Islands be adjudicated by the International Court of Justice, which led to a March 2001 ruling giving Bahrain sovereignty over the main island in dispute (Saad 2001).

In recent years, as relations inside the GCC improved and regional demand for gas increased, some elements of the GCC regional gas pipeline network have moved ahead. In December 1998 a state-backed corporation, the UAE Offsets Group (UOG), signed an agreement with Qatar to be the sole supplier and marketer of Qatari gas to the UAE and Oman. UOG then signed preliminary MOUs with Qatar, Oman, and Pakistan in June 1999. In December 2001, the project began in earnest when Qatar and the Dolphin Project joint venture, comprising the UOG and France's TotalFinaElf, signed a twenty-five-year development and production-sharing agreement to pipe as much as 21 Bcm per year of Qatari gas across the Gulf to Abu Dhabi by mid-2005.

Through the project, Qatari political links with the UAE and Oman strengthened, with Qatari gas flowing through a newly built subsea pipeline to the UAE built and operated by Dolphin Energy; the line extended to Oman and perhaps eventually to Pakistan. The pipeline project links Qatar to its neighbors in a manner that does not involve Saudi political, economic, or territorial participation, giving these three Gulf countries autonomy in a critical development that leaves out the Saudi Kingdom – an important political benefit for Qatar.

The push for the UOG's Dolphin Project was the result of the powerful backing of key players in the region. The fact that this project is actually advancing – unlike others proposed during the same time frame – was largely due to the leadership of UAE, Qatar, and Oman. The UOG's patron was Sheikh Mohammed Bin Zayed Al-Nahayan, chief of staff of the UAE Armed Forces and son of UAE President Sheikh Zayed Bin Sultan Al-Nahayan; in addition, the Dolphin Project clearly had the full support of the Qatari Emir and Omani Sultan Qaboos Bin Said (Barnett 2000).

In the lead-up to the MOU signings, the respective Gulf states worked to resolve long-standing border disputes. In May 1999, the UAE and Oman signed an agreement to demarcate their border at Umm Zummul, where the borders of Saudi Arabia, Oman, and the UAE meet. That border agreement was followed in June 1999 by Qatar and Saudi Arabia agreeing to delineate their shared 60 km land/sea border, which led to the final border accord signed between the two in March 2001. The UAE–Oman border agreement was formalized in December 2003. The resolution of the numerous border issues can be attributed to the leadership of *de facto* Saudi ruler Crown Price Abdullah Bin Abdul-Aziz Al-Saud, who was determined to settle these long-standing conflicts.

In a separate agreement, Qatar gave Dolphin the rights to build a 434 km underwater pipeline running from the Ras Laffan terminal to Tawilah in Abu Dhabi, allowing for surplus volumes of Qatari gas to be exported. In 2002, the Dolphin group awarded Foster Wheeler and Sofresid a $10 million upstream FEED contract, and started drilling the first of sixteen exploration wells. Most of the gas is expected to be consumed in Abu Dhabi for power and water generation, but some will be sold to Dubai for domestic industry.

In addition, Qatar Petroleum and Exxon-Mobil East Marketing Limited partnered in 2000 to form the Enhanced Gas Utility (EGU) project. This $1.2 billion project will develop North Field gas for domestic use as well as for export via pipeline to Bahrain and Kuwait. In 2002, an agreement was signed with Bahrain to provide from 5 to 8 Bcm of North Field gas per year as a part of a project to construct a regional pipeline grid. Under this agreement, gas deliveries were expected to start in 2006.

A gas sale and purchase agreement was also signed with Kuwait in July 2002, and a $500 million project to construct a 600 km underwater pipeline connecting Ras Laffan to Kuwait's Ras al-Zoor was unveiled. The pipeline would provide 10 Bcm of natural gas to Kuwait starting from 2005. However, the recall of the Saudi Ambassador to Doha in October 2002 following Saudi accusations that the Qatari government had allowed the Al-Jazeera television network to broadcast programms that slandered the Saudi royal family, including its founder, raised questions about whether the line to Kuwait will be completed (MEES 2004). Qatari officials expressed concerns at the time that the diplomatic row should not affect the 580 km subsea gas pipeline project that must cross Saudi waters in order to reach Kuwait.

Plans to extend the Oman pipeline leg to Pakistan remained stalled at the time of writing. Pakistan's financial difficulties and possible competition from gas imports to Pakistan from Iran weigh in the deliberations for moving the ambitious pipeline project forward (EIA 2004). In contrast to the large and established Japanese market, the Pakistani market is not well developed. In addition, questions remain about Pakistan's financial situation, the size and nature of future Pakistani gas demand, regulatory and legal structures for sales to Pakistan, and the stability of the Pakistani government.

A "Peace Pipeline" to Israel?

Another pipeline project, a line to extend to Israel, also remains on hold. The decades-old plan for a long-term gas supply arrangement to Israel may have been too ambitious a concept to put into practice given the political realities in the region and the pressure Doha felt from its GCC neighbors as well as other Middle East nations. The proposal came out of slightly improved relations between the GCC and Israel and the brightening prospects for a substantive Palestinian–Israeli peace in the mid-1990s. Indeed, the signing of the letter of intent between Qatar and Israel in November 1995 came two months after the GCC endorsed revoking aspects of the economic boycott on Israel and one month after the Qatari foreign minister expressed Doha's support for the cancellation of the primary economic boycott on Israel (Segal 1995).

In April 1996, the then Israeli Prime Minister Shimon Peres made the first official visit by an Israeli premier to Qatar, and an Israeli trade mission opened in Doha in the spring of 1996. However, a few months later, Israel declared that the letter of intent had expired and in November of that year Doha insisted that any concrete deal with Tel Aviv would depend upon progress in the Palestinian–Israeli peace process. Momentum on a Qatari–Israeli gas deal was further slowed when Qatar joined the other members of the Arab League in March 1997 in calling on an end to normalization of ties with Israel and the closure of mutual trade and representative offices as a result of escalating violence between Israelis and Palestinians in the West Bank and Gaza (Reuters 2000).

By November 2000, continued deterioration in Israeli–Palestinian relations prompted Qatar to close the Israeli trade mission following extreme pressure from Saudi Arabia, Syria, and others who were threatening to boycott the Organization of Islamic Conference (OIC) summit that was to be hosted by Doha later that month. That meeting, in particular, had been convened by the OIC to discuss Israeli violence following the onset of the second *Intifada*, which was spurred by then Israeli opposition leader Ariel Sharon's visit to the Al-Aqsa mosque in Jerusalem in late September 2000. Although Qatar had steadfastly refused to sever economic ties with Israel up to that point, Doha became uncomfortable at lending the appearance of tacit support of Israel during the renewed Palestinian uprising which was being viewed across the Arab world on regional satellite stations.

While the trade mission was closed in 2000, Israeli diplomats quietly remained in Doha and Qatar continued to maintain links, conducting discreet negotiations with Tel Aviv. In fact, in May 2003, Qatar raised the prospects of boosting its relations with Israel should progress be made in the Middle East peace process. In an interview with Al-Jazeera, Qatari Foreign Minister Sheikh Hamad Bin Jassem Al-Thani said: "We committed for a certain time to long talks with the Israelis because we must adopt practical steps to put an end to the killing between Israelis and Palestinians"(AFP 2003).

Although continuing Qatari–Israeli diplomatic relations mean that the pipeline project could some day be revived, it is unlikely that the project will move forward in the near term, given the deterioration of the Middle East peace process and seemingly bleak prospects for a peace agreement.

An LNG Boom

In the wake of Qatargas, Sheikh Hamad moved aggressively to open up the oil and gas sector, inviting in international oil majors into joint venture production deals, at a time when Saudi Arabia and others were reluctant to move quickly in this direction.

A debottleneck project on the three Qatargas trains, completed in 2002, brought each to a working capacity of over 2.5 mtpa. In 2001, Gas Natural of Spain contracted for 1.5 mtpa of this spare capacity from 2001 to 2009, of which almost two-thirds would be purchased on an f.o.b. basis.

By 2005, another debottleneck will bring total working capacity to 9.2 mtpa, over 3.2 mtpa greater than the original long-term supply contracts to Japan. Gas Natural contracted for another 1.45 mtpa for twenty years beginning in 2005. The overall cost of the two debottleneck projects is anticipated to be less that $200 million, a mere fraction of the original project costs.

Term contracts account for 100 percent of original design capacity; however, spare working capacity allows Qatargas to sell several spot cargos per year. Spot cargoes have reached major markets in Europe, Asia, and the United States by purchases from Gas Natural, Chubu, and CMS, respectively. It is interesting to note that such flexibility proved useful to the Japanese market during 2002 and 2003. Several LNG cargos were diverted to Japan from Spain to help mitigate possible power-generation shortages when Japan was forced to shut down its nuclear power plants due to safety concerns in 2002 and 2003.

Qatargas II, a separate two-train project with capacity of nearly 16 mtpa, will have the first train online by 2008 and the second by 2010. The $25 billion Qatargas II project, composed of Exxon Mobil (30 percent) and QP (70 percent), will be unique to the LNG market in several aspects. First, each train will have a capacity of up to 7.8 mtpa, substantially greater than the largest train currently used in Egypt at a capacity of only 5 mtpa. In addition, it is the first project in which a partner will be the sole buyer on a take-or-pay basis. Exxon Mobil and QP plan to jointly own and operate a receiving terminal in Milford Haven, Wales to take volumes from the project. At a cost of nearly $5 billion, a fleet of up to sixteen vessels with capacities of 200,000–230,000 m^3 is currently being built to accomplish this feat (*PIW* 2004). There are currently talks of Total as an additional partner to add an equally sized third train. In July 2003, a heads of agreement was signed by ConocoPhillips and QP to pursue the Qatargas III project, which will consist of a new LNG train and terminal to be constructed at the Ras Laffan Industrial City. ConocoPhillips will purchase the full volume and regasify and market 7.5 mtpa within the United States by 2008 or 2009. The company has also proposed an 180,000 b/d GTL plant.

Conclusion

The twenty-six-year delay between the discovery of the North Field in 1971 and the first exports of gas in 1997 was the product of domestic political and economic factors, as well as inter-state tensions and regional instability. During the 1970s, oil sales were booming and the North Field project was not deemed by the Emir to be suitably attractive to justify significant investment; the regeneration of the oil industry and finding additional oil reserves were the top priority. LNG projects required long lead times and high capital costs, meaning that Qatar faced great risks of becoming a debtor nation if such a project failed.

When oil revenues began to decline in the early 1980s and the impetus for gas development became more acute, a lack of institutional development – or, more simply, the vagaries of the Emir's one-man rule – stalled Qatar's LNG development plans. Meanwhile the "Tanker War" between Iran and Iraq in the Persian Gulf turned Japanese investors away from the region at a time when Japanese energy demand was also stagnant.

BP's withdrawal from Qatargas in January 1992 – based on its assessment of low returns and BP's weak cash position at the time – placed the project in jeopardy, but the engagement of Mobil later that year revived the enterprise, providing a strong signal to other investors about the security and stability of both the country and the project. Mobil was instrumental in rearranging the project organization to lower costs in a manner that could make the project internationally competitive. Qatargas thus became a joint project between QGPC, Mobil, Total, Marubeni, and Mitsui. American, French, and Japanese interests were all represented – Mobil's American flag, in particular, provided major security benefits to Qatar. The American troop presence in the region–and in Qatar in particular–was at an all-time high following the Gulf War in 1991.

Qatar had incentives to attract Mobil, as it hoped to strengthen its security relationship with the United States. The push to host US troops was supported by Sheikh Hamad, who in the aftermath of the 1991 Gulf War actively cultivated military ties with Washington as the Emirate's Defense Minister. American commercial participation in Qatargas, as well as US military support for Qatar's overall national security and for the security of the GCC, gave comfort to potential Japanese participants who had previously feared that too much political risk was associated with LNG exports from the Persian Gulf.

Japan, with a view to diversifying LNG sources and ensuring a new long-term supply source in the face of new buyer competition for LNG from South Korea and Taiwan, strongly supported the project. Tokyo provided the credit strength and commercial backing that was critical to the success of the Qatargas development. In Qatargas, as in previous Japanese LNG import projects, the *Sogo Shosha* acted as the "glue" to connect LNG users and the supplier as well as financial institutions.

The success of the Qatargas project can be linked in great measure to its traditional organization where Japanese firms dominated sales, financing and construction, tapping government-backed financial support. This kind of Japanese-led, comprehensive program has not been repeated on the same scale in the increasingly competitive and more flexible LNG market of the late 1990s. Japanese willingness to pay for secure LNG supplies appears to have reached a plateau, forcing suppliers to become more flexible in contract pricing and terms. Suppliers, under pressure from buyers, particularly in Korea and China, have increasingly switched to f.o.b. sales, forgoing additional margins from shipping services. The transition to this increased commercial flexibility is evidenced in Qatargas' marketing efforts for additional volumes from its debottleneck and expansion projects.

From the Qatari perspective, the shift in its energy export portfolio to natural gas has allowed it to move to a commodity for which Saudi Arabia plans a less dominating influence, since the Kingdom had no plans to export natural gas abroad. The move to be a major gas exporter fit with Qatar's desire to obtain greater independence from Saudi Arabia and to attain economic and security relationships that were outside direct Saudi control. Through its gas policy, first embraced twenty years ago, Qatar has established its own economic and military ties with Eastern and Western powers – and, in particular, strengthened its security relationship with the United States.

APPENDIX

Table 8.A *Timeline of important events*

1971		Discovery of the North West Dome (North Field) by Shell.
1974		Qatar General Petroleum Company (QGPC) established.
1977		Nationalization of Qatari oil industry.
		Japanese trading companies initiate contacts with QGPC.
1979		Oil production peaks and begins to decline (until 1986).
1980		Shell presents reports evaluating possible options for use of North Field.
1981		Japanese buyers sign first commitments for LNG from North West Shelf LNG (Australia).
1982		Decision reached to proceed on LNG JV, QGPC retains 70% Shell, BP, and CFP (Total) each offered 7.5% stake, Shell later withdraws.
1984		Qatargas officially established. Development of North Field officially decided by Qatar government. Only Marubeni participated from the Japanese group. Escalation of the "Tanker War" in the Gulf by Iran and Iraq.
1985		Mitsubishi and Mitsui and Japanese buyers sign long-term contracts with North West Shelf LNG.
1987		Phase 1 of North Field development started.
1989		Return of Mitsui to the Qatargas project
1990	Aug.	Iraq invades Kuwait; exodus of foreign contractors from region.
	Dec	Discussions on Phase II pipeline expected at GCC summit, distracted by Kuwait situation.
1991		Letter of Intent signed by Chubu for 4 mtpa deliveries from Qatargas.
		Total signs upstream PSC with QGPC.
	Sep.	Phase 1 production of North Field inaugurated.
1992	Jan.	Official retreat of BP from Qatargas project.
	May	Chubu Electric signs SPA for 4 mpta from 1997 to 2021.
	Aug.	Mobil announces entrance to Qatargas
		Qatar Shipping Company established.
	Sep.	Border disputes between Qatar and Saudi Arabia.
1993	Jan.	Final shareholders meeting for Qatargas.
	Apr.	First well drilled for technical evaluation.
	Sep.	Chubu exercises option to purchase additional 2 mtpa deliveries from train 3.
	Dec.	$2 billion loan signed by consortium of Japanese private banks.
1994	Jan	MITI backs JNOC $350 million financing for liquefaction plant and remainder of financing secured, led by JP Morgan.
1995	May	Drilling operations commenced.
	Jun.	Sheik Hamad takes power from his father, Emir Sheik Khalifa.
1996	Jul.	First gas from the North Field received onshore.
	Sep.	First condensate loaded for export.
	Nov.	First LNG vessel, *Al-Zubarah*, delivered to Qatar.
		Start up of LNG train 1, first LNG produced.
1997	Jan.	First LNG delivery to Chubu Electric.

REFERENCES

AFP (2003). "Qatar ready to boost ties wtih Israel if Mideast peace accelerates." *Agence France-Presse*, May 16

Al-Akim, Hassan Hamdan (2001). 'The Arabian Gulf at the new millennium: security challenges', in Joseph Kechichian (ed.), *Iran, Iraq and the Gulf Arab States*. New York: Palgrave

Aoki, Wataru (1995). "The Japanese approach to financing LNG projects." Doha Conference on Natural Gas, Doha, March 15

APS (1997). "Qatar – the LNG price." *APS Review of Gas Market Trends*, 49(17) October 27

Arab Oil and Gas Directory (1994). Paris: Arab Petroleum Research Center

Barnett, Neil (2000). "Dolphin project surges ahead." *The Middle East*, February

BP (2004). "Statistical Review of World Energy," available at http://*www.bp*.com

CEDIGAZ (2000). "CEDIGAZ News Report September 2000." November 16, 2001; available at http://www.ifp.fr/TXT/CE/CE400TH2.html

CERA (1992). *The New Wave: Global LNG in the 21st Century*. Boston, MA: Cambridge Energy Research Associates

Cordesman, Anthony H. (2003). *Saudi Arabia Enters the Twenty-First Century: The Political, Foreign Policy, Economic, and Energy Dimensions*. Westport, CT: Praeger

Crystal, Jill (1990). *Oil and Politics in the Gulf Rulers and Merchants in Kuwait and Qatar*. Cambridge and New York: Cambridge University Press

EIA (2004). "Country Analysis Brief: Qatar." Washington, DC: US Energy Information Administration

El-Shazly, Nadia El-Sayed (1998). *The Gulf Tanker War: Iran and Iraq's Maritime Swordplay*. London and, New York: Macmillan and St. Martin's Press

Feltham, Jeff (2002). "How Australia successfully develops LNG projects." Cross Border Gas Trade Conference, March 26–27,. Paris: IEA

FT (1996). "Qatar–Japan loan accord." *Financial Times*, London

Hillman, Dan (1994). "Special report on Qatar: Japan shares big LNG deal." *Lloyd's List International*, December 27

JCCME (1991). "Study of natural gas in Middle East countries." Japan Cooperation Center for Middle East

Kelly, J. B. (1980). *Arabia, the Gulf and the West*. London: Weidenfeld & Nicolson

MEED (1983). *Middle East Economic Digest*, August

(1995). "Qatar: Japanese sign up for LNG supplies." *Middle East Economic Digest*, February 10

MEES (1996). "Qatar says it foils *coup*." *Middle East Economic Survey*, February 26

(2004). "Saudi Arabia, Qatar commence talks aimed at improving diplomatic relations." *Middle East Economic Survey*, June 21

Oil & Gas Journal (1991). "North Field start delayed." *Oil & Gas Journal* February 25

(1992). "General Interest." *Oil & Gas Journal*. May 25

Ohashi, Tadahiko (1989). "Prospect of energy and Qatar LNG." *Tokyo Electric Monthly*, May

Oil Daily International (2004). "Iran accuses Qatar of overproducing gas." *Energy Intelligence Group*, April 24

OPEC "Statistical Review." Various years

Partin, John (1998). "Special Operation Forces in Operation Earnest Will, Prime Chance I." History and Research Office, USSOCCOM

PIW (1992). *Petroleum Intelligence Weekly*, June 22

(1994). "The second generation of LNG projects." *Petroleum Intelligence Weekly*, June 30

(2004). "Exxon takes a $25 billion bet on Qatar." *Petroleum Intelligence Weekly*, July 19

Reuters (1997). "Qatargas, Japan extend interim price deal through September," June 25

(2000). "Oman severs low-level ties with Israel." October 12

Saad, Rasha (2001). "Gulf Emirates settle dispute." *Al-Ahram Weekly*, March 22–28

Segal, Naomi (1995). "Israel and Qatar sign oil deal from Amman confab." *Jewish Telegraphic Agency* November 3

US Embassy Doha (1983). "Doing Business in Qatar"

WGI (1990). "Qatar." *World Gas Intelligence*, August 1

(1992a). "Competition comes to Qatar." *World Gas Intelligence*, June 1

(1992b). "Qatar *coup* raises stakes, poses challenges." *World Gas Intelligence*, September 1

(1993). "Qatar revs its engine but still needs finance." *World Gas Intelligence*, July 1

(1994). "Where there's a floor, must there be a ceiling?" *World Gas Intelligence*, June 17

9 Liquefied natural gas from Trinidad & Tobago: the Atlantic LNG project

Rob Shepherd and James Ball

Introduction

In 1992 Cabot LNG,[1] a relatively small Boston-based LNG importer and owner of the Everett LNG receiving terminal just north of Boston, approached the government of Trinidad & Tobago about developing a new LNG export project. Although three attempts had been made previously to develop LNG in Trinidad & Tobago, nothing had come of them and the government had largely concentrated on attracting intensive gas-based industries to the country. The industries had come but had not greatly prospered. Cabot's approach came soon after the government had decided to liberalize its economic policy; new sources of revenue were badly needed. Amoco and British Gas (BG) (both with significant gas prospects in Trinidad & Tobago) signed a memorandum of understanding (MOU) with Cabot, and the Trinidad & Tobago National Gas Company (NGC) to promote an LNG export project (Gas Matters 1993b). The group launched a feasibility study in 1993. Atlantic LNG, the JV company eventually set up to own and run the project, was formed in 1995. Cabot and Enagas of Spain pledged to purchase a total of 3 mtpa of LNG. Construction started in 1996. The first cargo (train 1), bound for

The authors would like to thank Gas Strategies Consulting for the structure charts (figures 9.8–9.12) used in this chapter and for research and assistance. Furthermore, they would like to thank all of those involved in the project, then and now, who have provided useful facts, historical points, and advice.

[1] The names of many companies referred to in this history have changed, and continued to do so through the writing of this chapter. While those of the Atlantic LNG players are, largely speaking, chronologically accurate in the text, it helps to know what the changes were: Amoco is now part of BP, Cabot became Tractebel, became Suez LNG which, at the time of final proofing, was in merger talks with Gaz de France (GdF). The Enagas interests in Trinidad were transferred to Repsol and those in the Spanish market to Gas Natural; today's Enagas is an unbundled operator of infrastructure. What was once Amoco's Trinidad exploration and production portfolio dedicated to LNG is now operated by bpTT, which is owned 70% by BP and 30% by Repsol. Of the other companies these are the main ones: Elf became Total; Exxon, ExxonMobil; Phillips, ConocoPhillips; and Agip, ENI.

Boston, was loaded at the end of April 1999. Design work and sales negotiations for a two-train expansion with a further 6.8 mtpa capacity (trains 2 and 3) were started in early 1999 and construction started in 2000. Train 2 started up in August 2002 and train 3 in May 2003. Train 4 is scheduled to begin operations in early 2006, while train 5 is still looking for approval. The development has been rapid by the standards of LNG projects, and judged a success for all parties involved.

This chapter sets out to explore why the venture was so successful and why less favorable outcomes were seen for competing projects. The question of competing projects in this case is quite complex, and indeed the relevance of different competing projects appears different for different stakeholders – the buyers of LNG, the government of Trinidad & Tobago, and the project promoters.

It is necessary, however, to emphasize that wonderful as hindsight is, the project decisions must be viewed in the context of the time at which they were made. For LNG, the early-to-mid-1990s was a very different time. The first projects in Algeria and Libya, launched in the 1960s and 1970s, had suffered a series of setbacks and market reversals (see chapter 3), and every subsequent attempt to launch an LNG export project in the Atlantic Basin had failed. In the 1990s the main exporter in the Atlantic Basin, Algeria, had only just begun revamping its own facilities after a period of lean demand. The LNG business was largely a Pacific affair (dominated by sales to Japan) in which the Middle East had gained a small role. The achievement of the promoters of Atlantic LNG was truly mold-breaking and, for very many in the LNG business, unexpected. This is not to diminish the achievements of the other Atlantic Basin project developed at a similar time, Nigeria LNG (NLNG), which is discussed below – for it, too, broke precedents. The LNG project launched in Trinidad & Tobago, however, had unique features both commercially and politically which were even more exceptional in the world as it was when the actions and decisions described in this chapter took place.

It also needs to be said that this project in many ways demonstrates that a host government can, via its policies, confer a competitive advantage to projects in its country *vis-à-vis* the policies of competing projects' host governments. Especially for the first project, the formative stage of a new LNG industry in a country, this can be a critical factor. LNG export projects tend to be less geopolitically complex than international pipeline projects and particularly less onerous than pipeline projects in which transit countries are involved. They are, however, technically and logistically more complex, which makes LNG projects more elaborate to manage. They generally present a challenge for the host government, which is faced with balancing the long-term benefits of a successful export project with the concessions and support needed (at least in the short term) to bring a project to life. LNG projects usually require preferential tax treatment compared with oil to make them economically viable, and often require favorable treatment when compared with gas for local use as well. Such concessions to multi-national companies are bound to be politically sensitive and require skilled negotiation to steer between the Scylla of offering too much and the Charybdis of a stillborn project. Furthermore, where there is local use and exports are a potential rival for the use of gas, a local debate usually surfaces over whether this precious domestic resource should be "wasted" on foreign customers. The host-country government will have to navigate this debate, often repeatedly. This debate arose in Trinidad & Tobago, and was resolved in favor of exports.

The Trinidad & Tobago government created a political and economic environment for the project that compared favorably with that faced by its would-be competitors, from its attitude towards outside investment to its political stability. Such factors were likely as important to the project's success as its commercial innovations.[2]

Historical Background

Oil was discovered in Trinidad & Tobago in 1886 and has been extracted on the island since 1907 (Geological Society of Trinidad & Tobago 2005). In fact, the steel drums characteristic of Caribbean music originated in Trinidad & Tobago through the excess of empty oil barrels discarded on the island. Since its inception, oil has been the mainstay of the island's economy. Gas was used only for oil recovery until the late 1950s, when Federation Chemicals pioneered the use of gas for ammonia production. Most of the oil and gas production now comes from fields in relatively shallow water off the east coast of the island (see the map in figure 9.1). A group led by Tenneco also discovered gas off the north coast of Trinidad in 1971. This gas lies under about 150 m of water and is much less rich in natural gas liquids than a typical east coast field.

---

[2] A more enlightened Algerian government policy in the 1980s might well have preserved the dominant position of Algerian LNG in the Atlantic market. Even if it hadn't, its new policy in the mid-1990s, which led to the plants being refurbished, came too late to prevent Nigeria and Trinidad filling the void in the market which opened up. Likewise, the various obstacles thrown in the way of the NLNG project by the Nigerian government, particularly in the early 1990s allowed the Trinidad & Tobago project to catch up and find a place in the market. The two successive Trinidad governments involved, by contrast, gave support when it was needed and stood out as the most hospitable of the three possibly contending LNG governments (Trinidad, Nigeria, Algeria) for LNG investment.

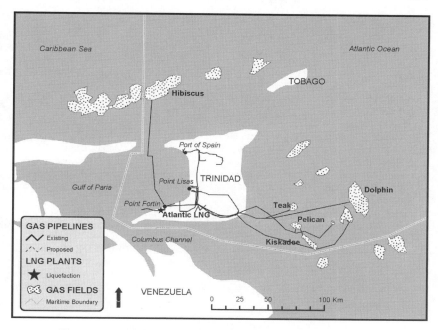

Figure 9.1. Trinidad & Tobago: gas infrastructure.

The first attempt to develop an LNG project in Trinidad occurred in the early 1970s (very early in the history of the LNG industry, which was born in 1964) when Amoco and the government spent two years negotiating with People's Gas of Chicago about the possibility of a project. Eventually the government decided that gas should be used to develop industry locally, and LNG disappeared from sight for a decade (Jobity and Racha 1999).

By the time of the first oil shock in 1973, following many years of low oil prices, the Trinidadian economy was in crisis with a large deficit, negligible foreign exchange reserves, and high unemployment (17 percent in 1970). As with many oil-producing countries at that time, Trinidad moved to take closer control of the industry, acquiring BP's operations in 1969 and Shell's in 1974. The National Gas Company of Trinidad & Tobago was formed in 1975 to develop the gas market and was granted monopoly rights for the purchase, transmission, and sale of gas within the country. Trinidad & Tobago never moved to complete nationalization of the upstream oil industry, however.

Table 9.1 *Gas-based projects in Trinidad & Tobago, 1985*

Company	Ownership	Start up (year)	Cost (million US$)	Management/Marketing
Iron and Steel Company of Trinidad & Tobago (ISCOTT)	100% government	1980	350.0	Local
Trinidad & Tobago Nitrogen company (TRINGENI)	51% government 49% W. R. Grace	1977	111.4	W. R. Grace: Management and Marketing
Fertilizers of Trinidad & Tobago (FERTRIN)	51% government 49% Amoco	1982	350.0	Amoco: Management and Marketing
Trinidad & Tobago Methanol company (TTMC)	100% government	1984	179.2	National Energy Corporation (Govt Owned)
Trinidad & Tobago Urea Company (TTUC)	100% government	1984	117.1	FERTRIN: Management Agrico Chemicals (US): Marketing

Source: Farrell (1987).

The increase in oil prices in 1973 and again in 1979 produced a huge cash windfall for the island and initiated rapid economic growth (see figure 3.7, p. 62). GDP grew from US$1.3 billion in 1973 to US$8.1 billion in 1982 and currency reserves reached US$3 billion in the same year (World Bank 2003). The government set out to encourage industries that were intensive users of gas by developing suitable infrastructure – in particular the industrial area and port facilities at Point Lisas – and by investing directly in the industries themselves, although generally supported by management contracts with international players. Five gas-based projects had been developed by 1985 (table 9.1) (Barclay 2003).

Trinidad & Tobago was very successful in attracting large-scale industry (proximity to the US market undoubtedly being a factor), but there are limits to the amount of gas that a small country can consume itself. Consumption leveled off at around 4 Bcm per year for most of the 1980s, but proven gas reserves stood at 310 Bcm (BP 2003), sufficient for about eighty years consumption at the then current rate. Faced with limited prospects of selling more gas, Tenneco attempted to promote an LNG project for the second time in the early 1980s. This was taken up by the government and discussed with several potential players. It was an

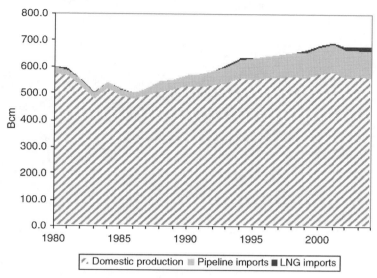

Figure 9.2. US gas supply and demand, 1980–2004.
Source: Alphatania (2004).

unfortunate moment; the oil price hike of 1979 had produced a world-wide recession in the early 1980s. Demand for gas fell in the United States (the main potential market for Trinidad LNG) and did not recover to 1980 levels for more than a decade (see figure 9.2).

While 1979 was a record year for US LNG imports, they declined rapidly thereafter and did not hit a higher level until a record of 14.5 Bcm per year (10.65 mtpa) was recorded in 2003. Shortly after 1979, the contracts for Algerian LNG (the sole source of LNG supply in the Atlantic Basin at that time) collapsed, victims of US market problems and Algeria's efforts to raise prices (see chapter 3). The United States was still left with an oversupply of indigenous gas which precipitated "deregulation" of the US gas industry as pipeline companies were allowed to abandon most of their long term take-or-pay contracts and seek abundant and cheaper unregulated gas (see figure 9.2). Nominal prices for newly discovered gas, which had under regulated wellhead pricing been as high as $10 per mmbtu, fell steadily and remained (on average) around or below $2 per mmbtu until the mid-1990s (see figure 9.3). These price levels were too low to make LNG a viable proposition, particularly as the projected costs of the Tenneco project were very high,

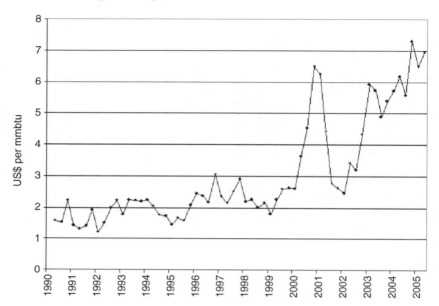

Figure 9.3. Henry Hub historic prices, 1990–2005, US$ per mmbtu.

Note: The Henry Hub, located at Erath, Louisiana, is the centralized point for natural gas futures trading in the United States. The Henry Hub offers shippers access to fourteen interconnecting pipeline systems that have markets in the Midwest, Northeast, Southeast, and Gulf Coast regions of the United States. In November 1989, the Henry Hub was selected by NYMEX as the official delivery mechanism for the world's first natural gas futures contract because of its interconnect ability and its proven track record in providing exceptional transportation service. Henry Hub prices quoted on NYMEX have since become the benchmark for US natural gas prices. Prices in regional markets vary depending on transport costs and transport bottlenecks from the Henry Hub. Such variation is known as "basis risk."

Source: NYMEX (2005).

based on north coast gas and the existing level of LNG plant cost (Jobity and Racha 1999). The second proposed LNG project came to nothing and faded away quietly in the early 1980s.[3]

The performance of the gas-consuming industries in Trinidad & Tobago provided little comfort, either. The steel plant was late to be

---

[3] This is not the place to discuss the history of US gas prices and regulation in detail; suffice it to say that while the price picture stayed in the $2.00–2.40 per mmbtu range

commissioned, experienced technical problems, and its output was subject to US anti-dumping duties. Investments in both ammonia and methanol plants turned out to be based on overly optimistic forecasts of price. These industries are very cyclical and only profitable in rare years (Barclay 2003). The difficult world economic climate of the early 1980s was not a propitious time for such investments.

To add to the pile of problems facing Trinidad & Tobago, oil prices collapsed in late 1985; the country fell into a seven-year recession. GDP fell by an average of 4.7 percent per year from 1982 to 1989. Unemployment rose from 9.9 percent in 1982 to an estimated 22 percent in 1990. By 1990, foreign exchange reserves had fallen to $492 million and external debt soared to $2.5 billion. In 1989 the government of Trinidad & Tobago approached international lending agencies for funding. As part of the loan conditions, it agreed to implement stabilization and structural adjustment programs (SAPs). The government set about liberalizing trade and foreign exchange, divesting state assets, and encouraging foreign investment. This program to implement the Washington Consensus of economic policy was in its early stages when the government published a Green Paper on energy policy in November 1992. The key elements were summarized by Amoco, a highly relevant international investor, as:

- Shift to natural gas to monetize the island's most plentiful resource
- Promote competition within the energy industry to maximize the government's take and to attract new business to Trinidad & Tobago with the country's abundant supplies of natural gas
- Privatize local industry to promote efficiency and repay national debt.

Mindful of this new attitude toward monetizing gas, Amoco had briefly flirted with a LNG project at the beginning of the 1990s – to supply Puerto Rico – but could not obtain satisfactory sales commitments. Such was the economic climate facing potential LNG project investors at the time that Atlantic LNG was being considered.

---

right into the late 1990s, the market situation in the mid-1990s was radically different to that at the beginning of the 1980s. At the time that this Tenneco project was envisaged, the gulf between projected cost and US price and market opening was too great. The opening seized upon by the Atlantic LNG partners almost fifteen years later was based on far better project economics and on the fact that LNG in Boston attracted a higher price than the rest of the US market right up through the 1990s when Henry Hub became the marker price. Even then, the old Tenneco north coast discoveries were not yet economic enough for inclusion in train 1 supply.

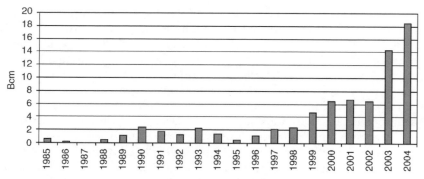

Figure 9.4. US LNG imports, 1985–2004.
Source: Alphatania (2004).

The Competitive Context and the Alternative Projects

After three false starts by Tenneco and Amoco, Cabot LNG initiated the Trinidad LNG project in 1992. That effort laid the groundwork for the Atlantic LNG project that exists today. Cabot was later joined in this endeavor by Amoco, BG, and NGC. Once these partners had formed the project company in 1995, they were joined by the Spanish oil and gas company, Repsol.

Cabot LNG, with its subsidiary company Distrigas, was a small part of a much larger company and a small player in the LNG business. It owned the Everett LNG terminal just north of Boston and sold gas in the highly seasonal New England market. The Everett terminal suffered from limited supply and was anxious to secure a new source of LNG. Only a trickle of Algerian gas (0.64 million tonnes in 1991) was finding its way into Boston, mainly in the winter to meet rising demand in the residential and commercial sectors (see figure 9.4). Since pipeline capacity into the northeast US states was limited, prices tended to rise quite sharply in the winter months to a level at which Algeria was prepared to supply. Two long-term contracts existed between Distrigas and Sonatrach, but LNG was supplied only when the prevailing price was affordable for Distrigas as well as acceptable to Sonatrach – a situation that usually existed only in the winter.

Demand was growing briskly in New England, from 9.9 Bcm in 1989 to 14.6 Bcm in 1992 (see figure 9.5). Without new supplies, Cabot faced a decline in market share. It also faced the threat that, if pipeline capacity into the northeast of the United States were significantly expanded, the

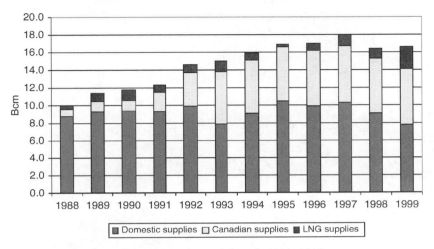

Figure 9.5. New England: gas demand, 1988–1999.
Source: EIA (1999).

premium price for gas in the winter would erode. If this happened, Cabot would risk losing its Algerian supply and would have greater difficulty buying new LNG. Since the company was dependent entirely on LNG for its business, this was a fairly stark proposition. Two new pipeline projects – the Portland Natural Gas Transmission System and the Sable Offshore Energy Project via the Maritimes and Northeast Pipeline from Canada – were under consideration (see the map in figure 9.6) (Department of Fossil Energy 1996). Cabot wanted to acquire LNG rapidly in an attempt to pre-empt some of the pipeline supply. Its main alternatives to Trinidad & Tobago were potential new LNG projects in Nigeria and Venezuela, and at one point Cabot signed up for Nigerian supply.

The driver for Amoco was the desire to monetize more gas resources in Trinidad; LNG, increasingly, looked like the best and only option. By adding the LNG route to its gas sales options, Amoco could diversify away from the methanol and ammonia price risk.[4]

Amoco was by far the dominant gas supplier to the island, with over 80 percent of the market. Gas demand on the island had reached 6.1

---

[4] As things turned out (with US prices soaring after startup in 1999) it is easy to assume today that Amoco expected higher net-backs from LNG. At the time, however, LNG looked decidedly marginal and at best likely to achieve a similar price to producers as rival island gas projects. The main prize at the time was seen as significant extra volumes of sales.

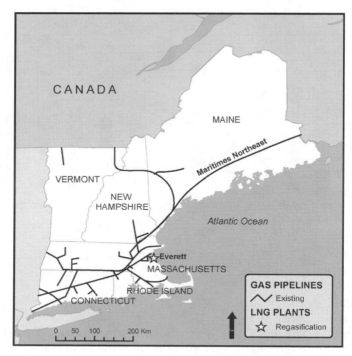

Figure 9.6. New England: natural gas infrastructure.

Bcm per year by 1993, with 1.4 Bcm per year being used for gas lift in Amoco's oil operations. Of the commercially traded gas, 1.3 Bcm per year was used for power generation and 3.4 Bcm per year by the various gas-consuming industries. The only non-Amoco supplies had been the Pelican field operated by state-owned Trintomar, which was in decline. However, the first 0.25 Bcm per year was now flowing from the Enron Kiskadee field under a new contract, signed in October 1992, which would build up to 1.6 Bcm per year, primarily to supply the new Caribbean Methanol Company plant scheduled to start up in 1994. Furthermore, BG signed a contract with NGC in September 1993 for the supply of up to 2.8 Bcm per year of gas from the Dolphin field, starting in 1996.

The situation – saturation of domestic markets and the entry of new suppliers – was a wake-up call for Amoco, which had become rather complacent about its position in Trinidad. It now realized that it could not expect to develop its full gas potential through island sales alone. Indeed, the desire of the government for competition in gas supply meant that Amoco's share of the local market was likely to be eroded further. In addition, gas sales prices on the island were largely tied to the highly volatile methanol and ammonia prices, with which Amoco was not very comfortable.

A further complication was that in order to minimize costs, Amoco had developed the habit of not proving gas reserves ahead of agreeing to sales contracts. Although Amoco believed at the time it was sitting on 226 Bcm of gas resources, its proven reserves were only 31 Bcm at the end of 1993, insufficient to fulfill in entirety its latest twenty-year NGC contract signed in 1991. It was, however, selling gas at well above contract volumes to compensate for the falling production from the Pelican field. Nevertheless, on the basis of higher reserve expectations, Amoco was very interested in developing the LNG option.

BG was in a similar frame of mind, although it had a weaker acreage position. It nonetheless hoped to prove more gas in the Dolphin field than it had sold and also held a stake in the north coast discoveries, which it had obtained when it acquired Tenneco's upstream activities in 1988. For neither upstream company was the prospect of more island sales a real alternative to LNG; the scale and timing made the two monetization routes complementary.

The People's National Movement (PNM) government under Patrick Manning also was anxious to see the development of LNG in addition to local industry. Although there were doubters in the country who thought that Trinidad would be better off concentrating on reserving gas for local development and employment-intensive projects, in practice Trinidad has been able to do both. As often happens in countries when a new monetization option is added, the prospect of LNG was a spur to exploration that discovered far more gas than was expected. At the same time that it encouraged LNG, the Trinidad government adopted a new policy that linked local gas prices to the market prices of the end-product chemicals produced with gas; in effect, this policy it has greatly reduced the risk of investing in downstream chemical plants by shifting the price risk to the gas producers (which in turn was why Amoco was keen to add a different market outlet to its sales portfolio). As a result, eight new chemical plants using gas feedstock have been commissioned since 1995, and three more are under construction. Trinidad is the leading regional producer of methanol and ammonia and its position has strengthened as US plants have shut their production since North American gas prices soared in 2002. (Those high prices have also lifted the price that Trinidad & Tobago gets when it sells LNG to the United States.) Gas consumption on the island is now in excess of 10 Bcm per year (1 bcf/d). The country has seen a long period of sustained economic growth.

The final actor, Spain's gas monopoly Enagas, (whose majority owner at the time, Repsol, would later join the project as a partner) was brought in only after the project had decided to increase its scale to reduce cost. Soon thereafter, Enagas successfully concluded a fast-track purchase deal for the expanded volumes. Spain was seeing rapid growth in gas demand, and the government was concerned about overdependence on Algeria, the source of almost two-thirds of its gas at the time. Enagas was therefore encouraged to find alternative sources of supply. Geographically, Spain is isolated from the European pipeline grid, and its neighbor France is a reluctant and expensive route for transporting gas from the north. These factors combined to focus Enagas on LNG.[5] Beginning with efforts to buy Nigerian LNG, when Nigerian gas deals were in limbo, Enagas turned to Trinidad. (Enagas would eventually procure LNG from both the Atlantic Basin and Nigeria.)

For LNG markets in the United States and Europe, the most obvious alternative projects to Atlantic LNG train 1 were Nigeria LNG and Venezuela LNG, both of which were being actively pursued at the same time. And, because the only viable market in the United States was seen as Cabot's small opening in the northeast, the pipelines from Canada to the northeast were also a threat to Atlantic's potential feasibility. In terms of partner perception at the time, this pipeline threat was a key driver. There was a strong feeling that unless they got LNG to Boston in the time window ending around 1998, both this market and its price premium would disappear. Also in the frame, especially at the beginning, was the fact that Cabot had signed up for LNG from Nigeria and had fought a long-drawn-out battle to obtain ownership of one of the three laid-up LNG ships which the US Maritime Administration (MarAd) had sold. When other contracted buyers rolled over their contracts after repeated delays by NLNG, Cabot cagily neither cancelled nor confirmed

---

[5] Spain had both LNG supply and the new pipeline supply through the GME pipeline from Algeria, which thus supplied almost two-thirds of its gas. Worried about diversity of supply, for supply security reasons, the Spanish government let it be known that it would tolerate no more than 60 percent of total gas supply coming from one country. With only a small quantity of expensive gas from Norway and domestic supply almost exhausted, Enagas had little choice but to seek alternative LNG supplies and it was an early customer of NLNG. When Nigeria suffered a series of politically driven delays in the early 1990s, Trinidad became an ideal addition to the supply slate. Trinidad's partners knew that they had to compete on price not only with other LNG, but also with Norwegian piped gas. Only later did others in the Spanish market, wishing to compete with Enagas (whose sales activities are now conducted by Gas Natural), take the LNG route to bypass the difficulties of accessing Enagas' pipelines. For more history on Enagas' pursuit of imports, see chapter 3.

its intentions (Gas Matters 1990).[6] This perceived pressure is why the Atlantic LNG partners acted to so quickly and broke so many LNG project precedents. In the event, Trinidad's LNG arrived in Boston first, but the pipelines were built anyway. Cabot failed to renew its NLNG contract and the ship it had secured in the MarAd battle became the *Matthew*. By a twist of fate, the *Matthew* delivered the first Atlantic LNG cargo, five months ahead of the first from Nigeria. Ultimately, NLNG landed its first cargo later in 1999 and quickly moved to firm up expansion plans. US oversupply – the "gas bubble" – had finally been used up by the end of the 1990s, and rising US prices were attracting new LNG suppliers. The market therefore was no real constraint on expansion. It is somewhat unclear, then, why Atlantic LNG fell behind Nigeria in its plans for building trains 2 and 3, even after it had beaten Nigeria to startup. We shall explore in depth the mould-breaking path taken by Atlantic LNG to market in 1999 and subsequent decisions on the expansion trains.

The Development of Atlantic LNG Trains

Train 1

When Cabot approached the Trinidad government in 1992, it had a requirement for about 2 mtpa of LNG, which is equivalent to a feed gas rate of some 3.1 Bcm. Initial discussions were held with NGC on behalf of the government, but by early 1993 BG and Amoco had joined in the discussions; clearly it was unrealistic to hope to develop an LNG facility without the cooperation of the major gas resource holders.

Development of a new greenfield LNG project is an undertaking of almost unprecedented complexity that requires, simultaneously, the development of major gas fields, the construction of large-scale liquefaction plants and ancillary facilities for the recovery of natural gas liquids, provision of port facilities and ships. Investment in the whole LNG chain typically runs into billions of dollars. The whole development is normally underwritten by long-term (twenty-year plus) take-or-pay sales contracts, with one or more overseas buyer. A new LNG project represents, above all, a management and organizational challenge even to the largest companies. Success critically depends on a supportive host government. More LNG projects have failed as a result

---

[6] This involved Shell chartering two of the ships from Argent Marine who bought them secure in the knowledge of the Shell charter, and Cabot agreeing to charter the ship it bought (then the *Gamma*, today the *Matthew*), to NLNG for half the time. This never materialized, as discussed in the text.

of management failures or lack of informed government support than for any other reason.

The group coming together in Trinidad had no experience in developing LNG export facilities. Cabot was a small importer of LNG and was owner of a laid-up 125,000m^3 LNG ship (then named the *Gamma*, now the *Matthew*) that had been made redundant by the failure of the Algerian trade more than a decade before, and was also half-chartered to Nigeria LNG (see p. 281 above).

BG had been a pioneer of LNG as a launch buyer. It was the recipient of the very first internationally traded LNG when it took the first cargo of LNG at its Canvey Island terminal in the United Kingdom in 1964 and had played a significant role in developing the world's first LNG ships. However, North Sea gas had been discovered in the United Kingdom as the first cargo of LNG arrived; imports dwindled to a trickle in the 1980s and ceased altogether in 1990. BG nevertheless still had one of the original ships, the *Methane Princess,* on charter to Enagas. In 1993 it also acquired two more ships that had spent twenty years working on the Alaska–Tokyo run for the Kenai LNG project before they became surplus when the Japanese required them to be replaced with two new ships. At the time, then, BG's only presence in LNG was as a ship owner.

Amoco and NGC had no LNG experience at all, although each had considerable technical experience within its own sphere and Amoco had a very successful track record of developing major international oil and gas projects.

Not surprisingly, it took the group time to develop leadership. The first task was to establish the basic technical and economic feasibility of a single-train plant with the relatively small capacity (even for a single train) of 2 mtpa. Conventional wisdom at that time was that a minimum economic scale for a new LNG plant was two or three trains with about a 7.5 mtpa total capacity. However, it looked most unlikely that there was a profitable market for such large quantities in the Americas or Europe, even if the gas had been available. Furthermore, the economic benchmarks for LNG at that time were all in the Pacific, where gas prices were substantially higher than they were likely to be even in the northeast of the Unitd States. The LNG price into Japan averaged $3.52 per mmbtu in 1993 whereas the US Henry Hub price was $2.12 per mmbtu (BP 2004). A clear impression at the time was that the project had to be robust down to US gas prices of $2 per mmbtu.

Technical scoping studies were carried out, and by the end of 1993 it was clear that a larger plant – closer to 3 mtpa – was needed. Therefore, more sales than Cabot's 2 mtpa were required at the LNG prices that could be expected. The associated gas liquids, present in the gas from the east coast fields, would almost certainly be critical to the project's economics. There was considerable nervousness about US gas prices. By 1992, the NYMEX futures contract based on Henry Hub in Louisiana provided the marker price for all gas in the United States. Gas prices at other US locations have a basis differential to Henry Hub; prices were sometimes lower at Lake Charles, Louisiana (the other operational US regasification terminal at the time) than at Henry Hub. In the northeast, however, winter gas prices often exceeded $3 per mmbtu, but were highly volatile. It was not clear whether a long-term contract based on volatile US market prices could be financed.

The clear tasks in 1994 were therefore to design the plant in such a way as to minimize costs and to find a buyer for the balance of the volume. Very little attention had been given at that point to how the project should be structured. Cabot and NGC were far smaller companies than either BG or Amoco, but no shareholdings had been agreed, not least because it had not been agreed what the role and scope of a project company should be, or even whether it should be a company or an unincorporated joint venture like the North West Shelf Project in Australia. Would all the companies participate in upstream gas supply – or, if not, how would the liquefaction company buy gas or choose between the competing ambitions of BG and Amoco? Did the project intend to sell gas freight-on-board (f.o.b.) or would it take responsibility for shipping and delivering LNG to its customers? Was the project even viable under current fiscal terms? The government offered various investment incentives to new industries; what package should the project seek?

Decision-making on these issues all progressed more or less in parallel before a final ownership structure was adopted. This approach ultimately turned out to be a key success factor for the project, although more experienced LNG promoters scoffed at the newcomers' approach.

Technical   The real technical success story of Atlantic LNG is cost reduction. The following section relies heavily on the paper given by David Jamieson, Paul Johnson, and Phil Redding of Atlantic LNG at the LNG 12 Conference in Perth in May 1998 (Jamieson, Johnson, and Redding 1998). As the authors describe in detail, much of the cost reduction was achieved by commercial ingenuity and management rather than technological innovation.

The most recent greenfield LNG plant to be commissioned at the time Atlantic LNG was in the design stage, was the three-train, 6 mtpa, North West Shelf project in Australia, which made its first delivery to Japan in

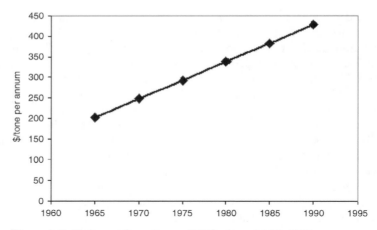

Figure 9.7. Unit cost for a 3 mtpa LNG plant, 1965–1990.
Source: Jamieson, Johnson, and Redding (1998).

1989 at a cost which was put at A$12 billion (about US$8 billion in 1989 USD). The real unit cost of LNG plants had been rising steadily since the first plant in 1964, rather surprisingly; the normal trend is that technical cost declines over time once the technology has become reasonably mature (see figure 9.7).

Initial analysis based on this trend suggested that the cost of a 2.3–2.5 mtpa LNG plant in Trinidad would be about US$1 billion, for the engineering, procurement, and construction (EPC) contract for the LNG plant itself, not the full project cost. If the plant were to cost that much, the project would not have been viable. To obtain an acceptable rate of return, it would be necessary to cut the cost to US$600 million. Feasibility work from experienced LNG contractors suggested that this would be very difficult to achieve, although the project's own analysis suggested that it should be possible. However, it also became apparent that there were major scale benefits from increasing the size to 3 mtpa. This gave some concern about the availability of additional market offtake for the larger plant and also about the adequacy of reserves (which were unproven at that stage). However, the larger size was chosen and used as the design basis developed with Kellogg (now) in Houston. By the time the Front-End Engineering and Design (FEED) contracts were let, the project had set a target of US$750 million for the EPC cost of a 3 mtpa plant.

Considerable thought went into how to reverse the rising cost trend and getting back to the lower costs of the earlier plants. Two factors appear to be the main contributors.

First, most LNG plants, particularly the more recent ones, had been built to serve the Japanese market. Japan has no real alternative source of gas to LNG (it has a minute quantity of indigenous gas). Thus, Japanese buyers placed far more emphasis on security and reliability of supply than on getting the lowest price. (Japanese power companies – which were the main buyers of LNG – have traditionally not been very price-sensitive because they are allowed to pass on their fuel costs in their electricity tariffs.) LNG plants to serve the Japanese market (over two-thirds the global LNG market at the time) were therefore built with very generous safety and capacity margins. It was quite common for LNG plants in the Pacific Basin to produce at 15 percent above their design capacity. (Australia's North West Shelf project, designed for 6 mtpa, produced 7 mtpa at the outset and was very simply debottlenecked for a total capacity of 7.5 mtpa.)

Secondly, there was very little competition to build LNG plants. Only thirteen LNG plant sites existed in 1994 and these plants had been built over a period of thirty years. There were only four major active contractors who built LNG plants – Kellogg, JGC, Bechtel, and Chiyoda, and they often worked as JVs (Kellogg with JGC and Bechtel with Chiyoda). If one of the contractors prepared the FEED, it generally acquired so much more detailed knowledge of the project than the competitors that it would almost inevitably win the EPC tender. Furthermore, for the last twenty years, all the new plants had used Air Products' APCI technology. Using this technology required purchasing a technology license from APCI and buying the core piece of equipment – the giant main spiral-wound heat exchanger that is at the heart of the process – as no other company could make it.

Amoco may not have had LNG experience, but it did have recent experience in cutting costs in complex gas projects from its North Sea operations. Amoco brought in an engineering manager for the project straight from a North Sea development project (David Jamieson), who mounted an assault on all design factors might inflate cost.

And as so often happens when fresh eyes set on an old problem, Amoco tackled the problem in a new way, with striking results. As a matter of design philosophy, it was established that a single large train would have acceptable reliability provided that the equipment was configured in a particular way. To minimize the risk of the whole train being shut down as a result of breakdown it had twin drives so that failure of a single machine would result only in the loss of half the capacity. This was a simple solution to a problem that had been solved so many times in the past by adding costly redundancy and was one of the reasons for the "at least two trains" rule that developers had imposed on themselves in the past. Unlike plants serving Japan, the planners decided that slightly lower standards of availability could be accepted because the buyers of Trinidad's gas had other sources of supply. This decision allowed a more vigorous attack on costs by keeping redundancy and complication to a minimum. Ironically this plant, like all of its predecessors, offered greater than nameplate capacity even as it maintained the innovative cost-reductions.

Of all the cost-reducing measures taken by the train 1 pioneers, none had as great an impact on costs as what is now called the "dual FEED" strategy.[7] This strategy was largely successful because the project was willing to accept a technology the rest of the industry had shunned for almost three decades and which, even as the plant was being built, was predicted to fail by those who should have known better. The commercial innovation of the process was the tendering strategy. The project's success in generating real competition between contractors had a dramatic effect. Key to the process was the principle that there were no favorites anywhere in the process.

The first shock was that Kellogg, after working with the project to prepare the design basis, did not win the competition to prepare the FEED; that went to a joint venture between Chiyoda and Hudson Engineering. In normal practice, this FEED would then have been put to tender and various contracting groups would bid slightly different prices and one would win. It was a sequential process and produced little competition except in lean times.

This time, things turned out differently. At this point the design was based on the APCI process, but while the Atlantic LNG partners were working on the design basis, Bechtel had just finished working in Alaska to refurbish and upgrade the Kenai LNG plant owned by Phillips and Marathon that had been operating since 1969. Phillips and Bechtel had realized the potential of the Phillips cascade technology used on the plant and decided to try to interest the industry in an optimized version. This development came rather late in the day for Trinidad, but two of the sponsors (Amoco and BG) were very interested to explore possible cost savings or other benefits to gain from an upgraded version of the old

---

[7] It should be noted that the NLNG project had also conducted a "dual FEED" process after if had been forced by the government to reject the first winning bid for political reasons, and needed to go quickly to construction once the FEED work was done. So here the projects were innovating in parallel, with Atlantic LNG improving on the NLNG process. Both achieved speed and efficiency and today dual FEED, with both the contractors paid for the FEED, is an accepted, albeit not always used, industry practice. The willingness to consider rival technologies made the Trinidad process more successful at reducing costs.

technology. The only way, at this rather late stage, to assess realistically the economics of the Phillips process was to ask Bechtel to carry out a parallel FEED exercise, and to pay for it. This would mean the project paying for two FEEDs and using only one. The extra cost was accepted and the second FEED ran in parallel with the first. Both FEED contractors had undertaken to submit full EPC bids following FEED. (Kellogg was also asked to bid on the basis of the APCI FEED.) The bidding process was highly competitive and was won by Bechtel, using the Phillips process. The project was built on budget and set something of a new marker in LNG plant costs. (Shell and ExxonMobil were also pursuing cost reductions by different routes in Oman and Qatar, and there is a lively debate in the industry about whose plant cost least; Trinidad certainly scores for its combination of manageable scale and low unit cost.) One clear strand of Trinidad's success was the determined delivery of a low-cost project, which was vital to its economic viability.

Marketing and Shipping Cabot was the initial driver for the project, but in many ways it did not provide a conventional market for a new LNG project, let alone an ideal one. Most LNG supplies had been sold to traditional utility buyers in East Asia or Europe. In Japan, this meant the power and gas distribution companies such as Tokyo Electric and Osaka Gas, in Korea, KOGAS, and the (partially or primarily state-owned) utilities such as GdF, Enagas (now Gas Natural) in Spain, or Snam (now ENI Gas and Power) in Italy. These companies are characteristically large and impeccably creditworthy. They historically purchased LNG on long-term take-or-pay contracts with prices determined at contract signing and then adjusted by contractually agreed oil-linked pricing formulae. Price formulae in most contracts are revisited every three – five years to ensure that prices are still in line with the market.

Cabot was very different. From the mid-1980s prices in the US gas market were set by the spot gas market price. By 1990, this market was deep and liquid enough for the NYMEX futures exchange to launch the Henry Hub gas futures contract, one of the most successful commodity trading contracts ever launched, and it quickly became the market against which all US – and, later, North American – gas prices were traded. By the mid-1990s, US gas prices had uncoupled from oil prices but were much more volatile than oil. All gas sold in the United States whether on short- or long-term contracts, had little alternative but to accept US gas market prices. Instruments did exist to allow prices to be hedged to provide a degree of risk management but this market was, and is, not liquid for a long period forward, certainly nothing approaching the normal life of an LNG contract.

Trinidad required a long-term take-or-pay sale for two main reasons. Although the US gas market is liquid, there is limited LNG-receiving capacity and a new project would have to be assured that it could always physically deliver gas to the market. Furthermore, the project wanted to obtain project finance and undoubtedly the lenders would insist on "normal" LNG contracting practice – that is, something more like the long-term Japanese and European contracts.

Cabot was prepared to negotiate a long-term take-or-pay contract provided that pricing was done on a net-back basis from its market in Boston. This clearly protected Cabot from price risk and overcame some of the concerns about Cabot's relative lack of creditworthiness. However, this approach did leave the project and its bankers with the need to make a forward estimate of US gas prices for the life of the contract. This was particularly critical, as Boston was seen as a high-price, niche market within the US market because of its high winter demand and high basis differential to the Henry Hub price. The project would not be viable on the Henry Hub price alone. This required an in-depth study of the market and the particular conditions in the Boston area. Fortunately both Amoco and BG (at the time a major shareholder and participant in National Gas Clearinghouse, now Dynegy) were major players in the US gas market and their experience, supported by consultant studies, provided the necessary confidence.

Since it had been established that the LNG plant would produce 3 mtpa, the search had started for another buyer. In reality, this meant a European buyer, as the price in the rest of the US market was too low and the next nearest LNG receiving facilities were in Europe.[8] This also provided a useful means to diversify market risk, as European buyers were more firmly in control of their markets and average prices were higher there. The established LNG buyers in Western Europe were the monopolies in France, Spain, Belgium, and Italy. Each country had a gas utility responsible for all the gas imports to the country – GdF in France, Enagas in Spain, Distrigaz in Belgium, and Snam in Italy. All these buyers had both pipeline and LNG options and thus

---

[8] It is easy today to see that other opportunities existed in theory in the United States But with speed of the essence and with other LNG promoters from the experienced Shell to Europe's Statoil having failed to break the regulatory logjam needed to open other terminals, the only real alternative at the time was Lake Charles in Louisiana where the price was too low and there was no ease of commercial agreement that the project enjoyed in Boston. Also, Europe had terminals with both plenty of capacity and creditworthy buyers able to pay a higher price than the US market then offered.

pricing for new LNG supplies would be highly competitive. Spain's options were limited, however, as the government had adopted a policy not to depend on one supplier for more than 60 percent of its gas. Algeria, its main pipeline and LNG supplier, was close to this limit. At that time, European gas market liberalization had not begun. Gas was purchased on long-term take-or-pay contracts with prices linked to oil product price (primarily fuel oil and gasoil), sometimes with an inflation or coal component. Prices in Europe were somewhat higher than at Henry Hub although lower than Boston (average price of Algerian LNG into Spain was $2.26 per mmbtu in 1994 when the Brent crude oil price averaged $15.81 per barrel, and $2.32 per mmbtu in 1995 when crude averaged $17.04 per barrel (*Gas Strategies* 2005). However, the shipping cost to Europe from Trinidad was also about $0.30 per mmbtu higher than to Boston.

The project, under some pressure to move quickly, went out looking for European buyers in the second half of 1994. The shareholders were almost as inexperienced at selling gas in Europe as they were in developing LNG. Amoco and BG both had substantial sales in the United Kingdom, but the UK market was isolated from mainland Europe and had significantly different characteristics. The project sought buyers who would take the lack of proven reserves on trust and who would be prepared to complete a deal in significantly less than the leisurely year-to-eighteen months that it usually took to negotiate a full gas sales contract in Europe. Furthermore, the ideal buyers would be prepared to buy from a company (Atlantic LNG) that did not yet exist, and whose exact shareholdings were unknown. This was all a pretty tall order in the mid-1990s.

Most European buyers had monopoly control over their markets and could plan well ahead so that they were not under time pressure to buy gas. They wanted proven gas from credible sellers. Not surprisingly, Atlantic LNG made little progress trying to sell gas in France or Italy. Spain was rather a different case. The Spanish market was relatively new and growing rapidly. It urgently needed new supplies to diversify from Algerian gas. Enagas had contracted to buy some NLNG, but the NLNG project kept missing deadlines and contracts were kept alive by rollovers by the buyers. Thus, even though Enagas had signed up for NLNG, at the time of its negotiations with the Trinidad partners the fate of that supply was uncertain. Trinidad supply would be welcome on suitable terms, and Enagas was willing to move quickly.

Furthermore, Cabot had a vision of much more flexible LNG trade in the Atlantic Basin. Cabot and Enagas, who had long had relations with each other as fellow buyers of Algerian LNG (not to mention as fellow would-be buyers of NLNG), rapidly established a letter of intent to cooperate on liftings and asked for considerable destination flexibility. Flexible destinations contrasted with most LNG sales, which require the LNG to be shipped to a defined unloading port, with any deviations to be agreed in advance with the seller (the so-called "destination clause"). Spain has much higher winter than summer demand, which Enagas, with very limited storage, was struggling to manage. Both Enagas and the project could see the advantage of placing gas in the deeper, more open, US market in summer even if this meant accepting a lower price.[9]

Enagas' parent, Repsol, also had ambitions to expand its upstream gas activities and saw an opportunity to gain a stake in the Trinidad project. By the summer of 1995, as delegates from the world LNG industry gathered in Birmingham for the LNG 11 conference, terms had been agreed for Enagas to buy 40 percent of the output and Cabot 60 percent. Destination flexibility terms were accepted, as was the ability of Enagas to take a stake in the LNG project. The sets of terms were agreed with unusual speed and, as part of the process, the shareholdings of a new company, Atlantic LNG of Trinidad & Tobago, were agreed – all in parallel. At the same time, uncertainty still surrounded NLNG's contracts and while this would soon end, it was significant that Trinidad's partners had secured their deal in this period.[10]

Both the Cabot and Enagas contracts were on an f.o.b. basis; Cabot had a ship and Enagas had shipping experience (as did BG). BG had, in any case already chartered some of its ships to Enagas. The partners could see benefits in delivered (d.e.s. or c.i.f.) sales, but Amoco, particularly, had had a rather unhappy experience with oil shipping and was doubtful about the commercial wisdom of owning and operating ships. After much debate it was decided to accept f.o.b. sales.

In summary, the marketing of Atlantic LNG train 1 was done remarkably rapidly by most LNG project standards and this speed was a significant contributor to the success of the project. At the time there

---

[9]   Spain's gas-fired electric power market had not yet taken off at this point. Furthermore this was the time when the Algerian LNG plants were undergoing refurbishment, cutting that source of winter supply, albeit temporarily. Enabling Enagas to take more of its volumes in the winter and Cabot to take more in the summer suited both parties and was the logic underlying the decision to give so much destination flexibility. In the end, however, the pattern was driven by price, not season, and most of the LNG goes to the United States, to all parties' benefit, especially Spain's. Thus one of the great commercial contributions of this project to modern LNG trading was arrived at by accident and the party willing to "suffer" US summer prices ended up the biggest gainer. Today in Spain, where the power sector is much bigger, we are approaching the time where the summer gas demand peak will be higher, as it has been for many years in Japan.

[10] For a contemporary account of the state of play between Atlantic LNG and Nigeria LNG at the time, see Gas Matters (1995a).

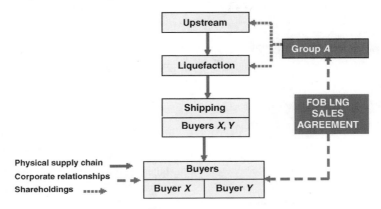

Figure 9.8. Integrated project with f.o.b. sales.

Note: Note that a similar structure where the sellers owned the shipping capacity (LNG tankers) would use c.i.f. or d.e.s. sales terms.

Source: Gas Strategies (2005).

was much agonizing about having a buyer as partner in the project (let alone two!) and whether the inevitable conflicts of interest could be managed. However, the presence of Cabot and later of Enagas gave considerable confidence in the marketing of the project. Far from being disadvantageous, the participation of the two buyers contributed to favorable sales terms and ultimately to the project's success.

Project Structure Perhaps the least successful feature of the Atlantic LNG train 1 development was the project structure. This is because it was easy to assemble at speed but very hard to expand, as the partners later discovered in the painful process of launching trains 2 and 3. That its participants have learned not to repeat the train 1 model underscores this point.

There have been three generic models for organizing LNG projects:

1. An *integrated structure*, in which the sponsors' shares in the project are in the upstream development and in the LNG plant; the project sells LNG, as shown in figure 9.8.
2. An *upstream transfer*, in which the upstream owner sells feed gas to a separate entity that runs the LNG plant which in turn sells LNG, as shown in figure 9.9.
3. A *tolling project*, in which the upstream owner retains title to the gas up to the point of sale and pays a tolling fee to the owners of the LNG plant for the liquefaction of the gas and its delivery, as shown in figure 9.10.

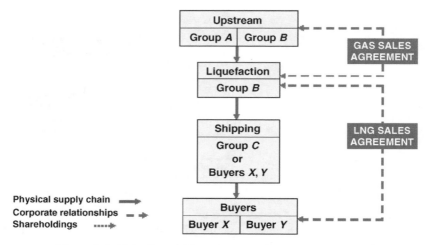

Figure 9.9. Transfer pricing arrangement.
Source: Gas Strategies (2005).

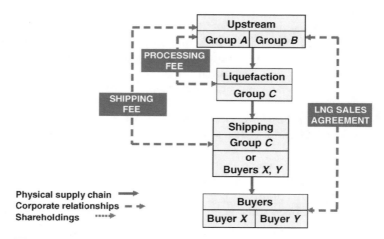

Figure 9.10. Tolling arrangement.
Source: Gas Strategies (2005).

Some form of each of these structures has been used successfully. The integrated structure (as in figure 9.8) has the advantage of avoiding the difficult issue of transfer pricing for the feed gas into the LNG plant. It is easiest to arrange where there is a single field that will be used to supply the plant and where all the potential sponsors already have a share in the upstream, although it is quite possible to have an integrated project for multiple fields as well.

The sale from the upstream into the LNG plant is perhaps the form found more than any other single type. It is simplest when there is a significant degree of common ownership between plant and upstream.

Tolling arrangements are rare. The Indonesian projects, however, have a quasi-tolling structure, in which the LNG plant is operated as a cost center and over the years a number of different gas fields have provided feed gas. This is particularly the case for PT Badak, at Bontang, Kalimantan. As of 2004, PT Badak is still the largest LNG facility in the world (see chapter 4). The fields receive a net-back from the LNG sales price. The Indonesians have also devised a satisfactory system for choosing which field's gas will provide the feed gas for the next expansion of the LNG plant. At Bontang, sales were coordinated by state company, Pertamina, centrally pooled, and grouped into "packages." If two different license areas (often with different operating groups) were in contention to provide feed gas to support new sales, then gas was taken from the two license areas pro rata to the quantity of reserves proved and certified by each license that had not been used for an earlier sales package. Thus, if license A had 60 Bcm of proven reserves not already committed to an earlier sales package and field B had 30 Bcm, then 66.67 percent of the supply for the next sales package would come from license A and 33.33 percent from license B. This encouraged exploration by creating a "reserves race" between competing license owners, which suited the Indonesian government very well.[11]

The situation in Trinidad was quite complicated, and no LNG precedent seemed entirely relevant. Two of the sponsors – Amoco and BG – had ambitions to supply gas from upstream; the other two did not. Neither NGC nor Cabot was financially very strong, but none of the partners was very clear about how they wished to finance the project.

The main issues to resolve were corporate form, shareholdings, and gas supply. The project started with a completely blank slate on all issues

---

[11] At the time, the upstream partners considered a modified Bontang structure as a way of both resolving reserves issues and inspiring more exploration but, while it was seriously considered it was not pursued, for a number of reasons. In hindsight, it is easier to see that geopolitical thinking at the time – by all of the stakeholders – could not fathom such a scheme working without state or state company compulsion (as is the case in Bontang). But Trinidad & Tobago's solid competitive investment environment was a product of the central government's aversion to taking a central role – either directly or via NGC – thus no one was eager to pursue an option which would require it. We now know that companies who can voluntarily impose on themselves the kind of project structures that later evolved with train 4 in Trinidad and with Egypt LNG (both explained later), can create a similar structure to Bontang's without the state compulsion or dominant ownership element. Hindsight is always clearer than foresight.

and the fact that they are partly interrelated made them difficult to resolve. As far as gas supply was concerned, it was agreed relatively early that the distant and deep-water gas off the north coast, where BG was the operator, should not be used for train 1 on economic grounds. Not only would this gas be expensive to develop but it also was very dry, with very little of the economically all-important associated gas liquids (NGLs), that were present in most of the east coast fields.[12] That left Amoco and BG east coast gas. Neither company had adequate proven reserves and therefore had no objective basis for deciding on their shares of upstream supply. Nor could they decide on a method of resolving the issue; neither company was really prepared to contemplate a formal reserves race where reserves proven by a specific date would set the basis for gas supply; this did not stop many abortive efforts during 1994 to agree upon shares before the reserves were established. Amoco had, nevertheless, an active appraisal program in 1994 that rapidly showed good results and proved adequate reserves for the whole project. BG did not drill any wells until the beginning of 1995 and, rather unfortunately for the company, drilled two dry holes in succession. This finally resolved the supply matter in Amoco's favor, as the project could not afford to wait while BG proved gas. Amoco therefore gained 100 percent of the supply for train 1 but agreed along the way that BG should have a right to supply 50 percent of the gas for the first expansion, and that north coast gas could be included.

The uncertainty over gas supply did not assist in resolving the corporate structure of the project, and then the shareholdings. The project toyed with an integrated structure but this would have required NGC and Cabot to be brought into the upstream and a system of cross-shares between BG and Amoco fields to be agreed upon. Clearly, shareholdings would depend to a considerable degree on the gas contributions of BG and Amoco. There was little stomach for the complex negotiations required to harmonize holdings in the gas fields and Cabot decided that, in any case, it had no experience in upstream gas and did not want to invest upstream.

The possibility of tolling was considered briefly, as it clearly provided one method of dealing with gas supply from different fields, but (as recorded above) neither BG nor Amoco wanted a reserves race or similar objective way of resolving gas supply. Also, the project looked economically marginal and there was considerable nervousness about setting a tolling fee. The tolling fee should be protected from gas price fluctuations but this would increase the price risk upstream and it was clearly

---

[12] The bonus of NGL revenues (NGLs can be sold like oil) can make or break some LNG project economics.

going to be difficult to agree on a fee. In the event, the attempt was not made.

By default, this left the only structure that stood a chance of being agreed reasonably quickly – the common form of gas sales into the plant from upstream. Even with the basic structure agreed upon, it was still necessary to decide five critical items:

1. The actual *corporate form* of the JV and which affiliates of the shareholder companies would actually hold the shares. These are largely taxation-driven issues and were settled in favor of a company – Atlantic LNG of Trinidad & Tobago – incorporated in Trinidad and Tobago.
2. The individual *percentage shareholdings* (including the option for Enagas to join, which then-parent Repsol later exercised).
3. The terms of the *JVAs* governing the management of the company.
4. The terms of *gas supply* to the project company.
5. The means of getting gas *from the fields to the plant*.

It was still not easy to resolve the shares each company should take in the project. Normally, BG and Amoco would have wanted their shareholdings to be roughly in proportion to their share of gas supply to the plant, but for a long time this was unknown and eventually turned out to be 100 percent Amoco. (This also raised the question of whether BG's upstream partners would be offered or would want a shareholding.) BG, with an eye to future expansion, did not want to opt out of the LNG plant. Amoco's original suggestion was that Amoco, BG, and Cabot own between 25 percent and 30 percent each, and NGC between 25 percent and 10 percent, in recognition of the fact that NGC was a little reluctant to commit too high a proportion of its resources to the project. However, it soon became apparent that Cabot was also unlikely to want such a large share (although Cabot kept its options open as long as possible) and that Amoco was going to be the major (if not the sole) supplier of gas. It took considerable iteration (not least when Enagas' parent Repsol negotiated its way into the project) to arrive at the current shareholdings: BP (formerly Amoco) (34 percent), BG (26 percent), Repsol (20 percent), Tractebel (formerly Cabot) (10 percent), and NGC (10 percent) (see table 9.2).

As a result of the protracted discussions on structure, it was relatively late in 1994 before the JVAs were drafted and active negotiation began (still before agreement on shareholdings and gas supply). This is inevitably a lengthy process and the JVA was not really settled until the terms of the Repsol entry were decided late in 1995 (Gas Matters 1995b). (As is common, the JVA and most of the other key agreements were agreed in

Table 9.2 *Ownership of upstream gas, LNG plants, and LNG sales*[a]

Train (Bcm)	Upstream (%)	LNG plants Owner	Share (%)	Owner	LNG sales all per annum (Bcm)	Contracted destination	
Train 1 4 per year	100	BP	10	NGC			
			10	Tractebel			
			20	Repsol	2.4	Tractebel	Boston
			26	BG	1.6	Enagas	Spain
			34	BP	1.9	BG	Elba Island
Train 2 4.1 per year	50	BG	32.5	BG	0.5	Tractebel	Boston
			25	Repsol	0.9	Repsol	Cartagena
		BP	42.5	BP			
Train 3 4 per year	50	BG	32.5	BG	1	BG	Elba Island Bilbao
			25	Repsol	1	Gas de Euskadi	Gas de Euskadi (1 Bcm)
		BP	42.5	BP	1.9	Repsol	BBE (1.1 Bcm) Repsol (0.6 Bcm)

Note:

[a] Current owners shown. Amoco was bought by BP and Cabot by Tractebel. The train 1 deliveries to Puerto Rico are contractually made by Tractebel, not Atlantic. Train 1 is owned by Atlantic LNG and trains 2 and 3 by a separate company: Atlantic 2/3, each with the shareholdings shown above. Orginal design capacities shown. Minor rounding discrepancies in totals. Indicates shipping organized by Enagas/Repsol.

Source: Gas Strategies (2005).

▨ Indicates Shipping Organised by Enagas/Repsol.

principle earlier, but signed in June 1996 as the final investment decision was taken.)

In the meantime, the project had no corporate entity to front sales negotiations or enter into contracts. In effect, the shareholders collectively stood behind any contracts by the project for surveys and then front-end engineering using a short agreement setting out each shareholders' liabilities.

With one LNG buyer and two shareholders holding only a share in the LNG plant, feed gas sales were always going to be on a strictly commercial, arm's-length basis. Both the government and Amoco had an interest in maximizing the into-plant gas price. For the government, taxation is greater on upstream profits than on the profits of the LNG plant. For Amoco, of course, having 100 percent of the supply but only 34 percent of the plant drove its preference. With a well-established local gas market, there were also perennial political sensitivities over gas price. Even if the local market is saturated, it can be difficult to see gas going for export at a significantly lower price than local industries pay. Fortunately local prices in Trinidad were not particularly high and this issue never became too difficult to resolve, although it was the subject of some controversy and considerable negotiation. It was established quite early that the price of feed gas should be linked to the price of LNG so that price risks were shared between upstream and LNG plant. The resulting structure is shown in figure 9.11.

Finally, there was the issue of the trans-island pipeline; gas landing on the east coast would have to be brought across the island to the LNG plant on the west coast. All gas transport on the island was carried out by NGC, which did not want to abandon this monopoly. The other partners and the potential lenders were anxious to achieve maximum security of supply and wanted a line dedicated to serving the LNG plant or assurances that there would always be adequate capacity available to provide all the feed gas the LNG plant required and that gas could not be diverted to island supply. In the end, it was decided that NGC should own the pipeline but lease the capacity to Amoco.

The resulting structure was clearly workable for train 1, but it was equally obvious that it would be difficult when it came to expansion as many of the original issues would be bound to resurface, particularly the gas supply issue and how economies of scale would be shared. This indeed proved to be a problem for trains 2 and 3. Ultimately, however, the train 1 project got itself to a position to go ahead remarkably quickly in spite of an above-average number of contentious issues. This was chiefly because it managed to carry on the broad sweep of activities in parallel (e.g. agreeing sales terms and letting engineering contracts before the

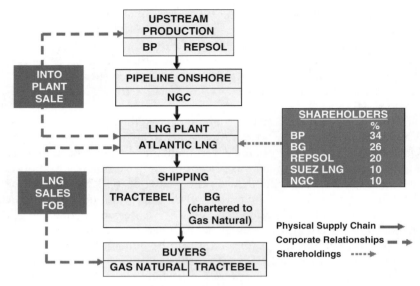

Figure 9.11. Atlantic LNG train 1 structure.
Source: Gas Strategies (2005).

company was formed, and by a degree of improvisation rather than waiting for complete resolution of problems before moving forward).

Financing   Once the structure of the project had been put in place, reserves were proven, long-term take-or-pay sales contracts were signed, and acceptable economic returns could be demonstrated, it was relatively straightforward to obtain financing. Gas projects, and particularly LNG projects, have a good track record and lenders are generally reasonably well disposed to them. The Trinidad project required finance, largely because the two smaller shareholders needed to raise money. For the larger investors it would have cost less to raise their own finance (as indeed happened for trains 2 and 3). Amoco, in particular, had a strong balance sheet and impeccable credit rating. However, a relatively modest 60:40 debt: equity ratio was all that the project sought.

The features of the financing that were specific to the project and relatively unfamiliar to lenders were the following:

1. Trinidad risk
2. US gas price risk
3. The Phillips Cascade technology
4. Inexperienced sponsors.

Trinidad and Tobago is a small country and therefore the level of exposure to the country risk was always going to be a factor. Trinidad has a democratic government and a good track record of orderly change of government following elections. The United States takes great interest in cementing its relations with the Caribbean and both the US Export-Import Bank and the Overseas Private Investment Corporation (OPIC) had significant appetite for Trinidad and Tobago risk. These two lenders provided political risk cover for the bulk of the loan ($571.4 million of the $600 million total debt) (OPIC 1998). This aspect of Trinidad & Tobago contrasted significantly with Nigeria, which attracted little political risk cover at the time, and Venezuela, which was much less attractive than Trinidad.

The sale to Spain used the conventional oil-linked indexation formula typical for European pipeline gas and was thus relatively familiar to the lenders. At the time, no long-term LNG deal with linkage to US gas prices (e.g. Henry Hub, whose NYMEX futures contract was then only a few years old) had been financed; there was no precedent at all. However, Amoco was the largest marketer of US gas and BG also had a major US gas trading operation (it was then part of the Natural Gas Clearing House, later called Dynegy) so both companies were active in and clearly understood the US gas market. This, combined with a positive consultants' report on the Boston market and its prices, re-assured the banks that the US price risk was understood and acceptable.[13] The net-back pricing mechanism removed virtually all price risk from Cabot, which was a distinct benefit. Without this, Cabot's credit risk as offtaker would have been of much greater concern. The liquidity of the market also gave comfort that the contracted gas volume could always be placed in the market (provided it could be landed) even if the price might be rather volatile.

The Phillips optimized Cascade process was subjected to considerable technical scrutiny. In its favor was the very successful record of the original Cascade process over nearly twenty-five years in Alaska and the proven competence of Phillips and Bechtel. Again, the risks were deemed acceptable.

Although none of the partners was experienced in building an LNG plant, they had taken advice from the leading contractors in the business and had recruited personnel who did have appropriate experience. Furthermore, both BG and Amoco had demonstrated strong track records managing major projects successfully, and managed to dispel the myth that LNG projects were uniquely technically difficult.

---

[13] Based on unpublished report from CERA, Boston, MA.

Although financing was relatively straightforward, limited recourse financing inevitably adds nearly a year to the schedule as due diligence is carried out and agreements are negotiated. Limited recourse financing shields corporate partners from project liabilities. As such, lenders evaluate project debt on the perceived risk of the project and its cash flows. It is not possible to secure financing until the shape of the project and the market are both fairly clear. Because Atlantic pulled so many things together in parallel, it was mid-1995 before there was sufficient clarity on reserves, sales, technology, and project structure, all of which came together over a relatively short period. Until this time, drafting an information memorandum to start the financing process was not a realistic proposition. Even so, various issues such as the Enagas/Repsol shareholding and in particular the project's agreement with the government had to be factored in along the way. The project was rather late in starting its negotiations with the government, and financing was clearly dependent both on the agreed fiscal terms and on the project receiving the wide range of government permissions required. Commitment from the banks was received by June 1996 in the form of Heads of Agreement (still at a fairly early stage of detailed loan negotiations), at which point the project made its final investment decision. Financial close was finally achieved in June 1997.

Government Agreement The project team came to negotiate with the government relatively late in 1995 when it tabled a "wish list" of terms for the agreement. The Manning government had been very supportive of the project in public, but until that point this had not been translated into concrete terms and there had been remarkably little discussion between project team and government during the formative stages of the project. The timing proved to be unfortunate as there was almost immediately a change in government. Premier Patrick Manning called an early election in November 1995 and both his ruling People's National Movement (PNM) and the United National Congress (UNC) won seventeen seats, the remaining two going to the National Alliance for Reconstruction (NAR). Within three days of the election, the UNC formed a government under premier Basadeo Panday in alliance with the NAR. Panday, the first Trinidadian prime minister of Indian descent, was also wedded to free market policies but had not actively supported the LNG project prior to his election, and was determined to examine it critically.

As in the case of most LNG projects, the economics of Atlantic LNG were expected to be marginal when the project was in the planning stages. The cost of liquefaction and shipping were substantial and the

LNG was to be exported to countries where there was competition from pipeline gas. The sponsors therefore sought some taxation relief as well as more general assurances from government. In principle, the government was supportive of Atlantic LNG. Furthermore, it had considerable experience in encouraging capital-intensive industries to invest in Trinidad. As a result the government had developed what amounted to a virtually standard package of fiscal incentives available through the Fiscal Incentives Act (Jobity and Racha 1999), including:

- A standard tax holiday of five–ten years
- Relief from taxes on dividends and other distribution
- Value added tax exemptions on imports, including capital imports
- Concessions on import duties
- Relief on withholding tax.

Because Atlantic LNG was seen as a pioneer industry (the first new LNG plant in the Western Hemisphere for thirty years) and with LNG prices expected to be low, it was granted a ten-year tax holiday.

Naturally, the project also needed a wide range of permits from government, many of which were individually negotiated rather than part of the overall government agreement. There was significant government interest in using local content and employment. LNG plants – and, indeed, offshore gas developments – are not major generators of employment when they are operating, although there are a substantial number of people involved in construction.[14]

The government agreement only came after a long and tough negotiation, and this was followed by a further negotiation between Amoco and the government to get permission for the upstream development and to gain assistance to secure a pipeline right of way across Trinidad to the LNG plant. In return, the government negotiated a reduction in island gas supply prices (a further reduction was obtained at the start of trains 2 and 3). The project loaded its first cargo into Cabot's *Matthew* in April 1999, six months ahead of NLNG, its closest rival.

---

[14] In this case, 140 permanent jobs were created and of these 120 were citizens of Trinidad & Tobago (1999 figures); the peak workforce during construction was about 3,000. Projects are normally more than willing to maximise local content provided it is competitive. Most local content assurances take the form of preference to local contractors when they offer competitive terms. Very often, however, local contractors will be at a disadvantage in terms of scale, experience, and creditworthiness as compared with their international competitors. Quite often these problems can be overcome by judicious joint venturing. As a result genuinely local content can be quite hard to define very precisely but is estimated at $150 million for Atlantic LNG train 1.

Atlantic LNG Trains 2 and 3

Amoco was keen to expand the project, and it was an open secret that the next trains would be the first of many expansion projects. During the course of appraising its reserves Amoco had found gas well in excess of that needed for train 1; BG also wanted to use its long-discovered, but undeveloped north coast reserves (the old Tenneco acreage). Proven reserves had reached 603 Bcm by January 2000, in strong contrast to the situation in 1994.

Internal discussion of an expansion started in 1997, but serious negotiations with the government over terms started only in June 1999 and the final approval to proceed was finally given in March 2000. The EPC contract was awarded to Bechtel only in August 2000 (although early construction had started in March) (Hunter and Andress 2002). The reasons for the extended time taken to bring the development forward were mainly due to unresolved issues of project structure from train 1 and partly due to negotiations with the government on revised terms.

Originally the project thought in terms of a single-train expansion of similar capacity to train 1, but as the market developed this was rapidly increased to two trains. Partner shares required complete renegotiation; in many ways, the expansion was like a whole new project. The difficulty in quickly moving to expansion illustrates the principal weaknesses in the train 1 project structure: the ad hoc way in which upstream gas supply had been decided and the different interests of the investors in the LNG plant. As we discuss below, this lesson was to be keenly remembered and remedied when BG later developed an LNG project in Egypt.

Marketing and Shipping By 1997, the market picture looked very different from 1993 and in many ways the market conditions were more attractive for new LNG supply. There was some sign of an upward trend in US prices (Henry Hub price averaged $2.53 per mmbtu in 1997 versus $1.88 eight years earlier) (BP 2004), which encouraged the hope that the famous US "gas bubble" of oversupply that had lasted for a decade had finally cleared. Events have since borne out that optimism.

There also appeared to be something of a window of opportunity to capture growth in the European market, as NLNG had run into more problems and Algeria was preoccupied with refurbishing its existing LNG plants and showed no sign of having expansion plans (Gas Matters 1993a). Other would-be suppliers – from Libya's long-underperforming LNG plant to other nascent newcomers – were not yet realistic prospects. Furthermore, the Middle East's new projects were focusing on what (at the time) were the more promising Asia Pacific markets. All would later turn their attention – and ships – towards the Atlantic Basin markets. At the time, however, Trinidad had the field largely to itself.

The European market was also changing. The European Union was determined to promote competition in gas and electricity markets. The United Kingdom had already (independently) taken this path, but many continental European countries were much less enthusiastic. The Spanish government, however, was one of the leaders in trying to open up its markets to competition. Amoco was taken over by BP in August 1998 (the deal was finally closed at the end of the year) and although Amoco and Repsol made the first moves, both positioning themselves to operate in a liberalized Spanish market, BP had also developed an independent strategic interest in securing a position there.

BP saw the liberalizing market as an opportunity to break the monopoly that state gas utilities (Enagas/Gas Natural in Spain's case) had on the final marketing of gas. BP was prepared to move further down the gas value chain and sell to large customers and power generators directly.

Repsol, as the major shareholder in monopoly distributor Enagas and also a shareholder in dominant marketer Gas Natural, saw its position under threat. Its main reactions were to diversify internationally (hence its initial interest in becoming part of the Trinidad project) but also to develop sales for gas-fired power. (In turn, Spain's electricity generators later sought entry into gas markets.) Repsol could develop its own direct position (as opposed to its indirect interest in Gas Natural, in which it was not even a controlling shareholder). Liberalization of the electricity market in Spain was clearly going to favor gas-fired combined cycle plants for virtually all new expansion, although at the time the country was virtually devoid of gas-fired power. While this promised rapid growth in gas demand, the new power pool into which the generators would bid to sell power was shrouded in uncertainty. There was considerable uncertainty as to how the pool would perform and where prices would settle; buying gas on the traditional basis with long-term prices indexed largely to oil products started to look very risky.

BP needed access to LNG terminal capacity if it was to sell gas directly into the Spanish market. However, regulated open access to the existing terminals, although offered in theory, was still some way off in practice.

The outcome was that BP and Repsol formed a JV to develop a new LNG terminal at Bilbao and an associated gas-fired power plant that would require about 0.8 mtpa of LNG. Agreement (in principle) between BP and Repsol was reached in July 1998 and the European

Union gave its approval in September. The Bilbao terminal had a novel structure – it provided terminal and regasification services only and did not get involved in buying LNG. Repsol committed, in principle, to take about 4 mtpa from the Trinidad expansion, this commitment, in effect, underpinned the work to develop it. Repsol intended to place the rest of the gas elsewhere in Spain. Gas Natural eventually took 0.64 mtpa and the Basque local distribution company based close to Bilbao (Gas de Euskadi) agreed to buy 0.7 mtpa (1 Bcm per year). Repsol retained the rest for its own use. While it was late in 1999 before arrangements were finalized and contracts completed, the existence of Repsol's commitment meant that this delay had no real impact on the project's critical path (*Gas Matters* 2000).

Although BG had earlier obtained an understanding that it would have the right to supply 50 percent of the gas to train 2, it took time proving sufficient reserves. It then targeted the improving US market and finally concluded a sale to El Paso for its 2.5 mtpa, which depended on re-opening the Elba Island terminal late in 1999. It is worth noting that while most LNG sellers in the world later beat a path to the US market, it was the Trinidad project that paved the way in renewing confidence in it. To this day its partners are the main importers of LNG into the United States.

To complete sales from train 2 and 3, Cabot resold 0.2 mtpa of its train 1 purchases to a new terminal and power plant in Puerto Rico – and then replaced these volumes with purchases from train 2. The Puerto Rico story is instructive in itself, as it demonstrates how the lack of destination restriction by the LNG seller and the flexibility offered by a "sink market" can permit the development of new satellite LNG markets. Cabot's position in the liquid US market allowed it to release volumes to Puerto Rico in a way that would have been very difficult for a traditional LNG project, where the buyers were totally dependent on LNG cargoes, without flexible supply alternatives. BP picked up this baton in an even more innovative fashion when it sold 0.75 mtpa to the Dominican Republic without indicating any source for the gas, even though it clearly intended to primarily use Trinidad LNG (*Gas Matters* 2000).

Amoco, which initiated the train 2 and 3 development, again demonstrated its reluctance to become involved in LNG shipping by selling all of its entitlement f.o.b., although BP has subsequently ordered ships and has used them to lift cargoes from Trinidad.

Clearly, a single-train expansion could have been launched earlier if Amoco and Repsol could have moved alone, but they were not free to do so. With a traditional LNG project – and even for Trinidad – the delay risked losing market opportunities to competitors (and arguably did so). By luck, the delays had less impact than they might have had at a different time. If anything, conditions improved during the delay and what opportunities Atlantic LNG lost to Nigeria in traditional utility sales, its partners more than made up with opportunities they created for themselves in the Caribbean, Spain, and Europe.[15]

Project Structure The biggest difficulties in expanding Atlantic LNG had to do with the project's structure and the diverging interests of the partners. Amoco and Repsol took the other shareholders by surprise when they announced that they were planning an expansion based on the Spanish market. The unexpected move also exposed the real divergences between the various shareholders. For both Amoco and BG, the primary drive behind investing in LNG was to develop gas discoveries, but BG had not yet proven the reserves it needed to fill half train 2 (it had gained a right to supply half train 2 as part of its acceptance of 100 percent Amoco supply to train 1). Repsol was partly driven by gaining access to reserves but was also interested in protecting itself from the threat to its Spanish market (outlined above). Cabot had no urgent need for more supply in its core market, and both Cabot and NGC relied on borrowing to fund train 1, which was not yet on stream (and thus not providing revenues to help fund another major round of borrowing). Both of the smaller companies had no direct interest in gas supply, and hence their main goal in any expansion would be to maximize the profit taken from the liquefaction services. This promised to make the negotiation of the prices for feed gas very difficult. Clearly BG, Cabot, and NGC saw little urgency, and without the agreement of these three it would not be possible for the Atlantic company to invest in another train.

A restructuring of Atlantic LNG's ownership for trains 2 and 3 would thus be needed. Both BG and Amoco wanted to find an easier and quicker way of deciding which company should supply gas to the plant,

---

[15] As with several of Atlantic LNG's developments, both unintended and intended good fortune fortuitously grew from its innovations. In this case, the unintended feature, at least for some partners, was the delay; the innovation was the partner's willingness to create market openings that had not appeared obvious before. Cabot flexibility paved the way for Puerto Rico sales, which inspired BP's Dominican sale; BG moved first to open the idle Elba terminal (with the El Paso sale) and then to buy all of the capacity and fill the previously almost idle Lake Charles terminal. BP and Repsol were the first of many LNG terminal/power station developments to be launched in Spain, bypassing the necessity of selling to Gas Natural or going through Enagas terminals. The train 2 delay probably also gave BG a better chance to develop its north coast gas.

and under what terms. Very few LNG plants in the world have supplies from more than one field or license area and therefore there were few precedents. The Bontang plant – owned by the Indonesian national oil company, Pertamina, and operated as a pure cost center – was a possible model. Bontang was supplied from PSCs that operated at several license blocks (which grew in number over the years) on the basis of reserves proven and not used by previous "sales packages." Pertamina made all sales with the active support of its PSC gas suppliers.

However, the Bontang model was not ideally suited to Atlantic LNG's circumstances. First, the Trinidad plant itself would have to earn an acceptable return, or no one would invest in it. Second, unlike Bontang, some partners had no upstream interest and there was no state oil company to drive the reserves' race or to impose the selection criteria. Third, the emerging flexible trade in the Atlantic Basin was creating new uncertainties and complexities in how the gas would be sold, and at what price. Finally, BP, BG, and to a degree Repsol had ambitions to create their own presence in the marketplace and optimize their own supply portfolios rather than necessarily continuing the rigid project structure based on links from supplier to market that were characteristic of the traditional LNG trade.

As the discussion on structure for train 2 and 3 evolved (along with changing market circumstances), the producers became attracted to a more conventional tolling structure, as shown in figure 9.10. The LNG plant would serve to process gas owned by the upstream gas suppliers, converting it into LNG for a defined fee. The plant owners' risk would be minimal as the suppliers would guarantee a level of throughput. The upstream owners would then sell the LNG individually. The risk of destructive head on competition between the sellers was much reduced in liquid gas markets. Prices for LNG cargoes would be determined by the broader US market – suppliers would not be competing based on price. Such an arrangement would still be quite difficult to manage in Asia, where no such pricing mechanism yet exists. This then, was yet another ground-breaking development which really paved the route from JV or project LNG sales to "branded LNG" (e.g. BG, BP, or Repsol gas, all produced in Trinidad).

There was little in this vision for trains 2 and 3 that appealed to Cabot and NGC, but BP and BG needed their support to proceed, as the expansions would share infrastructure with train 1. Eventually both smaller partners agreed to withdraw from investing in trains 2 and 3 in exchange for some financial compensation. It was still not possible to have a pure tolling arrangement as the sales plans did not exactly match the ownership of upstream gas – Repsol had gained only a small

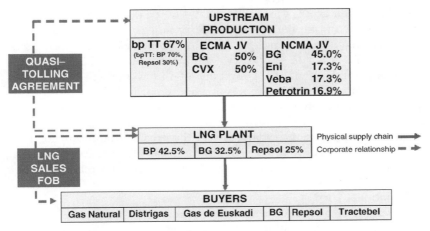

Figure 9.12. Atlantic LNG Trains 2 and 3 structures.
Source: Gas Strategies (2005).

foothold in gas supply when it joined the consortium and Cabot did buy some train 2 LNG. As a result, Atlantic 2/3 Company of Trinidad and Tobago Unlimited – whose shareholders are BP (42.5 percent), BG (32.5 percent), and Repsol (25 percent) – was set up to own the plant and also take ownership of the gas and become the f.o.b. seller (see figure 9.12). Nevertheless, the plant was paid a fixed fee as if it was a pure tolling entity and the commercial outcome was almost identical to a tolling arrangement. This solution was not achieved easily and the negotiation spread over three years (1998–2000) before it was resolved.

A pure tolling arrangement was finally adopted for train 4 which we do not fully cover in this chapter. Even before the train 4 structure was concluded, BG had launched in Egypt LNG (ELNG) – what we think deserves to be seen as a sort of "Trinidad graduation project." ELNG was not only a tolling structure, but could be (and has since been) easily expanded one train at a time, accommodating new investors in separate trains, and even new producers as needed.

Government Agreement In spite of the hard-fought terms agreed for train 1, there was still significant criticism in the Trinidad press of the terms granted to Atlantic LNG. By this stage, it was apparent that US prices were higher and train 1 would be more profitable than expected. Trains 2 and 3 would, in addition, benefit from economies of scale as they shared common facilities such as the jetty and storage capacity. Significantly, the project did not seek a tax holiday for the plant in this case. Nor, did the government ever renege on its earlier commitments; rather, it tried to improve its terms through each successive train-approval process. In February 2000, the Sustainable Economic Development Unit of the University of the West Indies Economics Department organized a symposium to attempt to influence the terms that would be negotiated for trains 2 and 3; the principal organizer of the forum, leading academic Dennis Pantin, raised concerns in the press. Although it was variously claimed that the project would provide $30–$48 billion in tax revenue over its twenty-year life, Pantin argued that there would be an opportunity loss of $3.3–$5 billion because Atlantic LNG would not be paying a fair market price for the gas (Gas Briefing International 2000).

When the Heads of Agreement was concluded a month later, BP and BG agreed to a concession – they reduced prices for gas supplied to NGC for sale in the island, reportedly from US$1.03 per mmbtu to US $0.91 per mmbtu (Gas Briefing International 2000). Local content was expected to be 25 percent and again there would be about 3,000 construction jobs at the peak.

Analysis of Alternative Projects

In many ways, the competitive environment faced by the promoters of train 1 in Trinidad could not have been more favorable; yet that outcome was hardly preordained. Nigeria LNG suffered several false starts at the beginning of the 1990s which offered Trinidad its vital window of opportunity despite the fact that the Caribbean project started later. Algeria, the long-dominant LNG supplier to the Atlantic and Mediterranean LNG markets, was relatively inactive in seeking out the new markets ultimately opened by Trinidad and Nigeria. Venezuela, just 160 km away, was seen in the early days of the project to be a competitor; however its challenge soon subsided in the country's political turmoil.

Nigeria LNG

The most active direct competitor to Atlantic LNG is – and was at the time – undoubtedly NLNG. LNG in Nigeria has a very checkered history. Despite having massive reserves of gas (3.4 Tcm), much of it associated with oil, relatively little gas was used in Nigeria and much of the associated gas was flared. This is both wasteful and environmentally damaging. The economic use of this gas is of strategic importance for the country, and LNG exports have long been considered an important means of commercializing this gas.

A LNG project from Nigeria was first proposed in 1964 in the very early days of the LNG industry. The proposal progressed in 1969 when market studies of the United States, Brazil, and Argentina were completed. As a result, attempts were made to develop two separate three-train projects. One was to be developed by BP and Shell at Bonny and the other by Elf, Agip and Phillips at Peterside on the other side of the Bonny River. The government was to be a major partner in both. Things moved fairly slowly (the Biafran Civil War ended only in 1970 and LNG was a very new and expensive technology) and in 1977 the government decided that the two projects should be merged to develop a six-train plant at Bonny. This plan was finally completed in 1978 when the sponsors signed a shareholders agreement and the government issued a Letter of Guarantee and Assurance. Shareholdings at that point were NNPC 60 percent, Shell 10 percent, BP 10 percent, Agip 7.5 percent, Phillips 7.5 percent, and Elf 5 percent. The plan at this stage was to produce 12 mtpa of LNG. Marketing was focused on the United States (Columbia LNG, with the Cove Point terminal; Southern LNG, Elba Island; Trunkline LNG, Lake Charles; and American Natural LNG) and Europe (a consortium of eight large utility buyers). Sales agreements were negotiated and initialed but the combination of the collapse of the Atlantic Basin LNG market in the early 1980s and a change in government in Nigeria[16] eventually stopped the project; the plant EPC contract was ready to sign and a government guarantee required for state NNPC's share to proceed. BP and Phillips failed to renew the shareholders' agreement in early 1982 and left and the company was liquidated.

In April 1982 the new Nigerian government commissioned consultants to carry out a feasibility study, which concluded that Nigeria would be well placed to supply the LNG market in Europe. Shell, Elf, and Agip were invited to participate in a new project and had all expressed interest by November 1983. Then, a month later, the government changed again. The new military government set up a task force to review

[16] Unlike the later quick review and approval of a previous government's LNG project which we saw in Trinidad, the new Nigerian government balked at the point when Phillips brought the partners an EPC contract to sign and asked the government to guarantee NNPC's share of the investment. It decided to review the whole project instead; this took so long that the market shifted and the project collapsed in the meantime. This historic lesson was one of several from Nigeria (listed in the following paragraphs) to later galvanise governments in Trinidad & Tobago to act with greater speed and in an investment-conducive manner.

previous LNG efforts and to make recommendations. The task force reported in March 1984 and an LNG working committee was established in March 1985. This was followed by the signature of a framework agreement in November 1985 by NNPC, Shell, Cleag (Elf), and Agip. Shell was made technical adviser and eventually the joint venture was incorporated in 1989 as Nigeria LNG Limited (NLNG). Shareholdings at that stage were NNPC 60 percent, Shell 20 percent, Agip 10 percent, and Elf 10 percent (Progress and Outlook for Nigerian LNG 1992).

From this point, the project moved steadily forward. The French Tealarc liquefaction process was chosen and accepted. (Technical adviser Shell accepted the process, albeit reluctantly, with the goal of generating some competition to the then monopoly in LNG liquefaction technology enjoyed by the Air Products' APCI process.) The scale of the two-train plant was reduced to 4 mtpa (5.7 Bcm per year). FEED was completed and the main EPC contract bids invited in October 1991. Bids were due in by May 1992 and award was expected in September 1992, which would have put the plant a few years ahead of Trinidad. Sales contracts were negotiated and agreed with Enagas (1 Bcm per year), GdF (0.5 Bcm per year), and Enel, the main Italian power company (3.5 Bcm per year), all on a c.i.f. basis. Cabot also negotiated a deal for 0.7 Bcm per year on f.o.b. terms. Cabot had a distinctly uneasy relationship with the Nigerian project, not least because it had long disputed the ownership of one of the second-hand ships, the *Gamma*, with a company that had an option to use the ship on long-term charter with Nigeria partners. The *Gamma* was one of three ships formerly owned by MarAd which became embroiled in a protracted legal battle over their fate.[17] Cabot eventually won ownership of the *Gamma* and arrived at an agreement to use the ship to carry its own Nigeria purchase volumes but with the ship's spare capacity leased to NLNG. There was none of the flexibility in destination that Cabot eventually negotiated in Trinidad; the full volume purchased by Cabot was destined for Boston alone.

The project had presciently acquired four second-hand LNG carriers in 1990 and was well on the way to amortizing their cost by chartering them to LNG suppliers in the Pacific while the Nigerian project was still taking shape.

The Nigerian partners also intended to raise limited recourse financing for the rest of the project and engaged the World Bank's commercial lending arm, the International Finance Corporation (IFC), to carry out an appraisal study by May 1992. However, this iteration of NLNG was also not to be. The government refused to support the award of the EPC

---

[17] To find a fuller, contemporaneous, account of this dispute see Gas Matters (1990).

contract and, for good measure, rejected what it saw as "Shell's" choice of liquefaction process (the Tealarc). At the same time, the government sacked all of the Nigerian board members of NLNG. It was in this period that Cabot, increasingly doubtful that the Nigerian project would proceed on schedule, approached the Trinidad & Tobago government.

NLNG was relaunched in December 1993 following substantial restructuring. It had become apparent that limited recourse financing would have been a totally unrealistic prospect in Nigeria at the time (because of the shareholding structure and perceived political risk). The IFC offered to support the project, which signaled much-needed credibility with the financial community. IFC support was contingent on a reduction of the NNPC share below 50 percent, as the IFC would finance only projects that were majority privately owned. The NNPC share was to be reduced to 49 percent, while the foreign group of companies would be raised to the same 49 percent total. Thus, Shell's share increased to 24 percent, Elf's to 15 percent, and Agip's remained at 10 percent. The IFC offered the balancing 2 percent. So, rather neatly for Nigerian sensibilities, foreign shareholders did not hold a majority in spite of NNPC having lost its overall majority (Etiebet 1993).

A new shareholders' agreement was in place at the time of the relaunch. The Tealarc process had been abandoned in favor of the almost universal APCI process (thus ending this particular challenge to APCI supremacy) and capacity was to be increased to 5.2 mtpa (7.15 Bcm per year). This meant a redesign – albeit this time on a fast track. Construction was slated to begin in the first quarter of 1995, with commercial operations set for 1999. In order to provide startup capital and to improve credibility with potential lenders, each partner was required to subscribe a significant proportion of its equity up-front to an escrow account. However, neither this move nor the entry of the IFC as shareholder made much difference, and no real progress was made with external financing.[18] Still, the escrow account proved very valuable when the shareholders eventually came to make their investment decisions (Montezemolo and Amu 1995). The final shareholdings settled at NNPC 49 percent, Shell 25.6 percent, Elf 15 percent, and Agip 10.4 percent. Nigerian desire to make real progress now outweighed any countervailing political sensibilities about foreign domination.

Throughout this tortuous process, the project tried as far as possible to hang on to the sales that it had agreed. Those of Enel and GdF

---

[18] Later in 1995 the IFC pulled out, alarmed over the human rights situation in Nigeria. Ken Saro-Wiwa and eight other dissidents were executed in November of that year (Gas Matters 1995b).

were retained and Enagas actually increased its commitment to 1.6 Bcm per year. For the time being, Cabot was still committed to take 0.7 Bcm per year. However, Enel could not commit irrevocably without the Italian government approving construction of a new receiving terminal at Montalto di Castro. The Italian government appeared to be in no hurry to decide.

In December 1994 NLNG signed a MOU with its preferred construction contractor. By March 1995, with the Italians still undecided and no financing in place, NLNG was in some danger of losing both its sales and its plant construction contract. The partners managed to rollover the engineering contract but the sales were not so simple this time; buyers' patience was running out. GdF agreed to extend the deadline to about November 1995 as did Enel. However Enel, not surprisingly, dropped its option to take an extra 1.1 Bcm per year. Botas of Turkey, where demand was also predicted to grow very rapidly over the next few years, was lined up for 1.2 Bcm per year to replace the lost Enel quantity. Cabot cannily suspended but did not cancel its contract, allowing it to delay a final decision until the viability of the project (and its alternatives) was clearer. Enel was given a deadline of 31 May 1995 to make a firm decision, but the Italian government still dawdled. NLNG said that it required Enel's decision was by the end of June; Enel, under pressure, finally went firm. It also explicitly ruled out making its contractual commitment conditional on the Italian authorities approving its terminal. This was to come back to haunt Enel later when approval for the terminal was refused, as was the backup terminal proposed by Snam at Monfalcone.

By the fall of 1995, Cabot was confident of Trinidad and wanted to gain full control of the *Gamma*. Cabot thus cancelled its contract with NLNG in November of that year.

All was not quite done; the final investment decision (FID) was postponed from September to November, when NLNG's board failed to decide, and the FID was finally made in December 1995. Still there was no financing, the escrow account contained nearly half the total funds required and thus the project proceeded on the basis of equity financing (Ollerenshaw 1996). In spite of making FID seven months ahead of Atlantic LNG, NLNG did not deliver its first cargo until October 1999, six months behind Atlantic LNG.

Undoubtedly, in 1992 the Nigerian project was well ahead of Atlantic LNG and had almost secured the important US niche market. It is equally clear that most of its problems were inflicted by the government which, by its lack of consistency and poor communication with its own national oil and gas company, contributed strongly to the failure of several incarnations of the project. Changes of government for many years were followed by total reappraisal of the project and more delay. Unrealistic ambitions for project finance contributed to the delays. However, in the later stages, the Shell-led management overcame several quite serious obstacles and finally did see the project to completion. It was still just in front of Trinidad, but it had allowed Trinidad to take over the Boston market (which was more critical for Trinidad than Nigeria) and capture a slice of the Spanish market that might otherwise have gone to Nigeria. This vital window for Trinidad had, several times in the early 1990s, been Nigeria's to lose.

When it came to expansion, however, Nigeria did not have the structural problems that encumbered Trinidad's trains 2 and 3. The existing partners were able to simply expand their project and sell as one unit. Still, some characteristically Nigerian problems continued to dog the project through 1997. In June, the energy minister, Dan Etete, announced that he had "sacked" the whole board of NLNG. However, Etete failed to take account of the fact that NNPC owned only 49 percent of the company and that he was not in a position to sack the whole board, only the NNPC members. The board fortunately, managed to survive and continue to develop the project.

The situation in Italy had not improved, however. Enel ran into environmental difficulties with its proposed receiving terminal at Montalto di Castro north of Rome and switched to its fallback option, Snam's proposed terminal at Monfalcone. Following the cancellation of this terminal after a local referendum in September 1996, Enel attempted to cancel its contract with NLNG. NLNG took the matter to arbitration and by March 1997 Enel had reversed its position and promised to honor the contract. Enel then had to make arrangements with GdF for most of the LNG to be taken into GdF's terminal at Montoir and then swapped for a combination of pipeline gas from Russia and Algerian LNG (the latter delivered to the one existing Italian LNG terminal at La Spezia). These arrangements were completed by the end of 1997, leaving NLNG free to contemplate expansion through a third train, in 1998 (*Gas Matters* 1997).

By February 1999, Enagas had committed to buy 2 mtpa, 70 percent of the output of train 3. The Technip, Kellogg, Snamprogetti, Japanese Gas Corporation (TSKJ) consortium was signed on train 3 as a carbon copy of trains 1 and 2; in June 1999 Transgas of Portugal bought the remaining 0.7 mtpa output. The third train started up at the end of November 2002. This was again three months behind Trinidad's train 2, although the Nigerian investment decision had been taken fifteen months earlier. Nevertheless, the total time required for Nigeria's expansion was far shorter than Atlantic's because it avoided Atlantic's structural difficulties. Train 3 for NLNG was simply more of the same. In this case, there was enough market to take both expansions, Spain's rapid market growth being a key factor. The more conservative Nigerian project sold to the traditional buyer (Spain's gas monopoly) and did not attempt to position itself for the liberalizing European gas market, let alone for breaking into the then increasingly promising US market – those opportunities were to come later.

Venezuela

The other LNG project that had the potential to thwart Atlantic's ambitions was in Venezuela, a mere stone's throw from Trinidad (see the map in figure 9.1). The genesis of the Venezuelan Cristobal Colon LNG project was a study conducted by Shell and Lagoven (a subsidiary of the national oil company PDVSA) in 1989 that identified potential commercial opportunities for LNG (although Venezuela had also toyed with the idea of an LNG project in the early days of LNG some twenty years earlier). By 1990, the country was sitting on resources (proven, probable, and possible) of 6.6 Tcm of gas, of which 0.9 Tcm was non-associated and the main target of LNG export proposals (Cristobal Colon Project 1992).

LNG proponents were stuck. On one hand they realized that foreign participation would be critical, but foreign participation was not permitted under the 1975 nationalization of Venezuela's oil and gas industry. LNG exports had become political hot potatoes, with strong opposition from those who objected to the reintroduction of foreign oil companies. However, the government was, in principle, prepared to reward foreign companies prepared to invest in the country's less desirable heavy crudes with the benefit of access to other hydrocarbons, including gas for export. Lagoven set out to select suitable JV partners and in June 1990 Shell, Exxon, and Mitsubishi were invited to take shares of 30 percent, 29 percent, and 8 percent, respectively in a proposed LNG project. Congressional approval would be needed to permit the establishment of the JV company. The initial feasibility study proposed a two-train 4.6 mtpa plant using 7.5 Bcm per annum of feed gas. The target market was the United States, for which three 127,000 m³ ships would be required (Urdaneta 1993).

The new JVs were given access to some rather unpromising reserves offshore the Paria peninsula in the east of the country. This appears to have been in part at least a concession to the opposition for letting foreign companies back in – they were offered reserves that were remote and difficult to develop. These were very close to and essentially of similar character to the Trinidad North Coast reserves which Atlantic

LNG was to reject for train 1 because they lacked associated liquids and were at the time too costly to develop.

The next three years (1990–1993) were spent trying to prove more reserves and to come up with a commercially viable development scheme. Negotiations were hampered by a well-publicized dispute between Shell and Exxon over the degree of access to Shell's technical LNG know how; still, some $30 million was spent over the three-year period. The scale was increased to 6 mtpa in an effort to achieve greater economies (a method of cost reduction rejected by the Trinidad partners who favored a one-train launch strategy so that they could serve smaller niche markets); an accord was signed between the companies in March 1993. The project was finally approved in August 1993 after long debate in Congress and the company (Sucre Gas) was formed early in 1994. The projected schedule – final approval by the partners was to occur in 1996 followed by the start of construction in 1997 – never materialized, and the project faded away.

The Venezuela project was burdened with low-quality gas, partly for political reasons. It also did not have access to the low-cost second-hand ships that Trinidad and Nigeria had. Marketing never made real headway. The prime focus was always on the United States and the project struggled with the expected low prices in that market. The rather high-priced niche at Boston would have been useful but would inevitably have been a small proportion of a 6 mtpa project. It was reported that the project was seeking prices of the order of $4.00 per mmbtu in 1993 (Gas Briefing International 1994) while NYMEX gas price averaged $2.12 per mmbtu at the time, which gives some insight as to what was needed to make it viable. European sales were not considered until much later.

Why did Trinidad overtake Venezuela? The Cristobal Colon project was an attempt to launch a conventional project in the Atlantic Basin in quite unconventional circumstances. By contrast, not only was the political and commercial climate in Trinidad more favorable, the Atlantic LNG partners pursued a market-driven one-train launch strategy rather than focusing on achieving cost reductions through scale economies. Still Nigeria's, NLNG was also a largely conventional LNG project and it eventually managed to launch. Venezuela, in the final analysis, simply reaffirms the geopolitical lessons of LNG in this period: its government more seriously hampered investors, both local and foreign, than either Nigeria or Trinidad. Nigeria's errors simply delayed NLNG and allowed Trinidad to proceed. Venezuela's policies actually derailed its own project.

Conclusion

Three key factors contributed to the success of Atlantic LNG train 1 compared with its competitors in Nigeria and Venezuela:

1. Trinidad's one-train launch strategy, tailored to market realities
2. Political considerations in Spain (to diversify supply sources) coupled with an unusual (for the era) willingness of sellers to offer buyer-driven flexibility of destination
3. Strong, and simply better, host-government support.

The one-train launch strategy combined small scale and low cost, essential for capturing the vital US niche market. The high-priced Boston market was quite small, and as a result it would form only a small portion of sales from the larger Nigerian and Venezuelan projects. Capturing that market, it was thought, required arriving with new gas supplies within a brief window of opportunity. Cabot's role as a key motivator for the Trinidad project provided Atlantic LNG with the firm relationship needed to access the Boston market, and revolutionary flexible sales arrangements matched well with Cabot's market position. The one-train design also allowed Atlantic LNG to move more quickly, with less time needed to firm up sales for larger volumes (as in Nigeria or Venezuela). Finally, the innovative design and project management tactics used by the project developers, unindoctrinated in the "standard" LNG model, allowed them to achieve the critical cost savings needed to make the single-train model economical.

The second key factor driving Trinidad's success (and also eventually Nigeria's), was the Spanish government's desire to diversify its gas supplies away from its near total dependence on Algeria.[19] Spain does have a small contract with Norway, which predates purchases from Trinidad and Nigeria. However, that gas must transit the whole of Europe, notably France, making it ultimately very expensive. LNG thus provided a far more attractive option. The ability to quickly sign up LNG sales into the rapidly growing Spanish gas market was also critical to both the timing and the perceived economic viability of the project. Conversely, Atlantic LNG had a crucial edge in Spain through its willingness to offer more flexibility in deliveries than any LNG buyer had ever enjoyed. Enagas (later Repsol) thus gained a seasonal swing advantage no other seller in the Spanish market could offer (Spain had

---

[19] The Spanish government has been trying for some time to keep the proportion of Algerian gas below 60 percent and besides Trinidad and Nigeria, Qatar and Oman are now regular suppliers; Egypt began LNG shipments in 2005.

almost no storage at the time and thus little ability to manage seasonal swing). Finally, offering Repsol access to the upstream benefits of the project also made Atlantic attractive to Spain. In short, Atlantic LNG was able to offer Spanish buyers unique benefits while gaining a much-needed offtake market.

The third major factor that drove Atlantic LNG to its early completion and success was Trinidad & Tobago's far more consistent host-government support which the country sustained through a change in governing party. The relatively stable environment in Trinidad stands in stark contrast to Nigeria and Venezuela. In Nigeria, NLNG suffered from random and unhelpful government intervention. In Venezuela, LNG developers found a government that struggled to gain internal acceptance of any foreign involvement. This difficult political environment yielded a political compromise – notably the offer of economically unfavorable reserves – that fatally weakened the chances of the project proceeding.

In retrospect, it is most apparent that the Nigerian government's undermining of NLNG allowed Trinidad to look much more reliable at a time when it was struggling to be taken seriously as an LNG provider. Determined management action by the NLNG partners eventually pulled the Nigerian project out of the fire, but by then Trinidad and Atlantic LNG were secure as a leading LNG supplier in the Atlantic Basin.

REFERENCES

Alphatania (2004). *LNG – The Commercial Imperatives.* http://www. alphatania. com
Barclay, L. A. (2003). *FDI-Facilitated Development: The Case of the Natural Gas Industry of Trinidad & Tobago.* Maastricht: United Nations University, Institute for New Technologies
BP (2003). *Statistical Review of World Energy*; available at http://www.bp.com (2004). *Statistical Review of World Energy*; available at http://www.bp.com
Cristobal Colon Project (1992). "Project brochure." Caracas
Department of Fossil Energy (1996). "North American gas trade." *Quarterly Focus*, 2nd quarter; available at http://www.fossil.energy.gov/programs/ gasregulation/analyses/Focus/2nd96foc.pdf
EIA (1999). "Natural Gas Annual." Washington, DC: US Energy Information Administration
Etiebet, Don Obot (1993). "Relaunch of the Nigeria LNG Limited project." Address by Hon. Minister of Petroleum and Mineral Resources, Lagos, December 16
Farrell, T. M. A. (1987). *Workshop on the Golden Calf: An Oil Exporter's Industrial Strategy, Technology Policy, and Project Planning during the Boom Years.* St. Augustine, Trinidad: Department of Economics University of the West Indies

Gas Briefing International (1994). *Gas Matters*, August 28, contact info@gas-matters.com for reprint

(2000). *Gas Matters*, March 28, contact info@gas-matters.com for reprint

Gas Matters (1990). contact info@gas-matters.com for reprint

(1993a). 28 January; contact info@gas-matters.com for reprint

(1993b). 28 February; contact info@gas-matters.com for reprint

(1995a). 28 June; contact info@gas-matters.com for reprint

(1995b). 28 November; contact info@gas-matters.com for reprint

(1997). 28 November; contact info@gas-matters.com for reprint

(2000). 28 October; contact info@gas-matters.com for reprint

Gas Strategies Consulting (2005). contact consult@gas-strategies.com for reprint. Also available at http://www.gas-strategies.com

Geological Society of Trinidad & Tobago (2005). available at www.gstt.org

Hunter, P. and D. Andress (2002). "Trinidad LNG – the second wave." Gastech, Doha, October 13–16

Jamieson, David, Paul Johnson, and Phil Redding (1998). "Targeting and achieving lower cost liquefaction plants." LNG 12 Conference, Perth; Des Plaines: Institute of Gas Technology, International Gas Union

Jobity, R. and S. Racha (1999). "The Atlantic LNG project: the state of play." Port of Spain: Central Bank of Trinidad and Tobago

Montezemolo, U. Cordero di and Thomas C. Amu (1995). "Status of the Nigeria LNG project." LNG 11 Conference, Birmingham, July 3–6; Des Plaines: Institute of Gas Technology, International Gas Union

NYMEX (2005). "New York Mercantile Exchange"; available at http://www.nymex.com

Ollerenshaw, Steve (1996). "Status of the Nigeria LNG project." LNG 12 Conference, Perth, July 3–6; Des Plaines: Institute of Gas Technology, International Gas Union

OPIC (1998). *Press Release*. Washington, DC: Overseas Private Investment Corporation; available at http://www.exim.gov

Progress and Outlook for Nigerian LNG (1992). Mediterranean Markets Conference

Urdaneta, R. (1993). "Cristobal Colon – the Venezuelan LNG project." Paris: Gastech, February 16–19

Word Bank (2003). *World Development Indicators*. Washington, DC: World Bank

10 Politics, markets, and the shift to gas: insights from the seven historical case studies

Mark H. Hayes and David G. Victor

Introduction

Most energy forecasts envision a shift to gas in the world energy system over the coming decades. To realize that vision will require tapping increasingly remote gas resources and shipping them to distant gas markets in other countries. Few analysts have explored the robustness of such projections in the real world where political and institutional factors exert strong influences on whether governments and private investors will be able to muster the capital for the long-distance pipelines and other infrastructure projects that are essential to a gas vision. Although gas has strong economic, technological, and environmental advantages over alternative energy sources, will the difficulty of securing contracts where legal institutions are weak – an attribute of nearly all the nations that are richest in gas resources – impede the outlook for global gas? Which gas resources and transportation infrastructures are likely to be developed? As gas infrastructures interconnect the world, what political consequences may follow? To help answer these questions, this study on the geopolitics of gas combines two tracks of research – one that employs seven historical case studies and another that rests on a quantitative model for projecting alternative futures for gas to 2040. Part II of this book has focused on the former – lessons from history – and this chapter examines the conclusions from the seven historical case studies presented in chapters 3–9.

We selected this sample of seven historical case studies with an eye to diversity in the factors that, as we hypothesized in chapter 2, would

We are grateful to Thomas Heller, Steven Krasner, Amy M. Jaffe, Joe Barnes, and Joshua House for comments on drafts, insightful discussions, and editorial assistance. We are particularly grateful to the authors of the case studies whose work this chapter attempts to synthesize; notably, we thank James Ball, Steven Lewis, David Mares, Fred von der Mehden, and Rob Shepherd for constructive critiques of earlier drafts and this chapter. Any mistakes reside with us.

explain why some international gas trade projects are built while others languish. These historical examples include ventures that transport gas in liquid form ("LNG") as well as by pipeline; they include projects that governments pursued when they controlled access to capital and set the rules in highly regulated markets, and cases where private investors were left to take risks in a more market-oriented context. We have probed projects that were first-of-a-kind and served largely virgin gas markets and projects that supplied markets that were already mature. The sample includes projects that span transit countries – and thus required cooperation of governments beyond simply the suppliers and users of the gas – as well as projects that exported gas directly from source country to a final market. Also presented are cases where international institutions such as multi-lateral trade agreements and development banks were omnipresent and those where they were scarce, as we thought such institutions might affect the prospects for inter-state cooperation. Each case study includes not just a probing of a built project but also an assessment of key alternatives that were contemplated seriously but not pursued at the time. This pairing of built and not built projects, as we discuss in further detail in chapter 2 where we introduce our case study methods, reflects efforts to avoid bias in the sample of studies – to ensure that our findings are not distorted by looking only at gas ventures that actually came into operation.

We focus this summary of our main findings on two topics. First, we examine the role of the state in orchestrating the construction of gas infrastructures. The international trade in gas arose during a period of state domination of most economies, and the provisions for state financing and programs to "create" demand for gas reflect that historical context. We explore the implications of the shift to a greater role for market forces. Second, we examine the fundamental challenge to governments and investors in cross-border gas trade: providing importing countries with the confidence that vital energy supplies will not be cut off and investors the surety needed to commit large sums of capital to projects that will be profitable only after many years of predictable operation. In the conclusion to this chapter we summarize our main arguments by revisiting the four main factors that we introduced in chapter 2 and which served to guide our selection of cases.

The Role of the State in Gas Trade

The international gas trade arose in the period of the late 1960s when states controlled most energy services. In the prevailing wisdom of the post-war era, infrastructures for energy supply, such as gas, were deemed too important to be left to the whims of the market. Through the 1980s European gas production, trade, and distribution were entrusted to national champion gas companies such as British Gas, Statoil in Norway, and Gaz de France (GdF). As consumption in European countries quickly outstripped local supplies, neighbors to the east (the Soviet Union) and across the Mediterranean (Algeria) soon became the two largest external suppliers of gas to Europe. A Soviet state ministry (GazExport) controlled gas exports. Algerian gas production was firmly in the grip of state-owned Sonatrach, the result of the wave of nationalization that would sweep other Arab energy exporters in the 1970s. North American gas markets, too, were state-dominated – with regulators in control of essentially all aspects of pricing, and contestable markets for gas largely non-existent. Elsewhere in the world, local monopolies and state firms were the main agents of gas production and supply.

The trend toward competitive gas markets began as part of the broader movement toward economic liberalization in the United States and the United Kingdom in the 1980s. In the United States government controls on wellhead prices were removed and gas producers began to compete to win buyers for their output – a competitive gas market was born. In the United Kingdom, state-owned British Gas was privatized and the sector was opened to competition. By the 1990s, gas markets in continental Europe, Latin America, and Asia began to follow, if tentatively, a path toward liberalization.

The seven case studies in chapters 3–9 span the past thirty years of gas trade and thus chronicle the shift from state control toward liberalized gas markets with an increasing role for private players. Today, nearly all major consuming markets have adopted plans to allow a greater role for the "invisible hand" of the market. However, this trend has been far from linear and homogeneous across the globe. Some governments, such as Russia, retain strict control of the gas market, where gas delivery remains the exclusive purview of a single state-controlled firm (Gazprom). Other countries, such as Bolivia and Argentina, have returned to state controls after brief experiments with more open markets.

We find it useful to imagine two archetypical worlds relating to the role of the state in gas markets. We define an "old world" of gas trade, where the state dominates the economy, including the provision of gas, and international trade in gas is backed by state-to-state agreements. In contrast we define the "new world" of gas trade as one where the role for the state shifts to the provider of market institutions that create the context for private firms to take risks and reap rewards from investment in costly gas infrastructure projects. These are ideal-types; no project operates solely in one of these "worlds," and most of the projects we studied combined elements of each. The "old world" often included substantial roles for private firms; the "new world" is often laden with state guarantees, subsidies, and other measures that dampen the pure expression of market forces. Nonetheless, we shall show that these two ideal types are useful in exposing the underlying forces at work, especially as more societies place increasing emphasis on markets as means of industrial organization. Here we focus on this shifting role for state and market – focusing first on the supply and then on the demand for gas.

The Role of the State in Gas Supply

The IEA's *World Energy Investment Outlook 2003* – the most recent comprehensive projection of its kind – envisions that about US$3 trillion will be needed over the next thirty years for the infrastructures to produce and move gas from fields upstream to final users (IEA 2003). Around two-thirds of that US$3 trillion will be required "upstream" for exploration, drilling, and the infrastructure of supply. Who will be most able to mobilize these resources, and what are the attributes of projects that are most likely to attract such large commitments of capital?

Our seven case studies show that while there is a shift to a greater role for private investment in new gas export projects, geography and politics have slowed the exit of the state. Much of this pattern simply reflects the desire of governments to preserve control over the rents that accrue from gas projects. Russia and Algeria maintain powerful state-owned companies (Gazprom and Sonatrach) that dominate gas production and concentrate revenues in the state and its favored partners. Even where private firms play a big role, host-country governments generally maintain sovereign controls over taxation, royalty treatment, and access to gas resources.

Still, there is relentless pressure for greater private participation in the upstream business. State-owned gas companies usually lack the access to capital and technology that are essential to the development of the most remote gas resources. Almost all the untapped huge gas resources in the world are located in countries that, today, confront this dilemma of industrial organization. On the one hand, state ownership and domination facilitate control over rents; on the other hand, state control and rent extraction are a powerful deterrent to private investors, especially when state terms are volatile and unpredictable.

This dilemma of industrial organization is especially evident in the LNG business, which is the most capital- and technology-intensive of gas infrastructures. The case studies on Qatar and Trinidad demonstrate successful models for attracting private players and building new gas export facilities (see chapters 8 and 9, respectively). The government of Qatar maintained a majority stake in Qatargas and subsequent LNG projects through Qatar Petroleum (QP). At the same time it attracted foreign investment by offering attractive terms for gas production from its massive North Field.

Trinidad, also, has created an environment that is attractive for private investment. When opportunities arose for private companies that were seeking to supply the US market with gas, Trinidad offered the easiest location to sink billions of dollars in capital with a reliable return for investors. Despite the fact that Trinidad's known gas reserves were smaller than many competing alternatives (e.g. neighboring Venezuela, Algeria, or Nigeria), the authors of the Trinidad case study in chapter 9 show that the government offered the most credible promises for an investor-friendly environment. Since the investment was large and lumpy, the attractiveness of that environment drew capital to Trinidad and temporarily foreclosed other possible LNG supply projects in the Atlantic Basin.

This finding is hardly remarkable in the era of "globalization," but it has immensely practical implications for how analysts assess the availability of gas resources. It appears that gas is enormously abundant in the world (USGS 2000); our findings suggest, however, that politics and institutions are as important as potential gas volumes in determining which resources can be exploited.

A cursory examination of the list of the top holders of the world's gas resources (table 10.1) suggests that the most of the potentially attractive gas resources are in countries where risks to investors are legion – the rule of law is weak and governments unstable. The coincidence of major gas resources and poor institutions poses a particular challenge in the "new world" of the global gas trade where private companies are expected to provide the bulk of capital and technology. Even as the direct role of host country governments in gas export projects diminishes, states still play a critical role in providing security and stability and in setting the institutional context within which these multi-billion dollar investments operate. The search for credible environments to invest explains, in part, why many of the largest gas resource holders have failed to become major gas producers and exporters. Whereas in oil there is a close relationship between the ranking of reserves and exports, in gas the correlation is weaker. In part, this divergence reflects geography. The cheapest way to move gas is by pipeline, and thus proximity to large markets is a valuable asset. (Notably, the proximity to the United States has pushed Canada to become the world's number two gas exporter yet does not appear on the ranking of top world reserves in table 10.1.) In part, however, we maintain

Table 10.1 *Top holders of world gas reserves, production, and exports, and their attractiveness to investors*

Country	Gas reserves and resources (Tcm)	Share of world total (%)	GIRI	Gas production (Bcm)	Total exports (Bcm)	Export rank
1 Russia	83.0	24.0	5.5	578.6	131.8	1
2 Iran	33.6	9.7	5.8	79.0	3.52	23
3 Saudi Arabia	32.4	9.4	7.2	61.0	–	–
4 United States	30.0	8.7	8.7	549.9	18.46	9
5 UAE	15.5	4.5	7.5	44.4	7.11	17
6 Turkmenistan	9.4	2.7	NA	55.1	4.92	20
7 Norway	8.9	2.6	9.2	73.4	68.4	3
8 Iraq	8.7	2.5	NA	2.4	–	–
9 Algeria	8.1	2.3	4.7	82.8	61.1	4
10 Venezuela	8.1	2.3	4.3	29.4	–	–
11 Indonesia	8.1	2.3	4.3	72.6	39.4	6
12 Australia	7.9	2.3	8.8	33.2	10.52	13
13 Qatar	6.4	1.8	7.5	30.8	19.2	8
14 Nigeria	6.3	1.8	2.8	19.2	11.8	12
15 Brazil	5.9	1.7	5.5	10.1	–	–
Rest of World	*73.9*	*21*				
World Total	*346.2*	*100*				

Note:
"Reserves and Resources" is the broadest measure of likely natural gas available in the country, which we obtain from the most recent comprehensive assessment by the United States Geological Survey's World Energy Assessment (USGS 2000). The USGS Assessment did not report resources for the US itself, which we draw from US Energy Information Agency (reserves) and other USGS reports (reserve growth and resources). GIRI is computed from the scores from the November 2002 edition of the *International Country Risk Guide* (*ICRG*), a well-known source of investment risk information for foreign investors (ICRG 2002). GIRI is a linear compilation of indices measuring government stability, investment profile, internal conflict, corruption, law and order, ethnic tensions, and bureaucratic quality. A high score of 10 denotes the best context for investment. Further detail on the GIRI calculation can be found in Hayes and Victor (2004) and chapters 2 and 12 herein. Total exports are for calendar year 2003 (BP 2004).
The USGS assessment merits updating, as evident especially in areas such as Qatar which have been the locus of intensive recent exploration.
NA = Not available.

that this looser relationship between resource potential and actual exports reflects variation in the contexts that explain where investors will actually risk capital to tap a resource.

Rather than look simply at potential volumes for gas supply, cost curves for gas production should be developed that combine the simple technical costs of recovery with factors that reflect the widely varying environment for hosting investments. In chapter 12 of this book our colleagues begin such an effort by exploring the effect on the optimal investment in gas infrastructures when the hurdle rates are partly adjusted to reflect the varying risks for long-term capital projects in different countries.

The Role of the State in "Creating" Gas Demand

All of the projects considered in this study involve large volumes of gas – typically 5–30 Bcm per year. For comparison, the energy content in 20 Bcm of gas is roughly equal to about 10 percent of all the energy consumed in Brazil, California, or Italy each year; it is about half the energy consumed in Singapore, and roughly equal to Hong Kong's total energy consumption.

The creators of these large projects have paid considerable attention to ensuring that demand for gas will rise in tandem with the surge in supply that occurs when a project begins operation. In all the cases where gas was to be delivered to a market that previously had little or no demand for gas – what we call a "virgin market" – government itself played a central role in creating the necessary demand for new volumes of gas. Absent this role by the state, none of these projects would have gone ahead at the same speed, or with the same volumes of deliveries. Even in cases where governments were liberalizing markets and adopting elements of the "new" gas world, they nonetheless often viewed one of their central functions as orchestrating the creation of demand. Table 10.2 summarizes the status of the target market, the role of the governments in orchestrating demand, and outcomes for each of the seven case studies.

The cases on Arun and the Qatar LNG projects show that the robust commitment of Japanese buyers to increase gas imports was essential to these projects moving forward (see chapters 3 and 8, respectively). In the first of these projects – Arun – the Japanese government (through MITI and J-EXIM) sent strong and credible signals to project investors by supporting the project with financial guarantees. Japanese trading companies (*Sogo Shosha*), while taking significant financial risks in launching these projects, acted under this "umbrella" of support from the government. Japan's energy system in the early 1970s was dominated by oil and coal; natural gas played a tiny role, but these investors knew that the Arun gas project would not founder for lack of demand because the

Table 10.2 *The role of the state in "creating gas demand"*

Chapter and case study	Target market and size[a]	Role of the state
3 The Transmed and Maghreb Projects: Gas for Europe from North Africa	*Italy*: virgin (South) and mature (North)	*Italy*: Government provides financial support via export credits; EBRD supports expansion of gas grid to Southern Italy. Alternative project to Spain fails because government does not support gas grid expansion.
4 Liquefied Natural Gas from Indonesia: The Arun project	*Japan*: virgin	*Japan*: MITI orchestrates purchasing by gas distributors and supports trading company investment.
5 Bypassing Ukraine: Russian Gas to Poland and Germany	*Poland*: virgin / *Germany*: mature	*Poland*: Government favors coal, and thus gas market fails to take off. *Germany*: Government plays schizophrenic role, but gas distributors find users for new supplies anyway.
6 Natural Gas Pipelines in the Southern Cone	*Argentina* (YABOG): mature / *Brazil* (GasBol): virgin / *Chile* (GasAndes or Transgas): virgin	*Argentina*: Government-owned gas company ensures use of gas purchased from Bolivia. *Brazil*: Brazilian government (with development banks) ensures Bolivian gas contracts but fails to create demand. *Chile*: Environmental regulations create market in favor of gas over alternative sources (coal, hydropower).
7 International Gas Trade in Central Asia: Turkmenistan, Iran, Russia, and Afghanistan	*Russia*: mature / *Iran*: mature / *Pakistan*: mature / *India*: largely virgin	*Russia*: Russian government and Gazprom use their dominant positions as the only large gas users to purchase gas at favorable prices. *Iran*: Iranian government provides financing for project via national oil and gas company. *Pakistan and India*: Neither government provides sufficient financial or political support for project.
8 Liquefied Natural Gas from Qatar: The Qatargas Project	*Japan*: mature	*Japan*: MITI supports project lending. Gas buyers (electric and gas utilities) granted monopoly service territories. Environmental regulations support gas.
9 Liquefied Natural Gas from Trinidad & Tobago: The Atlantic LNG Project	*United States*: mature / *Spain*: largely virgin.	*US*: Government plays no role. *Spain*: Gas supply diversification policy provides indirect assistance.

Note:
[a] "Virgin" markets depend on natural gas for less than 10 percent of primary energy supply.

central government would orchestrate the construction of receiving terminals, distribution pipelines, and power plants.[1] Twenty years later, when the Qatargas project was coming to fruition, MITI was weaker and its ability to orchestrate industrial investment had waned considerably; by then, however, a credible government commitment to create the needed demand for gas in Japan was less essential because a robust gas-using infrastructure already existed in Japan's key urban areas. (That infrastructure was not a gas transmission grid as in Europe or the United States but, rather, a network of LNG-receiving terminals, serving a cluster of relatively isolated local markets. Constraints on moving gas between those markets helped each local monopoly to protect its position, which in turn made it easier for the monopolists to commit with confidence to infrastructure projects that would yield a return only over long time horizons.) Despite its waning domestic influence, MITI and the Japanese government were critical in providing preferential terms for financing the Qatargas development.

Similarly, much of the variation in the outcomes of the two proposed projects to pipe gas across the Mediterranean in the late 1970s is also due to the starkly different roles that the Italian and Spanish governments took when confronted with the possibility of importing large volumes of gas (see chapter 3). Like Japan, in the 1970s the Italian government was actively seeking to diversify its oil-dominated energy system by importing gas and was willing to mobilize significant state resources to secure new energy supplies. Through its own export credit agencies, the Italian government provided support and guarantees for the bulk of financing that would be needed for the Transmed underwater pipeline project. State-owned ENI, a powerful and financially sound enterprise, used this credible state guarantee to orchestrate both the Transmed pipeline as well as the development of Italy's internal gas transmission grid (particularly in the southern part of the country). The state's commitment to guarantee ENI's returns allowed the firm to invest with confidence and to raise capital from international lenders. In contrast, Spain's government did

---

[1] The Japanese market was not completely virgin; like many industrial countries, Japan's major cities already had pipeline distribution systems in place to distribute "town gas"—a brew of aromatics, hydrogen, and carbon monoxide produced by heating coal. In some European cities, that network was used as the backbone for natural gas distribution systems, with technical changes (e.g. changes in the size of holes in burner nozzles, as the heat content and burning properties of natural gas are somewhat different from town gas). In Japan, the specifications of the old system were kept and the imported gas is blended with other fuels and ingredients to adjust its heat content to the specifications of the older town gas system. Nonetheless, town gas was a bit player in Japan's energy system and the vast majority of the infrastructure needed to get useful gas from tankers to final users was not in place when Japan began its shift to LNG.

not have a policy to expand gas consumption or imports in the late 1970s and early 1980s, and thus no state-owned or private player was able or willing to take the risks inherent in constructing a major gas import pipeline that would be economically viable only if it could deliver huge volumes of gas to final users in Spain.[2]

In general, gasification has not followed in cases where large volumes of gas have been readily available but governments have not orchestrated investment in infrastructures and other essential elements for assuring demand. Russian and German investors built a large pipeline across Belarus in the 1990s mainly to supply additional volumes of gas to the market where the investors thought that the risks were relatively low since the German market was already mature and a complex array of distribution pipelines was already in the ground (see chapter 5). To reach Germany the pipeline would also cross Poland, where the project backers also hoped to sell gas. Unlike most of the former Soviet client states that had shifted to gas when the Soviet Union built pipelines in the Cold War, gas played almost no role in Poland's coal-dominated energy system. The virgin market offered huge potential. In practice, however, the Polish gas market has not flourished mainly because gas was forced to compete with politically well-connected coal suppliers who were keen to scupper any advantage that might be given to gas. The Polish government, beholden to coal interests, was not a champion for gas; no entity in Poland was prepared to build the infrastructure and promote new policies that would be needed to confer an advantage for gas.

The seven case studies in chapters 3–9 sound caution about visions for rapid gasification in markets where gas delivery infrastructure does not already exist and where the state is not prepared to back the creation of the gas delivery infrastructure. Indeed, across all the case studies in this book the country that reveals the most rapid gasification is the one where the state played the most central role in determining energy choices: the Soviet Union. A decision from the center to favor gas in the 1950s, orchestrated through Soviet central planning, catapulted gas from just 1 percent of total primary energy supply in 1955 to 30 percent in 1980

---

[2] Italy had other advantages as well. The discovery of gas in the Po Valley in the North during the 1940s had spawned the creation of gas distribution networks around some of Italy's most lucrative northern markets; those networks were thus available for distribution of Algerian gas. Spain, by contrast, had virtually no gas infrastructure when it contemplated investment in Algerian export. Italy also received significant financial backing from the European Investment Bank (EIB) for the project, discussed below. In 1990, the situation changed and Spain became a hot gas market. New Spanish politics encouraged private investment in power-generation, and the favored technology for those plants was all gas-fired. Similar forces are at work in Chile, evinced in the Southern Cone case study (chapter 6).

(chapter 5). We do not claim that this role for the state is economically efficient or the only way to create a market, but we do note that in history this role for the state accounts for a large amount of the observed variation in the timing and completion of first-of-a-kind gas projects.

The case study of the Southern Cone (chapter 6) provides two contrasting examples of the potential role of the state in the context of liberalizing gas markets. The GasBol pipeline, connecting Bolivia to Brazil, was a favorite of both governments and the development banks. The Brazilian government, the World Bank and the Inter-American Development Bank (IADB) all sought to use the pipeline to encourage economic development and political stability in gas-rich Bolivia. Gas, it was hoped, would offer an alternative to drugs as Bolivia's top cash export. The development banks funded about half the project, and the Brazilian government forced state-owned Petrobrás to contract for the bulk of gas purchases from the pipeline and also encouraged the company to support investment in developing Bolivia's gas fields to help move the project forward. To ensure that the gas would be used – and to diversify Brazil's hydro-dominated electricity system that failed in years when rains were scarce – the Brazilian government introduced special subsidies and regulatory rules that, it hoped, would encourage potential gas users to build power plants, factories, and other investments in gas-using equipment. However, after catalyzing the development of the project, the Brazilian government did not continue to supply the incentives that favored gas, leaving Petrobrás with binding contracts for volumes of Bolivian gas it could not sell. The Brazilian government used state guarantees to advance its foreign policy goals (i.e. encouraging economic development in Bolivia) and found it convenient to externalize the cost of this policy to Petrobrás (and thus to Brazilian consumers via higher prices for other services Petrobrás provided). In this example, the government sought to orchestrate demand as it would in the "old" era of state-dominated energy markets; ultimately, however, it was unwilling to sustain a change in market rules and subsidies that would be needed to counteract the strong bias against using gas for power-generation.

The second example from the Southern Cone case study, the GasAndes pipeline from Argentina to Chile, illustrates the types of projects that seem most likely to proceed with the shift to the "new" world in which governments do not determine directly the prices and quantities of gas supplied and consumed. In this "new world," gas projects are most likely to emerge where distribution networks already exist or where private users are able to organize themselves to offer a credible demand for gas. The GasAndes project beat its competitor, Transgas, because it connected rich gas fields in Argentina to a small number of major buyers in Chile (power generators near Santiago). The liberalizing electric power market in Chile, along with the tighter air pollution regulations in badly polluted Santiago created favorable conditions for importing gas. Rather than simply serving large power plant consumers, the Transgas project sought a significant expansion of the gas distribution network around Santiago and in neighboring cities; it sought to spawn new gas distribution companies that would serve industrial and residential gas consumers, in addition to gas-fired power generators. Thus, the Transgas project would have been more costly, requiring a much longer period to recoup the investment and would require the alignment of a larger number of diverse interests. The backers of this vision sought a concession from the government to guarantee a return on its investment in the gas distribution grid. Favoring competitive markets, the Chilean government refused to provide such a concession and the Transgas project foundered, while the GasAndes project moved quickly ahead because it required coordinating only a small number of large gas users with shorter time horizons.

While the role of the state is critical in virgin gas markets, the Atlantic LNG project in Trinidad created a new mold for LNG projects to serve more developed gas-using markets. The Atlantic LNG project targeted the competitive Northeastern US gas market where gas prices were determined solely on the supply–demand balance, rather than linkages to oil prices, as had long been the case for other LNG projects. Lacking the kinds of long-term price assurances often provided to other LNG projects, Trinidad project managers employed innovative design and sales structures to ensure that the project could compete to deliver gas to its target market. The addition of the option to deliver gas to Spanish gas buyers further improved the long-term prospects for the Trinidad project. This shift to more flexible and more competitive contracting has come to define all subsequent LNG projects that have followed Atlantic LNG.

Contracting and Security of Supply in the Changing Gas World

The global trade in gas arose during the oil crises of the 1970s. Oil importers, especially in Europe and Japan, sought to supplant the suddenly expensive and unreliable supplies of oil with imports of natural gas. This shift, animated mainly by concerns about energy security, introduced severe challenges. First, importing governments needed to ensure that they did not replace oil with another insecure and volatile import. Second, a shift to gas would require building infrastructures (pipelines and LNG systems) that were even more costly than their oil equivalents. A long time horizon would be needed to justify these investments. The response to these two challenges was found in long-term contracts. For governments, these contracts promised to assure energy security; for investors in gas projects, such contracts created a context in which capital could be risked when returns were distant.

In this section we look at whether these two ambitions for long-term contracts have been realized. First, we examine the most simple and politically salient question of contracting for gas: were the promised volumes delivered, or have states deployed the "gas weapon" in a manner akin to the Arab embargo on oil? Second, we look at the role of long-term contracts as devices for managing financial risks, with attention to how the parties that invested in these projects mitigated their exposure. We probe whether such contracts were themselves credible, and the devices that parties have used when they feared that enforcement of long-term commitments would be imperfect.

The "Gas Weapon"?

The overriding concern in the "old world" of gas trade centered on assuring firm deliveries of contracted volumes. The long-term contract for guaranteed deliveries was specifically designed to mitigate these concerns. A take-or-pay sales clause was the keystone of the contractual relationship, committing the buyer to pay for a specified volume of gas (regardless of whether he actually takes delivery), usually over a period of twenty to thirty years. Pricing formulas included provisions for renegotiation (typically every three years) and were linked to prices for the oil products gas replaced in the end-user market, net of transportation costs; the amount left over was allocated among project developers and the host country. This so-called "net-back" pricing scheme was the status quo for long-distance gas trade – not only LNG but also for Russian and Algerian deliveries.[3] Japan has long indexed the price for its LNG imports to the JCC, a weighted index of Japanese oil import prices. Such oil-linked schemes created substantial fluctuations in gas prices, but governments and bankers were already familiar with these

---

[3] In only one example mentioned in these studies – Algeria's early LNG exports to Britain and to the US (chapter 3), contracts that dated to back to the in the late 1960s – was the gas delivered on a rate-of-return contract. Algerian shipments to the United States and Europe in the 1970s adopted full oil-linked pricing, similar to the net-back scheme, before pursuing a radical oil-export parity pricing scheme in the early 1980s. The Algerians returned to a more standard net-back pricing formula when oil prices collapsed in 1986.

risks, and gas was usually priced at a discount to the oil that it supplanted. (Of the seven cases in this book, only Atlantic LNG in Trinidad uses a contractual structure with flexible deliveries dictated partly by the price of gas in the United States). Prices might vary, but consistent volumes would be delivered.

Table 10.3 summarizes all instances from the seven case studies where gas deliveries have deviated substantially from the contracted terms; they include outright interruptions and provide a first snapshot of the situations where fears of insecure supplies have been realized.

Security of Supply Across all seven case studies we find just three instances where suppliers have reduced output below the contracted terms. The most dramatic example concerns Algeria, which stopped gas deliveries in the early 1980s in an effort to drive up prices for Italy, France, and other gas buyers. (These events are described in further detail in chapter 3.) This is the only example that is analogous with the "oil weapon" used during and after the Arab oil embargo – where an exporter unilaterally rejected existing contracts and expectations in an effort to tighten supply and drive up prices.[4]

All the other cases of supply interruption are more complicated and, mainly, do not simply reflect strategic efforts to drive up prices. Rather, they are the by-product of other factors, such as internal conflicts that spill over to disrupt exports. In 2001 uprisings in Aceh briefly stopped shipments from the project; the original deal with Japanese buyers that created the project had been predicated on the assumption that the Indonesian government would quell local uprisings in the Aceh region, but that deal was difficult to sustain in the face of Indonesia's severe internal strife. In 2004 Argentina unilaterally lowered the volume of gas it allowed for shipment to Chile; in the wake of an unexpected financial crisis, Argentina's government had frozen internal gas prices and found it politically expedient to cut exports rather than suffer the political consequences of the widespread domestic shortages that would have occurred if Argentina's producers had been free to send scarce local supplies to Chile where they would have fetched a premium export price.

Beyond these three examples – relatively few and short in duration when compared with the tens of decades of collective operations – the cases suggest that the "gas weapon" is rarely used because all major markets for gas are fundamentally contestable over the long term by

---

[4] Unlike the Arab oil embargo, however, Algeria's demands in the early 1980s did not have an overt political objective attached other than to increase the prices it received for its pipeline and LNG sales.

Table 10.3 *Contract interruptions, from the seven case studies*

Initiating party	Example
Supplier	1 Algeria (Sonatrach) (1981–1983): "Gas Battle" with Italy, Belgium, France, Spain, and the United States leads to refusal to ship gas via Transmed pipeline (Italy) and reduced volumes for LNG buyers (Belgium, France, Spain, and the United States). Outcome: Formula price increases for most buyers, US shipments nearly stopped.
	2 Rebels in Aceh province stop shipments from Arun LNG project in 2001. Outcome: Aceh rebellion suppressed and shipments resume.
	3 Argentine administrative policy forces a reduction in GasAndes pipeline supply to Chile (2004). Outcome: Argentina interprets its reduction in exports as allowable under the *force majeure* clause; Chile shifts to other fuels.
Transit country	1 Gazprom refuses to transport Turkmen gas to Europe (1997–1998). Outcome: Gazprom and its Russian partners get favorable terms and Turkmen gas is exported via Russia.
	2 Ukraine disputes with Gazprom over volume and payments for gas shipments (mid-1990s). Outcome: Ukraine secures extended transit contract with improved terms.
	3 Gazprom cuts supplies to Belarus (and to Europe via the BC) in pricing dispute with Belarus (2004). Outcome: Contract renegotiated and shipments resume.
	4 Gazprom cuts supplies to Ukraine (2005–2006). Outcome: Ukraine agrees to higher prices and sources additional (lower-priced) volumes of gas from Turkmenistan.
User	1 In 1981 US government refuses to allow LNG importers to accept shipments from Sonatrach to punish Algeria for its attempt to drive up prices. Outcome: Algeria loses most of its US market over the next decade.
	2 Argentina forces renegotiation of contracted deliveries from the YABOG pipeline, reducing volumes and prices taken from Bolivia (1987). Outcome: Contract is renegotiated and later pipeline is left empty.
	3 Brazil refuses to accept the full volume of gas it contracted from Bolivia via the Gasbol pipeline (2001). Outcome: Petrobrás absorbs penalties because the pipeline is part of Brazil's larger foreign policy strategy.
	4 Japan refuses to accept volumes and prices from Qatargas that are in line with historical LNG projects, but much more costly than contracts being signed by other LNG importers (1998). Outcome: Contracts renegotiated in Japan's favor.
	5 Turkey refuses to accept the large volumes of gas contracted through the Blue Stream pipeline from Russia because of macroeconomic troubles and a glut in the Turkish gas market (2002). Outcome: Russia accepts reduced contractual volumes and prices.

alternative suppliers or alternative fuel sources. Curtailing gas shipments causes harm to reputation; because gas projects come in large tranches and create lock-in effects, a potential supplier that is passed over for its poor reputation can find itself locked out of lucrative markets for a generation or longer. The studies suggest that governments are aware of this and that the "gas weapon" has come into play only when key decision-makers fail to keep their attention on their government's long-term reputation. The new government that took power in Algeria in 1980 focused on short-term political objectives rather than commercial stability. It sought a clean break from the past by abrogating the contracts that earlier technocrats had painstakingly assembled, and it sought for gas export prices what Algeria had already achieved (with OPEC's help) in oil.[5] The long-term costs to Algeria in reputation and in forgone gas revenues have been severe. Over the following decade Algeria lost the US LNG market as US buyers did not renew expiring contracts; previously the United States had been Algeria's largest buyer of LNG. European LNG customers also quickly looked elsewhere for gas supplies in the 1980s. The net cost of Algeria's "gas battle" ran quickly into billions, as over half of Algeria's costly LNG export facilities remained idle for nearly a decade. The damage to reputation has lingered longer, American and European gas buyers welcomed the opportunity to build LNG export projects in more stable Trinidad & Tobago in the 1990s; today, Trinidad & Tobago has supplanted Algeria as the dominant supplier of LNG to the United States. The Italian government and ENI did cave in to Algeria's demands and pay higher prices for Transmed pipeline gas in the early 1980s, as the Italians had already sunk its investment in the pipeline. However, future governments became much more wary of relying on Algerian gas supplies – building a diverse portfolio of supplies from Russia, Norway, and the Netherlands. Anecdotal evidence suggests that European buyers will not soon forget the checkered history of Algerian gas supply.

Users of gas are primed to be sensitive to the risk of gas curtailment, and thus any indication that such curtailment might occur usually yields swift effects on suppliers' reputations. The Polish government was extremely worried about dependence on Russia for gas and thus negotiated an alternative supply project with Norway, in parallel contracting for Russian gas from the cross-Belarus pipeline project. The Norway project fell apart

---

[5] The new government and new Sonatrach leadership also fundamentally misunderstood the commercial aspects of the gas market. They believed that lower shipments at higher prices was a sustainable model, as they had done via OPEC with oil. These new officials did not realize that gas required competitive pricing, otherwise there would be no demand at all.

because of unfavorable economics, but the Polish government rekindled the project when Russia's conflict with Belarus over gas pricing cut supplies to Poland for a brief period in early 2004. The Norwegian alternative – expensive, but viable – was a threat designed to focus Russia and Belarus on the potential long-term costs of their lack of discipline.

The two case studies of LNG projects supplying the Japanese market could be viewed as the most physically insecure of the seven gas supply projects examined. LNG tankers bound for Japan crossed thousands of miles of open ocean and dangerous straits. LNG tankers could have been attacked by pirates or terrorists; states hostile to Japan might have attempted to disrupt the sea lanes. Suppliers could, in principle, withhold supplies to drive up prices or to punish Japan politically. Such scenarios were examined closely by the Japanese government, and three factors explain why these dangers never materialized. First, just as Japan had few alternative LNG suppliers so, too, the suppliers had few alternative outlets for disposing their gas. Japan dominated the LNG market with more than half the total global consumption and, until very recently, there was no well-developed secondary market for redirecting cargoes to other users. Just as geography and sunk capital prevent pipeline routes from being redirected – thus binding even unreliable sellers to a particular market – so, too, the thinness of the world LNG market had a similar effect that bound most suppliers to security-conscious Japan. Second, Japan ensured stable supply by simply guaranteeing that it would pay the highest price in the marketplace. The first of these projects – Arun – remains among the most profitable (for developers) in LNG history. Given its willingness to pay a hefty premium for stable supplies, Japan Inc. shifted the burden to potential gas suppliers to show that they would be credible, long-term sellers. (The one instance of supply interruption concerning a Japanese LNG project – Arun in 2001 – occurred when the field was already in decline and Japan had ample alternative supplies. Still, the perception of Indonesia's instability has caused new buyers to choose Australia and Sakhalin (Russia) for new long-term contracts.) Third, Japan invested heavily in security – including gold plating of LNG operations – in an effort to protect against interruptions and to ensure very high levels of system reliability. In retrospect, that investment appears to have been costly, as a significant part of the reduction in LNG costs in the 1990s came from removing Japanese-mandated redundancies and other gold plating; however, that investment also helped to ensure LNG's admirable safety record. Japan also relied on the US security umbrella to protect the sea lanes.

The historical case studies provide some comfort to prospective gas importers who fear insecure supplies – especially those with diverse import infrastructures. Nevertheless, the experience of importers dependent on Algerian gas in the early 1980s is still a cautionary tale. Previous to the change in government in 1979, Algiers was sending all the right signals to gas buyers by offering long-term commitments to deliver gas at competitive prices. Circumstances changed rapidly when the new government took power in 1980, seeking to distinguish itself from its predecessor and emboldened in its aim to boost gas prices by the successes of the oil cartel. While the long-term results were disastrous for Algeria, historical lessons are not always well studied or applied. Shifts in political regimes – and the limited time horizons of leaders who aim to upset existing orders – may pose continued threats to stable gas exports.

Security of Supply and Transit Countries Analysts have given particular attention to the risks of insecure supply from pipeline projects that cross transit countries. The concern has been that while suppliers and users are bound together, transit countries could have disproportionate influence over outcomes and demand a disproportionate share of the revenue for themselves. Again, our studies suggest that interruptions due to behavior in transit countries are few and occur mainly as unintended by-products of broader disputes. In 1995, Ukraine suffered chaotic internal rule that made it difficult to collect revenues from gas users, as well as overriding hostility to Russia, and in 2004 the President of Belarus was locked in dispute with Russian President Putin and Gazprom over ownership of pipelines and pricing of gas. In 2005–2006 another bout of conflict between Russia and Ukraine spilled over into a brief reduction in gas volumes transiting the country. None of these cases involved simple disputes over transit fees as both countries had previously been part of the Soviet Union; both were large gas consumers built on the legacy of inexpensive Soviet gas.

As with suppliers, transit countries must contend with the fact that the transit fees they earn are linked to a service that is fundamentally contestable. In the original Transmed contract negotiations, Tunisia sought to use its geographical position along the most favorable pipeline route to demand a high take; it backed down when Algeria and Italy credibly explored an LNG export option that would have bypassed Tunisia completely and left it with zero transit fees. Tunisia could attempt to force renegotiation of its fee now that the pipeline is built, but such a move would jeopardize possible expansions.[6] (Almost all projects operate in

---

[6] Two expansions of the Transmed pipeline have been completed since its startup in 1983. Today, alternative pipelines bypassing Tunisia are feasible and moving forward. This is in part to avoid paying transit fees to Tunisia, but also to bypass the monopoly that ENI (Snam) holds on the route.

the context of constant chatter about expansion, which partly reflects the real prospects for expansion and partly is a tactic that keeps hosts and operators focused on the long term.) Once operational, if Tunisia were to block the Transmed gas shipments it would gain nothing itself. It has little domestic use for the gas, limited storage, and gas supplies would stop shortly after the blockage or diversion was detected. It might be feasible for Tunisia to extract a larger share of rents over the short term, but faced with such demands Algeria and its importers would certainly respond by focusing on other routes for the next phase of expansion.

In the case of the Ukraine and Belarus crises, the interruptions in 1995, 2004 and 2005–2006 created harmful consequences for reputation. Over the short term, both Ukraine and Belarus externalized their damage to Russia, which receives lower revenues for its exports and is seen as a less reliable supplier. Ukraine was able to demand higher transit fees because it controls nearly all of Russia's gas export capacity, but that loss in rents has spurred Gazprom to search for alternative export routes. For the West European market, Belarus was the easiest alternative because Russian trunk pipelines already crossed the eastern part of the country. But the souring of relations with Belarus has rekindled Russia's interest in the "NEGP" pipeline on the seabed of the Baltic, which would allow Russia to bypass all transit countries and allow shipments directly to the European Union. Barely four months after the Belarusian interruption Gazprom announced that it had lined up funding for the NEGP project in partnership with the German firm E.On. (E.On bought Ruhrgas in 2002 and, with that purchase, acquired a 6.4 percent stake in Gazprom, making it the largest non-Russian holder of Gazprom shares.) In 2006, after the second Ukrainian gas crisis, Gazprom reinvigorated the Baltic export route. For the potentially lucrative Turkish market, Russia built a pipeline directly across the Black Sea (The "Blue Stream" pipe) to avoid Ukraine and other transit countries. So far, it appears that Russia has not suffered much from the trouble of being upstream of unreliable transit countries because Europe's second-largest external supplier (Algeria) is perceived as even less reliable. Russia's real competitor is the rise of LNG imports into Europe, whose prospects have brightened considerably with the declining cost of LNG technology and the perennial interest by Germany and other Russia-dependent gas importers to diversify energy sources.

The case of Turkmen exports via Russia does provide a stark example of the leverage that a transit country can impose where there are no viable alternative export options in the near-to-medium term. In the mid-1990s Gazprom, as the sole owner of the pipelines that took Turkmen gas to Europe via Russia, halted Turkmen exports and demanded an increase in transit fees. Turkmenistan had little choice but to agree, as efforts to build viable export routes via Afghanistan and Iran had largely failed.

A Buyer's Weapon? For projects that ship large volumes of gas to markets, the "gas weapon" is equally available to users. Indeed, the case studies here involve more examples of interruptions and renegotiations of contracts instigated by users than suppliers or transit countries (Table 10.3). In some cases, these interruptions have been a by-product of misestimated demand, not a part of a grand strategy to reallocate rents or political power. Turkey, for example, forced renegotiation of the Blue Stream contracts when the expected bullish gas market in Turkey failed to meet expectations in the wake of macroeconomic troubles. Brazil, too, failed to absorb the large volumes it contracted from Bolivia. Only the Brazilian government's broader foreign policy concerns sustained Petrobrás' gas purchases from Bolivia.

Nevertheless, if a gas buyer has suitable energy supply alternatives *and* they are the sole buyer (as in a pipeline project), they are in a position of power to renegotiate prices. This monopsony power can be particularly acute as the operating costs of any project are a small fraction of the already sunk capital cost, thus suggesting that gas suppliers will continue deliveries for a fraction of the cost required to fully recover their investment. The implications for operations will be discussed further below; however, we note here three cases where gas buyers have used their power to shift the terms of the original contract bargain in their favor. First, in the early 1980s, the United States turned the "gas weapon" back on Algeria when it attempted to hold up supply. With adequate alternative supplies available in North America, the US Department of Energy refused to approve new Algerian contracts rather than allow US customers to pay the higher prices Algeria was demanding. In the late 1980s, Argentina unilaterally forced new contract terms on the YABOG pipeline, as increasing domestic production made Bolivian imports less necessary. Japanese buyers also had access to alternative suppliers in the late 1990s and used that leverage to bring the prices for shipments from Qatargas in line with the declining cost of contracted deliveries from other suppliers in the Asian region.

Credibility of Long-Term Commitments and the Management of Financial Risk

In both the "old" and "new" worlds, gas projects demand huge quantities of capital. Governments and private investors alike need assurance that their investments will yield a consistent return over the long life of the project. In the "old world" these projects were organized within state-to-state agreements with state-backed financing; governments, themselves, had a strong incentive to assure compliance because the gas trade was usually interwoven with many other international issues that affected the state-to-state relationship.

In the "new world" the capital and reputations at risk are private. As with any large investment where the preponderance of cost is sunk before operation begins, investors in gas supply infrastructures are exposed to what Raymond Vernon termed the "obsolescing bargain" (Vernon 1971). Before the project is built, potential investors are in the position of power, holding scarce capital and technologies required for the project. After a deal is struck between investors, gas buyers, and the host-country governments, capital is "sunk" into developing gas fields and constructing export infrastructures. Once built, a gas pipeline or LNG facility has no alternative use and the leverage for setting rules on taxes and prices shifts to the host-country government and to the gas buyers. Generally, a manager will continue to operate a project so long as the price it earns for its shipments (net of taxes and royalties) covers the continuing costs of operation – not necessarily allowing for the recovery of the initial investment or a suitable return on that investment. In gas pipeline and LNG projects, this risk is particularly acute. Compared with coal and oil, gas production and export projects are more capital-intensive,[7] requiring greater earnings over operating costs for a longer period to recover the initial investment.

The risk that gas buyers will not adhere to the full conditions of a contract is one aspect of the "obsolescing bargain" problem faced by investors in gas infrastructure projects. Table 10.3 includes several instances where buyers sought reduced prices after the full investment had been sunk. As these examples suggest, the "obsolescing bargain" is a real risk for investors. The ability of buyers to utilize their power to unilaterally adjust prices depends in large part on the availability of alternative energy supplies. In the "old world" single-partner relationships formed the bedrock of cross-border gas trade. In limited circumstances, such as those described above, buyers could unilaterally exercise power to reduce contract prices. Buyers could exercise this "weapon" (or monopsony power) only where suitable energy supply alternatives were available. Today, gas markets are evolving toward more flexible

---

[7] The IEA estimates that the average investment required to deliver gas from fields to end-users through 2030 would cost an average of $28 per metric ton of oil equivalent. Compare this to $22 required to build the capacity to deliver an incremental ton of oil, or $5 for the capacity to deliver an energy equivalent amount of coal (IEA 2003).

exchange, bringing with it a fundamental shift in the formation of prices and the ability and incentives for buyers to renege on price commitments. We revisit the impacts for security briefly at the end of this section, and it will be the subject of further discussion in chapters 11 and 12. We now turn to discuss the continuing challenges that investors will face in sinking capital in the countries that will supply the gas traded on world markets.

Most of the world's gas resources are in countries where institutions for enforcing commitments are weak, politicized, or non-existent. Yet typical gas export projects require devoting more than half of the capital investment in the export country itself – in field development, pipelines and processing equipment, and (for LNG) costly liquefaction facilities. Such investments are intrinsically immobile. Because the investor with sunk capital in a project will be willing to operate at much lower earnings than those agreed to in the original contract, host governments may be tempted to raise effective tax rates or engage in other "squeezing" of the project knowing that the investor has few options but to continue to operate. As discussed above, the long-term contestability of investment sites can exert a discipline on such behavior, but only when time horizons are suitably long and governments are actually able to implement distant-looking strategies – the problems in Algeria and Ukraine, among others, are evidence that such "squeezing" does occur.

Investors in gas supply projects are keenly aware of the motivations and opportunities for host-country governments to renege on contracts. All else equal, they prefer to operate in states that can most credibly signal their commitment to uphold original bargains. The most obvious way that a government signals its ability to sustain a commitment is through its own past actions, thereby establishing a reputation for being a stable and investment-friendly environment. Where these conditions do not exist investors demand higher rates of return and payback schedules that weight near-term payments over heavily discounted future streams.

Spiraling downward – the same countries deemed most risky by investors are arguably more likely to have governments that also heavily discount the benefits that might accrue from future investments. Where domestic and external disturbances are common (e.g. areas of civil unrest or war) the government is likely to place much greater importance on current payoffs (staying in power) relative to the promise of future projects.

Domestic politics can also limit the ability of governments to uphold the terms of agreement over the life of the project. Radical changes in government can lead to abrupt shifts in policy – as in Algeria or Iran in the late 1970s, or Bolivia in 2003. Host governments and government officials can change tax rates and property rights for their own personal enrichment, or to earn votes. Oil and gas resources are often viewed as a national heritage, and thus can be the focus of intense political rhetoric. The symbolism of "protecting the national interest" at the expense of "foreign profiteering" creates strong incentives for politicians and bureaucrats to renege on earlier commitments to gas project investors.

What can be done to overcome these obstacles? Here we examine the strategies that governments in supply countries can pursue themselves; later we examine the options available to private investors and through international institutions.

A host-country's governance structure is perhaps the strongest determinant of its ability to signal credibility in its commitments. North and Weingast (1989) showed that the establishment of the Bank of England in the late seventeenth century was an attempt by the British Crown to raise the credibility of its promises to repay loans from its wealthy citizens. The Crown needed new financing, particularly to prosecute a war against France. Wealthy capital holders, having suffered through a string of defaults, sought to ensure that they would be repaid this time. In part to address this issue the British Crown established a parliament composed of capital holders that assumed veto control over revenue collection and public spending. The Bank of England was created to coordinate state borrowing, using capital advanced by English citizens. Each loan was, in turn, backed by a specific tax allocation. If the Crown reneged on any of its loan obligations, future lending from the Bank would be withheld. The Bank of England was an early step toward a government with division of powers and a constitution to protect private property that is the foundation of the Western democratic and economic systems. Under this system, the constitution and an independent judiciary were intended to protect the long-term interests of the country (and its creditors) and guard against opportunistic behavior by any given political administration. Out of specific reciprocity, broader cooperation emerged (Axelrod 1984; Seabright 2004).

There is no exact analog to this structure for foreign investment in gas projects, but the Bank of England example suggests that governments might signal credibility by creating structures that limit their own freedom of action. Indeed, typical production-sharing agreements include visible promises to insulate the energy project from alterations in tax law and other adverse changes in context. But such agreements, in practice, are not immune to opportunism. Many analysts have imagined an ideal world in which institutions provide for the rule of law and the protection of property rights. That is a difficult task, especially as governments may only have a few years to demonstrate their credibility and earn visible rewards for painful reforms. Among the interim steps is transparency – simply publishing the receipt of government revenues and their allocation can signal seriousness that corruption and rent-seeking will be spotted and kept at bay.

The list of LNG-exporting countries shown in table 10.4, and the notable absentees from that list, provides insights into how governments signal the credibility demanded by investors. Whereas pipeline economics are highly sensitive to the geographical proximity to a particular user market, LNG export economics are less constrained and thus better illustrate the role of investor confidence. What matters for LNG is the availability of a large gas resource near a coastline and the proximity to any market – close enough to make shipping feasible, yet far enough to make LNG the preferred option to a pipeline. Such conditions are satisfied in most of the gas-rich countries shown in table 10.4.

Although gas-rich countries are numerous, only a select few have managed to secure the billions in capital required for new export projects. The success of Qatar, Trinidad & Tobago, and Brunei in the competition for LNG investment suggests that countries that are physically and economically small may have an advantage in creating an attractive investment environment. Trinidad established credibility with investors as a stable constitutional democracy with gas investment-friendly policies that survived a swing in political winds. Yet, the examples of Qatar and Brunei suggest that the division of powers and democratic governance is not the only path to investor confidence. The leaders of these countries have few checks on their near-absolute powers. Faced with declining revenues from oil exports, each of these countries adopted investment-friendly environments to develop gas exports. Revenues from gas sales quickly became critical to the economies of all three countries – accounting for over 10 percent of the total domestic economies in 2003. The prospects of concentrated benefits from LNG project investment were enough to encourage these governments to implement a set of laws to attract gas investors. In contrast, for larger countries with broader political landscapes – such as Venezuela or Iran – the demands on such resources are more complex to manage, which may make it more difficult for such nations to make credible any promises to protect foreign investment. Geographically, both of these countries juxtapose highly successful LNG exporters (Trinidad and Qatar); politically, they are quite different.

The nine other countries currently exporting LNG suggest that the focus and nimbleness that arise, especially in geographically small

Table 10.4 *LNG exporters, 2003*

		LNG Exports (2003)		GDP (2002)	LNG exports as share of GDP
Rank	Country	volume (Bcm)	value (billion USD)	value (billion USD)	(%)
1	Indonesia	35.7	4.1	172.9	2.4
2	Algeria	28.0	3.2	55.9	5.8
3	Malaysia	23.4	2.7	94.9	2.8
4	Qatar	19.2	2.2	17.5	12.7
5	Trinidad & Tobago	11.9	1.4	9.6	14.3
6	Nigeria	11.8	1.4	43.5	3.1
7	Australia	10.5	1.2	409.4	0.3
8	Brunei	9.7	1.1	4.7	24.0
9	Oman	9.2	1.1	20.3	5.2
10	UAE	7.1	0.8	71.0	1.2
11	United States	1.6	0.2	10,383.1	0.0
12	Libya	0.8	0.1	19.1	0.5

Note:
Value based on 2003 LNG exports (BP 2004) roughly approximated to $3 per mmbtu, estimated GDPs are market exchange rates (from EIA).

countries, is not the only path to attracting investment. Algeria and Indonesia developed their gas export industries largely in the 1970s under regimes that, at the time, welcomed foreign investment. In both cases, major LNG projects went ahead during periods of relative stability, and the attractiveness of both countries to new project investment declined considerably under political uncertainty. Host governments can also create (or allow) islands of investor-friendly stability in a sea that is otherwise opaque and daunting. Thus the first LNG projects in Russia moved forward on Sakhalin Island – physically far from Moscow and backed by commitments from a regional government that enjoyed autonomy from Moscow and had a strong vested interest in the sustainability of projects in its own territory.[8] Egypt and Nigeria have both created special zones for LNG investment.

Governments also have the option of structuring gas projects so that commitments are more readily self-enforcing, just as the seventeenth-century British Crown did when it reorganized public finances to promote reciprocity. Self-enforcing commitments are theoretically possible,

[8] A reassertion of power by the Kremlin in Moscow has upset the relative stability of the Sakhalin development.

but we do not observe any in practice. One strategy might be employed as a solution to deliver Iranian gas to energy-hungry India. The most economically feasible pipeline would transit Pakistan and deliver gas to that country as well. Given the tense relations between the two countries, India is concerned that Pakistan could withhold gas shipments as a weapon against it. The roughly $600 million USD in transit fees would help keep Pakistan in line, analogous to the claims that we have made with respect to Ukraine and Belarus. Restructuring the deal to include a power plant within Indian territory – to deliver electricity back across the border to an exclusively dependent segment of Pakistan – would magnify the potential benefits to Pakistan and raise the costs to Pakistan of reneging. An analogous arrangement, the Indus Waters Treaty, has facilitated the sharing of water between these two countries for over forty years, surviving two wars and near-continuous heated tensions over Kashmir (Sridharam 2000).

Ultimately, no constitutional or technical mechanism can eliminate the physical reality of sunk capital, and the dangers for investors are acute when a state is failing or collapses completely. Each of the state-based remedies to the commitment problem described above can be rendered impotent when governments are toppled or regional separatism supersedes federal powers. Where such risks exist the investor must search their own toolbox for remedies or perhaps turn to international institutions, options which we now discuss.

Private Solutions to the Commitment Problem   Oil and gas investors are no strangers to risk and are accustomed to operating where the state-provided safeguards against opportunism are few and even security protections are minimal. In these situations, investors also employ their own private mechanisms to maintain returns over the life of the project.

First and foremost, foreign investors can seek partners that can help to enforce commitment. The most common strategy is to establish a joint venture or partnership with a domestic company whose connections to the host-country government substitute for the weakness of national institutions and perhaps dampen the tendency for the "foreign" owners of a project to become a subject of political controversy. As the domestic player stands to benefit from the successful operation of the project, it will mobilize its political connections in times when the government may be otherwise inclined to change tax and royalty structures to squeeze equity and rents for itself. This strategy, however, is not without danger. Local partners can also be corrupt; their influence can be rendered impotent if political minds shift – just as ENI discovered when the

Algerian *coup* swept out not just the technocratic government, but also the leadership of their local partner Sonatrach.[9]

Foreign investors may also choose to employ technologies in a project that require special expertise to operate, rendering their investments unattractive for expropriation, just as retreating armies poison wells and burn depots to spoil the rents of territorial advance. European buyers of Soviet gas in the 1980s lent capital to the USSR for the construction of the massive inter-continental gas pipelines. However, the Europeans were quite sure that they would receive gas in repayment for the loans, as the bulk of capital they provided was in the form of the large steel pipelines that were useful only for shipping gas and Europe was the only viable export market at the time. (Some of the gas was also consumed internally within the Soviet Union, but Europe was the only proximate buyer who could pay in much-needed hard currency.) Such strategies provide some protection against outright expropriation by lowering the potential benefits to partner governments from reneging on their commitments.

Where the central government is unable to assure local security and deter civil unrest the investor may seek to make the project agreement self-enforcing by distributing benefits to local communities, giving them a stake in the continued operation of the project. Though not included in the case studies presented in this book, the recent LNG project in Nigeria and proposed projects in similarly fractured countries such as Venezuela and Egypt include fully developed plans to supply local communities with water, power, and health care. Gas projects may be less likely to create the ills of the "resource curse" that have plagued major exporters of oil (Karl 1997; Ross 1999). Because the capital commitments for gas projects are generally larger, investors' time horizons for gas projects are commensurately longer, giving them a greater stake in the stability of the community in which they are operating. Investors are also better protected from direct theft by locals, as gas lines are not easily tapped for resale on black markets. Contestation over the rents from gas projects remains a problem, however, and where governments fail to provide protection and the investor themself is unable to provide an effective remedy, solace may be found in special external institutions.

---

[9] Henisz (2002) examines investments in several sectors including energy, and shows that the risk of a local partner "squeezing" the profits from a foreign investor is in many cases greater than the risk of host-government opportunism.

A Role for External Institutions?   Where state-based and private mechanisms for enforcing contracts are inadequate, can governments and investors turn to outsiders, such as international institutions, to supply the function of enforcement? Our case studies suggest three possible roles for external institutions to provide assurances to investors.

First, investors and governments alike are seeking to protect themselves from each other – the investor fears that the government will squeeze or expropriate their investment, and the government fears that investors will demand too much of the rent for themselves. Both may engage an external institution that has a time horizon and a portfolio of engagement longer and broader than the individual project. Historically, the involvement of the World Bank or other multi-lateral lending agencies in a project in a resource-rich but institution-poor country has provided some leverage to protect the project investment. These multi-lateral lending agencies often provided other loans or support to the host-country government, and the banks used the threat of curtailment of these other services to sustain the agreed framework for the oil and gas project. In the Gasbol project, for example, the World Bank chose to provide financing as part of its broader agenda focused on Bolivian development and regional integration with Brazil. The strong position of the World Bank in these two countries, particularly Bolivia, provided a strong incentive for the governments to hold to the terms of the Gasbol contract. Similarly, investors may engage private banks to supply capital – even project builders with deep pockets could be drawn to that option because the host country may be reluctant to renege on commitments to banks with which they want to sustain broader lending relationships.

Second, international institutions may offer the possibility for governments to create broader linkages on their own. The gas export projects from Argentina to Chile probably required first that these historical enemies bury their swords and secure a broader political and trading relationship – codified and catalyzed through the Mercosur trading system. Similarly, détente allowed the creation of common security institutions in Europe that, in turn probably aided the investment in gas export projects from the USSR.[10]

---

[10]   An early hypothesis of this research was that pipelines could be a mechanism to promote peace and political integration through shared economic interests. The results of the seven case studies we have examined, along with cursory analysis of nearly all other cross-border gas pipelines, show no evidence that gas pipelines are a means to peace. As in the case of Argentina and Chile, peace and institutions preceded pipelines, rather

Third, an external institution can take a much more direct role in a gas export project by acting as a trustee for project revenues or an arbiter of disputes. Offshore escrow accounts have been employed in several oil and gas projects, including the Arun project in Indonesia. Generally, a trustee bank offshore receives the revenues and distributes it according to a fixed set of rules determined at the outset – e.g. operating costs are paid to project investors first, then royalties to the government, then debt repayment, etc. If the trustee is suitably independent, the ability of the host government to renege on the initial contractual terms is greatly reduced. This has been an effective structure where host countries have been willing to accept the impingement on national sovereignty that comes with it. In the 1970s, Algeria refused to accept such offshore escrow accounts, whereas the Indonesian government at the time embraced them as a very small price to pay for the very big prize of earnings from Arun and other LNG export projects.

An extension of the escrow account structure offers a promise to deliver project benefits to broader populations in exporting countries than often occurs. The Chad–Cameroon oil export pipeline, completed in 2003, was the first test of a structure that sought to manage the internal distribution of project royalties and taxes. In 1999, under pressure from the World Bank, Chad adopted the "Petroleum Revenues Management Law" which required that the bulk of the tax and royalties from the project be dedicated to education, health, and development purposes and created a external body charged with supervising these revenue allocations (Esty 2003). Again, the host country government is unlikely to accept such an arrangement except under external pressure and when other options are exhausted. In the Chad–Cameroon oil pipeline project, this trusteeship structure was imposed largely at the behest of the World Bank, in cooperation with project investors.[11] In 2006, when the government of Chad felt it no longer needed the World Bank's blessing, it abandoned the trusteeship with consequences that are still unfolding as this book went to press.

Some observers have speculated that a structure similar to that employed in Chad could be codified with agreements among the major gas importing countries, thereby requiring that all new export projects in

than the reverse. (Moreover, as in those two countries today, the pipelines can be a source of tension – Chile responded to Argentina's curtailments of gas in 2004 by exploring alternative energy strategies, which in turn amplified the animosities between the nations.)

[11] ExxonMobil sought World Bank involvement in the project to both protect them from contractual uncertainty and to provide some reputational shelter for partnering with a regime in Chad known for human rights abuses.

poorly governed states use trusteeship structures to control revenues coming from the export project to the host-country government – on the grounds that such external management would better deliver the benefits of the natural resource project to the people rather than the whims of the rulers. Such a code could mandate transparency on the use of revenues delivered to the state, or go further to direct the distribution of these revenues within the state, as the Chad model attempts to accomplish. Ceding control of gas revenues to an external body of trustees would impinge on traditional notions of sovereignty. Moreover any such approach would require cooperation from all the major international players in a particular resource field. That condition strikes us as difficult to satisfy, since some investors are always likely to defect, which would cause the whole arrangement to unravel. We expect that such arrangements, although impinging on sovereignty, are most likely to occur where the hosts themselves are most keen to demonstrate credibility – either because outsiders such as the World Bank insist on such arrangements as a condition for financing or because the host government is pursuing a long-term resource development strategy and knows that gas investors will demand risk premia in the absence of such confidence-creating mechanisms.

Implications for Gas Security   In discussing "gas security" there are dangers in drawing too close a parallel with oil, where security is mainly a function of the volumes that can be delivered to a fungible world market. Because gas is very costly to transport, and because new infrastructure connections take years to construct, gas supply security is assured in the short term only by having diverse routes for supply to final users. The infrastructure for moving specific volumes of gas to specific users – complemented with the ability to switch fuels – determines security for gas users that depend on imports. For example, in the early 1980s, Italy was able to respond to the cutoff of Algerian supply by sustaining shipments via already built long-distance pipelines from the Netherlands and Russia and increasing domestic production. Since the Transmed pipeline had not yet begun operation, Italy was in the fortunate position of not yet depending on the Algerian supply. The markets to which Algeria curtailed LNG supply (Belgium, France, Spain, and the United States) responded over the following decade by cutting Algerian gas imports dramatically; the US government simply refused to allow US buyers to sign new higher-priced contracts with Algeria. All of these LNG importers had other gas and energy supply alternatives. In the wake of the Arab oil embargo the Japanese government encouraged

LNG buyers to diversify their sources first away from the Middle East in the 1970s – LNG projects in Brunei and Arun were the products of this gas import policy. Later, Qatargas opened a new supply source for gas for Japan, providing additional diversity of LNG supply infrastructure. To a much lesser degree than with oil, gas security until now has not been merely a function of the sheer availability of volumes on the world market, although the emerging global LNG market with fluid spot pricing could make the analogy more appropriate at some point in the distant future. In this scenario, where many flexible supply alternatives are available, security concerns center mainly on prices signaled through interconnected global markets, not the absolute availability of volumes.

In a regulated environment it was clear where the gas came from and where it was going. It was thus relatively easy for governments and their bidders to tailor the terms of long-term contracts for political ends. When these original agreements became inconvenient, governments would adjust the terms through tacit actions that signaled the new expectations – for example, when the French and Italian governments decided to offer subsidies that sustained Algeria's shipments, and when a few governments caved in to Algeria's demands others followed. (For the United States, Algeria's gas was less essential, and the US government forbade any renegotiation of the Algerian contracts.)

As gas markets liberalize – especially in Europe, where countries are small and borders are numerous – directed gas trade is harder to sustain, especially as the forces of liberalization demand that gas traders abandon destination clauses and other schemes that create rigidity in gas markets. In this environment, the role of courts as enforcers has grown – made possible, in part, by legal reforms that have accompanied the shift to markets and given courts and quasi-judicial bodies, such as regulators, greater authority. In the "old world" the long-term contracts appeared to be keystones. In fact, those contracts were hard to enforce in courts as legal instruments. They were instruments for the coordinated sinking of capital – which, in turn, created partially reciprocal infrastructures that were largely self-enforcing – rather than strictly enforced legal instruments. In the "new world" where the length of contracts is shortening and the terms are more modest, the importance of legal enforceability is rising. Private players operate across borders and assume responsibilities for maintaining secure supplies and also seek to protect their financial interests. Removed from the protective arms of the state, these private companies often lack the suite of tools available to governments to coerce partners (both governments and private partners) to uphold their end of the contractual bargain.

We suggest three implications for gas security as the gas business shifts to the "new" world. First, the "new world," marked by multiple suppliers and users and fungibility of gas, can yield greater security for producers and users alike. However, realization of that security will require infrastructures that are "overbuilt" when compared with the point-to-point contracts that were typical of the "old" world. It is not clear that the market itself will deliver the incentives to attract such overbuilding, not least because private incumbents will generally benefit from scarcity in transportation infrastructures.

Second, in the "old" world the price of gas and the premium for security were combined into one final price and delivered by enterprises that were owned (or tightly regulated) by the state. In the "new world" those two functions may separate, which will make the costs of security more transparent and possibly harder to muster. Some entity will be required to supply the difference between the purely economic cost of gas supply and the cost of security, and consumers themselves may be prone to underinvest in the security portion.[12]

Third, large gas projects are typically very time-consuming to plan, license, construct, and commission. The pricing mechanism, alone, cannot bring new supplies on-line when there are disruptions in the existing system, when demand is misestimated, or other factors create a spike in price. Even as the "new" world shifts to a greater role for market forces, parties that are particularly keen on security may nonetheless demand "old-world" arrangements such as long-term contracts, dedicated pipelines, and point-to-point deliveries.

Conclusions

At the outset of the case study research, we selected four key factors – investment climate, transit countries, offtake risks, and geopolitical relationships – that, we thought, would affect the development of cross-border gas trade projects. A survey of the academic and trade literatures suggested that these four factors would be particularly important, and thus we selected case studies that allowed us to observe these factors in variation. We revisit each of those four key factors here, before offering broader conclusions on future gas geopolitics.

As expected, we found that investment climate was extremely important – especially in the shift to a greater role for private investors and competitive gas markets. However, we found that generic measures of

---

[12] For those familiar with electricity markets, the analog may be comparable to maintaining reserve requirements (excess production capacity) and excess transmission capacity.

investment climate – such as broad country risk indexes – are crude and generally unhelpful guides to the locations where investors are likely to sink their capital.[13] Gas projects are of such a scale that even in countries where broad risk measures are unattractive, special efforts are typically made to create investment zones and other unique arrangements that can provide the security that participants demand before putting billions in capital at stake.

Transit countries brought complexity, but we did not find broad evidence that states with pipelines crossing their borders were likely to act to "hold up" shipments for political or economic gain. Transit countries are constrained by the carrot of continuing revenues and the stick of becoming bypassed by an LNG tanker or an alternative pipeline route. The most successful examples of "hold up" involve pipelines delivering Russian and Central Asian gas to European markets. Russia exercised its leverage as Turkmenistan's only export route in the mid-1990s, refusing to ship its gas for nearly two years. Turkmenistan's response was ultimately limited as its only other viable export option crossed Iran, another major gas seller that was also looking for markets. In the mid-1990s Ukraine was also able to siphon gas from Russia's westbound pipelines. However, Ukraine's behavior was ultimately tempered by the knowledge that Russia could advance alternative export routes, with long-term erosion of Ukraine's transit fees. Transit countries appear to negotiate, as would be expected, to seek fees that approach the cost of the alternative route.

Our initial hypothesis was that projects that served well-developed markets would entail lower financial risks and allow speedier construction because a robust offtake market would allow easy absorption of new volumes. Instead, we found that the risks in the offtake market were

---

[13] Trinidad & Tobago, for example, was not an obvious winner for an investment in a new LNG project in the 1990s. Investment risk scores were not significantly better than those for Egypt, Nigeria, or even neighboring Venezuela. (According to the General Investment Risk Index (GIRI), in 1995 when Trinidad plans began to be solidified, Egypt scored 6.4, Nigeria 5.3, Venezuela 5.8, and Trinidad & Tobago 5.8. Lower scores indicate a lesser investment climate.) Despite weaknesses in other areas, the government of Trinidad & Tobago was able to create a context for this particular project that suitably assuaged investors. The managers of the Trinidad & Tobago project, in turn, were able to mobilize quickly on this government support. The authors of the Trinidad & Tobago case noted that "more LNG projects have failed as a result of management failures or lack of informed government support than any other cause" (see chapter 9). The author was arguing that the Atlantic LNG project in Trinidad & Tobago developed precisely because these two critical factors – government support and competent management – overcame a myriad of other obstacles that would have impeded development under less attentive oversight.

mainly a function of government energy policy. Was the importing country government willing to expend the political or economic resources needed to advance gas use?

Interestingly, we did not find that international institutions – such as trade agreements – played much of a role in the development of these gas trade projects. Rather, the massive scale of these projects suggests that they often operate outside pre-existing treaties and the imperative for energy trade can operate on its own logic (e.g. Soviet gas and oil exports to Western Europe). We did find that international financial institutions such as the World Bank have had an impact on projects in cases where they have been willing to supply substantial financial support for projects that, otherwise, would not be able to attract capital. The clearest example of that role, the Bolivia–Brazil gas pipeline, suggests that this is a costly way to interconnect countries since alternative capital avoided the project for sound reasons. In the early stages of this project we noted considerable enthusiasm for a "peace pipe" hypothesis – projects that, once constructed, would create interdependencies that could promote cooperation between linked countries. We found little evidence for that hypothesis.

In all, we draw two main conclusions for the geopolitical contours of a world that is shifting to gas. First, the countries and firms that become major players in the gas world will be those that combine access to resources with the ability to apply sound management and the proper institutional context for investment. We have shown that there is little correlation between the hegemons in proved gas reserves and those that actually deliver gas in market competition. This observation suggests that the traditional metrics for assigning power over natural resources requires much closer attention to subtle contextual and internal factors, with less focus on raw volumes of untapped resources. It also suggests that traditional concerns about politically motivated curtailments of resource shipments may apply less in the gas world than with other globally traded commodities.

Second, the role of the state in this world has been shifting dramatically over the last twenty years. In an earlier era, governments were at the center of all key commercial decisions – they assured contracts, and they "made" markets. Today, project developers increasingly expect that the role of the state is in setting the context but staying at arm's length. We have raised questions about whether that expectation is consistent with the assumption that a worldwide shift to gas will include the rapid gasification of relatively virgin markets as well as gasification in countries where there is no robust system for enforcing contracts and supplying capital. Traditionally the state has supplied those roles, but if the state moves to the shadows it is not clear that private investors will occupy that space – particularly the role of building gas grids. Conversely, more recent trends in Latin America and in the Former Soviet Union (FSU) suggest that retreat of the state may not proceed evenly in all regions of the world.

REFERENCES

Axelrod, Robert (1984). *The Evolution of Cooperation*. New York: Basic Books

BP (2004). *Statistical Review of World Energy*, available at http://www.bp.com

Esty, Benjamin C. (2003). "The Chad–Cameroon petroleum development and pipeline project." Boston, MA: Harvard Business School

Hayes, Mark H. and David G. Victor (2004). "Factors that explain investment in cross-border natural gas transport infrastructures: A research protocol for historical case studies". Working Paper, 8, Stanford, CA: Program on Energy and Sustainable Development

Henisz, Witold Jerzy (2002). *Politics and International Investment: Measuring Risks and Protecting Profits*. Northampton, MA: Edward Elgar

ICRG (2002). *International Country Risk Guide*. Political Risk Services (IBC USA, Inc.). New York: International Reports

IEA (2003). *World Energy Investment Outlook 2003*. Paris: International Energy Agency

Karl, Terry Lynn (1997). *The Paradox of Plenty: Oil Booms and Petro-States*. Berkeley, CA and London: University of California Press

North, Douglass Cecil and Barry R. Weingast (1989). "Constitutions and commitment: the evolution of institutions governing public choice in seventeenth-century England." *Journal of Economic History*, 49(4), pp. 803–832

Ross, Michael (1999). "The political economy of the resource curse." *World Politics*, 51, pp. 297–322

Seabright, Paul (2004). *The Company of Strangers: A Natural History of Economic Life*. Princeton, NJ: Princeton University Press

Sridharam, E. (2000). "Economic cooperation and security spill-overs: the case of India and Pakistan," in M. Krepon and C. Gagne (eds.), *Economic Confidence Building and Regional Security*. Washington, DC: The Henry L. Stimson Center

USGS (2000). "World Petroleum assessment." United States Geological Survey; available at http://energy.cr.usgs.gov/ oilgas/wep/

Vernon, Raymond (1971). *Sovereignty at Bay: The Multinational Spread of U.S. Enterprises*. New York: Basic Books

Part III

International gas trade economics

11 The Baker Institute World Gas Trade Model

Peter Hartley and Kenneth B. Medlock, III

Introduction

Natural gas increased from roughly 19 percent of world primary energy demand in 1980 to about 23 percent in 2002 (EIA 2004) and is now produced and consumed in forty-three countries around the world. Moreover, the International Energy Agency (IEA) (IEA 2004) predicts that world natural gas demand will be about 90 percent higher by 2030. It also projects that the share of gas in world primary energy demand will increase from 23 percent in 2002 to 25 percent in 2030, with gas potentially overtaking coal as the world's second largest energy source. The IEA predicts that the power sector will account for 60 percent of the increase in gas demand.

Much of current world production of natural gas comes from mature basins in the United States and the North Sea.[1] Russia, where production rivals that in the United States, currently accounts for almost one-quarter of world production but, unlike the United States, has substantial reserves that remain untapped. Furthermore, Russia and the countries of the Former Soviet Union (FSU)[2] rank first globally in undiscovered natural gas potential (USGS 2000). These countries already export considerable quantities of natural gas to Europe, and they are expected to become important suppliers to the growing needs in Asia.

The countries of the Middle East also have substantial natural gas resources, both proved and potential, which are relatively untapped. With the re-emerging interest in LNG, the Middle East is well

---

[1] Reported reserves in the United States have actually increased in each of the past few years. However, much of the increase has been in unconventional deposits that typically produce at lower rates, such as coal bed methane in the Rocky Mountains. Lower production rates, *ceteris paribus*, distribute cash flows more toward the future, thus lowering the NPV of such deposits. Unconventional deposits may also have higher per-unit costs of exploitation. Hence, as production shifts to unconventional deposits, the long-run market price must be higher to justify the capital outlay.

[2] Hereafter, these countries will be referred to collectively as the FSU.

positioned to become a major supplier given its proximity to growing markets for gas imports in South Asia and Europe. Particular interest in developing export projects in Qatar and Iran reflect those countries' massive reserves and strategic location to serve growing markets in both the East and the West.

Recent developments in natural gas markets around the world foreshadow a substantial expansion in global trade of natural gas. This portends a sweeping change in the manner in which natural gas is priced because natural gas markets have been, until recently, isolated from each other. Limited availability of regasification, shipping, and liquefaction capacity, as well as prohibitive costs, constrained the exploitation of remote gas deposits and inhibited the flow of LNG from one region of the globe to another. Asia was the early focus of the LNG business, and Japan remains by far the largest importer of LNG, followed by South Korea. However, with recent reductions in the costs associated with the movement of LNG to distant markets, new opportunities for LNG to compete in expanding world natural gas markets are rapidly emerging

The Baker Institute World Gas Trade Model

The Baker Institute World Gas Trade Model (BIWGTM) is a tool for examining the effects of economic and political influences on the global natural gas market within a framework grounded in geologic data and economic theory. The resource data underlying the model is based on an assessment produced by the United States Geological Survey (USGS 2000). The USGS data are combined with economic models of the demand for natural gas, which include important determinants of natural gas use such as the level of economic development, the price of natural gas, the price of competing fuels, and population growth. The costs of constructing new pipelines and LNG facilities have been estimated using data on previous and potential projects available from the EIA and industry sources.

The extent of regional detail reflects not only the availability of data but also the issues that will be later examined in case study scenarios. For large markets, such as China, the United States, India, and Japan, subregional detail has been created to gain more accurate results. In these cases, *intra*-country capacity constraints could have a significant effect on the current or likely future overall pattern of world trade in natural gas.

The BIWGTM is a dynamic spatial general equilibrium model. The solution algorithm is based on the software platform *Marketbuilder* from Altos Management Partners, a flexible modeling system widely used in the industry. The software calculates a dynamic spatial equilibrium where supply and demand is balanced at each location in each period such that all spatial and temporal arbitrage opportunities are eliminated.[3] The model thus seeks an equilibrium in which the sources of supply, the demand sinks, and the transportation links connecting them, are developed over time to maximize the net present value (NPV) of new supply and transportation projects while simultaneously accounting for the impact of these new developments on current and future prices. Output from the model includes regional natural gas prices, pipeline and LNG capacity additions and flows, growth in natural gas reserves from existing fields and undiscovered deposits, and regional production and demand.

Transportation links connecting markets transmit price signals as well as volumes of physical commodity. Thus, for example, building a new link to take gas to a market with high prices will raise prices to consumers from the exporting region and lower prices in the importing region. More generally, it is in this manner that markets become increasingly connected over time as profitable spatial arbitrage opportunities are exploited until they are eliminated. In a *global* natural gas market as predicted by the BIWGTM, events in one region of the world generally influence all other regions. For instance, political factors affecting relations between Russia and China will affect gas flows and prices throughout the world, not just in Northeast Asia.

Market structure in the BIWGTM

Current and projected increases in the demand for natural gas, as well as the desire on the part of producers to monetize stranded natural gas resources, have expanded the depth and geographical extent of both sides of the LNG market. Expanding the market alternatives available to both producers and consumers of natural gas reduces the risk of investing in infrastructure, thereby encouraging further development of the natural gas market. Moreover, with a greater number of available supply or demand alternatives and growth in the size of end-use markets located around the globe, the average distance between neighboring suppliers or neighboring demanders falls, increasing the opportunities

---

[3] The absence of intertemporal arbitrage opportunities within the model period is a necessary but not a sufficient condition for maximizing the present value of resource supply. Since future exploitation is always an alternative to current production, a maximizing solution also requires that a value of the resource beyond the model time horizon be specified. In our model, the required additional conditions are obtained by assuming that a "backstop" technology ultimately limits the price at which natural gas can be sold.

for price arbitrage. The resulting increase in trading opportunities increases market liquidity.

An increase in market liquidity could produce a relatively rapid shift in the market equilibrium away from long-term bilateral contracts to a world of multilateral trading and an increased number of commodity trades. The explanation is that market structure is partly endogenous. Expectations about the future evolution of the market influence investment and trading decisions today and these, in turn, further influence market developments tomorrow. Once market participants begin to expect a change in market structure, their investment decisions accelerate the change.[4]

The model examined in this chapter assumes that such a change in market structure has already occurred by treating LNG as a commodity that is traded somewhat analogously to the way oil is traded. Thus, while the near-term evolution of the market will most likely be dictated by contract rigidities, we have assumed that the market will evolve according to a long-term solution characterized by more flexibility. Long-term contracts are allowed to affect the risks borne by different parties, but not physical flows of gas. In essence, we assume that the gas market behaves as if contracted trades can be swapped with alternative shipments whenever such arrangements are cost-effective. Even today, this is generally true in the longer term, where any contracted flow that is not least cost can be, and usually is, replaced by swap arrangements that allow the financial terms of contracts to be satisfied regardless of where physical delivery actually occurs.[5] The financial arrangements in the contracts, however, will significantly affect risks and the ability to swap deliveries.[6]

Demand for Natural Gas

Economic growth, expanding power generation requirements, and environmental considerations are the primary explanations for projected rapid

---

[4] Brito and Hartley (2001) present a formal model of the evolution of the LNG market from a world of long-term bilateral contracts to one where LNG is traded more like the way that oil is traded today. A key implication of their analysis is that multiple equilibrium outcomes are possible, so that small changes in costs can dramatically change market structure.

[5] During industry review of this effort, it was generally agreed that this approach best captured the current transition of global LNG markets. Increasingly, deliveries are being made through swaps that allow producers to deliver to the lowest cost destinations relative to the location of their production facilities.

[6] In chapter 12, we use different discount rates in different regions to reflect varying degrees of political risk.

increases in natural gas demand. According to the EIA's *International Energy Outlook 2004* (EIA 2004), natural gas consumption in Europe is projected to rise by about 2.0 percent per annum in the next twenty years, as governments encourage natural gas as an alternative to more carbon-intensive fuels such as oil and coal. In North America, natural gas use is expected to rise about 1.4 percent per year, with growth in the power generation sector expected to rise even faster. Mexican demand is expected to rise by about 3.9 percent per year through 2025 as the Mexican government pursues policies to replace oil as a fuel for electricity-generation. Rapid economic growth in developing Asian countries is expected to result in increases in natural gas demand of about 3.5 percent per annum through 2025, with Chinese demand forecast to grow at an astounding 6.9 percent per year and Indian demand at 4.8 percent per year over the same time horizon. This growth will occur primarily for electricity-generation, but residential and commercial cooking and heating, and industrial demand, will also expand.

Demand for natural gas in developed economies has been spurred by increasingly stringent environmental controls. Natural gas is less polluting than coal or oil and does not present some of the problems, such as waste disposal, that are associated with nuclear power. Deregulation of wholesale electricity markets also has increased the demand for generating plants with smaller economies of scale, which has been met by the simultaneous development of combined cycle gas turbines (CCGT).[7] Prior to the development of CCGT, gas turbines had much lower capacities than coal or nuclear plants and were used only as peaking plants. CCGT technology, however, raised the thermal efficiency of gas plants and thus the economically efficient scale of operation. Consequently, for a given price of natural gas, CCGT plants operate for longer hours in the year than did the older-style gas turbines which, in turn, raises the demand for natural gas.

Developments in the transportation sector could accelerate projected trends as technologies that convert natural gas into transportation fuel could increase the demand for natural gas further. Already, compressed natural gas is used as fuel for mass-transit bus systems, taxicabs, and commercial vehicles in many large cities in the United States, Canada, and elsewhere. In addition, innovations in the development of hydrogen fuel cells target natural gas as a primary fuel source. The demand for transport fuels may also indirectly increase the demand for natural gas as

---

[7] Deregulation has increased competition in the provision of new electricity generation plants. As shown for example by Hartley and Kyle (1989), more competitive electricity markets favor more frequent construction of generating plants, with each new plant having a smaller capacity.

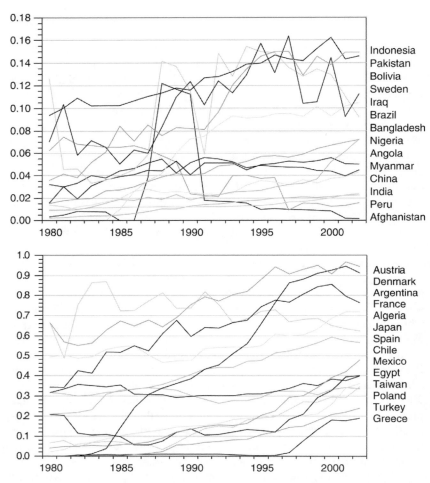

Figure 11.1. Historical demand for natural gas, selected countries, 1980–2004, Bcm/person. Note different axis scales. Countries are grouped according to increasing gas consumption levels.

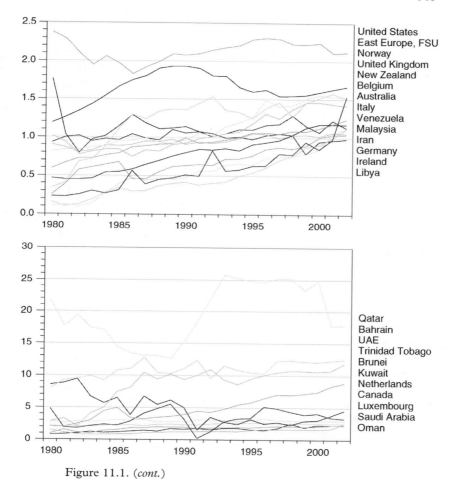

Figure 11.1. (*cont.*)

an input into the production of unconventional oil resources such as the Athabasca Tar Sands in Western Canada.[8]

---

[8] The tar sands in Alberta have oil potential estimated at about 1.7 trillion barrels of oil, of which approximately 300 billion barrels are thought to be recoverable at reasonable cost. Natural gas is used to produce the power, steam, and hydrogen needed to mine and process tar sands. The huge shovels that scoop up the sand operate on electricity, although the electricity plants also supply excess power to the grid while co-generated steam is used to separate the bitumen from the sand. Hydrogen separately produced from gas is used to process the bitumen into synthetic crude. Existing oil sands' operations use about 9.3 Bcm per year, but this is expected to increase to about 20.6 Bcm per year by 2010.

Conversely, further development of coal gasification, nuclear or renewable energy technologies may slow the increase in demand for natural gas as a fuel for generating electricity. Since CCGT for electricity generation have played a prominent role in expanding the demand for natural gas over the last twenty years, anything that disadvantages natural gas as a means of generating electricity could substantially slow projected growth in natural gas demand.

Figure 11.1 illustrates *per capita* annual natural gas consumption (in Bcm per person) for a sample of countries over the period 1980–2002.[9] Countries have been grouped into sets with similar levels of *per capita* consumption. As one moves from the top to the bottom chart the level of *per capita* gas consumption rises. Generally, *per capita* consumption tends to increase with the level of economic development, both as one moves from one panel to the next and within a given country over time. Resource endowments also play a major role. The largest *per capita* consumption is found in countries that are major producers, while some countries with smaller *per capita* consumption, such as Sweden, France, and Japan, generate a substantial proportion of their electricity from nuclear power plants.

The demand forecasts in the BIWGTM are based on the assumption that there are five major determinants for natural gas demand: population, economic development, resource endowments and other country-specific attributes, the relative price of different primary fuels, and new technological developments. In constructing the demand relationship, we first estimated models to extrapolate patterns of economic and population growth into the future.[10] Following Medlock and Soligo (2001), we then estimated total primary energy demand *per capita* as a function of the level of economic development. Finally, we estimated a function relating the *share* of natural gas in total primary energy to real energy prices and the level of economic development.[11]

An advantage of this multi-step approach is that theory can guide the choice of functional form at each stage. For example, by choosing a suitable functional form, we can constrain the share of natural gas in

---

[9] The data come from the EIA web site (www.eia.doe.gov).

[10] The estimation used data on population and economic growth from the World Bank supplemented by the well-known Summers and Heston data set (Summers and Heston 1995). The latter data have been used for a large number of studies on international economic growth and development. They are available at the Center for International Comparisons, the University of Pennsylvania, http://pwt.econ.upenn.edu/.

[11] Primary energy demand and natural gas demand data were obtained from the EIA web site: http://www.eia.doe.gov. The IEA web site (http://www.iea.org) provided international energy price data.

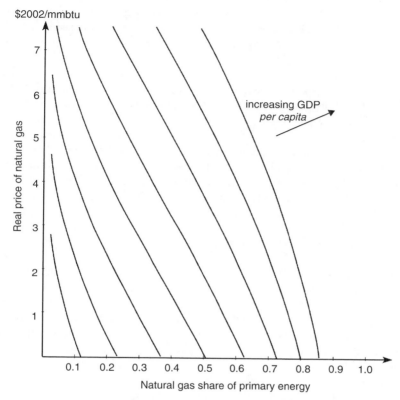

Figure 11.2. Long-run gas demand curve for different *per capita* GDP levels.

primary energy to lie between zero and one. This helps to ensure that demand forecasts that extend substantially beyond the sample period neither expand uncontrollably nor decline precipitously in the face of large out-of-sample changes in the exogenous variables. Although the focus of our analysis extends only through 2040, it is necessary to forecast demand over a much longer period. The reason is that investments depend on expected future prices; as we explain in more detail below, we assume that new technologies will compete with natural gas in the long term and ultimately establish a competitive ceiling for natural gas prices. The model time horizon needs to be large enough for this assumption to be realistic.

Figure 11.2 illustrates the resulting long-run gas demand curves for various levels of *per capita* real GDP. A detailed discussion of the methods used to generate these curves is given in the appendix (p. 389). The demand curves become more inelastic as the share of natural gas approaches zero or one. If the natural gas share were close to one, further declines in price could not greatly stimulate gas demand. Similarly, if the share is already close to zero, price increases will do little to further decrease gas demand.

In order to forecast natural gas demand, we need to forecast energy prices for competing commodities, population, and real GDP (in purchasing power parity, PPP, terms) for each country. (See appendix for a more detailed discussion of the multi-step approach used to forecast GDP, population, and natural gas demand.) While the price of natural gas will be calculated endogenously in the model to equate supplies to demands at each location, we include an exogenous forecast of the price of oil. In the base case, we assumed oil prices will follow the Reference Case forecast from the EIA's *International Energy Outlook* (*IEO*) (EIA 2004), which carries through 2025. Beyond 2025, we linked the oil price projection to a gas price that asymptotes to $5/mmbtu (the backstop price, see the discussion below) by 2100. In doing so, we take the ratio of the *IEO* world oil price and US wellhead price (both in $/mmbtu) in 2025, and hold it constant. This results in a long-run world oil price (in real 2000$) that rises from $27/barrel, or about $4.66/mmbtu, in 2025 to $31.20/barrel, or approximately $5.38/mmbtu, by 2100.

Our model of economic growth is based on the notion of *economic convergence*. In particular, capital and labor mobility, as well as the flow of trade in goods and services, should tend to increase economic growth rates in less developed regions relative to more developed ones. Holding things such as legal institutions and technologies fixed, returns to investment ought to be higher in locations where capital is relatively scarce. Therefore, firms have an incentive to increase investment in those locations rather than locations where capital is relatively abundant. Similarly, if workers can migrate, they also have an incentive to seek employment where their skills earn the highest real wage. Both capital and labor mobility ought therefore to raise *per capita* income growth rates in locations where *per capita* income is currently below average and reduce it in locations where *per capita* income is currently above the current average. Furthermore, even in the absence of international flows of capital and labor, trade in goods and services will tend to reduce differences in income. This result is commonly referred to as "factor price equalization." Regions with high payments to a particular factor of production will tend to import goods intensive in the use of that factor. This, in turn, will tend to raise factor payments in the exporting country while simultaneously reducing them in the importing one.

Yet another vehicle for convergence involves the diffusion of technology. Wealthier nations have a higher standard of living in part because they use more productive technologies. As those technologies spread into less developed nations, differences in productivity decline. As a result, the spread of technological innovations will also tend to produce convergence of living standards over time.

In our statistical analysis (see appendix), we use real GDP *per capita* adjusted for PPP differences as the basic measure of living standards. We also assume the United States as the leading country. In other words, we assume that the living standards in other countries will tend to converge toward those of the United States over the next century. Our empirical specification also assumes that US living standards (and, by extension, in other countries too as they approach the US level) will tend to increase over time but at a diminishing rate. The main motivation for this assumption is that, as the economy matures, economic activity shifts toward the service sector where past technological progress has been low, and foreseeable opportunities for future technological progress appear limited, relative to the manufacturing and agricultural sectors of the economy.

Finally, the demand curves included in the model were modified from curves such as those graphed in figure 11.2 in order to accommodate the potential adoption of "backstop" technologies. There are many substitutes for natural gas in generating electricity, ranging from hydroelectricity, diesel, and fuel oil for supplying peak power, to coal, nuclear, and newer renewable technologies such as wind or solar power for supplying base-load power. There also are substitutes for the other uses of natural gas. Indeed, prior to the widespread use of natural gas, many cities had plants to gasify coal and distribute it to industrial and household consumers.[12] Until the 1940s, almost all fuel gas distributed for residential or commercial use in the United States was produced by the gasification of coal or coke.

Although our statistical analysis suggests that, for the historical period we considered, coal did not compete with natural gas at the margin, coal–gas competition has intensified in recent years with the greater use of gas for electricity generation as a result of the development of CCGT. The competition may increase further in the next couple of decades, particularly as the integrated gasification combined cycle (IGCC) is

---

[12] Commercial gasification of coal began in 1792, while the first coal gasification company in the United States, the Baltimore Gas Company, was established in 1816.

developed. The estimated elasticity of demand incorporated into the model reflects the substitution possibilities between gas and other fuels that were available within the estimation period. However, this estimated elasticity does not reflect new technologies that may increase substitutability, particularly at higher prices for natural gas. For example, experimental IGCC electricity-generating plants are already in operation in the United States (at West Terra Haute, Indiana and Tampa, Florida) and overseas (Spain, the Netherlands, Germany, Japan, and India). In August 2004, the American Electric Power Company announced plans to build at least one commercial-scale IGCC plant. Current IGCC plants are dramatically cleaner than conventional coal-fired generating plants, producing only 3 percent of the sulfur, 18 percent of the nitrogen oxide, 50 percent of the mercury, and 80 percent of the CO_2 of an equivalent capacity conventional coal-fired plant without scrubbers. Using current technologies, generating electricity using IGCC is said to be competitive with natural gas CCGT in the United States at a natural gas price of \$3.50–\$4.00 per mmbtu (see, for example, documents available at http://www.netl.doe.gov, the National Energy Technology Laboratory, US Department of Energy). The inclusion of a backstop technology in the model allows for such a longer-term substitution possibility.

We allow for the possibility that new technologies could begin to displace natural gas substantially late in the model time horizon. In order to define the available backstop quantity, we must first define a "reference demand level" that the backstop is assumed to be capable of satisfying. Note that the reference demand is neither the *demand* forecast by the model nor the *level of backstop technology* actually deployed, both of which are calculated endogenously. Rather, the reference demand determines how much backstop supply is *available* at a given price in a given year.[13] To calculate the reference demand, we estimated natural gas demand using the method described above for a set of reference oil and natural gas prices. The backstop technology is first made available in 2020, when it can, at the maximum, meet only a very small portion of reference demand. To elaborate: in 2020, the backstop becomes available at a price of \$5/mmbtu, and can satisfy 0.625 percent of the reference demand for natural gas at a price of \$5.50/mmbtu and a maximum of 1.25 percent of the reference demand for a natural gas price of \$10/mmbtu or above.

---

[13] The quantities are somewhat arbitrary. They are chosen so that the backstop does not penetrate the market too rapidly, but is sufficient in later years to ensure that all demand can be satisfied between \$5.00 and \$5.50.

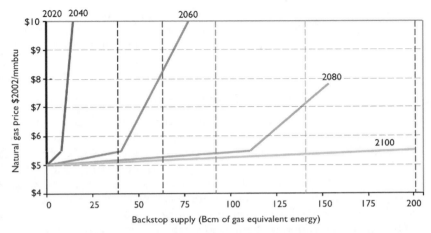

Figure 11.3. The hypothetical supply of a gas substitute, 2020-2100.

Note: 2020 supply is nearly coincident with the left axis.

In subsequent years, the backstop technology is assumed to become increasingly available.[14] The maximum quantity available is given by a Gompertz curve.[15] While the initial price at which the backstop technology can be supplied remains at $5/mmbtu (in 2002 prices), the percentages of reference demand assumed to be satisfied at a price of $5.50/mmbtu, or $10/mmbtu increase each year. In 2040, for example, the substitute technology is assumed to be capable of satisfying about 11.4 percent of the reference demand at a price of $5.50/mmbtu and about 22.8 percent at a price of $10/mmbtu. By 2100, the percentage of reference demand that can be satisfied by the backstop technology at a price of $5.50/mmbtu increases to 100 percent.[16] The supply curves for the backstop are illustrated in figure 11.3 for a location where the

---

[14] We allow the backstop to gradually displace natural gas because the type of energy consumed is related to installed capital and the cost of capital equipment that consumes natural gas as an input is sunk. Allowing capital stocks to be replaced at a reasonable rate would initially slow the growth of the backstop. However, a competitive backstop would slow, if not stop, the installation of natural gas capital equipment, so that the use of the backstop would begin to accelerate as older capital is continually replaced.

[15] The Gompertz function is given as $y = ab^{q^t}$. The various parameters determine the minimum (b) and maximum (a) values of y and the rate of ascent (q) through time (t). For the function used here, $a = 2.5$, $b = 0.005$, and $q = 0.9612$.

[16] This does not imply that natural gas is no longer consumed. Rather, all resources that can still be extracted and competitively supplied at a price of $5.50/mmbtu (in 2002 prices) will be used. Moreover, not all regions reach the backstop simultaneously. Areas with large deposits of natural gas tend to see exports fall but continue to consume natural gas domestically.

reference demand is 38.3 Bcm in 2020, 63.3 Bcm in 2040, 94.7 Bcm in 2060, 142.0 Bcm in 2080, and 202.8 Bcm in 2100. The vertical dashed lines in each case represent the reference case demands at this location in each year.

Current and Potential Supply Sources

To model the evolution of the world natural gas market, we must determine where new sources of supply are likely to be developed to meet the rising demand. We use, as the primary data source for this exercise, regional resource potential as given in the P-50 resource estimates from the *World Resource Assessment* of the United States Geological Survey (USGS 2000).[17] Resources are divided into three categories: proved reserves, growth in known reserves, and undiscovered resource.

The USGS data include both associated and nonassociated natural gas resources, estimates for both conventional and unconventional gas deposits in North America, and conventional gas deposits in the rest of the world.[18] The USGS estimates of reserve growth in existing fields and undiscovered resources uses a stochastic simulation of the success of past exploration and development in particular types of deposits in different regions.[19] The maps in figures 11.4 and 11.5 are constructed using the USGS database, and indicate, in particular, the significant role that Russia and the Middle East may play in supplying natural gas to the rest of the world in coming decades.

Capital Cost of Resource Development

The resource data for each field include estimates of minimum, median, and maximum depth as well as field size. Using data for the United

---

[17] We supplemented the USGS data with data from the Australian Bureau of Agricultural and Resource Economics (Dickson and Noble 2003) and Geosciences Australia (2001). In particular, Geosciences Australia used a methodology similar to that used by the USGS to assess the resource potential of Australian basins that were not assessed quantitatively by the USGS.

[18] The lack of unconventional resource estimates outside of North America is a function of the lack of exploration and development of commercial unconventional natural gas deposits in other regions of the world. Australia also already has some coal-bed methane (CBM) production. The Australian data sources referenced above provided estimates of economically viable CBM resources in the coalfields of eastern Australia. While the lack of such data for other regions underestimates the global resource potential, it is unlikely to have a substantial impact in the time horizon considered in this exercise. We would expect the massive quantities of economically accessible reserves of conventional natural gas outside North America and Australia to be exploited before the industry moves on to exploit substantial deposits of unconventional reserves.

[19] See USGS website (www.usgs.gov) for more details on their data.

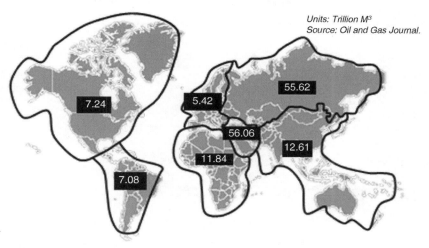

Units: Trillion M³
Source: Oil and Gas Journal.

World Total: 155.9 Trillion M³

North America: 4.6%   Eastern Europe/FSU: 35.7%   Western Europe: 3.5%
Middle East: 36.0%   Asia and Oceania : 8.0%   Africa: 7.6%   Central/South America: 4.6%

Figure 11.4. Proved natural gas reserves, by region, 2003.

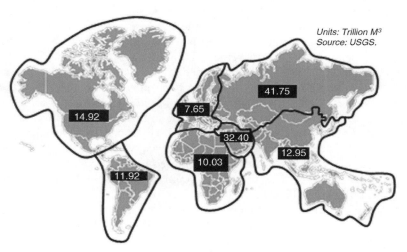

Units: Trillion M³
Source: USGS.

World Total: 131.6 Trillion M³

North America: 11.3%   Eastern Europe/FSU: 31.7%   Western Europe: 5.8%
Middle East: 24.6%   Asia and Oceania : 9.8%   Africa: 7.6%   Central/South America: 9.1%

Figure 11.5. Undiscovered natural gas, by region, 2000 estimates.

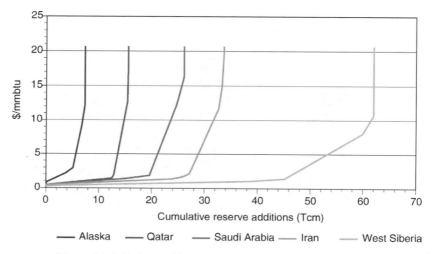

Figure 11.6. Estimated long-run cost of supply curves, selected regions.

States, Canada, and Mexico, we estimate equations relating the capital cost of development and operating and maintenance costs to the median estimate of recoverable reserves and the depth measures. The Modeling Subgroup of the National Petroleum Council (NPC) study (NPC 2003) of the North American natural gas market developed data for long-run marginal cost curves to be used in the *Marketbuilder* platform. These curves are characterized by three cost levels $\{c_1, c_2, c_3\}$ where c_1 is capital cost of developing the first incremental unit of gas, c_2 is the capital cost of the 75th percentile of the estimated median reserves, and c_3 is the capital cost of the median resource estimate. The approximate curves for the United States, Canada, and Mexico were based on proprietary industry information supplied by firms participating in the NPC study. While the NPC used many other variables in a discovery-process model to develop the cost estimates for basins in North America, we found that the three cost measures could be reasonably explained by the median estimate of recoverable reserves and the three depth measures – the minimum, maximum, and median depth of resources in the field. Total resource enters the equation as an inverse, implying that there are economies of scale in developing resources (for details on the estimation see the appendix).

The estimated equations were then used to construct long-run marginal capital costs curves for all resources outside of North America. Field depth and resource size were obtained from the USGS *World Resource Assessment* (USGS 2000). The resulting long-run marginal capital cost curve for the undiscovered resources in selected regions is depicted in figure 11.6.

Recent years have seen substantial declines in the costs of exploiting a given hydrocarbon resource. Advances in computer hardware, signal processing software, and remote sensing technology have all played a role. To allow for further technological change in the mining industry, the future costs of reserve additions are assumed to decline according to the rates used in the 2003 NPC study "Balancing Natural Gas Policy." Thus, the curves illustrated in figure 11.6 are valid only for the year 2002, which is the initial year of the model. Beyond 2002, all such curves will shift down by the assumed rate of technological innovation in finding and development costs.

Operating and Maintenance Costs

The NPC study also produced estimates of the operating and maintenance costs (O&M) associated with exploiting different fields in the United States, Canada, and Mexico. We also found that these costs were predictably related to resource size and depth measures.[20] As with capital costs, we included an inverse term in total resources to capture the economies of scale in exploiting resources. In contrast to the capital costs, however, we found a systematic relationship in the regional effects. Specifically, in the operating costs regression, the offshore regions of the United States and Mexico displayed higher costs. Hence, we included an indicator variable to capture the distinction between operating costs for onshore and offshore fields.

As with capital costs, the inverse term in total resources implies that there are some economies of scale in exploiting resources. In addition, we assumed that operating costs will decline at the rates contained in "Balancing Natural Gas Policy" (NPC 2003).

Transport Links and the World Natural Gas Market

About 73 percent of the world's proven gas reserves are located in the FSU and the Middle East, and moving those supplies to distant

---

[20] The estimate of O&M costs with respect to medium depth implies that costs decline up to a depth of around 1600 m. Since the minimum median depth in our North American data set is 400 m, while the average median depth is slightly over 2500 m, only about 26 percent of the fields show declining costs with increasing depth. Most of these are located in Western Canada, the Rockies, and northeast Mexico. Perhaps shallow deposits are correlated with other geological features, such as highly folded rock layers, that raise extraction costs.

consuming markets will present new technical, logistic, and economic challenges. Indeed, construction of transportation infrastructure is currently the major barrier to increased world natural gas consumption.[21]

In order to connect supply to demand, the model includes a simplified representation of existing pipeline links and all liquefaction and regasification terminals. Projects already under construction also are exogenously input into the model with the associated capacity becoming available at the expected startup date of the projects. In addition, transportation links can be added based on current investment cost, current and future prices – and, therefore, anticipated net benefits from the future flows. Supply sources compete for end-use markets via a specified range of transportation options thought to be feasible.[22] In particular, the model chooses the manner in which natural gas flows to consumers, either as LNG or via pipeline, in order to maximize the rents to the wellhead. Equivalently, the model seeks a solution that minimizes the discounted capital costs of expansion and the operating and maintenance costs of utilizing new and existing capacity. Hence, supplies earning the greatest rents (or with the highest "net-backs"), once all relevant costs of getting the resource to market have been taken into account, are extracted first. Supplies that are isolated from end-use markets or located in areas lacking prior infrastructure development are, therefore, disadvantaged due to the comparatively high cost of transportation.

Currently, most natural gas is transported by the well-developed pipeline infrastructures in North America and Europe that connect major consuming and producing regions. In Asia, LNG is the primary means of connecting end-users to supply, most of which originates in remote locations and must be transported in refrigerated vessels. International trade in LNG, though currently small relative to pipeline flows, has been occurring for over thirty years and involves shipments from close to a dozen countries.

---

[21] According to the IEA (2003), cumulative investments in the global natural gas industry of $3.1 trillion, or $105 billion per year, will be needed to meet rising demand for gas between 2001 and 2030. Exploration and development of gas fields are projected to require over half of this investment, with more than two-thirds of the new capacity replacing declining production in existing fields. Investment in LNG facilities is expected to double after 2020. Investment in Russia will be a critical factor to world gas supply. The IEA projects that investment in Russian infrastructure will need to exceed $330 billion over the next thirty years in order to meet domestic demands and for export to other industrialized countries. The average of $11 billion per year compares with Russian investment of $9 billion in gas fields and infrastructure in 2000.

[22] The model allows only for a limited number of transportation options to be specified in advance. However, once we have a solution for an assumed potential network, a new transportation option can be introduced when the price difference between two nodes suggests that it would be profitable to construct such a link.

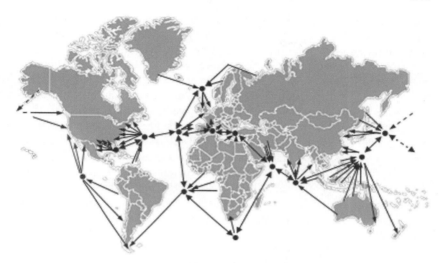

Figure 11.7. LNG transportation network.

A complicating factor in modeling investment in transportation links is that they are inherently discrete, linking a supply source with a particular demand sink. In order to accurately forecast the development of transportation links, one needs to consider a wide range of current and future potential options. It is very easy to bias the results by inadvertently precluding viable options. One way to minimize this problem is to model the transportation system using a "hub and spoke" framework. This breaks particular links down into notional transportation from a supply source to a regional hub and then from the regional hub to the demand sinks. Such an arrangement is less sensitive to the presence of any one link in the network. Swap agreements would be the physical analog of the "hub and spoke" arrangement in the model. Although one particular supplier linked in the model to a notional hub may have a contract with one particular demander linked to the same hub, the model solution will not be affected if any supplier to the hub in question fulfills the contract with the demander. In fact, such a "hub and spoke" representation ensures least cost flows and higher netbacks in an equilibrium solution. The map in figure 11.7 illustrates the "hub and spoke" framework for LNG proposed in the model.

Costs for development, construction, and operation and maintenance of transportation links are of critical importance to the model outcome. For example, further reductions in costs in liquefaction, shipping, and regasification would accelerate the development of a liquid market in natural gas. Thus, in order to model market evolution, estimates of liquefaction, shipping, and regasification costs are required.

The average capital costs for liquefaction for any potential project, as given in the IEA's *World Energy Investment Outlook* (*WEIO*) 2003 (IEA 2003), are $145.15/mcm (1,000 m^3) of annual throughput capacity. These costs, however, have been adjusted using various industry sources to reflect regional deviations from the average. The actual costs assumed in the model are given in figure 11.8. It should be noted that these costs are not the sole determinant of the decision to develop LNG liquefaction. In particular, differences in the feed gas costs, which are determined by the costs of developing reserves and which change through the model time horizon, serve either to offset or exacerbate the differences in liquefaction costs across regions. Therefore, the full cost to the tailgate of the liquefaction facility can differ substantially from project to project.

To construct shipping costs, we modified point-to-point data from industry sources. The costs (in $2002) are lease rates, which include an implicit return to capital as well as operating and maintenance expenses. They were available from various existing and proposed liquefaction locations to various existing and proposed regasification terminals. (See appendix for more details on the estimation as well as table 11.A, which lists the costs of movement along each "spoke.")

The capital costs of regasification included in the model vary by location, ranging from $36.02 to $130.31/mcm of annual throughput capacity. The variation in costs results from a variety of factors, one being variation in the cost of land. The estimates used in the model are generated by using costs in a number of reports (CERA 2002; IEA 2003), industry estimates, and the trigger prices for regasification terminals reported in EIA's *IEO* (EIA 2004). For all terminals outside the United States, except Japan, Taiwan, and Hong Kong, we used the cost for regasification reported in the WEIO (IEA 2003). For the United States, CERA reports a range of regasification costs by capacity in areas characterized as "Low-Cost" and "High-Cost," but they do not identify specific high- and low-cost areas. However, the EIA reports trigger prices for investment in regasification capacity in different regions of the United States. Using the CERA and other industry estimates, we fit a regression describing cost as a function of capacity. The EIA data were then used to identify where in the low-to-high-cost range different regions fall. In the United States, this ranks, in descending order of cost, the West Coast, the Northeast, South Atlantic, and the Gulf Coast region. The "high-cost" CERA estimates and industry estimates were also used for Japan, Taiwan, and Hong Kong.

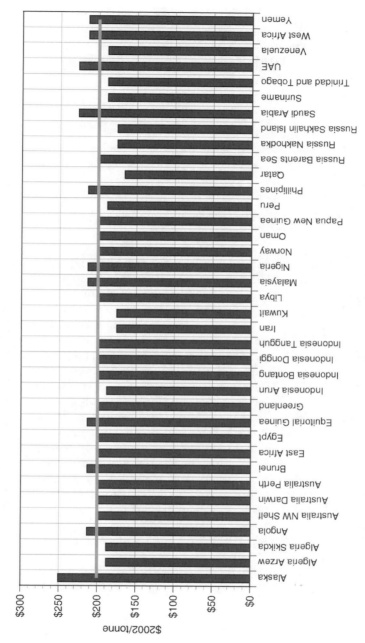

Figure 11.8. LNG liquefaction, capital costs per tonne annual production capacity.

Table 11.1 *Indicative LNG costs (excluding cost of feed gas), 2002,*
$/mmbtu

	Liquefaction($)	Shipping($)	Regasification($)	Total($)
Trinidad–Boston	0.82	0.25	0.69	1.75
Trinidad–Lake Charles	0.82	0.32	0.21	1.35
Algeria–Boston	0.82	0.45	0.69	1.96
Algeria–Lake Charles	0.82	0.63	0.22	1.66
Nigeria–Lake Charles	0.82	0.77	0.22	1.81
Qatar-Lake Charles	0.82	1.17	0.23	2.22
Qatar-Baja	0.82	1.32	0.28	2.41
NW Shelf–Baja	0.82	0.99	0.27	2.07
Norway–Cove Point	0.82	0.57	0.36	1.74

Source: EIA (2003a); various industry consultant reports, author's estimates.

Taken together, the required differential from liquefaction intake to
regasification tailgate falls between $2.54 and $3.09/mmbtu of annual
throughput capacity. Note, however, that the actual number will vary by
shipping distance and regasification location, and will change over time
as feed gas costs change and technological innovations occur in the LNG
value chain. Table 11.1 gives indicative costs for moving LNG between a
number of origination and destination pairs. Note that the costs reported
in table 11.1 *do not* include feed gas costs for liquefaction.

The costs in table 11.1 are indicative costs for 2000. We allow these
costs to change over time because, as a result of technological change,
there have been substantial declines in LNG capital costs, and further
declines are anticipated. In general, when infrastructure capital costs
decline the price differential required for flow between regions should
also fall. To accommodate this, we used the projected rate of cost
declines in liquefaction, shipping, and regasification as given in the
WEIO (IEA 2003). According to the WEIO, total capital costs for
liquefaction, shipping, and regasification have fallen from about $494/
mcm in 1995 to about $387/mcm in 2000, and will continue to fall
to about $292/mcm by 2010.[23] Figure 11.9 depicts the capital cost
estimates used through 2040.

We also use historical data to estimate the costs associated with
building pipelines. The regression analysis allowed us to estimate the

---

[23] In order to extrapolate this progress, we fit a regression equation of the form $Cost_t = \alpha + \beta \cdot \ln(Time)$ to the point estimates of past, current, and future costs for each piece of the
LNG "value chain" (liquefaction, shipping, and regasification).

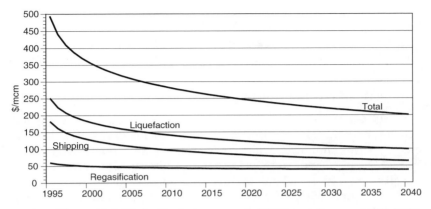

Figure 11.9. Technological progress in LNG capital costs, 1995–2040.

cost of any generic pipeline project based on miles, capacity, and geographical location. For example, the Gulfstream pipeline, extending from Mobile Bay, Alabama to Tampa Bay, Florida, is calculated according to the EIA data to have a capital cost of $108/mcm. The estimated value using our methodology is $113/mcm.

A rate-of-return calculation generated the tariffs on pipelines. Specifically, the tariff rate was calculated such that the present value of the tariff revenue at 50 percent capacity utilization, using the required return on investment (see next section) as a discount rate, just recovers the upfront capital cost in twenty years. As an example, suppose the weighted average cost of capital (WACC) is 8.4 percent. To recover an up-front outlay of $108/mcm (such as the Gulfstream pipeline) over a period of twenty years, the tariff would need to be about $0.46/mmbtu. However, pipeline capacity is not always fully utilized. In practice, the tariff typically allows some costs (for example, maintenance and fuel) always to be recovered, while another proportion is dependent upon capacity utilization. For example, any molecule of gas transported on a pipeline (such as the Gulfstream) may incur a charge of, say, $0.06 plus a 1.5 percent fuel charge. As capacity utilization rises from 0 percent to 100 percent, the tariff on the pipeline grows. This occurs because, as capacity becomes scarce, shippers bid up the price of using the pipeline. We set the parameters describing this scarcity premium such that at any load factor above 50 percent, the pipeline owner earns rents. In the case of the Gulfstream pipeline, the tariff rises to $0.46/mmbtu at 50 percent utilization, and $0.75/mmbtu at 92 percent utilization, which would be akin to a fully loaded rate. The tariff can then rise as high as $15/mmbtu at a load factor of 100 percent although this will not occur in an unconstrained long-run equilibrium. Such rents would more than compensate for capacity expansion, or alternative supply options would develop.

Required Returns on Investments

The BIWGTM solves not only for a spatial equilibrium of supply and demand in each year but also for new investments in resource development, transportation, liquefaction, and/or regasification capacity. The investments are assumed to yield a competitive rate of return, such that the NPV of the marginal unit of capacity is non-negative. The project life of all new investments is assumed to be 100 years, and the tax life is assumed to be twenty years. The tax levied on income earned from projects is assumed to be 40 percent, and property tax and insurance is assumed to be 2.5 percent.

The model uses a weighted average cost of capital to determine the NPV of each increment of new capital. The debt:equity ratio is allowed to differ across different categories of investment. Pipeline investments are taken to be the most highly levered (with 90 percent debt), reflecting the likelihood that pipeline transportation rates will be regulated and hence that the income stream will be very predictable. LNG investments are assumed to have a higher equity level (30 percent equity). Most of these will be undertaken only if a substantial fraction of the anticipated output is contracted in advance using bankable contracts. Mining investments are taken to be the most risky category, with an assumed debt ratio of only 40 percent. In addition to differing levels of leverage, the different categories of investments are assumed to have differing required rates of return on equity, again as a reflection of differing risks. Specifically, the required return on equity (ROE) for pipeline capacity is 12 percent (real), and the ROE on upstream investments is 15 percent (real). The real interest rate on debt is set at 8 percent for all projects. The assumptions regarding required returns are based on numerous meetings with industry reviewers.

For the reference case model, the ROE is assumed identical across regions. In chapter 12, we examine a modified model where rates of return also vary geographically to reflect differences in risks of investing in different countries. While the latter model is more realistic and will form the basis for our subsequent scenario analysis, we first examine the model with uniform rates so we can investigate the consequences of allowing required rates of return on investments to vary.

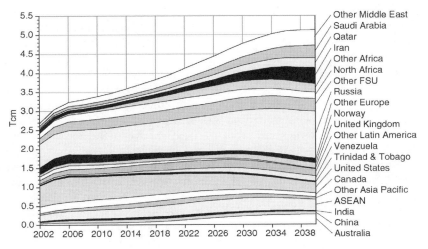

Figure 11.10. Gas supply projections:major countries or regions, 2002–2040.

The Base Case Solution

Figure 11.10 presents the supply projections in the Base Case. In many cases, these have been aggregated at the regional level to make the graph easier to read. Table 11.B in the appendix presents the supply data for a larger number of individual countries and a selection of years. Table 11.C presents results for demand. It is important to note that the base case represents the outcomes of a world in which there are no political constraints. Thus, by corollary, one could think of these results as occurring if the countries throughout the world shared relationships similar to those shared by Canada and the United States.

The model suggests, absent potential policy constraints, that Russia will play a pivotal role in price formation in a more flexible and inte-grated global natural gas market. Russia is projected to be the single largest producer of natural gas until 2040, although beyond 2038 the Middle East as a region (which, of course, is an aggregation of countries) becomes the largest global supplier. Russia is also strategically positioned to move large amounts of gas to consuming markets in both the Atlantic and the Pacific, giving it the potential to play an important role in linking prices between the two regions. In the base case, Eastern Siberian gas begins flowing into Northern China at the beginning of the 2010s and eventually flows into the Korean peninsula. Toward the end of the model time horizon, specifically 2035–2040, northeast Asian demand grows sufficiently to make the construction of a pipeline from Western Siberia to Eastern Siberia economic, and gas begins to flow into China from Western Siberia. Throughout the model period, Russia is also a very large supplier to Europe via pipeline. Once Russian pipeline gas is simultaneously flowing both east and west, production in the Western Siberian basin becomes the arbitrage point between Europe and Asia, thus linking gas prices in the two regions.

The model also indicates that Russia will enter the LNG export market in both the Pacific and the Atlantic Basins. In the Pacific Basin, production in the Sakhalin region is exported as LNG but also flows to Japan via pipeline beginning in 2010. In the Atlantic Basin, production in the Barents Sea eventually provides gas exports in the form of LNG beginning in the mid-2020s.[24] This ultimately provides another link between gas prices in North America, Europe, and Asia. Specifically, when gas is simultaneously flowing in all three directions out of Russia, the "net-back" price from sending the gas in any of the three directions has to be the same. Russia benefits not only from its location and size of resources but also because it was one of the first major gas exporters and has access to a sophisticated network of infrastructure already in place (see chapter 5).

Figure 11.10 also indicates that, in aggregate, the Middle East will become an important future supplier of natural gas, with production surpassing that of the United States in 2022 and North America as a whole in 2026. The largest exporters of the Middle Eastern region are Qatar, Iran, UAE, and (late in the time horizon), Saudi Arabia. The majority of these exports occur as LNG. However, barring from consideration any prohibitive political factors, pipeline infrastructure is developed to move Iranian gas through Pakistan to India. In addition, existing infrastructure is expanded to move gas from Iran to Europe though Turkey and Armenia.

Figure 11.11 gives the demand projections for the base case. (Note that quantity differences between figures 11.10 and 11.11 are due to natural gas used as fuel in the transportation process.) Interestingly, although Russia is the largest single national source for natural gas throughout most of the model period, figure 11.11 shows that Russia is simultaneously a large consumer. Demand growth in Iran and Saudi

---

[24] Production from the Barents Sea also will move to Europe via a pipeline through St. Petersburg from 2008.

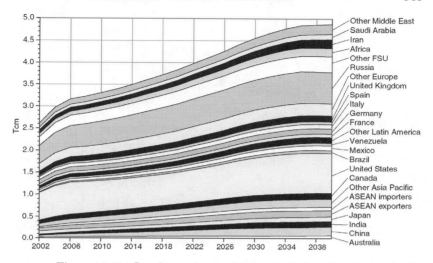

Figure 11.11. Gas demand, net of transport fuel and backstop supply, 2002–2040.

also limit exports from the Middle East. Thus, despite these countries' prominence in the future of global natural gas supply, their export capacity is limited by domestic requirements.

The largest-consuming regions are North America and Europe. North American demand, in particular, is large prior to the introduction of the backstop technology beginning in 2020. Japan, which is primarily dependent upon LNG supplies, also adopts the backstop technology relatively early. The model also projects that strong European demand growth will eventually lead to fairly aggressive adoption of the backstop technology, but not before it draws on Nigerian supplies via the Trans-Saharan pipeline (from Nigeria to Algeria), which is constructed in the beginning of the 2010s.

Figure 11.12 summarizes the implications of the above changes in supply and demand for international trade in natural gas via both pipeline and LNG; note that this figure consolidates trade within each of the identified regions. Figure 11.13 focuses on LNG imports alone, while Figure 11.14 graphs model projections for LNG exports.

The change in LNG imports is particularly striking. The United States surpasses Japan as the largest LNG importer by the end of the 2010s. Although Japan shifts marginally to pipeline imports with the development of a Sakhalin pipeline, North American production is increasingly unable to keep pace with North American demand. Price increases following the depletion of low-cost resources in North America

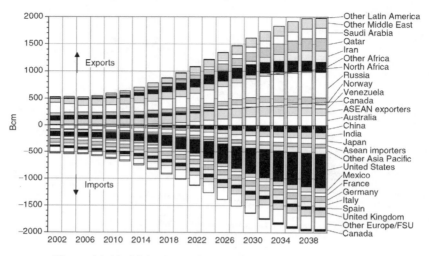

Figure 11.12. Major natural gas trades between regions, 2002–2040.

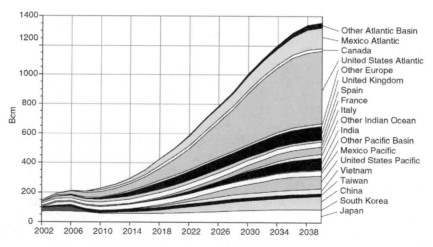

Figure 11.13. LNG importers, 2002–2040.

allow LNG to take an increasing share of the North American market and limit growth in demand. Beyond 2040, aggressive adoption of the backstop technology abates gas demand. Nevertheless, the United States becomes a premium region, drawing on gas supplies from around the

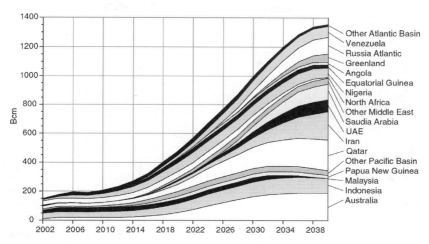

Figure 11.14. LNG exporters, 2002–2040.

world as imports of natural gas grow throughout the modeling period. Alaskan resources are an important source of future supply, as the model constructs capacity into Alberta beginning in 2014, but supply from Alaska neither collapses the North American price, nor eliminates the need for imported LNG.[25]

Mexico and Canada add to North American LNG imports by the end of the modeling horizon. Mexico (Pacific plus Atlantic imports) overtakes Japan as an importer of LNG at about the same time as the US, although some of that gas is actually destined for the US market.[26] Mexican domestic demand growth is stimulated by Mexican government policy favoring conversion of existing fuel oil facilities as well as targeting gas as the fuel for new plants. Early in the period, demand for natural gas in Canada is stimulated by the production of oil from tar

---

[25] Rather, Alaskan pipeline gas will replace declining Western Canadian Sedimentary Basin production, delaying further exploitation of marginal Canadian resources. While many analysts have predicted a substantial price impact of Alaskan supplies, the model results suggest that Alaskan gas will merely stabilize prices in the medium term. With a lead time approaching ten years, producers will have adequate time to adjust their behavior once an Alaskan project is announced. Intertemporal arbitrage in complete forward markets will then smooth the price impact of Alaskan supply.

[26] A substantial portion of the Mexican imports into Baja California, which will accelerate in the 2020s and 2030s, are also destined for the US West Coast. The model assumes that LNG regasification terminals are cheaper to build in Mexico than in southern California. The cost differential is more than enough to compensate for the additional costs of piping gas to California.

sands, while later in the model time horizon LNG imports into northeast Canada are stimulated by demand in the New England region.

Demand growth in Europe also outpaces indigenous production, making Europe the second largest importing region as a whole.[27] But, increasing availability of the backstop also causes European imports to level off by 2040. Europe imports via pipeline from Africa, the Middle East, and Russia as well as via LNG. The United Kingdom more or less matches Japan as an importer of LNG by 2020, while total European demand for LNG overtakes Japanese demand in the middle of the 2010s.

High demand growth in India and China also affect world trade. In the early part of the model period, both India and China obtain supplies from domestic sources. However, the model indicates that India and China will rival Japan as importers of LNG by 2030 even though LNG imports to China are limited to the southeast. Both countries also become large importers via pipeline.

Another notable feature of figure 11.12 is the very small impact of South America in global natural gas markets. The continent as a whole is neither a large importer nor a large exporter of natural gas at any time in the model horizon. There is, however, substantial trade in gas between countries within the continent. In particular, Brazil and Argentina eventually become large importers of regional pipeline gas as their domestic resources become relatively expensive.

Toward the end of the modeling period, the Middle East becomes the largest gas-exporting region, with Qatar being the leading exporter. Russia is a dominant exporter throughout the model period, In early years, Canada is a relatively large exporter to the United States, but its exports fade by the early 2020s, with its balance largely offset by the import of Alaskan gas in transit to the United States. The ASEAN exporting countries remain significant suppliers throughout the model period, although some ASEAN countries also become significant importers beginning in 2025. Australia also becomes a substantial exporter from 2025. The Australian share is particularly evident in the graph of LNG exporters (figure 11.14).

Qatar, Iran, and to a lesser extent Saudi Arabia and the UAE, become large exporters of LNG. Although Iraq is also a large exporter, it utilizes pipeline routes (both new and existing) to Syria and Turkey and on to Europe. For the period up to 2015, Indonesia, North Africa, Malaysia, Australia, Qatar, Nigeria, and Trinidad & Tobago all have significant

---

[27] Note that trade between two countries in "other Europe," for example, is not counted as inter-regional trade for the purposes of figure 11.13.

shares in LNG supply. But, by 2040, Qatar and Australia are the two largest LNG suppliers, followed in order by Iran, Russia, Indonesia, Saudi Arabia, the UAE, Venezuela, and Nigeria. The flow of LNG from the four largest suppliers makes up over half of all LNG supply in 2040. It is important, however, to note the scale of LNG exports. While these countries dominate LNG trade, they are not necessarily the largest suppliers of natural gas in the world. Russian exports by pipeline roughly equal the sum of the five largest LNG export volumes combined.

Qatar is an early leader in supplying LNG from the Middle East. Other resource-rich players lacking existing infrastructure needed to bear substantial fixed costs to enter the LNG market. Early entry would drive down prices and lead to inadequate returns on investment. Therefore, entry must be delayed until world demand in excess of alternative sources of supply is large enough to accommodate these incremental supplies. Thus, the principle of "first-mover advantage" plays a crucial role in the development of the LNG market. Consequently, Iranian LNG supplies do not enter the world market until 2016, Saudi Arabia does not begin to supply LNG until 2022, and Russian Barents Sea LNG exports begin only in 2024. However, all three of these countries are also better placed than is Qatar to supply large consumers via pipeline. Iran eventually supplies India and Turkey while Saudi Arabia supplies Egypt, Syria, and Jordan, via pipeline.

Figure 11.15 provides price projections for six locations. Henry Hub and Zeebrugge are already reference pricing nodes, and possibly Tokyo, Beijing, or Delhi could evolve as representative pricing nodes in Asia and Buenos Aires in South America. The most prominent feature of figure 11.15 is the convergence of prices over time as other countries become dependent upon LNG as their marginal source of natural gas, as Japan does today.

It is worth noting that near-term prices as predicted by the model do not correspond well to current market conditions. This is partially explained by some of our assumptions. For example, we use an EIA forecast of oil price that predates the 2005 increase in price. We also do not consider short-term financing constraints on producers that have resulted from the 2004–2005 turmoil in natural gas markets. In addition, factors such as the uncertainty associated with some gas developments in Russia and the reduced use of nuclear power plants in Japan, were not incorporated into the model. More generally, the price forecast produced by the model should be viewed as an average. Many types of short-term influences could produce random variations about that average. We have not modeled the uncertainties that lead to short-term variability. The possibility of these kinds of random fluctuations leads

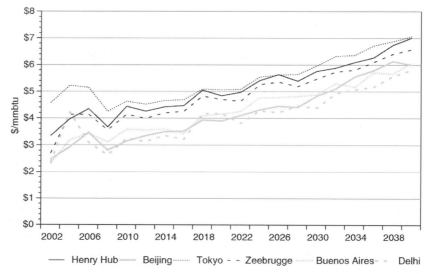

Figure 11.15. Selected regional price projections, 2002–2040
Y2000$/mmbtu.

to speculative behavior of market participants. Since the model calculates a "perfect foresight" equilibrium, near-term speculative behavior is
not captured.

Increasing use of the backstop technologies leads to a reduction in
forecast average prices beyond the model horizon. As end users substitute away from natural gas in the locations where gas becomes more
expensive, the cost of gas for the remaining users actually declines,
curtailing the demand for the backstop technologies. As a result of the
backstop technology, natural gas is eventually (late in the century)
consumed in large relative quantities only in regions where it is in relative
abundance, such as the Middle East, Russia, and Australia.

Concluding Remarks

We have presented an equilibrium model of the evolution of the world
market for natural gas over the next thrity years. The model is based
upon geologic and economic fundamentals and respects well-known
economic principles that resource extraction and trade should eliminate
profitable spatial and intertemporal arbitrage opportunities.

The model predicts widespread use of LNG and the extension of
major pipeline systems to span continents. This, in turn, links markets

for natural gas around the world. A consequence is that wholesale prices will tend to converge over time while regional shocks will have global consequences.

Another central finding is that Russia is destined to play a central role in linking the European and Asian markets for natural gas through the use and development of new and existing pipeline infrastructure. It is also likely that Russia will enter the LNG market in both the Atlantic and Pacific Basins. In fact, Russia is projected to be the largest single supplier of natural gas to global markets.

The Middle East will emerge as a key region in the LNG market, but may also supply gas via pipeline to growing markets in South Asia and Europe. Qatar and Iran, in particular, have substantial natural gas resources, both proved and potential, which are relatively untapped. In fact, the USGS estimates that about one-third of world natural gas potential lies in the region. Particular interest in developing LNG export projects in Qatar and Iran reflects those countries' massive reserves and strategic location to serve growing markets in both the East and the West.

Long-term, alternative energy sources will abate growing demand for natural gas. A reasonably good substitute for gas is available at a cost that is not dramatically higher than prices normally expected to prevail over the model horizon. Any long-term increase in gas prices above the $5/mmbtu range is likely to stimulate demand for these backstop technologies, thus emphasizing that natural gas is a "transition fuel." This is true of any depletable resource with an alternative whose cost is, at present, prohibitive. The central question for any transition fuel concerns its shelf life: just how long will natural gas be consumed? Demand for natural gas has been greatly stimulated in the short term by the expanding use of natural gas in electricity-generation. Moreover, most projections indicate that future natural gas demand growth will come primarily from the power-generation sector. There are, however, many alternative ways to generate electricity at comparable cost to CCGT, while other uses for natural gas can also be satisfied, for example, by "syngas" manufactured from coal. Indeed, before the widespread use of natural gas, coal gas was reticulated in many cities in the United States and Europe and provided many similar services to those provided by natural gas today.

APPENDIX: MODEL DETAILS

Estimating the Demand for Natural Gas

We use E_{it} to denote the consumption of primary energy in quadrillion Btu 1,000 population in country i and year t. We use the level of GDP *per capita* measured in PPP terms in 1995 real international dollars (denoted y_{it}) to proxy the level of economic development in country i and year t. We then estimate the following equation (estimated standard errors are indicated below each coefficient):[28]

$$E_{it} = a_i + 0.8228\,E_{it-1} + 0.4040\,y_{it} - 0.0145\,y_{it}^2 + \varepsilon_{it} \qquad (11A.1)$$
$$\phantom{E_{it} = a_i +} (0.0110) \qquad (0.0852) \quad (0.0051)$$

where the coefficients a_i are country-specific effects. The positive coefficient on y_{it} implies that *per capita* energy demand rises as the economy develops, but the negative coefficient on the quadratic term implies that the increase occurs at a declining rate.[29] This result is consistent with the notion that both the income elasticity of energy demand and the energy intensity of a country decline with the level of economic development.[30]

To estimate the own- and cross-price elasticities of demand, we used twenty-three years of data on twenty-nine OECD economies from the IEA *Energy Statistics and Balances for OECD Countries* that include prices of natural gas, oil, and coal. The econometric analysis did not reveal a significant effect of coal prices on the demand for natural gas once oil and gas prices had been included. As a result, coal prices were omitted from the analysis.[31] The estimated equation then related the share of natural gas in primary energy demand in country i and year t (θ_{it}^{NG}) to the real prices of natural gas and crude oil and the level of economic development measured by real GDP *per capita* (measured in PPP terms). The latter variable captures the idea that natural gas is a "premium fuel." Increased environmental regulation in wealthier economies encourages

---

[28] The cross-section time series model was estimated on 172 countries with an average of 18.7 years per country (resulting in 3,218 total observations). The shortest time series for any country was seven years while the longest was twenty-one years (1980–2001). Since the error term was autocorrelated, the lagged dependent variable was instrumented with $E_{it}-2$, $y_{it}-1$, and y_{it-1}^2. Autocorrelation in total energy services demand *per capita* could reflect dynamic interactions between energy supply and the overall level of economic activity. The within-country $R^2 = 0.8063$, while the between-country $R^2 = 0.9961$. The F-statistic for the test of joint statistical significance of the country-specific fixed effects was $F_{171,3043} = 2.77$, indicating that there are systematic country-specific differences that are not explained by the level of economic development.

[29] The quadratic only approximates the true relationship, in particular because we would not expect energy *per capita* to decline. Nevertheless, the quadratic in (11A.1) attains a maximum at a *per capita* income of more than \$1.136 million 1995 USA which is more than ten times any feasible *per capita* income level for any country in 2100.

[30] See Medlock and Soligo (2001) for more discussion of this issue.

[31] There is more than one plausible explanation for the lack of significance of coal prices. Two such arguments are: (1) since coal varies substantially in quality, coal prices are more difficult to measure and the series we used may therefore contain substantial error; and (2) coal became a close substitute for gas only when CCGT allowed gas to be used for base-load power-generation, and this occurred only in recent years. Previously, gas turbines competed with fuel oil to generate peak load power.

the use of cleaner burning natural gas, while higher wealth facilitates the large investments required to deliver gas supplies to customers. The functional form we estimated guarantees that the share, θ_{it}^{NG}, remains bounded between zero and one:[32]

$$\ln(-\ln \theta_{it}^{NG}) = b_i + \underset{(0.0149)}{0.8291}\ln(-\ln \theta_{it-1}^{NG}) + \underset{(0.0059)}{0.0335}\ln Png_{it}$$
$$\underset{(0.0059)}{-\,0.0302} \ln Poil_{it} - \underset{(0.0118)}{0.0677} \ln y_{it} + \xi_{it} \qquad (11A.2)$$

for country i in year t, where the country-specific effect b_i represents resource availabilities or other characteristics, and the variance of the error differs by country.

By differentiating (11A.2), we see that the elasticity of *per capita* natural gas demand with respect to its various arguments is:

$$\frac{\theta_{t-1}^{NG}}{\theta_t^{NG}}\frac{\partial\theta_t^{NG}}{\partial\theta_{t-1}^{NG}} = 0.8291 \frac{\ln \theta_t^{NG}}{\ln \theta_{t-1}^{NG}},$$

$$-\frac{Png_t}{\theta_t^{NG}}\frac{\partial\theta_t^{NG}}{\partial Png_t} = -0.0335 \ln \theta_t^{NG},$$

$$\frac{Poil_t}{\theta_t^{NG}}\frac{\partial\theta_t^{NG}}{\partial Poil_t} = -0.0302 \ln \theta_t^{NG}, \text{ and} \qquad (11A.3)$$

$$\frac{y_t}{\theta_t^{NG}}\frac{\partial\theta_t^{NG}}{\partial y_t} = -0.0677 \ln \theta_t^{NG}.$$

In particular, the functional form in (11A.2) implies that the elasticity of demand for natural gas with respect to prices and *per capita* GDP declines toward zero as θ^{NG} rises (recall that $\theta^{NG} < 1$, so $\ln \theta^{NG} < 0$). The lagged dependent variable on the right-hand side of (11A.2) implies that the long-run elasticity of demand with respect to the prices and *per capita* income will be approximately 5.85 times larger than the short-run elasticity.

[32] The combined cross-section time series model was estimated for twenty-nine countries with an average of 18.9 years per country (resulting in 548 total observations). Unlike the energy services demand equation, Hausman-tests did not suggest that the lagged dependent variable was endogenous, while allowing for a common first-order autoregressive structure across panels produced an estimated coefficient of only 0.0365. Hausman-tests also did not suggest that the real prices were endogenous to the natural gas share in any one country. Instead of using instrumental variables, we therefore focused on modeling heteroskedasticity using generalized least squares (GLS). Heterogeneity may be more important for the share equation because country-specific differences in resource endowments are likely to explain a substantial fraction of the variation in the data. The log likelihood of the cross-sectional time series model was 1054.247, while the chi-square statistic for testing whether the estimated coefficients are jointly significantly different from zero was 106,629.16 with thirty-two degrees of freedom.

In order to use (11A.2) and (11A.3) to forecast natural gas demand, we must also generate a forecast of *per capita* GDP and population. To forecast real *per capita* GDP, we estimate the following equation for real *per capita* GDP *growth*, defined as $y_{it} = \ln y_{it} - \ln y_{it-1}$ in country i in year t (estimated standard errors are in parentheses):[33]

$$y_{it} = c_i + 0.9362\, y_{it-1} + 0.9431(1/\ln y_{it-1}) - 6.1930(y_{it-1}/\ln y_{it-1})$$
$$\quad (0.0886) \qquad (0.1178) \qquad\qquad (0.7009)$$
$$\quad - 0.0152(\ln y_{it-1} - \ln y_{USt-1}) + \zeta_{it}$$
$$\quad (0.0030) \tag{11A.4}$$

where c_i is a country-specific constant effect (reflecting, for example, persistent differences in legal or political institutions), y_{it} is the level of real *per capita* GDP in PPP terms and y_{USt} is the corresponding US real *per capita* GDP in year t. The variance of the error term, ζ_{it}, is allowed to vary across countries. The negative coefficient on the difference between country i GDP *per capita* and US GDP *per capita* implies that *per capita* growth rates of other countries will tend to converge toward those of the United States over time. (Note that for the United States the fourth term takes a value of zero in all periods.) The positive coefficient on the inverse log level of *per capita* GDP ($1/\ln y_{it}$) implies that growth rates will tend to diminish as *per capita* GDP increases. Furthermore, the negative coefficient on the interaction term implies that growth rates will tend to become more persistent as the economy matures.[34]

Before we used (11A.4) to forecast future economic growth, we adjusted the country-specific constant terms c_i. The reason for doing so is that the constants reflect the average experience of a country over the sample period while the recent experience might be more salient for projecting future developments. We therefore calculated a value of c_i for each year from 1996 to 2002 by using the estimated coefficients from the regression and the actual data for each country. We then averaged these values with the estimated constant term, thereby giving increased weight to recent experience.

---

[33] The equation was estimated for 173 countries with an average sample of 37.6 years for each country and a maximum sample size of fifty-two years for any one country. The log likelihood of the cross-sectional time series model was 10513.88, while the chi-square statistic for testing whether the estimated coefficients together are significantly different from zero was 1311.39 with 176 degrees of freedom.

[34] Since $1/\ln y$ ranges from a maximum of 0.18 in the sample to a minimum of 0.085 out of sample, the *net* coefficient on the lagged dependent variable ranges from -0.186 to 0.4057, implying that the model is dynamically stable.

We also estimated a simple model where economic development reduces population growth rates.[35] Specifically, defining the approximate population growth rate in country i in year t as $P_{it} = \ln P_{it} - \ln P_{it-1}$ we estimated the following model (estimated standard errors of the coefficients are again in parentheses):[36]

$$P_{it} = d_i + 0.7882\, P_{it-1} + 1.57691/y_{it-1} + v_{it}$$
$$\phantom{P_{it} = d_i +}\ (0.0080)\phantom{\, P_{it-1} +}\ (0.1922) \tag{11A.5}$$

where, y_{it} is again the *per capita* real GDP, d_i is a country-specific-constant effect and the error terms for each country are again allowed to have different variances. In using the model to forecast, we modified the country-specific constants so that the implied average population growth from 2000 to 2015 matched the World Bank forecast average population growth over the same period. The motivation is that the World Bank forecast may be based on demographic considerations (particularly the current age profile of the population) that are not accounted for in (11A.5).

Estimating the Capital Costs and O&M Costs for Natural Gas

To determine capital costs we estimated the following three equations:

$$c_2 = -0.0207 + 0.00066\, MedD + 0.000014(MedD/Res)$$
$$\ (0.1998)\ (0.000075)\ (0.000002)$$
$$N = 316, R^2 = 0.427$$

$$c_1 = -0.0619 + 0.3838\, c_2 - 0.00009\, MinD + 0.000009(MedD/Res)$$
$$\ (0.1998)\ (0.0155)\ (0.000027)\ (0.000001)$$
$$N = 221, R^2 = 0.855$$

$$c_3 = -4.4073 + 6.4009\, c_2 - 0.00161\, MaxD + 0.000024(MaxD/Res)$$
$$\ (0.9912)\ (0.2516)\ (0.000229)\ (0.000006)$$
$$N = 221, R^2 = 0.859 \tag{11A.6}$$

---

[35] Many reasons could explain why birth rates decline as *per capita* incomes rise. As income rises, the opportunity cost of having children rises as more women enter the labor force and their wages rise. Moreover, children cost more to raise and educate. Initially, we examined a model where economic development at first raises population growth rates by bringing improved health care, water supplies, and other living standard advances that raise survival rates for children and increase life spans. We found, however, that the terms needed to allow for a rising initial population growth rate as a function of y added little to the within-sample explanatory value of the model once we also allowed for country-specific effects. In addition, these terms were irrelevant for projected out-of-sample population growth rates.

[36] The equation was estimated for 173 countries with an average sample of 38.1 years for each country and a maximum sample size of fifty-two years for any one country. The log likelihood of the cross-sectional time series model was 27864.99, while the chi-square

where *MedD*, *MinD*, and *MaxD* are, respectively, the median, minimum, and maximum well depth and *Res* the median estimate of the ultimately recoverable reserves from the field.

Each equation included a set of regional indicator variables. Since most of these coefficients are of little interest for applying the estimated equations internationally, they have not been reported. The constant terms as reported are chosen so that the equations fit the means of the reported variables ignoring regional effects. The complete equations with fixed regional effects are available from the authors. One regional effect of interest is the higher costs of exploiting Alaskan deposits, since the costs due to harsh weather are also likely to apply to other resources located above the Arctic circle. Unfortunately, we did not have $\{c_1, c_2, c_3\}$ for Alaska. Nevertheless, we added a premium for exploiting fields in the Barents Sea, Sakhalin, and Greenland to make them comparable to the Alaskan costs. Estimated standard errors are placed in parentheses below each coefficient. The equation for c_2 includes additional observations since only the median field depth was available for Canada, Mexico, and offshore fields in the United States.

The estimated regression for operating and maintenance costs is:

$$OM = 0.00972 + 0.32952 \cdot Off + 0.000027 \cdot MedD$$
$$(0.01786) \quad (0.01875) \qquad (0.000004) \qquad\qquad (11A.7)$$
$$+ 67.3652 \cdot (1/MedD) + 0.00356 \cdot (1/Res)$$
$$(14.2720) \qquad\qquad (0.00028)$$
$$N = 316, R^2 = 0.6436.$$

Estimating LNG Shipping Costs

To fit the shipping costs for point-to-point deliveries to the hub-and-spoke representation in figure 11.7, we regressed the point-to-point costs on a set of indicator variables for each of the hub flows implicitly included in each point-to-point route. For each liquefaction node i, there is just one hub where LNG is presumed to go initially, while each regasification terminal j also is assumed to obtain its LNG from just one hub. Let the associated shipping costs be β_i^L and β_j^R, respectively. In addition, let the total number of inter-hub routes be H and number them $h = 1, \ldots, H$, with associated shipping costs β_h. The cost on a particular route between i and j can then be written as:

---

statistic for testing whether the estimated coefficients together are significantly different from zero was 114349.55 with 174 degrees of freedom.

$$C_{ij} = \beta_i^L + \sum_{h=1}^{H} \beta_h D_h^{ij} + \beta_j^R \qquad (11A.8)$$

where D_h^{ij} is an indicator variable taking the value of one if the inter-hub route h is part of the shortest route between i and j and zero otherwise.

The original data set contained twenty-six different points of origination and multiple destinations, but not all origination and destination pairs are included. For example, data from Peru was available to only four delivery locales, whereas data from Qatar were available to thirty-two different delivery locales. We nevertheless could estimate the cost of shipping on each of the routes drawn in figure 11.7, except for the routes involving Argentina.[37] The results are given in table 11A.

Estimating Pipeline Capital Costs

The EIA has published project-specific data for fifty-two pipeline projects in the report "Expansion and Change on the US Natural Gas Pipeline Network – 2002" (EIA 2003b). We used these data to estimate a regression equation (with an R^2 of 0.690) that expresses the up-front cost per unit of capacity (also known as the specific capital cost, SCC) as a function of miles, capacity, and geography. OLS regression on the cross-section data yields the following estimates:

$$\ln(SCC_i) = -0.152 + 0.290 \cdot \ln(Miles_i) - 0.384 \cdot \ln(Capacity_i)$$
$$(0.514) \quad (0.072) \qquad\qquad (0.108)$$
$$+ 0.776 \cdot D_{Mountain,i} + 1.072 \cdot D_{Water,i} + 1.243 \cdot D_{Population,i}$$
$$(0.260) \qquad\qquad (0.323) \qquad\qquad (0.252)$$

$$(11A.9)$$

where the variables $D_{n,i}$ are indicator variables that take the value of one or zero. For example, if the project is in a mountainous region, is offshore, or crosses densely populated areas, then $D_{Mountain,i}$, $D_{Water,i}$, and $D_{Population,i}$, respectively, take the value of one. The positive coefficients indicate that an increase in length, crossing mountains, moving offshore, and/or developing in populous areas will raise the cost of a project. The negative coefficient on $\ln(Capacity)$ indicates that larger capacity results in *per-unit* cost reductions, which implies that there are economies of scale associated with pipeline construction.

---

[37] In the latter case, we pro-rated the shipping costs involving (respectively) Peru and Brazil on the basis of distances covered.

Table 11.A *Estimated LNG shipping costs for the route structure in figure 11.7*

Routes	Parameter estimate	Standard error
1 Liquefaction to Hub:		
UAE–Middle East	0.0562	0.0169
Qatar, Iran–Middle East	0.0619	0.0169
Oman–Middle East	0.0050	0.0169
Indonesia (Arun)–Indian Ocean	0.0000	0.0190
Indonesia (Bontang), Brunei, Malaysia–South Asia Pacific	0.0231	0.0190
Indonesia (Tangguh)–South Asia Pacific	0.0762	0.0190
Australia (Darwin)–South Asia Pacific	0.0727	0.0190
Australia (NW Shelf)–South Asia Pacific	0.0857	0.0190
Sakhalin–North Pacific	−0.0001	0.0199
Alaska–North Pacific	0.3451	0.0390
Peru, Bolivia–American South Pacific	0.1355	0.0423
Angola, Guinea, Nigeria, Brazil–South Atlantic	0.0554	0.0213
Trinidad & Tobago, Venezuela–North Atlantic	0.0620	0.0216
Barents Sea–North Sea	0.1028	0.0281
Norway–North Sea	0.0728	0.0281
Libya, Egypt–East Mediterranean	0.0283	0.0223
Algeria–West Mediterranean	0.0283	0.0223
2 Hub to regasification		
Indian Ocean–India East	0.1655	0.0251
Indian Ocean–India South	0.1680	0.0251
Indian Ocean–India West	0.1747	0.0251
South Asia Pacific–South China	0.2428	0.0248
South Asia Pacific–Taiwan	0.2034	0.0241
North Pacific–South Korea, South	0.0688	0.0271
North Pacific–South Korea, North	0.0841	0.0271
North Pacific–NE China	0.0903	0.0271
North Pacific–Japan	0.1134	0.0271
American South Pacific–Baja, S. California	0.1811	0.0278
American South Pacific–SW Mexico	0.2589	0.0278
Caribbean–Lake Charles, Louisiana Gulf	0.0200	0.0294
Caribbean–Freeport	0.0287	0.0294
Caribbean–Mexico (Altamira)	0.0327	0.0294
Caribbean–Florida	0.2273	0.0262
United States North Atlantic–New Brunswick	0.1327	0.0262
United States North Atlantic–Everett	0.1840	0.0262
United States North Atlantic–Cove Point	0.2180	0.0262
United States North Atlantic–Elba	0.2293	0.0262
United States North Atlantic–Humboldt	0.4690	0.0251
European North Atlantic–Portugal	0.1487	0.0210
European North Atlantic–NW Spain	0.2051	0.0209
European North Atlantic–France Atlantic	0.2082	0.0210
North Sea–Zeebrugge (Netherlands)	0.1769	0.0276

Table 11.A (*cont.*)

Routes	Parameter estimate	Standard error
North Sea–United Kingdom	0.1774	0.0276
West Mediterranean–SE Spain	0.1640	0.0204
West Mediterranean–Italy	0.1656	0.0205
West Mediterranean–France Mediterranean	0.1665	0.0205
East Mediterranean–Greece	0.1599	0.0201
East Mediterranean–Turkey	0.1847	0.0201
3 Hub to Hub		
Middle East–Indian Ocean	0.1349	0.0132
Indian Ocean–South Asia Pacific	0.2163	0.0131
South Asia Pacific–North Pacific	0.2645	0.0164
North Pacific–American South Pacific	0.4590	0.0230
United States North Atlantic–Caribbean	0.3033	0.0262
United States North Atlantic–European North Atlantic	0.2082	0.0142
European North Atlantic–South Atlantic	0.2560	0.0155
European North Atlantic–North Sea	0.0715	0.0225
European North Atlantic–West Mediterranean	0.1072	0.0109
West Mediterranean–East Mediterranean	0.0936	0.0135
East Mediterranean–Middle East	0.4500	0.0167

Note:
$R^2 = 0.9905$.

Table 11.B Gas supply projections, selected regions and years (Bcm)

	2002	2006	2010	2016	2020	2026	2030	2036	2040
AFRICA	**166.2**	**235.3**	**273.3**	**359.6**	**411.4**	**472.6**	**475.4**	**459.6**	**420.8**
Algeria	104.8	123.5	130.5	136.2	128.8	107.6	88.3	66.5	57.8
Angola	0.8	0.0	3.1	4.5	10.2	24.1	25.8	25.5	25.5
East Africa	0.0	0.0	0.8	2.8	3.7	4.8	5.9	12.5	13.3
Egypt	30.0	38.8	44.5	57.8	65.1	75.6	81.6	89.2	88.9
Libya	7.4	26.6	36.2	46.2	48.4	51.3	49.8	37.9	31.4
Morocco	0.0	0.0	0.0	0.0	0.0	0.0	0.0	0.0	0.0
Nigeria	17.3	29.4	36.8	71.9	104.2	150.4	167.9	176.7	162.3
Southern Africa	2.0	2.8	1.7	1.7	2.3	3.4	2.5	3.4	3.1
Tunisia	3.1	5.1	6.2	6.8	7.4	9.9	8.2	5.9	5.1
West Africa	0.0	0.8	2.8	5.4	7.6	7.6	7.9	7.6	5.9
West Central Coast Africa	1.1	6.2	10.8	26.1	33.4	38.2	37.1	33.7	27.8
ASIA-PACIFIC	**329.3**	**455.3**	**521.9**	**617.3**	**695.7**	**803.3**	**847.2**	**820.0**	**758.9**
Afghanistan	0.0	0.3	5.1	8.8	11.6	15.9	16.1	16.4	12.7
Australia	38.8	60.6	59.2	76.2	109.0	194.5	244.7	279.5	286.0
Bangladesh	10.8	20.1	30.3	34.8	35.1	32.3	27.2	18.4	14.4
Brunei	12.7	13.9	14.7	17.0	20.4	24.9	26.9	22.4	18.1
China	36.5	64.8	76.5	84.1	83.3	87.8	89.5	86.1	79.6
Hong Kong	0.0	0.0	0.0	0.0	0.0	0.0	0.0	0.0	0.0
India	28.9	37.4	43.9	54.9	57.2	49.8	39.4	29.4	22.7
Indonesia	83.3	93.2	98.5	114.7	135.4	168.5	189.4	197.9	186.6
Japan	2.5	2.3	1.7	1.7	1.7	0.8	0.6	0.3	0.3
Malaysia	56.1	73.9	80.4	88.9	91.7	92.9	89.5	72.5	58.6
Myanmar	7.1	11.9	19.8	26.9	28.6	28.9	26.6	17.6	13.9
New Zealand	5.1	7.1	6.8	6.2	4.5	2.8	2.0	1.7	1.1
Pakistan	23.8	31.1	43.0	52.7	54.1	36.8	26.9	18.1	14.7

Papua New Guinea	0.0	0.0	5.7	18.1	28.3	33.4	35.4	30.3	24.4
Philippines	2.0	3.7	4.2	7.1	13.3	18.4	19.8	20.7	17.3
Singapore	0.0	0.0	0.0	0.0	0.0	0.0	0.0	0.0	0.0
South Korea	0.0	0.0	0.0	0.0	0.0	0.0	0.0	0.0	0.0
Taiwan	2.5	2.8	2.0	1.1	0.8	0.8	0.8	0.6	0.6
Thailand	16.1	21.8	19.5	16.4	15.0	11.0	9.1	6.2	5.4
Vietnam/Laos/Cambodia	2.8	10.2	10.2	7.9	5.4	3.4	2.8	2.0	2.0
EUROPE	**339.5**	**409.5**	**374.3**	**317.4**	**275.8**	**235.9**	**248.3**	**278.9**	**285.1**
Austria	2.0	2.0	1.4	0.8	0.6	0.3	0.3	0.3	0.0
Balkans	5.4	8.8	7.4	4.8	3.4	2.0	1.4	1.1	0.8
Belgium and Luxembourg	0.0	0.0	0.0	0.0	0.0	0.0	0.0	0.0	0.0
Bulgaria	0.8	1.4	0.8	0.6	0.3	0.3	0.3	0.3	0.3
Czech Republic	1.7	2.0	1.4	0.8	0.6	0.3	0.3	0.3	0.3
Denmark (incl. Greenland)	5.4	6.5	5.9	4.0	2.8	2.5	10.5	42.2	66.0
Finland	0.0	0.0	0.0	0.0	0.0	0.0	0.0	0.0	0.0
France	2.0	2.3	1.7	1.1	1.4	5.4	11.6	14.7	11.3
Germany	21.8	28.6	26.9	25.8	23.5	17.0	13.0	7.9	5.4
Greece	0.0	0.0	0.0	0.0	0.0	0.0	0.0	0.0	0.0
Hungary	6.5	8.8	5.9	3.4	2.5	1.4	1.1	0.8	0.6
Ireland	0.8	1.7	1.1	0.6	0.6	0.3	0.3	0.3	0.0
Italy	23.2	28.3	22.7	21.5	19.0	12.2	8.5	5.1	5.7
Netherlands	78.4	92.0	89.8	74.5	58.6	37.7	27.5	16.4	12.7
Norway	64.3	75.6	77.9	85.2	88.3	104.5	129.1	153.2	150.6
Poland	9.3	14.2	10.8	5.9	4.2	2.5	2.0	1.4	1.1
Portugal	0.0	0.0	0.0	0.0	0.0	0.0	0.0	0.0	0.0
Romania	20.7	28.0	24.1	15.3	10.5	6.5	5.1	3.4	2.8
Slovakia	1.1	1.1	0.8	0.6	0.6	0.3	0.3	0.0	0.0
Spain	0.3	0.3	0.0	0.0	0.3	0.3	3.1	11.3	12.7
Sweden	0.0	0.0	0.0	0.0	0.0	0.0	0.0	0.0	0.0
Switzerland	0.0	0.0	0.0	0.0	0.0	0.0	0.0	0.0	0.0
United Kingdom	95.7	107.9	95.4	72.5	58.9	42.8	34.5	20.7	14.4

Table 11.B (*cont.*)

	2002	2006	2010	2016	2020	2026	2030	2036	2040
FSU	**808.2**	**902.4**	**981.7**	**1095.9**	**1192.1**	**1346.7**	**1473.3**	**1607.8**	**1649.7**
Armenia	0.0	0.0	0.0	0.0	0.0	0.0	0.0	0.0	0.0
Azerbaijan	9.6	22.1	26.3	28.6	32.0	45.9	60.0	75.6	78.7
Belarus	0.0	0.0	0.0	0.0	0.0	0.0	0.0	0.0	0.0
Estonia	0.0	0.0	0.0	0.0	0.0	0.0	0.0	0.0	0.0
Georgia	0.0	0.0	0.0	0.0	0.0	0.0	0.0	0.0	0.0
Kazakhstan	34.3	81.8	99.4	103.4	100.2	89.8	83.0	69.1	59.5
Kyrgyzstan	0.0	0.0	0.0	0.0	0.0	0.0	0.0	0.0	0.0
Latvia	0.0	0.0	0.0	0.0	0.0	0.0	0.0	0.0	0.0
Lithuania	0.0	0.0	0.0	0.0	0.0	0.0	0.0	0.0	0.0
Moldova	0.0	0.0	0.0	0.0	0.0	0.0	0.0	0.0	0.0
Russia	647.6	664.3	712.4	804.8	882.1	1013.7	1123.6	1259.5	1302.8
Tajikistan	0.0	0.0	0.0	0.0	0.0	0.0	0.0	0.0	0.0
Turkmenistan	46.2	46.7	48.1	54.9	67.1	91.7	108.7	137.1	157.4
Ukraine	19.5	35.4	42.8	51.0	56.6	52.4	46.2	28.3	22.7
Uzbekistan	51.3	52.4	53.0	53.2	53.8	53.2	51.8	38.5	28.6
MIDDLE EAST	**253.4**	**306.1**	**352.8**	**454.8**	**560.7**	**808.4**	**1014.0**	**1344.2**	**1475.6**
Bahrain	9.3	9.1	6.8	4.8	5.4	12.2	14.7	13.9	11.0
Iran	75.9	75.6	74.8	86.1	107.3	167.9	236.2	368.4	442.3
Iraq	2.0	21.5	46.7	83.0	105.6	133.9	145.5	152.6	148.9
Kuwait	9.9	10.8	25.2	42.5	47.0	48.1	48.1	47.9	42.5
Oman	12.2	8.2	6.2	12.5	19.0	28.9	30.9	36.8	39.6
Qatar	33.7	39.4	45.6	60.0	78.7	139.3	183.5	241.5	265.9
Saudi Arabia	63.4	73.6	75.6	91.2	115.0	171.9	224.8	310.6	344.3
Syria/Jordan	5.7	17.0	17.0	12.2	8.5	5.1	4.2	3.1	2.8
Turkey	0.8	2.5	1.7	0.8	0.6	0.6	0.3	0.3	0.3
UAE	40.5	46.7	49.0	54.4	60.3	76.5	98.3	141.6	148.9

Yemen	0.0	1.7	4.0	7.6	13.0	24.4	27.5	27.2	28.6
NORTH AMERICA	**794.0**	**919.7**	**848.6**	**802.2**	**737.6**	**641.1**	**570.3**	**464.7**	**425.6**
Canada	182.4	188.3	185.8	181.8	169.0	153.5	134.2	111.9	109.0
Mexico	35.1	39.9	28.3	25.2	28.6	29.4	28.6	19.0	15.0
United States	576.5	691.5	634.6	595.2	540.0	457.9	407.5	334.1	301.9
CENTRAL/SOUTH AMERICA	**118.6**	**162.0**	**194.8**	**241.3**	**281.7**	**340.6**	**368.4**	**361.9**	**352.0**
Argentina	36.2	41.9	43.0	43.9	42.8	43.3	42.5	31.1	25.2
Bolivia	5.1	14.2	16.4	20.4	21.8	27.8	29.2	26.9	24.1
Brazil	10.8	10.8	13.0	20.1	27.8	32.3	38.8	53.0	65.1
Central America	0.0	0.0	0.0	0.0	0.0	0.0	0.0	0.0	0.0
Chile	3.1	6.8	7.1	6.5	7.4	7.4	6.5	4.5	4.0
Colombia	6.8	9.3	26.1	34.8	35.7	34.5	32.8	25.2	20.1
Cuba	0.6	1.1	2.0	2.0	1.4	0.8	0.8	0.6	0.6
Ecuador	0.0	0.0	0.0	0.0	0.0	0.3	0.6	1.1	1.1
Other Caribbean	0.0	0.0	0.0	0.0	0.0	0.0	0.0	0.0	0.0
Paraguay	0.0	2.0	2.5	2.0	1.7	1.4	1.1	0.8	0.6
Peru	0.3	1.1	1.7	6.2	11.9	16.1	18.4	22.4	22.4
Suriname/Guyana/Fr. Guiana	0.0	2.0	6.5	13.3	17.8	20.7	21.0	20.4	15.3
Trinidad & Tobago	21.2	35.1	38.2	41.1	44.2	45.6	42.8	29.7	26.3
Uruguay	0.0	0.0	0.0	0.0	0.0	0.0	0.0	0.0	0.0
Venezuela	34.5	37.1	38.2	51.0	68.8	110.4	134.2	146.7	147.5
WORLD TOTAL	**2,809.6**	**3,390.3**	**3,547.8**	**3,888.1**	**4,154.6**	**4,648.7**	**4,997.0**	**5,337.1**	**5,367.4**

Table 11.C Gas demand projections, selected regions and years (Bcm)

	2002	2006	2010	2016	2020	2026	2030	2036	2040
AFRICA	**75.0**	**94.9**	**104.5**	**122.6**	**136.2**	**157.4**	**172.2**	**193.4**	**196.8**
Algeria	23.2	25.2	26.9	31.4	34.8	41.1	45.3	52.1	50.1
Angola	0.8	1.4	1.7	2.0	2.5	3.1	3.4	4.0	4.5
East Africa	0.0	0.0	0.0	0.3	0.3	0.3	0.3	0.3	0.3
Egypt	29.7	37.7	41.6	48.4	53.2	61.2	67.1	76.5	79.9
Libya	6.8	8.5	9.3	10.8	11.9	13.9	15.0	16.1	15.9
Morocco	0.6	1.4	1.7	2.0	2.3	2.5	2.5	2.5	2.5
Nigeria	6.2	7.6	8.2	10.5	11.9	14.4	16.4	19.3	21.0
Southern Africa	2.0	4.0	4.5	4.5	4.2	4.2	3.7	3.4	2.8
Tunisia	4.5	5.9	6.8	8.2	9.3	11.0	12.2	12.7	13.3
West Africa	0.0	0.8	2.0	2.8	3.4	3.7	3.7	3.7	3.4
West Central Coast Africa	1.1	2.0	2.0	2.0	2.3	2.3	2.5	2.8	2.8
ASIA-PACIFIC	**346.0**	**458.4**	**517.3**	**614.2**	**686.1**	**800.8**	**861.4**	**903.9**	**904.4**
Afghanistan	0.3	0.3	0.3	0.3	0.3	0.6	0.6	0.6	0.8
Australia	27.2	37.7	40.8	46.2	50.7	56.3	59.7	64.3	66.5
Bangladesh	10.5	13.9	15.9	18.7	20.4	23.2	24.6	25.8	26.3
Brunei	2.0	2.3	2.3	2.5	2.5	2.5	2.8	3.1	3.1
China	37.7	61.7	76.2	104.2	127.1	165.1	183.5	196.2	201.9
Hong Kong	0.8	1.1	0.8	0.8	0.8	0.8	0.8	0.6	0.6
India	27.5	42.2	65.4	84.1	95.7	113.0	121.8	129.1	129.7
Indonesia	37.1	46.2	49.3	54.4	57.8	62.9	66.0	65.4	63.1
Japan	76.7	77.3	70.5	73.9	79.3	92.0	100.2	105.9	105.1
Malaysia	30.9	38.2	41.9	48.1	52.4	59.5	63.7	64.8	63.7
Myanmar	2.3	3.1	3.7	4.2	4.5	5.1	5.4	5.4	5.4
New Zealand	5.1	6.5	6.8	7.1	7.4	7.6	7.6	7.1	6.8
Pakistan	23.5	30.6	33.7	39.4	43.3	49.8	55.2	63.7	61.4

Papua New Guinea	0.0	0.3	0.3	0.3	0.3	0.3	0.3	0.3	0.3
Philippines	2.0	3.4	4.0	4.8	5.7	6.5	7.4	7.9	8.2
Singapore	1.1	2.5	2.8	3.4	3.7	4.0	4.2	3.7	3.4
South Korea	24.9	33.1	35.4	43.3	49.3	57.5	62.3	63.7	63.7
Taiwan	8.5	15.0	17.0	19.5	20.7	21.5	21.5	20.7	19.8
Thailand	25.2	33.4	36.0	38.8	40.2	42.2	41.3	40.5	39.6
Vietnam/Laos/Cambodia	2.8	9.9	14.4	20.4	24.1	29.7	32.3	34.8	35.1
EUROPE	**528.1**	**623.2**	**632.6**	**673.1**	**705.1**	**746.1**	**769.4**	**788.9**	**777.6**
Austria	8.8	10.2	10.2	11.0	11.6	12.2	12.5	13.0	13.0
Balkans	5.1	7.4	7.6	7.9	8.5	8.8	8.8	8.2	7.9
Belgium and Luxembourg	18.7	21.2	21.0	21.8	22.4	23.2	23.8	24.9	24.6
Bulgaria	5.4	4.8	4.2	4.2	4.5	5.1	5.4	5.4	5.4
Czech Republic	9.9	10.8	10.2	10.8	11.3	11.9	12.5	13.3	13.6
Denmark (incl. Greenland)	5.9	7.6	7.9	8.5	8.8	9.1	9.3	9.3	9.3
Finland	5.1	6.5	6.5	7.1	7.6	8.8	9.3	9.1	9.1
France	50.1	59.5	58.3	60.9	63.1	67.7	71.9	77.0	77.0
Germany	93.7	105.3	102.2	105.3	108.7	113.3	116.7	120.3	119.5
Greece	2.3	3.7	4.0	4.8	5.7	7.1	7.9	7.9	7.9
Hungary	13.9	16.1	17.0	19.3	21.2	23.5	24.4	24.9	24.6
Ireland	4.8	7.1	7.9	8.5	8.5	9.1	9.3	9.6	9.6
Italy	73.6	81.0	81.8	88.1	92.9	98.3	100.5	101.9	100.2
Netherlands	46.4	53.0	54.4	57.5	59.7	61.2	62.6	63.7	62.3
Norway	8.2	11.3	11.9	12.7	13.6	14.2	14.4	15.0	15.0
Poland	13.9	17.8	18.1	19.8	21.5	24.1	24.6	24.9	24.4
Portugal	3.4	6.8	8.2	9.6	10.5	11.0	11.3	11.3	11.3
Romania	19.3	19.3	19.0	20.7	22.7	25.8	26.6	27.5	27.2
Slovakia	7.9	8.8	8.8	9.1	9.3	9.6	9.6	9.6	9.3
Spain	24.1	40.5	46.4	54.1	58.3	62.6	63.4	64.6	64.0
Sweden	1.1	1.7	1.4	1.4	1.4	1.4	1.4	1.7	1.7
Switzerland	3.4	4.2	4.0	4.0	4.0	4.2	4.5	4.8	4.8
United Kingdom	103.9	119.2	121.5	126.0	129.4	134.5	138.8	141.3	136.2

Table 11.C (*cont.*)

	2002	2006	2010	2016	2020	2026	2030	2036	2040
FSU	**632.6**	**756.1**	**807.6**	**884.6**	**937.8**	**1016.3**	**1061.9**	**1083.4**	**1057.1**
Armenia	1.1	1.7	1.7	1.7	1.7	1.7	2.0	2.0	1.7
Azerbaijan	9.9	15.3	18.1	21.8	24.1	27.5	29.7	33.1	33.4
Belarus	18.1	21.0	21.5	22.1	22.7	23.8	24.1	22.9	22.1
Estonia	1.4	2.3	2.5	3.1	3.4	4.0	4.2	4.2	4.2
Georgia	1.4	2.5	3.1	3.7	4.2	4.5	4.8	5.1	4.8
Kazakhstan	16.7	21.2	22.7	25.2	27.5	30.9	32.8	35.7	37.4
Kyrgyzstan	2.3	3.4	4.2	5.4	5.9	7.1	7.9	8.2	8.2
Latvia	1.7	2.3	2.3	2.5	2.8	3.4	3.4	3.4	3.4
Lithuania	3.1	3.7	3.7	4.0	4.2	4.8	4.8	4.8	4.8
Moldova	2.3	3.1	3.4	3.7	4.0	4.0	4.0	4.0	3.7
Russia	427.6	510.8	546.8	598.0	632.0	681.0	710.7	715.3	688.4
Tajikistan	1.4	1.7	1.7	1.7	2.0	2.0	2.3	2.3	2.3
Turkmenistan	12.2	15.9	18.1	21.2	23.5	26.9	29.2	33.1	35.7
Ukraine	85.2	99.7	102.8	109.0	113.5	120.6	121.5	119.5	116.7
Uzbekistan	48.1	51.8	54.9	61.2	66.0	74.2	80.1	89.8	90.0
MIDDLE EAST	**250.3**	**288.8**	**301.0**	**334.4**	**364.7**	**416.0**	**453.3**	**507.7**	**536.0**
Bahrain	9.6	10.2	10.8	11.9	13.0	15.0	16.4	18.4	17.8
Iran	86.6	90.0	91.2	103.9	116.9	139.6	156.6	182.6	199.6
Iraq	1.7	3.1	3.4	5.4	7.4	11.0	14.2	18.7	21.5
Kuwait	9.3	10.5	10.5	10.8	11.6	13.0	14.2	15.9	17.0
Oman	6.8	8.5	9.6	11.0	12.2	13.9	15.3	17.0	18.4
Qatar	11.6	12.7	13.0	13.3	13.6	14.2	14.4	15.0	15.3
Saudi Arabia	61.4	72.5	75.6	82.4	88.1	97.4	104.5	115.0	122.0
Syria/Jordan	5.7	7.9	7.4	7.9	8.8	10.2	11.0	12.7	13.6

Turkey	19.3	27.2	30.3	36.0	40.5	47.3	52.1	56.9	55.2
UAE	37.9	46.4	48.7	50.7	51.5	52.7	53.0	53.0	53.2
Yemen	0.0	0.0	0.6	1.1	1.4	1.7	2.0	2.0	2.3
NORTH AMERICA	**783.8**	**922.6**	**904.7**	**916.9**	**939.0**	**1031.3**	**1101.8**	**1170.9**	*1159.0*
Canada	87.2	109.9	112.4	117.5	120.9	128.8	135.1	139.3	136.5
Mexico	45.6	57.5	60.9	69.9	76.5	87.2	95.4	105.9	109.6
United States	651.0	755.2	731.4	729.4	741.6	815.2	871.6	925.7	912.9
CENTRAL/SOUTH AMERICA	**107.3**	**136.8**	**149.5**	**172.4**	**189.2**	**216.3**	**231.6**	**251.5**	**261.1**
Argentina	30.9	36.2	39.4	45.9	50.7	58.3	62.3	67.1	68.5
Bolivia	1.1	1.7	2.3	2.5	2.8	3.4	3.7	4.0	4.0
Brazil	14.2	26.1	30.6	37.9	42.5	50.7	55.2	62.3	66.5
Central America	0.0	0.3	0.3	0.3	0.3	0.3	0.3	0.3	0.3
Chile	7.1	9.6	10.5	11.0	11.6	12.5	12.5	13.0	13.0
Colombia	5.4	7.6	8.5	9.3	10.2	11.0	11.9	12.2	10.8
Cuba	0.3	0.8	0.8	0.8	0.8	0.8	0.6	0.6	0.6
Ecuador	0.3	0.3	0.3	0.3	0.3	0.3	0.3	0.3	0.3
Other Caribbean	0.6	1.1	1.1	1.1	1.4	1.4	1.7	2.0	2.3
Paraguay	0.0	0.0	0.0	0.3	0.3	0.3	0.3	0.3	0.3
Peru	0.3	0.8	1.1	1.7	2.0	2.3	2.5	2.8	3.1
Suriname/Guyana/Fr. Guiana	0.0	0.0	0.3	0.6	0.6	0.8	0.8	0.8	0.8
Trinidad & Tobago	12.5	15.0	17.3	20.1	22.1	25.2	27.5	28.3	28.9
Uruguay	0.0	0.0	0.0	0.0	0.0	0.0	0.0	0.0	0.0
Venezuela	34.8	37.1	37.4	40.5	43.9	48.7	52.1	57.5	61.4
WORLD TOTAL	**2,723.5**	**3,280.8**	**3,417.0**	**3,718.5**	**3,958.1**	**4,384.3**	**4,651.8**	**4,899.3**	**4,891.4**

REFERENCES

Brito, Dagobert and Peter R. Hartley (2001). "Using Sakhalin natural gas in Japan," in *New Energy Technologies in the Natural Gas Sector: A Policy Framework for Japan*; available at http://www.rice.edu/energy/publications/newenergytechnologies_gassectors.html

CERA (2002). *The New Wave: Global LNG in the 21st Century*. Cambridge, MA: Cambridge Energy Research Associates

Dickson, Andrew and Ken Noble (2003). "Eastern Australia's gas supply and demand balance," *APPEA Journal*, Australian Petroleum Production and Exploration Association 43, pp. 135–145

EIA (2003a). "The global liquefied natural gas market: status and outlook." Washington DC: US Energy Information Administration

　(2003b). "Expansion and Change on the US Natural Gas Pipeline Network – 2002." Washington, DC: US Energy Information Association

　(2004). *International Energy Outlook 2004*. Washington, DC: US Energy Information Administration

Geosciences Australia (2001). *Oil and Gas Resources of Australia*

Hartley, Peter R. and Albert S. Kyle (1989). "Equilibrium investment in an industry with moderate investment economies of scale." *Economic Journal*, 99, pp. 392–407

IEA (2003). *World Energy Investment Outlook WEIO, 2003 Insights*. Paris: International Energy Agency

Medlock, Kenneth B., III and Ronald Soligo (2001). "Economic development and end-use energy demand." *Energy Journal*, 22(2), pp. 77–105

NPC (2003). "Balancing natural gas policy." Washington, DC: National Petroleum Council: available at http://www.npc.org

Summers, R., A. Heston *et al.* (1995). *The Penn World Table* (Mark 5.6a). Philadephia, DA: Centre for International comparisons at the university of Pennsylvania; available at http://put.econ.upenn.edu

USGS (2000). *United States Geological Survey World Petroleum Assessment*. Washington, DC: United States Geological Survey

12 Political and economic influences on the future world market for natural gas

Peter Hartley and Kenneth B. Medlock, III

Introduction

The base case model, discussed in chapter 11, assumed uniform rates of return across countries but allowed for different rates of return on different categories of investment. Specifically, we assumed that pipeline investments were least risky, followed by LNG regasification and lique-faction terminals, and then by mining projects (or exploration and development). The risk associated with pipeline investment is low as regulation often keeps the costs associated with transporting gas via pipeline quite stable. By contrast, since LNG liquefaction and regasification terminals embody less mature technologies, their costs of construction are likely to be more variable. Some of the risks associated with LNG, however, may be ameliorated by "bankable" contracts for LNG sales that limit variability in returns. The resource-mining projects are most risky because there is substantial geological uncertainty (such as initial reserve assessment, ultimate recoverability, and so forth), as well as economic uncertainty resulting from variation in commodity prices.

Assuming that rates of return on a given category of investment are uniform across countries ignores political factors that can greatly affect the risks of investing in different countries. These differing risks are a major reason that resources in some countries remain undeveloped. The relatively small amount of capital currently invested in such countries should make the return to capital relatively large and attract new investments, but the political risks may more than offset the higher expected return.

The reference case examined in this chapter allows rates of return on a given category of investment to vary across countries. The different

The authors thank David G. Victor and Mark H. Hayes for the GIRI numbers discussed below and for suggesting some scenarios based on a distillation of lessons learned from the case studies.

"risk-adjusted" rates of return in each country reflect various political factors – such as government stability, bureaucratic quality, corruption, internal conflict, and ethnic tensions. Although economic and geologic fundamentals may attract potential investors to certain locations, political factors such as these may reduce expected returns and discourage investments. All other features of the Baker Institute World Gas Trade Model (BIWGTM) remain unchanged from the base case. The reader therefore is referred to chapter 11 for details on how demand and supply and infrastructure costs were calculated.

After developing the reference case, we consider three scenarios. The first of which is a case in which selected political actions apart from the factors that are reflected in discount rates could prevent the development of certain projects. In particular, we consider a case where political barriers prevent the development of pipeline infrastructure from Russia to Northeast Asia.

We then examine two scenarios that illustrate how different economic assumptions can affect forecast outcomes. In particular, our forecasts embody conjectures about economic growth in different countries and the availability of alternative energy technologies that could compete with gas for market share. We consider two particular variations on these assumptions: one in which there is higher demand resulting from more rapid economic growth in China and another where more aggressive development of the backstop technology, such as integrated gas combined cycle (IGCC), erodes long-term demand for natural gas. Economic growth in China is of current interest since it has been cited as the major reason for recent surges in the world demand for raw materials and energy. We examine the effects of more rapid adoption of an alternative to natural gas because much of the recent growth in natural gas demand has been for power-generation and further developments in coal gasification, solar, wind, and other technologies could limit that source of demand growth.

The reference case reveals that variable rates of return influence which countries will emerge as key producers in the short-to-medium term. The particular variations we examine tend to disadvantage Iran to the largest extent. Longer term, those countries with large resource endowments eventually become the primary sources of global supply.

With regard to the scenario analyses, three central results emerge. First, a Northeast Asian natural gas pipeline network, or absence thereof, plays a pivotal role in natural gas price formation in Northeast Asia, and also for prices around the globe. Second, Chinese demand growth will prove critical to LNG developments, with Japan, South Korea, and the United States being most greatly affected on the demand side and Russia on the supply side. Third, the rapid emergence of alternative technologies would highlight principles of first-mover advantage and prevent gas resource monetization in some cases.

Calculating Risk-Adjusted Returns

We used two sources of information to calculate risk-adjusted returns for gas investments. The first is a composite measure of political risk borne by a private investor in each host country constructed using data from the *International Country Risk Guide (ICRG)*, published monthly by the PRS Group, Inc. The second is a data series on the "risk premium on lending" obtained from the World Bank (World Bank 2004). These two data sources were used to derive a set of country-specific risk premiums for investments in gas infrastructure relative to the United States. These differential risk premiums were then added to the real rates of return required on each type of gas investment in the United States to derive corresponding real rates of return for each country.

As in the selection of cases described in chapter 2, we constructed a "General Investment Risk Index" (GIRI) using a sub-set of the political risk variables tabulated in the ICRG. The index measures the risks for privately financed projects. Indeed, the ICRG data set is designed to help guide private investors. However, the large-scale, cross-border projects we are modeling involve strategic and foreign relations between countries in addition to domestic tax, regulatory and subsidy policies, or loan guarantees. Government stability and sovereign risk are thus likely to be the critical measures of risk.

The seven criteria extracted from the ICRG dataset were as follows:[1]

1. **Government Stability**: "A measure of the government's ability to carry out its declared program(s) and its ability to stay in office. This will depend on the type of governance, the cohesion of the government and the governing party or parties, the closeness of the next election, the government's command of the legislature, popular approval of government policies, and so on." **Scored 0–10, with lower scores for higher risks.**
2. **Investment Profile**: "This is a measure of the government's attitude to inward investment as determined by the assessment of four subcomponents: the risk to operations (scored from zero [very high risk] to four [very low risk]); taxation (scored from zero to three),

---

[1] Criteria definitions listed below are obtained from Howell (2001). Components were selected from the *ICRG* tables based on an expert assessment of their relative importance for an investor in gas infrastructure. Relative weights of the different components have been retained from the *ICRG* index.

repatriation (scored from zero to three), and labor costs (scored from zero to two)." **Scored 0–20 (double weighting for each sub-component), with lower scores for higher risks.**

3. **Internal Conflict**: "This is an assessment of political violence in the country and its actual or potential impact on governance. The highest rating is given to those countries where there is no armed opposition to the government, and the government does not engage in arbitrary violence, direct or indirect, against its own people. The lowest rating is given to a country embroiled in an ongoing civil war." Intermediate ratings take into account kidnapping and terrorist threats. **Scored 0–10, with lower scores for higher risks.**

4. **Corruption**: Incorporates "the most common form of corruption" such as bribes and protection payments, but is more focused on "actual or potential corruption in the form of excessive patronage, nepotism . . . and suspiciously close ties between politics and business." **Scored 0–10, with lower scores for indicating higher levels of corruption.**

5. **Law and Order**: "Law and Order are assessed separately, with each sub-component comprising [zero–seven] points. The Law sub-component is an assessment of the strength and impartiality of the legal system, while the Order sub-component is an assessment of popular observance of the law." **Scored 0–20, with lower scores indicating a less established legal system.**

6. **Ethnic Tensions**: "This component measures the degree of tension within a country attributable to racial, nationality, or language divisions." This may be particularly important where an infrastructure investment may span a particular ethnic enclave, creating potential for shutdown due to uprisings or hold up. **Scored 0–10, with lower scores for higher risks.**

7. **Bureaucratic Quality**: "The institutional strength and quality of the bureaucracy is another shock absorber that tends to minimize the revisions of policy when governments change. Therefore, high points are given to countries where the bureaucracy has the strength and expertise to govern without drastic changes in policy or interruptions in government services." **Scored 0–20, lower scores indicating a less efficient bureaucracy with greater political interference.**

The values of the above variables for November 2002 (the latest month that was available) were then summed and divided by 10 to give a total score from 0 to 10, with lower numbers corresponding to higher risk. The resulting index number for each country is referred to as the "General Investment Risk Index" (GIRI).

We used data on the risk premium on lending from the World Bank *World Development Indicators* to convert the GIRI score to a required rate of return (World Bank 2004). While the risk premium on lending reported by the World Bank is not specific to natural gas investments, it does reflect the relative risks associated with investments across countries. Regressing the average risk premium from 1999–2003 on the GIRI scores yields a rule by which GIRI scores can be mapped to interest rates.[2] This allows the factors underlying the GIRI scores, which are targeted to measuring political risks relevant to the natural gas industry, to be converted to an interest rate. In addition, while the World Bank data are available for only sixty-five countries, the GIRI scores are available for 140 countries. The regression therefore allows the World Bank data to be extended to the additional countries. The results of the regression are as follows (standard errors in parentheses):[3]

$$\rho = 15.001 - 1.359 GIRI$$
$$(3.015)(0.442). \tag{12.1}$$

From the regression analysis, we see that a lower GIRI score, which by construction corresponds to higher risk, is associated with a higher country risk premium, and the relationship is statistically significant. For example, GIRI scores range from 0 to 10, indicating that the country risk premium, ρ, will range from 15.0 to 1.4. This provides a fairly wide range of required returns on investment across countries. The risk premium in each country, which is given in table 12.A in the appendix, is the predicted value from the regression (Equation 12.1) for that country's GIRI. To obtain a country's return on equity for a given investment category, we then add the calculated risk premium for that country *relative to the United States* to the required return on equity in the United States for that type of investment.

The leverage for each type of investment is taken to be the same in each country.[4] A primary justification for assuming that some types of

[2] The main motivation for using an average risk premium as the dependent variable in this regression is that it helps minimize the effect of short-term macroeconomic instabilities. In addition, many countries have incomplete time series. Using the average of the non-missing values in a five-year window produces a larger sample.

[3] The number of observations was sixty-five, the $R^2 = 0.131$ and the t-test for the significance of the slope coefficient has a p-value of 0.003.

[4] Thus, given the debt:equity ratios assumed for each project type, the risk adjustment affects the required return on pipelines least, followed by LNG infrastructure, and finally mining operations.

investments are more highly levered is that returns on those investments are usually regulated. On the one hand, a lower variability of cash flow in a regulated activity raises its debt capacity. On the other hand, regulation also limits the extent to which average returns can rise. In reality, the debt capacity of similar types of projects may vary across countries. However, absent data on these variations we chose to leave them uniform.

We also do not allow country risk premiums to affect the return to debt. There are a number of justifications for assuming a uniform return to debt but a variable equity return. First, debt financing is either backed by government guarantees (in the case of national energy companies, for example) or by the balance sheet of the firm undertaking the project. Accordingly, the premium on debt primarily reflects default risk and not project risk. Second, many of these projects include government guarantees, export credits, and other complex financing arrangements that lower investor exposure and reduce any risk premium that third parties may otherwise require. Nevertheless, equity returns, being a residual claim, are vulnerable to *ex post* changes in rules. Debt returns, being a legal obligation, are much less vulnerable to such sovereign risks. Indeed, one reason that large international firms finance a substantial part of the investment via borrowing is precisely because the bond contracts are enforceable in US courts. Third, the World Bank data reflect currency risk among other factors. While many of the large international energy bond deals are syndicated in the United States under US law and floated in US dollars, currency risk will affect the return to equity to the extent that earnings are exchanged for dollars before repatriation.

Our approach is deliberately conservative. We limit the impact of variation in returns because the model generates long-term forecasts. Serious questions can be raised about the predictability of future risk premiums. For example, what would people have said in 1985 about the likely risk premium relevant for investing in China in 2005?

We also do not want to overstate the empirical relevance of our scenario. There are many other plausible ways of altering risk premiums to account for political risk factors. The strongest argument for our approach is that a uniform change of some sort is easier to comprehend. If many relative values are changed at once, it is more difficult to understand what outcome may be due to which particular variable change. Our approach allows the political risk premiums to magnify existing risks in a simple and systematic way. Moreover, by applying the adjustment to equity returns only, we highlight how political factors can differentially affect incentives to invest in pipeline versus LNG versus resource developments.

The Reference Case Solution (Adjusting for Risk)

By way of comparison to the base case, in the near term (through roughly the middle of the 2010) the risk-adjusted rates make little discernible difference to supply, both across countries and over time. As time progresses, however, adjusting for risk renders global supply slightly lower in the reference case relative to the base case, while the composition of supply by country also changes. Figure 12.1 indicates the supply projections in the reference case by regional grouping.

In general, adjusting for risk by using higher required rates of return on investment increases natural gas prices and reduces demand across all regions and countries (see figure 12.1). This occurs as producers with-hold supplies until prices are driven up to support the higher returns on investment.

On the supply side, adjusting for risk most noticeably reduces production in Iran and, to a lesser extent, in Russia.[5] Russia, however, continues to play a pivotal role in the global natural gas market. It supplies large amounts of gas to consuming markets in both the Atlantic and Pacific Basins by both pipeline and LNG. As in the base case (where returns are uniform), East Siberian gas begins flowing into Northern China at the beginning of the 2010s and eventually into the Korean peninsula. Furthermore, in the 2030s, northeast Asian demand again grows sufficiently to draw supply from as far as West Siberia. In contrast to the base case, however, the reference case indicates the construction of a pipeline linking West Siberia to East Siberia much earlier, allowing East Siberian supplies to flow *west* from 2012 to the mid-2020s. This development reflects in part a response to a reduced supply of pipeline gas from Iran into Europe. Another contributing factor is the increased supply of LNG from Australia, particularly during the decade from 2020–2030. Much of this Australian gas is shipped to Northeast Asia as higher required returns in Russia generally raise prices in those markets.

As regards international trade in natural gas, the greatest change is a reduction in exports from Iran (see figure 12.1 – Natural gas trade). There are other discernible impacts as well. For example, Russia sees its exports grow more slowly, whereas Australia, a relatively low-risk supplier, exports more natural gas earlier in the model time horizon. In addition, Canadian exports to the United States are more robust for a

---

[5] Although table 12.1 indicates that the risk premium in Iran is smaller than in Russia, Iran has less infrastructure already in place and hence the higher required return has a larger effect on overall export capacity.

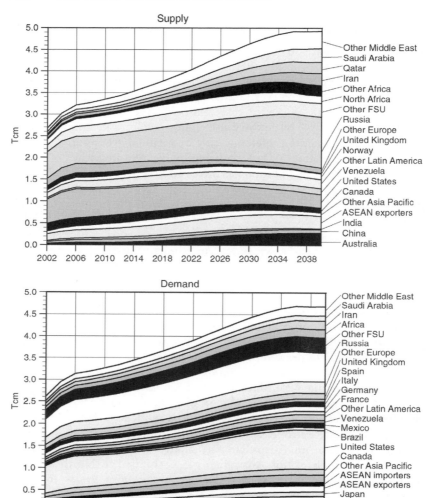

Figure 12.1. Reference case results, 2002–2040 – supply and demand.

longer period. This occurs because LNG imports into the United States (Pacific and Atlantic Coasts) are noticeably lower after adjusting for risk. When equity returns are uniform, as in the base case, substantial LNG supplies come from high-risk regions such as Iran, Nigeria, Angola, and

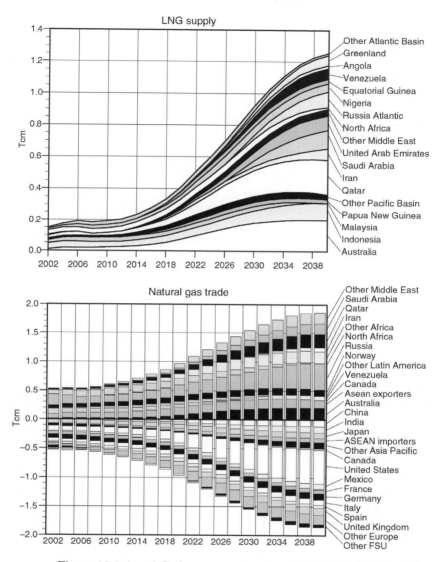

Figure 12.1 (*cont.*) Reference case results, 2002–2040. LNG supply and natural gas trade.

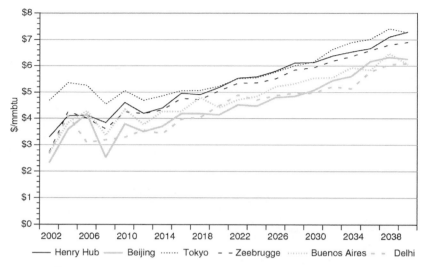

Figure 12.2. Reference case selected prices, 2002– 2040.

Venezuela. Higher risk delays investment in these regions, which in turn reduces LNG supply. Thus, the United States must turn to other sources, most notably pipeline imports from Canada, to sate demand.

In contrast to the United States, LNG imports into China are slightly higher in the reference case. Raising the required returns on investing in pipelines from Russia to China makes LNG more attractive at the margin. This is particularly so when a relatively low-risk supplier, such as Australia, can supply LNG to China at a relatively low cost. In fact, Australia gains a larger overall market share of LNG exports at the expense of Iran, Nigeria, and Angola (all relatively high-risk areas). In an intertemporal equilibrium, projects in the latter countries are delayed until prices rise sufficiently to allow investments to earn the higher required rates of return.

Since higher rates of return delay investments and reduce available supply, prices are generally higher in the reference case relative to the base case, rising above $7/mmbtu in both Tokyo and at the Henry Hub before 2040 (see figure 12.2). Another discernible difference is that the dispersion in prices across locations is somewhat lower in the reference case. In particular, prices in Beijing and Delhi are closer to prices in the other areas. In the base case, each of these regions receives supplies from relatively high-risk areas (Beijing by pipe from Russia, and Delhi by pipe from Iran), which keeps prices relatively low. A higher risk premium on those infrastructure developments, as in the reference case, delays those supplies coming to market. The resulting higher prices in China and India attract more LNG imports, more closely connecting their prices to those of other countries competing for LNG. Prices at Zeebrugge and the Henry Hub are also somewhat closer in most years in the reference case. Since Europe receives much of its gas supplies from Russia and North Africa in the base case, higher risk in these regions will delay investments and raise prices. This, in turn, will increase competition in the Atlantic Basin for LNG supplies, and more closely link prices in North America and Europe as LNG suppliers arbitrage between the two markets.

There is also an indication that the cycles in prices are somewhat shorter in the reference case relative to the base case. With higher required rates of return, investments will generally be smaller and more frequent.[6] This in turn will lead to the more frequent price fluctuations.

Political Scenario: No Pipelines from Russia to Northeast Asia

In this section we examine a politically motivated deviation from the reference case. Specifically, we investigate the effect of disputes that prevent the construction of critical international pipelines in Northeast Asia. Obviously, countries that would otherwise benefit from such pipelines are affected by their absence. In general, both the exporting and the importing country are worse off, although the welfare losses need not be shared equally as they depend on alternative sources of supply for the importing country and alternative export markets for the exporting country. In addition, while the effect of eliminating large international pipelines will influence those nations directly involved, we also find that there are secondary effects on countries *not* directly involved in the projects.

Eastern Siberia has substantial gas reserves and undiscovered potential. South Korea and Japan have substantial demand, with virtually no indigenous reserves. Although China has some domestic gas resource, most of it is not well positioned to serve demand, particularly in the southeast, absent significant infrastructure development. Moreover, Chinese demand will soon outstrip available domestic supplies, leading

---

[6] This conclusion follows, for example, from the theoretical model discussed in Hartley and Kyle (1989).

to a substantial appetite for gas imports. In terms of geography and economic and geological fundamentals, the relationship between Russia and Northeast Asia resembles the relationships between regions in North America such as Alberta and Chicago, or South Texas and Miami, that currently are linked by long-haul pipelines covering distances not too dissimilar from Kovytka (Russia) to South Korea. This, in fact, is brought to bear in the reference case as early in the model time horizon reserves in East Siberia can satisfy Northeast Asian demand at a price that is competitive with imported LNG. Toward the end of the time horizon, the cost of adding to East Siberian reserves exceeds the cost of shipping gas from West Siberia, which results in gas flowing from West Siberia into the then developed Northeast Asian pipeline grid. Thus, in the reference case, pipeline gas from Russia supplies a substantial fraction of Northeast Asian demand.

Political relations between Canada and the United States and between states within the United States are much closer and more stable than relations between Russia, China, North Korea, and South Korea. Accordingly, political tensions could easily stymie development of a pipeline connecting East Siberian gas resources to China. Moreover, any pipeline from Russia to South Korea would most likely have to pass through North Korea, making it an unlikely event for some time.

The first scenario disallows any pipelines connecting Russia to China or Russia to South Korea. We also rule out the pipeline from Uzbekistan to China because it provides an alternative route, albeit indirect, for gas sales from the Volga–Urals region in Russia to China. The scenario assumes, however, that a pipeline can still be built from Sakhalin Island to Japan.

In the absence of a pipeline connecting East Siberia to China and Korea, Russian producers will seek alternative outlets for their gas. Two options include constructing a pipeline to Nahodka to export gas as LNG or constructing a pipeline from East Siberia to Europe via West Siberia.

Although a pipeline to Nahodka is possible, the model predicts that this will not happen. LNG supplies from Southeast Asia and Australia and pipeline supplies from West China have lower costs. Instead, East Siberian gas is eventually transported to the West.

Pipeline gas exports to Japan from Sakhalin Island also increase relative to the reference case. Eliminating the pipelines from Nahodka to South Korea and Nahodka to Northeast China renders the pipeline from Sakhalin to Nahodka uneconomic, thus freeing up additional Sakhalin gas for export to Japan.

While Russia is the major supplier disadvantaged by not allowing the Russia–China and Russia–Korea pipelines, other countries affected include Saudi Arabia, Nigeria, and Iraq (see figure 12.3). Increased Russian pipeline exports to Europe displace some exports from these countries.

Despite increased exports to Europe, Russian production is lower absent pipeline infrastructure to Asia. For East Siberian supplies to be monetized they must be either be moved to Western Siberia to access existing infrastructure or they must be moved to Nahodka for liquefaction. The former option disadvantages East Siberian resources relative to other supply options due to the cost of long-haul transportation, and the latter option is very capital-intensive as both pipeline and liquefaction infrastructure must be built. Thus, while East Siberian resources are eventually exploited, they are not exploited to the same extent as in the reference case.

Since China has proved reserves and geologic potential, the elimination of cheap pipeline imports from Russia results in an expansion of Chinese domestic production. The opportunities to replace imports with domestic supply are, however, somewhat limited. Domestic supply responds positively early in the time horizon and even more strongly from around 2016–2030, but by the mid-2030s geological factors limit Chinese domestic supply.

Prominent among the countries where domestic production responds positively to the absence of Northeast Asian pipelines are Australia, the United States, and Indonesia in the short to medium term, and Iran, Qatar, and Azerbaijan in the longer term. Several of these countries are well placed to supply more LNG to South Korea and China. As Northeast Asia turns to LNG, increased competition for LNG drives up prices everywhere. At the margin, this favors more costly production. In some countries, the supply response is better characterized as a shift in the intertemporal pattern of production rather than a change in aggregate supply. Although higher prices accelerate production outside of East Siberia in the short run, the faster rate of resource depletion also raises the cost of developing future supply. This then encourages the development of East Siberian supplies, but at a later date. Examples where production is accelerated include Norway, Bahrain, Venezuela, Brazil, and Turkmenistan.[7]

---

[7] In another scenario that we do not report in detail, we ruled out the Pakistan–India pipeline in addition to the pipelines from Russia to China and South Korea. The Pakistan–India pipeline also carries substantial gas in the reference case solution and is another project that would be vulnerable to political disruption. The general pattern of

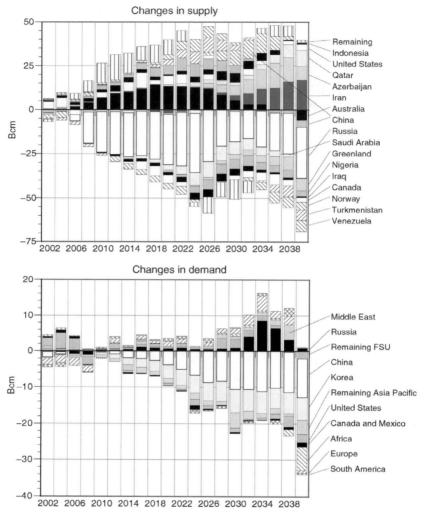

Figure 12.3. No pipelines from Russia to northeast Asia: results, 2002–2040 – changes in total gas supply and demand.

supply response is similar in the two cases, although responses from each country tend to be larger when the Pakistan–India pipeline also is ruled out. Particularly noteworthy is that US production is considerably higher beyond 2028. As we note below, India also becomes a large importer of LNG in this scenario, and the higher LNG prices encourage more US domestic production and fewer LNG imports.

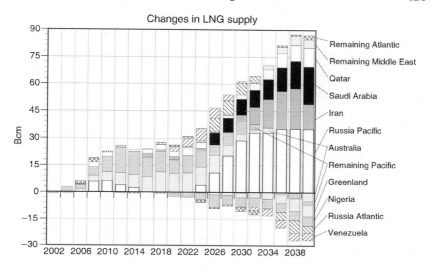

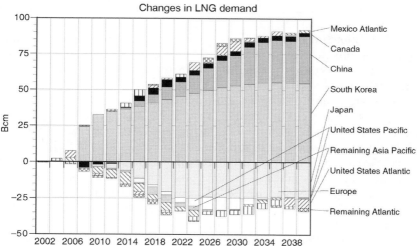

Figure 12.3 (*cont.*) No pipelines from Russia to northeast Asia: results, 2002–2040 – changes in LNG supply and demand.

Relative to the reference case, China and South Korea substantially increase their LNG import capacity (see figure 12.3). One consequence is a large expansion of LNG exports in the Russian Pacific relative to the reference case (see figure 12.3). The increase occurs later than LNG expansions in Australia and Southeast Asia, which partially fill the void left by a reduction in Russian pipeline gas supply to Northeast Asia. As prices rise, Sakhalin LNG becomes increasingly profitable, and LNG exports from Sakhalin Island grow substantially in the later time periods. The absence of a pipeline from Sakhalin to China and South Korea, via Nahodka, also helps to facilitate the increase in LNG supply from Sakhalin. At first glance, the increased export of LNG in the Russian Pacific might appear inconsistent with the notion underlying the original experiment. If China, Japan, and South Korea decline to import gas via pipeline from Russia, why would they import Russian gas as LNG instead? The answer lies in the real option that LNG imports provide. A pipeline will connect countries as supplier and customer much more firmly than LNG, and could require agreement from transit countries. Importing countries relying on LNG have an option to turn to alternative suppliers. This option does not exist with pipelines.

Higher LNG prices relative to the reference case also encourage the flow of pipeline gas from Malaysia to mainland Southeast Asia in addition to increased export of LNG from Papua New Guinea, Brunei, Indonesia, Australia, and Middle Eastern countries such as Iran, Saudi Arabia, Qatar, and Oman (see figure 12.3).[8] As noted above, overall Saudi production falls as increased competition from Russian pipeline gas in Europe decreases the demand for Saudi exports via pipe through Syria and Turkey, but some of the displaced resource reappears as increased LNG.

Restricted pipeline construction in Northeast Asia also affects the Americas. Increased competition for Pacific Basin LNG supplies reduces LNG imports into the US Pacific coast. However, LNG imports into the US Atlantic coast and Canada increase. This is facilitated by increased exports of LNG from Russia to the Atlantic Basin as the absence of export outlets to the East pushes gas volumes to the West.

An increase in Venezuelan LNG exports, which are supported by higher prices for LNG relative to the reference case, contributes to the rise in US Atlantic Basin LNG imports. As Asian markets attract LNG supplies, some Middle Eastern production that flows to the Atlantic in the reference case flows to the Pacific instead. South American, West African, and even Russian LNG expand to fill the void in the Atlantic.

---

[8] In the scenario where the Pakistan–India pipeline also is ruled out, India becomes a larger importer of LNG than China from 2026–2038. India can still import gas via pipeline from the East, however, and in consequence Thailand also imports more LNG when the Pakistan–India pipeline also is ruled out. On the other hand, the United Kingdom, Belgium, Italy, and France import less LNG than when only Northeast Asian pipelines are constrained.

We also see that Mexican LNG imports from the Atlantic Basin decline. This is facilitated by increased production in northern South America, which allows more aggressive development of pipeline import infrastructure into Mexico through Central America.[9]

Global demand changes by less than one quadrillion Btus (approximately 26 Bcm[10]) in most years relative to the reference case, indicating that the marginal supplies from Russia are capturing market share without having a significant impact on price (see figure 12.3). Nevertheless, China and South Korea do not find perfect substitutes for the lost Russian imports, and demand in those countries declines. We do see, however, a modest increase in demand in Russia, Ukraine, Belarus, Azerbaijan, Uzbekistan, Germany, and other European countries that import gas from Russia. This occurs because East Siberian gas raises volumes flowing through Western Russia and lowers prices in Russia relative to the reference case.

Figure 12.4 indicates the price changes relative to the reference case for all of the scenarios being considered. We see that reduced pipeline imports of natural gas to China from Eastern Russia raise gas prices in Beijing, as China must rely on LNG to meet demand.[11] Tokyo also sees slightly higher prices on average while in Zeebrugge average prices over the whole period decline slightly (in real terms). Another point worth noting is that the expanded LNG trade that results from a lack of Northeast Asian pipelines more closely links prices in a greater number of markets to arbitrage points lying offshore, thereby causing more rapid convergence of prices.[12]

Economic Scenario 1: Higher Chinese Demand Growth

In our first alternative economic scenario, we increase demand growth in China by allowing for more rapid economic progress. Specifically, we assume that the recent experience in China carries more weight in

[9] In the scenario where the Pakistan–India pipeline also is ruled out, demand in India also declines relative to the reference case, while demand in Pakistan increases. Demand changes in the United Kingdom and Germany also become more consistently positive. Also, while the United States shows somewhat larger declines in consumption from 2014–2026, US demand actually expands relative to the reference case from 2032–2040.

[10] Assuming 36,000 Btus per m³ of natural gas.

[11] The large swings in prices result from shifts in the timing of large infrastructure investments.

[12] If the Pakistan–India pipeline also is ruled out, prices in New Delhi and Beijing increase by a similar amount from 2024. The difference in price changes in the remaining cities also becomes much less volatile from 2024 as the even greater role of LNG trade in the world gas market helps to link prices across regions.

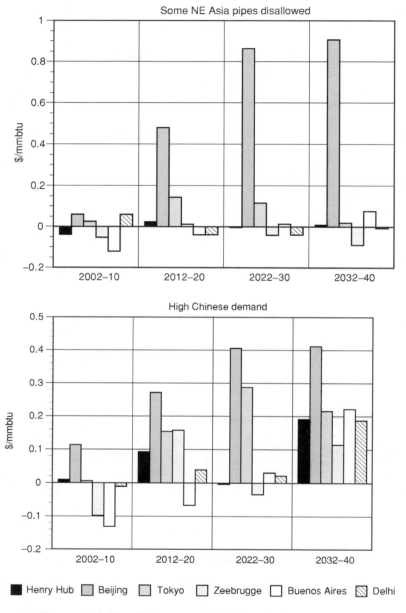

Figure 12.4. Decadal average price changes from the reference case, 2002–2040 – *top*: some northeast Asia pipes disallowed and *below*: high Chinese demand.

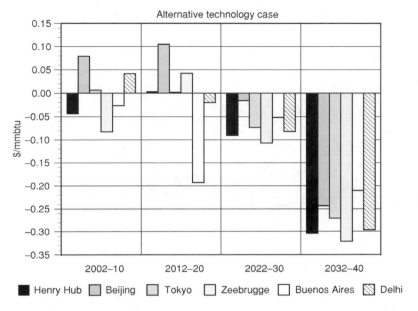

Figure 12.4 (*cont.*) Decadal average price changes from the reference case, 2002–2040 – alternative technology case.

determining future economic growth.[13] Average annual real GDP growth in China from 2002–2040 is 3.4 percent in the reference case, compared with 5.1 percent in the high-growth case. In the reference case, the average annual real GDP growth rates, by decade, are 4.7 percent from 2002–2010, 3.3 percent from 2010–2020, 3.0 percent from 2020–2030, and 2.4 percent from 2030–2040. By contrast, in the high-growth case they are 6.9 percent from 2002–2010, 5.5 percent from 2010–2020, 4.4 percent from 2020–2030, and 3.2 percent from 2030–2040.

Figure 12.5 shows the major changes in demand across the globe resulting from the higher Chinese economic growth. Not surprisingly, higher Chinese demand for natural gas is the dominant feature of figure 12.5. In fact, demand in almost all other countries is reduced, largely because increased demand for LNG from China raises the price of LNG

[13] In technical terms, we chose a country-specific coefficient for China in the growth equation (estimated in chapter 11) to reflect China's recent growth experience more than its sample average one. Data from 2002–2005 indicate that China has continued to grow at high rates, but there may still be room for doubt that those high rates can continue for many decades, particularly in the absence of fundamental reform in the Chinese political and legal framework.

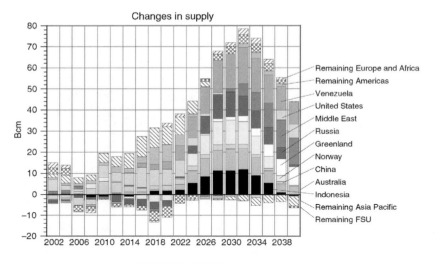

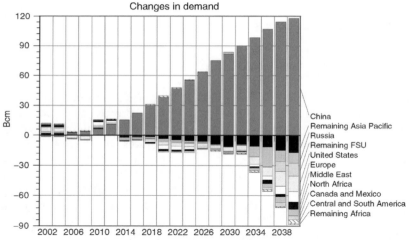

Figure 12.5. Higher Chinese demand growth results, 2002–2040 – changes in total gas supply and demand.

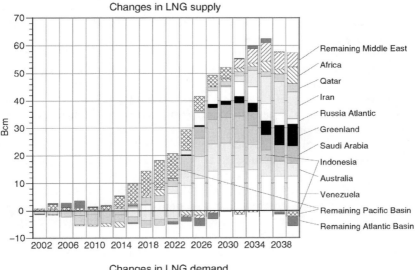

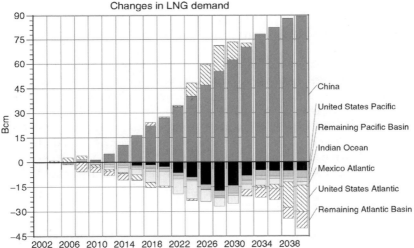

Figure 12.5 (*cont.*) Higher Chinese demand growth results, 2002–2040 – changes in LNG supply and demand.

globally, thereby reducing the call on gas elsewhere across the globe. The largest demand reductions occur in the marginal suppliers to China (Russia, Uzbekistan, Kazakhstan, and Iran) and the closest competitors for imports to China (Japan and South Korea, and the United States). Higher prices in China are transmitted more directly to these countries.

Demand also falls in Egypt and Algeria because increased Russian exports to the East raise the demand for North African gas in Europe, thus raising prices in both North Africa and Europe.

We also see in figure 12.5 that the increases in demand in China begin to slow in the later time periods despite the higher rate of economic growth. This results from the direct effect on demand of price increases and more rapid adoption of the backstop technology. Since the demand shock originates in China, it is perhaps not surprising that the greatest change in the use of the backstop technology also occurs in China. Other countries that respond to higher prices by using the backstop earlier than in the reference case include Russia, the United States, Uzbekistan, Kazakhstan, Azerbaijan, and Egypt.

The reductions in demand from other countries are insufficient to accommodate the increased Chinese demand absent an increase in global production. The most significant increases in supply tend to come from those countries that can supply LNG to the global market (see figure 12.5). Moreover, the countries that increase production tend to be distributed across the globe, indicating the intricate relationships that may evolve between supply and demand in a global market. For example, while it is not surprising that increased demand in China prompts increased production in Russia, Australia, and Indonesia, with the latter two increasing exports of LNG, it is more surprising to see strong supply responses from Venezuela, and Norway. The diversion of Russian and Middle Eastern resources toward China allows both Venezuela and Norway to capture market share in the Atlantic Basin markets.

Increased demand for LNG drives up prices to varying degrees everywhere, thereby encouraging additional production.[14] In addition to Russia, Australia, Indonesia, Venezuela and Norway, we also see production increases in Papua New Guinea, Greenland, Qatar, and Algeria, all of whom, in the reference case, are major LNG exporters. There are also notable increases in production in the United States, Mexico and, not surprisingly, China.

Figure 12.5 indicates that, in most periods, the *net* changes in total natural gas supply (where net changes are defined as the sum of supply increases minus the sum of supply decreases across cases) substantially

---

[14] Although some countries reduce supply in some years, each of these countries increases supply in other years. Hence, the reductions are best thought of as intertemporal shifts in the pattern of production rather than overall declines. The relatively large "remaining" category of supply increases in these years also implies that many countries exploit their reserves more heavily in the early years, although the supply change in any one country in any one year is not large.

exceed the net changes in LNG supply over the same period.[15] This can happen only if there are increased pipeline flows. Conversely, when the net change in LNG supply is larger, as in the late 2030s, higher prices encourage export to China in particular.

Much of the increased LNG supply is ultimately destined for China, where we see a large increase in LNG imports relative to the reference case (see figure 12.5). Chinese LNG imports slow beyond 2030, partly due to increased use of the backstop technology but also because increased imports of pipeline gas from Russia reduce the need for incremental LNG.

Higher demand for Pacific Basin LNG resulting from increased Chinese imports negatively impacts some other large Pacific Basin LNG importers. In particular, imports into the US Pacific decline. It is interesting, however, that imports into the US Atlantic rise. This occurs as the "arbitrage point" in the United States gas pipeline network shifts further west, allowing some Atlantic Basin LNG (through displacement of supplies from Alaska, Alberta, and the San Juan and Permian Basins) to indirectly satisfy demand in the western United States. Increased imports in the US Atlantic, in turn, negatively affect other Atlantic Basin LNG importers, such as Italy, the United Kingdom, Belgium, Canada, and Mexico.

At first glance, it is somewhat surprising to see South Korean imports of LNG rise, which occurs despite lower demand in South Korea. The explanation is that pipeline flows from Russia do not penetrate the Korean peninsula as heavily as in the reference case. Higher Chinese demand, and flow of East Siberian resources into China, would require more rapid extraction, and hence depletion, in East Siberia in order to achieve the same level of pipeline flows to South Korea. This would, however, raise the cost of pipeline gas to South Korea, which makes LNG a less costly marginal source of supply.

As seen in figure 12.4, higher Chinese growth drives up gas prices around the world, particularly beyond 2010. In addition, while the largest impact is on prices in Beijing, followed by Tokyo, the increasing integration of the world gas market through greater LNG trade leads to similar price increases in all locations beyond the mid-2030s.

---

[15] A similar argument applies to each country considered individually. For example, the relatively large changes in Iranian LNG exports in the 2030s are not matched by a similar increase in overall Iranian production. The additional LNG comes largely from a reduction in pipeline exports from Iran.

Economic Scenario 2: Alternative Technology

The final scenario examines the effects of a negative change in the demand for natural gas. Specifically, we assume that alternative technology becomes available just as in the other cases, but at a lower price of $4/mmbtu. Such an outcome might occur, for example, if a breakthrough in coal gasification, nuclear power, solar technology, or some other technology for generating electricity reduces the demand for natural gas as an input into electricity-generation.

The new technology path has two main effects. As the technology enters the market, it takes away market share from natural gas, which directly reduces gas demand. Because the alternative technology has a lower cost, it also produces a lower long-term price for natural gas. Rational producers, knowing that future prices will be lower, exploit gas resources more aggressively in the near term.[16] This transfers the lower future prices back to earlier periods, although time discounting diminishes the impact as we move further from the year in which the cost of the alternative technology effectively pegs the gas price. In addition, some gas that would have been produced in the reference case never gets produced under the alternative technology assumption, simply because prices are never high enough to justify development.

Figure 12.6 illustrates how the alternative technology case changes the demand for the backstop technology up to 2040. Countries with the largest changes have been separately identified, while countries with smaller changes have been grouped into regional categories. The type of pattern we see in Russia could result if increased adoption of the backstop in natural gas importing markets displaces gas back to the producing country. Aside from resulting in fewer resources being developed, this lowers the price of gas in Russia and makes it competitive with the alternative for a longer period of time. In fact, with more rapid adoption of the alternative technology, long-term import requirements to supply-deficit locations are diminished, and natural gas is primarily consumed only in locations where it is relatively abundant.

Relative to the reference case, we see that aggregate gas supply declines after 2020 (see figure 12.7). Prior to 2020, however, it increases in

---

[16] This is a basic result of the depletable resource economics. If there exists an alternative that can be made available at a lower price, the opportunity cost of mining the depletable resource is reduced. If one thinks of the depletable resource as an asset, lower long-term prices will render some of the resource valueless. Thus, we shall maximize the value of the portion of the asset that is economically competitive by extracting as much as we can in the finite time it will be used.

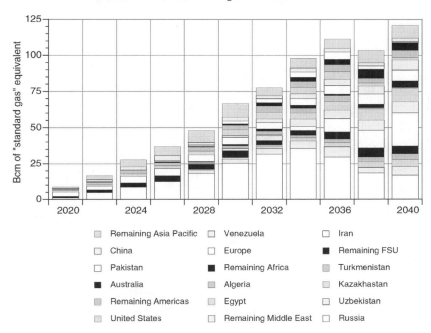

Figure 12.6. Changes in backstop demand, alternative technology case, 2020–2040.

most years as production is accelerated. In a few countries – notably Iran, Venezuela, and Norway – supply expands substantially. As with previous scenarios, these expansions result primarily from local substitutions between suppliers. For example, Iran expands exports in the near term by replacing resources from Saudi Arabia since development in Saudi Arabia is more sensitive to the lower prices. Thus, Saudi Arabia's ability to monetize its gas resources is severely diminished when an alternative technology enters the market at a lower price.

In Iran, the increase in production appears primarily as LNG. This occurs as the development of Iranian supply is shifted forward in time relative to the reference case.[17] Since most of the expanding LNG sources ship into the Atlantic Basin, marginal suppliers in that basin,

[17] It is worth noting here that in the reference case Iranian production does grow in years beyond 2040. However, we do not focus on those results as the analysis here is concerned only with years up to 2040.

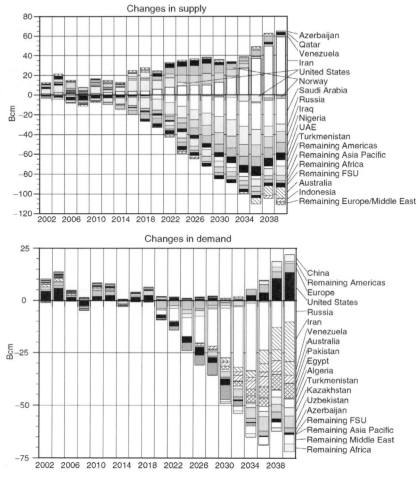

Figure 12.7. Alternative technology case results, 2002–2040 – changes in total gas supply and demand.

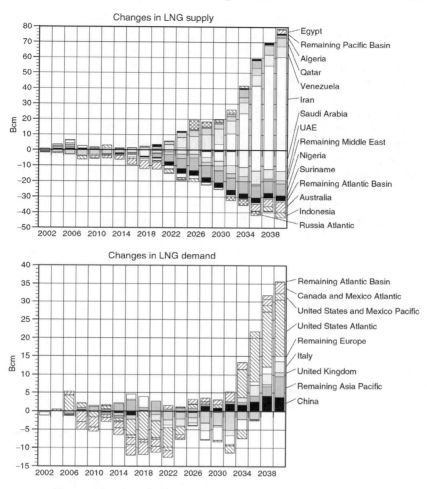

Figure 12.7 (*cont.*) Alternative technology case results, 2002–2040 – changes in LNG supply and demand.

such as Nigeria, reduce output. The changes in supply from major Pacific Basin LNG suppliers, such as Australia and Indonesia, are generally smaller and increase in some years while decreasing in others. Some of the expanded Middle East supply, however, is transported to the Pacific Basin as Japan and China increase LNG imports somewhat, particularly from the mid-2020s.

While the United States imports less LNG between the mid-2010s and the mid-2020s, it imports more in other years, and substantially so into the Atlantic coast after the mid-2030s. Some other Atlantic Basin importers, particularly the United Kingdom and Ireland show reduced LNG imports in most years. Italy, Belgium, Spain, Mexico, and Argentina display a more variable pattern of responses with LNG imports increasing in some years and declining in others.

As indicated in figure 12.4, prices in the alternative technology case are not affected systematically until after 2020, at which point they begin a steady decline relative to the reference case. Increasing adoption of the backstop technology, as seen in figure 12.6, facilitates this steady decline.

On a more speculative note, the more rapid adoption of alternative technologies could also prove to be a long-run impediment to the likelihood that a natural gas cartel could develop. In particular, it could reduce global reliance on a few regions (Russia and the Middle East) with an abundance of natural gas supply.

Concluding Remarks

Although the basic patterns of natural gas supply and demand in the reference case do not differ dramatically from those in the base case, some interesting generalizations can be made about demonstrated impacts. First, since higher required returns delay new investments but do not affect the use of existing infrastructure, supply is reduced most in countries with high required returns and little infrastructure in place. Second, the decrease in production from regions with high risk is compensated by an increase in higher cost supply from relatively low-risk developed countries, which tends to raise price everywhere. Third, the resulting higher prices tend to reduce demand in every region.

To indicate the types of analyses that can be performed with the BIWGTM, we chose three scenarios that could be compared to the reference case. We compared to the reference case because, as the World Bank data and regression analysis of the GIRI data show, required returns vary considerably from one country to the next and political risk plays a significant role in determining these return differentials. To the extent that these political risks remain fixed through time, it is more realistic to construct alternative scenarios taking those risks into account.

The first scenario prohibits the development of a pipeline network in Northeast Asia, thereby precluding the flow of gas from East Siberia to China and the Korean peninsula and constraining the development of

East Siberian reserves. With this pipeline option eliminated, a larger percentage of the resources must flow to the West, which raises the costs of getting them to market. Thus, East Siberian development must be delayed until prices increase sufficiently to support the necessary infrastructure. In addition, Northeast Asia turns increasingly to LNG to sate demand, which raises LNG prices everywhere and stimulates increased production from marginal suppliers of LNG, particularly in the Pacific Basin.

We then considered two scenarios that examined changes in assumptions regarding economic variables affecting the demand for natural gas. In the first, we allowed China to grow at a faster rate, which substantially raises long-term gas demand. This demand is met by both increased pipeline imports from Russia and increased LNG imports. The net effect is an increase in global prices, which promotes increased production by major LNG suppliers as well as demand reductions by many LNG-importing nations, particularly the United States, Japan, and South Korea.

The second demand-side scenario postulated a more rapid adoption of a competing backstop technology, by assuming that it will be available at a lower price. This accelerates production in many regions and generally lowers price beyond 2020. Interestingly, LNG flows are slightly higher than in the reference case, driven largely by acceleration of production in Iran. Another key point is that the presence of a low-cost backstop gives increased importance to first movers and prevents some producers, such as Saudi Arabia, from monetizing their resources. Eventually, substitution to the backstop results in natural gas being consumed primarily in regions where it is produced.

While the scenarios examined here are by no means exhaustive, they indicate the types of impacts that perturbations could have on the development of a global gas market. The experiments confirm predictions that increased gas trade will enhance interactions between regional gas markets and promote arbitrage and global pricing over time. For example, it is apparent that supply infrastructure and demand growth in Northeast Asia will significantly influence the developing global market for natural gas. In addition, given the role of electricity-generation in expanding gas demand, alternative technologies could dramatically alter the evolution of the gas market. This highlights the role of natural gas as a transition fuel. Further research could focus on combinations of scenarios of particular interest to policy-makers. One such example might be the formation of a "gas–OPEC" combined with political barriers to key pipeline routes.

APPENDIX

Table 12.A *Risk premium adjustments*

Country	GIRI	Predicted premium	Relative to United States	Country	GIRI	Predicted premium	Relative to United States
Albania	5.8	7.19	3.96	Algeria	4.7	8.60	5.38
Angola	5.2	7.98	4.76	Argentina	5.3	7.87	4.64
Armenia	5.3	7.87	4.64	Australia	8.8	3.05	−0.17
Austria	9.1	2.66	−0.57	Azerbaijan	5.7	7.30	4.08
Bahamas	8.1	4.01	0.79	Bahrain	7.6	4.64	1.42
Bangladesh	4.5	8.88	5.66	Belarus	5.5	7.58	4.36
Belgium	8.5	3.50	0.28	Bolivia	5.8	7.13	3.91
Botswana	7.0	5.49	2.27	Brazil	5.5	7.58	4.36
Brunei	8.5	3.39	0.17	Bulgaria	6.9	5.60	2.38
Burkina Faso	5.8	7.19	3.96	Cameroon	4.3	9.11	5.89
Canada	8.9	2.94	−0.28	Chile	8.0	4.18	0.96
China	6.5	6.17	2.94	Colombia	5.2	7.98	4.76
Congo Rep.	5.2	7.98	4.76	Congo, Dem. Rep.	2.9	11.04	7.82
Costa Rica	6.8	5.77	2.55	Côte d'Ivoire	3.9	9.73	6.51
Croatia	7.6	4.69	1.47	Cuba	6.3	6.45	3.23
Cyprus	8.2	3.90	0.68	Czech Republic	7.6	4.64	1.42
Denmark	9.2	2.49	−0.74	Dominican Republic	5.2	7.98	4.76
Ecuador	5.0	8.21	4.98	Egypt	6.3	6.39	3.17
El Salvador	5.8	7.19	3.96	Estonia	6.8	5.71	2.49
Ethiopia	5.3	7.75	4.53	Finland	9.8	1.75	−1.47
France	7.8	4.41	1.19	Gabon	5.5	7.47	4.25
Gambia, The	6.6	6.00	2.78	Germany	8.8	3.11	−0.11
Ghana	5.0	8.15	4.93	Greece	7.2	5.20	1.98
Guatemala	5.5	7.53	4.30	Guinea	5.2	7.98	4.76
Guinea–Bissau	4.0	9.51	6.29	Guyana	5.4	7.64	4.42
Haiti	3.7	10.02	6.80	Honduras	5.7	7.30	4.08
Hong Kong	8.2	3.84	0.62	Hungary	8.1	3.96	0.74
Iceland	9.5	2.09	−1.13	India	6.1	6.73	3.51
Indonesia	4.3	9.22	6.00	Iran	5.8	7.19	3.96
Iraq	3.1	10.81	7.59	Ireland	9.5	2.15	−1.08
Israel	7.0	5.43	2.21	Italy	7.4	4.92	1.70
Jamaica	6.0	6.90	3.68	Japan	9.0	2.77	−0.45
Jordan	6.8	5.71	2.49	Kazakhstan	6.5	6.22	3.00
Kenya	4.8	8.49	5.27	Kuwait	7.2	5.20	1.98
Latvia	7.3	5.15	1.93	Lebanon	6.3	6.51	3.28
Liberia	3.8	9.85	6.63	Libya	5.7	7.24	4.02
Lithuania	7.0	5.49	2.27	Luxembourg	9.6	1.98	−1.25

Table 12.A (*cont.*)

Country	GIRI	Predicted premium	Relative to United States	Country	GIRI	Predicted premium	Relative to United States
Madagascar	4.8	8.49	5.27	Malawi	5.3	7.81	4.59
Malaysia	6.8	5.77	2.55	Mali	5.0	8.26	5.04
Malta	8.4	3.62	0.40	Mexico	6.2	6.62	3.40
Moldova	6.3	6.39	3.17	Mongolia	6.7	5.94	2.72
Morocco	7.4	4.98	1.76	Mozambique	5.4	7.64	4.42
Myanmar	4.3	9.17	5.95	Namibia	7.3	5.15	1.93
Netherlands	9.0	2.71	−0.51	New Zealand	9.2	2.49	−0.74
Nicaragua	5.3	7.81	4.59	Niger	4.8	8.54	5.32
Nigeria	2.8	11.21	7.99	North Korea	5.4	7.64	4.41
Norway	9.2	2.49	−0.74	Oman	7.5	4.81	1.59
Pakistan	5.1	8.04	4.81	Panama	6.3	6.51	3.28
Papua New Guinea	5.0	8.21	4.98	Paraguay	4.6	8.71	5.49
Peru	5.0	8.21	4.98	Philippines	6.3	6.39	3.17
Poland	7.7	4.58	1.36	Portugal	8.3	3.67	0.45
Qatar	7.5	4.86	1.64	Romania	5.8	7.07	3.85
Russia	5.5	7.53	4.30	Saudi Arabia	7.2	5.26	2.04
Senegal	5.1	8.04	4.81	Sierra Leone	4.5	8.83	5.61
Singapore	9.6	1.98	−1.25	Slovakia	7.5	4.81	1.59
Slovenia	7.8	4.47	1.25	Somalia	2.3	11.89	8.66
South Africa	5.5	7.47	4.25	South Korea	7.1	5.37	2.15
Spain	8.3	3.67	0.45	Sri Lanka	5.6	7.41	4.19
Sudan	4.1	9.45	6.23	Suriname	5.5	7.53	4.30
Sweden	9.4	2.20	−1.02	Switzerland	9.1	2.66	−0.57
Syria	6.5	6.22	3.00	Taiwan	7.7	4.58	1.36
Tanzania	6.0	6.90	3.68	Thailand	6.8	5.77	2.55
Togo	4.3	9.17	5.95	Trinidad & Tobago	6.0	6.85	3.62
Tunisia	7.0	5.54	2.32	Turkey	5.7	7.24	4.02
United Kingdom	9.0	2.71	−0.51	United States	8.7	3.22	0.00
Uganda	6.0	6.85	3.62	Ukraine	5.0	8.26	5.04
UAE	7.5	4.81	1.59	Uruguay	6.4	6.34	3.11
Venezuela	4.3	9.22	6.00	Vietnam	6.4	6.28	3.06
Yemen, Rep.	4.9	8.37	5.15	Yugoslavia	5.0	8.15	4.93
Zambia	5.0	8.21	4.98	Zimbabwe	3.0	10.98	7.76

REFERENCES

Howell, L. D. (2001). *The Handbook of Country and Political Risk Analysis.* East Syracuse, NY: PRS Group

Hartley, Peter R. and Albert S. Kyle (1989). "Equilibrium investment in an industry with moderate investment economies of scale." *Economic Journal,* 99, pp. 392–407

ICRG (2002). *International Country Risk Guide. Political Risk Services* (IBC USA, Inc.). New York: International Reports

World Bank (2004), World Development Indicators, available at www.worldbank.org.

13　Market structure in the new gas economy: is cartelization possible?

Amy M. Jaffe and Ronald Soligo

Introduction

Significant growth in trade in natural gas has been a major feature of international energy markets in recent years (see figure 1.3, p. 11). As discussed in earlier chapters in this volume, such growth is expected to accelerate in the coming decades. The increasing importance of natural gas to the major modern economies is raising new concerns regarding the security of gas supplies and the potential formation of a gas cartel similar to the Organization of Petroleum Exporting Countries (OPEC) that currently dominates oil markets. Presently, OPEC's mandate does not cover condensates, natural gas, and other petroleum-based liquids that are not technically defined as crude oil. However, many of the members of OPEC are major players in international gas markets. As growing natural gas use increasingly impinges on market share for oil in the mix of world primary energy demand, OPEC members will be tempted to consider cartelization of their gas sales activities. This chapter investigates the feasibility of the formation of a natural gas cartel and the potential limitations to any monopoly power wielded by such a group.

In considering the possibility of the rise of a gas cartel, this chapter will also postulate consumer country responses to the new reality of a gas-fed world. As gas becomes a more important input to industrialized economies and the volume of gas traded in international markets increases, large consuming countries will begin to focus more and more attention on the security and availability of their gas supplies. Concern for maintaining a secure supply of reasonably priced natural gas, which up to now has taken a back seat to its sister fuel, will increasingly be viewed as a vital national interest. This change is bound to influence the "geopolitics of natural gas."

The authors thank Stacy Eller, Peter Hartley, and Kenneth Medlock for their help with this chapter.

439

The discussion in this chapter is divided into six sections. The first deals with the concentration of gas resources and exports. We then discuss the security of gas supply relative to its geographical location and concentration of supply. The remaining sections investigate the options for the creation and policies of a potential gas-OPEC, taking into consideration the formative activities of the Gas Exporting Countries Forum (GECF), which held its first meeting in May 2001, as well as studies of the historical experience of OPEC in oil markets.

In studying the issues related to the future structure of the natural gas market, we observe that the overall distribution of world natural gas reserves is more concentrated than the distribution of oil resources, in the sense that the countries with the largest gas reserves have a larger share of total world reserves than is the case for oil. For example, the two countries with the largest gas reserves – Russia and Iran – have roughly 45 percent of world natural gas reserves, while the two countries with the largest oil reserves – Saudi Arabia and Iraq – have 36 percent of world oil reserves. On the other hand, the regional concentration of gas resources is more diverse. Middle East countries hold only 36 percent of natural gas reserves, as opposed to 65 percent of oil reserves. The FSU represents a second equally important region for gas production and exports.

Despite the concentration in gas reserves, an examination of the current situation in world natural gas markets indicates that it will take many years to work off a plethora of supplies from within major consuming regions and small competitive fringe producers, thwarting the formation of an effective gas cartel in the short term.

Furthermore, this chapter argues that the GECF has too many members with competing interests to constrain effectively new capacity expansion projects in the immediate term. Thus it is likely to be at least twenty years before the GECF could assert sustained monopoly power in world gas markets. It might be possible, however, for a large gas producer(s) to gain short-term rents in particular markets by manipulating the availability of immediate supplies.

Over the longer term, however, we show that gas exports may eventually become concentrated in the hands of just a few major producers. To the extent that a cartel is possible, constraining capacity expansion will be a more effective mechanism for managing production and enforcing compliance than using production quotas where members are producing below their capacity. This reflects the very high initial cost of development of production capacity.

As world LNG markets become more liquid, it will be feasible for the emergence of a "swing producer" to emerge in the spot LNG trade. In the intermediate term, Qatar is best positioned to assume this role due to its current plans to add quickly to its spare export capacity and its relatively greater financial freedom given its small population compared to its resource wealth. In the longer term, Russia may play a critical price arbitrage role between eastern and western markets, with the potential to extract rents from its dominant position in the market, but its ability to play a role as swing producer will be constrained by its large population, high costs, and more diversified industry that includes a mix of private and public companies.

The Distribution of Gas Reserves and Exports

In order to understand how the world's major powers will respond to the increased dependence on gas as a fuel, it is important to start with an analysis of the availability and location of world gas resources. A comparison with oil can illuminate the discussion. As is the case with oil, the locations of the largest gas deposits are not coincident with the locations of the largest demand centers. This lack of coincidence has necessitated significant international movements of both oil and gas. Future growth in the relative use of gas will result in even more international trade in both pipeline gas and LNG.

It is often said that gas resources are more varied and dispersed than oil and therefore sufficient concentration does not exist for the effective creation of a gas cartel. However, the facts are more nuanced – tables 13.1 and 13.2 show the geographical distribution of natural gas reserves and net exports for both oil and natural gas.

On a reserves basis, distribution of gas resources is indeed highly concentrated at the top of the distribution, with 45 percent of natural gas reserves lying in only two countries – Russia and Iran. Oil reserves are actually slightly less concentrated – as we have seen, the two countries with the largest reserves (Saudi Arabia and Iraq) hold 36 percent of the world total. A similar relationship holds when comparing the three- and four-country concentration ratios. However, the five-country concentration ratio is roughly the same for oil and gas – in both cases the top five countries hold 62 percent of total world reserves. Going further down the list shows that gas reserves are slightly less concentrated than oil reserves. For example, the ten countries with the largest reserves hold 81 percent of oil reserves but only 76 percent of gas reserves.

An important difference in terms of the geographical concentration is that while the largest oil reserves are all in Middle East countries, the largest gas reserves are in Russia. Middle East countries are still very important, holding 36 percent of natural gas reserves – as opposed to 65 percent of oil reserves. Also the specific countries in the Middle East that

Table 13.1. *Distribution of oil and gas reserves, 2003*

		Oil				Natural gas	
Rank	Country	Share (%)	Cumulative share (%)		Country	Share (%)	Cumulative share (%)
1	Saudi Arabia	25.3	25.3		Russia	30.5	30.5
2	Iraq	11.1	36.4		Iran	14.8	45.3
3	Iran	9.7	46.1		Qatar	9.2	54.5
4	Kuwait	9.6	55.6		Saudi Arabia	4.1	58.6
5	UAE	6.1	61.7		UAE	3.9	62.4
6	Russia	5.7	67.4		United States	3.4	65.8
7	Venezuela	5.1	72.5		Algeria	2.9	68.7
8	Nigeria	3.1	75.6		Venezuela	2.7	71.4
9	Libya	2.9	78.5		Nigeria	2.3	73.7
10	China	2.3	80.8		Iraq	2.0	75.7
11	United States	2.2	83.0		Indonesia	1.7	77.3
12	Other FSU	2.0	85.1		Australia	1.6	79.0
13	Qatar	1.9	87.0		Norway	1.4	80.4
14	Mexico	1.7	88.6		Malaysia	1.4	81.7
15	Algeria	1.3	89.9		Turkmenistan	1.3	83.0
16	Brazil	0.9	90.8		Uzbekistan	1.2	84.2
17	Norway	0.9	91.7		Kazakhstan	1.2	85.4
18	Angola	0.9	92.6		Netherlands	1.1	86.5
19	Indonesia	0.6	93.1		Canada	1.1	87.6
20	Oman	0.6	93.7		Egypt	1.1	88.7
21	Canada	0.5	94.2		China	1.0	89.7
	Rest of world	6.8	100.0		**Rest of world**	10.3	100.0

Note:
[a] Data are from the EIA website, http://www.eia.doe.gov. Gas reserves are from *Oil & Gas Journal* (2004). Oil reserves are from *World Oil* (Gulf 2004). The Oil & Gas Journal estimates include some 174.8 billion barrels of bitumen from Alberta's oil sands not included in the *World Oil* estimates. Including those reserves puts Canada in second place after Saudi Arabia. IEA's estimates put Russia in second place, with 14.3% of the world's oil reserves.
Source: EIA (2004).

have the largest gas reserves – Iran and Qatar – are different from those with the largest oil reserves – Saudi Arabia and Iraq. Saudi Arabia, Iran, and the UAE are in the top five spots in both the gas and oil lists. Thus, the gas world is less concentrated in the sense that there are two geographically separate regions of high reserves, as opposed to oil where the Middle East is of unparalleled importance and, within the Middle East, oil and gas reserves are distributed in different proportions.

Resource concentration only tells part of the story, however. The market power of a country will be reflected in its share of total output – or

Table 13.2. *Distribution of net exports of oil and gas, 2002*

		Oil[a]			Gas	
	Country	Share (%)	Cumulative share (%)	Country	Share (%)	Cumulative Share (%)
1	Saudi Arabia	17.8	17.8	Russia	28.8	28.8
2	Russia	12.6	30.4	Canada	15.9	44.7
3	Norway	7.8	38.2	Norway	9.6	54.3
4	Venezuela	5.9	44.1	Algeria	9.2	63.5
5	Iran	5.4	49.5	Turkmenistan	6.6	70.1
6	UAE	5.1	54.6	Indonesia	5.7	75.8
7	Nigeria	4.5	59.1	Netherlands	4.1	79.9
8	Kuwait	4.4	63.5	Malaysia	3.2	83.1
9	Mexico	4.1	67.6	Qatar	2.9	86.0
10	Iraq	3.9	71.5	Uzbekistan	1.8	87.8
11	Algeria	3.4	74.9	Australia	1.5	89.3
12	Libya	2.9	77.8	Brunei	1.4	90.7
13	Canada	2.2	80.0	United Kingdom	1.3	92.0
14	Oman	2.1	82.1	Nigeria	1.2	93.2
15	Angola	2.1	84.2	Oman	1.3	94.5
16	Qatar	2.0	86.2	UAE	1.1	95.6
17	United Kingdom	2.0	88.2	Burma	1.0	96.6
18	Kazakhstan	1.8	90.0	Argentina	0.9	97.5
19	Argentina	1.0	91.0	Trindad	0.8	98.3
20	Colombia	0.8	91.8	Bolivia	0.8	99.1

Note:
[a] Net oil exports include petroleum products as well as crude.
Source: EIA (2005).

more importantly, exports. We employ exports rather than production as a measure of the dominance of countries in world markets since market power is more likely to be related to its share of total internationally traded gas and oil than its share of total output. For example, the United States is among the largest producers of both oil and gas, but is a net importer of both. The smaller Gulf producers, on the other hand, have more modest output levels but are significant players in the export markets.

Table 13.2 shows the distribution of current net exports. Again, contrary to popular perception, the geographical concentration of gas exports is higher than that for oil. Saudi Arabia, the largest exporter of oil, has 17.8 percent of the export market while Russia, the largest gas exporter, has 28.8 percent. The largest four oil exporters have only a 44.1 percent share while the largest four gas exporters have a 63.5 percent share.

Table 13.3. *Reserve and production shares for oil and gas*

	Oil		Gas		Ratios P/R	
	Production (%)	Reserves (%)	Production (%)	Reserves (%)	Oil	Gas
North America	19.8	4.4	30.8	4.6	4.5	6.7
Central and South America	9.4	7.3	4.4	4.5	1.3	1.0
Western Europe	9.0	1.6	11.3	3.5	5.6	3.2
Eastern Europe and FSU	11.6	7.9	28.0	35.7	1.5	0.8
Middle East	29.1	64.7	9.3	36.0	0.4	0.3
Africa	10.5	9.3	5.3	7.6	1.1	0.7
Asia and Oceania	10.7	4.7	11.0	8.1	2.3	1.4

Note:
P = Production, R = Reserves.
Source: EIA (2004, 2005).

The higher concentration of gas exports is due to the relatively undeveloped state of gas relative to oil markets as well as the low level of LNG as compared with pipelines. For example, the largest gas exporters – Russia and Canada – are countries connected by pipeline to large gas consumers – Europe and the United States – with a well-developed gas distribution infrastructure.

Table 13.3 compares the share of reserves and production of various regions for both oil and natural gas and shows the ratio of the production share to the reserve share, which gives some indication of the degree to which a region's reserves are being exploited.

North America and Western Europe are areas where gas reserves are being fully developed. These two areas have only 8.1 percent of gas reserves, but produce 42.1 percent of gas output. For oil, they have 6 percent of reserves and produce 28.8 percent of output. The Middle East is an area where gas resources are underexploited even relative to oil. While the Middle Eastern share of gas reserves is 36 percent, their share of output is only 9.3 percent. Africa and Eastern Europe and the FSU (mainly Russia) are also areas where resources are relatively underdeveloped. In these regions, gas production has largely been geared to provide for local domestic consumption and export to nearby consumer countries that can be easily connected by pipeline. As the costs of LNG production and transport continue to fall, more countries will develop their gas resources and join the likes of current exporters Indonesia, Algeria, Malaysia, and Australia.

Security of Supply: Geographic Location

The concentration of oil resources in the Middle East has been a major feature of international oil markets for over thirty years. While there are many volatile areas around the world that produce oil, there is no other area with the same concentration of production as the Middle East. The probability that there would be simultaneous disruptions in several oil-producing areas outside the Middle East that could knock out significant oil supplies is relatively small. By contrast, markets tend to think of the Middle East as an area where events in one country can easily impinge on the fortunes of others. In general, these perceptions of interdependence suggest that events in the Middle East will appear to (as they have in recent history) threaten large quantities of oil and hence produce larger price reactions than one would expect from disruptions or instability in other non-Middle East-producing areas. Moreover, growing dependence on oil from one supply region, in this case the Middle East, strengthens the monopoly power of those suppliers with consequences for longer-run prices.

With respect to natural gas, tables 13.1 and 13.3 show that the locations of gas reserves are more diversified regionally than oil. Even to the extent that political disturbances in the Middle East can easily spread from one country to another, such disturbances will likely have a smaller effect on gas markets than on oil markets. This is particularly true in the near term as several major Middle East gas reserve holders, – notably, Saudi Arabia, Iran, and Iraq – face economic and political constraints that will likely prevent them from becoming major exporters for some time. The fact that large reserves are located in Russia is a major source of geographic diversification and stability for world gas markets. Russia has its own areas of conflict but these regions are distant from the location of gas reserves. In addition, potentially destabilizing incidents in the Middle East and Russia are unlikely to be correlated.

In terms of energy markets as a whole, the relative shift from oil to gas in energy consumption will be helpful in diversifying the geographic concentration of energy supply. Not only are the two major gas–resource and gas-producing regions – the Middle East and the former Soviet Union – not contiguous, but within the Middle East region, gas reserves are not concentrated in the same countries as oil reserves. Iran and Qatar have 69 percent of Middle East gas reserves, but only 17.9 percent of oil. Saudi Arabia and Iraq account for only 56.3 percent of regional oil reserves, but only 16.9 percent of regional gas reserves.

The Potential for a Gas Cartel

In May 2001, the GECF held its first ministerial meeting in Tehran with the aim of enhancing consultation and coordination among gas producers. The meeting included representatives from Algeria, Brunei, Iran, Indonesia, Malaysia, Nigeria, Oman, Qatar, Russia, Norway, and Turkmenistan. Although the GECF ministers' announcement emphasized that they did not intend to pursue a production-sharing agreement and quota system during the initial meeting, certain individual members of the group have debated the merits of exercising some form of market influence or control (MEES 2001). Such ideas have been gaining momentum since the group's first session.

A second official ministerial meeting of GECF was held in 2002 in Algiers and was attended by thirteen countries including Bolivia, Egypt, Libya, and Venezuela, which did not attend the first meeting in Tehran. Norway and Turkmenistan did not attend the second meeting. In 2003, the GECF held a third ministerial meeting in Doha, with fourteen members in attendance including representatives from Algeria, Brunei, Egypt, Indonesia, Iran, Libya, Malaysia, Nigeria, Oman, Qatar, Russia, Trinidad & Tobago, the UAE, Venezuela, and one observer, Norway. The 2003 grouping held a subsequent meeting in Cairo in 2004 and agreed to establish an executive bureau.

Producer associations, both national and international, are quite common. They serve as a forum to discuss common problems and provide useful information to members. They can also serve a useful public function of lobbying for regulatory changes to enhance the development of their industry. These associations can also work against the public interest, if they collaborate to raise prices or lobby for regulatory changes that restrict competition. It remains unclear what sort of association the GECF will become.

Ostensibly, the Forum is to focus on "promoting policy discussion and exploring avenues of technical cooperation" (Aïssaoui 2002). Yet, more than half of the fourteen participants in the GECF are members of OPEC and several other GECF participants have occasionally provided varying support for production sharing cutbacks implemented by OPEC.

The GECF has already tried, unsuccessfully, to exercise some collective influence in the European market. The first example was its attempt to create a unified response to liberalization in Europe. At the second official meeting of GECF in Algiers in early 2002 a working group, including Russia and Algeria, was set up to discuss gas supply issues with the European Union. Following such working group sessions, Algeria and Russia made clear that they wanted to band with other gas exporters to resist EU attempts to outlaw destination clauses that prevent buyers from reselling gas (PIW 2002). The option to resell gas is a pivotal mechanism for market arbitrage and efficiency that can restrict sellers from segregating markets and exercising monopolistic influence (Soligo and Jaffe 2000).

In another example, Egypt, at the third Ministerial meeting of GECF in Doha in February 2003, proposed that the exporter group initiate a gas pricing change in Europe by ending the link to crude oil prices in hopes to create better market penetration for gas (PIW 2003). Both of these proposals have so far not advanced further, and a gas cartel remains at a theoretical stage.

Lessons from Oil Markets

Cartels are difficult to create and maintain, and especially so when there are more than just a few members. The reasons are well known. The cartel must decide how much to restrict output below the level that would be collectively produced in the absence of the cartel. Allocating production quotas among members is difficult because each member has different needs, ambitions, and uncertain bargaining power. Once agreement is reached, however, each member can benefit at the expense of others by cheating on the quota. The larger the number of members and more liquid the market, the more difficult it is to detect who is doing the cheating. There is also the problem of how the cartel can punish a cheater, even if caught. Finally, the cartel must deter entry into the industry; otherwise its share of the market will shrink along with its power to set price or other market conditions.

OPEC is generally considered a textbook case of a cartel, although there remains considerable disagreement on its efficacy. Mabro (1998) surveys the literature and points out the myriad of explanations – other than OPEC manipulation – that have been offered for major swings in oil prices, as well as the many models that have been put forth to explain OPEC behavior. As Smith (2003a, 2003b) shows, the debate continues. Despite the ambiguity regarding just how much market power OPEC or Saudi Arabia has exhibited at any particular time, several facts remain clear. Oil prices are significantly above the marginal costs of production in some of the largest OPEC producers (Adelman 1995). It is also accepted that in situations where investment in capacity lags growth in demand, OPEC can temporarily raise prices by modestly restricting output. It is also understood that Saudi Arabia has at times fulfilled a special role in maintaining price discipline within OPEC. By maintaining excess capacity, Saudi Arabia is a "swing producer" that can flood the market and drive down oil prices to punish members who may exceed their quotas on the one hand and increase production to moderate price increases, and hence limit new entry by fringe producers, on the other (Harvard 2003).

Moreover, it is clear that any cartel would be more effective at raising and maintaining prices if it controlled the capacity growth of its members as opposed to trying to persuade individual producers to produce less than their capacity. Maintaining excess gas production capacity is extremely expensive. Excess capacity will, of course, occur from time to time as demand fluctuates, but the ability to set prices in the longer term would be facilitated by coordinating capacity expansion even more so than output levels.

Over the years, Saudi Arabia's enormous reserves and high oil revenue earnings capability relative to its population have facilitated its role as OPEC disciplinarian. For example, Saudi Arabia has oversupplied oil markets twice in face of stiff market competition – once in 1985 when non-OPEC production was on a sharp upward path and again in 1997 when Venezuela embarked on an aggressive policy to increase its market share. The 1985 price decline lasted for several years although it should be noted that some authors, citing interviews and documents from the Reagan administration, have suggested that the prolonged depression of prices was also engineered, in collaboration with the United States, in order to deny revenue to the Soviet Union so as to put stress on their ability to match the growing US defense expenditures of the Reagan era and finance the war in Afghanistan (Schweizer 1994). It is not clear that Saudi Arabia could execute the same sort of policy today given its much larger population and revenue needs, and its growing public debt (Morse and Richard 2002). In addition, the revival of the Russian oil industry and future re-emergence of Iraq as a significant oil exporter may diminish the Saudi role as the dominant force in oil markets.

The need to control capacity expansion and the dominant role of Saudi Arabia as an enforcer came together in the late 1990s in the Saudi reaction to Venezuelan capacity expansion. Venezuela had been actively expanding its oil production capacity through an opening up to foreign direct investment (FDI) by American oil companies initiated in 1992. The program was expected to take Venezuela's oil production as high as 7 million b/d by 2010, a level almost rivaling Saudi Arabia's output. For a period of many months in 1998–1999, Saudi Arabia publicly warned Venezuela to stop overproducing and to abandon its plans to expand its oil market share. It threatened to initiate an oil price war to eliminate the incentives for continued investment in Venezuela and to "punish" the Venezuelan government. Venezuela failed to heed Saudi warnings, and as markets softened in 1998, Saudi Arabia refused to cut back its production as oil prices moved into free fall. When oil prices reached a low of $8 a barrel in 1999, Venezuela was forced to concede. Ironically, in part related to internal financial troubles, Venezuela experienced a change in government, and the new government immediately trimmed back plans to expand oil production capacity. In fact, continued political unrest in Venezuela, in the aftermath of the financial débâcle stimulated by the 1998 oil price crash, led to an oil workers' strike that significantly set back Venezuela's state oil industry. Venezuela's production capacity fell from 3.7 million b/d prior to the election of Hugo Chavez in 1999 to just over 2 million b/d today (2005), contributing dramatically to the tightening of oil markets in recent years and related high prices (Bird 1997, 1998). A John F. Kennedy School of Government, Harvard University executive seminar report on "Oil and Security" in May 2003 concluded that this Saudi strategy, "has been costly for countries attempting to challenge the position of Saudi Arabia. The Saudis have responded aggressively and ruthlessly to protect their leading role in the world market" (Harvard 2003).

Ironically, OPEC's ability to limit capacity expansion has been aided by sanctions levied by Western countries against several members – Iran, Iraq, and Libya – which, among other effects, discouraged investment in these key producing countries (O'Sullivan 2003). Without those sanctions, it is unlikely that OPEC could have controlled capacity expansion to the level of success seen in recent years (Soligo, Jaffe, and Mieszkowski 1997). There were other factors limiting investment in capacity: For example, the rapidly expanding populations in many OPEC countries created intense pressures on state treasuries for expanded social services, leaving less money to be spent on oil sector expansion (Jaffe 2004).

In the late 1980s, OPEC had planned capacity expansions to a total of 32.95 million b/d targeted for 1995, but by early 1997, OPEC capacity had reached only 29 million b/d. Iran, Libya, and Iraq all failed to achieve their production targets.[1] All these factors have contributed to a general stagnation of OPEC capacity since the late 1990s. In fact, as

---

[1] Iran had aimed to reach 4 million b/d, Libya 1.6 million b/d, and Iraq 4.5 million b/d, but were constrained at 3.8 million b/d, 1.4 million b/d, and 1.2 million b/d, respectively; see Jaffe (1997).

Table 13.4. *OPEC production and spare capacity, 1979–2003*

Member country Capacity	1979	1983	1990	1997	1998	2000	2001	2003
Saudi Arabia	10.84	11.30	8.00	9.65	9.50	9.50	9.90	10.15
Iran	7.00	3.00	3.10	3.70	3.70	3.75	3.80	3.80
Iraq	4.00	1.50	3.60	2.30	2.80	2.90	3.05	2.20
Kuwait	3.34	2.80	2.40	2.40	2.40	2.40	2.40	2.50
UAE	2.50	2.90	2.20	2.40	2.40	2.40	2.45	2.50
Qatar	0.65	0.65	0.40	0.71	0.72	0.73	0.75	0.75
Venezuela	2.40	2.50	2.60	3.45	3.30	2.98	3.10	2.50
Nigeria	2.50	2.40	1.80	2.00	2.05	2.10	2.30	2.30
Indonesia	1.80	1.60	1.25	1.40	1.35	1.35	1.30	1.15
Libya	2.50	2.00	1.50	1.45	1.45	1.45	1.45	1.45
Algeria	1.23	1.10	0.75	0.88	0.88	0.88	0.88	1.15
Total Capacity	**38.76**	**31.75**	**27.60**	**30.34**	**30.55**	**30.44**	**31.38**	**30.45**
Total Production (Call on OPEC)	34.01	16.65	22.20	27.59	25.85	30.04	28.23	29.20
Spare Capacity	4.75	15.10	5.40	2.75	4.70	0.40	3.15	1.25

Source: Baker Institute estimates; Hetco Trading; *Petroleum Intelligence Weekly.*

table 13.4 shows, OPEC capacity has actually fallen since 1979, not increased.

Modeling OPEC as the Dominant-Firm Model: Applications to OPEC and a Potential Gas-OPEC

There are a number of different ways in which economists have attempted to model OPEC in order to explain its behavior. The "dominant-firm" model is one that captures some important aspects of OPEC. The model divides industry producers into one large firm (or cartel) and many other smaller firms that can be called the "competitive fringe." Figure 13.1, drawn from Perloff (2004) illustrates the model.

The world demand curve for oil is given by the curve labeled D. The supply curve of the competitive fringe is given by S^f. The demand curve facing the dominant firm (OPEC) is the residual demand curve constructed by taking, for each price, total world demand and fringe supply. That curve, shown as D^r in figure 13.1, gives the amount of oil that OPEC can sell at each price. Having monopoly power, OPEC will then maximize its profits by setting output at the point where marginal revenue is equal to marginal cost. In figure 13.1, MR^r is the cartel's marginal revenue curve while MC^d shows its marginal cost curve. OPEC

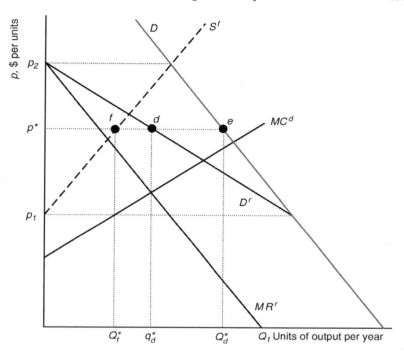

Figure 13.1. Dominant-firm equilibrium.
Source: drawn from Perloff (2004).

produces q_d^*, and sets price equal to P^*. The fringe produces Q_f^* and total output is Q_d^*.

The market power of the cartel with monopoly power is measured by the extent to which it can set price above marginal cost and is given by the equation:

$$\frac{P}{MC} = \frac{1}{1 + (1/\varepsilon_d)}$$

Market power is determined by the elasticity of demand facing the cartel – which is a weighted average of the elasticity of aggregate demand and the elasticity of fringe supply, where the weights are the inverse of the market share of the dominant firm and the ratio of outputs of fringe producers to that of the dominant firm, respectively. It is given by the equation:

$$\varepsilon_d = \varepsilon \times (Q_d/q_d) + \varepsilon_f \times (Q_d - q_d)/q_d$$

where: ε_d is the elasticity of the residual demand curve;
ε is the elasticity of the aggregate demand curve;
ε_f is the elasticity of the competitive fringe.

Holding all else constant, the pricing power of OPEC is enhanced the more inelastic the aggregate demand curve, the more inelastic the fringe supply, and the larger OPEC's market share.

This model is useful to the analysis of OPEC, because it highlights the importance of the competitive fringe, as well as other factors, in limiting the market power of OPEC. Efforts to raise prices by restricting cartel output will be limited if the higher prices result in a large increase in supply from non-OPEC members or in large decreases in oil consumption. The mid-1980s demonstrated the importance of both of these factors when, in response to the sharp oil price increases in the early and late 1970s, non-OPEC production increased rapidly at the same time that demand decreased – in part, because consumers learned how to economize on energy. The fall in demand was further aggravated by the recession that occurred at the same time.

The dominant-firm framework can also be used to gain insight as to the future path of oil prices. The IEA, in its *World Energy Outlook (WEO)*, and other forecasters project that non-OPEC production could reach peak levels as early as 2010 (Deffeyes 2001; IEA 2002). This might be interpreted to suggest that the elasticity of supply of the fringe will be reduced in the future – there will be a smaller supply response by non-OPEC producers if prices should increase in the future as compared with the past. As discussed above, a reduction in the supply elasticity of the fringe will reduce the elasticity of demand facing OPEC for its oil and increase OPEC's market power. So as the potential for increasing fringe supplies over time diminishes, the result will be to give OPEC (Saudi Arabia or the OPEC core) more pricing power.

Many forecasts of future world oil markets contend that OPEC's share of the world oil market will markedly increase in the coming decades. For example, the IEA estimates that OPEC's share of total supply will increase from 38 percent in 2000 to 48 percent in 2020. This increase in market share would in and of itself increase the monopoly power of OPEC. However, as Gately points out, IEA projections for OPEC supply are calculated as a residual between world demand and non-OPEC supply (Gately 1995, 2001, 2004). These estimates do not take into consideration whether incentives will be in place for OPEC to actually increase its supply to the high forecasted levels. Indeed, Gately argues that the IEA forecasts that OPEC will meet rising demand are not consistent with the interests of OPEC producers themselves (Gately 2004). A firm with monopoly power has no incentive to produce where the marginal revenue of output is negative. Gately argues that that is precisely what is implied for OPEC by the IEA forecasts.

Gately's work suggests that the IEA may be overly optimistic about future oil prices, which are assumed to remain flat to 2010 and then gradually increase. Indeed, the recent rise in oil prices is already inconsistent with IEA assumptions, although it is still not clear whether current prices are a short-term aberration or a glimpse of what lies ahead.

It is important to note that Gately does not discuss the issue of whether OPEC members can agree to future quotas. So while it may be in their collective interest to restrict future output, it is not certain that they will be able to cooperate to do so. In favor of Gately's thesis is the fact that, in a growing market, each member country will be able to increase output even if its share remains unchanged. Collusion is generally easier in a non-zero-sum environment. However, if one or more major OPEC members were to make a large drive towards rapid capacity expansion, this would make it more difficult for the producer group to reach strong agreements.

Prospects for a Gas-OPEC

The requirements for an effective cartel are that there should be a relatively small number of producers who control a substantial share of the market and that this group must be able to establish and enforce production quotas, control capacity expansion, and restrict entry of new producers at the fringe. Controlling capacity expansion is a preferred way of restricting the output of cartel members since capacity will limit the ability to cheat and the extent of actual production cheating.[2] New entrants, or capacity expansion by existing producers who are not in the cartel, will undermine the effectiveness of the cartel unless their size is small relative to market growth.

The data in table 13.2 showing country shares of the gas export market suggest that the GECF could evolve into an institution with market power similar to that of OPEC. Seven counties, fewer than the membership of OPEC, currently account for almost 80 percent of the gas export market! That suggests that there are already a sufficient number of producers to form a price-setting cartel. However, three of

[2] Authors' interviews with the organizers and participants of GECF, Vienna, September 2003.

those seven – Canada, Norway, and the Netherlands – would be unlikely to join a gas producers' cartel given their ties to the industrialized West and thereby conflicting interests. The remaining four exporters would control only 50 percent of exports. Still, adding the next three largest exporters (Malaysia, Qatar, and Uzbekistan) would yield a 58 percent market share. Without Russia, however, the share of the remaining six countries falls to only 30 percent – probably too little to wield much market power. Russian cooperation with the GECF would be critical for any cartel's success.

However, while concentration of current exports is fairly high, the potential for a significant increase in output and exports from other countries is also very large and, therefore, we are led to conclude that the prospects for an effective cartel in the short term are weak. Table 13.1 showed that there were a large number of countries with significant gas reserves – say with at least 1 percent of the world's reserves. With a reduction in transport costs and the further development of a gas market, many of these reserves will be developed without significant price increases. In the context of the dominant-firm model, the elasticity of supply of fringe producers is quite large, thus limiting the pricing power of a small group of producers – even a group including Russia.

Moreover, the politics of creating a gas-OPEC from among the membership of the GECF is not currently favorable. The membership list is large and therefore politically cumbersome. Additionally, many current members of the GECF have differing views on what the group's goals should be. As already noted, several major gas exporters such as Canada, Australia, Norway, and Trinidad & Tobago have strong ties to the industrialized West and therefore would be unlikely to work as key participants in cartelization policies.

Also hindering the GECF is the fact that several members are accelerating LNG development projects quickly to take advantage of first-mover opportunities in the market and therefore have no interest in cartelizing project development at this time (see chapters 8 and 9). Qatar's Minister of Energy and Industry and Second Deputy Prime Minister Abdullah Bin Hamad al-Attiyah stated at a public conclave that there will never be a gas-OPEC because Qatar would not be party to such a grouping. "There are many uncertainties and challenges we have to deal with on a global scale, which makes the producer–consumer cooperation essential," he noted in a speech at the James A. Baker III Institute for Public Policy on May 26, 2004.[3] In fact, Qatar and fellow

---

[3] Baker Institute Report; available at http://bakerinstitute.org/Pubs/report_22.pdf.

GECF member Iran have a brewing conflict over output in a field that straddles their national borders. In April 2004, Iran's deputy Oil Minister Hadi Nejad-Hosseinian openly accused Qatar of overproducing gas at its giant North Field which straddles Iranian territory and warned that if Qatar continued to avoid discussions on regulating offshore production, Iran will find "other ways and means of resolving the issue" (Energy Compass 2004).

However, eventually, as in oil, gas production in the fringe will peak, and the market power of the cartel will at that time be enhanced. The timing of these events will be determined by the rate at which gas demand grows and gas reserves both within the cartel and in the competitive fringe are developed. But given political changes that might happen over the coming twenty years, it is too soon to conclude that a gas-OPEC could not possibly emerge in the future. As the number of key players in the gas world narrows as expected beyond 2025, the chances for producer collaboration will be enhanced. However, a number of factors remain that could undermine the market power of such a cartel.

One challenge is the competition of gas with other fuels. Unlike oil where there are few substitutes in the transportation sector, natural gas must compete with coal, oil, hydroelectric power, and nuclear power for its market share. In terms of the dominant-firm model, the existence of many substitutes for gas increases the elasticity of demand for gas, in both the aggregate and for cartel output. A higher elasticity of demand will translate into reduced market power for any cartel. Improvements in the safety of nuclear power and reductions in the cost of clean-coal technologies will, over time, lower the upper limit to gas (and potentially oil[4]) prices that a cartel can set without triggering massive defections to alternative energy sources. But it must be remembered that a lag is likely to exist between the time at which a gas cartel can assert its power to accrue rents and the time it will take natural gas users to make the capital investment to shift to facilities that can utilize alternative fuels.

The interdependence between gas and oil markets presents an additional challenge for a gas producers' group. There will be an overlap of members who already participate in the OPEC oil cartel and those who would be members of a gas cartel. But there will be some countries that will be a member of only one group or the other. As the gas market develops further and gas supplies become a more readily

---

[4] Radical cost reductions in nuclear power or in syncrude production from coal could, over the long term, introduce a viable competitor to oil in the transport sector. Hydogen, used in fuel cells and produced from nuclear power, might be the energy carrier for such a transport system.

available alternative to oil in many parts of the world, price competition between gas and oil may increase. This could complicate the politics of both cartel organizations since the largest gas producers are not necessarily the countries with the largest oil production potential. Gas-on-oil competition between new major gas producers and the major oil producers in particular growth markets such as China or Japan could cause market share rivalries and political tensions that could weaken the market power of both organizations. Cooperation between the two cartels would be difficult because a larger number of members in the larger coalition would make it unwieldy. On the other hand, Russia will be a major player in both markets and the link between oil and gas prices may induce it to join – or at least cooperate – with OPEC.

Certain OPEC oil countries have recognized this possible future connection between oil and gas. In the official communiqué of the second summit of Heads of State and Government of OPEC member countries on September 28, 2000, OPEC recognized a group interest in promoting both oil and gas use, as opposed to just oil use. The OPEC document said the cartel should seek to promote the "use of both oil and gas in circumstances where they can be substituted for other fuels that are recognized as being damaging to the global environment."[5] This language was interpreted by analysts to mean that OPEC heads of state were concerning themselves with the future of regulating gas sales and prices, as well as just oil markets.

As an aside, it should be noted that from the point of view of oil consumers, the prospect of growing competition between oil and gas on a worldwide basis would be welcomed. To the extent that Gately is correct that OPEC will not have the incentives to produce the quantity of oil that is forecast by IEA projections, the growth of gas production and exports will ameliorate some of the bullish price effects on oil that are implicit in his analysis (assuming that some of the incremental gas substitutes for oil).

Privatization of gas reserves and the gas transport network in producer countries may also present an impediment to the formation of a successful gas cartel. It will be easier for national, state-owned, producers to participate in a cartel than for privately owned firms that might have different objectives from the state. If a number of private Russian gas producers emerge, it will be more difficult to reconcile their conflicting corporate ambitions with OPEC-related production quotas.

---

[5] Communiqué, available at www.opec.org. Analysts commented at the meeting that this reference was the result of exploratory OPEC discussion of the idea to draw natural gas into its portfolio. (See LaFranchi 2000.)

On the other hand, the experience of the Texas Railroad commission – which pro-rationed production shares in Texas with a significant impact on US oil prices in the 1960s – suggests that such coordination among private actors is not impossible. Nonetheless, Russia's participation in a gas cartel will be facilitated to the extent that Gazprom maintains its monopoly in gas production and transmission. However, even if ownership of production is liberalized, continued Gazprom control of transmission capacity alone could provide the company (or the state) a mechanism force producers to cooperate (Baker Institute 2004).

Liberalization of energy markets in consumer countries will also hinder cartel development to the extent that it fosters competition not only between gas and other energy sources but also between different sources of gas. From the perspective of an importing country, having different, competing sources of gas effectively increases the elasticity of demand facing a cartel and reduces its market power. For example, even Algeria and Russia's limited goals to roll back EU strictures on resale contracts proved too difficult in the European context given competitive pipeline supply from Northern Europe and a variety of new LNG suppliers such as Nigeria and Egypt. Moreover, Algeria itself was conflicted because of the attractive opportunity to expand its market share via the Italian pipeline system into nascent Eastern European markets – for which it needed Italian cooperation – thus weakening its leverage to hold fast to the destination clauses.

Controlling capacity expansion is probably more important to an effective gas cartel than it is for oil. The very high costs of building the infrastructure for a gas project puts great pressure on owners to fully utilize their capacity. But controlling capacity investments will be difficult. Cartel members would have to agree to some system of staggering new capacity investment projects. Countries that were required to postpone such investments would be penalized in the sense that they would not be able to benefit immediately from the revenues that would be generated by monetizing those reserves. Also, many countries face pressing needs for development funds and will be subject to pressures to exploit their resources as quickly as possible. A fair system of staggering investments would require that those countries at the head of the queue would compensate those who were relegated to positions further on down. Such cross-country payments add an additional layer of complexity to a gas cartel and increase the difficulty of reaching consensus. Most countries would prefer to develop resources within their own boundaries rather than depend on promises of payments from other members.

An effective cartel requires an ability to enforce discipline among members to prevent cheating on quotas. As we have seen, in OPEC this role has been performed by Saudi Arabia who maintains excess capacity so that it can be the swing producer – to moderate price increases to discourage new entrants and to lower prices in order to punish transgressors.

The role of swing producer will be much more costly for a gas producer because of the much higher fixed costs associated with gas projects. For gas, the swing producer would have to maintain excess liquefaction and LNG tanker capacity (or gas pipeline capacity as well extra production and storage capacity). Given the costs, such a role may not be attractive and consequently could go unfilled. As Fawzi (2004) points out:

In the oil industry, it is estimated that a 1 percent capacity surplus in world-wide oil production (assuming an investment of $3,000 per daily barrel) would cost about $2.2 billion. By contrast, creating a 1 percent surplus in world-wide gas production, assuming that the entire 1 percent was brought to market as LNG, would have a price tag of about $13.8 billion (in field development, liquefaction and tankers).

An option is to have a core group in the cartel that would act collectively as swing producers so as to spread the costs over a larger number of members. But such a plan would mean that the costs of decision making would increase. Moreover, the potential for agreement would diminish as the number of members increased. The need for collective action would result in a weaker cartel than having a single country fulfill the role of swing producer. The absence of any swing producer would require that the cartel find other ways to enforce agreements; otherwise it would become irrelevant if faced with cheating, which is very likely.

To the extent that one country would fulfill the role of swing producer, the likely candidates for such a role in a gas cartel would be the countries with the largest reserves. Two such candidates are Russia or Qatar, although in each case there are factors that may inhibit them from playing such a role.

There are several reasons why Russia might not play the role of swing producer. First, the cost of excess capacity includes the opportunity cost of forgone public revenues from gas production and export – the value of the public goods and services that are not produced as a result of excess capacity. Russia has a very large population and many developmental and social needs. There will be great pressure over the next several years to produce at capacity in order to generate as much government revenues as possible. Second, gas production might in the future be undertaken with participation by privately owned companies, since the state monopoly Gazprom might not be able to meet demand inside

Russia and in European markets on its own. Since it would not be in the interest of private companies to maintain excess capacity some mechanism would have to be developed to force them to do so. As discussed above, private ownership is not a bar to cartelization but regulating private firms is not as easy as dealing with a single state monopoly. The retention of control of the export infrastructure by the government or government enterprise could provide the impetus for production-sharing rules.[6]

In theory, Qatar may be better placed to play the role of swing producer, even though its reserves are substantially smaller than Russia's. Qatar's reserves are large relative to its population and the need to maintain output to generate adequate revenue is not as urgent as in the case of Russia. In addition, Qatar will export LNG and is geographically well placed to move supplies to all three major markets in Asia, Europe, and the United States. Finally, given its first-mover advantages and prolific reserves, Qatar "has the lowest exploration and development costs for gas of any region in the world" (Fawzi 2004).

However, according to projections from the BIWGTM (see chapter 11 and table 13.5), Qatar will have a relatively modest share of world gas exports, in the 3–8 percent range until 2030. Still, its share of LNG exports will be approximately 10 percent which, given the inflexibility of pipeline gas, may be sufficient to give Qatar enough leverage to influence world gas prices.

Other large reserve holders – such as Saudi Arabia, Iran, and Iraq – are unlikely candidates for the swing producer role because they will not become significant exporters until after 2030. Nigeria, despite its modest reserves, is predicted to have a significant share of world exports by 2020 (6.6 percent). This share, driven by LNG exports to the United States, will increase to 7 percent by 2030. Nigeria is unlikely to be a swing producer, however, because of its large population and pressing revenue needs.

Table 13.5 shows projected exports as computed by the BIWGTM. As shown in table 13.5, the model predicts that gas development in Russia will continue to be a pivotal factor in global gas market development (see chapter 11). Russia has the advantage that it lies between two of the world's largest energy consuming areas – Europe to the West and East Asia to the East. It is geographically positioned to reach these markets easily by pipeline. Its largest potential gas supply competitors –

---

[6] For a more detailed discussion of the future options for the Russian gas industry, see the US–Russia Commercial Energy Summit Executive Seminar Report, available at http://www.bakerinstitute.org.

Table 13.5. *Projected share of total gas exports by country, 2010–2040*

	2010 (%)	2020 (%)	2030 (%)	2040 (%)
Russia	15.71	16.18	17.35	19.54
Kazakhstan	8.11	5.17	2.21	0.71
Turkmenistan	3.17	3.11	3.65	4.55
Canada	7.56	3.14	–	–
Algeria	11.03	6.72	1.89	0.20
Nigeria	2.99	6.64	7.04	5.33
Angola	0.17	0.55	1.04	0.79
Indonesia	5.03	5.40	5.55	4.50
Malaysia	3.98	2.69	1.03	–
Brunei	1.32	1.28	1.12	0.56
Australia	1.88	4.10	8.46	8.09
Iran	–	–	3.17	8.69
Qatar	3.47	4.68	7.87	9.50
Saudi Arabia	0.00	1.65	5.28	8.13
Norway	7.05	5.40	5.30	5.11
Greenland	–	–	–	2.12
Trinidad & Tobago	2.22	1.55	0.65	–
Venezuela	–	1.63	3.68	3.15
Rest of World	**26.31**	**30.10**	**24.69**	**19.00**

Source: Chapter 11, BIWGTM results.

primarily in the Middle East – must rely on more costly, long-haul LNG shipments to compete in those markets.

Table 13.5 shows that Russia's share of the gas export market will decline from current levels (28 percent) but will remain the highest worldwide even out to 2040. It has, and will continue to have, such a commanding share of the gas trade that Russia alone could exert some monopoly power. The export share from other countries in the FSU– primarily Turkmenistan and Kazakhstan, whose export routes are currently controlled by Russia – will increase significantly in the short run from a current combined level of 7.6 percent to 11.3 percent by 2010, and then will decline gradually.

Because other LNG suppliers are closer to end-user markets and pipeline gas competitors, BIWGTM projects that Qatar's share will hover around 3–4 percent of the export market until after 2020 despite its massive resource base. Iran and Saudi Arabia, as indicated above, will be late developers. Iran is not expected to be an exporter until after 2025; Saudi Arabia is projected to begin exporting earlier, but will have only 1.7 percent of the market by 2020.

The results of BIWGTM are based on the assumption that the pattern and level of investments in gas development and production are motivated by strictly economic criteria – in particular, that investment occurs where and when it is most efficient. The economic attractiveness of Russian pipeline gas relative to distant LNG promotes a modeling outcome with Russian gas coming online to a far greater extent than the resources of the Middle East. For the next twenty years, Russia's capability to exercise significant market power will be limited to its ability to appropriate the difference in costs between its pipeline gas and the higher cost of LNG from the Middle East and Africa. In the context of our earlier discussion of the dominant-firm model, the elasticity of supply of the fringe – in this case, including LNG capacity from the Middle East and Africa – is relatively inelastic over a small range of prices. But once prices reach the level that would cover the difference of higher LNG costs, supply from the competitive fringe becomes very elastic, essentially eliminating any power that Russian exporters would have to raise prices further.

Over the longer term, as gas production capacity peaks in the various regions with more limited gas production potentials – including regions in or near industrialized economies – cooperation between LNG suppliers and Russia could become increasingly attractive. BIWGTM predicts that the export share of OPEC countries plus Russia will grow over the next several decades (see chapter 11). By 2020, the model predicts that Russia, in combination with Algeria, Nigeria, Indonesia, Qatar, and Venezuela will account for 42.9 percent of world exports, potentially giving this group considerable market power. By 2030, this group, plus Iran and Saudi Arabia, will account for 51.8 percent of total exports and by 2040 the group will have a share of 59.1 percent. Russia's incentive to cooperate with these other producers that are members of OPEC is enhanced by the fact that oil and gas are close substitutes in several market segments, and overall market power could be strengthened by cooperating on pricing for both fuels. Thus, it might be in Russian interests to collude with all OPEC members to coordinate and attempt to set prices for both oil and natural gas.

Conclusion

The foregoing discussion suggests that any gas producer group is unlikely to exercise significant market power in the near term. While Russia has a large share of the export market currently, its sales are directed at Europe where there are several alternative sources of supply – especially from North Africa and Northern Europe. In the intermediate term, starting around 2020, Russia's dominance is predicted to decline but a small group consisting of Russia, and several members of OPEC (Algeria, Nigeria, Indonesia, Qatar, Iran, Saudi Arabia, and Venezuela) could command close to 50 percent of the export market.

Initially, the ability of this group – or a sub-set of it – to set prices will be constrained by the fact that there are many countries with sufficient undeveloped resources to provide for many competing sources of supply – assuming that price levels are suitably attractive. However, eventually, a point will be reached in the long term – say, beyond 2025 – when many of the alternative supplies will have peaked, and those countries endowed with the largest reserves will be in a very strong market position. In these conditions, it is easy to imagine a scenario where it is in Russia's interest to cooperate with OPEC to at least limit gas-on-oil competition. The extent to which this small group of oil and gas exporters will be able to exercise monopoly power will be determined, among other factors, by technological improvements that will affect the cost and attractiveness of other competing fuels, such as coal, nuclear, or renewable energy.

Options available to consumer countries to forestall the development of such a gas cartel are limited and well known. Energy sector deregulation – permitting utilities freedom in setting prices, in choice of technology, and in contracting with fuel suppliers – effectively increases the elasticity of utility gas demand and limits the market power of gas sellers. Consuming countries can also actively promote technologies that will increase competition between gas and alternative energy sources. The potential emergence of significant monopoly power by gas exporters is at least a decade or two away, permitting a realistic time frame for pursuing new technologies with the potential to replace natural gas should it become subject to the influence of a gas cartel.

REFERENCES

Adelman, M. A. (1995). *The Genie Out of the Bottle: World Oil since 1970.* Cambridge, MA: MIT Press
Aïssaoui, Ali (2002). "Gas-exporting countries: towards 'cartelization'?" *Oxford Energy Forum* 45(32)
Baker Institute (2004). "The energy dimension in the Russian global strategy." Houston: James A. Baker III Institute for Public Policy; available at http://www.bakerinstitute.org
Bird, David (1998). "Saudis subdue doubters by plowing ahead with crude production." *The Oil Daily*, January 8
    (1997). "Saudis not about to concede any markets." Dow Jones & Co, October 16
Deffeyes, Kenneth (2001). *Hubbert's Peak*. Princeton, NJ: Princeton University Press

Energy Compass (2004). "Iran accuses Qatar of overproducing gas." April 30; available at http://www.energyintel.com

EIA (2004). "World proved oil and natural gas, most recent estimates." Energy Information Administration; available at http://www.eia.doe.gov; accessed on February 20

(2005). "International Energy Annual 2003." Energy Information Administration; available at http://www.eia.doe.gov; accessed on August 19

Fawzi, Aloulou (2004). "Qatar LNG 2010 and the US gas market: setting a new global cost benchmark." US Department of Energy, Washington, DC: Energy Information Administration, July

Gately, Dermot (1995). "Strategies for OPEC's pricing and output decisions." *The Energy Journal*, 16(3), pp. 1–38

(2001). "How plausible is the consensus projection of oil below $25 and Persian Gulf oil capacity and output doubling by 2020?" *The Energy Journal*, 22(4), pp. 1–27

(2004). "OPEC's incentives for faster growth." *The Energy Journal*, 25(2), pp. 75–96

Gulf (2004). "World oil." Gulf Publishing Co., September, pp. 225–229

Harvard (2003). "Rapporteur's report." Harvard University Oil and Security Executive Session, May 14. Environment and Natural Resources Program. Cambridge, MA: Belfer Center for Science and International Affairs

IEA (2002). *World Energy Outlook*. Paris: International Energy Agency

Jaffe, Amy M. (1997). "Political, economic, social, cultural, and religious trends in the Middle East and the Gulf and their impact on energy supply, security and pricing: main study." Houston: James A. Baker III Institute for Public Policy; available at http://www.bakerinstitute.org

(2004), "Geopolitics of Oil." *Encyclopedia of Energy*, New York:Elsevier

LaFranchi, Howard (2000). "OPEC hopes to settle price swings." *Christian Science Monitor*, September 27

Mabro, Robert (1998). "OPEC behavior 1960–1998: a review of the literature." *Journal of Energy Literature*, 4(1), pp. 3–27

MEES (2001). "Gas Exporters Forum holds first annual meeting in Tehran." *Middle East Economic Survey*, 44(22), May 28

Morse, Ed and James Richard (2002). "The battle for energy dominance." *Foreign Affairs*, March–April

Oil & Gas Journal (2004). "World oil and gas reserves." 102(47) December 20

O'Sullivan, Meghan L. (2003). "Shrewd sanctions: statecraft and state sponsors of terrorism." Washington, DC: Brookings Institution Press

Perloff, Jeffrey M (2004). *Microeconomics*, 3rd edn. New York: Pearson Education, Inc.

PIW (2002). "Club house: Yusufov proposes gas exporter club." *Petroleum Intelligence Weekly*, March 14

(2003). "Mixed reviews for Egypt's pricing plan." *Petroleum Intelligence Weekly*, February 12

Schweizer, Peter (1994). *Victory: The Reagan Administration's Secret Strategy that Hastened the Collapse of the Soviet Union*. New York: Atlantic Monthly Press

Smith, James L. (2003a). "Inscrutable OPEC?: behavioral tests of the cartel hypothesis." WP-2003–005, MIT CEEPR Working Papers; available at http://web.mit.edu/ceepr/www/workingpapers.htm

    (2003b). "Distinguishable patterns of competition, collusion, and parallel action." WP-2003-006, MIT CEEPR Working Papers; available at http://web.mit.edu/ceepr/www/workingpapers.htm

Soligo, Ronald, Amy M. Jaffe and Peter Mieszkowski (1997). "Energy security." Baker Institute Working Paper; available at http://www.bakerinstitute.org

Soligo, Ronald and Amy M. Jaffe (2000). "A note on Saudi Arabian price discrimination." *Energy Journal*, 21(1), January

Part IV

Implications

14 Conclusions

Amy M. Jaffe, Mark H. Hayes, and David G. Victor

Natural gas is rapidly gaining in geopolitical importance. Over the last hundred years, gas has grown from a marginal fuel consumed for specialized purposes in regionally disconnected markets to a commodity that is transported globally and used in many different economic sectors. In the last forty years, especially, natural gas has become a fuel of choice for consumers seeking its relatively low environmental impact, especially for electric power-generation. Over the next thirty years, world demand for gas is expected to double, surpassing coal as the world's number two energy source and potentially overtaking oil's share in many large industrialized economies.

The vision for a world shifting to gas is not constrained by the physical abundance of the resource. The world's known ("proved") gas reserves are sufficient for nearly seventy years of production at today's levels; the total base of potential conventional gas resources is estimated to be at least twice as large.[1] Like oil, however, the richest gas deposits are far from the areas where demand for gas is expected to rise most rapidly. About three-quarters of the world's proven gas reserves are located in the Former Soviet Union (FSU) and the Middle East.

The integration of gas markets is the by-product of a steady and cumulative improvement in technologies for long-distance transportation of gas – pipelines and LNG. Regional and local gas trading networks are based on pipeline interconnections, and very-long-distance transportation is increasingly the province of LNG. International trade in LNG has been occurring for over forty years and involves shipments from close to a dozen countries. In the 1990s, roughly 5 percent of world natural gas consumption moved as LNG, but this is expected to rise with higher demand for imported gas, particularly in North America, as

---

[1] Reserve estimates are from BP (2005) and resource estimates are from USGS (2000), consistent with sources quoted earlier in this text. USGS "conventional" resource estimates include associated and non-associated natural gas, but do not include vast potential gas production from CBM or methane hydrates.

locally available sources become depleted. Indeed, construction of transportation infrastructure is currently the major barrier to increased world natural gas consumption. Simulations of the gas future presented in chapters 11 and 12 suggest the need for truly massive investments in gas trade infrastructures, both pipeline and LNG, over the coming thirty-five years. These results are supported by previous studies cited in chapter 1, such as the IEA's *World Energy Outlook*, which suggests that cumulative investment needs in the global natural gas supply chain between 2001 and 2030 will total $3.1 trillion, or $105 billion per year.

This book has investigated the geopolitical roots and consequences of a shift to gas. We looked historically through seven case studies that illuminated how firms and governments have mobilized capital and managed international gas trading infrastructures – both pipelines and LNG (see chapters 3–9). The case studies concentrated on countries that lack the stable legal and political environments that are often seen as essential to attracting private investors. The expansion of gas as a global fuel depends in large part on success in attracting investment within such political, institutional, and economic environments as most of the world's gas is located in such countries. The studies covered projects in Algeria, Indonesia, Russia, the Southern Cone of Latin America, Turkmenistan, Qatar, and Trinidad & Tobago (see the introduction in chapter 2 and the summary of case studies in chapter 10).

In addition to the perspective of history, we also peered ahead to the possible futures for the next thirty-five years. To aid in that effort, the book presented results from a new model of world gas trade. It offered a base case (chapter 11) as well as several scenarios that examine the impacts on the global market of various geopolitical, economic, and technological factors on the development of gas infrastructure (chapter 12). Looking to the future, we also explored the important geopolitical topic that is already rising in attention: whether major gas exporters could form a cartel akin to OPEC's scheme for oil (chapter 13).

In this conclusion, we identify four broad findings from the study. First, we find that an *integrated global gas market* is emerging, in which events in any individual region or country will affect all regions. Second, we conclude that the role of governments in the development of natural gas markets is changing dramatically – away from the direct providers of capital and infrastructure and toward *facilitators of markets* in which private firms and investors take most of the risks. Third, we argue that among the many geopolitical aspects of a global gas market will be growing attention to *supply security*. Finally, we discuss the many ways that a rapid shift to a prominent global gas market could falter. We find that a key risk to the gas future is that governments may not create a context in which investors will be willing to invest the huge sums of capital needed for an expanding global gas infrastructure. Our study highlights the importance of the *internal governance* as a key factor in determining which gas-rich countries see their resources developed most profitably.

Emergence of an Integrated, Global Gas Market

This book has considered the implications of a major shift from a world of regionally isolated natural gas markets to a new more interdependent, increasingly global, marketplace for gas. The driving forces for this shift to a global gas market include the increasing preference for gas as a fuel, technological advances that are reducing the cost of producing and delivering gas to markets, and liberalization of gas markets. The rising importance of gas as a primary energy source brings with it concerns about gas pricing and security of gas supply. Globalization of the natural gas trade will have significant ramifications for consumers and gas producers alike. Just as policy-makers in large consuming countries have focused on the macroeconomic effects of variable oil prices, similar concerns are already evident about natural gas prices as the fuel begins to play a larger role in world economies. Producing countries will also have to worry about income effects of global natural gas pricing trends.

Results from the study's economic modeling suggest that the shift to a global market will render each major consuming or producing area vulnerable to events in any region. The timing of major gas export projects coming online, as well as discontinuities in supply or demand, will ripple throughout a global market. For example, as shown in the scenario runs of the model presented in chapter 12, in a world of fully integrated natural gas markets, gas users in Japan will have a vested interest in stability of South American gas reaching the US West coast; those in the United States will have concern about natural gas policy in Africa and Russia, and the European Union will be compelled to monitor the political situation in gas-producing regions as remote as the Russian Far East and Venezuela.

Major consuming countries will have to learn to adjust to the interdependencies of a global gas market. In the past, policy-makers in large gas-importing countries have focused on key supply relationships – such as the large pipelines from Algeria and the Soviet Union that fed Europe or the multitude of pipelines that sent gas from Bolivia to Brazil and from Argentina to Chile (see chapters 3, 5, and 6, respectively). Sustained attention from governments will continue to be critical to creating an attractive environment for these massive capital investments. However, a narrow focus on one-off trading relationships is unlikely to prove an effective means to providing supply security in a future where a much more fungible global market will set prices in all major markets and determine the movement of gas supplies.

Our research conclusions suggest that Russia will play a pivotal role in price formation in this new, more flexible and integrated global natural gas market (chapter 11). Russia was one of the first major gas exporters to the European market, it controls a huge pipeline network that serves greater Europe, and it is already the largest exporter of natural gas worldwide (see chapter 5). In addition to gas deposits that it controls directly, Russia also exerts strong leverage on price and export quantities from the rich gas deposits of land-locked Turkmenistan (see chapter 7). If economics alone were to determine gas exports, more than half of total European demand after 2020 would come from Russian suppliers. Already, policy-makers in the European Union are debating the ramifications of depending on Russia for over one-quarter of its supply (see chapters 5 and 10). Russia's rich deposits of gas in Eastern Siberia are also well situated for export to China – an outcome that the model suggests would occur over the next ten years if economic factors reigned alone. Strategically positioned to move large amounts of gas both east and west, the presence of low-cost Russian pipeline gas in both Asia and Europe could serve to link Asian and European gas prices. The model also suggests that Russia will also eventually enter the LNG trade in both the Atlantic and Pacific, via the Barents Sea and Sakhalin, respectively, providing an additional link between gas prices in North America, Europe, and Asia.

Several nations in the Middle East – such as Qatar, Iran and Saudi Arabia – are also geographically situated to become swing suppliers that could interconnect regional gas markets into a global system of gas trading. The rise of this role has been delayed, partly, by the large fixed costs for the new infrastructure that will be needed to carry their gas to the lucrative European and Asian markets. As global gas demand rises, these new supplies from the Middle East will become an important hub for flexibility in global markets. In an attempt to dominate this future opportunity, Qatar (and, to a lesser degree, Iran) is making massive investments in LNG. Interestingly, Qatar's rise was contemplated and could have happened ten years earlier it had if not been for the distraction of political controversies with its neighbors and concern by major LNG users (notably Japan) about the risks of relying on gas tankers that had to traverse the dangerous waters of the Persian Gulf (see chapter 8). Abundant Turkmen gas may also be slow to come to market due to political and economic barriers in moving that gas across rival Russia (see chapter 7).

The international gas industry is already responding to this integration of supplies and major gas consuming regions. As liquidity in the market and the number of available supply alternatives have grown, so have the opportunities for price arbitrage. Traditionally, the risks associated with multi-billion dollar LNG projects have been secured through bilateral contracts between suppliers and users of gas that, by design, provided security by not allowing flexibility in source or destination. LNG tankers were like "floating pipelines." This book includes a study of one of the first LNG projects to adopt that model – the export from Arun in Indonesia to Japan (see chapter 4). The book also documents the first project designed to "break the mold" and create flexibility in destination: the LNG export project from Trinidad & Tobago allows project operators to export gas to Europe or the United States, depending on where the prices are most attractive (see chapter 9). In this new model, multi-national gas companies with access to vast amounts of capital are investing in major natural gas infrastructure projects without the security of fully finalized sales for total output volumes. Instead, companies are counting on their own ability to identify end-use markets at some future time, closer in line to the investment pattern that characterizes development of multi-billion dollar oil fields. Expectations of a premium, liquid market for gas in the United States are a key factor encouraging this change, as is liberalization of certain European markets which permit gas sellers to bypass European state gas monopolies and sell directly to large gas customers and power generators (see chapter 9).

The modeling work suggests that the US market will remain a premium region as North American production fails to keep pace with demand, and high prices pull gas supplies from around the world. New supplies from Alaska are also likely to play a role, but they will not eliminate the need for imported LNG (see chapter 11). LNG is also forcing a change in how US policy-makers and gas buyers think about the factors that govern the supply of gas in the US market and formation of prices. At present, only 4 percent of US gas supplies come from LNG, although some projections envision that fraction rising to one-fifth of all supplies in the next twenty years. Much of the US political debate on LNG has focused on the safety and siting of regasification terminals, and much of the conventional wisdom assumes that once these terminals are built, they will be filled to capacity to quench the US thirst for gas imports. In reality, despite record high gas prices in the United States at the time of writing (mid-2005), the existing five LNG terminals are running half-empty because gas net-backs (net profits once transport costs are considered) are even higher in Europe and much of the available LNG in the Atlantic Basin (where all current US terminals are located) is being drawn to European markets. In the Atlantic Basin, as the authors of the case study on Trinidad & Tobago's LNG projects demonstrate, an interconnected gas market has already taken shape (see chapter 9).

New Market Structures and the Changing Roles for Governments

Throughout most of the historical development of the gas industry, governments have played the central role in creating markets for gas, as well as in directing gas supply projects. Government-owned enterprises have built and operated the infrastructures that were essential to distributing the large volumes of gas. Government-to-government agreements, usually backed with government-controlled financing, have been the essential cement for the producer–consumer relationship. Historically, governments absorbed and managed nearly all the risks of major international gas supply arrangements.

However, as market liberalization takes hold in many key gas consuming countries and global trading of natural gas expands, the role of government is changing – away from builder, operator, and financier of gas projects and toward regulator and creator of the context for private investment. The historical case studies in chapters 3–9 show how this shift to a market-oriented structure – which itself is part of a broader trend in the organization of modern states and economies – will affect the incentives to create new gas transportation networks that are essential if the world is to continue its rapid shift to gas.

The case studies demonstrate that governments have played the central role in "creating" demand for new import volumes of gas. Absent the state, very few, if any, of these projects would have been able to move ahead at the same speed, or with the same volumes of deliveries.

Studies of the first-of-a-kind LNG export projects from Arun in Indonesia (1970s) and Qatar (mid-1990s) to Japan show the importance of a willing government to orchestrate the investment – in these cases, the government of Japan and a small coalition of Japanese buyers. The first of these projects – Arun – rested on the willingness of the Japanese government (through MITI and J-EXIM) to orchestrate the purchase of the gas and the timely construction of an infrastructure for utilizing it. The Japanese government provided crucial financial support as Japanese trading companies launched the Arun venture. The government's interest was rooted in its high priority on energy security and a desire to diversify energy supplies away from coal and oil. In the Japanese context, as an island nation, the government supported construction of an infrastructure that was not a gas pipeline transmission grid (as seen in Europe) but, rather, a network of LNG-receiving terminals, serving a cluster of relatively isolated local markets. Constraints on moving gas between those markets helped each local monopoly protect its position and thus invest with confidence in long-term returns. Lack of similar US government backing for proposed sales of Arun gas to California meant that contracts to that market languished in the face of Japanese insistence that it be given the right of first refusal on any increased gas exports from the Arun field (see chapter 4).

Similarly, the role of the Japanese government and its coalition of gas buyers was important to Mobil Corporation's ability to get the Qatargas project off the ground in 1987. Although the strength of MITI and other crucial arms of the Japanese government had weakened considerably as part of a broader effort to expand the role for market forces in the Japanese economy, the role of a Japanese buying consortium with access to existing import infrastructure was critical to Qatargas' success in gaining financial backing and sufficient sales contracts. The timing of the project coincided with a reduction in Japanese concerns about the political stability of energy supplies from the Persian Gulf, derived in no small part from rising US military presence in that region (see chapter 8).

In the same vein, much of the variation in the outcomes of the two proposed projects to pipe gas across the Mediterranean in the late 1970s is also due to the starkly different roles that the Italian and Spanish governments took towards the prospects of starting to import large volumes of gas. Like Japan, Italy was actively seeking gas imports and was willing to mobilize significant state resources to secure new energy supplies. Through its own export credit agencies, the government provided the bulk of financing for the Transmed pipeline project. The state-owned energy firm ENI was positioned at that time to orchestrate the Trans-Mediterranean ("Transmed") pipeline project as well as the development of Italy's domestic gas transmission grid. State backing allowed ENI to invest with confidence and provided cover for international lending. Spain, on the other hand, did not have supporting policies in place, and thus could not lead successful development of a major gas import project in the 1970s and 1980s (see chapter 3).

Importantly, other case studies show that the ready availability of large volumes of gas is not enough to create demand for gas in end-user markets. In markets where the state has avoided a central role in supporting infrastructure expansion, rapid gasification has not taken place. In the 1990s in Poland, for example, a large pipeline from Russia was constructed mainly to supply additional volumes of gas to the German market. Because it crossed Polish territory, large volumes were also available to Poland, yet the Polish market has used very little of that available gas, despite take-or-pay contracts for Polish delivery. The Polish gas market stalled in large part because the Polish government did not support gas and thus no entity in Poland was prepared to build the infrastructure needed to distribute it. Coal represented a plentiful – and politically entrenched – fuel source (see chapter 5).

The instance of most rapid gasification that is observed in any of the case studies is the one where the state played the most central role: the Soviet Union. A decision from the center to favor gas in the 1950s, orchestrated through central planning, catapulted gas from just 1 percent of total primary energy supply in 1955 to nearly 30 percent in 1980 (see chapter 5). Of course, state intervention is usually neither the most economically efficient nor the only way to create a market, but these case studies suggest that state intervention accounts for much of the observed variation in initial gas projects. Moreover, the importance of governments in creating demand historically should sound a note of caution about visions for rapid gasification in settings where gas delivery and domestic market infrastructure do not already exist and where the state is not prepared to back the creation of the gas delivery infrastructure.

The historical case studies also show that intervention of the state and other supporters of gas projects can backfire in the absence of a strong commercial rationale. The GasBol pipeline, connecting Bolivia to Brazil, was a favorite of both governments and multi-national development banks looking to support market reform, transparency, and intra-regional trade in the aftermath of a bi-lateral peace treaty. Under pressure from multi-national organizations, market liberalizers and domestic trade groups, the Brazilian government forced state-owned Petrobrás to contract for the bulk of gas purchases from the pipeline and also encouraged the company to provide financial support for the investments in field development in Bolivia to be sure that the project went forward. But the failure of demand for gas in Brazil to materialize – in part due to the inability of the Brazilian government to create a regulatory context that would allow gas-fired power plants to sell their electricity – meant that GasBol could not survive financially. Petrobrás was left on the hook for volumes of gas it could not sell (see chapter 6).

The GasAndes pipeline from Argentina to Chile indicates the type of project that seems likely to emerge when governments themselves do not absorb the risks associated with building a gas market. The GasAndes project, a relatively small pipeline to connect gas fields in Argentina to a small number of power-generators near Santiago, Chile, beat its competitor, Transgas, because it was able to find private sector buyers and environmentally driven government support for a limited, strictly commercially viable project. The liberalizing electric power market in Chile, along with the tighter air pollution regulations in badly polluted Santiago, created favorable conditions for the project.

In contrast, the Transgas project sought to build a much more elaborate gas distribution network around Santiago, seeking to supply gas to new distribution companies that would serve industrial and residential gas consumers in addition to new gas-fired power-generators. The rival project, GasAndes, sought to supply just large electricity plants in Santiago directly. The Transgas project was more costly, and payback would have occurred over a longer period and with greater uncertainty. Transgas sought a concession from the government to allow it to recover investments in the gas distribution grid. When the government made it clear that it would not provide such concessions, the GasAndes project moved quickly ahead (see chapter 6).

On the supply side, the role of government in managing and absorbing risk has been equally important. Even where private firms have actually made the investments in developing gas fields and in building the transmission infrastructure, governments have been essential guarantors of long-term contracts that, historically, have underpinned most large-scale gas infrastructure investment. In the past, investor risk has been mitigated by "take-or-pay" contracts. But new, more flexible contracting is being pressed upon the industry as gas markets become more global and commoditized. Gas-on-gas competition, new gas resale contract clauses, and joint investor/host-country marketing strategies are creating a new market structure for gas.

As the role of the state weakens, the key anchoring role for gas projects is shifting toward the private sector. In the "old world," governments had deep pockets and a strategic vision that was organized around serving national markets and developing national resources. The development and implementation of this vision was often inseparable from the state-owned and state-supported enterprises whose charge it was to supply energy to the national market. In that world, cross-border gas trade projects were national ventures (see, especially, chapters 3, 4, 5, and 7).

In the "new world," a handful of large energy companies with deep pockets and a similar strategic vision are taking over the role as creator and guarantor of the implementation process. These players are largely private, but they also include national energy companies that are now playing a larger role in the international marketplace – Gazprom, CNOOC (China National Offshore Oil Corp.), Petrobrás, Petronas, and others. This shift to large energy companies, however, is likely to mean that infrastructure development will increasingly be driven by commercial interests rather than national energy security objectives.

The advent of new, more commercially oriented players dominating the gas scene will also change the nature of how contracts are negotiated and enforced. In the regulated, state-controlled environment, it was relatively easy for governments and their bidders to tailor the terms of gas trade agreements for political ends. But as gas markets liberalize – especially in Europe, where countries are small and borders are frequent – directed gas trade is harder to sustain, especially as provisions such as destination clauses are undone. In the emerging commercially driven environment, the role of courts as enforcers has grown – made possible, in part, by legal reforms that have accompanied the shift to markets and given courts and quasi-judicial bodies (such as regulators) greater authority. Although the industry press is just now focusing on the implications of this trend, the studies in this book suggest that this shift has been under way for more than a decade (see chapters 3 and 9, respectively).

Ironically, the importance of existing contracts may lie less in their enforceability but, rather, in their ability to tap a first-mover advantage. By facilitating the creation of sunk infrastructure costs, existing relationships act as a deterrent to others and a binding agent for the project investors. Once Italy had partnered with Algeria and had begun to lay pipe, huge incentives were created to continue cooperation (see chapter 3). Russia's contract with Poland partly deterred alternative (more costly) suppliers to that market. The ultimate deterrent to Norwegian supplies to Poland was the fact "on the ground" of Russia's pipeline (see chapter 5).

With the exception of Russia, various case studies show that private commercial players have been better placed to position themselves as first-movers than state gas concerns. Owners of Trinidad LNG were able to push Algeria's Sonatrach from lucrative US east coast markets by producing at lower costs (see chapter 9). Nimble GasAndes beat out slow-paced Transgas, which had hoped to tap government support to create a market (see chapter 6). A topic that remains to be explored is whether government-owned entities will be able to act as strategic players in the more competitive gas world or whether private commercial firms will be able to organize competitive supplies to get to market more effectively, thereby leaving state monopolies to wait for long-term market growth to make space for them to enter without the pressure of innovation nimbleness, and strategy.

Global Gas and Security of Supply

The shift from the highly structured world of government-backed bilateral contracts with oil-linked pricing formulas to a new world of private, market-related gas contracts raises questions about national security of supply. Private sector participants have different interests from countries; they cannot be expected automatically to consider the energy security concerns of client nations as they are driven mainly by commercial pressures. Moreover, some gas exporters may explore the prospects for creating a gas-exporting cartel similar to OPEC.

The studies presented in this book suggest that concern for maintaining a secure supply of reasonably priced natural gas, a topic that has been eclipsed by the same questions applied to oil, will increasingly be viewed as a vital national interest. In the past, gas consumers have feared interruption in vital gas supplies for a variety of reasons, such as contract disputes between Algeria and its customers (chapter 3), political unrest in Indonesia (chapter 4), and transit-country risk such as those associated with transporting Russian gas to Europe through Ukraine and Belarus (chapter 5). In addition to fears of supply interruption, major gas consuming countries or regions worry that a key exporter, such as Russia (to Europe) or group of exporters, could exercise monopoly power to extract inflated rents for their product.

Key gas-exporting countries have already been engaged in nascent efforts to create a gas cartel. In May 2001, the GECF held its first ministerial meeting in Tehran, with the aim of enhancing coordination among gas producers. Although the GECF ministers announced that they did not intend to manage production or set quotas, some members of the group are exploring their possible leverage over current and future gas markets. By its third session in Doha, Qatar, GECF had swelled to fourteen members: Algeria, Brunei, Egypt, Indonesia, Iran, Libya, Malaysia, Nigeria, Oman, Qatar, Russia, Trinidad & Tobago, the UAE, and Venezuela (and one observer, Norway).

The GECF has already tried, unsuccessfully, to exercise some collective influence in the European market. GECF helped to catalyze formation of a working group headed by Russia and Algeria who sought to resist EU attempts to outlaw destination clauses that prevent contracted gas buyers from reselling to third parties. (The option to resell gas is a pivotal mechanism for market arbitrage and efficiency, as it helps to prevent the segregation of markets that allows gas sellers to exert monopoly power.) In another example, Egypt has sought a change in gas pricing systems that would end the link to crude oil prices with the aim of easing the penetration of gas into European markets.

These efforts have generated little practical effect on gas markets, and an exporters' cartel remains still a theoretical prospect rather than a real present danger. Chapter 13 shows that the GECF has too many members with diverging interests to exert effective constraints on gas export capacity in the intermediate term. There are a large and growing number of suppliers in international gas markets, and the existence of this diverse, competitive fringe of alternative suppliers does not favor cartelization. Moreover, large LNG and pipeline projects are marked by huge capital costs and relatively low operating costs, which put a premium on full operation once the equipment is in service.

Over the long term, gas exports may eventually concentrate in the hands of just a few major producers, which could make it more feasible for a group of gas suppliers to restrain capacity expansion to gain higher rents. The overall distribution of world natural gas reserves is more concentrated than the distribution of oil reserves. The two countries with the largest gas reserves – Russia and Iran – have roughly 45 percent of world natural gas reserves while the two countries with the largest oil reserves – Saudi Arabia and Iraq – have just 36 percent of world oil reserves. The five-country concentration ratio for the two fuels is roughly the same at 62 percent. However, the regional concentration of gas resources is more diverse. Middle East countries hold only 36 percent of natural gas reserves, as opposed to 65 percent of oil reserves. The Former Soviet Union represents a second equally important region for gas production and exports (see chapter 13). However, we can already see evidence that gas export market share is less tightly correlated with reserve base than in the case of oil. Chapter 10 argues that the countries most likely to become exporters are those that are able to combine prodigious gas resources with a business environment that favors private investment; those same conditions could impede the successful implementation of an effective cartel.

Historically, some well-positioned gas suppliers have been able to extract short-term rents in particular markets by manipulating supplies into markets where alternative supplies are not available. Algeria used this position to force higher prices on the Italian and French markets in the 1970s, but Algeria quickly suffered when circumstances changed. Over the long term, Algeria has paid a high cost due to the reputation it gained as an unreliable supplier (see chapter 3). The same Algerian effort to lift prices also contributed to its loss of share in the US market, which created an opening that new export projects from Trinidad & Tobago eventually filled (see chapter 9).

As the case studies show, diversity of supply is an important protection from the rent-seeking behavior both of both gas exporters and transit countries. When Ukraine first interrupted Russian gas exports in 1995, European buyers who redoubled their efforts to diversify found many alternative suppliers, confirming the importance of policies (including market reforms) that encourage multiple supply sources (see chapters 5 and 10).

We expect that the globalization of gas markets will increase the diversity of supplies and reduce the risk that any single supplier (or even a cartel) could exert influence over gas supplies and prices. The shift from administered to competitive gas markets introduces new uncertainties, but it also provides some security benefits. Where the market reigns, shortages yield higher prices that in turn yield demand response (curtailment or fuel-switching) or attract new supplies. In contrast, where prices are administered, or determined via rigid oil price linkages, users do not see the signal of shortage. Privatization of resources and export networks in key supply areas such as Russia may also make it more difficult for governments to coordinate rent-seeking supply restraints. Without this privatization of resources, a group of key national exporters could, over the coming decades, exercise market power to gain monopoly rents as chapter 13 warns.

Risks to the Greater Gas Vision

For many analysts, the assumption that the world will shift to gas is rooted in current trend lines and models whose strength is their ability to represent fundamental economic potentials. By those reckonings, the future for gas is bright. But the real world depends on many political and social factors beyond trend lines and economic potentials, and some of those could turn sour for gas. We focus on four such factors that, by way of conclusion, help to illuminate the geopolitical forces that could stall the dash to gas.

First, the vision for gas depends enormously on investor confidence and the supply of vast sums of financial and intellectual capital. A plethora of studies has confirmed that world gas resources are abundant (see chapters 1 and 2). Gas projects are as capital-intensive as, if not more than, those for oil, and most of the capital needed for typical LNG and pipeline export projects is required in the country or region where the gas deposits are located. The richest gas deposits are generally located in countries that traditionally have not been attractive for private investors. The capital-intensive nature of gas and the long payback periods typical of gas projects (twenty years or longer for some of the most complex projects) means that the gas future probably hinges on whether the major gas players will be able to justify spending on gas projects in some less than hospitable investment contexts.

We argued in chapter 10 that the countries that are likely to become large exporters are not simply those with large amounts of gas but, rather, those that combine gas resources with an attractive investment environment. Thus, Trinidad & Tobago has become the largest LNG supplier to the United States while gas-rich and proximate Venezuela, where it is harder for private firms to commit capital with confidence, remains on the sidelines (see chapter 9). In the Persian Gulf, Qatar has attracted far more gas investment than all other nations because it has offered an attractive environment for investors (see chapter 8). For the moment, it appears enough countries are offering settings for large-scale gas extraction and export projects that this fear of a slowdown in gas development will not become a reality. However, circumstances can change quickly. Whole regions, such as the volatile Middle East, can become embroiled in war and other deterrents to investors; key gas exporting countries, such as Russia, can become distracted by other political priorities; countries that are the darlings of investors can switch when new regimes take power, as happened in Algeria in 1981 (see chapter 3).

Second, developers of gas resources may run foul of problems with the governance of host countries, often called the "resource curse," that has historically afflicted countries that become largely dependent on revenues from natural resource exports. Historical experience shows that many countries that are rich in natural resources have nonetheless failed to sustain economic growth because of poor governance, including fiscal management. When the sale of natural resources accounts for a large fraction of a society's economic activity, politics becomes focused on disputes about allocating and seizing the revenues from such exports; harm to indigenous communities often proliferates; good governance, focused on the society's broader long-term interests, is difficult to sustain. Such problems are evident worldwide across many extractive industries from Bolivia to Indonesia and Russia. The Arun case study concludes, for example, that NGOs and social discontent had less impact on Arun development in the 1970s because critics had yet to organize themselves sufficiently on a political basis to provide significant impediments to the Arun operation. By 1998, however, agitation in Aceh where Arun is located became so severe that gas export operations were temporarily suspended and led finally to full-scale central government military action against local armed groups (see chapter 4).

The Arun case may be a telling sign of an era coming to an end – an era where developers of these resources faced much less external scrutiny on their operations and where states themselves directed many resource development projects. It is plausible to argue that neither of those two conditions will hold in the future. With the advent of revenue management schemes for oil (and gas) export projects in Azerbaijan and on the Chad–Cameroon pipeline, it is plausible to expect that most gas projects could some day face similar intervention. Democratization and the spread of information have put new powers in the hands of people and NGOs and have eroded the assumption that private investors can speak directly to governments who will do their bidding.[2] In Bolivia, as in Arun, indigenous groups have developed their own independent influences on policies that have been strong enough to derail investors.

Third, visions for gasification may also run foul of political difficulties in the countries that are the major users of gas. Questions have arisen, in particular, around the siting of major gas infrastructures amid growing worries about terrorism. In the United States, politicians have focused particular attention on LNG regasification terminals, which are essential if the vision for a global gas market driven by rising US imports is to be realized. Community resistance has stalled LNG regasification terminal siting in nearly every part of the US market – except the Gulf coast where public acceptance of industrial facilities is generally much higher than in the rest of the country. Since ample regasification is critical for LNG supply and arbitrage, sustained difficulties in siting these import facilities will hamper the gas future.

However, policy makers and gas buyers should realize that regasification import capacity will not be the only determinant of how much LNG is actually delivered to the US over time. As we discuss in the first section of this chapter, the emergence of an integrated, global gas market will mean that prices and supplies in one locale will increasingly become a function of the machinations of markets in other locales. Historically, long-term contracts were the keystone to financing LNG project development. Increasingly, however, these long-term contracts are not

---

[2] Unocal's 2005 extra-judicial settlement with a group representing an indigenous population in Burma further supports this line of argument. The settlement avoided a final opinion in a case brought by the indigenous group alleging that Unocal was aware of the Burmese military's use of slave labor to aid construction of a gas export pipeline to Thailand in the 1990s.

determining the physical flows of LNG. As a larger number of regasification facilities are constructed, particularly terminals serving deeply liquid domestic gas markets in the United States and the United Kingdom, the opportunities for arbitrage between markets continues to grow. Arbitrage itself drives price convergence across regions – and also determines the destinations of LNG cargoes. Thus, gas buyers and energy policy-makers in importing countries will increasingly need to be aware of gas market conditions beyond their borders and their direct supply relationships. Gas prices and the destinations of LNG cargoes will be determined by the development of global gas supplies and the demand conditions in numerous end-user markets.

Fourth, and finally, the case studies also underscore that since around 1990 much of the "dash to gas" has depended on expectations about electric power markets. Conventional wisdom holds that gas is favored for electricity; from the middle 1980s through the late 1990s that was, indeed, the experience in England and Wales, the United States, and several other markets. In many regions, gas gained its advantage because of tighter environmental rules. It also gained, however, because liberalization created additional pressure to select the least-cost options. Increasingly efficient gas-fired turbines are well adapted to competitive markets, because of their relatively low capital cost and the short lead time required for construction. But close attention must be given to markets where gas-fired generation is not the current low-marginal cost supplier or where electricity demand might be constrained by other factors.

In Brazil, a darling for potential investors in the 1990s, the collapse of economic growth, combined with dominance of incumbent hydropower and an unfavorable implementation of regulatory rules, has impeded the entry of gas (see chapter 4). In Poland, the dominance of incumbent coal-fired power plants, the vast oversupply of electric-generating capacity, and the lack of strong government incentives for gas have made it difficult for Russian gas to enter the market (see chapter 5).

It is not yet clear whether gasification in other emerging markets (such as China and India) will follow the examples set in the United States and United Kingdom (where electrification and liberalization favored gas for electricity) or Poland and Brazil where governments failed to institute the incentives for a push to gas. We end, thus, with a note of caution on the crucial connections between markets for gas and the final suppliers of energy services. In the late 1990s nearly every new power plant ordered in the United States was gas-fired; after 2002, with gas prices expected to sustain historically unprecedented levels for the remainder of the decade, the order books for new gas plants have thinned, and US power-generators are looking with fresh eyes at new coal and nuclear plants and are expanding investment in renewable energy. Oil products have secured a dominant position in energy systems because these energy-rich liquid fuels, with their high energy density and flexibility, presently have no viable competitor for providing transportation services. In electric power, however, gas confronts many viable alternatives.

REFERENCES

BP (2005). *Statistical Review of World Energy*; availabhle at http://www.bp.com
USGS (2000) *World Petroleum Assessment*. Washington, DC: United States Geological Survey

Appendix: technical notes

Nadejda M. Victor

For any country, a variety of statistical sources for natural gas exist: (1) the IEA produces detailed statistics on gas production and export/import and consumption by sectors; (2) Eurostat, the European Union's statistical body, produces less detailed but more up-to-date statistics on gas use and supply in the member countries; (3) for each country, government bodies produce their own national statistics using their own definitions; (4) national or other gas/oil companies report either their own or national statistics, using potentially yet another set of definitions. Thermal conversion factors measuring the equivalent heating content of various fuels can also be different. In the United States, the common practice is to use the gross or upper end of the range of heat-content values for a specific product. In Europe, net or lower end heat-content values are typically used. The difference is the amount of energy that is consumed to vaporize the water created during the combustion process, and this difference is typically 2–10 percent, depending on the specific fuel. As the definitions, units, and conversion factors are different in different data sources, it is very important to present the approach that was used in our gas study.

Natural gas comprises gases occurring in deposits, whether liquefied or gaseous, consisting mainly of methane (see table A.1). It includes both "non-associated" gas originating from fields producing hydrocarbons only in gaseous form, and "associated" gas produced in association with crude oil as well as methane recovered from coal mines (CBM). Gas production is measured after purification and extraction of NGLs and sulfur. Quantities reinjected, vented, or flared are not included in production statistics. Data in m^3 are usually measured at 15°C and at 760 mmHg, known as Standard Conditions or the amount of gas required to fill a volume of $1m^3$ under Standard Conditions of temperature, pressure, and water vapor. Nevertheless, in the FSU countries Standard Conditions are different and are measured at 20°C, rather than 15° and that makes the national estimations for gas volumes about 7% higher than comparable heat contents for European or US volumes.

Table A.1 *Typical composition of natural gas*

Gas		%
Methane	CH$_4$	70–90
Ethane	C$_2$H$_6$	0–20
Propane	C$_3$H$_8$	0–20
Butane	C$_4$H$_{10}$	
Carbon dioxide	CO$_2$	0–8
Oxygen	O$_2$	0–0.2
Nitrogen	N$_2$	0–5
Hydrogen sulfide	H$_2$S	0–5
Rare gases	A, He, Ne, Xe	Trace

Source: Naturalgas.org.

Thus, in order to precisely define what we mean by "natural gas" some attributes of the gas need to be measured. Such characteristics include gas temperature, density, pressure, compression factor, and calorific value, as well as the knowledge about some of its minor components in addition to methane – e.g. water, liquid hydrocarbons, and carbon dioxide. A typical composition of natural gas is presented in table A.1.

The energy value of a unit of natural gas (1m^3 at Standard Conditions) can vary depending on the composition of the gas, and cannot be measured directly. Calculation of the energy value of natural gas is thus a two-step process requiring both the measurement of the volume and the calorific value of the gas (via combustion).

With respect to the above, individual countries have adopted different approaches to the issue of gas quality, reflecting their different gas sources and the historical development of their respective national markets. As a result, there is no uniform gas quality specification for gas produced, transported, and distributed across national boundaries.

To account for the differences in quality between types of natural gas in different countries the IEA has applied specific conversion factors supplied by national administrations for the main flows or uses (i.e. production, imports, exports, consumption). The IEA has two primary methods of obtaining these data. It sends out annual questionnaires to each OECD member country to collect the data. The data for non-OECD countries are collected via other international organizations (i.e. UN, Organización Latinoamericana de Energíal, OLADE); close cooperation with national statistical bodies; direct contacts with energy consultants and companies; publications; and questionnaires for UN-ECE countries). National natural gas data are collected in the following energy units: in Terajoules (TJ) based on Gross Calorific Value (GCV);[1] and in million m^3 meters under Standard Conditions. Conversion is presented by specific conversion factors in kJ/cm for indigenous gas production, gas imports, gas exports, and inland gas consumption.

To account for the differences in quality between types of gas, we apply specific conversion factors that are based on IEA data. Throughout the text we present figures in billion m^3 (Bcm) of natural gas, unless otherwise specified, and based on an average GCV of gas consumed, produced, exported, and imported for each observed country, as reported in the annual national gas reports and produced by the IEA. As far as possible, the data represent standard m^3 (measured at 15°C).

Data for FSU countries are adjusted to account for the different reporting standards described above. Thus, as our data are derived directly from Btus[2] using the average calorific values of gas consumed, produced, exported, and imported for each country, it does not necessarily equate with gas volumes expressed in specific national terms.

The term "Conversion Factor" has two uses. First, as a calorific value, in order to convert quantities expressed in physical volume (Bcm) units to energy units (Btu) and, secondly as a scaling factor to convert one form of energy unit to another (e.g. Btu to Mtoe). Table A.2 shows the conversion factors that we used in our study to convert one form of energy unit to another. Table A.3 shows the conversion factors to convert gas quantities expressed in Bcm to Btu. The values in Table A.2 are not exact coefficients or conversion factors, since they can express only a mean value of the heat content without respect to gas quality or different standards' measurement. For example, the average calorific value of gas produced in Argentina is reported as 36,913 Btu/cm. This, for example, equates to 1 Mtoe equaling 1.075 Bcm of natural gas. Table A.3 lists the values that we have used for different countries in assembling this book.

---

[1] The calorific value of a fuel is a measure of its value for heating purposes, and it is expressed in terms of the heat released from a specified unit quantity under defined conditions of complete combustion. The calorific value is sometimes called the heating value of the fuel. Two measures of calorific value are possible: net calorific value (NCV) and gross calorific value (GCV), also termed as the low heating value (LHV) and high heating value (HHV). The GCV is the total quantity of heat released during combustion when all water formed by the combustion is returned to the liquid state. The NCV is the total quantity of heat released during combustion when all water formed by the combustion reaction remains in the vapor state, thus the NCV is less than the GCV. For natural gas, this difference is approximately 9–10 per cent, for oils and coals the difference is approximately 5 per cent. NCVs give the amount of useful heat on combustion, rather than the total heat theoretically available. Thus, NCVs generally form a better basis by which to compare the energy contents of different fuels.

[2] A Btu is the amount of energy required to raise 1 lb of water 1°F.

Table A.2 *Natural gas and LNG conversion factors*

From:	To:					
	Bcm natural gas	billion ft³ natural gas	Mtoe	million tonnes LNG	trillion Btu	MBOE
	Multiply by					
1 Bcm natural gas	1	35.3	0.9	0.73	36	6.29
1 billion ft³ natural gas	0.028	1	0.026	0.021	1.03	0.18
1 Mtoe	1.111	39.2	1	0.805	40.4	7.33
1 million tonnes LNG	1.38	48.7	1.23	1	52	8.68
1 trillion Btu	0.028	0.98	0.025	0.02	1	0.17
1 MBOE	0.16	5.61	0.14	0.12	5.8	1

Source: BP (2003).

Table A.3 *Conversion coefficients of natural gas, from m³ into Btu, for the key countries included in this book*

Country	Production (Btu/m³)	Imports (Btu/m³)	Exports (Btu/m³)	Consumption (Btu/m³)
Algeria	39,808	–	39,808	39,808
Argentina	36,913	36,913	36,913	36,913
Bolivia	36,908	–	36,908	36,908
Brazil	36,737	36,737	–	36,737
Chile	37,068	37,068	37,068	37,068
Indonesia	38,481	–	38,481	38,481
Italy	36,096	36,131	36,113	36,118
Japan	38,843	36,860	–	36,933
Russia[a]	33,303	33,290	33,303	33,303
Spain	40,292	40,272	–	40,272
Trinidad & Tobago	36,905	–	36,905	36,905
Turkmenistan[a]	33,410	33,410	33,410	33,410
United States	36,984	36,984	36,984	36,984

Note:
[a] Turkmenistan and Russia data were adjusted for difference in Standard Conditions of temperature.
Source: IEA; author's calculations.

REFERENCES

BP (2003). *Statistical Review of World Energy*; available at http://www.bp.com

Index